To all those who have taught me to love.

Florence Montreynaud

LOVE

A Century of Love and Passion

Florence Montrcynaud

Preface by Yves Simon

EVERGREEN

First Meeting:

Declaration of Love:

Wedding:

When:

Where:

Witnesses:

Honeymoon:

&

TABLE OF CONTENTS

Preface

THE TWENTIETH CENTURY HAS TRULY BEEN A CENTURY OF EXCESS. From Hiroshima to the first men on the moon, the latter part of the millennium has seen humanity devise its own comfort and extinction, scan thousands of faces daily without recording a single one, and become compassionate over a distant earthquake while ignoring the body stretched on the pavement at one's door. Love has not escaped our appetite for "all or nothing", our frenzied quest to love a little by embracing everything. Totalitarian temptations there were aplenty. Now we are compelled to create another, the temptation to cram everything into the fragile sentiment of love: marriage, the couple, passion, sex and eternity.

Invented early in the twentieth century, the metaphor of total love seems the greatest torture yet inflicted on our imagination. Unconsciously *formatted* by this insensate desire, we relentlessly dream of its enaction, though every minute of every day is there to tell us that this cannot be.

Florence Montreynaud traces the development of this folly: a century of epic love with its heroes and victims, saints and symbols. These are couples who crossed the firmament of their times like comets, rich in infinite emotion, the creators of an unprecedented syntax of love. "Unprecedented" because gestures, sentiments and words have their own history. And from the very dawn of the twentieth century, our time has invented a new *Code of Love*. It is a code commensurate with its own exorbitant desire: God is dead, long live love! For us, the imperative is not "thou shalt love thy neighbour", but "thou shalt love love". This new credo, the liturgy of modern times, has drawn into its orbit the largest religious community in the world. In the intimacy of the embrace, its devotees officiate, crucify, and deify. The great revealed religions are holed below the waterline! People believe, genuflect and worship *en masse*! Arrogant love weighs on our lives like the tables of the law, with laws such as no god would ever dare impose. We submit to their injunctions like the followers of a tyrannical guru, love's fools, whose invisible dictator commands our very instant. The worshippers are writers and artists, and the role-models, from Julien Sorel to Scarlett O'Hara, form the substrata of our daily divagations.

The one-dimensional man of our century mutters endless prayers to a diaphanous idol. The idol can wear whatever visage chance commends, provided only that it resonate with ancient memory and finds itself decreed the "one", the elect.

What do they say, these witnesses, the victims, the members of the voyage? Is their experience privileged? Certainly. The entry ticket seems available to everyone, but behind the frippery democracy of the façade is a redoubtable process of selection. The pretenders are many, but the inheritors of the kingdom are a caste apart. Tyrannical, tender, legitimate, febrile, passionate, sublime, mad: such are the adjectives hurled out by the initiates as they proffer to the excluded their history of revelation. For this is an encounter with the most mysterious of alchemies. Those who return transmuted speak of treasure and refulgence, like survivors of a voyage to the beyond, and profess strange yearnings compounded with terror and dismay. In this fusion of two secret selves, is each selected to drive the other mad? Chosen such that his or her absence depopulates the world? Did Zelda kill Scott? Or vice-versa?

"I have suicided you, my love," wrote Serge Gainsbourg. One thing is certain: nobody returns unscathed. Love is a revolution, there is a before and after. For the fortunate ones, the revolution is permanent, and theirs is the silence of bliss. Or they make believe, for what could be more reassuring than to convince the loveless that one loves? For the others, love condones, nay commands, transgressions public and private. A princess marries a fisherman, a banker an usherette. Lift up your hearts, lift your souls: love marks human beings with its seal, relieves them of their burdens, sacralising their secular being.

But eternity is not what it was. We realists have remodelled it; it has been tailored to private requirements. Quantum theory has taught us that the meaning of an object of perception is given by the observer's gaze. Don Juan is no longer an exclusively masculine personality; the women's revolution has carried him into the other camp and feminised him. Love's enterprise is no longer predatory, the conquest of one person by another; it is a contract between two people, in which respect gazes upon regard. This reciprocity is what gives the enterprise its meaning: the instant when love is born of the intimacy played out between two persons of equal power and equal stakes. Malraux famously predicted "a spiritual event on a planetary scale that will leave its mark on the twenty-first century". His prediction has, perhaps, brought about new forms of emotional behaviour. In these, the body of the other, as instrument of my pleasure, is less important than the world of the other, in which *both* may rejoice. "I want to live with you," means "I want to live *with* your body and *in* your world". In a universe fraught with crisis, despair and ever-present violence, the sacred has taken up residence in bodies and relationships. Between individualism and collectivism, the experience of love may thus become a common faith, in which revelation is that of partner to partner. Without reference to some exacting external divinity (this is a spirituality without religion), I sacrifice my predation. I no longer kneel before you to win your body (which I already possess); I kneel to pray to you.

Duration let there be, but one to which heart and soul can attain! Pornography was the instant of sex, raised to extremity, and exclusive of more duration than was required to exhaust the powers of fantasy. The new code has redefined that instant, placing it at the heart of love and its fulfilment. Sound the knell of the spectacle-as-duration, the new eternity has arrived! Eternity is renewable, and love-time is one's gift to oneself. It is a private time, standardised by what medicine permits and society prescribes. These successive existences are the *sine qua non* for deferring death. Golden and silver anniversaries now take their place in the museum of conventions, and the love of one's life is multiplied by three or four different lives. The exceptional beloved has given way to quotidian figures, with whom one enjoys an unceremonious intimacy. With the addition of a personal dimension, internalised in each of us, which makes of love the primary *locus* of meaning, the point at which human and divine conjoin in a new pact. From this unprecedented form of belief, a new and modern grandeur can arise.

Only recently has Western love broken free of a religion that claimed to bring a message of love and created the marriage of convenience. Would this not be a paradoxical moment to arrive at a marriage of faith?

YVES SIMON

Introduction

"The second greatest pleasure after love is talking about it."
(LOUISE LABÉ, *Debate on Folly and Love*, 1555)

Love has a history. The notion of love entertained by a society is the product of a long process of development and constitutes one of the cultural pillars of its organisation. To be sure, all those who discover themselves through love reinvent it in their own image. Their voyages of supposed discovery are enacted as if alone in the world. The expression of feelings, the discovery of bodies and sexual practices, everything, in fact, which they spontaneously and freely experience, is conditioned by the milieu and time in which they live. "I love you" is at once unique as emotion and period-specific as to form.

LOVE STORIES. This book tells almost one hundred great and moving love stories, one for every year from 1900 to 1998, together with brief notes in the right-hand column about other couples. For each year, a second section touches on a social phenomenon connected with love.

Any choice comprises an element of subjectivity. The couples that I have included have in one way or another left their mark on the twentieth century. Their fame may be national or universal, instant, belated, or posthumous. Their influence is felt today at the intersection of the history of mentalities and ideas with that of social and cultural phenomena, and it is undeniable. In my quest for a varied and meaningful list, I have studied hundreds of biographies. My criteria were twofold. In the couples I chose, both partners, either together or separately, accomplished something significant. And together they continue to act as role models in shaping the general public's perception of twentieth-century love.

Most of these people are "exceptional", but behind the myth lived figures of flesh and blood. In the pleasures and pains, sometimes extreme, often moving, that they lived through, we perceive qualities that cast light on our own love lives and help us to understand and move forward.

COUPLES OF EQUALS. The couples in this book were exceptional in a second sense. Most of them consisted of two individuals of equal merit, each eminent in their particular field, who greatly respected and assisted each other. Thus Albert Einstein saw in Mileva Marić a woman as strong and independent as himself, fully his equal, though force of circumstance quickly prised them apart.

History abounds with wonderfully devoted wives, but devoted husbands are somewhat rarer on the ground. The emergence of the "couple of equals" therefore seems to me one of the twentieth century's major advances in the area of relations between men and women. This concept was once unthinkable. Early in the twentieth century it was revolutionary, and it remains unacceptable in a majority of countries today. In the West it arose when it when men no longer dared present the inferiority of "woman" as an article of faith, "demonstrated" by the fall of Eve. How *could* such a notion arise while women were denied access to the language of erudition and were not permitted to study under the same conditions as men? Slowly and reluctantly, mind-sets and societies began to change. The process began in the mid-nineteenth century and owed much to the courage of pioneering women and the generosity of certain audacious men. As I have shown in *Women in the Twentieth Century*,[1] women have gradually been afforded the dignity of historical subjects and have progressed towards equal rights with men.

While writing this book on love, I again encountered some of the exceptional women whose lives and contribution to our culture I had related. I have broadened my knowledge of the men who counted in their lives and studied the nature and development of their relationships. The individuals who formed the couples that I have selected are, therefore, already familiar to me. I have read their books, seen or heard their works, reflected on their ideas. Where possible I have consulted archives, questioned witnesses and compared sources of information. It took considerable time to extract the essential from ever-expanding bibliographies and a degree of detach-

1. Florence Montreynaud, *Le XXe Siècle des femmes* (Nathan, 1989, republished 1995).

ment to escape the extremes of blind admiration and excessively judgemental attitudes. The end product is a "portrait" of each couple in their grandeur and their intimacy, emphasising their originality and their contribution to history or culture, alongside their daily lives, passions and torments.

WHO ARE THEY? The year in which each couple is presented marked a milestone in the history of their love (a meeting or a marriage) or the beginning of their collaboration, for example, a joint project of some kind. Their geographical origins are varied: twenty-six countries [2] from five continents, with another eighteen countries [3] in the right-hand column. The clear predominance of Western countries is a deliberate editorial choice. These couples used their talents in a wide range of mainly artistic activities: cinema, literature, photography, music, song, dance, theatre, art and sculpture, as well as business, journalism, politics, science and sport. Sometimes they worked together so closely that history refers to them collectively, as "the Curies" or "the Klarsfelds", for example. More often, each is known by their own name: Galina Vishnevskaya and Mstislav Rostropovich, Jean Tinguely and Niki de Saint-Phalle, Elsa Morante and Alberto Moravia, Kurt Weill and Lotte Lenya. In the title of each section, the uninterrupted stroke of the ampersand comes to symbolise their union. In Wagner's opera, Tristan and Isolde sing of the "tender little word *and*", which is the "love-tie" between the names of lovers.[4] Since the time of Adam and Eve, legends, myths and novels have placed the man's name first: David and Bathsheba, Theseus and Ariadne, Paul and Virginie. Rare examples of the reverse include the Egyptian deities Isis and Osiris and the American gangsters Bonnie & Clyde. In this volume, precedence alternates.

LOVE FOR LIFE? Some of these love stories lasted a few years, some for a lifetime. Some were stormy (Richard Burton and Liz Taylor being the best known of many) and a few were peaceful (Paul Newman and Joanne Woodward or Andrei Sakharov and Elena Bonner). Some confirmed the *Song of Songs*, and proved that "love is strong as death"; Benjamin Britten refused the ultimate accolade of burial in Westminster Abbey because he preferred to lie in the cemetery at Aldeburgh next to his lifelong companion Peter Pears.

Over half the couples in this book have something in common with their fictional or mythical predecessors: they are childless (three couples are too young for this judgement to be made[5]). The forty-five couples who are (or were) parents had an average of two children, though this is an average to which the seven Pitoëffs and five Roosevelts made a notable contribution. Some couples chose to remain childless in order to devote themselves to their work, such as Beatrice and Sidney Webb, others for health reasons, such as Leonard and Virginia Woolf. For others, childlessness was a matter of principle: Salvador Dalí declared that "every son of a genius is a cretin". Others suffered from infertility, such as Clark Gable and Carole Lombard and Katia Ricciarelli and Pippo Baudo.

A WHOLLY HUMAN RELATIONSHIP. Twenty-four centuries ago, Demosthenes defined the Greek male ideal: *hetairai* for conversation, wives for children, and prostitutes for pleasure. Nothing, however, is known about the female ideal; the voice of those who have been mute throughout history has only recently begun to be heard. In the twentieth century, more and more women have rejected the idea of defining their status in relation to a man, and some of them have renounced marriage or motherhood in order to pursue their own fulfilment. Demosthenes' rule is still followed by some men, but others (not just men) have broken new ground, seeking to live a full monogamous relationship at all levels.

Success in a couple is a rare and mysterious phenomenon. It is also difficult to appraise. Experience teaches one to be suspicious of celebrities posing as devoted lovers; posthumous publications often reveal what lay concealed behind the official façade. Nobody ever heard Elsa Triolet complain during her lifetime, yet the woman who inspired Louis Aragon's magnificent love poems considered herself "unloved".

Despite the spread of feminist ideas of justice and equality, our society is still dominated by sexual stereotypes that ensure the survival of traditional power relationships within the couple.

2. Argentina, Austria, Belgium, Bulgaria, Canada, Czechoslovakia, Denmark, France, Germany, Great Britain, Greece, India, Italy, Japan, Mexico, Norway, New Zealand, Philippines, Poland, Russia, South Africa, Spain, Sweden, Switzerland, USA, Yugoslavia.

3. Australia, Bolivia, Chile, China, Dubai, Egypt, Finland, Hungary, Iran, Ireland, Israel, Jordan, Latvia, Monaco, Netherlands, Palestine, Peru, Portugal.

4. Richard Wagner, *Tristan & Isoldo*, II, 2.

5. Bob Kersee and Jackie Joyner, Prince Naruhito and Princess Masako, Roberto Alagna and Angela Gheorgiu.

The pressure of such norms adds to the difficulties encountered by two people who try to lessen the tension or bridge the gulf between their individual callings and their love lives. When a woman emerges from her supporting role in the shadow of a great man, she has to improvise a status in society. A husband can find it very difficult to accept his wife's success, as the experience of Margarethe von Trotta and many other women artists testifies. Neither man nor woman can achieve full potential without help, reassurance and, above all, trust. Love can release unexpected resources and bestow the courage to explore one's intuitions and attain one's own standards. In a happy couple, the favourable image reflected in the other's eyes confirms and reassures.

♡ ♡ ♡

STORIES ABOUT LOVE. This volume examines nearly one hundred phenomena relating to love (one for each year): feelings, sexuality, morals, laws, and symbolic types. These sections trace the development of love in our time and show its new place in Western life. In each case an issue is explored. This may be an issue particular to the twentieth century (the effects of the Russian Revolution on love and marriage, or the controversial concept of "sexual liberation" in the sixties). Or it may be a subject which, though timeless, has a historical anchor point (the kiss in 1927, when the controversial lipstick Rouge Baiser was launched, or the love letter in 1942, when war was imposing separations). Different stages of love are described in different sections: meeting, falling in love, terms of endearment, the "first time", marriage or cohabitation, daily life, quarrels, the chance to "rebuild one's life", the death of a loved one, love in old age. The main sexual practices are described, along with sex education, sex surveys, Western and Eastern eroticism, aphrodisiacs, pleasure, tenderness and other such things.

6. Edgar Morin, *Les Stars*, Galilée, 1984.

Edgar Morin[6] has demonstrated that film stars serve to initiate their audiences in the techniques of love. Nathalie Heinich,[7] studying the structure of female identity in fiction, has analysed the different models with which women identify. I therefore felt that I should give a prominent place to the products of the Western imagination. Historically, love is inextricably linked with the novel. Literature, cinema and television illustrate certain characters from the myths of our culture: Pygmalion, Don Juan and Romeo and Juliet. These representations contribute to sentimental and sexual education, are the inspiration for techniques of seduction and serve as erotic role models where information is lacking. Many adolescents, partially or completely ignorant of these matters, were long tormented by unanswered questions, some serious, some utterly frivolous: why does the kiss of a starlet leave no trace of lipstick? What really happens after the kiss, during the fade-out, and before you see the slightly dishevelled lovers in bed?

7. Nathalie Heinich, *Etats de femme, L'identité féminine dans la fiction occidentale*, Gallimard, 1996.

DOMINANT ROLE MODELS. When one's knowledge of love is confined to fictional images, one can easily be taken in by a world of appearances in which bodies are perfect, stories fascinating and heroes unattainable. The influence of pornography in Western culture has led to the inclusion of a certain "dosage" of soft porn in popular cinema. With the exception of children's films, almost every film of the last thirty-odd years has included a sex scene; this is a cliché as inevitable as the sunset was in the traveller's tales of yesteryear. But what does it represent? What does it give us to see? The answer is, generally, a small self-centred world with no thought of contraception or AIDS; a man without fears or shortcomings, a woman who is always "ready"; and two orgasms going off in tandem like synchronised cuckoo-clocks. In short, a sexual relationship both clinical and magical. The norms thus imposed have two functions. On the one hand they reassure those who conform. On the other, their very existence suggests the possibility of transgression, and with it a new source of pleasure and stimulation.

Before they learn, in reaction, to build their lives from the materials of their own imagination, adolescents (more or less unwittingly) undergo a form of conditioning. Thus the characters in Yves Simon's novel *La Dérive des sentiments* "made loving gestures, but were all too well aware that they sometimes borrowed them from chapters in novels or sequences in films. And so they wondered whether everyone whispered borrowed words, as they did".[8] Is there anything left for lovers to invent? Long ago, Montaigne noted: "All we do is quote one another." Perhaps

8. Yves Simon, *La Dérive des sentiments*, Grasset, 1991.

the women poets of the early twentieth century, whose predecessors were few and largely unknown to them, were freer. The paradigm of love poetry was then the love of man for woman, and the woman poet was compelled to be original.

♡ ♡ ♡

MARRIAGE AS A SOCIAL REGULATION. Historians of mentalities have charted the rise of romantic love; before them, anthropologists showed how human groups ritualised sexual disorder in an attempt to control it. Methods of control were instituted to channel the subversive energies released by love and sexuality. The most important of these is marriage. In the West, before the twentieth century, what we call love was by no means the defining attribute of the married couple. In medieval courtly love, "there [could] be no love within marriage", whereas Tristan and Isolde were borne down by the toils of passion. Montaigne went further: "a good marriage, if any there be, refuses the company and condition of love".

In the past, the couple was essentially an economic partnership, and a "good marriage" was a marriage of expedience. In predominantly rural societies, where each generation was duty bound to transmit what it had inherited, the very foundations of the community were at stake in every marriage. Marriage was not a matter of personal choice, but of family strategy and economic interests. The need for solidarity between generations long overlay the notion of the couple as a distinct social entity possessed of its own intimacy; this notion emerged for the first time in the West in the twentieth century. Until then, marriage had been a contract negotiated by two families and signified or reinforced an alliance between two clans. This is still the case outside the West. Sometimes arranged as soon as the child is born, marriage procures a substantial dowry for the woman's family in Africa and for the man's in India. If the husband/wife brings no wealth, s/he must be healthy and industrious, for their new family relies on this influx of strength and stamina.

When the couple and the family were essential for personal survival, it was a weakness to remain unmarried; even today, in poor countries, childlessness implies poverty in old age. The assumption by the community of tasks that once fell to the family, such as education, has combined with the advent of social security to alter traditional family responsibilities. And the family has, in consequence, become less utilitarian in its significance.

MARRIAGE CAME BEFORE LOVE. To this day, when a wedding occurs in Korea, the Sudan or Bangladesh, in an immigrant community of Turks in Germany or of Pakistanis in Britain, the husband and wife have not, for the most part, met; they encounter each other for the first time on their wedding day. So, too, in the West in former times. The partner is chosen by others; love has nothing to do with it. Marital sex is associated much more with reproduction and carrying on the family line than with pleasure. Where divorce or renunciation are unacceptable, the marriage union is indissoluble. The conjugal relationship drew much of its solidity ("till death us do part" says the Christian ritual) from the gendering of domestic and other tasks, which inevitably enhanced the couple's mutual dependence. Arranged marriages are no barrier to love, as the (rare) example of the Duc de Saint-Simon shows. In 1695, at the age of twenty, he contracted an arranged marriage with a girl of seventeen. Their happiness lasted more than fifty years, and the couple was renowned for its perfect harmony. With time and luck, the marriage of convenience could give rise to a form of love, though the relationship seems to us more akin to friendship, since the approved model of married life implied mutual respect, physical modesty and emotional reserve. The wedding of Queen Victoria and Prince Albert in 1840 thus came to mark the dawn of new era, in which morality was exalted in marital bliss.

Under no circumstances could love be considered a reason for marriage, since it was perceived in the guise of passion, and passion might disturb the social order. In the Middle Ages, transgressors (the rebellious young, or the widow persisting with an incongruous choice) were severely punished or even banished.[9] Passion was a torrent liable, in either sense, to shift its bed. How could it form the basis for a lifelong union? "If you marry for love," the Provençal saying has it, "you will have good nights and bad days."

9. Hanna Zaremska, *Les Bannis au Moyen Age*, Aubier, 1996. In today's India: Catherine Weinberger-Thomas, *Cendres d'immortalité, La Crémation des veuves en Inde*, Seuil, 1996.

THE DAWN OF THE MARRIAGE OF LOVE. Today, in the West, the couple is based on love; marrying for love has become a norm that is gradually spreading to the rest of the world. Why? There has been a revolution of sensibility. Its consequence is a completely new phenomenon: a bond at once intimate and public between two individuals.

With urbanisation and the rise of the middle classes, each generation inherited less property (less land and equipment) and more culture (knowledge and skills). The importance of the marriage contract diminished in consequence. Strategic alliances between families declined, and there arose those individual aspirations which, having defined Western modernity for the last two hundred years, are now spreading to other cultures.

10. Edmund Leites, *The Puritan Conscience and Modern Sexuality*, 1986; *Passion and Happiness*, Cerf, 1989. Eric Fuchs, *Sexual Desire and Love: Origins and History of the Christian Ethic of Sexuality and Marriage*, 1990.

Protestantism was a factor in the rise of the marriage of love.[10] The compulsory celibacy of the Catholic priest reflected ill on sexuality even within the Catholic marriage. By contrast, the union between the Protestant minister and his wife, modelled on that of Martin Luther and Katharine von Bora, became a highly respected form of Christian life from the seventeenth century onwards. The English Puritans of Cromwell's milieu broke with tradition; their spiritual heirs, the founding fathers of the United States, followed in their footsteps. Both believed that sexual pleasure was important to the success of married life, which should be "the anteroom of heaven". "Choose thy love, love thy choice", was their motto. The purpose of marriage went beyond mutual help and encouragement; it was happiness, to which sensual love evidently contributed. This was a significant innovation.

LOVE COMPATIBLE WITH VIRILITY. In mid-eighteenth century Europe, it began to be accepted that mutual love could form the basis of marriage. Artists depicted the ideal of romantic love, and couples, sensitive to the "elective affinities" of Goethe's novel, were formed by personal decision. Simultaneous with this significant cultural change was a transformation in the masculine perception of love. Till then, love had been a weakness incompatible with virility. The conventions of chivalry contrasted the manly prowess of the hero with the softness and effeminacy of the lover. Men achieved status by demonstrating their valour on the battlefield. The difficulty of "reconciling" career and love, so central to our time, would have seemed incomprehensible; military glory was a self-evident duty.

Respectable women were raised in ignorance of things bodily and made a cult of virginity. In marriage, they had to submit to the man's desire, and if they were frustrated, they could do little but dream of love. Female adultery was considered an intolerable blow to a husband's honour and severely condemned, while the infidelities of men were largely tolerated. But in the second half of the nineteenth century, voices were raised against the "double standards" that allowed men everything and women nothing. The emancipation of women was then just beginning and highlighted the injustice of the situation. Later on, marital love gained in importance, adultery was seen as a breach of trust rather an attaint to honour, and mutual fidelity became possible.

THE TRIUMPH OF THE MARRIAGE OF LOVE. Progress was slow, but began to accelerate at the beginning of the twentieth century. A close relationship within marriage became the priority, and marriage based on mutual feeling, "the marriage of inclination", became the norm.

The development of the marriage of love was favoured by the institution of divorce. This is not the paradox it seems. Since the contract could be broken, one no longer had to believe in "marrying for ever" and the meaning of the undertaking altered. On the one hand, Western countries, despite Catholic resistance, legalised divorce; the Naquet Law in France dates from 1884, while in Ireland divorce law reached the statute book only in 1997. On the other, there arose a further component of secular modern life: the civil marriage, an agreement between two individuals, revocable by definition, and devoid of transcendental overtones.

Did the arranged marriage sink, like so many other traditional values, in the great shipwreck of the First World War? In the twenties, marriages of expediency began to seem immoral, marriages of convenience mediocre, and it was no longer a matter of pride if one failed to find a partner by one's own efforts. Love, that redoubtable passion whose presence in society was tolerated only in regulated forms, was promoted in a few short decades to the status of *sine qua non* of a successful marriage. This abrupt reversal of tradition was reflected in changing feelings about the marital or family home. Throughout the twentieth century, it has increasingly been perceived as a refuge from the implacable outside world and, in particular, as the place where emotions receive their expression. With the enhanced value accorded to intimacy, a person's love life has increasingly become a private affair. When a man and woman are allowed to choose freely, their mutual commitment is strictly their own business, even if a wedding subsequently makes it official and public. This new entity is increasingly independent of the extended family and rests on economic foundations of its own making. Simultaneous with the rise of individualism and the perception of the couple as a refuge, we have seen a new trend: society and the state are increasingly reluctant to intervene in private life. The combined effect of these two phenomena goes some way towards explaining the spectacular fall in Western marriage statistics during the last third of the Twentieth Century.[11]

11. Sabine Chalvon Demersay, "L'Union libre", in *Encyclopedia Universalis*, Universalia 1995, pp 408–411.

EXPORTING THE "MARRIAGE OF LOVE". Many Africans and Asians still see in "Western" manifestations of love a weakness that they would be ashamed to emulate; for them, "love sick" is a state that smacks of sorcery. In societies where it is important not to "lose face", everyone is required to master their emotions, and saying "I love you", holding hands or kissing in public demonstrates a deplorable want of modesty.

In Japan, where "I love you" essentially means "I desire you", the advent of the marriage of love has nonetheless wrought a change in the status of sex. A new generation in other parts of the world is following in the footsteps of Europe and North America, asserting its right to decide its own destiny rather than allow the family to prescribe it. "Down with arranged marriages! Long live romantic love!" cry the young in China, where Maoist repression is being overthrown in an emotional and sexual revolution. "This," they argue, "is not Westernisation, but modernisation." For the young people of South Korea, another country undergoing a process of transformation, it is "democratisation". The traditional family provides for burdensome vertical relationships founded on filial piety. Young Koreans are seeking to replace it (or combine it) with the horizontal relationship of the couple, which they perceive as liberating. While older people criticise their "individualism", young people are expressing a desire for successful marriages based on love, communication, and a more equitable sharing out of responsibilities.

THE SACRALISATION OF PROFANE LOVE. In a convergent development, caused by the rise in secularism and the decline in religious faith, love is increasingly dissociated from things sacred. In the past, Christians saw human love as a humble reflection of God's all-embracing love; today it is more and more an end in itself. This process of humanisation has contributed to the advent of the modern love-centred lifestyle. But this is accompanied by a spiritual investment; love has become the great prize in the quest for meaning, as if it were sufficient to justify life as a whole. Popular culture associates love with the sentimental delights of paradise on earth, symbolised by the honeymoon in a dream location. If the consequence is an unhappy housewife, she shall seek consolation in dreams of love. This is a revolution unprecedented in human history. Since time immemorial, love has been elbowed to the edge of society; now, in the twentieth century, it has been raised to the status of a universal myth. Now it is the great thing in life, particularly for women, and a prerequisite of personal success. Collectively, it is turning into an ideology with overtones of religion: at a time when Christianity is in free fall and traditional religious values are losing their appeal, the fervour once invested in faith seems to have been channelled into expectations of love. In love is vested an almost messianic hope. If "Prince Charming" or "Miss Right" are the new saviours, whose love "fulfils" us by finally giving a meaning to our lives, are we not becoming our own gods? Are we not expecting too much of love? An entire culture labours to convince us of its omnipotent magic. "Without love, one is nothing," sings Edith Piaf. But does it follow that, *with* love, we can be anything and everything?

A SHAKY FOUNDATION. Gambling on happiness and a freely chosen partner, modern Western couples seek to build their union on a feeling. But is this not a case of building on sand? The traditional union was associated with duration and even eternity, while love, though it comprises moments of great intensity, is a precarious state. "I shall always love you" we promise, but who can guarantee the permanence of their love? Feelings are dependent upon the psychological and moral development of each of the partners and are revealed by experience and maturity for what they are: unstable and sometimes short-lived. They are often weaker than reason, duty or interest, the "cement" of traditional unions, and weaker again when not consolidated by social standards. Since their parents have not made the decision for them, husband and wife have only themselves to blame if their love does not last. They choose each other and marry or live together because they love each other. If love fades or sexual attraction wanes, should the couple then separate? If they don't, on what is the union now based?

Despite the gloomy predictions, the alliance of love and marriage, so long frowned on as "unnatural", has not brought about any major social disasters. The new convention governing reasons for getting married excludes considerations of expediency, but do they never play a part (conscious or not) in the choice of marriage partner? Even if one chooses to believe that Cupid's arrow strikes at random, and that a prince may marry a shepherdess, are not social constraints generally internalised? Modern love is construed as disinterested; doomed to proclaim its freedom from the shackles of expediency, it can find its justification only in itself. "Because it was him, because it was me": Montaigne's explanation for his friendship with La Boétie, which we would now call love, has the mysterious resonance of the obvious.

THE RIGHTS OF MAN OR HUMAN RIGHTS? In the twentieth century, the marriage of love has become one of the spheres in which personal freedom is exercised. As such, it has joined the ranks of human rights. But for a long time this right was confined to men. The ideal of two kinds of freedom consisting together in equality was legally untenable while the law deemed the married woman a minor (until 1938 in France) or confined suffrage rights to men (until 1971 in Switzerland). And the new freedom arose in a profoundly inequitable society with highly gendered roles. The prevailing ideology of love conditioned women to sacrifice themselves in its name and devote themselves to husband and child. "What is your preferred occupation?" Proust is the only man ever to have replied "loving". Many of the women of his time viewed love as a semi-mystical revelation, which contributed to the perpetuation of "double standards". Marriage afforded them a public identity *via* their husband's, but it repressed their own; Miss Mary Smith lost, in fact, if not in law, her family and even her Christian name by becoming Mrs John Jones.

12. Norbert Elias, *The Changing Balance of Power Between the Sexes, Theory, Culture and Society,* Vol 4, No. 2–3, June 1987 (quoted by Nathalie Heinich, op cit).

THE CONTRACEPTIVE REVOLUTION. According to Norbert Elias,[12] who analysed "the process of civilisation", the greatest revolution in Western society during twentieth-century history was the acquisition by women of an autonomous identity, separate from that of father or husband. This emancipation, associated with the figure of the free woman, can be partly explained by the increased independence of women, who in the twentieth century have been able to study and exercise professions. Modern female contraception has also played a decisive role. The very widespread availability of the pill and coil is one of the most important events in the history of love, indeed in history.

The two world wars were not as influential as one might believe. The images of heroic women and mixed comradeship faded, and relations between men and women slipped back to earlier norms. After such vast upheavals, the traditional roles seemed somehow reassuring. Almost everywhere in the West, the turning point occurred between 1965 and 1975. This was not an overnight change perceptible to the people of the time, but the harbinger of social transformation. The major statistical trends began to shift: births and marriages decreased, divorces increased, premarital sex became widespread, and people married and had their first child later. These changes were followed, in some countries later than others, by laws on contraception, divorce, abortion, marriage, the sharing of parental responsibilities, the changing of a woman's name and so on, which brought law into line with life. This great process remains incomplete today. It was accompanied by a restructuring and re-evaluation of relations between men and women, while the couple itself mutated to become part of an increasingly complex and mobile society.

The last thirty-odd years, therefore, have seen a revolution unprecedented in the history of humankind whose consequences are still unclear. In most Western countries, modern contraception and legal abortion have given women rights over their own bodies. New methods make it possible for young women to control their own destinies. They, no less than their male contemporaries, can look forward to the future; they can choose their lifestyles free of the inhibitions that restrained their mothers and grandmothers. Above all, they are free from the fear of unwanted pregnancy, which has weighed throughout history on all fertile women.

VIOLENCE AGAINST WOMEN. In traditional societies, a woman's body does not belong to her. The family guards the daughter's virginity; after marrying, she becomes her husband's property. Every year, two million young girls are mutilated by clitoral circumcision, which not only deprives them of sexual pleasure for the duration of their lives but also causes physical and mental suffering and can lead to serious health problems. In the West, violence by men towards women remains very widespread and was long deemed socially acceptable. In cases of rape, incest, unwanted pregnancy, cruelty in marriage or sexual harassment at work, the blame fell on the woman; she was more sinner ("she was asking for it!") than victim and had to bear the consequences alone. This hate-filled, aggressive chauvinism helped to organise and perpetuate male superiority. Thanks to feminists of both sexes, it has gradually been destabilised, analysed and opposed; in our day, public opinion seems less inclined to tolerate it. But it remains full of life, ready to surface at the slightest incident. Under the cover of fantasy, in pornography and in the hands of certain *agents provocateurs* who protest their artistic licence, it still enjoys free rein.

Traditional sexual behaviour has also been challenged. Those who make the challenge – mainly women – seek alternative models which aim to eliminate the increasing eroticisation of men's violence and women's passivity. What makes men's urges irresistible when women can "master" theirs? Until the eighteenth century, the contrary view prevailed: a woman's desires were considered insatiable. During this period, thousands of European women were condemned for their "satanic" sexuality and burnt as witches[13]. By contrast, a spell – a knot tied in lace – was enough to upset the fragile mechanics of the male erection, and aphrodisiacs, then as now, were in great demand.

13. Guy Bechtel, *La Sorcière en l'Occident, La Destruction de la sorcellerie en Europe des origines aux grands bûchers*, Plon, 1997.

THE "RIGHT" TO PLEASURE. Today, wherever the marriage of love has triumphed, one of the professed aims of the couple is the pleasure and happiness of both partners. The voiceless women of the past were resigned to submission; when their descendants finally made themselves heard, the aspirations that they voiced were unheard of. When female pleasure became legitimate, frustrated wives were finally able to express their grievances. Norbert Elias argues that women's demands have always been the driving force in the history of the couple.

Sexual understanding has thus become one of the conditions of conjugal harmony, and sexual incompatibility can justify a separation. For centuries, sexuality was associated with the devil. Now the pendulum has swung in the other direction, and it is glorified and promoted in the West as the means to all kinds of self-discovery. On the one hand we have neurotically repressive religious fundamentalists, on the other pseudo-libertarians yearning for a new May 1968; the world as reflected in the media, public debate and advertising presents a confusing spectacle. What anguish lies behind this collective preoccupation, this obsession, with sexuality?

The more public the manifestations of sex, the shyer love becomes. Perhaps we are witnessing the end of a process: the ebbing away of the myth of love that prevailed immediately after the Second World War and has gradually been eroded as its dangers became obvious. In the fifties, particularly in the United States, the excessive idealisation of love led to a reliance upon the life of the couple that was ultimately stifling. The feminist Betty Friedan analysed it, inveighing against the "feminine mystique" by which women were imprisoned in middle-class homes, while the novelist Albert Cohen waxed lyrical about it in *The Lord's Beautiful One*. The conclusion is obvious: lacking the oxygen of contact with the outside world, relations within a couple will wither away. The romantic fusion does not lead to a creative life: we can witness an extreme case in the suicide pacts of exalted nineteenth-century lovers.

14. Julia Kristeva in Augustin Barbara, *Les Couples mixtes*, Bayard, 1993.

15. Interview with Philippe Sollers and Julia Kristeva by Philippe Lançon, *Libération*, 5 August 1996.

An egalitarian "We". Living "for" or "through" another is written into the tradition of self-abnegation that has for so long stood between women and fulfilment. At present we tend instead towards Julia Kristeva's view of the couple as "the meeting of two freedoms",[14] and perceive love in the terms given by her husband Philippe Sollers, as "the full recognition of the other as other".[15] New models are being essayed, in which each partner lives "with" the other while maintaining their own independence and living "for" themselves too; this can mean living separately. Such was the life lived by Jean-Paul Sartre and Simone de Beauvoir, who deemed themselves no less authentically a couple for the fact that they never breakfasted together. What right have we to judge otherwise? A couple needs only its own authority.

Via negotiation and individual resistance, the modern dialogue of love is building new forms of relationships; they are more consensual and inflect the balance of power in new ways. Thanks to feminism, women have more or less established their rights, and though they have not attained anything like true equality with men, they are asserting themselves and their voices are more often heard. The "we" of a modern couple has a richer, more diverse and no doubt less stable meaning than in the time of "Mr and Mrs John Jones". The law has abolished the "head of the household", and the age of "partners" has begun. Its ideal is the trust and freedom of perpetual dialogue.

Like any cultural and social phenomenon, love and the couple are continuously evolving. Measuring the considerable distance travelled to date, believers in human progress count on egalitarian relationships tomorrow or the day after. The couple of the future already exists. It was defined in 1969 by a Swedish minister (the Nordic countries are the pioneers in this field) as "the voluntary union of two independent people". One might expect its foundations to be lucidity and equality, but its watchword is, more than ever, love.

As long as ye both shall live? Another phenomenon particular to the twentieth century is the staggering increase in life expectancy: it reached fifty years in 1900 and has risen by about thirty years over the course of this century. The possible duration of a marriage has therefore increased considerably, though the incidence of separations makes golden weddings a rarity still. Longevity has nonetheless increased the number of elderly couples, who are enjoying a higher publicity profile now that the taboo on love in the autumn of life is lifting. Love is possible at any age, though the fact is not widely acknowledged.

"Till death us do part" runs the marriage service; but today it is more often life, with its jolts and switchbacks, that parts us. Late-twentieth-century Westerners are more aware of this when they make their commitment; they know that love is less and less often "for life". But this remains the dream of many, who, like the Surrealists, celebrate love as "the great promise that survives being kept". The wisest, or the most disabused, prefer to talk about "routes that coincide".

And yet the myth of the "great love of one's life" survives, propped up by a culture of mass sentimentality breeding mad hopes, childish dreams, and fantastic plans. People exaggerate their passion and convince themselves that it will last. If it could, would it still be called passion? Too much is expected of love, and more is required of the couple than it can bestow. Those who demand too much of married life are ill-equipped to overcome its first trials and disappointments. Then, when trials come, instead of striving to surmount them, the couple splits up, and each goes in quest of another, of the right, the perfect lover, the one who, unlike the unsatisfactory incumbent, will answer every expectation ...

"I rejoice that you exist." The poet Rainer Maria Rilke wrote these words at the beginning of the century. Today, the philosopher André Comte-Sponville analyses them thus: "To love, one must be ready to accept two forms of solitude: one's own and that of the other. To love is to say: 'yes, I love you as you are'. Even if you do not fulfil my dreams and hopes, the reality of you rejoices me more than my dreams".[16]

16. André Comte-Sponville, interview in *Marie-Claire*, September 1994.

One cannot give love unless one has received it as a child and learnt to love oneself. The earliest caresses, endearments and tenderness sow the seeds. Later meetings, attachments and complicities bring forth flower and fruit.

There is only one love. Filial or parental, brotherly or sisterly, familial or friendly, sexual or emotional, passionate or reasoned, love for a woman or for a man, for the other, for God or humanity, for the living or the dead, for abstract things such as country and nature, or for words, animals and things, love is one; all love is born of the zest for life. All love helps us to live. Loving, according to Alain, "is finding one's riches outside oneself".[17] Loving also means making room within oneself to welcome the other. Loving is knowing (the word used in the Bible). It is waking each day to a renewed sense of wonder.

In Italian, one way of saying "I love you" is "I wish you well". As André Comte-Sponville writes, with reference to Spinoza: "Love is a joy that accompanies the idea of its cause. 'Your existence fills me with joy', is a declaration of love that expects nothing from the other person".[18] I love you; I do not worship you, because you are not a god. But I cherish you as a human being; no other body moves me as your body does. You dwell in my thoughts, but in the most intimate embrace I neither possess you nor belong to you. A foretaste of eternity, infinity at the heart of the finite, the love that I bear you leaves intact the mystery that is you.

Nothing can ever be taken for granted. If we are not inured to happiness, if the sense of wonder has not deserted us, we may hope to attain the secret that grants joy to the body and peace to the soul.

FLORENCE MONTREYNAUD

17. Alain, *Elements de philosophie*.

18. André Comte-Sponville, *Petit Traité des grandes vertus*, PUF, 1995.

Albert & Elisabeth of Belgium

A love match: this popular royal couple found fame during the Great War.

A keen sportsman, Albert of Belgium had a passion for speed. Elisabeth loved to accompany him (above: in the Bois de la Cambre, in Brussels).

FACING PAGE
The queen was very interested in the arts. In 1934, with one of the first cameras for amateur photographers.

On 2 October 1900, Elisabeth, a young fragile-looking girl glowing with happiness, the daughter of the Duke of Bavaria, married Prince Albert of Belgium in Munich. He was the nephew of Léopold II, an unpopular king without a male heir, and was preparing to succeed him. She was twenty-four; he was twenty-five. The couple first met in 1897 in Paris. Their wedding was a true European society event. The newspapers described the bride's satin dress and its four-metre-long train beaded with myrtle bouquets (a symbol of bliss) in great detail. The couple made a jubilant "Triumphal Entry" into Brussels. The first appearance of the smiling princess delighted the Belgians, who never ceased to show her and her husband affection and respect.

The early years of the marriage were content. A son, Leopold, was born in 1901, followed by Charles in 1903 and their daughter Marie-José in 1906. Prince Albert was a quiet, shy, cultured, multilingual man. From adolescence he had been fascinated by automobiles, speed, and machines in general. A keen sportsman, he also became an experienced mountaineer. Princess Elisabeth, an excellent musician, surrounded herself with artists such as the musician Eugène Isaÿe, the tenor Ernest Van Dyck and the poet Emile Verhaeren. She showed a dignity and refinement that won the praise of all who

met her. The happy couple delighted in each other's company and enjoyed long walks together.

AN IDEAL ROYAL COUPLE. When Albert, in the spring of 1909, travelled to the Congo, which the Belgian Parliament had just voted to annex, he remembered to bring back some bird feathers to trim his wife's hats. When he returned, the princess, who was anxious to see him, surprised him by waiting for him in Tenerife.

Soon after that, Léopold II died and Albert I ascended the throne on 23 December 1909.

Albert and Elisabeth made an ideal royal couple. They were intelligent and brave, and aware of their responsibilities; they were interested in modern things and also sensitive to public opinion. They organised competitions to encourage bird breeding and horticulture. The queen brought art to the Laeken Palace and set up numerous well-known medical, social, and artistic foundations. Dinners they hosted brought together eminent scientists such as Marie Curie, Paul Langevin, Albert Einstein, Ernest Rutherford, and Maurice de Broglie, and writers such as Paul Claudel and Jean Cocteau.

On 1 August 1914, the queen translated into German the king's last letter to the Emperor Wilhelm II in favour of peace. War, however, broke out and after sending their children to England, the couple both enlisted. They spent the four years of war in the part of Belgium that remained free, around the Yser River. Albert, who soon gained the nickname the "Knight King", took command of the Belgian Army and spent his time at the front, taking care to preserve his soldiers' lives. The queen organised a network of ambulances to evacuate the wounded, saving many thousands of soldiers. Elisabeth, who had often helped her father in his clinic in Bavaria, set up one hospital in the Royal Palace in Brussels and then another in the Hôtel Océan, in La Panne, a fishing village on the North Sea coast where the couple had a villa. She helped with the operations and gently dressed wounds, taking time to spare a kind word for everyone. The 20,000 wounded soldiers who were cared for in the Hôtel Océan remembered her slender frame and periwinkle-blue eyes with tenderness. And thanks to her, the artistic life was not neglected at the front.

In July 1918, at an invitation from George V of Great Britain, the intrepid Belgian royal couple caused a sensation by landing at Folkestone from Calais in two seaplanes. The end of the war provided the opportunity for another triumphal entry into Brussels, on horseback, on 22 November 1918. The country now had to be rebuilt. The prestige which the "Knight King" enjoyed allowed him to overcome the political divisions and pass the law on votes for all men. The king and queen were very popular and their photograph had pride of place in every home. They travelled widely and visited the United States and Brazil. In 1923 the queen was in Luxor with her eldest son when the tomb of Pharaoh Tut-Ankh-Amen was opened. She then visited the Valley of Kings with the egyptologist Jean Cappart, to whom Albert slipped this message before the departure: "If there is anything dangerous, don't tell the queen; she will want to go there." In 1925 the couple celebrated their silver wedding anniversary in the Indies and the queen, who regretted not having visited the Congo, travelled there in 1928.

ALWAYS HAPPY, ALWAYS TOGETHER. Throughout 1930, Belgium celebrated its centenary with great ceremony and the king and queen, happy as ever, went everywhere together. They made one more long trip, to the Middle East in 1933. But tragedy struck the following year: on 17 February 1934, at Marche-les-Dames, Albert, aged fifty-nine, suffered a fatal fall while climbing. Belgium mourned its king and gave him a grand funeral. The throne was ascended by Léopold III, who had married Princess Astrid of Sweden.

The Queen was inconsolable, but another tragedy brought her out of her solitude, when in May 1935 Queen Astrid died in an automobile accident. Léopold and his three children came to live at the Laeken Palace. Elisabeth once again opened her piano, got out her violin, invited artists into her home, and organised children's festivals. By the Second World War she was President of Honour of the Red Cross. Many times the queen intervened with the occupying forces on behalf of imprisoned Belgians and Jews under threat of deportation. After the war she took up her wide range of activities again, re-launched the music competition that bore her name and continued to travel with just as much pleasure. At sixty-nine she visited Poland, and at eighty-two she went back to the Congo and also visited the Soviet Union, getting as far as Uzbekistan; she then celebrated Easter in Palestine. At the age of eighty-five, accompanied by her daughter Marie-José, she realised her final dream, which was to visit China. She died on 23 November 1965. Her memory lives on in the famous Reine-Elisabeth music competition.

AUSTRIA-HUNGARY. **Archduke François-Ferdinand of Habsburg, nephew of Emperor François-Joseph and heir to the throne, marries Countess Sophie Chotek. Solemnised with a woman of a lesser rank, this morganatic marriage (the adjective derives from a German word meaning "morning gift") meant that neither the Archduchess nor her children could enjoy dynastic rights. It was the assassination of the Archduke and his wife in Sarajevo on 28 June 1914 that triggered the First World War.**

FRANCE. **The poet Lucie Delarue marries the Egyptian Doctor Joseph-Charles Mardrus. They had met less than one month previously and on the following day, he asked her father for her hand in marriage. He had translated the *Thousand and One Nights* into French, and the first volume had just been published. According to his wishes, the couple wed dressed as cyclists, wearing tartan jackets and boaters. The wedding night traumatised the young woman, who from then on saw "the brutal expression of an instinct" in male sexuality. She flatly refused to bear children and enjoyed celebrated love affairs with women, the first of these being...**

IMAGES
The Lovers' Postcards

Words and pictures: using appropriate stereotypes to convey emotions.

"Your soul and my soul share the same ardour of love. May a tender kiss unite our hearts from above." "Our hearts' leaning together delights us / And sweet happiness with joy unites us." These are two messages of love from a vast number which accompanied a literary genre that flourished from 1900 onwards: the lovers' postcard. In a somewhat stilted formula these quintessential expressions of love took root in popular Western society, despite the diversity of cultures, and allowed lovers to express their sentiments in a recognized and acceptable way.

Lucien loves Marie-Louise, who returns his love in good measure. Otto is sighing for Eva, John dreams of nothing but Maggie. But how could one express to the other the feelings that set the heart a-beating, in words that please? In Paris, Berlin or London, in the cities or in the villages, the embarrassment felt when the time came to declare one's love was identical. The young man, of course, had to make the first move. Rare indeed were those lovers who could write letters (cf. p. 202). To express one's love would

be to move too quickly. The course of correspondence must pass through stages, as the tradition of love required. The man in love, often shy, did not rush his lady friend; and when he was away from her, postcards, with their wide range of sentiments, messages and colours, allowed him to carry on his conversation in a way that everyone could see. First there were cards that expressed the hope that the love may be allowed to grow though a meeting; then a second type of message declared budding love, a third confessed passionate love, and finally (why not?) a marriage proposal. Words expressed the whole of this process, reinforcing the figures' feelings and the symbols that surrounded them, such as flowers with hidden meaning, like "heart's-ease" and "forget-me-not".

But why this detour, when pre-viously seduction had progressed without any help other than public holidays and individual people's imaginations? Three social aspects which combined at the beginning of this century can explain the development of lovers' postcards: the increased use of the postcard as a means of communication, urbanisation in the Western world, and the resulting decrease in traditional festivals which had provided young people with opportunities to get together.

FROM THE ROMANTIC ENGRAVING TO THE POSTCARD. The illustrated postcard was first produced in Austria in 1869 and subsequently spread right across Europe. In France the World Exhibition, held in Paris in 1900, and the First World War, sped up its development (it became less "proper" and more "risqué", and was circulated under cover). It was at the turn of the century that the first lovers' postcards appeared, some with a few lines of verse. Before spreading across Europe and the United States, it seems this type of communication first appeared in France. It's hardly surprising that lovers' epistles should develop so dramatically in a country that boasted of its legendary skill in the art of "love" and preserved countless examples of romantic art within their homes. However, millions of these post-

cards were issued in countries that had very different iconographic and romantic traditions, such as post-Victorian England, the Puritan United States and even Germany. Adapted to cater for sensitivity and local traditions, they certainly show the diversity of moral standards which existed before the progressive standardisation of Western behaviour began.

AN IDEAL PICTURE OF LOVE AND LOVERS. Urbanization affected the whole of Europe. Festivals such as May Day or Harvest-home were not the same in the cities. Meetings at popular gatherings were now arranged by friends or colleagues, particularly at dances, and couples came together without having rubbed shoulders since childhood. To please each other, they had to play on an illusion: the figure in boater and jacket on the postcards was an image that the man in love wished to convey to the young lady whom he desired. She would be flattered by this portrayal of a couple. She would not dare to show

herself in "real life" in the way in which she was projected on the cards, any more than he would; but she could dream of the carefully codified and "proper" poses of false shyness, seductive smile, and half-pensive, half-naughty expression. All these images were "correct" for the period in question, despite a few innocent kisses being shown.

Here are lovers transformed into smartly-dressed modern-day heroes, exchanging their feelings through words of love from serialised novels (popular literature developed to educate at the same time as to entertain) or from speech boxes in silent films. On the postcards a young man and a young lady, well-dressed and with neat hair, look at each other and smile. They show to the world at large the tilt of their heads, their gentle swaying walk, their abandonment to their tender feelings. Their stereotypical poses and expressions, far from spoiling the message, actually enhance it. This is because they have nothing in common with the people whose "sweet nothings" they

are conveying, because they belong to a world which is unreal, as well as to the world of love. They may seem flat and banal; on the vast number of cards sent the themes and figures change little, as indeed do the poetic pictures and sentences. In reality, lovers did not have the vocabulary needed to speak of love, which was all the more reason for writing. Ready-written messages loosened their tongue-tied awkwardness. By appealing to a language which was not their own and which seemed to them carefully chosen, by borrowing for an instant the rather stiff image of the figures, they overcame their shyness and gained a little confidence in themselves, without betraying their feelings.

Lovers' postcards lasted until the 1870s, and were then replaced by St Valentine's cards, sent on 14 February, an Anglo-Saxon tradition that developed in the West during the twentieth century (cf. p. 248).

1900

... the rich American Natalie Barney in 1903. Mardrus, tired of being the "Prince Consort" of a fashionable woman, left her in 1914 and asked for a divorce, but he continued to help and protect her.

♡ ♡ ♡

IV _ Et pour vous acquitter, en payant votre écot
Que chacune de vous me permette un bécot!

Anton Chekhov & Olga Knipper

When the great Russian writer finally found love, he had only six years to live.

With his pince-nez and pepper-and-salt goatee beard, Anton Pavlovich Chekhov charmed women with his humour, weakness, and melancholy. But if one of them asked him to make a commitment, he shied away: "Sure, I want to get married," he wrote to a friend, "but give me a wife who isn't on the horizon of my life every day, like the moon, with her in Moscow and me in the countryside." The Russian writer's notebooks, novels, and letters are full of misogynous, but also misanthropic writings. "Women take away men's youth, but they're not getting mine." "If you are frightened of loneliness, don't get married!" "The world is beautiful. One thing only is bad: us." There are many testimonies to his coldness, which

FACING PAGE
Chekhov and Olga Knipper surrounded by their friends from the Moscow Arts Theatre in 1899. Amongst them are the directors Stanislavski and Meyerhold.

was "like an unchanging crystal inside him". It was said that he "could be kind and generous without loving, tender and caring without attaching himself".

What transformed Chekhov, the most important playwright of his time, was a talented actress of German origin, Olga Leonardovna Knipper, who took the principal role in his last plays. He was forty-one and she ten years younger when they married in secret on 25 May 1901, after a two-year relationship.

AN ACTRESS WHO INSPIRED HIM. Theatre had been a passion for Chekhov since his poverty-stricken and loveless childhood at Taganrog near the Sea of Azov. He became a doctor, and his novels, tales, and short stories gradually became very successful, although his first plays were failures. Discouraged by the failure of *The Seagull* at St Petersburg in 1896, he hid himself away in his country retreat.

It was here that the Moscow Arts Theatre Troupe, with its director Konstantin Stanislavski, suggested that he take up the play again. The Moscow première, on 17 October 1898, was a great success. The part of Irina Arkadina was played by Olga Knipper, a dark-haired actress with an expressive face, a penetrating look, and thin lips. Chekhov stated that he was captivated by "her voice, her dignity, her sincerity". It was a great shock to him to discover, at his age, a passionate love for this brilliant, intelligent woman, who was bursting with health and vitality.

As doctors had advised him to move to the dry, mild climate of the Crimea, Chekhov decided to set up in Yalta, where he had a house built. It was here that he wrote his last works, plays and long novels. He was in love with an actress, and he wrote roles for her. On 26 October 1899, she created the part of Elena Andreevna in *Uncle Vanya*, and on 31 January 1901, the role of Masha in *The Three Sisters*.

"My health has become that of an old man," he wrote to her. "It means that with me you will receive not a husband, but a grandfather." He knew he was doomed. "I'm terribly afraid of marriage ceremonies," he stated, "the customary celebrations, and the champagne you have to hold in your hand with a vacant smile on your face." To mystify their friends and acquaintances, they both organised a great dinner at which they did not appear, getting married instead at the time. They then went to a strange destination for a honeymoon: a sanatorium near the town of Ufa, where Chekhov underwent a course of treatment. He had been spitting blood; tuberculosis, which had already carried off his brother, had been troubling him since 1885.

SEPARATED BY ILLNESS. After the holiday at the sanatorium, the couple returned to Yalta but as soon as the season started, Olga had to return to the theatre and they did not meet again until summertime. Being married did not mean that they lived together, at least in winter, because the harsh Moscow climate would then have been fatal to the sick man and Olga Knipper had no intention of refusing a role to stay with him in the Crimea. "I would be terribly bored," she wrote to him, "I would pace up and down the room and nag, nag, nag." Chekhov, who had previously wanted to marry a "distant friend", complained about his loneliness: "I am bored, terribly bored, without you ..." He spent his time writing *The Cherry Orchard* for her, a play in which the heroine's first name is Lyubov, a word which means "love".

He was envious of her freshness, her spirit, her liveliness, her health. He desperately wanted a child, but he was not to experience that joy. When she wrote to him of her sorrow at neglecting him, he supported her, forgave her, comforted her: "Not once since our wedding have I criticised you over your acting; on the contrary, I have rejoiced that you are working, that you have an aim in life. ... It is not your fault that you can't live with me in wintertime. On the contrary, we both

make very suitable marriage partners, because neither of us prevents the other from working." And further: "If we are not together, it is neither my fault nor yours, but that of the devil who sowed germs in me and a love of art in you." Love, a deep and dispassionate love, changed him and also altered his view of the world. In the short story *Gooseberries*, one of his last masterpieces, he wrote: "If our life has a meaning, an aim, it has nothing to do with our personal happiness, but something wiser and greater."

Although it was winter, the doctors allowed him to leave Yalta, and he once again found the theatre, and his wife. The actress gave a triumphant performance in *The Cherry Orchard*, the première of which took place on 17 January 1904. In May, seeing that he was losing the fight, she accompanied him to Germany, to the spa town of Badenweiler in the Black Forest, where he died on 2 July. Olga Knipper-Chekhova lived until 1959 and remained the principal actress of the Arts Theatre for the rest of her life, acting in plays by Gorki, Ibsen and of course her late husband. In 1943 she acted for the last time the role of Lyubov Ranyevskaya, which she had created thirty-nine years before, in *The Cherry Orchard*. "To play Chekhov," she said, "you have to love human beings as he did, with all their faults and weaknesses."

1901

UNITED STATES. **The Union of Christian Women for Temperance launches a national campaign against kissing on the lips, which was prohibited on the grounds that it was very unhygienic. The President of the Union, Dr Anna Hatfield, recommended that if this "barbaric and unhealthy" practice could not be avoided, then at least the mouth should be washed out thoroughly with disinfectant beforehand.**

The Marriage Ceremony

The rituals of marriage combine tradition and modernity. Recent additions are photographs, the white dress, and the honeymoon.

The first wedding-gift list appeared in the United States in 1901. The idea, credited to Herman Winkle, a china shop salesman in Rochester, Minnesota, was taken up by other businesses and developed by department stores during the thirties. Sending out their list allowed the future husband and wife to set up their home according to their taste. Another typically American custom was for friends and parents of the future bride to give her a "wedding shower" of small presents that could all be used in the bathroom or kitchen.

The wedding present display, a common practice in Western middle classes, satisfied the curiosity of the wedding guests and others invited to view. Traditionally, a wedding has been a time of consumption as well as consummation, a break with all that is everyday. Bringing together two family groups rather than just two individuals, the wedding is the business of the girl's family who "give her away" to another family. The ceremony, particular to every culture, solemnises the young girl's (occasionally the young man's) transfer to another home, complete with trousseau, household linen and clothes, and a dowry. The public celebration underlines the importance of the commitment, which is unbreakable in countries where divorce is not recognised.

The day before, the groom bids farewell to his bachelorhood with his friends, who go out of their way to get him drunk and bait him. In several countries, this custom endures for both future bride and groom; in Sweden both are paraded blindfold by their same-sex friends and taken to the strangest of places.

In Anglo-Saxon cultures, the best man plays an important part in organising the wedding; he is responsible for bringing the rings, the wearing of which by both partners goes back to the end of the nineteenth century.

In Orthodox cultures, the exchange of rings occurs at the moment of engagement. In Germany, the engaged couple wear the ring on their left hand and transfer it to the third finger of the right hand on the wedding day. Although the tradition of the engagement ring, which symbolises a promise of marriage, goes back to the Middle Ages, the custom of using diamonds only dates from the nineteenth century. Another innovation which quickly became a ritual is posing for the photographer, a key figure in the wedding ceremony. The wedding photograph is kept in a conspicuous place. In France, the wedding bouquet, consisting of orange-blossom and flower buds as well as a wax crown, was kept in a prominent place under a glass dome. This custom lasted until the Second World War.

THE PERFECT DAY. Religious feasts have always fascinated people, even those who practise no religion (cf. p. 298). Communist Russia created "marriage centres" where Mendelssohn's *Wedding March* was played and an address by the mayor replaced the sermon. "Long live the bride!" cried the onlookers; she was the centre of the celebration, her beautiful white gown contrasting with the groom in a sombre suit. The glamour of the long dress helped it survive the shorter hemline trends of the twenties and now, at the end of the twentieth century, many fashion show parades still end with a wedding dress. Previously (and even now in Asia) the dress was red, the colour of celebration and joy. The choice of white, a symbol of purity, only dates from the

nineteenth century, but the meaning remains: it is still the most beautiful dress of all, and one that is worn only once.

In Anglo-Saxon tradition, the bride has to wear "something old, something new, something borrowed, something blue". The first two things symbolise the passing from the old state to the new, the borrowed item ties the bride to the community, and the colour blue is associated with fidelity.

All around the world the wedding procession is accompanied by much noise, car horns replacing the gun volleys designed to chase away evil spirits. In the same way, cars decorated with flowers and knots of white ribbon have replaced horses with flower-covered harnesses pulling richly decorated carriages.

In Orthodox marriage ceremonies, the couple each wear a crown of metal or leaves; Jews stand under a canopy that symbolises divine protection. But beyond the ceremonies, it is the exchange of vows in front of witnesses that characterises marriages everywhere. Couples in ancient Rome joined their right hands together. For Catholics, it is a sacrament which the couple confer on each other, the priest being responsible for receiving the celebrated "I will" from each of them. Opposition to the match can be expressed up until the last minute, something which is often used as a dramatic device in films.

The tradition of the gold ring placed on the woman's finger symbolises an eternal bond, the choice of the third finger of the left hand stemming from the ancient Greek belief that it was the heart finger because it contained the love vein! The couple are now together "for better and for worse, until death do [us] part". When the husband lifts the veil and kisses his wife, the kiss seals their union in everyone's eyes; this had already become a custom in Roman times, as had the throwing

of wheat (later replaced by rice) over the couple as a symbol of fertility.

A UNION BETWEEN TWO FAMILIES. The union between the two families is confirmed by the wedding feast. There is much eating, drinking and singing, and toasts are proposed. The bride cuts the ceremonial cake and offers the first piece to her husband. A tradition with strong sexual links concerns the bride's garter, which is stolen during the meal by the best man; it may be sold by auction or torn into small pieces which are distributed among the men. In the same way, the bride may tear her veil and give pieces to the guests.

In the United States, pots and cans tied to the bumper of their car prevent the newly-weds from escaping quietly; this harks back to the European "hullabaloo", a noisy demonstration of jokes and interruptions throughout the wedding night.

"Alone at last!" After the wedding night (cf. pp. 134 and 294), the transition to everyday life is marked by the honeymoon, a custom which emerged in the nineteenth century, starting the couple's new life with a period of happiness.

RUSSIA. **The mystic summer of the poet Aleksandr Blok, madly in love with Lyuba, the young girl who lived next door and whose father was the celebrated scientist Dmitrii Mendeleyev. He rode on his white horse to see "the young girl in a pink dress with heavy gold braid", for whom he wrote *Verses about the Beautiful Lady*. Their wedding took place in 1903. Some months later, poet Andrei Byely fell in love with Lyuba. This new love, sometimes reciprocated and sometimes not, led Blok to break off relations with Byely and grow distant from his wife, although he continued to love her. Shattered by her rejection, the Beautiful Lady's "hot-blooded but timid knight" turned into a cynic whose poetry expressed a deep melancholy from that time on.**

A grand traditional wedding feast.

Gustav
& Alma Mahler

The last of the romantic composers married the inspiration behind early twentieth-century Vienna.

At the turn of the century, Vienna was the centre of a passionate artistic and intellectual life. After a long career as a conductor in various cities, Gustav Mahler had directed the Court Opera there since 1897 with a tireless zeal, making demands that were often difficult to satisfy. The last of the great romantics, still little known as a composer, he wrote symphonies and lieder with an intensely powerful lyricism that ranks them among the century's masterpieces.

In 1901, at a dinner with Bertha Zuckerkandl, hostess of a famous Viennese salon, he met Alma Schindler, who, at twenty-two, was nineteen years younger than him, and whose beauty and personality made her the highlight of the receptions of the day. Musically gifted, she dreamed of becoming an orchestra conductor and had already written over a hundred lieder. She was the daughter of the great Austrian painter Emil Schindler, who died when she was thirteen. Very fond of her father, she suffered greatly when her mother married his pupil Carl Moll. She began her career as a "genius snatcher" at the age of eighteen, with her declaration of love for Gustav Klimt, the leader of the young Austrian artists' movement known as The Secession. She provoked passion in Max Burckhard, the director of the Burgtheater, and in her composition teacher Alexander von Zemlinksy (who trained the future founders of the New Vienna School, Arnold Schoenberg, Alban Berg and Anton Webern).

SILENCE MUST REIGN. When they married, in 1902, Mahler insisted that she give up her music. Believing that "a house full of composers would be ridiculous", he allotted her one job only: "to make him happy". Convinced of his own genius, he wrote to her while they were engaged: "You must give yourself to me unconditionally, you must submit your future life to

my needs and desire nothing but my love. ... From now on, your music is mine." By accepting the marriage, the young woman who wanted to win fame sacrificed herself instead. Mahler, above all else, was the most prominent personality in Viennese cultural life. It was this she admired in him, not his music, which she only appreciated very much later. Mahler was a Jew and his wife was not: she, being steeped in the racist thinking of the period, believed that a Jew could not be a creative being.

But from the day of their wedding she devoted herself to his work, the demands of which dictated their daily family life. In winter, Mahler was fully occupied with his heavy workload as Director of the Opera. In summer he would compose at Maiernigg, in the chalet he had built and which had got him into debt. The young Alma, who needed to be seen by others in order to "blossom", was consigned to solitude. Even though she maintained the silence that her musician husband demanded of her, she could not stifle her voice in her diary: "I am barely a day over twenty, and my life is all mapped out: the children, Gustav; Gustav, the children." Two daughters were born: Maria, known as Putzi, in 1902 (conceived out of wedlock) and Anna in 1904.

Rebelling in silence, she copied out parts of her husband's works, or played them on the piano between pregnancies (she suffered several miscarriages). The fifth symphony was dedicated to Alma ("To my dear Almschi, my courageous and faithful companion"), who suffered attacks of nerves and lamented her vanished hopes. Mahler, isolated behind his work, did not understand her. She wrote to him: "I often feel that I have had my wings clipped. Gustav, why have you chained me, a bird wild with flights and dazzling colours, when a plain white goose would have suited you just as well?" He answered: "You are a goose."

In 1907 Putzi, at the age of five, died of diphtheria, but the couple were not brought together by their grief. Mahler, whose health was failing, had endless problems with the Vienna Opera and in that year left its directorship for that of the Metropolitan Opera in New York; from then on, they visited the city every year.

THE CHILD AND THE GODDESS. To cure her depression, Alma took courses of treatment in spa towns. In 1909 she met a young German architect named Walter Gropius, the future creator of the Bauhaus, who brought her the passion and tenderness that she needed. Protected by her mother, she met him by devious means and started a passionate correspondence with him. Mahler discovered their relationship in 1910 when, after a mistake by Gropius, he received a letter sent by him to Alma. The boot was on the other foot! The tyrant was now a "great sick child", afflicted and terrified by the idea of losing his "goddess". Alma, now the dominant one, chose to stay with him. She wrote to Gropius: "If I leave, he'll die; if I stay, he'll live." Mahler consulted a much-talked-about Viennese doctor, Sigmund Freud, who reminded him that he had prevented his wife from composing. After that he discovered her

music with admiration and encouraged her to compose again. He had five of her earlier lieder published, at the same time as his *Symphony of a Thousand*, which he dedicated to her.

He was growing steadily weaker, and was too frail to accompany his wife when one of her lieder was played for the first time in New York in Spring 1911. She took care of him with love and devotion, but without losing touch with Gropius. The return trip was very trying and Mahler arrived back in Vienna to die there on 18 May 1911, leaving "Almschi" his unfinished tenth symphony. The young widow, aged thirty-two, once again became a "Muse". After a scandalous love affair with the painter Oskar Kokoschka, seven years her junior, she went back to Gropius and married him in 1915. Their daughter Manon, who was her favourite, was born in 1920 and died of polio in 1935. After that Gropius withdrew gracefully so that the famous Austrian writer Franz Werfel, a Jew ten years younger than Alma, would take his place. They married in 1929. Nazism and the war drove them to France and then to the United States, where he died in 1945 and she in 1964. Although she was Werfel's widow, Alma remains above all else the widow of Mahler.

IRELAND. **Maud Gonne performs in the play *Cathleen Ni Houlihan*, written by William Butler Yeats, who had loved her since 1889 with a wild and hopeless love. She was his inspiration for the love poems in *Wind among the Reeds* (1899), and the theatrical characters such as the violent and passionate queen in *On the Banks of Baile* (1904). Yeats' mystic cosmos was very far removed from the militant nationalism pursued by Maud Gonne. Coming from a rich family and highly gifted as a speaker, she gained her independence by becoming an actress. From her brief marriage to the militant John Macbride, the future founder of Amnesty International Sean Macbride was born in 1904. Still affected by Maud Gonne, Yeats then fell in love with her daughter Isolde. In 1917 he asked her to marry him, but she refused.**

Morals
The Scandalous Claudine

A "naïve little savage" marries an "old-debauchee" who pushes her into a lesbian affair.

"Surely there is something not right in our household. Renaud doesn't know anything any more; how could he know?" Such is the beginning of *Claudine At Home*, the third and most successful volume in the best-selling *Claudine* series. The name of the author, Willy, conceals the collaboration between this well-known Parisian journalist and his wife, who later found fame under her own name of Colette. The subject matter in the series is largely autobiographical.

When they married, in 1893, she was twenty and he thirty-four. The first book, *Claudine at School* (1900), describes the rebellion of the "little savage" who in the second book

Claudine in Paris (1901) threw herself into love with all the fury of someone desperate to give of herself. In the end she sought submission: "To obey, a humiliation which I have never suffered, I would write of as something savoured. ... My liberty weighs heavy on me, my independence exasperates me; what I look for ... [is] a master. Free women are not women." Contempt

for things feminine drives the heroine to show herself as something both male and female, laying heavy emphasis on her short hair and "coarse" gestures. Although the tale of emotional awakening was a common genre at the time, the destiny of Claudine, first young girl and then young woman, free without being "emancipated", who discovered love within marriage, is exceptional. It's not a question of the destiny allotted to girls, the house and the children! The house is not Claudine's, but her husband's; nothing is said about motherhood, and she finds its substitute in her cat, which she calls "my Ba-bee".

PLEASURE AND PERVERSITY. Claudine is eighteen and Renaud forty. Even before their marriage she offers herself to him, but he makes her wait. "With excessive care for his own happiness – and mine? – he kept us locked in a suffocating good behaviour." Finally the wedding night arrives. She begs him to hurry up and describes her own reactions "from my quivering revolt to my panic-stricken consent, to the shameful groaning of the pleasure which I wanted to keep through sinful pride". It is a strange introduction which ends with the "merciless" husband, who stupefies and humiliates her; but it is an effective

one. "Renaud showed me the secret of sensual pleasure given and felt, and I have kept it, I enjoy it with a passion, like a child with a deadly weapon."

What a difference between them! For him, "sensual pleasure is born of desire, of perversity, of light-hearted curiosity, of a libertine kind of insistence. Pleasure for him is happy, gentle, easy, while it strikes me down, casts me into a mysterious despair." While she appears as "an obedient child filled with wonderment", the old "husband-daddy" soon turns out to be a debauched voyeur who pushes her into a relationship with the beautiful Rézi. At a time when stories of male homosexuality made him shiver with horror, he defended female homosexuality: "You can do anything, you others. It is charming, and of no importance. … It's between yourselves, you pretty little animals, a … comfort from us, a diversion which calms you."

In reality Colette, after her initial adventure with the American Georgie Raoul-Duval, had other lesbian relationships, including a long-standing friendship with another rich American, Natalie Clifford Barney. When she left her husband in 1906, tired of his unfaithfulness, she lived with the Marquess of Belboeuf. In *The Vagabond* (1910), she wrote with a gentleness that Willy could never attain: "For him, two women locked together will always be just a naughty pair, not the melancholy and touching picture of two frailties who might find refuge in each other's arms to sleep there, cry there, and flee the many evils of man and taste better than any pleasure the bitter ecstasy of feeling equal, lowly, forgotten."

THE REAL SCANDAL. Claudine was ashamed of her husband, and scandalised by him: "What strange kind of affair had he in mind, to push me towards Rézi, to put on all my finery for her?" For her, love or desire is "the good natural law", and "vice is the evil that one creates without pleasure".

In his preface to *Claudine at School*, Willy wrote: "Well, this little Claudine, who is almost a child of nature, seems to me (O Rousseau!) almost innocent in her naïve perversity." The naïve girl appears more cheeky than perverse, or perhaps coloured with a perversity so candid that it ceases to be perversity; what is important to her is pleasure, which all senses can obtain. A celebration of this sort of sensuality was to follow in Colette's next work. By contrast, Willy is a libertine, more attracted by desire than by love; a pervert in that his sexuality was linked to the degradation of the other person; a debauchee who concealed his anguish at his impotence and his very end-of-century fear of the vampire-woman. Proud of the extraordinary success of the Claudine novels, he carried on openly in public with his wife and the actress Polaire, wanting to make people believe that there was a relationship between them.

The great success of the series was largely due to the homosexual episodes, but the real scandal was in the relationship of the legitimate couple, very similar to that which the writers enjoyed. In *My First Experiences* (1936), Colette recalls her marriage to this "corrupter". She who gave herself with confidence still feels dirty and guilty; she regrets "her patience, her long, slow and complete tacit consent". In *The Vagabond* she breaks completely with the light-heartedness of her previous books and tells of a painful inner rebuilding process. Claudine's renunciation of childhood and the androgynous ideal appears in *The Tendrils of the Vine* (1908), Colette's first major book. "What I have lost … is my beautiful pride, the secret certainty of being a precious child, of feeling within me the extraordinary soul of an intelligent man, a woman in love, a soul fit for making my little body shine forth. … I have lost almost all that, to become, after all is said and done, merely a woman."

1902

PARIS. **The first performance of Claude Debussy's opera *Pelléas et Mélisande*, the libretto of which was taken from a play by Maurice Maeterlinck. The old King Golaud meets Mélisande, a mysterious young girl with long fair hair, in the forest, brings her back and marries her. His half-brother Pelléas, a young dreamer "and mad besides", is taken by her. Wild with jealousy, Golaud kills Pelléas and Mélisande takes her own life. This masterpiece of French lyric art contains, in the fourth act, one of the greatest of all love duets. On a par with Tristan and Isolde or Romeo and Juliet, Pelléas and Mélisande are a modern representation of the pair of mythical lovers whose love is inextricably linked with death.**

SEM

Pierre Marie & Curie

The work of two great scientists, who were also a very close couple, was crowned with the Nobel Prize.

In 1903 Pierre and Marie Curie, together with Henri Becquerel, received the Nobel Prize for Physics for their work on radioactivity. Already well known among scientists, the Curies became public celebrities. For them, however, the glory was a "disaster"; both as shy as each other, and consumed by the same passion for research, they suffered greatly being constantly distracted, seeing their laboratory attacked by intruders, and having their modest Paris house invaded by journalists and photographers. The burden of social demands which weighed on them was added to by an ever-increasing volume of mail to which they dedicated their Sundays.

When they met in 1894, they were both working on a study of magnetism. At thirty-five, Pierre Curie was one of the great hopes in French physics. Tall and brown-haired, with a distinguished, nonchalant air, he had a fine, angular face lit by soft, dreamy brown eyes. His education, which he received at home from his remarkably progressive parents, strengthened his fiercely independent character and at the same time developed his love for nature. He immediately fell in love with the refined, almost austere twenty-seven-year-old Pole who shared his altruistic faith in science.

Marie Sklodowska had penetrating grey eyes and her fair hair framed a high forehead. A disappointment in love when she was working as a governess in Poland strengthened her resolve to study in France. Encouraged by her father, she arrived in Paris in 1891 where she led an austere life wholly devoted to work. As well as achieving a degree in mathematics, she was the first woman in France to obtain a degree in physics.

For the only time in his life, as he said later, Pierre Curie acted without a shadow of a doubt

when he asked her to marry him. She, however, hesitated, despite their fruitful scientific dialogue and the humanist values they shared; she also found it difficult to make a final break with her family and homeland. Having exhausted all his arguments, he offered to go and live with her in Poland; but it was she who chose to remain in France. "Our friendship," she wrote, "has become more and more precious to us. We both understand that we could not find a better companion in life."

Their wedding, which was celebrated in Paris on 26 July 1895, was very simple; there was no great ceremony, no ring, no white dress. The bride wore a blue dress which she could have worn in the laboratory. The young couple then mounted their bicycles and spent their honeymoon travelling along the roads of France. Every summer they covered the whole country in this way. They had two children, Irène in 1897 and Eve in 1904.

THE LABORATORY FORMS THE HEART OF THEIR LIFE TOGETHER. Their great voyage of discovery together was in the field of radioactivity, the word being coined by Marie Curie together with the names of the two elements discovered by them in 1898, polonium and radium. For her doctorate (which made her the first woman Doctor of Science at the Sorbonne), she chose to study the nature of the rays discovered by Becquerel. Her husband accompanied her in her research; he was more the physicist, the brilliant inventor of the apparatus necessary for the experiments, and she was the chemist, handling many tonnes of ore. Their work, however, was carried out together; their notes, in their own distinctive handwriting, testify to this, and their many publications generally carry both their names.

BELOW
French stamp, 1938.

FACING PAGE
Marie and Pierre Curie with their daughter Irène.

The laboratory was the centre of their lives: a run-down and dusty shed, baking hot in summer and icy in winter, at the Paris School of Industrial Physics and Chemistry. They sometimes returned in the evening to admire in the darkness the strange blue glow of the radium. They were desperately short of money and also of time, as they had to teach in order to finance their research. Pierre Curie, who was too independent to belong to the teacher training college, studied for many years for the chair in physics and chemistry at the Sorbonne; he only aquired the position in 1904.

Their only need was their work. At home they had as little furniture as possible (which resolved the problem of housework to some extent), and no social life; their evenings were spent working together facing each other across the bench. They were never apart. Doctor Curie, Pierre's father, lived with them and helped them raise their daughters.

A JOINT VENTURE STOPPED IN ITS PRIME. The money from the Nobel Prize improved their material situation but not their health, which was affected by chemical compounds and radioactivity. Then, in 1906, tragedy struck: Pierre was killed on 19 April, knocked down by a horse-drawn carriage as he crossed the Rue Dauphine. Life stopped for Marie Curie that day, and, as though turned to stone, she forbade any mention of her husband's name in her presence. However, she wrote him letters about her work and their daughters for several years. "The poor little orphan," she lamented over Irène, "the poor child of our great love!" She wrote a biography of her husband and also published his complete scientific works.

A pioneer once more, she was nominated at the Sorbonne for her husband's chair, and took up his text book in 1906, at the very sentence where he had left off. The couple's faithful friends, the Borels and the Perrins, surrounded Marie and her family with their love, particularly in 1911 when the "Langevin Affair" blew up: Marie Curie (such a scandal!) had an affair with the scholar Paul Langevin, who was married. Some newspapers loosed their fury against "the husband-stealer" and "the foreigner" in the same year as she was awarded a second Nobel prize, for chemistry this time, for her discovery of radium. The rest of her life was devoted to work.

During the First World War, she and her daughter Irène became famous for tirelessly travelling the roads near to the front with the "petites curies", carriages equipped with radiological equipment for the wounded. In 1918 her doggedness was rewarded with the opening of the Radium Institute, which had always been her and Pierre's dream. Before dying of leu-

1903

IRELAND. The wedding of Francis Skeffington and Hannah Sheehy, both of whom from that time on bore the name Sheehy-Skeffington in order to show that marriage was not a barrier between the sexes. They fought together for women's rights and for Irish independence, while at the same time disapproving of revolutionary violence. During the nationalist Easter uprising in 1916, Francis witnessed the killing of a young unarmed man by British soldiers; a captain, who was later declared mad, had had him arrested and shot without a trial. His wife refused the compensation of £10,000 offered by the British army.

♡ ♡ ♡

kaemia in 1934, she had the delight of helping with the discovery of artificial radioactivity by another pair of pioneering scholars: Irène and Frédéric Joliot-Curie (cf. p. 170).

In 1995, France bestowed the supreme honour on the Curies when their remains were moved to the "Pantheon" and their picture appeared on the new five hundred franc note.

♡ ♡ ♡

MORALS
Love According to Ellen Key

Glorifying both love and motherhood, Ellen Key proposed that the accepted role of the couple be changed so that husband and wife have equal status and children's rights are respected.

"To change the world through love" was the goal of the internationally-known Swedish lecturer and journalist Ellen Key. In 1903 the publication of her book *Lifslinjer* (Lifelines), in which she denounces the hypocrisy of marriage, caused much controversy. The repercussions were considerable, because the first volume was soon translated, under the more attractive title *Love and Marriage*, into ten European languages, and even appeared in Japanese in 1958.

Ellen Key, who shared the prevailing belief of the time that women were biologically and intellectually inferior, professed that women should be able to blossom freely by setting up a home, choosing to become mothers, and raising the next generation. She proclaimed the sanctity of motherhood, but in the name of children's rights, a very new idea at that time. She discouraged those who did not feel that "sublime calling". She even went so far as to agree to a woman leaving a man and giving him his freedom if she was unable to reconcile love, children, and work.

Love, which she viewed as something almost mystic, was for her "woman's gift par excellence". It sanctified every union, whether or not it was legal. Criticising "free love" in the libertarian sense, she asserted that she was "fighting for

freedom of love, because although the first expression has come to mean all kinds of sexual licence, the second only defines freedom for the one type of love worthy of bearing the name." She proposed a new law on marriage: it should be civil and not religious, because in her eyes Christianity could not be reconciled with the laws of evolution. It would be forbidden in cases of hereditary illness; the spouses must be of age, the difference between their ages should not be more than twenty-five years, and women would retain their personal rights.

CRITICISM FROM FEMINISTS AND CONSERVATIVES. Even dealing with sex, love, and marriage was enough to get an unmarried woman accused of immorality in a country where, in 1880, prison sentences were still passed for blasphemy. Ellen Key was therefore attacked by conservatives who accused her of defending free love and atheism. Admired abroad as a great feminist, and often invited to give lectures, particularly in Germany, she was criticised by Swedish feminists. She did not accept the standard of sexual abstinence that some of them proposed, and was herself opposed to the ideas of Frederika Bremer who wanted to increase the scope of paid work for women so that they could become independent of, and equal to, men. For Ellen Key, femininity was the equivalent of maternity, although she herself never bore a child. Coming from a well-to-do family, she never went to school, and learned German and French at home. In 1880, needing to make a living, she became a teacher. In the summer of 1895 she looked after

her nephews and nieces and concluded from that experience that a mother could not hold down both housework and a paid job. In *The Delinquent Force of Women* (1896) and particularly in *The Century of the Child* (1900), her most famous book, translated into eleven languages, she launched an attack on conventional marriage in which the man "settled down" after a debauched youth by marrying an ignorant girl. She insisted that marriage should become more "moral", so that children could grow up in a healthy and harmonious atmosphere. "Give them the right to live their full individual childhood with a mother and father who are themselves living a full individual life."

Ellen Key used bold feminist arguments. Love, she said, must serve as a moral basis for marriage. It presupposed equality, while the laws relating to marriage were based on a "master and subject" relationship. "Men say pretty things about the wife's noble task, and about the power of love which levels everything. Let's ask one of these men if for him love would compensate for the need to beg for money for his personal needs, or the housekeeping, from his wife! Would love be a consolation for loss of control over his property, his civil rights, even his name?"

NEW SUGGESTIONS AND ACCEPTED IDEAS. However, Ellen Key adopted accepted ideas when asserting that love produced the best children, frowning on mixed marriages because of racist thoughts, and claiming that "the difference in sexual character between a man and a woman" makes polygamy the right of one and destines the other to love ...

More original are her ideas on reproduction, which is considered solely from a social viewpoint and implies that the woman "regains her status in the home". As the ideal age for conceiving a child, according to her, was twenty for the mother and twenty-five for the father, young people should remain virgins until then. She was therefore in favour of marriages at a younger age than the average for that time, but she put together a very progressive condition indeed; that divorce should be freely available. "Then," she said, "people will always look to please each other, as they did when they were engaged." Married women should be freed from any work outside the home and their domestic work seen as a paid duty. The father would be required to supply one half of the child's maintenance. Society would give the mother an allowance for the other half, up to a limit of four children, the number reckoned to be sufficient for society. Beyond that, children would be the responsibility of their parents. She regretted that "the woman of the day" was limited to two children.

Another remarkable stance was that she judged adulterers purely from the children's point of view. A man or woman guilty of adultery was not by that token a bad father or bad mother. Asserting that "the duty of parents towards their children was to remain young and truly alive", she found it pointless for them to sacrifice "the chances of happiness offered by a new love". Mixing the prejudices of her time with some utopian suggestions, Ellen Key developed her ideas in articles and during lecture tours in Sweden and abroad. Her thoughts influenced novelists such as the Norwegian Sigrid Undset, some German feminists and the founders of the Swedish People's Democracy.

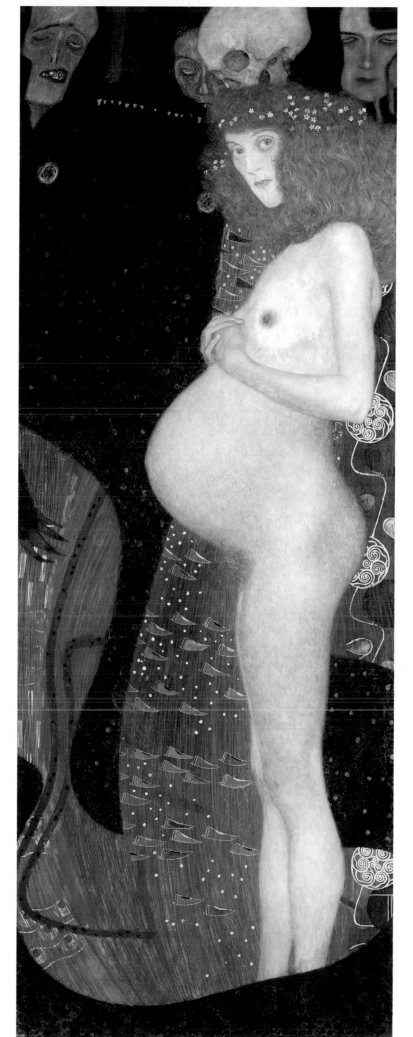

1903

FRANCE. **The publication of *Cervelines*, Colette Yver's first novel. The heroine is a brilliant woman whom a man tries to persuade to give up her career and independence to marry him; wishing to put herself to the test, she dedicates herself to nothing but housework for a week ... and ends by refusing him! It was thanks to this book that the writer met her husband, Auguste Huzard, who worked with her publisher. After that she wrote several successful novels, particularly *The Princesses of Science*. Curiously, all her other heroines give up their careers to become their husband's "Girl Fridays", but the sequel to the tale showed that the choice, imposed by the customs of the time, was an unjust sacrifice.**

Hope, Gustav Klimt, 1903. For Ellen Key, femininity was the same as motherhood.

La Duse & D'Annunzio

The great Italian tragic actress left the scandalous writer because she wanted to be more than just his "inspiration".

"There can be no response to this letter." With these words, in July 1904, Eleonora Duse ended her relationship with the writer Gabriele D'Annunzio. After ten years of passion, the great actress had reached the end of her strength and finally lost faith in him.

Their meeting, in September 1894 in Venice, was an encounter between two Italian "superstars" who were well-known throughout Europe. The writer was thirty-one and Eleonora Duse, or "La Duse", as she was known, thirty-six and as famous as her French rival, the "divine" Sarah Bernhardt. D'Annunzio was attracted to women older than himself and La Duse nick-

named him "mi figlio" (my son). At the time, she was enjoying a break in Venice between two highly successful tours. She delighted her audiences in both the classical repertoire such as Shakespeare's plays, and in modern works – she created Ibsen's new female roles – and became the idol of the European avant-garde intellectuals. Her greatest role remains that of *La Dame aux Camélias*, by Dumas the Younger. Her unique beauty came across warm and vibrant, with great powers of seduction. Her beautiful, expressive hands and deep voice made her a truly remarkable actress.

D'Annunzio, a society poet, had a doubtful reputation at the time; his works portrayed the intoxications and the torments of soul and flesh which, together with his writing, characterised his life. His particular life-style, independence, and erudition enabled him to show both flattery and hatred with equal ease. A small man with "unfortunate" teeth and premature baldness, this prince of words seduced as readily as he talked, aided by his rich Tuscan accent. He was incapable of resisting the promises of pleasure and his mistresses were as numerous as they were passionate. He fathered five children, two of them illegitimate.

La Duse, between two love affairs, had a brief marriage which produced a daughter, Enrichetta, born in 1882. Having sent her to boarding school, La Duse frequently snatched her away, overcome by crises of guilt which always vanished as quickly as they arose.

When she met D'Annunzio, she had just read his book *The Triumph of Death*, and felt herself caught in a trap. She wrote to her then lover: "Each of us poor women thinks we have discovered words for ourselves; but that blasted D'Annunzio knows them all." And later: "I would rather die in a corner than love the likes of him." After emerging as a poet while still very young, D'Annunzio, using a highly exaggerated style, published a trilogy of scandalous novels entitled *The Child of Sensuality* ("to whom," said Romain Rolland, "women opened their dreams if they couldn't open their beds"), *The Intruder*, and *The Triumph of Death*. This last work features the myth of the "superman", inspired by Nietzsche and adopted again, later on, in fascism.

IN THRALL TO HIS LOVE. "D'Annunzio! I hate him, but I love him," she wrote. Did she sense that this seducer loved to evoke passion's destructive effects in his mistresses so that he could exploit them in literature?

Whatever the truth of that, she, like others, succumbed, fired with enthusiasm by the "treaty of alliance" sealed by them both for the theatre of their dreams: he would create, for her alone, a work "which could never be equalled". La Duse, a child of the theatre, was businesslike as well as passionate: she founded troupes, directed rehearsals and dragged her entire circle of friends around Europe and America. There she financed and played the roles that her lover wrote for her: *Songs of a Spring Morning*, *The Dead City*, and *Francesca da Rimini*.

Despite mocking and sometimes biting criticism, her love gave her the courage to perform in theatres that were sometimes almost empty. She remained faithful to their "pact" to the very end, while he deceived her openly; in fact she pushed the denial so far as to say "I'm ready to smother Eleonora to make La Duse work like a slave."

There was also a financial reason why La Duse was pushed onto what she called "the accursed stage": the poet, who confessed to having "a deep and ruinous passion" for beautiful things, pursued his extravagant lifestyle without any scruples. It was with him that she developed her stage roles, in his villa in Tuscany or in seaside holiday villas.

For ten years, periods of absence, with separations that tore her apart, were followed by ecstatic reunions. After each new conquest, he went back to her. She wanted to break away, but allowed herself to be seduced again. They bombarded each other with letters and telegrams from one country to another, from one town to another; and when they lived together, they even sent each other letters from one room to another. His complete opus, with one or two exceptions, was dedicated to her. When his novel *The Fire* was published in 1899, readers identified the ageing heroine rejected by her lover as La Duse. Despite her sadness, she held her head high, asserting that she wanted the book published because of her love of art. As for D'Annunzio, he acknowledged his cruelty with the cynical comment: "I've given her everything, even suffering." He spoke through the hero in *The Intruder*, saying: "Why, in every man who loves and desires, is there a germ of that loathsome sadistic perversion?"

La Duse, ruined, exhausted by her travels, and sick, was, as it were, imprisoned by her love. But in 1904, when D'Annunzio gave the principal role in *The Girl From Jorio* to his latest mistress, and told La Duse in a letter that she had not fulfilled "his desire for the carnal life", she finally found the strength to break free. Rejecting his promises of "devotion, admiration and tenderness", she was no longer satisfied with the role of "the inspiration for a great poet" that he foisted on her.

She comforted herself with love affairs, with both men and women, and retired from the theatre in 1909. She became interested in cinema and wrote scripts for this "new art". Then, in 1917, at the age of fifty-eight, she made a triumphant return to the theatre. D'Annunzio sent her a spray of flowers and their letters started again, tender and affectionate this time.

HIS COMPLETE WORKS DEDICATED TO HER. D'Annunzio, meanwhile, pursued his quest for "the violent life". In 1910, he escaped from his creditors by hiding in luxurious exile in Paris, thanks to the generosity of mistresses of doubtful reputation, such as Liane de Pougy, the painter Romaine Brooks and the dancer Ida Rubinstein.

1904

ZURICH. **A love affair starts between the married Swiss psychoanalyst Carl Gustav Jung, a pupil of Freud (cf. p. 46), and his patient Sabina Spielrein, a young Russian from Rostov-on-Don, who had been sent to Zurich for treatment after being diagnosed as mentally ill. When he made her break off the relationship, she complained to Freud, and Jung was forced to admit that he had not properly mastered the analytical technique of counter-transference with this patient, his training case. Finally cured by Jung, she married, had a daughter and became a psychoanalyst herself. Before returning to Rostov in 1923, she corresponded with him again in 1917 and 1918 through a series of passionate letters in which she described the imaginary son she dreamed of having with him.**

"The person whom you love has every right against you, even the right not to love you."

ROMAIN ROLLAND
Jean-Christophe

A convinced nationalist, he returned to Italy in 1915 to fight in the war, as a pilot. He fought with great courage and was wounded, losing his right eye. In 1919 he seized the disputed town of Fiume, which he wanted to establish as an independent republic; Mussolini was to copy this dictatorship and develop it. D'Annunzio and La Duse remained tied together by memories; and when she died in 1924, she declared "I forgive him everything, because I loved him."

Death finally claimed D'Annunzio in 1938 when, with pen in hand, he was rewriting the dedication of his complete works to La Duse.

♡ ♡ ♡

THE LAW
Remarriage after Divorce

Remarriage between a divorced person and their "accomplice in adultery" was finally authorised by French civil law in 1904. The law, however, is peppered with restrictions on remarriage.

In France, the law of 15 December 1904, replacing Article 298 of the Civil Code, finally authorised the "accomplices" of adulterers to marry after the divorce of one (or both) of the parties. The Naquet Law of 1884 authorised divorce on grounds of misdemeanour, but added: "If adultery constitutes the grounds therefore, the guilty person (be they man or woman) may not marry their accomplice." The argument put forward was still essentially moral: adultery must remain a misdemeanour and could not lead to marriage after divorce. For some time therefore, the law permitted divorce but punished "guilty" lovers by forbidding them to legitimise not only their love but also the children born of it. This difficulty was sometimes overcome in practice by not mentioning the name of the "accomplice" during the separation process; this left the option of remarriage open.

In the West, for example in the Austrian law of 1868, the dissolution procedure was always seen as a punishment for a misdemeanour; the idea of separation for an objective reason or by mutual consent only became prevalent in the second half of the twentieth century.

England was the exception: right from the first Divorce Law, in 1857, married people "guilty" of adultery were permitted to marry their accomplices. In fact, commentators stated that "one is thought to be lacking in honour if, after having seduced a married woman, one does not make restitution for one's misdemeanour by marrying her".

The laws that included this ban gradually fell into disuse, and were eventually repealed everywhere in Europe during the twentieth century; in some cases, however, they endured, lasting until 1952 in Belgium.

The various legal provisions show clearly that the issue most often at stake was the husband-wife-lover "triangle". In most countries, in fact, the wife's adultery was treated still more severely than the husband's. In England, equality between spouses on this subject was not established until 1923. In France it had to wait until 1975. On the other hand, the Dutch Civil Code of 1838 made no distinction between a husband's adultery and a wife's adultery; neither did the German and Austrian laws of the nineteenth century.

DIVORCE AND PUNISHMENT. The Romans recognised divorce for adultery and punishment for "accomplices". The Code of the Emperor Justinian, in the sixth century, forbade the adulterous woman to marry her accomplice, on pain of death for him and forced entry into a nunnery for her. In other countries, the laws of so-called "barbarian" peoples also allowed adulterous wives or husbands to be sent away, and forbade remarriage with accomplices.

Different religions have adopted different solutions. While divorce and remarriage are permissible for liberal Jews, Orthodox Christians and Protestants, they are not for Catholics, who maintain that holy matrimony remains an insoluble sacrament, whatever the circumstances. However, if one goes back to the early Middle Ages, one notices that some Anglo-Saxon Penitential Books allowed husbands to remarry. Theodore's even specified that a guilty woman could marry again after two years' penance. Usually, church doctrine and canon law did not allow a man to remarry, but permitted him to send the adulterous wife away; however, the numerous calls to order demanding that this principle be respected indicate that it was not well observed!

In modern times Scandinavian countries, which have allowed divorce for longer than their European neighbours, initially forbade remarriage of a guilty couple. In Denmark, the Code of King Christian IV (1684) provided that a woman guilty of adultery could only remarry with the king's permission, after waiting for three years and upon production of a certificate testifying to her "good Christian conduct". If she did remarry, she was then forbidden to live in her former husband's parish, district or town. In Sweden, the Code of 1734 specified that the spouse against whom divorce had been pronounced for adultery could not remarry unless

IRELAND. **On 16 June, James Joyce meets Nora Barnacle on a street in Dublin. He was twenty-two and she twenty, and the attraction between them was immediate. This red-haired, anti-authoritarian girl blatantly acquiesced to a sexual relationship, something which no respectable young girl did at that time. Rebelling against the social order, and still not married, they left for Switzerland, where Joyce taught English. She supported him in his writing career until she died.** *Ulysses*, **Joyce's masterpiece, a clever parody of the** *Odyssey*, **takes place on 16 June 1904 in Dublin. The book, published in 1922 and banned on grounds of obscenity, ends with the famous monologue by Molly Bloom, wife of the hero: "He asked me if I wanted to say yes ... I drew him to me so that he could feel my breasts all perfumed yes, his heart was beating like mad and yes, I said yes, I really wanted it to be yes."**

Separation, Edvard Munch. The pain suffered by the couple is illustrated by Munch, who specialised in studies of despair. He wrote: "I shall paint beings who breathe, who feel, who suffer, who love."

his or her former spouse had re-married or died. This ban, however, could be lifted with the consent of the former spouse and with the king's permission.

MORE REMARRIED DIVORCEES THAN REMARRIED WIDOWS. Although divorce is a sign that a particular marriage has failed, it does not mean that those who resort to it despair of marriage in general. Indeed, today most people who divorce marry again; in England, more than two thirds do. The rate of remarriage after divorce is higher for people of equal ages everywhere than that of remarriage after the death of a spouse. The phenomenon persists despite the decline in the number of marriages (cf. p. 298), and the percentage of marriages containing at least one divorced person is steadily increasing. It is lowest (less than 10 per cent) in countries where divorce has only recently been instituted, such as Italy, Spain and Portugal; in countries where civil marriage developed earliest (cf. p. 370) it is over one quarter, and in England and Denmark almost one third of marriages contains at least one divorced person.

In all cases of remarriage after divorce, whether or not there has been adultery, the woman is required to respect a certain period of time known in French as "délai de viduité" (minimum legal period of widowhood). In German it is known simply as "Wartezeit" (waiting time). The expressions have been borrowed from widowhood. Except in unusual cases where the time period is reduced or repealed, it begins from the date of the divorce and ends if a child is born. It is fixed, depending on the country in question, at ten months or three hundred days, the official duration of a pregnancy, and is intended to overcome any biological (and therefore legal) uncertainty about the identity of any child's father.

Apart from adultery, there is another bar to remarriage after divorce, designed to overcome the problem of incest among allied families (cf. p. 230). The law forbids marriage between relatives after widowhood, for example between a mother-in-law and a son-in-law. But does it allow marriage between former relatives after a divorce? Can a divorced man marry his ex-wife's sister? Can a divorced woman marry her former father-in-law? The interpretation of the ban on incest between relatives varies from one country to another. In some cases, such remarriage is possible, but in other countries it remains banned.

Albert Einstein
& Mileva Marić

Albert Einstein published fundamental discoveries in the field of physics, the fruit of his collaboration with his wife and former fellow student Mileva Marić.

A key date in the history of science is 1905. It was in that year that a little-known twenty-six-year-old civil servant in Bern published, in an academic review, three fundamental discoveries in different areas of physics, the most important of these being the special theory of relativity. Although we know that E = mc² and that Einstein was one of the greatest geniuses in the history of mankind, only few people know that he undertook his research with his wife, Mileva Marić, whom he admired for her intelligence and freedom of spirit. Biographies of Einstein, which barely mention her, cast her in the traditional role of the companion who freed the great man from practical matters and took care of the children, which indeed she did. However, thanks to several publications, particularly the anthology of their letters, she has now been revealed as a remarkable woman. "I am alone with everything, except you," Einstein wrote to her on 3 October 1900. "How happy I am to have found in you my complete equal, someone as strong and independent as myself."

THEY STUDIED AND RESEARCHED TOGETHER. They met in 1896, the year when they both entered the Polytechnicum, the State Polytechnic of Zurich; he was twenty-seven and she twenty. Born in Ulm, in Southern Germany, Albert Einstein grew up in Munich where his father ran the family electrical equipment business. Fascinated by electrodynamics, he decided to become an engineer, but failed the "poly" entrance exam in 1895.

Mileva Marić, the daughter of a minor civil servant, originated from Voivodina, a Serb area then under Hungarian domination. Very intelligent, she obtained special permission to help with the science courses at Zagreb Boys' School, and then went to study in Zurich. At that time some Swiss educational establishments played a pioneering role in welcoming young foreign

women, although they, like every other educational establishment, gave a better education to their male pupils.

Mileva Marić, the only woman in the mathematics department at the Polytechnicum, was more mature and thoughtful than Albert Einstein. Her quiet, resolute character contrasted sharply with the young man's cheerful, indecisive personality. Neither of them was very attractive. She walked with a limp, a legacy of congenital coxalgia, while he always sported scruffy clothes and dishevelled hair. Although she never fully mastered German, her native language being Serbo-Croat, she was a master at solving mathematical problems. She understood her companion's genius; and he admired her remarkable personality and independent spirit. They studied for their examinations together and shared the same passion for science. In their leisure time they made music: she was a singer, he played the violin.

In 1900 Einstein passed the "poly" degree, while Mileva Marić failed. The next year, she suffered another setback; she discovered that she was pregnant, and failed her exams a second time. As both families had opposed the idea of their marrying – he was a Jew and she was not considered good enough – this illegitimate child was a disaster, as neither of them had any guaranteed income. However much Einstein wrote to his beloved: "I will not leave you and I will make it so that everything comes right", how could he find work with such an "immoral" record? Their daughter Lieserl (her name a diminutive form of Elisabeth) was born early in 1902 and they were forced to give her up for adoption. In June 1902 Einstein, who had taken Swiss nationality, found work in the Patent Office in Bern, and they married on 6 January 1903. A son, Hans Albert, was born in 1904, followed by Eduard in 1910. Although it cannot be determined precisely what part each played in the

1905 discoveries, it is certain that they were the fruit of a collaboration. Einstein believed his wife to be very special and clever, while she enriched his research with her own instincts and other mathematical formulae. Apart from this work, she coped alone with the house and children, despite her disability, even taking in lodgers to increase their income. Little by little, however, financial worries and their second son's mental illness became more pressing than her personal ambitions. Einstein, who later became renowned for his humour and pacifist leanings, appeared to behave like a big selfish child, indifferent to his family and not anxious to communicate with them, when out of the public gaze. As Mileva grew more and more frustrated, their relationship turned sour.

FAME AND MISFORTUNE. Einstein became famous, accepting work abroad despite his wife's desire to stay in Zurich. In 1911 he taught in Prague, and was then appointed as a lecturer at the Zurich Polytechnic. In 1913 he was offered a prestigious position at the Prussian Academy of Science, and the directorship of the Berlin Institute of Physics. They moved again, to Berlin, in April 1914; but in August, when war broke out, Mileva was in Switzerland with the children and refused to return to Berlin. It was this separation that finally tore the couple apart. Einstein started a relationship with his cousin Elsa, who was five years older. A very caring person, with conformist leanings, she understood nothing about science, but found great favour with the family. A divorce was granted in 1919 and Einstein remarried immediately. He had a bad relationship with his elder son, and paid no attention at all to the younger for the rest of his days. He sent very little money to Mileva, who was forced to fall back on teaching to make ends meet.

UNITED STATES. **Jack London, aged twenty-nine, marries Charmian Kittredge, aged thirty-four. He, a self-made man and militant socialist, led a life of adventure before writing the novels that made him famous, such as *Call of the Wild* (1903). She was one of the "new women" who worked in a "male" job as a secretary and typist, practised sports reserved for men, and, as an advocate of free love, had numerous lovers. Both feminists, they campaigned for voting rights for women and viewed their marriage as a union of equals, between friends and lovers. She inspired in him a new type of heroine, who was fearless and sporting, and refused to allow men and women to be judged differently from a sexual viewpoint. Curious about everything, the couple sailed around the Pacific, and she kept a diary of their eventful journeys, descriptions of which feature in his books.**

Mileva Marić, as a student, in 1914.
In Berlin, with her two sons.

Mileva Marić's troubled, frustrated life had a sad end. She did not marry again and, until her death in 1948, looked after her mentally ill son, who was subject to fits of violent rage. The eldest son emigrated to the United States (where his father lived from 1933 onwards and where he died in glory in 1955) and became Professor of Hydraulic Engineering at the University of Berkeley, California.

When Einstein was awarded the Nobel Prize for Physics, in November 1921, he went to Zurich to give the money to Mileva Marić; was this perhaps an acknowledgement of what he owed her? Even though he never allowed her to be fully herself, she was the only one whom he loved and admired. It was with her that he wished to live outside the traditional bourgeois bounds and be a "Philistine"; but in truth he failed her, despite the noble intentions that he expressed in his early love letters.

♡ ♡ ♡

Freud, Sexuality and Love

Sexuality is a reality from early childhood, asserts the founder of psychoanalysis, whose discoveries caused a scandal.

In his *Three Essays on the Theory of Sexuality* (1905), Sigmund Freud put together a theory based on his discoveries on child sexuality and on the sexual nature of the traumas, both real and imagined, which lie at the root of all forms of neurosis. Without passing any moral judgements, he argues in his description of sexual aberrations and perversions that they stem from urges that are at work in every human being. According to his point of view, sexuality exists from birth; he distinguishes between genitality, which manifests itself at puberty, and sexuality, which expresses itself in children and passes through oral, anal, and phallic stages.

Psychoanalysis, as distinct from reproduction or pathology (cf. p. 62), opened up a vast new field in the study of sexuality. According to Freud, all human beings are, to varying degrees, neurotic; this is the price to pay for "becoming civilised". Although he gained a following in Europe, his revolutionary ideas caused a scandal. In 1933 the Nazis burned his books publicly in Berlin, and reading them was also banned in Russia (cf. p. 122).

A doctor specialising in neurology, he began practising in Vienna in 1886, receiving "nervous" patients whose troubles did not appear to have any physiological cause. Influenced by Charcot, a well-known French doctor specialising in hysteria, he worked with Josef Breuer, whose "catharsis" method used suggestion through hypnosis. After that he used the "psychoanalysis" technique – the word dates from 1896 – which consisted of free association of images, memories, and ideas. This allowed him to discover "the great road to the subconscious" in dreams, and the symbolic substitutes for desires repressed by social and moral demands in missed acts (slips or lapses) or in nervous symptoms (hurts, phobias or obsessions). From 1905 onwards, Freud defined libido as the biological and psychological energy behind sexual urges; he defined "repression" as the unconscious defence mechanism which uses the *ego* to ward off the temptations of libido. For him, sexuality in childhood was determined by the Oedipus complex; the child, in love with the parent of the opposite sex, is determined to kill off the parent of the same sex. Transference onto the psychoanalyst, that is, the attribution of feelings by the patient to the person treating him, replicates the original conflict that triggered the neurosis.

Freud, Salvador Dalí, 1938.

FACING PAGE
The Great Head,
Alfred Kubin, 1899.

"PENIS ENVY". 1905 was also the year in which Freud formed an association with the Swiss doctor Carl Gustav Jung, who was seen as his "heir apparent" before breaking with him in 1914. The Freudian movement subsequently suffered many more splits; most of the "heretics" differed on the interpretation of libido, such as Alfred Adler who denied its sexual nature, and particularly Jung who expanded it into a universal energy, introducing concepts of "collective subconscious" and "biological prototypes". Freud, breaking away from the idea of a feminine nature, asserted that this nature was no more than a form of libido, essentially phallic. A young boy, on discovering that a girl has no penis, sees this "lack" as a threat of castration. The young girl, unaware of the existence of her vagina, feels deprived of the penis and "envies" it. These theories were refuted from the 1920s onwards by Melanie Klein and the "English School" who maintained that there were two forms of libido, masculine and feminine. The feminist movement of the 1970s was violently opposed to the notion of "penis envy" and the precedence given by Freud to vaginal pleasures over clitoral pleasures. Acknowledging that there were "major differences in sexual development between men and women", Freud admitted that he had failed to address the question of female sexuality, writing in 1926 that for him, it was "a vast dark continent". He believed that perversion was marked by obsessive symptoms or regression to childish stages of sexual development. "The desire to make the object of the sexual desire suffer – or the opposite sentiment, the desire to make oneself suffer – is the commonest and most widespread form of perversion," he wrote in his *Three Essays*. He defined the sex act as "a form of aggression that leads to the closest form of union", and was

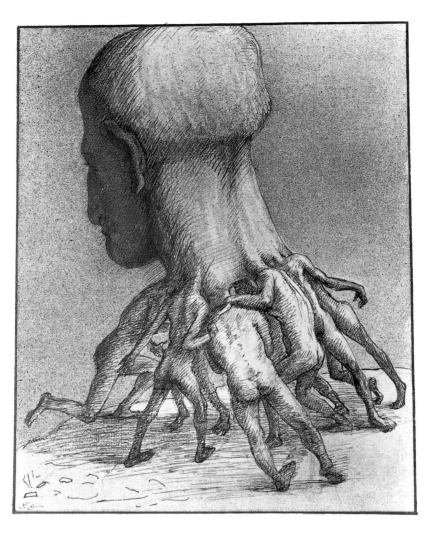

interested more by masochism rather than sadism.

FREUD AND LOVE. In 1905, interviewed during an investigation into "the reforming of marriage lines", he came down in favour of "a greater degree of sexual freedom". According to him, marriage was harmful to women who were "forced to solemnise it at a very young age, and therefore at a stage of total intellectual immaturity, and who were forced moreover by social demands to enter into marriage with no knowledge of love life". A man of science with a well-ordered life, Freud believed that love should be defined as "the cohesion of everything that exists". He was a bashful and jealous lover, as witness the 900 impassioned letters that he wrote to Martha Bernays during their engagement. It was for her that he abandoned pure research; as they were both poor, he

had to set up a practice to earn enough to marry her. Before their wedding in 1886, he confirmed her role: "I believe that you and I are in agreement in believing that running a home, and caring for and educating children, requires all of a person's attention, and excludes almost every opportunity for earning money." The Freuds were a classic bourgeois couple, modest, discreet, and together: "I am always in agreement with my wife, and I am grateful to her above all else for her many wonderful qualities and our successful children, and because she has always been very close to the norm, and very rarely ill," he wrote in 1912.

He had a special relationship with Anna, the youngest of his six children, who specialised in psychoanalysis of children. Anna organised the family's move to London in 1938, when Freud decided to move into exile so that he could "die free".

1905

BERLIN. **The German Helene Stöcker, feminist and exponent of the theory of free love, founds the League for the Protection of Mothers and Sexual Reform. While opening homes for unmarried mothers and their children, she insisted that men as well as women should bear the consequences of their sexual behaviour. She believed that it was love and not marriage that legitimised relations between the sexes. The League's demands included freely available contraception, sexual education at an early stage, and the abolition of Section 218 of the Penal Code which prohibited abortion.**

Emma Goldman & Alexander Berkman

"Free love" blossomed, followed by a life-long companionship, between two famous American anarchists.

Pittsburgh, 1906: Alexander Berkman, a thirty-five-year-old anarchist, was released from prison. He had spent fourteen years behind bars, sentenced for an assassination attempt on Henry Frick, a steelworks manager who had fiercely repressed a strike. The papers talked of Berkman's "honeymoon" with the companion he had found again, the celebrated speaker Emma Goldman, a militant campaigner for "free love" and editor of the monthly anarchist magazine *Mother Earth*.

Berkman was free, but the ghosts of the past would not leave him in peace. He had left a very young woman, whom he nicknamed "my little sparkler"; he came back to find a hardened fighter whose life-style he deplored. In the troubled, irritable man who came out of prison, Emma Goldman had great difficulty recognising the barrel-chested, determined young man with thick hair who had charmed her with his humour and insatiable zest for life since they met in New York in 1889.

At the time, she was twenty and he nineteen. They were both Russian émigrés from the town of Kovno (later Kaunas) in Lithuania. They took as their role models the literary heroes of Chernyshevsky's novel *What Is to Be Done?* As workers battling against capitalist exploitation, they followed the anarchist vision, which was to reject authoritarianism, social hierarchies, the state and religion, and applaud the coming of a society of equals where small organisations worked together in freedom, sharing a common ideal of dignity and justice.

After their first night together, she wrote in her *Memoirs*, "My heart was overflowing with love for Sasha and I was sure that our lives were inextricably linked together". But while her lover was determined to dedicate himself fully to the cause, the pretty young blonde, curly-haired, blue-eyed Emma Goldman also loved life and wanted everything, even revolution, to be invested with beauty. When she decided that she could love two men at once and took a young artist as a lover, Berkman "who could be so hard but yet have such tender caresses", reacted "with dignity and magnanimity". He declared that he loved her passionately as a woman, but that he valued her even more as a comrade. They were responsible for the attack of 1892. In order to obtain money to buy a gun, she tried prostitution; a passer-by laughed at her inexperience and slipped her ten dollars.

The assassination attempt failed. Berkman was "buried alive" in prison, wrote Goldman, who also spent a year behind bars. After that, she flatly rejected violence as a means of action. She left for Vienna, to train as a nurse and midwife. On returning to the United States, she staged several conference tours around the country, speaking eloquently on social injustice, the revolt of women, and plays by Shaw, Ibsen, and Strindberg. She rose up against the "illusion based on agreement" of which marriage consisted, and advocated "free love" while herself enjoying several passionate love affairs. For the anarchists, ideal love existed only between two equals. A world away from the puritanical views of some feminists who rejected both men and sexuality, she asserted that "women should be free to drink from the fountain of life". She advocated voluntary motherhood and contraception, which later earned both herself and Margaret Sanger a prison sentence. Emma Goldman herself was unable to bear children; an operation would have remedied the problem, but she refused it.

TIED FOR LIFE BY AN ASSASSINATION ATTEMPT. Although they were no longer intimate and Berkman sought the company of younger women, only death would sever the relationship between these two militants. In her *Memoirs*, Goldman explained why the assassination attempt tied them together for ever. "The memory, which was stronger even than the pain, was the one thing that held me back. This act which he perpetrated, and for which he paid so dearly, was the only thing that still tied me to him; but it was, I soon learned, a shackle that would bind me until my dying day. The memory of our youth and our love would probably disappear, but never would I be able to pluck from my heart the memory of those fourteen years of martyrdom." This link, a mixture of mutual concern and blazing arguments, survived both a series of separations and the jealousy which Goldman suffered when Berkman went to live with another woman in 1923. She herself had many lovers, often much younger than she, with whom she did not live up to her ideal of "free love". "Hungry for love", to use her own words, she suffered from an emotional deficit that stemmed from her childhood, and she expected too much of men.

RUSSIA. **Alexandra and Vladimir Kollontai separate. The aristocratic revolutionary (cf. p. 122), born of the old conservative nobility, wrote later in her** *Memoirs*: **"We did not separate because we ceased to love each other, but because I was being suffocated by the environment that being married would not let me leave behind." All through her life she scandalised people with her wild behaviour and numerous love affairs. The men whom she loved included the famous militant Pavel Dybenko; her relationship with him, for a few months in 1917, embodied the typical revolutionary couple.**

ARGENTINA. **The police in Buenos Aires reinstates an 1889 decree which punished any man who complimented a woman in the street with a fine of fifty pesos. This step was the inspiration for the tango song** *Cuidado con los cincuenta!* **(A gaffe will cost you fifty.)**

♡ ♡ ♡

ISOLATED BY CLARITY. In 1914, they headed the opposition against America going to war. Arrested in June 1917, they were sentenced to two years in prison for their campaign against conscription, and the ill-treatment that Berkman suffered there finally ruined his health. In December 1919 they were exiled to Russia, where they were welcomed as heroes; but as they travelled about that country, they discovered "the reality of the tyranny concealed behind the show of things revolutionary". He became very ill, and she cared for him; it was with him, when he placed his trust in Lenin, that she saw things clearly. However, the crushing of the sailors' revolt in Kronstadt in 1921 made them decide to leave, with "their faith shipwrecked". They travelled about Europe as stateless people, rejected by many of their friends, who continued to be spurred on by the Revolution. The right-wing press used their opposition to the Bolsheviks in their propaganda effort. In order to return to the United States, Emma Goldman contracted a marriage of convenience with her old anarchist friend James Colton, a Welsh miner. She also took British nationality, but was only allowed to stay in Britain for a brief period in 1934. Her life revolved around conference tours in Europe and Canada, using Saint-Tropez as her home base. It was there that she wrote her life story, aided by Berkman who was living in Nice. Very ill, and driven to despair by the rise of fascism, he committed suicide in 1936. She survived him by four years, saved from despair by an appeal from the anarchists in Barcelona. She expended her last strength in the fight against Franco and in trying to help her Spanish comrades in the Spanish civil war.

♡ ♡ ♡

The Exquisite Pleasure of Physical Pain from a Beautiful Woman

Those who imitate Sacher-Masoch endure pain to attain enjoyment. They want to be enslaved while still taking the lead in the sex act.

In 1906, eleven years after the death of the Austrian knight Sacher-Masoch, Wanda de Sacher-Masoch, his first wife, published a book entitled *Confessions of My Life*, which caused a scandal. This disturbing account, published in French translation the following year, is a study in how real life and fiction can become entangled. The author, who describes herself as a wife and mother beyond reproach, condemned the practices in which she had participated, "the sweet pleasure found in pain, and all those strange sensations which I understood so little".

No doubt masochism existed before Masoch, but the word did not appear until 1886 when the book *Psychopathia Sexualis*, written by German psychiatrist Richard von Krafft-Ebing (cf. p. 62), used it; he defined it as "a sexual tendency which associates pleasure with pain and sometimes with humiliation". Sacher-Masoch saw the whole world, including relations between men and women, as being under the shadow of evil and destruction; and for him, love was "the war of the sexes". When the word "masochism" became widely used during the 1890s, he protested against his work being used to describe a "medical case".

Leopold von Sacher-Masoch was born in Galicia, a Polish province in the Austrian Empire; his father was a chief of police and his mother a Ukrainian. It was from her that the name Masoch came. In adolescence he read the lives of the martyrs, and particularly of their sufferings, "with a sweet painful pleasure". In 1869 he formed a relationship with Fanny Pistor, a married woman, and together with her signed a contract in which he undertook to "be her slave" and "carry out to the letter all her wishes and commands" for six months. He turned this adventure into the novel *Venus in Furs* (1870), in which the heroine, Wanda de Dunajew, declared: "Every person needs someone to torment them. Some have a dog; myself, I have a lover." Severin, the hero of the famous novel, defined the quest in this way: "I find myself strangely attracted to pain, and nothing fans the flame of my passion like a beautiful woman's tyranny, cruelty and, above all, infidelity."

His many successful novels all

show the same obsession, featuring as the central character a woman, dressed in furs and armed with a whip, who makes the man her slave. The woman may be called Dragomira, Mardonna or Warwara, but it is always the same Venus, a surreal figure with a body as cold and hard as marble. The minute descriptions of her clothes and the analysis of her gestures spoil the novels with a rather overworked form of symbolism.

No matter how much the heroine wields her whip and issues orders, she remains a sex object manipulated by a man. In *The Separated Woman*, Julian wants to educate Anna, who is weak and liable to prejudice, to make her a mistress who "lives only to satisfy her whims and fancies, deceives and belittles him, and devours his life like a vampire". The author turns the scale of values upside down, giving the faithful wife the lowest rank and championing the adulterous woman. He also praises the separated woman, who dares to leave her husband in order to enjoy her love affairs. He exalts the woman who concludes a contract with the man demanding his submission.

DELIGHTFUL, SENSUAL TORTURE. It was this role that Sacher-Masoch wanted to foist upon Angelika Aurora Rümelin, whom he married in 1873. This admirer, born in 1845, wrote to him and signed her letters "Wanda", the name of the heroine in *Venus in Furs*. By entering his life, she recalls in her *Confessions*, she entered his game as well, keeping the name of Wanda. He gave her ... a fur as a wedding present, and for Christmas he gave her ... another fur. He commanded her to whip him, saying: "It's a delight for me to be abused by a woman."

He suggested, after spending all his money on furs and clothes for her, that she manage the finances. He undertook to obey her in a writ-

ten contract: "From now on," he said to her, "you are my mistress and I am your slave. Give the order and I will obey you always." He searched continually, in his longing for Greek antiquity and paganism, for what he called "the Grecian", something which would allow him to fulfill his supreme erotic dream of "being in the arms of a woman who calls on the man with whom she deceives me and has me whipped by him". It was for this reason that he begged his wife to take a lover, calling her ideas on love "mean-minded and petit-bourgeois". When he finally saw her being kissed by a man, he told her: "It was a dreadful moment, an unspeakable torture; but in that torture I found such a pleasure as I have never tasted before." He arranged meetings for her through classified advertisements, including one just ten days after she had given birth. He dressed her in finery, covered her in furs, kissed her feet in a gesture of humility, and watched her go ... and was greatly frustrated if she returned without "success". Finally she snapped, saying that she was overwhelmed by disgust and hatred for her husband. For his part, he was well aware of the impossible role he asked her to play, stating: "If this woman was in

my life, she would not feature in my books."

Enter Armand Rosenthal, a French journalist and admirer of Sacher-Masoch, who fell in love with Wanda. When Masoch pushed her into an affair with him, she finally broke away and in 1892 left with the Frenchman for Paris, overjoyed at having found her freedom. "No more to put on a fur, no more to wield a whip!" she exulted. The divorce was granted in 1886, with her as the guilty party because of her adultery! In the same year, Sacher-Masoch was received in Paris with great pomp and made a member of the Legion of Honour.

AN EXTREME FORM OF EROTICISM. Sigmund Freud (cf. p. 46) saw masochism as a form of sadism which the subject directs against himself. He combined sadism and masochism together, but it is unlikely that one is the inverse of the other. As the Masochs show, the masochistic man compels the woman to participate in scenes of masochistic behaviour. This however is not the case with the woman described in *The Story of O* (cf. p. 252) who accepts pain as a part of love. What the two authors have in common is the torture equipment – whips, masks, chains and so on – normally associated with relationships of domination and submission. This is how they appear in books, films, and the later fashion of black leather clothes (cf. p. 382), which shows the influence that these practices had on the public, albeit in a watered-down and altered form.

In the extreme form of eroticism practised by Masoch and those who imitated him, the sufferings that the hero wishes to inflict upon himself, however severe, remain under his control; they depend upon a contract which ritualises the ordeals endured and limits the torture.

1906

FRANCE. **The Protestant philosopher Jacques Maritain and his wife Raïsa Oumansoff, a Russian Jew, convert to Catholicism. Married in 1904 after a whirlwind romance, they had no children.**
On 2 October 1912 they took a "final vow of chastity". He said: "We wanted to make room for meditation and union with God ... We feel ... that the depth and strength of our love for each other will go on increasing for ever." This absolute commitment, based on their remarkable insistence upon truth, united them for life and strengthened their intellectual and spiritual communion with each other. The couple exerted a considerable influence between the two world wars.

♡ ♡ ♡

ABOVE
The Empress of the Flesh dominates men.

FACING PAGE
The Riding Whip, Alastair, 1905.

Gertrude Stein
& Alice Toklas

Two Americans in Paris; a long relationship, a mixture of writing and love at the centre of contemporary cultural life.

In 1907, thirty-year-old Alice Toklas, passing through Paris on a journey across Europe, met Gertrude Stein, three years her senior, who had lived there since 1903. Both were daughters of Californian middle-class families, who provided them with a small income. "She was large and heavy," recalled Toklas, who had small, delicate hands and a beautiful face. "She had a certain physical beauty, and great power." As Gertrude Stein's first book, *Three Lives*, was about to be published, Alice Toklas offered to correct the proofs; she soon became indispensable, and the two women were inseparable from that time on. The literary salon at 27 rue de Fleurus, where they received artists and writers, was one of the most important of the twentieth century. Toklas, who greatly admired Stein's genius, was her first reader, her typist, her muse, and her lover. Stein would call her from the kitchen to make her read her newest creation, and she used shopping lists or other raw material from Toklas's life in her works. Introduced as her "secretary" or "companion", Toklas played the traditional role of the artist's wife, relieving Stein of practical cares and enabling her to dedicate herself to her work.

"She was wonderful, and she was mine, which was also wonderful," wrote Stein, who signed her notebooks "Gertrice/Altrude", a mixture of their names. She had other lesbian affairs, but it is only in *QED*, which recounts the first, that she expresses herself openly on the subject. Her love poems, published after her death, record her private life with Toklas in a complicated cryptic style. "Tender button" can be easily identified, but use of the word "cow", as an obscure symbol for a female orgasm, is much less clear. The manuscript of the famous poem "A / Rose is a / Rose is a / Rose is a / Rose" includes a final line: "She is my rose."

Stein's rich, serious, authoritative voice and loud, hearty laugh contrasted sharply with Toklas's reticence,

acerbic wit, tanned appearance, thin frame and soft whispering voice. Their discreet relationship, similar to that of the famous Paris publishers Adrienne Monnier and Sylvia Beach, whom they often visited, was markedly different from the overt lesbianism of their colourful friend Natalie Barney, the rich American Paris nicknamed "Bonheur-Des-Dames". She rejected many other social standards, including fidelity, but her relationship with the painter Romaine Brooks lasted for fifty years, and her cult of friendship earned her the faithfulness of lovers such as the poet Lucie Delarue-Mardrus (cf. p. 27).

UNRECOGNISED GENIUS. Gertrude Stein came to Paris with her brother Leo, who wished to be a painter. Fascinated by the avant-garde, they collected paintings by artists then unknown. She purchased the first picture sold by Marie Laurencin, *Apollinaire and His Friends*. She supported Matisse and especially Picasso, who became her lifelong friend and painted a famous portrait of her in 1905. When she cropped her hair, he exclaimed with disgust: "What about my portrait?"

Unlike many other women, Gertrude Stein had faith in her own genius, ranking herself with Picasso or Einstein; but although her desire was to find fame as a writer, she suffered from what she believed was an unfair lack of recognition. In 1914 she was delighted to be hailed by the *New York Times* as "a literary cubist", having sought to introduce into literature the break made by abstract art. Her determined wish was to introduce a "continuous present" tense into English by using duplication, but the result was difficult to understand or even read. She worked furiously every day, but could not find a publisher.

After the war, during which Gertrude Stein and Alice Toklas used their van to bring aid to the wounded, they opened their salon to young American writers whom Stein christened "the lost generation". Stein was

ABOVE
Gertrude Stein (in the foreground) and Alice Toklas, photographed by Cecil Beaton.

FACING PAGE
Enemy Fat, Romaine Brooks.

a friend of Sherwood Anderson, F. Scott Fitzgerald (cf. p. 108), and Ernest Hemingway, who greatly admired her and maintained that she taught him the art of writing. "She directed the conversation," said American journalist Janet Flanner. "She directed everything, in every way. She talked, while Alice served the tea. One might say that she delivered a speech, while Alice supplemented it with footnotes." While the men talked with Stein, Toklas's duty was to keep their wives entertained by talking about cooking and other "women's" matters.

They spent their summers in a rented villa in the village of Bilignin, near Belley in Ain Province; there they received many visitors.

PARADOXICAL FAME. Toklas dealt with the printing of Gertrude Stein's works, at her expense. The publication in 1933 of *The Autobiography of Alice B. Toklas* was a turning-point in their lives: Stein at last found success with a witty, lively book written in an understandable language, in which she told, through Toklas, of their life

NEW YORK. **Maxim Gorki, the famous Russian writer, campaigns in the West against borrowing by Russia. The Russian government wanted to stop him entering the United States at all costs. Believing that the American prudish attitude would bring him publicity, the Russian envoy indicated to the press that the woman travelling with him, the writer and former actress Maria Andreeva, was not actually his wife. Rich and generous, and actually married to an army general, she had left her husband to give herself over to revolutionary activities. American intellectuals, anxious to appear moral, gave the writer a frosty reception, and hotel staff refused to welcome the scandalous, illegitimate couple, who were instead put up by sympathisers. The move brought Gorki enormous publicity, and he and his companion posed for photographers in the street, both sitting on their suitcases!**

and friendships with artists. In 1934 she made a highly successful conference tour of the United States, accompanied by Toklas, whom one journalist described as "her strange, birdlike shadow". Some of their friends, however, believed that the book showed them in a bad light, and protested; Braque and Hemingway even went so far as to break off their relationship.

War broke out while they were in Bilignin. They decided to stay there, and were not persecuted despite their Jewish background. When France was liberated they returned to Paris, welcoming American soldiers making a "pilgrimage" to visit the famous couple. Stein's death in 1946 left Toklas devastated. She said: "I'd imagined that we would go together – a bomb, a shipwreck perhaps – anything but this." Impoverished, she survived thanks to the generosity of friends, as she had no rights to the collection of pictures.

On her death-bed, Stein asked Toklas to publish all her manuscripts. Toklas dedicated herself to that task and wrote books herself, most notably two cookery books and her *Memoirs*, which ended with the account of Stein's death and included her famous last words: "'What is the answer?' I remained silent. 'In that case,' she said, 'what is the question?'" After her death in 1967, Alice Toklas was buried together with her friend in Paris's Père-Lachaise cemetery. She had converted to Catholicism in the hope of being reunited with her beloved in Heaven.

♡ ♡ ♡

Morals
Before Marriage …

In a book years ahead of its time, French socialist Léon Blum campaigned for equality of sexual freedom for young men and women.

"To allow and indeed arrange freedom for girls before marriage" was Léon Blum's suggestion in his essay *On Marriage* (1907), which portrayed marriage as "necessary and beneficial" but "out of adjustment". The future politician, then a jurist with the Council of State, was pursuing a career as a writer. His book, notable for its impartiality and many significant anecdotes, was very successful but was immediately condemned as "immoral", foreshadowing the scandal triggered in 1922 by Victor Margueritte's novel *La Garçonne* (*The Scarlet Woman*).

Blum claimed to have been inspired by *Amoureuse* (1891), a play written by his friend Georges de Porto-Riche, in which the heroine suggests that young girls should love first and marry later. Many feminists of the time criticised the "suffocation" of women in marriage; the heroine of Marcelle Tinayre's first novel, *Before Love* (1896) cries out, "I have a right to be loved. If I can't find it in mar-

riage, then … This 'then' occupied all my thoughts from then on."

Recalling that the Civil Code fixed a girl's marriageable age at fifteen years (cf. p. 286), Léon Blum believed girls to be "quite capable of enjoying love at that age". The "love initiation" for both girls and young men should be with an experienced partner; in this way, a girl would discover the pleasures of sex without the risk of pregnancy, and a young man would find a "protective and motherly mistress … [who] would take care of all his shyness and clumsiness". Neither men nor women should marry without going through "sexual apprenticeship"; only after that would they be ready to accept monogamy. In order for marriage to become "synonymous with both carnal and moral delight" it was important "not to embark upon it until instinct has been satisfied", that is, after tasting passion, pleasure, and disappointment. In this way the rate of adultery would be reduced. To be sure, infidelity would not disappear, but it would be less of a drama for not being compounded with lies.

Why virginity? The writer of this explosive book was thirty-five; married since 1896, he described himself in his dedication to his wife as "a happy man". Inspired by Balzac, he criticised Tolstoy's suggestion, born of his longing for lost innocence and condemnation of sensuality, that both boys and girls should be kept "in the dark" until the wedding day. A socialist, optimist, and utopian, Blum was concerned for the happiness of the human race, but he was not as progressive as Charles Fourier, who wanted to free women from the "economic yoke" of men by educating them and giving them charge over their own bodies. Blum's secular view of marriage – "Relieve it of all its ceremony and mystique … see it as a positive and determined relationship" – ran contrary to the trend of that time, which regarded the couple as sacred.

Another dominant trend of that time was encouraging men to repress their sexual activity (cf. p. 134) and, above all, denying women's sexual appetite completely. Among the bourgeoisie, this was achieved by preserving the girls' virginity until their wedding and delaying the awakening of desire. This gave rise to the ideal of the "pure woman", a pure white bird who suspected nothing until her wedding night, even though society balls, with waltz and tango, allowed her to discover emotions and sensations. This ignorance was less widespread in the country, where girls were allowed some freedom to meet with young men, although traditions varied between regions. In the towns and cities, premarital sex was common; the birth dates of first children born at the beginning of the century show that one in four married women was pregnant on her wedding day.

Why preserve the virginity of young girls? asked Blum. It risked producing an obsession or, worse still, bargaining among families. "I would like young girls to give in freely to their instincts, to follow their desires to the end, to give themselves if they wish, but I would hate ... for them to be fearful instead of chaste."

It is hardly surprising that these suggestions provoked violent reactions, not only from Blum's anti-Semite and anti-Dreyfusard enemies but also from women, many of whom considered the book too feminist. Even the great socialist Jean Jaurès was, despite his humanist views, shocked by its bold ideas and casual tone.

SEXUALITY AND EQUALITY. Blum saw sex as the coming together of two active desires. This was a revolutionary idea, quite contrary to the dominant view that defined sex as the coming together of the active desire of the man and the benevolent passiveness of the woman. The concept of "consent" was based on this view.

After becoming President of the Council in 1936, Blum had *On Marriage* republished, stating in the preface that the book contained "some important truths". Was he thinking of his description of a future world, with equal education for both sexes, sex education, and opportunities for divorce by mutual consent? "Then," he wrote, "girls will earn their living; they will not live with their parents or lovers, but have their own homes." They would be open in their relationships with men and live in equality and freedom, without false guilt or preoccupation with appearance. Children would be desirable, because reproduction would become "voluntary and premeditated". It would be pointless marrying to legitimise children; they would enjoy the same rights whatever the circumstances of their birth.

On Marriage, which Pétain's extreme right defined as a "sex manual for dogs", remains a very modern work in many respects. Its main argument, in favour of sexual freedom for young girls, was gradually realised with the advent of more reliable contraception in the 1970s. Only then did the number of women sexually active before marriage increase noticeably, although it remained less than the number of men (cf. p. 310). But as long as a girl who enjoys several "adventures" is censured and a young man who behaves thus is given the flattering title of Don Juan (cf. p. 194), Blum's dream of equality is still far from becoming a reality.

Young Girl,
Egon Schiele, 1913.

PARIS. **The beginning of a stormy relationship between two highly gifted and sensitive artists, the painter Marie Laurencin and the poet Guillaume Apollinaire. They spurred each other on with their mutual love. Her picture *Apollinaire and His Friends* (1908) showed them both, together with Picasso and Fernande Olivier. He expressed his love and pain in a series of splendid poems, published in *Alcohols* (1913) and *Caligrammes* (1918). He criticised her for being a "cold lover", while she preferred tenderness to savage desire. The "poorly beloved", as he defined himself, was a violent man, jealous and unfaithful, who dreamed about love rather than practising it. She left him in June 1912, but they continued corresponding until Apollinaire's death in 1918. She died in 1956 and was granted her wish to be buried with Apollinaire's letters placed on her breast.**

♡ ♡ ♡

Madame Edwards
& José María Sert

"Misia", one of the great oracles of Paris artistic and literary life, appeared openly in public with a fabulously rich Catalonian painter.

Portrait of Misia Godebska,
Pierre Bonnard, 1908.

FACING PAGE
The Serts in 1931, in front of one of the frescoes at the Waldorf Astoria, New York.

Madame Marie Edwards, known affectionately as Misia or Missia, was as beautiful as a bouquet of blooming roses with her white dress, full face and large chignon of red hair. Artists who met her and fell in love with her included Vuillard and Renoir, who painted numerous portraits of her, and the Catalonian painter José María Sert who met her in Paris in 1908.

The French called her "La Polonaise" because of her Polish father, the sculptor Cyprien Godebski. Motherless, she was raised in Belgium by her grandmother, the widow of the famous cellist Servais, before moving to Paris. She was thirty-six, living apart from her husband, and José María Sert y Badía was three years younger. From a family of immensely wealthy mill-owners, this seducer with his strong Spanish accent was in fact small, squat and unattractive, and the frescos that he painted for multi-millionaires' living rooms earned him the nickname "Tiepolo du Ritz". A Paris resident since 1900, he specialised in enormous murals, using a powerful – some would say heavy – style that combined baroque with imitations of neo-classical sculpture. The King of Spain chose him to decorate the cathedral at Vich, near Barcelona. Extravagant, courteous, and cultured, he was a source of immediate delight to Madame Edwards. When he left for Rome and asked her to go with him, she accepted, albeit hesitantly.

Misia herself led a life full of passion without knowing love or even displaying her sensuality. Seductive-looking and very popular, she shared the opinion of women in "polite society" that sexual conquests were the preserve of the demi-mondaine. But here was a man who encouraged her sensuality to blossom! She had been unaware of him during her two marriages, to Thadée Natanson, Director of *Revue Blanche*, and then the rich, unrefined, depraved Alfred Edwards. Edwards, mad with desire for her, brought about Natanson's ruin, arranged the divorce and married Misia in 1905; and she exchanged, as she wrote in her *Memoirs*, a "delightful, refined and cultured friend" for a man who turned her into "the worst spoilt brat in the world". She moved from the world of artistic and literary avant-garde into a world of journalists and actors; but the move was short-lived, because Edwards soon met a young actress and demanded a divorce, although he continued to support Misia to a considerable degree.

THE FASHIONABLE WOMAN AND THE SUCCESSFUL PAINTER. During their lovers' holiday in Rome, Sert showed himself to be a remarkable "guide" in more ways than one. After that, they travelled widely and returned to Italy every year to visit their friends in Venice. Misia loved his extravagance; he wore a cape and sombrero, drank heavily, and snorted cocaine. On their return to Paris, they appeared in public together with a

total disregard for convention, marrying only in 1920. They went together to the première of Mussorgsky's opera *Boris Godounov*, staged by Sergei Diaghilev with the great Chaliapine. She won the heart of the homosexual "Diag" with her spirit and charm, and later became his confidante, the only woman who ever got close to him. After becoming the leading light of *Revue Blanche*, she became the soul of the Russian Ballet, the troupe that he directed, and their success made her the trendsetter of the time. Always in the vanguard, she played a leading role in many "artistic battles"; after her portrayal in Alfred Jarry's *Ubu Roi* (1896), scandals did not scare her, although few were as notorious as the review of Stravinsky's *The Rite of Spring* in 1913.

A PASSIONATE LIFE WITH A SAD END. As an adviser, a patron of the arts and an oracle, she produced no works herself, but was the inspiration for others. Writers and musicians dedicated their works to her; she posed for painters; she was one of the few women who understood the music of her time, able to sight-read new scores on the piano; and she secretly gave money to Stravinsky for many years. She introduced artists encouraged by herself to Diaghilev, and it was through her that he met Jean Cocteau, Maurice Ravel, Claude Debussy and ... Sert.

Did love cloud Misia's sound judgement? She admired Sert greatly and contributed to his international reputation. He pleased rich people with the grandiose atmosphere he lent to their living rooms. In 1924 he staged a remarkably successful exhibition in New York and received an order from the Waldorf Astoria Hotel for frescos which earned him the highest ever payment for a wall painting. He earned millions and spent them with great gusto. His great work, the decoration of the cathedral at Vich, was destroyed during the civil war, but he set about remaking it in 1941.

Life with him was exciting. "You must admit, Jojo makes the rest of them look quite tame," Misia said to her close friend Coco Chanel. In Paris, they lived in a suite in the Hotel Meurice, which Sert transformed into a kind of luxurious "Aladdin's Cave". Although he said that his wife was the only woman who understood and supported him, he was unfaithful on many occasions. In 1925, at age fifty, he

1908

UNITED STATES. Publication of *The Link*, autobiography of Neith Boyce, who had been married to Hutchins Hapgood since 1899. These two writers belonged to New York's radical and intellectual Greenwich Village set. Influenced by Havelock Ellis and Ellen Key (cf. pp. 62 and 38), they shared housework and the education of their children, so that both could write. Although as feminists they believed in sexual freedom in "open" marriages, they battled with the horrors of jealousy and possessiveness, the hero of *The Link* finding nothing unusual in taking advantage of a freedom that he denied his wife. Hapgood took up the same theme, defending ...

met a beautiful twenty-year-old Russian named Roussadana Mdivani, known as Roussy. Misia, who had no children, felt a genuine affection for this young woman and showered her with presents; all three were censured for drug-taking. Later, they provided the inspiration for Cocteau's play *The Sacred Monsters* (1940). Although Sert had promised never to leave her, Misia accepted a divorce with good grace in 1927.

After that, her life was no longer one long festival. The Paris fashion switched to the Swedish Ballet; and in 1929, Diaghilev died in her arms in Venice. She took comfort in morphine. After Roussy's death, in 1938, Misia became the object of Sert's affections again, although he went from one affair to another and commissions took him all over the world. In 1945, after finally finishing the decoration at Vich, he asked her to join him so that she would be the first to see his life's work finished. By the time she arrived, however, he was dead.

"With him," she wrote, "went my whole reason for living." She survived a further five years, however, blind and addicted to morphine. She was buried in the small cemetery at Valvins, near Paris, where in 1898 the young, beautiful Misia Natanson had walked behind Stéphane Mallarmé's coffin accompanied by her artist and writer friends.

♡ ♡ ♡

"They Wrote of Love"

Female poets, such as Marguerite Burnat-Provins, worship lovers' bodies and glorify love's ardour.

The only reason for her love for Sylvius was: "Because you are you." She loved his mixture of power, gentleness, manly strength, steadfastness, and tenderness, "the ardour of your powerful body and the warm softness of your skin". She used nature as the inspiration for the description of his handsomeness: "Your legs, firm as the maple tree's trunk / With which mine entwine, / Like the curling branches of hops." In the tender warmth of his caresses, her will buckles and gives way: "Passive and naked, I was a queen crowned with the living crown of your entwined fingers", and finally, nightfall darkens and hides all that is around them. "Let the horizon close up at your smile!"

"She" was Marguerite Burnat-Provins. She wrote *A Book for You* for her lover, whom she called Sylvius, "as a memory of our times of sweet, sensual pleasure". This poet, who began as a wood carver, discovered writing through love and passion. Born in Arras, Marguerite Provins studied art in Paris and there met her first husband,

The female body, "the field of enjoyment and the garden of ecstasy". Tomb in the Staglieno cemetery, Genoa, Italy, photograph by Isolde Ohlbaum.

Adolphe Burnat, a young architect from Vaud, with whom she lived in Switzerland. In 1906 Paul de Kalbermatten entered her life; they married in 1910 and lived happily. *A Book for You*, written in unusual poetic prose, with long, flowing lyrical phrases, was successfully published in 1908.

She described her desire to possess him totally, "When you sleep, do you love me still?" and the sting of jealousy; the temptation to be hurt and suffer at his hands, "Do me evil with your large hands, / Do me evil with your strength which commands", she wrote in *Summer Song* (1910); the fantasy of sharing death which would ensure passion in eternity; separation, and the anticipation of a reunion: "I shall offer you my loins like a polished table, where the fruit of my open heart, richer than the choicest apple, waits to feed you and quench your thirst."

"At last, a woman speaks!" was the reaction of many male members of the literary world. In his preface to the second edition of *A Book for You*, writer Henry Bataille applauded "this brave move by a woman ... beautiful in her shamelessness, rich in her daring". For him, the book "contained the most impassioned confession that one could imagine". But to assert that "the cry of physical adoration, without veil and without double standards, had never before been uttered by a woman" is to forget the writings of the great lovers of the past, such as the letters of Héloïse and Abelard, or the impassioned sonnets of Louise Labé.

EROTICISM AND FASCINATION. At the beginning of the twentieth century writings on love, pleasure, and desire seemed the preserve of men; women who dared to produce such writings risked provoking righteous indignation. It must be admitted, however, that when erotic literature is undervalued or misunderstood, it is poorly judged. In France, literary tradition has allowed a certain measure of tolerance; the law condemned Flaubert's *Madame Bovary* and Baudelaire's *Les Fleurs du Mal*, but not Zola's novels which, thanks to the scandal they generated, were very successful in France and beyond. Things that shock people's "good taste" are easily likened to pornography, but eroticism is something quite different; it calls on the imagination, it excites, it mixes anticipation and desire.

The aesthetics of "La Belle Epoque" were full of erotic images. However, the dizzy round of pleasures with which the 1900s have become associated conceals a preoccupation with the *femme fatale* (cf. p. 88) and all-consuming femininity, at once desired and feared. The seductive "new Eve" was a malevolent siren, and "modern style" eroticism deadly and mixed with magic, mysticism, and the shadow of the occult. For many artists and writers, love was haunted by sin, castration, and death.

Certainly there is a great difference between the morbid description of marriage in *The Dance of Death* by the Swede August Strindberg (1901) and the free sexuality celebrated by the Austrian Arthur Schnitzler in *The Ring Dance* (1897). Some writers, such as Otto Weininger, embraced a radical form of misogyny, expressing a wish to flee all relations with the opposite sex; others praised androgyny, while the devotees of the "new woman", who criticised the conventional, essentially negative portrayal of female sexuality, wanted real relationships to develop between human beings.

Male or female writers? The identities become blurred when women produce and invert male stereotypes: Rachilde, who was partial to macabre and disturbing subjects, caused a scandal by doing this in *Monsieur Venus* (1884) in which the hero is a man-figure dominated by a woman; or when men use female pseudonyms, such as Pierre Louÿs who dedicated his shocking *Songs of Bilitis* (1894) to an imaginary Greek poet, similar to Sappho. Sapphism, the name then given to lesbianism, was in vogue in Paris, having been cultivated by wealthy foreigners such as Renée Vivien, a sensitive poet obsessed by the figure of the androgyne. What a contrast between her joyless eroticism, where lust bruises the spirit, and the powerful, allegorical sensuality of Colette (cf. p. 34)! Colette, in an erotic scene from *The Tendrils of the Vine*, describes herself as "tied to your bed by a fiery ribbon of pleasure", while the lover sees "inescapable pleasure pulsing under my skin, from my tightened throat to my curled feet".

AN INVITATION TO PLEASURE. Women therefore broke with the hatred of the body and the fear of sexuality which characterised the "decadent" form of aesthetics, and novelists such as Colette, or poets such as the Italian Ada Negri, author of the famous *Book of Mara* (1919), or the Hungarian Anna Lesznai, whose cosmic poetry extolled the ecstasy of love in which the ego can enjoy communion with nature (*Eden*, 1918), all show different perspectives.

Many writers at the beginning of the century focussed on the "invitation to pleasure". Anna de Noailles specifically mentioned this, albeit discreetly, in her first book *The Immeasurable Heart*, which appeared in 1901: "Drink the well of pleasure dry; it is the only wisdom. ... Live, my heart; be immeasurable in the desire, / the dizzy heights of delight you can impart." In poetic images that allowed her to be more daring, she felt "the thorn and the sweet honey of a crude caress / slide into the depths of her heart". Her heroines lived "sweet pleasures of love" (the title of one of her poetry collections) with a desire to dominate men. Another new trend was the campaign for "the right to pleasure", the title of a novel by Odette Dulac (1908). New also was the woman free of prejudice, who organises her love life according to her desires: in *The Fickle One* (1903) by Marie Régnier (alias Gérard d'Houville), the heroine undresses "without embarrassment" and the man is "so amazed by her calm joy and satisfaction" that he dares not go near her or even touch her!

Contemporary poets of Marguerite Burnat-Provins, who like her are unfairly forgotten, also exalted female love, such as Hélène Picard: "Oh! the beloved whom I await in the shadow, / Oh unknown evenings! / The desire which rises while the will sinks / Into a pair of bare arms" (*The Eternal Moment*, 1907). Marie Dauguet stated that she preferred "vertigo to pleasure" and proclaimed that her greatest delight was "To remain there, standing, on the firmament's edge / With my soul open, my flesh offered in a pledge." (*The Pastorals*, 1908). Happy in love, happy at home, she portrayed the body of a lover with a kind of cosmic lyricism. Finally, the Belgian poet Marie Nizet, whose collection *For Axel* dates from the same period but was not published until after her death in 1924, describes "the mouth of freshness, delight and fire" of the man she loves, and also celebrates her own body: "I love you, my body, which was his desire / His field of enjoyment, his garden of ecstasy and fire."

1908

... his own case, in *The Story of a Lover* (1919). Despite their difference in attitude to sexual morals, this avant-garde couple managed to lead a life of passion while preserving each other's individuality and independence.

NORWAY. Performance of *The Game of Life*, a play by Knut Hamsun who, after a wretched childhood, became a famous writer (*Hunger*, 1890). At the age of forty-nine, he fell in love with his interpreter, twenty-six-year-old Marie Anderson, wishing to snatch her away from the corruption of the city and the theatre. They married, had four children, and set up a country home at Nörholm, south of Oslo. A farmer and writer, Hamsun cultivated the soil and reared animals. While he wrote, in a cabin in the forest, she provided a calm existence and gave him the peace he needed. Their life together was happy, and he was awarded the Nobel Prize for literature in 1920. His last years, however, were unhappy; his marriage broke down and he suffered a nervous condition which led him to sympathise with Nazism.

♡ ♡ ♡

Beatrice & Sidney Webb

Two British intellectuals who exerted a profound influence on political life and thought.

In 1909 increasing unemployment was a problem in Great Britain, and a report on the trend was submitted by a Committee of Enquiry, appointed by the government to reform the poor laws. Minority members, however, including Beatrice Webb, submitted an alternative report, published by the Fabian Society, which at the time was involved with promulgating the ideas that foreshadowed the future welfare state. The Fabian Society, founded in 1884, was an important school of thought named after the Roman general Fabius Cunctator, and was a group of political and intellectual militants, artists and philanthropists who proclaimed a reformist socialism free from the shadow of Marx. It was in this context that Beatrice and Sidney Webb worked together. Sidney Webb was introduced to the Society by George Bernard Shaw, and became one of the chief sources of its ideas. The Fabian Society subsequently formed the framework of the British Labour Party through the foundation, by the Webbs, of the London School of Economics in 1900 and the *New Statesman* in 1913; both of these organisations still carry considerable prestige today. A feminist sub-group provided many militants for the suffragette movement.

A REAL INTELLECTUAL PARTNERSHIP. The eighth of nine girls, Beatrice Potter was the daughter of an intellectual who led a famous literary salon, and a businessman who, most unusually for that time, believed women to be superior to men. Beatrice did not study, but gained an education of her own from guests of the family salon; her passion for collecting information, for example, came from sociologist Herbert Spencer. Demanding and headstrong, with a puritanical outlook on life, she suffered a miserable adolescence. Horrified by poverty and destitution, she satisfied her need for an ideal by giving herself wholeheartedly to social work, first as a benefactress and then by carrying out research into the co-operative movement.

She had an unfortunate love affair with the liberal politician Joseph Chamberlain, a widower twenty-two years her senior; he was anxious to marry again, but only an intellectual. At thirty-two she met Sidney Webb, one year younger, who fell head over heels in love with her. They had become acquainted through their published works, and already admired each other.

The son of a London clerk and a hairdressing salon owner, Sidney Webb was a tireless worker. His ability to read quickly and his remarkable memory made him, according to his friend George Bernard Shaw, "the most capable man in England". He was different from Beatrice Potter not only in social status, but in stature; she was tall and beautiful, he quite undistinguished. She was artistic and liable to depressions and bouts of anorexia, while he was characterised by his even temperament and lack of imagination.

Having been warned that physical pleasure meant very little to her, he persuaded her nevertheless to marry him; together they could accomplish much, he said. On their wedding day, 23 July 1892, she wrote: "We are both only second-class minds, but we are remarkably well-matched." She saw herself as the architect, the philosophical researcher, while he was the practical one who "got things done". One year after their wedding, she wrote: "My husband and I grow closer with every day. A wonderful pact, is marriage: intimate love, tenderness, sharing of ideas, and companionship in work." She also described their way of "thinking together":

"We throw ideas at each other, and each of us stands back, appreciating and producing ideas in their turn. And we are not content if the conclusion does not fully satisfy us both."

"OVERT DOGMATISM". The Webbs formed a classic intellectual partnership, and this image was the driving force behind their work. Tireless workers, with no children to distract them, they wrote many thousands of pages together, and Beatrice kept a diary rich in valuable observations about the times. Among their publications were *The History of Trade Unionism* (1894), *Industrial Democracy* (1897), *English Local Authorities* (1906–1910), and *Constitution for a Socialist Commonwealth* (1920). While Sidney enjoyed studying statistics and administrative and political papers, Beatrice preferred direct investigation of London slums, dangerous workshops or mines.

The Webbs were the source of innumerable social reforms, private members' bills and political concepts that have continued to develop throughout the twentieth century. In the ideal state that they envisaged, governed by an administrative élite drawn from the middle classes, large-scale public service departments would meet the needs of individuals, and an improved social environment would make them healthier, more noble in attitude, and better workers.

Their personal goal was to live "as simply and as healthily as possible, to accomplish a maximum of work with a bare minimum of personal luxury". Beatrice's money, one thousand pounds from annual rents, allowed them to live in a comfortable house and to travel. Their salon at Grosvenor Road, Westminster, was one of the best known in London; members of the Balfour government, in particular, visited them.

"Their open-minded dogmatism", as Leonard Woolf described it (cf. p. 102) and the selfishness born of their lifelong dedication to work, earned them few friends. H. G. Wells (cf. p. 78), who was a Fabian until their great split in 1908, painted a very unfavourable portrait of them in *The New Machiavelli*; but they remained very close to George Bernard Shaw and his wife Charlotte.

Sidney Webb was elected Deputy Leader of the Labour Party in 1922 and played an active part in Ramsay MacDonald's government in 1924. In 1929 he was made a baron – although Beatrice refused the title Lady – and became Secretary of State to the Colonies. In 1931, however, both disillusioned with the progress of socialism in Britain, they helped to bring down the Labour Government; instead, they turned their affections to the Soviet Union, particularly Beatrice whose need for ideological causes was turning

1909

RUSSIA. **Moishe Segal, who became painter Marc Chagall, falls in love with Bella Rosenfeld, daughter of a Vitebsk jeweller. They parted in 1910 and promised to wait for each other; he left for Paris, where he became connected with the avant-garde school in Montparnasse. He returned to Vitebsk shortly before the war and they married in 1915. Their only daughter, Ida, was born in 1916. After being touched by revolutionary fervour, he gave up supporting political movements and settled in Paris with his family in 1923. He exalted the beauty of his "loving muse" in splendid portraits, and his pictures of lovers flying through the air illustrated his desire to "soar skywards" in love shared. In 1941 they took refuge in New York, where Bella died in 1944. Deeply grieved, he gave a canvas that brought together everything of significance in their world the title *Around Her*.**

♡ ♡ ♡

her into a fanatic. In 1932, on a trip lasting several months, they took at face value everything they were shown. In *Soviet Communism: A New Civilisation* (1935), she showed this form of socialism as the answer to all their dreams. From that time on, nothing could sway their blind faith.

♡ ♡ ♡

SEXOLOGY
Havelock Ellis and Sex without Sin

The English pioneer in sex psychology, Henry Havelock Ellis developed progressive ideas on marriage, pleasure for women and homosexuality.

Do "sexual problems" exist? Henry Havelock Ellis, the British author of the vast anthology of cases entitled *Studies in Sexual Psychology*, aimed to show that the very concept of "normality" was in fact absurd. Like

the Swedish writer Ellen Key (cf. p. 38), he exerted a profound influence on progressive thinkers of his time. The six volumes of his *Studies*, his most famous work, were published between 1897 and 1910, and devoured by readers in the United States and Europe; the German translation of the first volume was actually published one year before the original, and a French translation appeared in stages between 1908 and 1935. Ellis, who sat at the crossroads of psychology, biology and sociology, had begun by studying medicine but spent his working life studying

sexual behaviour, opening up the field that was to become known as sexology (cf. p. 114). His pioneering work was hailed as such by Freud (cf. p. 46), whose genius he recognised without being influenced by his thought.

Joseph Wortis, a pupil of Ellis' analysed by Freud, relates in his recollections their opinions of each other. Freud was convinced that Ellis, to be driven to carry out such research, must have a sexual problem. "You could say the same thing of me," Freud added, "but I would answer firstly that it's not your business, and secondly that it's not true." When Wortis mentioned Freud's suggestion to Ellis, Ellis retorted: "His belief that my interest in sex is caused by a perversion doesn't bother me. I can think of many people obsessed with sex, who obviously do have a problem. I'm quite prepared to admit that it's not true of Freud. But neither is it true of me!"

FRIGIDITY AND IMPOTENCE CAUSED BY CIVILISATION. Doctors studying sexual problems treated the pathological aspects first of all. German psychiatrist Richard von Krafft-Ebing, in *Psychopathia Sexualis* (1886) coined the words sadism and masochism, and described the distress that sexual behaviour could cause; however, he wrote the "sensitive" passages in Latin! For him, "a sexual pervert was an unfortunate, but not a criminal"; aberrant sexual behaviour was not a perversion or vice, but a distortion of instinct and therefore a problem in that area.

The first volume of Ellis's *Studies* deals with "sexual inversion", the name given by him to what was subsequently called homosexuality

(cf. p. 114). For him, it was innate, and as such should not be punishable by law. He described masturbation as "auto-eroticism" believing it to be a form of relaxation and a good way for adolescents to discover their sexuality.

The discovery in the nineteenth century that fertilisation is not linked to a woman's pleasure levels lent further strength to male egoism and hostility towards the clitoris, which as a result was considered useless. Victorians denied that sexual desire existed in women and were suspicious of sex in general. In a book published in 1865, which became an authority in Britain, the American doctor William Acton asserted, that female sexuality was compensated for by childbirth and domestic life. He therefore suggested that men should limit their sexual activity to one act of intercourse every seven to ten days and practise quick coition to "keep themselves together". Ellis, on the other hand, believed that abstinence was unhealthy because sex, life's central function, was "simple, natural, pure and good". In the West, as individualist thought developed, the progressive fringe looked to free itself from Victorian restraints and stand up for the right to pleasure.

In 1894 Ellis noted that there were a great many "relatively impotent" men, and defined premature ejaculation not as an illness but as "a legacy of civilisation". In 1908 Freud also noted the increased frequency of this problem, as well as the problem of frigidity in women, which he attributed to "our civilised sexual morals". He agreed with the conclusion of the first feminists, such as Elizabeth Blackwell (the first woman doctor in the United

States, in 1845), who blamed frigidity on education; in an effort to encourage girls to preserve their virginity until marriage, they had been made to associate sex with sin.

To become an authority on sex? In his *Memoirs*, Ellis describes himself as a mild, passive man, attracted by strong women. "I am considered an authority on sex, which has amused a few of my close female friends," he wrote. It appears that he himself suffered from premature ejaculation. From 1884 to 1889, he had a major love affair with Olive Schreiner, the author of *Story of an African Farm*. Lying naked in an embrace was enough for him, he recalled; and undoubtedly he had no full sexual relations with her, or with Edith Lees, another writer, whom he married in 1891. After becoming a lesbian, she was one of his cases for the *Studies*. He

dedicated about one hundred pages to his own sexual leanings, to which he gave the name "undinism" or "urolagnia"; he derived his pleasure from seeing a woman urinating.

Although Edith Lees wanted children, Ellis decided that she should not have them, for what he called eugenic reasons (cases of mental instability in her family) and for practical reasons; they were poor and he had no wish to be distracted from his work. They lived apart, he in London and she in Cornwall. Ellis had another affair in 1915, with the American feminist Margaret Sanger who was spending a year of exile in Europe.

Although he helped his readers rid themselves of much fear and ignorance, Havelock Ellis nevertheless held some of the prejudices of his time, believing

ABOVE
Woman in Repose,
Gustav Klimt, 1913.

LEFT
Self-Portrait of the Artist Masturbating,
Egon Schiele, 1911.

that genius was the exclusive preserve of men and childbirth the high point of a woman's life. He condoned male sexual aggression, describing it as "a normal outworking of the sexual instinct". Like Freud and most of his contemporaries, he believed that the sexual organs were primitive, and therefore ugly; but contrary to Freud's assertions, he maintained that the clitoris was the main source of sensation in the female and advised men to devote plenty of time to "erotic preludes".

Ellis believed that a husband and wife should be economically independent. He was in favour of "trial marriages" before a couple entered into a lasting commitment, and also believed that some people needed variety, psychological or emotional faithfulness appearing more important than sexual fidelity. However, in his own marriage, both partners took a dim view of the other's freedoms ...

Henry Havelock Ellis appointed himself to the almost divine mission of enlightening the world on the various aspects of sex and dispelling guilt which often accompanied it. His last book was a lyrical celebration entitled *The Dance of Life* (1923). He left behind an interesting explanation for the general fascination for erotic subjects, saying: "Adults need erotic literature just as children need fairy tales."

Coquetry. In an article entitled *The Psychology of Coquetry*, German philosopher Georg Simmel describes the game and fine art of coquetry, which he defines as a feminine attitude consisting of refusing everything while maintaining an attitude of acceptance. He distinguished it from a desire to please, and acknowledged in it the attraction of the secret, the hidden, the furtive. He produced a discerning analysis of eroticism, showing how a person in love can derive "more joy from the first secret hand-hold than from the total giving of the self that follows", and how "the kiss, or even the simple awareness of being loved in return, can surpass all the stronger sexual joys".

♡ ♡ ♡

Sonia & Robert Delaunay

Two major avant-garde painters combined their artistic and amorous fortunes. For them, colour was life.

The Eiffel Tower as a wedding present! It was the canvas that painter Robert Delaunay gave to his wife Sonia, also a painter, in 1910. *The Tower Speaks to the Universe* was the first in a long series inspired in him by this symbol of modernity. Painted in the year the two artists met, it bears the inscription "Movement, Depth 1909, France, Russia".

Sarah Stern, also known as Sonia Terk, was born in the Ukraine in 1885. She was raised in St Petersburg by her uncle and aunt Terk, members of the well-to-do French-speaking bourgeoisie. After two years studying art in Karlsruhe, she set up in Paris in 1906, and, in order to stay longer than was right for a young girl of the time, contracted a marriage of convenience with an enthusiastic German modern art collector, a homosexual named Wilhelm Uhde. It was he who introduced her to the world of art and artists, such as Picasso, and in particular Robert Delaunay, with whom she fell passionately in love. She divorced in order to marry him. They married at twenty-five and were tied together by a love which lasted a lifetime.

Robert, a Parisian, was also raised by an uncle and aunt. Unlike Sonia, who internalised her passion and intensity and thus preserved a wise, studious appearance, Robert was fiery and difficult to deal with. At seventeen he was hired as an apprentice in a theatre set workshop to paint large surfaces; two years later, he was showing impressionist canvases at the Independent Art Exhibition.

A MARRIAGE OF COLOUR. Thanks to the income from Sonia's Russian inheritance, the young couple were not short of money. They lived in Paris's Rue des Grands-Augustins, in an apartment with workshop; its ceilings were decorated by Sonia. When Charles, their only son, was born in 1911, she produced her first abstract work, a cover consisting of pieces of coloured cloth, for his crib. Both Robert and Sonia were fascinated by modernity, speed, railways, motor cars, and aircraft. For Robert, the Eiffel Tower was his "emancipated muse", his "Eve of the future". He painted it continually, in his own particular way, from many different angles at the same time.

The life of Sonia, the avant-garde artist whose friends included Marie Laurencin and Hans Arp, revolved around Robert; it was he who talked, he who got carried away with his enthusiasm, his frustrations. To Sonia, Robert represented "life in all its impetuousness, all its violence, all its beauty". He was also a brilliant theorist, and as such fascinated her. Reading Chevreul's book *The Simultaneous Contrast of Colours* (1839) inspired in Robert the concept of "simultaneity" which consisted of producing form and movement through the interaction of juxtaposed areas of colour. They both illustrated this concept in their paintings, which were most notable for their rounded bands of colour. Robert and Sonia were the best example of many artistic couples with equal values, who worked together and combined art and love (cf. p. 72).

Their move into poetry led them to meet Blaise Cendrars, for whom Sonia illustrated *Prose on the Trans-Siberian and Petite Jehanne of France* (1913), and

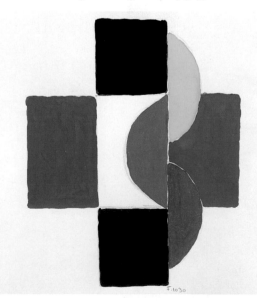

ABOVE
In front of *Helix*,
Robert Delaunay, 1923.

RIGHT
Composition,
Sonia Delaunay, 1962.

FACING PAGE
Dancer and *Dress Simultaneous*,
Sonia Delaunay, 1917.

Guillaume Apollinaire, who christened their style "Orphism". He lived with them for two months, praising Robert's masterpiece *La Ville de Paris* and writing a poem for his first abstract series *The Windows*, while Sonia painted her *Electric Prisms*. Everything around them was "simultaneous": their friends' poems, Sonia's collages, and the dresses or suits designed by her and worn by the whole of their happy band of artists on evenings out at the Bal Bullier. Their paintings were exhibited, both separately and together, in Paris, Berlin, Munich, London and New York. In 1913 Paul Klee published an important article by Robert on the subject of light in the German review *Der Sturm*.

Their family life was spoilt by Robert's rages, but Sonia put up with his difficult personality and her smile never wavered. An artist, a lover and a mother combined, she was a secretive woman, marvellous at organising, who always ensured that her husband was comfortable, and made sure that he did not overwork or neglect himself during his intense bursts of creativity. Her motto was: "Nothing is done through chance; everything is done through love."

FREE FORM AND COLOUR. When war broke out in August 1914 they were in Portugal; they decided to stay there, since Robert was unfit for military service. They visited avant-garde artists both in Portugal and in Madrid, where they set up next. Here Sonia opened "Casa Sonia", a shop where bold Madrilenians came to try on "simultaneous" coats and dresses.

On their return to Paris in 1921 they once again found themselves at the centre of a whirl of artists and theorists, including Marc Chagall and the surrealist and Dadaist poets Tristan Tzara, Joseph Delteil, Philippe Soupault and others. Her income cut off by the Russian revolution, Sonia became a set designer and artist, and used her dazzling sense of colour to create costumes and pieces of scenery with equal zest. She designed innumerable styles of clothes, swimsuits and costumes for the Russian ballet, and brought colour to interior décor as well, being hailed as the star of the 1925 International Exhibition of Decorative and Industrial Art. She

worked with silk manufacturers in Lyon and opened a business; and when the slump forced her to close it, she continued working for herself.

The Delaunays were a team. They created costumes for ballet and cinema, and Robert, in his turn, experimented with different materials. In the thirties, he

ST PETERSBURG. **The wedding of two great Russian poets, Anna Akhmatova and Nikolai Gumilëv. During their Paris honeymoon Akhmatova met up with Modigliani who drew numerous sketches of her, but Akhmatova and Gumilëv are only known as a couple from what their poems tell of them. He was looking for his ideal woman, but Akhmatova was too sophisticated, too sensitive: "I believed her to be pleasant / I wanted her to be fantastic." A difficult husband who, she wrote, hated the sound of babies crying – their son Lev was born in 1912 – he remained a mystery to her. He preferred the great historical poems and criticised the lyrical style of his wife, who found freedom in writing "under the sharp stiletto of pain". They parted in 1918 and their lives were broken by the Revolution; Gumilëv was shot in 1921, and Akhmatova was forced to remain silent while her works were circulated "underground".**

moved into architecture and thus closer to his wife's work, and in 1935 they both had a stand at the Exhibition of Light. For the 1937 Exhibition, Robert designed the vast decoration for the Palace of Aeronautics and the House of Railways. In 1938, both of them decorated the sculpture hall in the Tuileries Gallery. Robert, however, fell ill, although he still held talk sessions with young painters and architects, and in 1939 organised the first

Réalités Nouvelles exhibition. After Robert's death, in 1941, Sonia dedicated herself to publicising her husband's works while at the same time continuing her relentless activity: she produced mosaics, stained-glass windows, wallpaper, playing cards, decorations and posters. She also took up painting again, and in fact never stopped creating or continuing to liberate form and colour, until her death in 1979.

♡ ♡ ♡

Eastern Eroticism

The "art of the bedroom", the product of a sophisticated culture, suggests that men should exercise self-control so that lovers can reach mutual cosmic ecstasy.

All that western cultures remember of Tantrism is the supposed sex-orgies, despite the continued publication since 1910 of the *Principles of Tantra*, translated from Sanskrit into English by Arthur Avalon. The famous Kama Sutra, the Hindu text translated many times over since the end of the nineteenth century, has become known for the acrobatic positions (cf. p. 314) adopted during lovemaking by princes and courtiers. Westeners fantasise about the bound feet of Chinese women, and look through the eyes of tourists at the carvings of erotic scenes in the Indian temples at Khajuraho, slipping surreptitious glances at "daring" Japanese etchings and Persian miniatures. The West has developed a scientific discussion of sex and gives priority to speed and efficiency; this has led many people to reduce sex to a function and look to orgasm as a means of relieving their tensions. Eastern eroticism, on the other hand, is the product of a sophisticated culture, an art based on slow, tender caresses; although it too adopts a masculine point of view, it recognises the difference between male and female pleasures and advocates a different type of enjoyment, suggesting that the man show self-control and restrain himself before ejaculating.

SEX LINKED WITH THE SACRED. In the West, sex has been devoid of religious overtones since the time of Plato. In Judaeo-Christianity it has become associated with sin, a combination unknown elsewhere. In the East, meanwhile, even Japanese Buddhism, which advocates the renouncing of everything that might hinder the path to enlightenment, does not condemn the pleasures of "this fleeting world".

Away from the West, sex is linked with the sacred everywhere; human love is a reflection of divine communion, and the sex act is an

echo of the cosmic creation process. Its aim is to produce ecstasy rather than reproduce the species. Through meditation and self-control, it aims to reconcile the masculine and feminine within the self in order to attain harmony. The knowledge of sex, which is at once a fleshly ritual and an out-of-body experience, is acquired through practice; the art is to hold back the "seed", thus transforming it into a source of light and distributing the energy throughout the body. Desire is denied, repressed, or held back, because to master desire supposes that it has been acknowledged. The man's sexual power increases with every orgasm that does not produce ejaculation, and this mastery of himself brings him inimitable pleasure, freedom from the temporal, and even, the Taoists believe, immortality.

Of the three monotheistic religions, Islam is the only one that links "drinking deep of love" with spiritual ecstasy, and seeing in a sexual union an act of worship of the Creator. As sexual pleasure gives a foretaste of the delights of Heaven, the Moslem man is duty bound to bring his wife that pleasure, at the same time gaining strength and courage himself.

China, Japan, India, and the Arab world all give manuals on "the art of the bedroom" to new lovers and young married couples belonging to a certain social and cultural élite; examples include the Chinese classic *Jin Ping Mei (The Flower in the Golden Vase)* and *The Thousand*

and One Nights. Before eventually adopting a more puritan view of sex, these societies developed an erotic art unparalleled by anything in the West, with the sole exception of the *Song of Songs* (cf. p. 264).

Most western people are unaware that in India the lingam, the phallic representation of the god Shiva, is actually a "pillar of chastity" because it "holds back its seed"; that the *Kama Sutra* recommends "continency" during the three nights following the wedding and preaches gentleness, tenderness and refinement: "The woman should be seen as a flower and treated in such a way that her beautiful scent spreads without her closing up."

In Eastern art the image of the vulva, which has aroused so much fear and hypocrisy in the West, is praised and represented as a lotus flower, a peach or an apricot.

Tantrism, a series of physical and psychological practices that have influenced Hinduism and some forms of Buddhism, is a form of yoga that carries a shift of empha-sis from orgasm to ecstasy and concentrates on the female aspect of sexual energy (*shakti*); the *yoni* (vulva) is active and the *lingam* (penis) passive. During their embrace, which represents cosmic union, the man and the woman, sitting face to face in the lotus position, cease to move: "united in total harmony, they are transported by the enlightenment and pass together into Nirvana".

THE UNION OF HEAVEN AND EARTH. In Chinese Taoism, the union of the female element, which proceeds from the earth, and the masculine element, which appears in the sky, brings the lovers a peace which allows them to share in the infinite energy of the cosmos. It brings their Yin and Yang energy-flows together in a complete harmony, which leads to the discovery of Tao. To reach this harmony requires the sex act to be long-drawn-out, without the man ejaculating from his "jade stalk"; to do this will reduce his vitality. Instead, he has to allow the woman the greatest possible measure of enjoyment, in order for her to produce "the rose of pleasure", that is, the essence of Yin, with which the man then becomes impregnated; this in turn increases his own "Yang". "The Yin awakes slowly and is satisfied slowly, while the Yang awakes quickly and withdraws readily."

Over time, however, the East has allowed some of its traditions to be lost. In China, long before the Maoist revolution, the puritan form of Confucianism destroyed or censored the so-called "pillow treaties"; and from the eighteenth century onwards, Islam greatly increased the number of things prohibited, painting the woman as the devil's advocate who must be veiled in order to protect the faithful from her wiles.

Since the 1980s, the West has been discovering traditional Eastern eroticism and offering seminars where formulae for "opening" one's body, in order to allow sexual energy to circulate, are taught. But the sculptures of Khajuraho, who smile the smile of the initiated, seem to be asking: Can the sexual be separated from the sacred?

THE KISS, by Constantin Brancusi, a Romanian sculptor living in Paris, is put on exhibition for the first time; a block of stone, which showed two almost identical busts, side by side, differing only in the length of the woman's hair. The joining of the mouths and eyes, and the entwining of the arms, appear to symbolise two becoming one, a theme which Brancusi had touched on before. He placed the sculpture in Paris's Montparnasse cemetery, for the monument to Tatyana Rachevksaya who committed suicide after an unhappy love affair. Brancusi said: "I wanted to remember not only the picture of that unique couple, but all the unknown couples of this world who have loved each other before suffering the agonies of separation."

Chundra-Lela, *Dominique Jouvet-Magron.*

Alexandra David-Néel & Philippe Néel

A "singular marriage", as described by this spirited adventurer who travelled across Asia while writing a remarkable travel diary for her husband.

On 9 August 1911, Alexandra David-Néel, a journalist and Orientalist, left Tunis for Marseille, from where she sailed for Ceylon and the Indies. The tall form of her husband Philippe Néel gradually grew smaller and fainter as the quay receded. It would be January 1926 before they met again, back in Marseilles.

Alexandra David, born in 1868, was always closer to her French, Protestant socialist father than to her Belgian Catholic mother. As a proud and secretive adolescent, she ran away first to Italy, then to England, and it was only lack of money that forced her to return. At twenty she went to live in London and then Paris, where she was introduced to Indian and Chinese philosophies. After an initial voyage to Ceylon and the Indies, she published articles on Asia; but as these did not earn her enough to live on, she embarked on a career as an opera singer – she had a beautiful soprano voice – which led her to the Hanoi Opera where she appeared in 1895.

It was in Tunis, on a tour, that she met Philippe Néel. Born in 1861 at Alès, in Gard, the son of a Jersey clergyman, this gentle, refined man was the chief engineer for the Tunisian railway system. In keeping with his "Don Juan" reputation, he seduced Alexandra and made her his mistress after inviting her onto his yacht *L'Hirondelle*. Always independent, Alexandra had previously lived with the composer Jean Haustont, maintaining a friendship and correspondence with him after leaving him in 1900.

A "MARRIAGE OF SPITE". She settled in Tunis, where she first ran the casino and then dedicated herself to studying journalism. She published texts on Tibetan mysticism, Buddhism and Taoism, as well as articles campaigning for social justice and equality between the sexes. She explored the south of Tunisia and Algeria. When she dis-covered that Philippe had kept her letters together with those of his former mistresses, all of whom he had seduced on board *L'Hirondelle*, she went into a violent rage.

They married, in spite of that, on 4 August 1904. "It was a singular marriage," she was to say, "we married more out of spite than out of affection." Although she believed that "the ideal place ... to set up home [is] a garden with two residences", they nevertheless shared the same house. They had no children.

Philippe responded to his wife's uncompromising views and search for absolute truth with a coolness that infuriated her. She very soon grew tired of their daily life. Philippe, who was frequently depressed, continued to have affairs, and Alexandra invariably made a scene; however, as she travelled to every corner of Europe during this period, it was usually by letter. In 1906 Philippe remarked: "You don't love me any more, my poor dear one; too often you have told me 'I love only myself.' And he added: "I've tried to give you what I could of myself, and all the comfort I could."

Alexandra, a member of the feminist movement, expressed in her writings her frustration at being unable to meet all his needs, as well as her abhorrence for sexual relations. Meanwhile, her tireless work was winning her recognition as an Orientalist. She was ready for the great voyage.

A PRECIOUS CORRESPONDENCE. As soon as she left, she started writing to her husband, requesting that he keep the letters safe, which he duly did. Together, these letters made up a diary of a fascinating voyage; and it was through the diary that an exceptional relationship, quite out of the ordinary, developed between them.

In 1912, she sent him the first of her many requests for money: five thousand francs from his own capital. Clearly she believed it "strange to ask someone to give money to the thing that most upset him". Philippe was worried by his wife's "increasing interest in mysticism" and the length of her voyage. "Perhaps I'm mad, ungrateful, selfish, whatever you like," she replied, "and the dream will consume me, as you say. But I cannot come back." In 1917 she wrote to him: "I have always wanted to come back ... but not to the life of struggles and ambition that you describe. I really want to live with you, provided I can get up at three and go to bed at nine, and shut myself away for a week or two without either of us disturbing the other."

Christened "the lamp of wisdom" by a Tibetan ruler, she followed her spiritual quest to the Indies, China, Korea, and Japan. But it was the Himalayas, and particularly Tibet, then closed to foreigners, that attracted her. She was the first Westerner to enter the territory in 1924, disguised as a beggar and accompanied by a young lama, Aphur Yongden, whom she hired in Sikkim in 1913 and legally adopted in 1929. He was her

1911

PARIS. **Mistinguett and Maurice Chevalier dance the "amazing waltz" at the Folies Bergère, and the music-hall queen with the famous "legs" remarks on the debutant actor's "pretty little mouth". She was thirty-five, he thirteen years younger. Taken prisoner during the war, he was freed thanks to Mistinguett's intervention with King Alphonse XIII of Spain, her then lover. She made him work with her again, but the relationship was a stormy one. "I loved him too much to want to understand him," she confided. "He didn't give me much, but I will feel his absence for the rest of my life." After their split, she dedicated her anthem "My Man" to him. He left for the United States, where he very soon found stardom, in 1927; but in his** *Memoirs*, **he commented on the talents of "Miss" and her "sexiness, cheeky humour and Parisian style".**

The "Lamp of Wisdom" surrounded by proud Tibetans in 1921.

constant companion, acting as her servant, secretary, companion-in-adventure and student. She compelled him to take a vow of chastity.

Meanwhile, Philippe Néel left Tunisia for Algeria and settled in Bône. He sent her a letter, which reached her on her journey back, intimating that he had learned to live without her. She never joined him again.

Her return to Marseille, in 1925, was a triumphant one. The publication of *A Parisian Woman's Voyage to Lhasa* brought her worldwide fame. In 1929 she set up home in Digne, in the Southern Alps, and named her house *Samten Dzong* (fortress of meditation). She saw her husband from time to time, and they retained a mutual affection and respect for each other.

When she left again for China in 1937, her correspondence with her husband, and her requests for money, began again. This time she was forced to flee the Japanese invasion, and remained stranded in Western China until 1945 because of the war.

Philippe Néel died in 1941; with his death, thirty years of correspondence came to an end, but she continued writing letters to him nevertheless. In their "singular marriage" he had been her best friend, her protector and the privileged witness to a remarkable adventure.

Alexandra David-Néel died in Digne in 1969, having lived her life according to the Buddhist verses that she kept as her watchword: "Be to yourself your own light. Be to yourself your own refuge."

♡ ♡ ♡

SOCIETY
The Painter Couples

The combination of painting and love, of art and marriage, was an innovation of the twentieth century.

1911 saw the beginning of two major artistic trends of the twentieth century, one in Moscow, the other in Munich. Painter couples were actively involved in both.

The *Blaue Reiter* (Blue Knight), which was the foundation of German expressionism, was started by the Russian painter Vasili Kandinski, who was also the theorist in the group. With him were his German companion Gabriele Münter, and a Russian couple Alexei Yavlenski and Marianna Verefkina. In 1908 and 1909 all four lived together, painting, at Murnau, near Munich. Tragically, however, the war put an end to the *Blaue Reiter*, as some of its German members were killed or injured. The Russians had to leave the country: Yavlenski and Verefkina settled in Switzerland, while Münter and Kandinski separated in 1916. In 1937 the Nazis mounted a major exhibition in Munich, called "Degenerate Art", which brought all these pioneers' works together.

WORKING TOGETHER. At the turn of the century, painter couples were living and working together in the avant-garde quarters of every major European city. Most had met while studying at art schools, which had only recently begun to accept women. Was painting more conducive to love than other art forms? Maybe, but it was difficult nevertheless for female painters who married and had children to carry on working; it must be remembered that in an artistic household the wife had to meet the practical needs and thus favour the husband's creativity, which took priority over her

own. For this reason many women chose the more lucrative area of decorative art, designing textiles, fashions, wallpaper or theatre scenery, and illustrating books or posters.

This was the case with Robert and Sonia Delaunay (cf. p. 66), one of the best-known painter couples, and their friends Hans Arp and Sophie Taeuber (cf. p. 93) who helped found the Dada group in Zurich in 1916. Hans was also a sculptor and poet: Sophie danced, made puppets, and produced innovative designs for wallpaper and embroidery. For a long time she was

Alexander Rodchenko and Varvara Stepanova.

overshadowed by her husband, although they both influenced each other with an understanding so deep that they created joint works: collages, paintings, embroideries, and even "duo-sculptures".

In Moscow it was another couple, Mikhail Larionov and Natalya Goncharova, who launched neo-primitivism, and subsequently Rayonism, with *The Donkey's Tail*. Both born in 1881, they met in 1898 and spent their whole lives together, becoming involved in all the avant-garde's struggles; they were the driving force behind the development of modern Russian art, although they left Russia in 1915. Their movement, known as Rayonism, which published its manifesto in 1911, was one of the earliest expressions of abstract art; the paintings used rays of colour reflected from the surfaces of objects, rather than the objects themselves, to convey expression. Larionov and Goncharova pursued both theoretical reflection and artistic practice together; their pictures were similar, although his were more ironic and hers more emotional. They settled in Paris in 1917, where Goncharova worked with the Russian Ballet, but they did not become wealthy.

In Russia, the beginning of the century was a remarkable period of artistic development, enriched by Western influence and the discovery of popular culture. For the first time the country produced an artistic movement that brought about a worldwide change. Its founders were anxious to distance themselves from the French influence in Russia and turn to native sources of inspiration.

These radical intellectuals and innovative artists included several young women. Often from well-to-do environments, these emancipated women wore their hair short, smoked, and retained their maiden names after marriage; there is nothing traditionally "feminine" in their works. They played a key role in subjective painting, an art considered unimportant until then, and were able to express themselves in designing theatre scenery and costumes. Following on from Goncharova, they designed dresses and materials, attempting to "bring art down into the streets". Getting their talent acknowledged was not, however, easy; the avant-garde ideologies, particularly futurism, placed emphasis on "masculine" values, giving women a subordinate role and considering subjective arts to be "minor". Some artists' dogmatism and puritanical views were accompanied by a fascination for violence, as notable for its use of military metaphors as for being described as "avant-garde".

JOINT ADVENTURES IN ART. In 1917, many of these young artists welcomed the October Revolution and became channels for propagating the "proletarian culture". Couples very often shared the same workshop, embarked on adventures in art together and explored many fields, sometimes producing works together, such as collages. Alexander Rodchenko, the driving force behind constructivism, was best known as a photographer, but was also a painter, sculptor, and typographer; his wife, Varvara Stepanova, was a painter, model maker, and stage designer, and produced prints for fabrics. The other couples included Lyubov Popova and Alexander Vesnin, and Olga Rozanova who produced books together with her husband Alexei Kruchenykh, creating collages inspired by his poems. The intense artistic activity of this period influenced the whole of the country's visual culture until the Stalinist freeze, which started in the 1930s and showed in art as "socialist realism".

In the West, other painter couples in a typically twentieth-century mould included Vanessa Bell and Duncan Grant in England (cf. p. 83) and the Swedes Isaac Grünewald and Sigrid Hjertén; in Paris, meanwhile, Diego Rivera had numerous painter companions before returning to Mexico where he married Frida Kahlo (cf. p. 137). Later came Maria Elena Vieira da Silva and Arpad Szenes (cf. p. 151) and, in the United States, Yves Tanguy and Kay Sage (cf. p. 183), and Jackson Pollock and Lee Krasner (cf. p. 203).

Cover of the magazine *Der Blaue Reiter*, Vasili Kandinski, 1912.

SPRINGTIME, a painting by Marcel Duchamp, is exhibited. The young man and young slender woman holding up the tree represent the artist and his sister Suzanne. They are a picture of alchemical incest or "conjunction of opposites", which produces the androgyne, a common theme in Duchamp's work. Duchamp painted the picture on the occasion of his sister's wedding to chemist Charles Desmares, and gave it to the young couple. A painter herself, Suzanne Duchamp was married again in 1919, this time to the painter Jean Crotti, and both were involved in the Dadaist movement. The two other Duchamp brothers were also artists: Gaston, a painter, was known as Jacques Villon, and Raymond Duchamp-Villon was a sculptor.

"Marriage: an honourable estate consisting of a master, a mistress and two slaves, all in two people".

AMBROSE BIERCE
The Devil's Dictionary

Katherine Mansfield
& John Middleton Murry

A young, exalted love lived out through writing, between a novelist and a literary critic.

"A young love, the brightest and best love in this world," was how Katherine Mansfield, at the end of her short life, described her relationship with John Middleton Murry. After they met in December 1911, he published her novels in *Rhythm*, the avant-garde literary review that he edited. She was beautiful, he was handsome, and they were both brilliant and progressive in their thinking. In 1909 Katherine, pregnant at the time, had married George Bowden, but left him immediately. She desperately wanted a child, but suffered a miscarriage and would never bear one. In August 1912 Murry left his classical studies at Oxford, and a promising university career, to live with her in London.

John Middleton Murry had, ever since his poverty-stricken childhood, been plagued by feelings of insecurity. An introvert, he spent his whole life hiding from reality by developing friendships with writers; but in truth he was fascinated by their works rather than by them. He became a famous literary critic, introducing Marcel Proust and André Gide to the British public.

Katherine Mansfield – born Katherine Beauchamp, she took her grandmother's maiden name – grew up in a well-to-do family in New Zealand. That country's healthy climate and beautiful landscapes left a permanent mark on her. Somewhat fragile-looking, she soon turned out to be very sensitive and independent-minded. Sent to London with her two sisters to study at age thirteen, she was an admirer of Oscar Wilde and the "decadents", passionately fond of music, and an excellent cello player. At eighteen she was called back to New Zealand by her parents, but managed to return to London two years later. She cut her hair short, adopted an avant-garde hairstyle and published her novels while holding down several part-time jobs. It was the start of a new life.

THEY WROTE AT THE SAME TABLE. Literary life, in those last happy months before the war, was exciting. In July 1914, Murry was the witness to the wedding of D. H. Lawrence and Frieda Weekley, née von Richthofen (see right). The two couples were very good friends. In autumn 1914, Katherine Mansfield had an affair with the French writer Francis Carco. "I knew that she would come back," Murry wrote subsequently, "I had this deep-rooted belief that our love would stay ever green." Later she had an affair with the pacifist thinker Bertrand Russell, and Murry became involved with Dorothy Brett and then with Lady Ottoline Morrell. Their love, however, persisted.

In September 1915 Katherine Mansfield's younger brother came from New Zealand to fight in the war, and perished at the front one month later. Their reminiscences plunged her into a deep longing for her childhood, which from then on was the inspiration for many

of her stories. In 1915 the novella *Bliss* was published in *The English Review*, and John Middleton Murry became a columnist in the *Times Literary Supplement*. In 1916 they stayed in a villa at Bandol, in the South of France, where they wrote together at the same table: she produced *Prelude*, published in 1918 by the Hogarth Press (cf. p. 102), and he wrote an essay on Dostoevsky. On their return to London, they were often to be seen in intellectual circles, particularly the Bloomsbury Group, which was centred around Virginia Woolf. The esteem in which these two women held each other was not however free from rivalry.

TIED BY A KIND OF MYSTERY. In December 1917, Katherine Mansfield suffered the first attacks of the tuberculosis that eventually killed her. She began writing at a frenzied pace, staying in England or on the Côte d'Azur. In April 1918 she married Murry, as she put it, "purely for convenience". He edited *Je ne parle pas français*, which conjured up the "seamy side of Paris" that she had seen with Carco, and early in 1919, while lecturing at Oxford, became director of the prestigious literary magazine *The Athenaeum*; each issue carried a review signed KM.

When apart, they wrote every day. She described herself, "turning the envelope that she had received inside out to sniff the inside, screwing up her eyes to see the bottom, shaking it in the hope that one of your eyelashes or perhaps a little wink from you might still be in there." As she became more ill, she became more sensitive, as her diary shows: "To live with a lack of concern is to live in the only real hell that I know." "One reason for writing is this: you have to make a declaration of your love." She even hurled an accusation at her husband: "Neither of us is normal. I have too much vitality, and you don't have enough." In 1921, during a long stay in Montana, Switzerland, she wrote *On the Bay* and finished *The Garden Party*; the publication of this book established her as the best novelist of her generation.

"Why can some people not separate? They cannot do it, they are tied by a kind of mystery," she wrote in the last pages of her diary. Murry was then living with poet Vivien Locke-Ellis and Katherine took refuge in the community led by George Gurdjieff, in the priory at Avon, near Fontainebleau, where she lay down beside the cow shed to benefit from "the curative vapours of the cows". She beseeched her husband to join her, and died in his arms on 9 January 1923 at the early age of thirty-five.

Haunted by the memory of Katherine, John Middleton Murry published all her works, including her diary, which he prefaced: "The glass through which she saw life was as clear as crystal, and the quality of her works was consistent with her quality of life." He pursued his

1912

GREAT BRITAIN. **Frieda Weekley leaves her English husband, three children and comfortable life to run away with novelist David Herbert Lawrence (cf. p. 142), six years her junior. This blonde-haired German was as strong-minded and impulsive as the stunted, red-haired Lawrence was clumsy and mentally troubled. They married in 1914 and stayed in Cornwall with John Middleton Murry and Katherine Mansfield (see this page), who witnessed the violent quarrels that erupted between them. For Lawrence, love was a coming together of forces, and he described his wife as a "new, all-consuming mother".**
In 1919 they left the country and spent their life travelling the world. He died in 1930 and she had his ashes scattered in New Mexico, which Mabel Dodge (cf. p. 79) had helped them discover.

"He desired her as she was, and not as she would have liked to be."

EDITH WHARTON
The Reef

♡ ♡ ♡

literary career, becoming involved in the Pacifist movement, and in 1924 married twenty-two-year-old Violet Le Maistre, who cultivated her striking resemblance to his first wife. Their daughter, Katherine, was born in 1925. "I always had the impression," Murry wrote, "that Violet's daughter was actually Katherine's daughter, and that is why I gave her that name." Violet rejected her and, when she was stricken with tuberculosis in 1926, told her husband: "I wanted you to love me as much as you loved her. How can you, unless I go the same way?"

Two months after Violet's death, in 1931, Murry married his housekeeper Ada Elizabeth Cockbayne, despite his friends' warnings about her; she brought him misery with her jealousy and violence. In 1930 he wrote: "To refuse love, that's a disaster; to accept it, that's also a disaster," and finally found happiness with his fourth and last marriage, to Mary Gamble.

♡ ♡ ♡

MYTH
Pygmalion

The myth of the artist in love with his creation turns into reality in a love relationship that carries the seeds of its own death.

George Bernard Shaw's well-known play *Pygmalion*, published in 1912, was inspired by one of the best-known love myths, the story of the Cypriot sculptor Pygmalion and his creation, Galatea. Among the various versions, Ovid's story in *Metamorphoses* relates that Pygmalion carved an ivory statue that represented his ideal woman; he considered it his companion, dressed it, adorned it, laid it on his bed. He prayed to Aphrodite to give him a woman just like the statue, and his prayer was answered: Galatea came to life and soon proved to be a disappointment in the flesh. According to another version, Galatea, from the moment the breath was blown into her, complained about Pygmalion's beard and commanded him to cut it. In his haste, Pygmalion cut his chin; the drops of blood that fell to the ground turned into red roses, which have since become sacrificial symbols of love.

This myth of love linked with artistic creativity has spread throughout the West and inspired many works, more or less faithful to the original story line, such as Shaw's play. Shaw, a staunch socialist (cf. p. 60) and winner of the Nobel Prize for Literature in 1925, excelled himself in his comedies of manners, attacking the absurd and ridiculous aspects of society with an acerbic wit. *Pygmalion*, like all his plays, illustrates his watchword "make them think by making them laugh".

AN ARTIFICIAL CREATURE. Shaw's play, set in London, features Professor Higgins, a specialist in phonetics, who wagers that he can transform a common girl with a coarse accent into a duchess. Shaw portrays Eliza Doolittle, an eighteen-year-old flower seller, as a young girl so disgustingly dirty that even

her hair is "mouse-grey", and Henry Higgins as a man of some forty years, "passionately interested in all that lends itself to scientific study, caring little for himself or for others, or for their feelings". The professor turns the young Eliza into a kind of automated snob; through a course of lessons, she loses her cockney accent and mannerisms, and instead acquires a worldly veneer and an aristocratic manner of speaking. Unlike the myth, however, Higgins does not fall in love with his creation, although she yearns in vain for him. He sees her merely as a successful experiment, and not a person worthy of love. Eliza, now elegant and distinguished, is condemned to a life of incomprehension and loneliness, and resigns herself to living in hopelessness with the professor.

Often adapted for the cinema, the play was turned into the successful musical comedy *My Fair Lady* and subsequently, a film of the

same name starring Rex Harrison and Audrey Hepburn (1964). It was produced by George Cukor, who often dealt with this theme, for example in *A Star Is Born*. The end of the film is more optimistic than the end of the play, for the professor discovers that he can no longer live without Eliza and finally sees her for the woman she is. A more recent illustration of the myth, the American film *Pretty Woman*, features a businessman who turns a low-born young prostitute into a beautiful doll that he can marry. Proust analysed men of this type, those enslaved by the dream of an ideal woman, when he said: "The woman loved is but an artificial creature, whom the man gradually forces the real woman to resemble".

LOVE AND POSSESSIVENESS. The name "Pygmalion" has passed into modern language to mean a type of man who wishes to fashion a woman, his junior and socially and culturally inferior, to suit his desires. Their love-relationship is marked by condescension on the part of the man and admiration from the woman. The Pygmalion type, who wishes to "lift" her up to his level, sees her as an extension of himself, a kind of Adam's rib deprived of independence. He cannot conceive of her as a person, with her own future, with whom he could form a relationship of equality.

Many possessive men hide a Pygmalion inside. Certainly, love relationships often have a degree of possessiveness; but when it becomes too strong, the relationship invariably dies when Galatea finds her own way in life, because it is then that she escapes from the prison of destiny built for her.

In a world where social and economic power is often wielded by men, a woman in a situation of authority, who wants to "model" a young man whom she loves, is a rare phenomenon. A famous example, however, is Edith Piaf (cf. p. 224) and her succession of young lovers whom she endeavoured to turn into singers.

The world of cinema abounds in Pygmalion-Galatea couples, bringing together producers and stars as with David Selznick and Jennifer Jones, or directors and actresses such as Joseph von Sternberg and Marlene Dietrich, or Roger Vadim and Brigitte Bardot. In literature we

find Willy and Claudine (cf. p. 34). In the world of dance, choreographers often show Pygmalion tendencies, as did Sergei Diaghilev, director of the Russian Ballet, who lost Nijinsky's dancing genius when, in 1913, he could not bear to see his creation leave him to marry a ballerina. George Balanchine, who was styled as a "body sculptor", chose very young girls with long legs and necks as his subjects; in love with his creations, he married five successive highly talented dancers. Like the Cypriot sculptor, he chose their clothes and the perfume that best suited their personality, dismissing his last muse, Suzanne Farrell, when she dared to marry in 1969.

To assume the title of "creator" is to run the risk of behaving like a "sorcerer's apprentice", soon overtaken by the human that he has cre-

Pygmalion and Galatea,
J. L. Gérôme.

FACING PAGE
Self-Portrait
of George Bernard Shaw.

ated, like Mary Shelley's Frankenstein. This theme also appears in the Jewish myth of Golem, who, created by a rabbi, escapes from his creator and wreaks havoc, which leads his creator to destroy him.

Galatea always ends by escaping from the power of her Pygmalion, who has become lost in his artistic pride. To wish to rank oneself with God is ignore one of the foundations of Judaeo-Christian culture, namely the truth that the Creator has made man in His image through an act of love, not of power, by giving him both free will and the capacity to exercise it.

1912

PARIS. **The Café de Paris witnesses the beginning of the phenomenal success enjoyed by the dancers Irene and Vernon Castle. (Their life is recounted in H. C. Potter's 1939 film *The Story of Vernon and Irene Castle*, the last film to feature the famous dancing duo Fred Astaire and Ginger Rogers.) He was English and she American; she persuaded him, a comic actor, to leave the theatre and take up dance. They were an ideal couple, their grace and elegance providing a marvellous blend of movement and sensuality. They were much in fashion in Europe and then in the United States, where they enjoyed great success with music-hall dances such as the castle-walk, the two-step, the tango, the foxtrot and the polka. Vernon Castle trained as a pilot during the war, and in 1918 was appointed a flying instructor in Texas, where he was killed during an air show.**

H. G. Wells
& Rebecca West

A passionate but stormy relationship between a famous British writer and a young, brilliant journalist.

1913 saw the beginning of the relationship between Rebecca West, a young feminist journalist, and the British novelist Herbert George Wells. He expressed a desire to meet her after reading her caustic review of his novel *Marriage*; but fearing that she thought little of him, he remained aloof and thus left her in despair. "You," she wrote, "are like a person who lights fires of delight everywhere but is terrified of flames." A letter from Wells, sent after he read an article written by her on Spain, read: "You are a marvellous writer; can we please be friends again." In fact they became not just friends, but lovers, and soon Rebecca

West had a child. Their son Anthony, born on 4 August 1914, the day that Great Britain went to war, bore his mother an intense grudge for his illegitimate status.

Rebecca West was the pseudonym, taken from Ibsen's play *Rosmersholm*, of Cicily Isabel Fairfield. She came from a poor family, her father having walked out when she was nine. Wells, who was self-taught, first found major success with *The Time Machine* (1895), and he was the inventor, along with Jules Verne, of the science fiction genre. *The Invisible Man* and *The War of the Worlds* are still literary classics, but whole collections of his prolific works – philosophical treatises, social novels and social critiques – do not command a wide reading public today. Always short of money, he accepted every request to write an article, produced one book a year, and travelled widely.

THE JAGUAR AND THE PANTHER. When they met, Wells, warm and good-humoured, had not yet become an embittered prophet. He divided his time between his house in Essex, his London apartment and wherever his mistress of the moment lived. He had no desire to leave his wife Jane, who provided him with material support, or their sons George and Frank, born in 1901 and 1903. A

very sensuous man, he had many short-lived affairs, and his wife allowed him complete freedom on condition that he kept up the appearances of a respectable family man. He was attracted by women of superior intelligence, but he did not treat them as equals and spent very little time with them, as his work took priority over everything. In 1907 he had an affair with Dorothy Richardson, whom he encouraged to write and who eventually became a novelist. In 1909, he caused a scandal amongst the Fabian socialists by seducing Amber Reeves, twenty years his junior and the daughter of two of his friends; when she became pregnant, he pushed her into marrying another man. His friends Beatrice and Sidney Webb (cf. p. 60) also severed contact with him.

Rebecca West was twenty-six years younger than H. G. Wells. He loved her "clear, open, forceful and above all generous spirit". She dreamed up stories in which he was a jaguar and she a panther, and whose adventures he sketched in his letters. One delightful drawing by Wells shows the two big cats, swollen with pride, saying to each other: "You should have heard my speech!" The caption asks: "Can love exist between two people of this type?"

Rebecca West lived near London and, at Wells' request, moved several times. She wrote articles, but apart from a few discreet journeys with Wells, she spent her time waiting for him uneasily while the maidservants looked on with disapproving glares. When the couple travelled to Italy or Spain, she passed herself off as the great man's secretary. Her position as "number two" was all the more humiliating because Wells kept nothing whatsoever hidden from his wife. He reacted to Rebecca's outbursts of frustration, or to the fears that the war-time air-raids inflicted on her and her son, by accusing her of "painting everything black".

NEW YORK. A scandalous affair between Mabel Dodge, the rich owner of a much-frequented literary salon, and the journalist and militant revolutionary John Reed, eight years her junior. Eccentric and charming, she had a great gift for making friends. Already married twice, she finally discovered love: "At last I knew that there could be a honeymoon." She was, however, unable to accept Reed's worldwide travels and passion for politics, and wanted him all to herself. After six months of life with her, he fled: "I love you more than life, but I don't want to be a slave."
He later married journalist Louise Bryant, witnessing the Russian Revolution together with her, and wrote the famous Ten Days that Shook the World before dying of typhus in Moscow in 1920. Mabel Dodge settled in Taos, New Mexico, where she kept open house for her friends; she married a Pueblo Indian and finally found peace.

♡ ♡ ♡

In 1918, when she published her first novel, *The Return of the Soldier*, and decided to settle in London with her son, she wrote that she felt "like a nun newly released from a convent". She wrote other novels, which showed the impossibility of reconciling a search for happiness with honesty in a relationship. She worked on the prestigious magazine *Time and Tide*, and also gave conferences. In the literary world, where their affair was known and indeed approved of, people sought the company of this intelligent and witty couple.

WORLDWIDE FAME. The war had a tremendous impact on Wells, who ceased to write novels thereafter. An advocate of socialism, he wanted to become a social reformer, using writing as a means of propaganda. He proposed the creation of a new world state, directed by an élite, as the only way of avoiding another conflict, indeed the only way ahead for humanity, whose future seemed "a race between education and disaster". As he grew old he became cantankerous, obsessed with power, and his thoughts turned to totalitarianism. His fame

increased and his *Outline of History* (1920) was a commercial success. In 1920 he visited the Soviet Union, had a meeting with Lenin, and met Gorki's secretary Baroness Moura Boudberg; he spent a night with her. He had many other conquests, most notably in 1921 in the United States with the militant feminist Margaret Sanger, but it was in 1923, when a young Austrian journalist attempted suicide in Wells's London residence and caused a major scandal, that Rebecca West finally decided to leave him. In 1930, she married banker Henry Maxwell Andrews and from then on her life was comfortable. Ever the feminist, she published novels and important reports, most notably on Yugoslavia in 1941 (*The Black Sheep and the Grey Falcon*) and on the Nuremburg Trials. She was made a Dame in 1949.

Wells's fame is worldwide. As president of the International Pen Club, he had conversations with Roosevelt and Stalin in 1934 on the future of the world. After a turbulent affair with French journalist Odette Keun, he at long last settled down with Moura Boudberg, who became his companion in 1931.

Why did so many brilliant women, such as the writer Winifred Holtby, show such fascination for this man? When Holtby learned in 1930 that a serious illness had left her little time to live, she immediately paid H. G. Wells a visit, as she did not, as she wrote, "wish to die without meeting him". Their conversation gave her "more pleasure than anything else in [her] life". Did Wells's secret lie in Moura Boudberg's response to W. Somerset Maugham? When he asked her whether she was attracted by his intelligence or by his sense of humour, she answered: "Not at all. It was because his body smelled of honey ..."

♡ ♡ ♡

SENSUALITY
The Tango

"A sad thought dancing" that migrated from the brothels of Buenos Aires to the European dance halls.

The tango, which originated from Argentina, caused a great sensation and replaced the waltz as Europe's most popular dance. Heavy with erotic overtones, it was the expression of a dramatic perception of love and life.

In 1913 newspapers in Paris, London, Berlin, and even New York alternated sketches of tangoing figures with heated arguments about this foreign cultural intrusion with its lustful swaying walk. While the British aristocracy was divided on the subject, Emperor Wilhelm II banned German officers from dancing the tango, although he could not stop it from becoming very popular in Berlin during the war. Both in Paris and Milan, Argentine teachers opened tango schools; even in diluted form, the dance seemed to attract scandal wherever it went.

A REVOLUTION. The tango brought a revolution to dancing couples: interrupted movement. First, they both stood still; then the man remained standing while the woman danced and postured about him; and then it was the other way round. The tango allowed improvisation, which gave it an advantage over the waltz or the mazurka. Unpredictable in its nature, it was danced "with life before you" as the *Portegnes* (the natives of Buenos Aires) put it, and a rhythm that seemed to command, "respect the beat more than your mother!" Other innovations were that the

man danced without stepping back, as he was not supposed to expose his back to a possible enemy; and the woman, to make the movements easier, wore a dress with side-slits or a short skirt over petticoats with starched flounces. The man decided his partner's steps while holding her tightly round the waist. However, although the dancers did hold each other close, it was not out of lust, but to avoid treading on other dancers' feet ...

This practical consideration was not noticed by the archbishop of Paris, who banned the dance in 1912. For "right-thinking" people, two bodies holding each other tightly to the beat of a slow, heady melody, imitating physical possession, seemed the height of shamelessness. The various dance positions were shown in postcards, and some critics compared them to the thirty-two positions of making love (cf. p. 314). The very word *tango*, which described a shade of orange, became a symbol of depravity for some poor souls.

Quite different from the happy tumult or cheerful eroticism of other dances (cf. p. 130), the sad, nostalgic music of the tango, a Spanish word of uncertain derivation, expresses darkness and pain. It was born during the displacement of poor émigrés at the end of the nineteenth century, at a time when half of the population of Buenos Aires was Italian and Argentina was the sixth most powerful nation in the world. Economically it depended on Great Britain, but for culture, its rulers looked to Paris.

LEFT
Dance in Baden-Baden, Max Beckmann.

FACING PAGE
The Archangel's Tango, Kees van Dongen

Originally played in brothels, the first tangos were pornographic and, as such, revolting to "decent" people, who associated them with inner suburban brawls. A mixture of the music of the pampas' gauchos (whose *milonga* was a country version of the tango), black rhythms, Caribbean tunes, the Italian *canzonetta*, Arab-Andalusian melodies and so on, the dance that accompanied this novel, anti-authoritarian music was a provocative one. The tango gave the Argentineans a feeling of pride and national identity. Like jazz, it spread right across the world; the South American musicians with their satin smocks and plastered-down jet-black hair became as much a stereotype as the "frenzied" black jazz orchestras.

Only when the dance was exported to Europe and came back stripped of its panache was it allowed in Argentinean bars, legitimised by its popularity in Paris. But in passing from the brothel to the chic night club, the tango changed its repertoire; the lewd overtones of the early versions were often replaced by a harmless sentimentalism, while the bourgeois piano accompanied the traditional bandoneon, a kind of small six sided accordion.

VIOLENCE AND PESSIMISM. The best-known singer of the time was Carlos Gardel, who made several tours of Europe and remains a national legend in Argentina to this day. Before his death in an air crash in 1935, he made films in Hollywood, with numbers featuring the tango; these were all the rage after Rudolph Valentino's famous caricatured exotic scene in *The Four Horsemen of the Apocalypse* (1921).

"Without hope, I drink to forget your love": in Pascual Contursi's *Mi Noche Triste* (My Sad Night) sung by Gardel in 1917, the man who bemoans his abandonment is a lout

whose "lost girl" has "left his soul bruised and thorns in his heart". The words of the tango, which recreate the world of the "bad lads" of the Rio de la Plata, contain none of the sickly sentimentality associated with it by the foreign public. In these songs life is a robber, sex a delusion, women liars; only the mother is a haven of forgiveness. Originating from the seedy quarters of the cities, the tango expresses a longing for sympathy and love "My life has brought me many chicks, but a real woman I have never had" – while showing at the same time a feeling of inferiority in the man who is unsure of himself and fearful of being ridiculed. "I ran away to keep from crying / Ten years ago I was mad for her," sang Azucena Maizani, one of the few women singers in this masculine world, in *Esta Noche Emborracho* (Tonight I Get Drunk) in 1928. Despair, sometimes suicidal, born of love, as well as violence, repressed homosexuality and chauvinism, are all themes blended together in a myth and glorified in the film *Last Tango in Paris* (cf. p. 328).

Several great writers have written tango songs, but the greatest and most profound lyricist is Enrique Santos Discépolo. The man who defined the tango as "a sad thought dancing", "a mixture of anger, pain, faith, and absence" sings of love, death, and paradise lost in radically pessimistic poems that express the despair of the thirties, that "infamous decade" where hopes of democracy gave way to *coups d'état* and electoral fraud. Faced with shattered dreams, "All is a lie, nothing is love / the world buggers you about as it turns." Love is always a punishment: "Why was I taught to love / If to love is to cast all your dreams into the sea?"

"All is dead, that I know," were the final words of *Sur*, a song by Homero Manzi and Anibal Troilo, artists of the golden age of the forties. Another favourite tango theme was the idea that time flies, bearing everything away. The fall of Peron (cf. p. 216) in 1955, marked the end of an era; but with each new generation the tango reappears. Astor Piazzolla (died 1992) was one of the most recent artists to revive it.

1913

PUBLICATION of Alain-Fournier's novel *Le Grand Meaulnes*, a unique book about a young writer killed in action in September 1914. He was inspired to write it by his love for a tall blonde girl whom he likened to a "scape of white lilac". He saw her one day in June 1905, "a day as fixed and beautiful as my death day". This inaccessible creature, "so beautiful that to look at her was to suffer", was his inspiration for the character of Yvonne de Galais in a strange story of innocence and desire that recounts a vain search for a mysterious young girl, the heartbreak of an impossible desire, and the dream of a happiness that makes him different from others.

"To think that I have wasted years of my life, that I have longed for death, that the greatest love that I have ever known has been for a woman who did not please, who was not in my style!"

MARCEL PROUST
Swann in Love (last words)

Madame Caillaux Kills Calmette

When the wife of the Minister of Finance shot dead the director of the daily newspaper "Le Figaro", she acted out of love and to save her honour. She was acquitted.

Joseph and Henriette Caillaux during the trial.

Late in the afternoon of Monday, 16 March 1914, a smartly-dressed woman entered the editorial office of *Le Figaro*, in Paris's Rue Drouot, and requested a meeting with the director. The woman was the wife of Minister of Finance Joseph Caillaux. Scarcely had she been introduced to the director, Gaston Calmette, when she produced a pistol from inside her muff and fired, fatally wounding him. Arrested immediately afterwards, she declared: "That's the only way to finish it. There's no justice in France." For several weeks, the paper had been waging a campaign against Caillaux, attacking both his political stance and his private life, with a viciousness that is hard to imagine in this age of much stiffer defamation laws.

Joseph Caillaux, a millionaire and left-wing republican, was, as Maurice Barrès later said, "the most hated man in France". With his bald head and contemptuous monocled stare, this grand-bourgeois was both exceptionally intelligent and supremely proud and arrogant. "Born of millionaire parents, the son of a minister, and an inspector of finances with an impeccable academic record" was how he was described at his wife's trial. At thirty-six he was made Minister of Finance, and at forty-eight he was leading the government.

The pressure of the criticism forced him to resign in 1912. He was anxious for France to enjoy the benefits of a modern tax system and had income tax voted in during 1909. A reasoned pacifist, convinced that France's future lay not in revenge but in alliance with Germany, he negotiated with the Germans after their coup in Agadir in 1911, and by ceding the Congo to them, managed to maintain peace.

In January 1914 he was elected president of the Radical Party, France's most powerful party, and then became Minister of Finance again. In the run-up to the 1914 elections, he was seen, by the right, as the man to get rid of. *Le Figaro*, under the directorship of Gaston

Calmette, launched a relentless campaign against him; in three months, one hundred and ten articles attacked him with insults and slanderous accusations. On 10 March, Calmette announced his intention to publish one of Caillaux's private letters; and on 13 March, *Le Figaro* featured the first of a series of letters addressed to "Henriette" and signed "Your little Jo".

FEAR OF DISHONOUR. "Henriette" was Calmette's killer. Daughter of a rich architect, Henriette Rainouard was divorced in 1908 and then, secretly, became mistress to the married Caillaux. In 1909 Madame Caillaux discovered the affair and seized her husband's letters to his "beloved Riri". Wanting at all costs to avoid a scandal in the run-up to the 1910 elections, Caillaux made amends, and his wife burned the letters in his presence. Immediately after his re-election, however, he demanded a divorce, which was pronounced with him as the guilty party in March 1911. He was then able to marry Henriette, in October 1911.

Caillaux's first wife was careful to take photographs of all the compromising letters, which then fell into the hands of the politician's sworn enemies. When their publication was announced, Henriette Caillaux, fearful of being dishonoured in her family's eyes, panicked at the scandal that was about to break. On the morning of 16 March 1914, Joseph Caillaux visited the Élysées Palace to request President Raymond Poincaré to intervene. Poincaré, as he recalled later in his *Memoirs*, tried to reassure him, saying that Calmette was a gentleman who would not stoop so low. However Madame Caillaux, in desperation, bought a pistol and wrote a letter for her husband, stating that she would not tolerate the publication of private letters and would administer justice herself.

A LOVER'S REACTION. All the murder did was increase the scandal, as the couple's private life was thrust firmly into the public gaze. Caillaux resigned from the government. The right-wing press claimed that he had provided his wife with the weapon and that he should have challenged Calmette to a duel. In the papers, the whole sensational business provided the "trial of the century", causing much more excitement than the distant international crisis brewing in the Balkans. The Sarthe region remained faithful to its elected member and the wives of the local woodcutters sent flowers to Madame Caillaux in prison. Caillaux was re-elected a deputy without opposition, but he took no part in the new government, which he would normally have led.

The trial opened on 20 July 1914 before the Paris Court of Assizes, with an all-male jury whose job was to state whether the murderer should be granted mitigating circumstances. Fair-haired and well-rounded,

smartly dressed and sporting a silken hat topped with two feathers, Henriette Caillaux was defended by the esteemed lawyer Fernand

Labori, who had defended Captain Dreyfus. He explained that Madame Caillaux had been "subjected to a pressure under which no respectable woman could have failed to buckle". The publication of intimate letters written by her lover was an intolerable affront to her respectability, stated Mr Labori, who read several passages from the letters to the jury. When his client heard the words "I love you and I am yours. A million kisses I rain on your beautiful body", she fainted.

The accused declared that she had wished to defend her husband "exactly as he would have defended me". Her crime appeared, therefore, to be a reaction by a woman in love. At that time, women were viewed as being gentle but impetuous, swayed constantly by their nerves and emotions; the opinion was that their outbursts could remain civilised as long as they stayed within the protection of the home but they could, left to their own devices in the outside world, fall prey to uncontrollable impulses.

Henriette Caillaux was acquitted on 28 July 1914, on the same day that Austria-Hungary declared war on Serbia. The government got the couple out of the public eye by sending Joseph Caillaux on a study trip to Brazil.

On their return, the extreme right-wing group Action Française launched a campaign of hate and violence against the "killer couple". The hatred continued unabated. During the First World War, Caillaux became the political symbol of pacifism which, in 1917, was made tantamount to treason; he was arrested in January 1918, accused of collaboration with the enemy, and sentenced to three years' imprisonment. After an amnesty, however, he resumed his political career; he became a minister and then a senator, but never reached the heady heights to which he could still have aspired.

GREAT BRITAIN. **The start of the affair between the painters Vanessa Bell and Duncan Grant, six years her junior. Both were members of the famous Bloomsbury Group (cf. p. 102). The sister of Virginia, who married Leonard Woolf, Vanessa Bell was the wife of art critic Clive Bell and had two children by him, although their marriage had become just a friendship. In 1916 Duncan Grant and Vanessa Bell settled in Sussex. Convinced of Grant's genius, Bell lacked confidence in herself, although he encouraged and supported her. After the birth of their daughter Angelica in 1918, they ceased to be sexually intimate (Grant was in fact a homosexual), but their intense emotional and artistic exchanges lasted until Vanessa Bell's death in 1961. Although Grant was the more famous during their lifetime, both are well known for their works today.**

♡ ♡ ♡

Anguish
Separation

As millions of young men went off to war, letters remained the only link between the soldier and his beloved. Sometimes, however, the telegraph boy brought awful news …

On the streets of Berlin, the soldiers left to cries of "Nach Paris!" (To Paris!), convinced that they would soon get the better of the "effeminate" French. Paris responded with an equally thunderous "To Berlin!", but in the provinces, where the wives, children, and elderly left behind made no effort to hide their tears, the enthusiasm was far less apparent. It was crying, suffering, hardship, loneliness, death, and wounds that characterised this war, which everyone hoped would be the last, the "war to end all wars".

The men were at the front, but the women were left behind. The men fought for victory or defended their homeland; the women dressed the wounds and worked the soil. The only remaining line between them was the thin line of the postal service, a channel of intimacy often violated by censors. Some loves died, others were born. More than ever before, there were two worlds: that of the men on one side, and that of the women and children on the other, and the relationship between the two worlds changed as time went on. The absence of so many young men caused great social upheavals; Russia, for example, mobilised 10 million soldiers between 1914 and 1917.

HOPE AND HORROR IN THE TRENCHES. When war broke out, on 2 August 1914, very few anticipated that it would be long and agonising. By November, however, it was evident that it would last. The conflict zone settled along a front 500 miles long, which stretched from Flanders to the Russian front. Men dug trenches and lived there in the mud, with attacks, bloody hand-to-hand fights, choking gases, cold, and horror.

The national hero, the soldier, was weakened through being torn from his familiar world, and separated from his beloved, whom he beseeched: "Wait for me! Write to me! Give me courage!" Looking at her photograph, that precious gift from her to him, he dreamed and worried. Letters were their only link. There were letters that the soldier waited for, called for, read and re-read; and there were letters that he wrote back, to kill time, overcome boredom or put off fear, to his wife, mother or *marraine de guerre*. The *marraine* was a very French phenomenon, a female pen-friend, young or old, whose role was to gladden the hearts of valiant soldiers with a little affection; she chose one soldier, often through a small advertisement placed in the paper, and wrote to him, knitted him socks and scarves, sent him food parcels. Often a relationship – friendship or love? – began through the letters, allowing the soldier to dream of a "happy place" far away (Apollinaire's letters, for example, are well known), and led the *marraine* to fear for him and devote herself to him, as indeed did every woman in her family circle.

While some of these correspondences led to weddings, other weddings were held hastily under flags, or while soldiers were on furlough, legitimising the fruit of a union born of drunkenness or of fear at leaving for the front. Many taboos fell while the thunder lasted, and many young women gave themselves for the soldier and for the homeland in a single burst of passion, only to find themselves pregnant from the military "advance" some time later. In France, a law dated 4 April 1915 allowed marriage by proxy for soldiers, under a national flag; and on 19 August, the law was extended to prisoners of war. This deviation from a basic principle of French civil law allowed many women official status

and rights to state aid; after all, the life of those left behind was hard too.

HOPE AND PAIN AT HOME. All across Europe, the men left in August, at harvest time; and it was the women who courageously replaced them in the fields. In the cities, however, businesses and shops closed, and unemployment was rife, particularly in traditionally female professions such as sewing or shop-keeping. Every country brought in a soldiers' wives' allowance, the most generous being that of Britain; France and Germany saw it as a means of boosting the morale of the soldiers, who were racked with guilt at leaving their families without means. Living costs were high, priority for raw materials went to the war effort, and people went hungry and cold in consequence. In the city and in the country, everything revolved around the news from the front. In every house the postman's arrival was anxiously awaited – at last! a card, a letter or a photograph of the soldier in uniform, oh so dashing! provided he was not wounded – and simultaneously feared, because he could just as easily be bringing the awful telegram that told of the death of a husband, a brother, a son, a father. Many women who lived through that time developed a lifelong fear of postmen and telegraph boys.

Most information on the war itself was concealed by the censors. Names of dead or missing could not be published. Soon, in the areas invaded by the Germans (Belgium and northern and eastern France), a flood of refugees from all areas took to the roads. Women were exposed to violence, forced labour, and even rape. Although the rapes were quite rightly condemned as barbaric, children born of them posed a problem both moral and legal for the French authorities: should they accept these little unwanted ones, who

Soldat,
La Patrie compte
sur toi; garde
lui toutes tes
forces...........
Résiste aux
séductions de la
rue où te guette
la maladie aussi
dangereuse que
la guerre......
Elle conduit ses
victimes à la
déchéance et
à la mort sans
utilité, sans
honneur.......

Steinlen 1916

HOPITAL

1914

The novel *Maria Chapdelaine* is published after the accidental death of its author Louis Hémon, who spent many years living with the country people in Quebec. Inspired by their harsh life, lived in harmony with an imposing landscape, the novel relates the long-held secret expectations of a young girl. During the bilberry harvest, love blossoms between Maria Chapdelaine and François Paradis, a woodcutter. The young man promises to return at Christmas, but is caught in a storm and disappears for ever. As "peasants never die from sorrows of love", Maria Chapdelaine, resigned to life, agrees to marry her neighbour.

Guillaume Apollinaire sends Lou, his mistress, a series of exaggerated erotic poems: "The propelling cannons thrust forth / Impregnate the lovestruck earth / Time in brutal moments passes, / Love is like war, both to new things give birth".

They left for "the war to end all wars" armed with recommendations.

bore the title of "young vipers"? Could abortion be tolerated in these cases? The Church was faced with difficult questions on the subject. should the children be placed in orphanages and have their education

paid for by the Germans once the war was over – and won? Journalists and deputies argued long on this issue.

Leave, that welcome relief for the hearts of couples torn apart by war, also carried its own fears and imaginings. The bawdy tales told by the soldiers, and the campaigns

waged in the French press against those who, "left behind", were unsettled by their sudden independence, made many wives suspicious. Wives and fiancées grew fearful of being forgotten, and their greatest fear was often the woman at the wounded soldier's bedside: the nurse or "angel in white" (cf. p. 92).

Ruth St Denis
& Ted Shawn

These two dancers' great work, the Denishawn School, opened the United States to modern dance and cultural diversity.

Ruth St Denis and Ted Shawn performing the *Egyptian Ballet*, 1914.

As a child, Ruth Dennis was always on the move, wild with the sheer joy of living. Born in 1879, she grew up in a Bohemian family on a New Jersey farm; her mother, a qualified but non-practising doctor, had mystical tendencies, and her father was quiet, dreamy, and intellectual. Ruth took dancing lessons in New York, and made her first public appearance at fifteen, after changing her surname to St Denis, in variety shows and private concerts. In 1904, inspired by an advertising poster for Egyptian cigarettes, she decided to adopt an oriental style. She caused a sensation by whirling about on stage in a sari or draped in long floating veils, enveloped in the heady smoke of burning incense. She found success in 1906 with *Radha*, an Indian ballet, which was followed by *Incense*, *The Cobras*, and *Egypta*. From 1906 to 1909 she performed in Europe, and returned to the United States, crowned with international success, to tour there.

In 1913, Ruth was looking for a show dancer with whom she could perform figures from the "maxixe", then in fashion together with the tango. The dancer recommended to her was Ted Shawn, twelve years her junior. Born in Kansas in 1891, the son of a brilliant journalist father and cultured mother, he grew up in Denver where, while studying to become a priest, an attack of diphtheria left his legs temporarily paralysed. He learned to dance as part of his rehabilitation, and it was then that he discovered his remarkable talent; unfortunately, however, he also discovered the deep-rooted social prejudice against male dancers. He saw Ruth St Denis perform in Denver in *Incense* and immediately understood her efforts to combine religion with art.

The harmony between them was instant. she hired him and they left on tour. They were both tall, strong and energetic, and with her he fell in love for the first time. "I drank from the well of love," she wrote, "with profound thanks, touched by his beautiful, child-like, captivating eyes." Ted's proposal of marriage, however, overwhelmed her. "Why should I get married?" she said. Dismayed at reducing what she perceived as a quasi-cosmic union to a mere contract, finalised on a sheet of paper, she nevertheless decided to marry him, for propriety, in 1914.

DENISHAWN: MUCH MORE THAN A SCHOOL. "There were four people in our marriage," wrote Ruth; "the male in me and the female in Ted were just as alive and demanding as we ourselves." She spoiled him, while he confessed to being homosexual. Their union was stormy, although it never ceased to be both passionate and tender. They had no children because she wanted none; her maternal instinct was reserved for her pupils. In 1915 they both founded, behind a grove of eucalyptus trees in the hills above Los Angeles, a dance school

which they named Denishawn. All modern dance in the United States has its origins in Denishawn, where the courses were held in the open air in front of huge mirrors. Several great dancers trained there, including Martha Graham, who enrolled in 1916, Doris Humphrey and Charles Weidman. For fifteen years Denishawn was a place of collective creation, love, and freedom; it was financed wholly by pupils' fees and income from tours, without any grants or subsidies. Ted, a great organiser, dealt with all the administrative matters, while Ruth enriched it with her warm, shimmering movements, sun worship sequences, and unfailing humour. All forms of dance were taught, as well as other art forms (music, weaving, costume design) and other dancers, including Hawaiian and Japanese sword dancers, pupils of Jaques-Dalcroze, and artists from nearby Hollywood, also taught there. "It was much more than a school," wrote Ruth; "it was the life-style we all wanted."

Their ballet performances included solo acts from them as well as joint sequences. Ted Shawn, a prolific choreographer, invented and popularised the modern-style male dance routine. He brought dance and sport together and devised a series of movements for the male body that did away with the effeminate dancer image. In 1918 he opened his own studio in Los Angeles, aided by Martha Graham; he created *Gnossienne* and *Xochitl*, and established himself as a solo performer. He gave triumphant performances at Carnegie Hall in 1929, and again in Europe in 1930, particularly in *Orpheus*.

"JOINED TOGETHER AT SOUL LEVEL". To get away from it all, the couple bought a bungalow in Eagle Rock; they named it *Tedruth*, a combination of their first names, and there Ted Shawn wrote *Pioneer and Prophet*, a major book on his wife's artistic life. Tedruth was burnt down shortly afterwards; the disaster symbolised the breakdown, already apparent, of the love between them. Although they did not divorce, Ruth reproached herself for "upsetting the order of marriage without the honesty and dignity of a divorce". After a few frustrating affairs, she went on to enjoy other, more harmonious love relationships.

Ted Shawn did not create any dance patterns for women. "He couldn't fulfil his destiny and help me to fulfil mine at the same time," noted Ruth St Denis. She needed "emotional contrasts that produced creative beauty", and often left on tour with her troupe, both to get afloat again financially and to maintain contact with the general public. For Ruth, dance was both experimental and popular: "I share with Isadora Duncan the honour of having brought dance to the concert halls, and of dancing with symphony orchestras," she said.

They carried on working together, but despite Den-

1915

Moscow. **Elsa Kagan (later Elsa Triolet, cf. p. 140) introduces the futurist poet Vladimir Mayakovsky to her sister Lili, a red-haired, sensitive, fragile sculptor and dancer. Married to the rich Osip Brik, she lived in a society that was both cultured and brilliant. The couple were very struck by the genius of the poor poet and the thundering tone and savage humour of his poems. "Wound about with flames, I remain on the inextinguishable log / Of my unbelievable love," he wrote in 1916. Lili Brik, who shared that love with him, was his inspiration, his lover and his life's great passion. Mayakovsky, who lived life at white heat, worshipped the true and all-consuming love born of mutual freedom; but it was Brik's magnanimity that kept relations between the three of them sweet. The affair finished in 1925, but a deep-rooted friendship kept them together until the poet shot himself in 1930. After the suicide, Lili Brik dedicated herself to defending his good name.**

♡ ♡ ♡

ishawn finding a new home in New York, and the highly successful 1925 tour of Asia, from which Ruth brought back *White Jade*, the gulf between them widened. However, they remained, as she put it, "joined together at soul level, a bond which could never be broken". In 1931 Denishawn closed and its two founders danced together for the last time, in New York. Ted Shawn founded a dance school and festival at Jacob's Pillow, Massachusetts, while continuing to tour. Ruth St Denis, who amassed many honours, published her memoirs, *A Life*

Unfinished, in 1939, and settled in Hollywood in 1942. She taught, gave conferences, spoke on the radio and appeared on television; and still she went on dancing.

In 1964 the legend of Denishawn was revived when Ruth St Denis and Ted Shawn celebrated their golden wedding anniversary with a dance: she was eighty-six and he seventy-four. She died in 1968, and he survived her by four years. They left the New York Library a great wealth of documents, particularly many thousands of photographs taken by these two truly great performers.

Myth
The "Femme Fatale"

The man-eater, the bloodthirsty black-clad vamp hungry for riches and obsessed with sex, haunts the imagination.

As the war, that awful consumer and mangler of men, mowed them down by the thousand in the trenches, a myth grew up alongside the reality: the vampire woman, who sucked on the blood of men. A new form of the deadly seductress, who haunted the imagination of men in the West, the vamp (an American abbreviation of "vampire"), brought men a pleasure which was both intensely sensual and deadly. The first "vamp" to appear in cinema was played by the Danish actress Asta Nielsen in a 1912 film, but it was in 1915 that the character type became popular with the appearance of two famous films. In *A Fool There Was*, the American actress Theda Bara, whose name was an anagram of *Arab Death*, appears in a long-drawn-out kissing scene as the first ghoul (female vampire) who "drinks" the soul of her lover. In *The Vampires*, a serial film by Louis Feuillade, the French actress Musidora plays a hotel sneak thief clad in a cowl and black leotard; with her supple, corset-less body, she is an embodiment of guiltless eroticism. The film was greatly welcomed by a public traumatised by the horrors

and absurdity of war. In 1917, in a climate that very much favoured imagined betrayal, the French courts condemned to death the famous Dutch dancer, adventuress, and spy Mata Hari; the story was told in the cinema by Greta Garbo and later by Marlene Dietrich.

THE MAN-EATER. "If I love you, better look out!" Carmen's threat has echoed ever since the success of Bizet's opera in 1875. The sublime spectacle of lovers dying together, one of the favourite themes of the nineteenth century, disappeared together with romantic illusions. Enter, in its place, "the war of the sexes" and the venomous seductress dressed in black, harbinger of death or disease such as the dreaded syphilis! With her accessories of

long black gloves and cigarette-holder, and her symbol, the serpent, which decorated Sarah Bernhardt's jewels, the "femme fatale" produced mixed feelings of fascination and horror everywhere.

Surrounded by tendrils of climbing plants, the woman who symbolised Art Nouveau uncoils the trap of her luxuriant hair, a symbol of animal sensuality. This "new" woman, however, has long been around; examples of her also include the Biblical man-killers Salome and Judith, reinterpreted by Gustav Klimt, Oscar Wilde and Gustave Moreau, the threatening images of the sphinx or Medusa, and the devilish Amazons featured in the novels of Gabriele D'Annunzio and Octave Mirbeau. Many writers and artists of that time saw woman as an Other, foreign and strange to them, and combined their yearning for an ideal figure as saintly as a mother with a deep-rooted hatred for real women, who had to be content with their role of "muse" without campaigning for equality with men.

At the turn of the century, when thoughts were very much preoccupied with the End of the World, a chorus of male voices arose prophesying the suicide of mankind. In a

Pornocrates, Félicien Rops. The femme fatale has the man-pig on a lead.

FACING PAGE
Drawing of Erté for *L'Illustration*.

world of people dedicated to living solitary lives, any contact between the sexes produced obsessive thoughts of cruelty, castration and death. The "femme", a seductress with a heart of stone and an ice-cold, calculating eroticism, a bloodthirsty praying mantis hungry for riches and obsessed with sex, terrified men with the apparent superiority of her sexual enjoyment. Efforts were made to exorcise fears of this man-eater by depicting in paintings the dream of a gentle, passive woman, preferably sleeping or dead. In *Sex and Character* (1903), Otto Weininger advocates chastity, stating that men must renounce all sexual activity to escape from the grip of woman. Every seductress appears fearsome, redoubtable; and that is why Mata Hari was executed and Lulu, in Pabst's famous 1929 film, murdered. Calling for the

death of a woman, or the extinction of the species, is a clear demonstration of despair by men whose hatred of women is but one face of self-hatred and contempt for their own feminine attributes.

LOVE IS ALWAYS FATAL TO MEN. Men are terrified by the "femme fatale", but there is no "homme fatal" for women, since the "Latin lover" (cf. p. 118) does not make his conquests at their expense. According to tradition, woman, as the Angel Gabriel announces to Mary, fulfils her destiny by "being with child and giving birth". The Prince Charming of the fairy tales brings the sleeping beauty back to life, and restores her sexuality with a kiss. The black-clad woman, however, confronts the man with a face of death – his death. Evil and malevolent, she preys on men whom she transforms into

puppets (as in Pierre Louÿs' novel *The Woman and the Puppet*) or into pigs (Circe and Ulysses' companions). As the Greek siren or the German Lorelei, she lures navigators to their deaths on the rocks with her voice. As love is incompatible with glory, which was the classic hero's only aspiration, seduction by a woman was always fatal to the man who was distracted (the original meaning of *seduced*) by it. In the West, woman has been "deadly" since the time of Eve, the temptress, or even Lilith, the demoness depicted in Jewish mythology as Adam's first wife. After unsuccessfully claiming equality with the man, she exacts her revenge by bringing a curse on the human race.

For half a century vamps, and later tarts, abounded in the cinema. After the adventure roles played by Marlene Dietrich, the character type was featured even more in the "black" American films of the 1940s (Rita Hayworth in *Gilda*, or Barbara Stanwyck in *Double Indemnity*, cf. p. 168). It was shown in the caricatures created by the larger-than-life Mae West, or through the delightful Betty Boop (cf. p. 160), before Marilyn Monroe transformed the man-eater into a charmer and fortune-hunter.

The vamp disappeared in the 1950s, when the emancipation of women allowed the creation of more complex and subtle personalities and her cold, destructive character began to appear absurd. The sexual energy concentrated in her became shared by other female personalities. In the 1980s, however, she reappeared, after the panic caused by "new women" and the fear of AIDS; the word "fatal" appeared in several film titles, particularly *Fatal Attraction* (cf. p. 390), while Sharon Stone, in *Basic Instinct* (1991) kills with an ice-pick that is an end-of-century version of the dagger wielded by the first vamps.

1915

First hearing of Manuel de Falla's music to the ballet *The Sorcerer's Love*, composed at the request of dancer Pastora Imperio, who created it in Madrid. Adopted subsequently by the famous Argentina Ballet, it finally found success in Paris in 1928. The gipsy girl Candelas once loved a man whose jealousy brought her misfortune. Although he is now dead, his ghost comes back to haunt her, forbids her to love the handsome Carmelo and appears between the lovers whenever they are about to embrace. While Candelas consults the keepers of the tradition, who perform some incantations, a young gipsy girl offers to confront the ghost; she distracts him while the lovers, together at last, exchange the kiss that frees them from the evil spell and demonstrates that love must conquer death.

George & Ludmilla Pitoëff

The theatre was their life, their passion. They loved each other with a pure and demanding love. Both on stage and in their life together, they searched for the absolute.

It was in 1916 that George Pitoëff discovered his young wife Ludmilla's acting talent. He was thirty-two, she only twenty, and they had been married for a year. After training in the Moscow Theatre, George came to Paris, where he met Ludmilla in 1914. When he asked for her hand in marriage, he warned her: "It will be difficult, because I want to live the high life." Ludmilla Smanova was the daughter of a senior civil servant in Tbilisi, Georgia, where George's father directed the theatre. The young couple spent the war years in Geneva, where their older children were born and where, against almost impossible odds, George founded a troupe in which he was both director and principal actor. They settled in Paris for good in 1922.

Both spoke French with a Russian accent that they never lost, despite their great talent. George was small and sickly, a dark, mysterious personality with a tortured body and a harsh, halting voice; so great and powerful was his fervour that he would embody, rather than simply play, a character. Ludmilla, whom Jean Cocteau described as "a breath disguised as a woman", transformed her roles with her glowing purity and indomitable fragility; small, sometimes mischievous and sometimes serious, with enormous dark eyes and a crystal-clear voice, she considered herself to be just a beginner and kept herself in the shadow of her husband, as his partner and his inspiration. He told her: "Without you, I would not be what I am. Without me, you would not be what you are."

IN LOVE WITH THE ABSOLUTE. Preoccupied by their shared passion for the theatre and their intense inner life, they seemed to sleepwalk through daily life. Even their endless money problems never troubled them, as they shared the same dreams and both saw art as an "absolute". Their house contained very little furniture apart from Ludmilla's piano, George's books and their children's toys (they had seven children, five daughters and two sons, one of whom, Sacha Pitoëff, born in 1920, also became a famous actor). The only thing important to them was unadorned décor and theatre scenery, which Ludmilla often brightened with her large, colourful shawls and which George transformed through his ingenious light effects.

They acted in several different Paris theatres and toured Europe many times. George wore himself out with his constant creativity, staging more than two hundred plays from Shakespeare to Pirandello. He also introduced the works of Chekhov, Maeterlinck, Strindberg, Ibsen, and contemporary French writers such as Anouilh. Their lack of money, however, sometimes forced them to stage quite mediocre plays; and in addition, George's work was often misunderstood and sometimes severely criticised. He was accused of making his productions revolve around his wife. Ludmilla's talent, however, became more and more evident; whenever she took on a role she began quietly and slowly, "like a growing blade of wheat", but ended

by appearing completely absorbed in the stark, lyrical emotion that radiated from her. Their love, so tender and so absolute, touched all their contemporaries, and for Cocteau, they represented "the true beauty that cannot be seen". One journalist reported: "When Pitoëff says 'Ludmilla', his voice opens up a little paradise of gentleness and love." When pregnant, she acted right up until the last possible moment; but in 1922 a car accident took her away from the stage, and Georges Pitoëff wrote sadly to Jacques Hébertot, director of the Théâtre des Champs-Elysées: "The tour is going very well, but it's the last time I shall act without Ludmilla. With her, I shall act as much as you want." Similarly, when she acted without him in another theatre, he was miserable and would go, with his head cast down, to look for her at the stage door.

THE CARTEL. Tired of moving from one stage to another, they founded the famous "Cartel", with Charles Dullin, Louis Jouvet and Gaston Baty, on 6 July 1927. The name symbolised this avant-garde theatre's aesthetic requirements, its search for truth, its creativity, and its attempts to reach the pinnacle of emotion with a minimum of means, combining freedom of subject matter with discipline of form.

In 1934 George Bernard Shaw's *Saint Joan* was the Pitoëffs' crowning success. The weakness transformed by faith into strength was personified in Ludmilla, who in this role seemed imbued by a remarkable, mystic quality that never left her. She preferred contemplative roles in which she could attempt the impossible, aspire to reach the absolute. She was remarkable as Medea, as Lady Macbeth, as Lechy in Claudel's *The Exchange*, as Nora in Ibsen's *The Doll's House*, and in Jules Supervielle's *Beauty in the Wood*.

By 1935 it was evident that the couple were drifting apart. Ludmilla took refuge in a tortured form of mysticism and abandoned the theatre. Her brooding, running away, solitary trips to an Alpine village, and long periods spent away meditating, alienated her from her husband. He, in the meantime, became ill with heart

trouble, which eventually killed him in 1939. Both George and Ludmilla came back together to realise one of their oldest dreams, to play opposite each other in *Romeo and Juliet*; however, they were too old for the roles, and the show was not a success. George could not understand his mistake, and grew bitter. Failure was always very painful for him, even though his loving wife and children always supported him in his struggles. His last productions were, however, perfect, such as Ibsen's *The People's Enemy*, and particularly Chekhov's *The Seagull*, in which Ludmilla shone brighter than ever.

When war broke out they left for Switzerland, where George suffered a fatal heart attack. Ludmilla returned to Paris, broken-hearted. She tried to act again but left for the United States, where she directed a school of dramatic art in Hollywood. After the war she returned to France, weakened by illness. She did, however, play Sheriff's *Miss Mabel* once again, before her death in 1951. Her daughter Svetlana quoted her last words: "It's so good to be alive, to live simply."

1916

LONDON. **The end of the relationship between Lady Ottoline Morrell, tall, red-haired, generous and unconventional – she had numerous writers and artists as lovers, and kept a famous literary salon – and philosopher and logician Bertrand Russell, whose writings on religion she influenced. Russell's genius had been recognised at a very early stage; he made a fundamental contribution to the philosophy of knowledge, but his four marriages and numerous affairs led the puritans to hold him in contempt. In 1916 he met Dora Black, who shared his libertarian ideas, and married her in 1921. In 1929 his famous book *Marriage and Morals*, got him banned from teaching mathematical logic at New York City College; it was believed that the writer of such a book would corrupt youth with his "sexual immorality".**

♡ ♡ ♡

Anguish
Angels in White – or Demons?

A gentle woman in white soothes the pain of a wounded soldier. This patriotic pair contrasts violently with the wives in affairs with "shirkers" behind their husbands' backs.

The First World War, for everybody, meant pain. For the millions of wounded it also meant loneliness, fear of being maimed for life or sent back to the front after recovery, and the mental pain born of suffering far from home and alone – at least, almost alone, because the bedside of the wounded soldier was attended by a guardian angel. Either a military or Red Cross nurse, she fought her own personal war. Always devoted and motherly, she was sometimes a little more than that, particularly in the mind of the wounded soldier, or of the wife who could not provide the care.

Love was certainly around in those painful times, but took a form different from that which beautified the days of peace. First of all, it moved to a rhythm of separation, reunion and brief encounters; it was often felt in situations of absence and worry. The man by whose side you had slept every night for years was suddenly gone. In the trenches, the soldier dreamed of the woman he loved, remembering the closeness of her body. And then, more and more often, he was wounded, and transferred to military hospital.

THE LADY IN WHITE. The soldier awakes from the anaesthetic, not knowing where he is, aware only that he is in pain. By his side an angel, dressed completely in white, wipes his brow and speaks words of comfort. Later, he discovers perhaps that he has lost an arm or a leg. Still a man, but now as dependent as a boy, he is in need of maternal care. The women dear to him are far away, and only occasional visits are possible. He is suffering and fearful. He dreams that the angel in white will follow him when he leaves, perhaps marry him. Sometimes his desires are more specific, more physical in nature. Will she respond? In reality, it seems, it happened only very rarely, but sometimes the dream turned true, as Ernest Hemingway relates in his partly autobiographical *A Farewell to Arms*. An eighteen-year-old American soldier, wounded in Italy in 1918, he fell in love with Agnes von Kurowski, a twenty-five-year-old nurse on whom the character of Catherine Barkley is based. Similarly, the parents of Doris Lessing, born in 1919, met in a hospital while her mother cared for her father, who had had a leg amputated.

Together, the wounded soldier and the nurse form a couple that symbolises a patriotic union between two complementary archetypes, the defender of the homeland and the ever-devoted woman. Meanwhile another type of couple fed the soldiers' imaginations, that of the adulterous woman and the "shirker", described in newspaper articles or by novelists' pens.

AFFAIRS ON THE HOME FRONT? Apart from the torments that racked the soldiers – the enemy, the mud, the rats, the shells, and so on – there was a question that haunted them: what were their wives doing? At the start of the war these women were brave, ready for anything, even to enlist; in Germany, in fact, the Na-

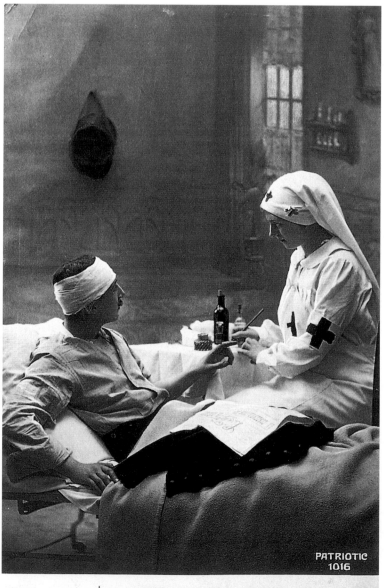

LA LETTRE AUX PARENTS

tional Women's Service was recognised as an auxiliary army by the authorities and provided them with assistance and supplies. Similarly, in Britain some female volunteers became local police officers. In France, where the authorities did not fulfil the demands of the League of Recruits founded by Jack de Bussy, the middle classes lived out their fantasies by wearing pseudo-military clothing. Colette recalls with some humour the disappointment of some soldiers on leave, hungry for gentleness and femininity, who instead encountered these "soldier girls" who had been left behind but nevertheless sported forage caps, greatcoats and false military decorations.

During 1916 the picture of the young woman devoted to her uniformed husband or lover was gradually replaced by a less favourable picture: that of the happy spendthrift who had been given independence by her wages from the munitions factory. The truth, however, was quite different; what actually happened was that governments decided to make use of female labour, and instead of independent women wearing silk stockings and indulging themselves in shops and cafés there were hordes of low-paid munitions workers who laboured in dangerous and tiring conditions with gunpowder stains on their hands. Nevertheless they became the pet hate of some journalists, whose writings caused considerable anxiety for the men at the front, as indeed did the sights that greeted them when they returned on leave. For what did they see? Women doing men's jobs, driving trams, buses and taxis. In the country, some women even held the office of mayor if no man was available. The papers continually criticised this "world in reverse", stating that it was all due to an act of sexual revenge by women. The novelists followed on from the journalists, de-

LA GUERRE ILLUSTRÉE

DECEMBRE 1917

scribing wives who gave themselves over to sinful pleasures while the men risked their lives for their country; indeed, they showed them as something even worse than a "shirker" or "whippersnapper" too young to be called to the front! One of the most successful French postwar novels, Raymond Radiguet's *The Devil Inside* (1923), was inspired by the author's adventures, at age fourteen, with a married woman of twenty-four whom he met in a train in 1917. Paul Morand saw this book as "an outrageous picture of a holiday amongst a forest of wooden crosses", which seemed to him "an attack on the moral state of the nation"; much the same thing had been said, in fact, when the press denounced the "self-indulgent" and

"unfaithful" women during the war. Behind individual people's misfortunes, the nation's honour was at stake. In France, in fact, the courts dealt very severely with adulterous women, whereas in crimes of passion, killers who had been at the front were treated very leniently. In Britain, women were watched and threatened with loss of state allowances for bad conduct; while in Germany the punishment was a prison sentence or a fine.

The war not only ripped men apart from women, but also put them into two separate worlds with a division more rigid than before. In such a male-oriented society, the supreme bond was between comrades, the manly brotherhood of soldiers.

1916

ZURICH. **The first meeting between French cubist sculptor and painter Hans Arp and Swiss dancer and painter Sophie Taeuber. Both were actively involved in the Dadaist movement. Married in 1921, they settled in Meudon, near Paris, in 1928 and lived in peace and harmony. Their works contain one recurring theme, the contrast between sharp and round. For him, sexuality was "the essential channel of bringing together the material and the spiritual". Their relationship was so close that they produced joint works, including collages, paintings, embroideries and even "duo-sculptures" (*Conjugal Sculpture*, 1937, and *Milestone*, 1938). As with their close friends the Delaunays (cf. p. 66), the wife's work was initially eclipsed by the husband's, although they influenced each other. Hans Arp produced further duo sculptures with the works left by Sophie Taeuber after her death in an accident in 1943.**

Female worker in a munitions factory.

Amedeo Modigliani & Jeanne Hébuterne

A great love in Montparnasse, remarkable works of art and a tragic end.

In July 1917 Florence-born Amedeo Modigliani, who had studied in Florence and Venice and arrived in Paris in 1906 aged twenty-two, met a nineteen-year-old girl named Jeanne Hébuterne. After visiting the artists of Montmartre, he felt no affinity with either the Fauvists or the Cubists, but in 1909 he settled in Montparnasse and began sculpting grotesquely elongated women's heads, becoming a personal friend of Romanian sculptor Brancusi and artists such as Utrillo and Soutine. Recognised much later as one of the twentieth century's greatest artists, he lived his life in poverty. Sick and racked with tuberculosis, he went on wild drinking binges, smoked hashish and snorted cocaine with his artist friends. In 1913 he gave up sculpture and turned to painting. During his few remaining years he produced some 200 canvasses and innumerable sketches, his sole subject being the human face. Indifferent to all sense of depth, he concentrated instead on lines, which gave his paintings great powers of expression; he stretched the faces out, as it were, painting them in elongated form viewed from the front, and their almond-shaped, pupil-less, shining eyes conveyed an expression of "tacit acceptance of life". This expression, for him, was the essence of his subjects. When war broke out he wanted to enlist, but was rejected on health grounds. At the time he was having a tempestuous affair with English journalist Beatrice Hastings, whom he painted in a series of magnificent portraits. After they parted early in 1917, Modigliani painted his first series of female nudes and became involved with the young Pole Leopold Zborowski, who became not so much an agent – he only managed to sell a few of his works – as a faithful friend and supporter.

LOVE AND MISERY. Jeanne Hébuterne was the daughter of a middle-class Catholic family in Paris; her father was an accountant. Nicknamed "Coconut" because of her very pale complexion and light brown hair, she was small and shy, with a beautiful even face, large, wide eyes and hair in two plaits that she sometimes wore around her head like a crown. As her brother was an artist, she gained permission to study at the School of Decorative Art and the Colarossi Academy. Her staunch Catholic parents were opposed to her relationship with the poor, foreign, Jewish painter; but she defied their ban, broke away from her family environment and moved in with him in Montparnasse, in two tiny narrow rooms at the top of a steep staircase.

The love between Modigliani and Jeanne Hébuterne touched all their friends. André Salmon contrasted the young girl's angelic softness with her companion's explosive outbursts. Others described the strange, almost mystical look in her dreamy eyes, and Chana Orloff produced a sculpture of her made entirely of wood. From the first, their household was a truly artistic one, as Jeanne also sketched and painted; her self-portrait and pencil sketch of Modigliani were widely acclaimed. She became his inspiration, his true Beatrice, as he described her, quoting Dante. His magnificent portraits of her, which echoed the sophisticated elegance of the Siena and Florentine masters, depicted her with heavily plaited or sugar-loaf hair, or wearing a hat, all accentuating her swan-like neck and the graceful poise of her hands.

The theme of the painter in love with his model who inspires his masterpieces appears frequently in the history of art. Famous examples are Picasso (cf. p. 97) and Dalí (cf. p. 144). Montparnasse, at that time, abounded in such relationships, like the photographer Man Ray and the beautiful Kiki in 1921, or the Japanese painter Fujita and Fernande Barrey and later Youki (see right).

Artistic life went on despite the war. On 3 December 1917 Modigliani's first exhibition was previewed in Berthe Weil's gallery. Someone, however, called the police, who ordered the "indecent" paintings to be taken down, as the female nudes displayed ... pubic hair!

In March 1918 the Germans bombed Paris, and Zborowski pooled his resources to take his artist friends to the Midi region. Modigliani and Jeanne made the

journey with Soutine and Fujita, and their daughter Jeanne was born in Nice on 29 November 1918. The painter, meanwhile, grew close to Blaise Cendrars and Léopold Survage, painting by day and doing the rounds of the bars by night. The couple later returned to Paris, leaving their six-month-old daughter with a wet-nurse.

THE ULTIMATE SACRIFICE. When Jeanne's second pregnancy was confirmed, Modigliani wrote: "I promise today, 7 July 1919, to marry Miss Jane (sic) Hébuterne as

PARIS. **One night, in Montparnasse's La Rotonde café, Japanese painter Fujita falls head-over-heels in love with a beautiful girl with short brown hair. Her name was Fernande Barrey, and she was also a painter. They married thirteen days later. In 1922, when Fujita had found fame, another thunderbolt turned his life around when he met Lucie Badoul, whom he nicknamed Youki ("Pink Snow" in Japanese). He painted her nude, depicting her as a "snow goddess", and left his wife to live a life of luxury with her. They parted in 1930, however, after both being distracted by new loves. Youki lived for many happy but poverty-stricken years with the great poet Robert Desnos, who was arrested by the Gestapo in February 1944 and deported to a labour camp where he died.**

"To love is to see a man as God created him, and in a way that his parents have not."

MARINA TSVETAYEVA
Land Signs

Jeanne aged twenty, posing for her lover.

soon as the papers arrive." Nothing more is known about it, although Thora Klinkowström, who posed for her in late 1919 and described Jeanne as "a fragile little woman who looked out on the world with terrified eyes and treated me with deep suspicion", reported that Modigliani described her as "his wife". His health, meanwhile, fluctuated wildly, and he alternated between deep depressions and bursts of wild enthusiasm. In his creative fervour he painted numerous portraits of close relations and his only self-portrait; but tragically he died on 24 January 1920, when Jeanne was in the last month of her pregnancy. She went back to her family and, preferring death to life without him, killed herself two days later, at three in the morning, by throwing herself from the window of her bedroom. He was thirty-six years old, and she only twenty-two. The painter Chantal Quenneville, who recalled her as "that young girl so gifted and so totally in love with Modigliani", also recalled seeing in the studio "sketches of Jeanne that showed her with her long plaits, stabbing herself in the chest with a long stiletto. Did she foresee her own death?"

A great procession accompanied the painter's coffin to the Père Lachaise cemetery. Jeanne Hébuterne's parents forbade her to be buried with him and only ten years later did they allow her remains to be moved.

The couple's tombstone bears an inscription in Italian, which describes the painter as "snatched by death when he had reached the heights of glory", and Jeanne as "Amedeo Modigliani's devoted companion, who made the ultimate sacrifice for him".

♡ ♡ ♡

SOCIETY
Revolution in Marriage

The new Soviet power liberalises marriage and divorce laws as never before. The consequences are disastrous.

In a country racked by civil war and surrounded by the Allies, the Bolsheviks, who seized power on 25 October 1917 (7 November 1917 in the western calendar) carried revolution into every corner of life, including the law, with remarkable speed. On 19 and 20 December 1917, two decrees were published, one on divorce, the other on marriage. Soviet Russia became the first country in the world to liberalise divorce in this way, granting it automatically in cases of mutual consent, with all connotations of guilt removed. Marriage in church was abolished, and only civil marriage was recognised, which did not even exist in many countries at that time (cf. p. 370). The ceremony was greatly simplified, and marriage itself was bereft of the concept of joint estate that had guaranteed the woman's personal inheritance. These measures were summarised and extended in the Family Code of 16 December 1918, under the editorship of Alexandra Kollontai (cf. p. 122). This code brought in absolute equality between the spouses and with regard to children; marital rights were abolished, and the husband could not impose his residence, his nationality or even his name upon his wife. Women were granted absolute equality of civil rights. Other radical changes introduced by the revolutionaries were complete freedom of abortion (1920) and the abolition in 1921 of the distinction between legitimate and illegitimate children; all children enjoyed the same rights. The 1926 Code went further still and equated cohabitation with registry office marriage, calling it a "de facto union". Divorce, too, was made simpler: a unilateral request, which could even be made by letter, was sufficient.

"THE REVOLUTION SOLVES PROBLEMS BETWEEN THE SEXES". Individuals, not so much set free as torn from the old structures, were granted rights and freedoms that they had never claimed and which therefore only left them bewildered. On top of this, the upheavals occurred in a society that was falling apart anyway: the revolution was, after all, a counterblast to the famine in the land and the mass killings at the front. The new masters of the state – intellectuals from the cities – used the law as one of their revolutionary tools without letting it reflect any moral developments in the predominantly peasant population. This population was saddled with the task of making the intellectuals' utopia become a reality.

The nineteenth-century ideologists Karl Marx, Friedrich Engels and August Bebel, so accurate in their economic analyses, said remarkably little about the future of relations between the sexes. They believed that the revolution would create new economic relations, and led in turn to new social and human relations; but in placing so much emphasis on the proletariat, they paid no attention to the problems in relationships common to all classes. They believed that marriage was based not on material constraints, but on natural inclination; it should, therefore, end when feeling ended, although they believed that divorce should remain very much the exception. According to Marx, one of the social revolution's main tasks was to abolish marriage and the traditional family and replace it with the "socialist community". Engels, however, saw the proletarian couple as the ideal unit, believing that love was the only reason for a poor man and woman to live together while the bourgeois marriage remained based on money and self-interest. For Engels, the bourgeois family was intrinsically immoral, as was capitalism, since it encouraged adultery by married women and prostitution by working women. August Bebel was the only one to take marriage and its duties seriously; he was one of the first to identify exploitation of women as one foundation of the capitalist society, but he too saw revolution as the only solution.

In a country torn apart by poverty, famine and alcoholism, women and children were the first victims of the new order; it created great instability amongst couples and a reluctance to bring children into the world.

THE ADVERSE EFFECTS OF FREEDOM. As a result of this new freedom, unwanted children were aborted, murdered and, most frequently, aban-

Soviet propaganda invites women to fight for socialism and against religion.

FACING PAGE
A gang of abandoned and hungry children, a world away from the glowing but hackneyed slogans of the revolution.

doned. These abandoned children formed gangs and survived by living a life of crime. The freedom had another adverse effect in that divorce by simple request, the "post-card divorce", bred very cynical attitudes in people. The "de facto" marriage was aimed at protecting women against short-lived affairs and compelling men to finance the needs of any children, but when the man disappeared it was very difficult to establish proof of the relationship or take out affiliation proceedings. In 1935 there was almost one divorce for every two marriages in the cities, but such was the shortage of housing that divorced couples were forced to live together anyway.

Ignorance and sexual prejudice were widespread, and it was inevitable, against the background of extreme economic hardship, that the question of sex would add to the frustration. The revolution shattered the old family framework, and Stalin's reactionary approach upset the situation even more by forcing the backward peasant society into a

frantic industrialisation process. In 1936 divorce was made more complicated and costly and in 1944 the "de facto" union was abolished and divorce made almost impossible. Unmarried mothers lost the right to commence affiliation proceedings or even receive a state allowance and illegitimate children lost their equality of status. It was not until 1965, long after Stalin's death, that divorce was once again simplified and made less expensive; the 1968 Family Code made divorce by mutual consent possible again, with maintenance contributions for children being deducted from the father's salary.

In Western Europe in 1917, the proletariat and left-wing intellectuals, horrified by the slaughter of the Great War, idealised the new Russia. William Reich wrote: "In our struggle against the reactionary marriage laws, we will always refer to the laws of the Soviets." However, he was later to denounce "the suffocating effect of the Soviet sexual revolution" (cf. p. 122).

ROME. **Pablo Picasso, already a famous painter, meets Olga Khokhlova of the Russian Ballet. After the première of the ballet *Parade* in Paris, he followed the company to Spain where he introduced the beautiful brown-haired dancer to his family. They married in Paris in 1918, with Apollinaire, Cocteau and Max Jacob as witnesses. Misia Sert (cf. p. 56) was godmother to their son Pablo, born in 1921. Picasso painted several beautiful neoclassical portraits of his wife, but became more and more irritated with the bourgeois yoke which she tried to impose on him. Although they parted in 1935, she refused to divorce him.**
Love played a major role in Picasso's works. The women who featured in his life one after the other, Marie-Thérèse Walter (1927), Dora Maar (1936), Françoise Gilot (1946) and Jacqueline Roque (1954), each gave him a fresh burst of inspiration.

♡ ♡ ♡

Karen Blixen & Denys Finch Hatton

A meeting in the wilds of Africa between a weaver of words and a man both seductive and inscrutable.

In 1918, a Danish baroness met an adventurous British aristocrat in Kenya. Both had left their homeland, disenchanted with their environment and drawn by the wide, open spaces.

Karen Dinesen had been born thirty-three years earlier at the family estate of Rungstedlund, near Copenhagen. Her father had lived for some years in America, amongst the Wisconsin Indians, coming back to take care of his land and pursue a political career. Although he was often away, he had a great influence on the young Karen, who listened enraptured to the tales of his travels. She was ten years old when he committed suicide, and she never lost the feeling of abandonment that followed.

Karen, clever and witty, studied art and soon began writing stories. She enjoyed a good relationship with her two cousins Hans and Bror Blixen, twin sons of a Swedish baron, who led an exciting life of festivals and hunts. She fell in love with Hans, although he did not reciprocate her feelings. From 1910 to 1912 she lived in Paris and then in Italy; when she returned, she agreed to

FACING PAGE
The cover of
Out of Africa.

marry Bror Blixen, who was both less brilliant and less cultured than his brother. She persuaded him to leave Denmark and settle instead in Kenya, on a coffee plantation at the foot of the Ngong Hills near Nairobi. He left first and she followed, and they were married in Mombasa on the day after her arrival in January 1914.

Although they shared a fascination with the wilds of Africa and its animals, that in itself did not provide a solid foundation for their marriage; Bror Blixen turned out to be a desperado, quite incapable of managing money and, indeed, the plantation. He infected his wife with syphilis, and although he was relatively unaffected by it, it caused her great suffering throughout her life.

A PASSION FOR AFRICA. On 5 April 1918, Bror and Karen met Denys Finch Hatton, a British officer on leave, while visiting friends. He was thirty-one and had fought bravely since his call-up in 1914; in him, Karen Blixen saw her "ideal man". He was handsome, intelligent, somewhat eccentric, refined, aesthetic, and an accomplished sportsman. After studying at Eton and becoming disillusioned with life in England, he left for Kenya where he settled in 1911, making his living as a businessman and safari hunter. On his return to Kenya in 1919, he became so close to the Blixens that the baron introduced him as "my best friend and my wife's lover".

Meanwhile, the plantation had gone bankrupt, and the owners had already accepted several attempts at reopening it; its management was transferred from Bror to Karen, who was more competent. In 1920 Bror left the Ngong plantation for good, and shortly afterwards demanded a divorce, ostensibly because his wife had not borne him any children. She did, however, retain what was most important to her: her title of baroness.

Between his travels Denys Finch Hatton lived with Karen Blixen, but he was anxious to preserve his independence and reluctant to commit himself permanently. He called the shots and, as Karen wrote, "was always happy on the farm, because he only visited when he wanted to".

Her book *Out of Africa* (1937), in which her literary creative skills evoke the real atmosphere of the plantation, makes only a passing reference to Denys Finch Hatton; her letters, on the other hand, express the full power of her passion for him: "It seems to me that I am tied to Denys for ever, impelled to worship the ground he walks on." When he left on safari or to visit Europe, it was as though he took with him "the sweet smell of roses and the light of the full moon", and when he returned, "it was as though he brought me fresh air and light".

Did they plan to marry? No matter how much she

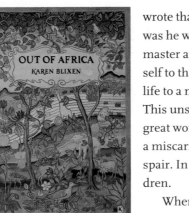

wrote that she had given up the idea, it was he who wanted to remain his own master and she who had to resign herself to that, saying: "I've dedicated my life to a man who can't be tied down." This unstable relationship caused her great worry, and in 1922 she suffered a miscarriage which drove her to despair. In fact, she never had any children.

When together, they lived in perfect harmony, as Sidney Pollack's 1986 film *Out of Africa*, inspired by their relationship, shows. A true Scheherazade, she enchanted him with the stories that she told him; he in turn encouraged her to discover the Bible and the Greek poets. They looked after the plantation together and went on safari following lion and leopard tracks; he took her in his aeroplane on flights over the mountains. Together they loved Africa and recognised the worth of its civilisation. They chose a place to be buried together, on the side of a hill overlooking the plantation, surrounded by the imposing scenery that they loved so much.

HEARTBREAK AND RUIN. Ruined by drought and by the fall in coffee prices, Karen Blixen was forced to give up running the plantation. She dreamed of buying it back, but Denys wanted nothing to do with it. "There is nothing I can do to help you," he wrote to her in 1930. The plantation was sold and Karen, sick at heart, was forced to return to Denmark, although she wanted for all she was worth to stay in Kenya. The closer she got to her lover, the more he pushed her away, unable to bear her demands for affection. They argued frequently and their last meeting, in May 1931, ended in a violent quarrel. A few days after leaving Karen, Denys Finch Hatton was at the controls of his aircraft when it suffered a mechanical failure and crashed; he died in the fire that followed. He was buried in the place that they had chosen, but remains alone there; Karen Blixen, after her death in 1962, was buried under a beech tree in the park at Rungstedlund. Karen Blixen made no mention of Denys Finch Hatton in any further letters, or in *Out of Africa*; it was as though she wanted to forget the split and idealise their love for all time. Reduced to despair by the loss of everything she loved, fearful for the future and believing that her life had been "completely wasted", she attempted suicide, but was saved.

She spent the rest of her life in Denmark, becoming a world-famous writer under the name of Isak Dinesen and later Karen Blixen. The magic quality of her writing brought to life the Africa that she loved so much, and in Denmark, where her artistic merit was late in being recognised, she has now become a national celebrity.

HOLLYWOOD. **Marion Davies, protégée of American newspaper magnate William Randolph Hearst, first appears on the cinema screen. This beautiful, intelligent and spirited blonde was twenty-one years old and he fifty-five. Hearst was married, and his wife refused a divorce. Marion Davies enjoyed several successful screen appearances, although her career folded in 1937 when Hearst broke with MGM. He suffered financial ruin in 1929 and she sold her jewels to help him back on his feet. It was for her that he had the magnificent castle built at San Simeon in California, but when he died aged eighty-eight, no mention of her appeared in his will. "I don't feel strongly about that," she said, "because with him I tasted happiness." Hearst tried in vain to get Orson Welles's 1941 film *Citizen Kane*, based on his life story, banned. "Rosebud", which is one of the key words in the film, is probably the name given by Hearst to an intimate part of his mistress's body.**

SEXOLOGY
Married Love

Marie Stopes' successful book caused a scandal through advocating sexual fulfilment for women and birth control.

In 1918 a book called *Married Love*, subtitled "A New Contribution to the Solution of Sexual Difficulties", was published in London; it caused a scandal and enjoyed overwhelming success. It sold a million copies and was translated into many languages; the French language version, *L' Amour et Le Mariage*, appeared in 1919. In 1935 the work appeared on a list, drawn up by American universities, of the most influential books published in the last fifty years.

The author, Marie Stopes, wrote the book after her first marriage, annulled in 1916 on grounds of non-consummation, failed. This seductive, very feminine lady was a doctor, not of medicine but of botany, specialising in plant fossils, and she broke many taboos to become an ardent supporter of sexual fulfilment for women and for contraception or "birth control". In 1918 she married Major Humphrey Verdon-Roe, a rich businessman who supported her. She saw "the key to happiness in the home and in the human race" in a woman "who had no more children than she and her husband had the means and the strength to raise in comfort". Two sons were born of this marriage.

The separation of pleasure and procreation evoked reactions of horror from "right-minded" people, as this was one of the keys to the liberation of women. The only solution offered by the nineteenth-century feminists who had denounced the double sexual standard of "everything's allowed for men, but nothing for women" was abstinence. For them, sexuality was a dangerous power and the "ideal woman" an angel of purity. At the beginning of the twentieth century, however, female sexuality began to be viewed in a more positive light, thanks to the first generation of woman doctors. The militant neo-Malthusians, socialists and feminists, however, spoke out against the damage caused by too many pregnancies and secret abortions.

THE PIONEER OF THE DIAPHRAGM. Marie Stopes was of the eugenist view, very widely held at the time, which stated that poor people had too many children and thus aggravated their poverty. She dedicated another of her books, *Wise Parenthood*, to "everybody who wishes to see our race grow and become more beautiful". The originality of *Married Love* lay in its championing sexual fulfilment for women and calling upon men to make this easier. Influenced by Havelock Ellis (cf. p. 62) and Ellen Key (cf. p. 38), she used, despite her scientific training, a style that was more lyrical than precise, with florid descriptions, such as that of woman's desire: "waves of wonder break within her, heavy with the rich aroma of the innumerable experiences that the human race has tasted since the early days of pleasure when love's flower first was new".

Similarly, her desire was to improve the quality of sex in marriage with "moves of exquisite gentleness" or a "delightful game of love"; in more prosaic terms, she suggested replacing the missionary position (cf. p. 314) with a side-by-side position, and reaching orgasm through mutual masturbation. Thinking, wrongly as it turned out, that the woman's desire peaked every fifteen days, just before menstruation and in the middle of the cycle, she thought it normal for a woman to ask her husband for repeated sex at these times.

Knowledge of sex and reproduction was very primitive at the time. It was not until 1929 that the discovery by the Japanese gynaecologist Ogino that ovulation occurs in the middle of the cycle led to the practice of periodic abstinence that bears his name. The commonest form of contraception at the time was withdrawal (where the man ejaculates outside the vagina). Marie Stopes roundly condemned both that practice and the condom, asserting that

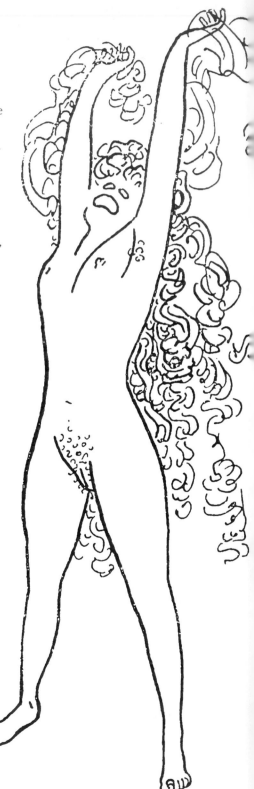

1918

HOLLYWOOD. **Screen star Charlie Chaplin, aged twenty-nine, marries sixteen-year-old débutante Mildred Harris. Two years later, she demanded a divorce. In 1924 he married actress Lita Grey, then also sixteen. After the birth of their two sons, she demanded a divorce in 1927 and her revelations provoked a scandal; indeed, the private life of the creator of "Charlie" shocked puritan America. In 1928 the French surrealists leapt to his defence, arguing In Louis Aragon's manifesto** *Hands Off Before Love!* **that he was a genius.**
In 1936 Chaplin married Paulette Goddard, the star of his masterpiece *Modern Times,* **but divorced yet again in 1942. He finally found stability with Oona O'Neill, whom he married in 1943 when he was fifty-four and she eighteen. Refusing to return to the United States, they lived happily in Switzerland with their eight children, one of whom was the future actress Geraldine Chaplin.**

♡ ♡ ♡

the woman "derives great enjoyment from the partial absorption of semen by the vaginal membranes". She became the pioneer of the pessary, a small rubber seal inserted into the vagina (the cap, which fits over the neck of the uterus, or the wider diaphragm).

Marie Stopes, hailed as a "sex prophet", was loved by the public and became convinced that she had been given a mission. Her many books brought her great success, as well as fierce opposition, with numerous lawsuits which however only succeeded in spreading her ideas more widely. On 17 March 1921 she and her husband opened the Mother's Clinic, where nurses gave advice on birth control, in the poor London suburb of Islington. The lack of scientific presentation in the results of the consultations discredited her in the eyes of doctors, while her growing arrogance and dogmatism made co-operation between her and the militant neo-Malthusians, who themselves opened numerous clinics, impossible.

THE SPREAD OF BIRTH CONTROL. The various methods of birth control spread slowly throughout Northern Europe, while Roman Catholic countries kept the prohibition on them the longest (France until 1967). The first sex information centre was opened in Amsterdam in 1882 by Aletta Jacobs, the first woman doctor in the Netherlands. In Sweden, where contraception was illegal until 1938, the greatest exponent of the method was Elise Ottesen-Jensen (cf. p. 218). In Germany, the League for Sexual Reform opened its first office in Hamburg in 1924.

In the United States it was nurse Margaret Sanger, following in the footsteps of the anarchist Emma Goldman (cf. p. 48), who gave "advice" to poor mothers before opening the first birth control clinic in Brooklyn in 1916; there she distributed diaphragms smuggled in from Europe, which earned the pioneering nurse a prison sentence. Brilliant and controversial, she was first a friend and then a rival of Marie Stopes, particularly within

How can female sexual enjoyment be reconciled with birth control?

the International Family Planning Movement.

Attitudes in Britain and America evolved very differently. In 1931, the British Labour government approved official clinics "to teach birth control methods to married women for whom pregnancy could be medically dangerous". In the same year in the United States, where birth control propaganda was still banned, the publisher of *Married Love* was prosecuted for obscenity, even though all the information relating to birth control had been edited out. Notwithstanding, the book continued to cause a stir!

ANGUISH
The War Widows

So many men dead, so many loves broken. No wonder relations were different in the new marriages that followed.

Eight million dead, 27 million wounded and 6 million of them permanent invalids, 4 million widows, 8 million orphans: this was the ghastly legacy of the Great War in Europe. A whole generation of men had been sacrificed, and every family mourned at least one dead person. The consequence of all this was broken homes, shattered dreams, love-songs frozen in time, widows shrouded in mourning clothes, fiancées ever faithful to the memory of a dead beloved, young girls resigned to becoming "old maids" or agreeing, out of dedication, to marry a " ruined man".

As soon as the great conflict started, widows began to appear, veiled in the black clothes of deep mourning. In Belgium, Italy, Germany, Britain, Australia, and the United States, from 1917 onwards, death notices were delivered to shattered families in their thousands. When a soldier died a long way from home, it was rare for his body to be repatriated; he had to be mourned without a funeral, without a gravestone. In the French countryside the mayor (provided he was not "under the flag") brought the fateful notice himself. In Paris, special workers or widows of great tact brought their condolences with the awful news. An occasional consolation in the form of a military cross or posthumous nomination, the dead soldier's personal property if it could be retrieved, or the glorious distinction "died for his country", was all that those left had to show for the lives lost. Vera Brittain, who lost her fiancé and her only brother in the war, expressed this pain and her misgivings on the morality of war in her well-known book *Testament of Youth* (1933).

THE WIDOWS' WEEDS. The war widows and the mothers who gave their sons for the homeland, sublime and dignified in their black clothes, were the very image of sacrifice. But how horribly significant this image in the light of such carnage! Some villages saw all their men go off to war and saw very few, sometimes none, return; they had been sent off with a bare minimum of training as foot soldiers straight to the front line. In France, the classes of 1914 and 1915 lost 29 per cent of their male members. How could a woman live in the country without a man? The women could not always work the land by themselves and some left the villages altogether. In the Vosges area, some tried to survive by planting fir trees; today, these trees have grown into thickets, dense with foliage, called "widows clumps".

After more than four years of war, some women did find their husbands again, wounded or mutilated, and always distressed; so many men had been traumatised and were plagued with anguish, depression and horrible nightmares. After such a long separation, it was difficult to adapt to life with a wife and children. What did families know of the effects of war on soldiers, except that, as one woman said: "I let them have a lamb, and I got a wolf back"? After so many years of being incited to violence, many men became alcoholics and wife-beaters.

And the others, those who knew not even whether their husbands were dead, suffered too. The "unknown soldier" of the tombs had a mother, and perhaps a wife or fiancée who waited in vain for his return, without ever discovering how or where he had died, as Bertrand Tavernier recounts in his 1989 film *Life and Nothing Else*. Quite apart from the pain and problems with children, there was financial hard-ship, despite the introduction of a pensions system. In 1921 there were 520,000 assisted war widows in Germany, but the scale of the need was vast and the aid very limited. Large groups were set up to defend widows' rights, and some years later associations for remarried war widows appeared, claiming the right to continue drawing their pension. (The same demands were made in Britain after the Second World War). In France, 230,000 of the 630,000 war widows had married again by 1928, because in spite of the agony of irretrievable loss and the family circle's opposition to remarriage, life had to go on and the time to marry came round again. It was a less happy, less affluent time, but it came nevertheless.

YOUNG GIRLS FOR OFFER. So many young men killed in the prime of life: in Britain there were 2 million more women than men, a state of affairs which greatly upset the balance of relations between the sexes. Apart from the widows more or less

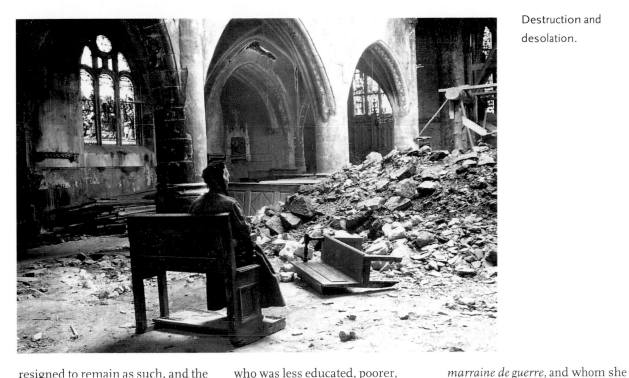

Destruction and desolation.

1919

The wedding of Marjorie Dumont to Lieutenant R. W. Meade becomes the first to be celebrated in an aircraft. The ceremony was held on board a massive bomber at Houston, Texas, before a crowd of 10,000 spectators. On a more sporting note, the first parachute wedding was celebrated in 1940, when Arno Rudolphi and Ann Hayward married in the air. They were surrounded by the minister who officiated, the witnesses, and four musicians, each carrying their own parachute, in a combined jump over Flushing Meadows Park in New York.

"And then, sly arch-lover that he was, he said the subtlest thing of all: that the lover was nearer the divine than the beloved, for the God was in the one but not in the other."

THOMAS MANN
Death in Venice

resigned to remain as such, and the fiancées, the "white widows" who remained faithful to the memory of their dead beloved (which included several posthumous marriages), other young girls were lacking in suitors, and those who were around often fell far short of previous ideals. In order to get married, many had to be content with a man who was less educated, poorer, shorter or in poor health. Others, meanwhile, said "We could only refuse". All were invited to show their allegiance to their homeland by marrying an invalided soldier. Marie Laparcerie, in her book *How to Find a Husband after the War* (1915), describes a young girl's love for a *poilu* for whom she acted as *marraine de guerre*, and whom she married even though he had lost an arm. This girl was "the good fairy who gave him hope, joy and a taste for life". This angel's mission is also described in *Guide To Propriety*, attributed to Liselotte (1919); according to her, those who gladly married war-wounded men would taste "the deep joy that is born of fulfilling a great duty". Vera Brittain recalls reading a classified advertisement in *The Times* that said: "Lady, fiancé killed, would be happy to marry an officer blinded or otherwise maimed by the War". What sort of relationship, one asks, would develop between a crippled man and a wife-cum-nurse on whom he depended daily?

The long years of male absence, which lead to so many women's hopes being stifled, sometimes led to an explosion of independence. Some "emancipated" women were intent on preserving the independence, incompatible with marriage, that they had found during the war. Some of those who worked in men's jobs and went out without chaperons now had a different view of marriage. Anxious not to be classed as their husband's servant, they wished instead to be treated as friends and companions.

Scott & Zelda Fitzgerald

Both in their heyday and in their final dejection, the Fitzgeralds were the epitome of the "Roaring Twenties".

The wedding of nineteen-year-old Zelda Sayre and twenty-three-year-old Francis Scott Fitzgerald in New York in April 1920 coincided with the beginning of the "Roaring Twenties" that they seemed to personify. Their life at the time was a celebration: both fair-haired, blue-eyed, brilliant and good-looking, they were loved for their charm and extravagance, and nobody condemned them for their drunkenness. Fitzgerald enjoyed phenomenal success with his first novel, *This Side of Paradise*, and a whole generation of youth identified with its hero and his romantic loves.

F. Scott Fitzgerald owed everything, and above all his marriage, to that novel. When he asked Zelda to marry him in 1918, she answered that he would have to be successful for her to marry him. He had met her in July of that year, at a party in Montgomery, Alabama, while his regiment was billeted in the town: although he undertook military training, the Armistice was signed before he sailed for Europe. The daughter of an Alabama Supreme Court judge, she, like him, wanted to become rich and famous. Mischievous, resourceful, indifferent to opinion and typically "sassy", she was as sure of herself as he was insecure.

Scott – he detested the name Francis because of its similarity to Frances – grew up in a middle-class family in St Paul, Minnesota, and was haunted by his father's failure in business; for him, glory, money, and the conquest of Zelda were all inextricably linked. This Southern beauty drove him mad with jealousy and he tried to drown the jealousy in drink, particularly when Zelda left him in June 1919 because his success was "late in coming". It was then that he decided to channel everything into writing a novel, and therefore into finding his love again. "It wouldn't bother me if she died," he wrote; "but I can't bear the thought of her marrying someone else."

LIFE IS CRAZY. The couple led a wild life all through the 1920s, in California, New York, Paris, on the Côte d'Azur, and Italy, and scarcely slowed down even to look after their daughter Scottie, who was born in 1921. They got drunk every night, tried to outdo each other's outrageous stunts, got themselves thrown out of hotels for damage or disturbing the peace and went on wild midnight car rides. Zelda, with her short hair and scandalous behaviour, was the epitome of the flapper, the cheeky, young, short-haired "tart" so typical of the Roaring Twenties. When a friend reproached her for her lifestyle, she answered: "We don't believe in things that last."

Scott and Zelda Fitzgerald swung between violent quarrels and reconciliations. Although she, like Scott, was insanely jealous, Zelda was not averse to flirting. In the summer of 1924 she had a romance with a French pilot, but Scott managed to dissuade her from divorcing him. These beginnings of disillusionment are reflected in *The Great Gatsby* (1925), often considered his greatest novel.

Zelda, meanwhile, complained of sexual frustration; Ernest Hemingway, in *A Moveable Feast*, recalls having great difficulty in reassuring Scott after Zelda convinced him that the way he was built, he could never make any woman happy. Although she hurt him by accusing him of being homosexual, she on the other hand enjoyed several lesbian relationships, which drove him crazy with anger.

DEMOLITION AND DERELICTION. Scott also suffered through being unable to make Zelda, who did not recognise her true worth, share his literary ambitions. There were more quarrels when he wanted to shut himself away to concentrate on producing works other than novels, which he scorned even though he wrote them quickly and in large numbers to meet their constant financial needs. When Scott was busy working, Zelda grew bored and ran off; the worry that this caused Scott interfered with his writing. She could not bear being just the wife of a great novelist; in fact she herself wrote several novels but abandoned them in humiliation when the magazine editors insisted that they be signed by both Scott and Zelda. In 1928 she decided to become a professional dancer, imposing an extremely punishing regime on herself, but all it produced was more quarrels. Her mental health began to suffer and she developed schizophrenia; and in April 1930, after suffering hallucinations that triggered suicidal thoughts, she was committed to mental hospitals several times in France, Switzerland and finally the United States.

"All life is a demolition process." This is the opening sentence of *The Crack*, F. Scott Fitzgerald's autobiography written in 1936. "We have destroyed each other," he wrote in a letter to Zelda. Times of togetherness were invariably followed by separations, and tenderness by

1920

PARIS. **American writer Ezra Pound meets American violinist Olga Rudge; their daughter Mary is born in 1925. Pound, however, was already married and refused to leave his wife, who bore him a son in 1926. A highly cultured poet and essayist, and an admirer of Mussolini, he divided his time between his family in Paris and Venice, where he lived with Olga who became a musicologist and contributed to the rediscovery of Antonio Vivaldi. Pound's support for the Fascist regime earned him an enforced stay in a Washington psychiatric hospital in 1946, and Olga Rudge spent all her time and energy trying to clear his name of the serious accusations levelled against him. After he was freed in 1958, they moved together to Venice and she encouraged him to write, particularly his masterpiece *Cantos*. The couple are buried together in Venice's San Michele cemetery.**

♡ ♡ ♡

heartbreak and pain. Greatly distressed by Zelda's accusation that he was homosexual, Scott, for the first time, started affairs with other women. He refused to do what she asked him on medical grounds – stop drinking and go for therapy – because he feared that it would harm his creative capabilities.

Zelda tried to fight her husband on his home ground. In 1932 she sent his publisher the manuscript for a novel. Scott managed to read it and, noticing that it contained many echoes of his current work, *Tender Is the Night*, felt a dreadful sense of betrayal; the similarity was not surprising, however, given that both novels were inspired by their experiences of life. Nevertheless he ordered the passages that showed him as too severe to be rewritten, because, as he wrote, "my books have made a legend out of her". Zelda's novel, a minor work entitled *Save Me the Waltz* (1932), was a failure.

When Zelda announced her intention to write on the subject of madness, Scott, who was writing his own novel on that subject, flew into a rage and threw a vicious accusation at her, saying: "You pick up the crumbs that I drop from the dinner table, and make them into

books." He ordered her to stop writing, and bitterly she gave in, devoting herself to painting instead. In 1934, driven to distraction by Zelda's worsening mental state and the failure of *Tender Is the Night*, Scott abandoned himself utterly to drink. He had several affairs during this dark time, including, in 1937, a relationship with Sheilah Graham, whose resemblance to a young Zelda attracted him to her. However, he could never bring himself to leave his wife, calling her "my invalid".

Zelda and Scott never stopped writing to each other. Their meetings, however, became briefer, more uneasy and less frequent; in 1939, during a stay in Cuba, Scott went on a binge while Zelda suffered a spiritual crisis. They never saw each other again. Scott suffered a fatal heart attack in Hollywood in September 1940, while staying with his mistress; his work, all but forgotten at the time, was not discovered until the 1950s.

Zelda Fitzgerald died in 1948 in a fire in the hospital where she was a patient. She was buried beside Scott. Remembering the "Roaring Twenties", their wild years, she had written: "At that time, scarcely any form of life was not depicted with the poetic and moving glory of his pen".

♡ ♡ ♡

Morals
Jules and Jim: The Trio

"My heart is pulled between the two of them": a triangle of friendship and love, with all the delights and risks of a three-way relationship.

The inspiration for the 1953 novel *Jules and Jim* was provided by a three-way love that was created during the summer of 1920. The character of Jim is a representation of the author, Henri-Pierre Roché, known simply as Pierre. Tall and thin, interested in everything, this well-dressed, charming lover of art was a friend of artists and art collectors. Gertrude Stein, to whom he introduced Picasso, said simply: "He knew everybody." His life was ruled by two passions: art and women. François Truffaut said that this "twentieth-century Don Juan" had countless affairs, most of them simultaneous, keeping accounts of them all in his diary.

"Jules" was Pierre's friend, the German writer Franz Hessel. Since their first meeting in Montparnasse

in 1906, they had discussed literature and art, and shared everything, even women, such as painter Marie Laurencin, without jealousy or rivalry. Franz, who was small, rotund, mild and sensitive, was in fact looking for a mother-love, and in the autumn of 1912 he met Helen Grund. She, like him, was from the Berlin bourgeoisie; she had come to Montparnasse to study painting, and was tall and slender with large blue eyes. A powerful, free-thinking woman who hated mediocrity in any shape or form, she was both provocative and unpredictable. Like Kathe in the novel, she had "a smile like an ancient statue" and both Franz and Pierre fell in love with her. Although Franz warned his friend "not that one", Pierre and Helen were married the following summer in Berlin.

A BALANCED MORALITY WITHOUT PERVERSITY. The friends were separated by the war, but in 1920 Helen wrote to Pierre: "Franz needs you." On 10 August, Pierre arrived in the

village near Munich where the Hessels were living with their two sons. Franz later wrote of this reunion: "At the very moment their eyes met, a destiny was sealed". At the time, he was forty, Helen thirty-four, and Pierre forty-one. Helen, with her modern, trouser-clad figure and short hair, was the embodiment of the emancipated woman of the twenties. She had lovers and saw her husband as "a big playboy" who had become like a brother and confidant to her.

For Pierre, Helen was life itself, with both its power and its danger. A passionate three-way relationship began, governed by a morality that was completely egalitarian, transparent, and free, without any shadows of perversity. "What others called sin, was for us just a glistening butterfly," wrote Franz Hessel in his novel *Parisian Romance*. Pierre, meanwhile, wrote in his diary: "The three of us, on Franz's bed, with Helen between the two of us, passed round a huge, mild cigar." In *Jules and Jim*, Jim asks:

"Who possesses a woman more, the one who has her or the one who looks upon her?" Jules replies: "The answer must be both of them."

Pierre admired Franz's total lack of jealousy, although he himself was jealous. As for Helen, her diary shows that she was looking for an "ideal union" and had decided to invent "a new kind of love". She was trying to find a balance between herself and the two men, and drew many triangles containing their three names.

Franz did not stand up to Helen enough, but Pierre, an altogether stronger personality, persuaded her to go out to work; as a result, she became a journalist. Whenever he was away, she sent him passionate letters: "This paper is your skin. This ink is my blood. I'm pressing hard to make it go in."

The three-way relationship began to go

Henri-Pierre Roché's "trio", as shown in François Truffaut's 1962 cinema film by Jeanne Moreau (Catherine), Oskar Werner (Jules) and Henri Serre (Jim).

sour, and Pierre wrote: "... the three twos remain, and the three, that might come back". In 1925 Helen, in order to be closer to Pierre, moved to Paris with Franz's sons; and while Franz, left destitute by the split, earned a living as a translator in Berlin, she became a fashion correspondent. Although Pierre wanted to keep his independence, she demanded his exclusive attention and left him when he fathered a child with another woman. She went straight back to Franz and ordered him never to see his friend again.

Franz died in Provence in 1941, leaving an unfinished novel on the love between Helen and Pierre; in it, he wrote that "they were made for each other". *Jules and Jim*, on the other hand, ends with the lovers dying, their end hastened by the capricious heroine who is a kind of modern "femme fatale".

Truffaut, when he discovered this novel which he later adapted for the cinema, was fascinated by "the almost shocking nature of the scenes described, which was

however purified by the innocence of the people involved".

ONE OF THE COMMONEST SEXUAL FANTASIES. The avant-garde artistic movement contains other examples of three-way love relationships. In the Bloomsbury Group (cf. pp. 83 and 102), the painter Dora Carrington, who had lived with the homosexual writer Lytton Strachey since 1917, married journalist Ralph Partridge. This three-way household was remarkably stable, despite a few "incidents", and when Strachey died in 1932, Carrington's despair drove her to suicide. Another famous trio consisted of the French poet Paul Eluard, his wife Gala (who later married Salvador Dalí, cf. p. 144), and the German painter Max Ernst, who moved in with the Eluards near Paris in 1922. The two friends were not rivals, but loved each other through Gala who did not, however, take well to her "double love". The trio lasted until April 1924 when Eluard, on an impulse, left for Tahiti. Gala left to look for him, Ernst accompanied her, and the Eluards were eventually reunited in Saigon. When they returned, Ernst moved out.

After the excitement born of discovering new pleasures wears off, it is rare for the sex trio to last long. Usually a relationship between two of the partners carries them away, and the third person is left nursing the wounds.

FRANCE. **The start of a secret and agonised affair between the writer Paul Valéry and Catherine Pozzi, who came from the very rich Paris bourgeoisie. Separated from the playwright Edouard Bourdet, whose son Claude she bore, this highly sensitive and much-revered woman, known as "Karin", believed that she could find her ideal partner in the famous and brilliant writer of *The Young Fate*. However, she found it very difficult to admit to herself that this poor, married man made many compromises and in truth cared more for his career. Nevertheless, their fruitful intellectual conversations and explosive love upset their lives. It revived Valéry's writing, leading him to produce *Charms*, *Eupalinos* (dedicated to Karin), and *The Soul and the Dance*, based on their passion. Catherine Pozzi decided to end the relationship in 1928, but when she died in 1934 she left a diary and six magnificent poems inspired by her love. These poems are amongst the most beautiful ever written in French.**

"I have never been unfaithful to my wife. There is no point: I love her."

GEORGES DUHAMEL,
The Life and Adventures of Salavin

♡ ♡ ♡

Isadora Duncan
& Sergei Esenin

A stormy relationship between one of the greatest dancers of the twentieth century and a brilliant, alcoholic, violent Russian poet.

"A rose in full bloom, whose petals of flesh snap shut on their prey", was how Isadora Duncan was described at the time of her meeting with Russian poet Sergei Esenin in Moscow in 1921. At forty-three, the American dancer had already found worldwide fame; beautiful and shapely, with shining blue eyes and henna-tinted hair, she was immediately captivated by the angelic charm of the handsome, fair-haired, twenty-six-year-old who was the *enfant terrible* of revolutionary Russia. As famous as the great Mayakovsky, he wrote in one of his poems: "There is only passion. Love does not exist."

They were both rebels, hungry for the absolute, who showed exceptional talent at an early age. Isadora Duncan, anxious to rediscover the purity that had invested Greek art, cast off the yoke of classical dance and, following in the footsteps of Loïe Fuller, contributed to a completely new dance form. Misunderstood in her native America, she was however widely acclaimed in Europe, enjoying success there from 1900 onwards. Alone on the stage, with hair hanging loose and feet bare, her agile body moved freely under the light material of her costumes as she improvised new dance routines. Living "unfettered by limits" – her motto – she set herself the task of "delivering people from their chains to help them find out about themselves and discover the element of the divine in them". Gabriele D'Annunzio, with whom she had an affair in 1912, called her "The Goddess of Nature".

An opponent of marriage, she vowed never to let herself "be reduced to that degrading state"; she led a highly eventful life full of emotion. She had a daughter by English theatre director Edward Gordon Craig in 1906 and a son by the rich American Paris Eugene

Poster by
Kees van Dongen.

Singer in 1911. Tragically, however, the children drowned in the Seine in 1913. In desperation she started an affair with a complete stranger, having a third child by him, but this child lived only a few days.

Esenin, who came from a peasant family in the Ryazan area, was filled with memories of his country upbringing and drew his inspiration from nature. He was twenty when he arrived in Paris, where the great poets welcomed him: his first collection of verse appeared in 1916 and brought him immediate success. He welcomed the revolution with great enthusiasm, viewing it as a kind of new cosmic spirituality, but later became disillusioned and tried to hide in drink and debauchery. He had many affairs with women and, in all probability, with men. In 1917 he married the actress Zinaïda Raikh, but left her when she was pregnant with their second child. Driven to despair by the harsh reality of the poverty, dictatorship and civil war that the revolution triggered, he poured out the poems of his cycle *Confessions of a Hooligan*, both in night clubs and on the pages of the literary journals. His works, banned by Stalin, remained very popular nevertheless and were officially recognised again in the 1960s.

"Esenin loves nothing!" During her first visit to Russia in January 1905, Isadora Duncan had been greatly moved by the image of the sledges bearing the coffins of demonstrators shot after the "Bloody Sunday" uprising. Impassioned by her experience of Bolshevism, she saw it as the coming of a new world order. In April 1921 she arrived in Moscow to open a dance school there at the invitation of Commissioner (Minister) for Instruction Lunacharski. In the economic chaos of the time, money was very short and "Comrade" Duncan was given the task of raising it.

When she met Esenin, she knew only a few words of Russian and he spoke nothing but Russian; they communicated using gestures and their own special language. Their passion, however, did not stop him drinking, and when drunk, he flew into frightening fits of rage. Sometimes tender and loving, sometimes tyrannical, he would beat her, insult and revile her, and then ask for forgiveness. She merely accepted everything. On 3 May 1922 she married him to allow him to leave the country and accompany her on the tour that she was undertaking to raise money. In Berlin they met Gorki, who wrote: "Esenin loves nothing. That, perhaps, is the secret of his power." For him, "this renowned woman, loved by millions of cultured Europeans, appeared beside the extraordinary poet from Ryazan as the perfect symbol of something he simply didn't need."

"THE RED DANCER AND HER GIGOLO". Esenin, who was homesick, was not at all happy to be seen merely as "the dancer's young husband". In October 1922 Isadora Duncan gave a series of performances in the United States and shocked the American puritans by praising the Soviet Union as "a land of freedom". The press, meanwhile,

described the odd couple rather derogatorily as "the red dancer and her gigolo". The drunkenness of Esenin, who was hailed as "the greatest Russian poet since Pushkin", scandalised the United States, which was under the banner of prohibition at the time. He wrote magnificent poems but suffered greatly through his inability to communicate with her. Their marriage was a failure: "In this woman I searched for happiness / And quite by accident, I found my downfall." After another spree of violence in Paris in February 1923, he was expelled from France. Isadora Duncan went on supporting him.

In September 1923 they returned to Moscow. Ravaged by alcohol, he took up his debauched life-style again while continuing to write heart-rending verses. Perhaps she read the lines that he wrote in hospital: "You alone, I shall not forget you / Even if I love another / With another, or with still another / I shall speak of you, my dear / Shall I tell her that once I called you dear?" At this time he was writing profusely, his talent at its peak. After his disappointing tour of the West, he sang the praises of revolutionary Russia and wrote some marvellous lyric poems. They separated, and Isadora Duncan made a major tour of southern Russia, staging a triumphant final per-

formance with the Bolshoi Ballet. In December 1924, however, she left the country and demanded a divorce.

Esenin began to suffer hallucinations and at-

1921

PARIS. **Igor Stravinsky, composer of the famous *Rite of Spring* ballet (1913, cf. p. 57) is introduced to Vera de Bosset, costume designer for the Russian Ballet, by Sergei Diaghilev at a dinner. Both were Russian émigrés. Diaghilev had given the beautiful, tall, and sunny de Bosset the task of cheering up the composer, who was downcast after being rejected by Coco Chanel. An affair followed, in secret, because Stravinsky was married with four children. His wife Ekaterina died in 1939 and in the following year, he married Vera in the United States, where they lived from then on. They understood each other on a deep level and lived together happily; Vera was as calm as Stravinsky was anxious. Until Stravinsky's death in 1971, they both led a very active and cosmopolitan life; she painted, and he composed several masterpieces.**

tacks of madness. In June 1925 he married Sophie Tolstoy, the grand-daughter of Leo Tolstoy, but he could not forget Isadora Duncan. "I remember you saying to me / The good years shall pass / And you will forget me, my dear / With another at last". He described himself as "sadly in love with another" and concluded "My heart will remember you, even with another." On 27 December 1925, in Leningrad, Sergei Esenin booked into the England Hotel and requested the room that he had occupied with the dancer in February 1922. He wrote a poem of farewell to a friend with his own blood, and hanged himself.

Two years later, in Nice, Isadora Duncan was strangled by her scarf when its fringe caught in the spokes of a car wheel as she was setting out on a journey.

♡ ♡ ♡

Sexology
The "Third Sex"

Magnus Hirschfeld established sexuality as a scientific subject and proposed a biological explanation for homosexuality.

Thanks to Magnus Hirschfeld, a German doctor and one of the principal founders of "sexual science", sexology – the word in English means "the branch of science that deals with sexual life and relationships, especially in human beings" – became a discipline in its own right, following on from the pioneering work of Henry Havelock Ellis (cf. p. 62). For a long time, however, it was not considered "respectable"; those who researched it were ridiculed, vilified, and accused of being "pornographic" and "amoral". Hirschfeld, who was hated by the extreme right and the anti-Semitic movements, was attacked several times, most notably in Munich in 1920.

He did not confine his studies to the sphere of genital function; that would have reduced sexuality to procreation. Instead, his desire was to produce a whole sexual sociology dealing also with ethical and legal questions. He published a series of major sexological reviews and innovative books, for example on transvestism (1910) and on aphrodisiacs (1926).

The world-famous Institute of Sexology, which he founded in Berlin in 1918, had many thousands of files and books, as well as documents and objects brought back from Hirschfeld's frequent travels. He was one of the first to treat homosexuality scientifically, rather than from a moral standpoint, at a time when the "unnatural" acts of "inverts" were attributed to moral degeneracy and as such roundly condemned. Since 1897 he had been organising a petition against Article 275 of the Penal Code, which punished any sexual act between men with a five-year prison sentence. This article was abolished in part in 1929. "I'm not spreading propaganda in favour of homosexuality," he said, "I'm just opening the eyes of those who are attracted to people of the same sex, and campaigning against their condemnation by society."

NOT AN ILLNESS TO BE CURED, NOR A PERVERSION TO BE PUNISHED. The word "homosexual" was used publicly for the first time in 1869 by the Hungarian-born doctor Karoly Maria Benkert. Formed from the Greek prefix *homo*, meaning "same", it appeared in several different European languages at the end of the nineteenth century. Since his first study, *Sappho and Socrates*, in 1896, Hirschfeld defined homosexuality as a natural form of sexuality; he attributed it to a congenital make-up that could not be changed despite being linked to glandular secretions. For him, it was neither an illness to be cured nor a perversion to be punished. He explained the very wide variety of forms of sexual behaviour in terms of the bisexual nature of the embryo and the action of sex hormones, which had been discovered at the end of the nine-teenth century. Increased or decreased levels of masculine elements in women, or of feminine elements in men, led to the so-called "intermediate stages" between men and women. The homosexual was therefore a "type of intermediate stage", which he called "the third sex" (the title of a 1905 book the subject of which was developed further in *Homosexuality in Men and Women*, published in 1914).

Hirschfeld was interested in Freud's research (cf. p. 46); Freud worked with him in producing his review and described him as a "charming colleague, able to sublimate his homosexuality completely". They took entirely different standpoints, however, and Hirschfeld split with Freud in 1911. From the psychoanalytical point of view, homosexuality was the outworking of a neurosis that determined a person's sexuality at an early stage; the person's relationship with his parents, and particularly with the opposite-sex parent, made it impossible to transfer in adulthood from a narcissistic attitude to one centred on a person of the opposite sex. All through the twentieth century, the two interpretations have alternated: is it innate or acquired? Is it a genetic inclination or does it stem from too strong a relationship with the opposite-sex parent? Clearly the first interpretation would relieve families of much guilt and reassure anyone who might be scared of becoming "contaminated". Nevertheless, nobody has yet been able to identify a "homosexual gene".

Sexology, from its very beginnings, has been closely linked with eugenism and "social hygiene", that is, an ideal based on quality of population, as opposed to the quantity-based ideal defended by the neo-Malthusians. Its exponents seek to argue a medical viewpoint in preference to a moral or religious one. Nobody questions the "natural" difference, accentuated by culture, between "active" masculine sexuality and passive "feminine" sexuality.

"SEXUAL REFORM". The opening conference of the World League for Sexual Reform was held in London in 1929. Hirschfeld presided, supported by the English doctor Norman Haire, Henry Havelock Ellis, and the Swiss psychiatrist Auguste Forel, who practised sterilisation for eugenic purposes. The League established its aim as "the moral and physical enrichment of sexual life". Its programme included political and sexual equality for men and women, full availability of contraception and abortion and scientific sex education. The militants of "sexual reform" believed sexual problems to be pathological phenomena rather than crimes, vices or sins. For them, sexual acts between responsible, consenting adults were essentially private; the only criminal acts were those that infringed the rights of others.

The League spread from Berlin and London right across Europe. Interest was greatest in Germany, where left-wing intellectuals such as Kurt Hiller and Wilhelm Reich, and the feminist Helene Stöcker, who founded the League for the Protection of Mothers and Sexual Reform in 1905, demanded that laws be adapted to reflect developments in morals. In France, on the other hand, the repressive 1920 law allowed Eugène and Jeanne Humbert to be imprisoned for spreading propaganda in favour of contraception. Most of the action was taken

by men, with rare exceptions, such as Berty Albrecht (the future leader of the French Resistance) who launched the magazine *Sexual Problems* in 1933. The militants' view of sexual activity was often dictated by the extent of its effects on women, particularly in cases of illegitimate pregnancies. In England, feminists were opposed to sexual reform, favouring instead the protection of women against the violence and perversion of men. While anarchists demonstrated that repression of sexual activity was an

essential tool for wielding control over society, nobody questioned that heterosexuality was the norm.

On 6 May 1933, the Nazis burnt all the files and books belonging to the Institute of Sexology. Hirschfeld was exiled to France, and sexology was branded a "Jewish science" by the Nazis, who used this biological explanation to justify their extermination of homosexuals. It was not until 1993 that the World Health Organisation (WHO) removed homosexuality from its list of recognised mental illnesses.

UNITED STATES. **Ruth Hale, a journalist married to Heywood Broun, a colleague, battles with the State Department to have her passport issued in her own name instead of her husband's. She founded the Lucy Stone League, named after a well-known feminist, and campaigned for married women to be allowed to keep their maiden name. The struggle was in vain. In France, in fact, a married name is only a "name of habitual use", since according to the Law of 6 Fructidor Year II, never repealed, "no citizen may bear a first name or surname other than those entered on his or her certificate of birth". In many cultures, married women bear both names coupled together: in Spain and Latin America they are linked by the conjunction *de*. In Germany a 1986 law (cf. p. 385) allowed couples to choose a common name, which could be that of either or both partners, with a uniting hyphen, at the time of their wedding.**

♡ ♡ ♡

Masculine elements in a woman: painter Peter Abelen's wife, photographed by August Sander.

Lila Bell Acheson
& DeWitt Wallace

The founders
of *The Reader's
Digest*, one
of the greatest
successes
in publishing
history.

The first edition of the *Reader's Digest* was published in New York in February 1922. This monthly pocket-size magazine contained a series of previously published articles reproduced in abridged form. The publication was the brainchild of DeWitt Wallace, who was supported by his wife Lila Bell Acheson. Both aged thirty-three, and both from a Presbyterian background, they had married a few months before on 15 October 1921; they never had

children. Their temperaments complemented each other. Lila Bell Acheson, a small woman with brown hair and blue eyes, was open-minded, optimistic and dynamic; her father was a preacher from Manitoba who emigrated to the North-Western United States, and she had worked in a number of social projects with the Young Women's Christian Association (YWCA).

DeWitt Wallace, the son of an academic from St

Paul, Minnesota, was looked upon as a disgrace by his family, firstly because his schooling was considered to be mediocre and secondly because he made his fortune in the business world. Shy and retiring, he described himself as an ordinary man, even though he was interested in everything and had a great capacity for work. He met his future wife while working with her brother, and had the good fortune to meet her again after the war. Wounded in October 1918 at the front in Lorraine, he spent his period of convalescence avidly reading magazines.

THE READER'S
DIGEST

THIRTY-ONE ARTICLES EACH MONTH
FROM LEADING MAGAZINES ⟶ EACH
ARTICLE OF ENDURING VALUE AND
INTEREST, IN CONDENSED AND
COMPACT FORM
⁓

FEBRUARY 1922

A JOINT WORK. "He had the genius," one of their relatives subsequently remarked, "but it was his wife who revealed it." Wallace's desire was to create a magazine for everyone who wanted to learn and better themselves in the process, but no publisher was willing to take the risk. His wife encouraged him to launch with a loan. Just before their wedding he sent out several thousand letters offering the magazine at a fixed subscription, and when they returned from their honeymoon the cheques had flooded in; indeed, the flow has not stopped since. The first issue of *Reader's Digest*, produced in February 1922 with a circulation of 5,000, found the right formula straight away; it contained no fiction, photography or colour, only factual articles of "enduring value and interest", reproduced by Wallace "in condensed and compact form" without losing their content, and interspersed with short interesting or amusing stories. It contained no advertising, as Wallace firmly believed that advertising was harmful; in fact the first advertisements did not appear until 1955, and then only to avoid an increase in the subscription rate. The first articles included: "How to Stay Mentally Young", "Love: Luxury or Necessity?", and "The Ravages of Tobacco".

They set up their office in their house at Pleasantville, a small town one hour's drive from New York. To save money, DeWitt Wallace read in the public library, copying his selected articles onto sheets of yellow paper. While he reproduced them on his portable typewriter, Lila Bell Acheson played the piano. During those early years, in order to produce each issue without being disturbed, they spent a week in a hotel, staying in neighbouring rooms each with an armful of magazines. In order to avoid distracting each other, they communicated by little notes slipped under the door. Soon, the *Reader's Digest* began to include original articles; in 1935 Wallace, after having a car accident, commissioned one encouraging drivers to take care, and from December 1934

onwards the Digest began publishing condensed books. Lila Bell Acheson produced the editorial until 1938 and was also responsible for the artwork on the cover. DeWitt Wallace always placed his wife's name before his own, although she was less involved with the publication and instead concentrated more on building and decorating their new offices, also in Pleasantville.

The magazine, with its familiar symbol of Pegasus, the winged horse, went from 30,000 subscribers in 1926 to 290,000 in 1929. In ten years the circulation had reached 1.8 million copies, and in 1939 the total number exceeded 3 million. The first foreign edition was published in Great Britain in 1938, and editions in Spanish, Portuguese, Swedish and other languages soon appeared. The *Reader's Digest* became the greatest success in the history of journalism: now, at the end of the twentieth century, it has forty-eight publications in nineteen languages and 28 million copies each month in more than 200 countries. (In Great Britain, for example, the *Reader's Digest* has a circulation of just under 1.5 million). The condensed books club, which now sells twenty million volumes per year in ten languages, was founded in 1950; the *Reader's Digest* also produces and publishes full-length books and compact discs. With its commendation of courage, loyalty and patriotism, the *Reader's Digest* also promoted the "American Dream" with its unshakeable faith in progress and the conviction that material needs would always be satisfied if one worked hard enough.

GENEROUS PATRONS. With a fortune estimated in 1980 at $500 million, the Wallaces showed themselves to be generous patrons. Lila Bell Acheson's numerous passions included dance, music, flowers, birds, Egyptian art and impressionist paintings, and she also commissioned the restoration of Monet's house and garden at Giverny. She bought numerous paintings, putting them on display in the Reader's Digest Group's various offices. "Works of art," she explained, "are like a husband. I've become a collector because I've discovered that I simply can't live without them."

In memory of their great generosity, the periodicals room in the New York Public Library is named after DeWitt Wallace, and a new wing of the Metropolitan Museum of Art bears the name of Lila Bell Acheson. She, in fact, left the museum enough money to allow the magnificent bouquets of flowers decorating the entrance to be replaced every week, so that it could reflect

1922

FRANCE. **Marcel Sembat, the Socialist deputy and one-time minister in the Poincaré government, dies in an accident in Chamonix aged sixty. He had been married to the painter and sculptor Georgette Agutte, who was fifty-five, and together they made a very close, but childless, couple. Georgette Agutte received all the visitors, stayed close to the body to write up her will, and then killed herself with a bullet in the head. She had introduced Matisse, Marquet and Picasso to her husband, and herself had Fauvist tendencies. Both were great lovers of modern art, and purchased from Matisse a sketch and watercolour produced by him in preparation for his famous painting *The Dance*. Their impressive art collection, which was left to the state, is now on display in the Agutte-Sembat rooms at the Grenoble Museum.**

♡ ♡ ♡

living beauty as well as art. In addition, she offered scholarships to young artists while her husband offered them to students of journalism. In 1973, at the age of eighty-four, the Wallaces finally retired, although they carried on their philanthropic activities; he died in 1981, and she survived him by three years.

"I have a perfect wife," he declared at the festival staged in 1972 to mark the fiftieth anniversary of their joint work. "When I married her, she liked to have a good time... We have spent all our time working, without ever going out, but she knew that this was what I wanted."

♡ ♡ ♡

The Latin Lover

In the cinema, Rudolph Valentino was the most famous of a long line of Mediterranean seducers known as "Latin lovers".

The reason why actors of Mediterranean appearance have been successful ever since the beginnings of cinema is partly a technical one: dark hair shows better on black and white film than fair hair. The ideal lovers of the cinema screen were, for that reason, Italian, like Rudolph Valentino, the star of the silent screen in the twenties; Spanish or Latin American, like the Mexican Ramon Navarro or the Argentinian

Carlos Gardel, star of the tango (cf. p. 80); or French, like the thirties romantic hero Charles Boyer (cf. p. 352), Maurice Chevalier, or Louis Jourdan. Of the characters that they played, the greatest seducer of them all was the matador: this was one of Valentino's best-known roles, in *Blood and Sand* (1922). During the bullfights, the female spectators, delirious with delight, rained flowers on the matador who earned himself the title of "superman" by killing the bull; on the screen it was the Latin lover, with his handsome appearance, dark skin and jet-black pupils, who excited wild feelings and dreams of love in the women who

admired and indeed worshipped him.

Although the Latin lover, like the "femme fatale" (cf. p. 88), became associated with black, he was not her masculine equivalent. Although he captured many women's hearts, he did not lead them to their doom; rather, he was content to seduce them with his magnetic personality and noble qualities and leave them with an indelible memory of him. A cultural legacy of old Europe, this type of fiery-eyed, hot-blooded, proud man, who dominated women with the full power of his sensuality, corresponds in Latin American and particularly Mexican culture with the traditional virility expressed in machismo (a word derived from the Spanish *macho*, meaning male).

A YOUNG GOD OF LOVE. Although Rudolph Valentino was not the first of the Latin lovers of the cinema screen, it was he who embodied all their characteristics. Born in a small village in southern Italy, he emigrated to the United States in 1913 at eighteen. After working in a string of jobs in New York, he became a host in the "chic" nightclubs and a high-class gigolo. In 1917 he arrived in Hollywood; starting as an extra, he quickly rose to land the starring role in Rex Ingram's successful film *The Four Horsemen of the Apocalypse* in 1921. In a scene that remains famous to this day, he holds the heroine tightly and passionately to him and leads her in a tango that ends with him giving her an ardent kiss.

During the five years that he had left, Valentino made fourteen

The irresistible Valentino captivates Vilma Banky in *Son of the Sheik*.

films in all. With his mixture of feminine languor and male braggadocio, he made the "bad type" highly fashionable. *The Sheik* (1921), which shows the heroine as being half-willing despite her resistance, confirmed his reputation as a "great lover" and made a fortune for Paramount Films. "Divine Rudy" received thousands of love letters: as a passionate or sentimental lover, an enterprising seducer whom none could resist, he embodied a great many women's dreams. This prince of a thousand and one nights, with his unlikely roles, extravagant costumes, dark eyes, and carefully slicked-back hair, brought them dreams, fantasies and a way of escape from everyday life.

Although Valentino was almost worshipped as a sex god, his private life was so strange that his opponents accused him of being impotent or homosexual. Certainly he was married twice, but on both occasions it was to one of the Russian star Anna Nazimova's circle of lesbian lovers. His first wife, the actress Jean Acker, sent him away on their wedding night in 1919; he subsequently demanded a divorce on grounds of non-consummation. Valentino was then won over by Natasha Rambova, an American costume designer who had chosen a Russian pseudonym; although her attitude was motherly, she was more interested in her career than in him. He married her in Mexico in 1922, but one week later, on his return to Los Angeles, he was arrested for bigamy; quite rightly so, as he had not respected the mandatory one year after his divorce before marrying again. He was advised to declare that the marriage to Madame Rambova had not been consummated either. That, of course, begged the question: was it consummated or not? A new scandal broke, with more questions about his virility. After they separated in 1924, Valentino took up pub-

RUDOLPH VALENTINO

Rudolph Valentino

licly with Pola Negri, a beautiful brunette famous for wearing sumptuous turbans, who came to Hollywood after becoming a star of the German cinema.

Valentino died of peritonitis in New York on 23 September 1926. Forty thousand people watched the funeral; Pola Negri's awesome show of grief, the riots that broke out during the service and left many people injured, the numerous faints and the attempts at suicide, were truly memorable. Similar scenes of mass hysteria were witnessed after the untimely death of Carlos Gardel in 1935 and that of James Dean in 1955.

As in ancient tradition, the hero was elevated to a kind of glowing immortality after his death and a posthumous "cult of personality" developed around Valentino. The "god of love" lived on in his films and photographs and in biographies. Two films, both named *Valentino*, celebrated the myth: one produced by Lewis Allen in 1951, starring Anthony Dexter, and the second produced by Ken Russell, and starring Rudolph Nureyev, in 1977.

THE LATIN LOVER SEDUCES STILL. Rudolph Valentino once said: "I give women the material to help them embroider their dreams." With his slender, well-kept body and made-up face with languorous expressions, this Latin lover with all the poise and grace of a dancer seems very effeminate for a "sex symbol" today. The reason for this is because he has been succeeded by another male type, embodied by Clark Gable (cf. p. 172). The thing about him that still moves people is his fragile, youthful appearance, which causes a desire to protect him; in fact his second wife saw him as "a small, sad boy".

Valentino died before the advent of talking pictures, which put in the shade many actors whose voices were poor; this was the case with the other great seducer of the time, Greta Garbo's partner John Gilbert. The theatrical, sometimes highly exaggerated antics of the stars of the silent screen makes Latin lovers seem outdated and somewhat ridiculous here in the 1990s.

1922

UNITED STATES. **The wedding of Margaret Sanger, the recently divorced militant supporter of birth control, and J. Noah Slee, a fabulously rich industrialist and oil magnate. Anxious to avoid the pitfalls of marriage, Margaret Sanger made it a condition that Slee respect her independence. He kept his promise and indeed supported her cause financially. In 1937, after getting the obscenity laws changed to exclude documents relating to contraception, she left New York and they both retired to the house they had built in Tucson, Arizona. In 1926, Margaret Sanger published *Happiness in Marriage*.**

"A great love? I think, myself, that a great love is when two people manage to support each other all through life and remain devoted and faithful to each other."

KAREL ČAPEK
The Fabric of the Absolute

Anna de Noailles & Maurice Barrès

A secret love between two famous people of the time: an all-consuming passion by a man obsessed with the absolute and a woman more coquette than sensual.

On 15 December 1923 Maurice Barrès, the famous writer and politician, died suddenly of a heart attack at his Paris home aged sixty-one. "You died one evening as the day was ending. ... / You were sleepy, I suffered and fell, cruelly deprived / And worse than death is having survived." The writer who suffered the dreadful pain of surviving him was the poet Anna de Noailles; she had been tied to him by a secret passion that remained unknown to the general public for several decades. It was a passion that suited their images: he self-controlled, restrained and strict, and she lively, brilliant and unpredictable. In a letter written shortly before his death, he dedicated his works to her: "One day I would like your name, my life's dream and closely guarded secret, to be written on the first page of something that might survive from your friend."

Anna de Noailles's first novel, *New Hope*, caused a scandal when published in 1903; it was the story of a woman who expected passion. It was also in 1903, in painter Jacques-Emile Blanche's studio on 26 April, that something described by the painter who witnessed it as "love at first sight", occurred between Anna and Maurice Barrès. The young woman, born Anna de Brancovan, was twenty-seven at the time. Her father was a Romanian prince, and her mother a Greek princess, and she was raised in Paris in a very cultured home frequently visited by aristocrats, writers, and artists. Small, fragile-looking and very beautiful, with large greenish eyes and long black hair, she married Count Mathieu de Noailles in 1899; their only son, Anne-Jules, was born the following year. The couple had progressive ideas and were supporters of Dreyfus. Anna de Noailles's first collection of poems, *The Unfathomable Heart* (1901), brought her great success.

Maurice Barrès was fourteen years older than Anna. A dandy, originally from the bourgeois of the Lorraine region, he married Paule Couche in 1891; she, a devout Catholic, was devoted to her husband's career and to educating their son Philippe. Barrès's trilogy *The Cult of I* (*Under Barbarian Eyes* published in 1888, *A Free Man* published in 1889, and *Bérénice's Garden*

in 1891) brought him success. Idolised by youth, an ardent nationalist, and an anti-Dreyfusard, he was elected a deputy in 1906 and became a member of the Académie Française in the same year.

THE POWER OF LOVE. Anna de Noailles's passion was to please; she loved to be surrounded, flattered, praised. She was not greatly sensual, but instead she delighted in tantalising men, driving them wild with her flirtatious behaviour. In 1909 the young poet Charles Demange, Maurice Barrès's nephew, killed himself after love for her drove him to despair.

"I want the absolute, and nothing else." Barrès's passion for Anna de Noailles was powerful and exclusive; he was insanely jealous and wrote to her almost every day. Although Anna had split with Mathieu, she refused to commit adultery with Barrès. In fact, she found the physical side of love repulsive, and in 1906 had ordered her husband to sleep in a separate bedroom, while imposing a regime of "courtly" love on Barrès. He accepted it "with head bowed". However, the almost daily visits from the writer upset the Count, who could no longer bear his wife's many friends, these visitors whom he described as "cannibals".

Barrès's jealousy, meanwhile, increased: "I was born too suspicious, and you were born too clever." He criticised her writings, saying: "She has genius, but no talent", and her faults: "all the aloofness and pride of a nightingale". However, he never ceased to desire her, love her, idealise her: "You were never more noble, more divine than on that day, with your cheek flushed, your hair loose, and a tender, sensuous expression on your proud face." In 1907 he left her because of the pain that her remoteness caused him, and avoided her for some time afterwards.

In 1912 the Noailles announced that they were separating amicably. The war brought Barrès and the Countess close together at official demonstrations, and on 7 March 1917 she finally gave in to him. She sang of her happiness: "I love you, / Stranger who takes all, and has given me all", and described their "close, fierce and barbaric union" and "desired, supreme, wild passion". A poem from the 1920 collection *The Eternal Forces* is called "Pleasure", and reads: "The temporal being draws alongside eternity / Fullness, desert, destruction, long, long pause ... / Passing from premature death to sudden brightness."

She preferred the writer and poet in him to the great nationalist speaker, and sometimes he would abandon his patriotic outbursts to make her his "muse": she was the inspiration for his works, from *The Spartan Voyage* (1906), which was dedicated to her, to *A Garden on the Oronte* (1922), a tale of love and death, affirming the cleansing power of love.

THE ROCK AND THE KINGFISHER. After a few happy years, Barrès's morbid jealousy reared its ugly head again. In July 1921, when Anna dared to reveal to him her very brief affair with Edmond Rostand in 1914, he was devastated, describing himself to a friend "like a beast groaning in a trap with its legs smashed". The letters that they exchanged were heavy with criticism, but also bright with adoration.

In September 1921, Anna experienced another "love at first sight" when she met the dazzling Maurice

1923

MEXICO. **The American photographer Edward Weston takes a series of superb pictures of his companion, the beautiful Tina Modotti, naked on the terrace of their house. Both were already married when they met in Hollywood in 1920; she was a young actress of Italian origin and he was already a well-known photographer. She posed for him, and he persuaded her to become a photographer also. After the death of her husband, she left with Weston for Mexico, where they lived a life of passion together and met with other artists and political militants. Turning their backs on pictorial art, they turned instead to abstract art, and she also became a social reporter. Weston returned to his family in 1926 and after his departure Tina Modotti became a fighter for the revolutionary cause. Today, both are considered to be truly great photographers.**

Anna de Noailles
on her divan.

FACING PAGE
Maurice Barrès amidst
the ruins of Baalbek.

Alfred Stieglitz & Georgia O'Keeffe

A photographer who played a key role in the artistic life of the United States and one of America's greatest painters.

Georgia O'Keeffe painting a flower, photographed by Alfred Stieglitz in 1918.

FACING PAGE
Stieglitz, posing in front of a painting by his wife, photographed by Imogen Cunningham.

The relationship between Alfred Stieglitz and Georgia O'Keeffe is one of the most important in the history of American art. He was sixty and she thirty-seven when they married in 1924, eight years after their first meeting. (Stieglitz had been married at that time, with a daughter.) The son of a wealthy New Jersey businessman, he studied engineering in Berlin but made his career in photography, becoming the pioneer in that field in the United States. "Photography is my passion," he stated, "and the search for truth is my obsession." In an effort to have photography recognised as an art in its own right, he staged a series of avant-garde exhibitions and in 1902 founded both the Photo-Secession movement and the magazine *Camera Work*. He also introduced modern art to his country: in Gallery 291, on New York's Fifth Avenue, he exhibited between 1905 and 1917 works by European artists such as Constantin Brancusi, Henri Matisse, Pablo Picasso, and Georges Braque. After that, however, he concentrated more on American artists.

His photographs were very striking; he became well-known for his New York and Paris winter scenes, his glowing landscape paintings of Lake George, near New York, where he owned a house, and his magnificent portraits.

ORIGINALITY AND INDEPENDENCE. "I never do anything in imitation of anyone, anything that does not come from right within me. I myself am my only judge." The words were Stieglitz's, but it was an attitude shared by both artists. At the age of twenty-nine, Georgia O'Keeffe, a teacher of art from a Wisconsin family who settled in Virginia in 1903, decided to break the bonds of her academic training. She showed a series of abstract drawings to a friend, who in turn showed them to Stieglitz. He was wildly enthusiastic about them, saying "At last, the creative force of a woman's work, on paper!" He exhibited them, and then fell in love with the painter. In the spring of 1917 she moved into a studio in New York; she painted, and he began constantly photographing her. He photographed her at work or at rest, naked or dressed, with all the details of her body, particularly her long, thin hands, accentuated; 500 plates of a beauty that masked the scandal some of them provoked. Stieglitz recalled one occasion when some friends expressed a wish that he use their wives for a model instead. "She was highly amused. She said, 'If they knew what sort of relationship was needed to achieve results like this, they wouldn't have asked!'"

Far from being enslaved by the misogynist prejudices of his time, Stieglitz was conscious of Georgia

O'Keeffe's worth and encouraged her to dedicate herself to painting. They set up home together in the autumn of 1918 and married after his divorce was finalised. They had no children. They divided their time between New York and Lake George, where the splendid scenery inspired both of them to produce masterpieces. They exhibited their works together and Georgia's paintings quickly became known. Using abstract or fantastic formations, she depicted landscapes, skyscrapers, shellfish or skeletons, all of which made up a symbolic universe, heavy with sexual overtones, which expressed a form of cosmic mysticism. In addition to this she began, in the

year of their wedding, to paint flowers with curves of fascinating sensuality. Despite her feminist leanings, she refused to be placed within the confines of erotic feminist art and challenged the critics whose interpretations placed too much emphasis on that aspect of her painting.

Although she preferred to be alone, she took part in her husband's social functions with good grace. She was at once ambitious and able to keep herself in the background, as this 1923 letter witnesses: "I like to be the first, as long as I'm recognised; that's why Stieglitz and I work together so well, because with him I feel that I am the first. And when he is there, and other people are

1924

CAPRI. **German philosopher Walter Benjamin, shortly after his meeting with Asya Lacis, writes to his friend Gershom Sholem: "I have met a revolutionary from Riga, one of the most outstanding women I have ever encountered." She was a theatre producer; she told him about the Moscow theatre, and he showed her the world of literature. Together, they wrote a text on Naples (1925) and went back to Moscow in 1926, and thence to Berlin in 1928. Benjamin's love for Asya Lacis produced a "powerful change" in him. *One Way* (1928), one of his most important works, carries this dedication: "This street is named Asya Lacis Street, after the one who engineered it and thrust it into the author's soul." Asya Lacis was released in 1948, after ten years in a labour camp, only to find that Walter Benjamin had died in 1940. As a Jew in hiding in France, fearful of falling into the hands of the Gestapo, he had committed suicide on the Spanish border.**

♡ ♡ ♡

present, he is the centre and I count myself as nothing." Open to new experiences, she had a tremendous zest for life and for discovering the world. "I'm divided," she wrote in 1932, "between my husband and life with him, and something outside of that life." On returning to Lake George after one of her numerous trips, she wrote: "It's marvellous to be here and be with my wonderful Stieglitz. He is magnificent ... he is the most magnificent person in the world. It amazes me that I survived without him for so long."

In 1917 she visited New Mexico, being struck particularly by piles of bones in the desert; she painted them and he photographed them. She often spent the summer there and after Stieglitz's death in 1946 moved near to Albuquerque, surviving him by forty years. Here, she created some remarkable paintings of desert scenes.

MUTUAL RESPECT AND INFLUENCE. Alfred Stieglitz and Georgia O'Keeffe inspired and influenced each other; they also both loved to attach themselves to objects, paying attention to particular details. "Stieglitz has made the sky into something that looks just like what I did with colour before," she wrote in 1924. "He has consciously produced something that I have most often produced subconsciously." She who could only paint when alone watched him working with fascination, comparing him to a beaver. "His work always surprises me. You get the impression that he can't do anything more, and then, suddenly, he's achieved something more." According to Georgia, Stieglitz was always photographing himself, so to speak, through his subjects, and Stieglitz confirmed that when he wrote: "My photographs of clouds are equivalents of my inner self as I have been forged by the experiences of life." The psychoanalyst Julia Kristeva explained that when Georgia O'Keeffe painted her shellfish and flowers, she was doing something similar: "transposing the unknown force lines of her inner world into something that could be known".

Shortly before Stieglitz died, Georgia O'Keeffe wrote in a letter: "I see Alfred as an old man for whom I feel a great affection, a man who is growing older... he looks so pale and tired that it frightens me. Apart from the affection that I feel for him personally, I think that he has been a major part of one element of my universe. I'm happy to be able to make him feel that I'm holding his hand to encourage him along his path in life." Their love for each other was enriched by their love for life. At the age of seventy-four, Stieglitz wrote that "life is very beautiful... To affirm that is to catch the joy of deep living. Whoever has created, even once, must believe that for all time."

♡ ♡ ♡

WRITINGS
The Sentimental Novel

In Barbara Cartland's "rose romances", a pure young girl waits for love to bring her life's great adventure.

As pretty as she is innocent, Mona wanders through the dark, perverted jungle of London's streets before finding refuge in the arms of a duke who marries her. That is the story line of *Jigsaw*, Barbara Cartland's first successful novel. Mona was followed by a long series of pure young girls, all waiting for love, whose names all ended in an "a". Barbara Cartland's total of 600 published novels has beaten the previous record set by Delly's 108 "rose romances"; and although their titles vary as widely as *Love Duel, A Kiss in the Desert, Love's Flame* or *Lucky in Love*, all of them could be subtitled *The Triumph of Love*. Most of her

novels are set in the English Regency period (the early nineteenth century); this allows her to use the richest and most sumptuous of backgrounds, and makes her heroines' virginity more believable.

Barbara Cartland, born in 1901, is famous for her tremendous zest for life and the excessively long false eyebrows and pink clothes that offset her turquoise-blue eyes. She dictates her books and can produce a novel in fifteen days, with a plot that keeps the heart racing right up until the final embrace. Her works are among the most widely read and translated in the world; and it is estimated that by the end of the twentieth century, 550 million copies of her novels will have been sold. In France, where the vast majority of her readers are women, over a million a year are purchased and Barbara Cartland is the author whose books are borrowed most frequently from libraries. Before the war, French women also read similar novels by Delly and Max de Veuzit.

LOVE WILL FILL THE EMPTY SPACE. Since the 1950s, other writers of serial love stories, such as Anne and Serge Golon, the creators of *Angélique, Marquess of Angels*, Guy des Cars, and Americans such as Danielle Steel and Belva Plain, have fed the dreams of millions of women.

Novels celebrating love's triumph have been a successful literary genre since ancient times, relating the adventures of a prince or princess at the mercy of Fate. After travelling widely – the exotic is an essential ingredient – and overcoming all the obstacles, the heroes return to their homeland to marry and produce a large family.

The modern sentimental novel resembles the traditional fairy tale: the young girl is beautiful, fragile and gentle, with golden hair, and her Prince Charming has all the appeal of a Latin lover (cf. p. 118). Everything conspires to keep them apart, but after falling head-over-heels in love at their first meeting and then going their separate ways to many fascinating places, they are reunited in the inevitable happy ending, the wedding. The man represents the ideal about whom many women dream: strong and brave like the classic hero, but also loving and sensitive. The plot, rich in sudden or unexpected developments, always includes the machinations of a rival over whom the heroine triumphs thanks to the hero's sincerity and devotion. The key moment is the man's protestation of love, the "I love you" that real men find so difficult to utter (cf. p. 152). In *Helga's Irresistible Charm* (1986), Barbara Cartland has the duke say, fifteen pages from the end: "You are one who loves me for myself, and the one whom I love because you are all that I desire, all that I need, and will stay with me as long as I shall live." The kisses in Barbara Cartland's novels, although fiery, remain innocent, with only a suggestion of sexuality. The same applies to Delly's novels, of which this sentence is typical: "He embraced her, and she awoke pregnant."

Both innocent and ignorant, the motherless heroine of the popular novel invites hostility and jealousy from other women. As soon as fate brings her into the presence of a

man, love becomes evident, even though the characters have to pass through several stages to discover each other. Love, therefore, seems to be the only adventure that a woman can live through; she must not cultivate any ambition other than being loved by a glamorous man older than herself, as she can only find her true identity and true happiness in submission. Encouraged by this type of portrayal, traditional female sentimentality is therefore based on an expectation that love will finally come and fill up all the empty space. The "rose-water" novels of the nineteenth century offered their poverty-stricken readers the hope that one day they would escape from the factory thanks to the love of a rich man. For this reason, the left-wing press vilified these books for providing female workers with illusions, their "second bread".

HARLEQUIN: AWAY FROM IT ALL. He rules the world, she reigns supreme in his heart. The same role division is found in the works of Canadian publisher Harlequin, which began production in 1949: the man always has a job that greatly enhances his status, while the woman is invariably his junior. Even though changes in morals allow the sexual theme to be described more explicitly, the heroine never exists to satisfy herself; she is like a blank page, waiting to be written on, so to speak, by a man's desire. In the well-managed plot, the first kiss always occurs somewhere between pages 50 and 100, and the "sensual" scene some fifty pages beyond that.

Harlequin has enjoyed huge success: more than 200 million Harlequin books are now sold each year in twenty-five languages (in France alone, 500 titles and 20 million books are sold yearly). The Hungarians hold the record for sales per head of population, with eleven million volumes sold annu-

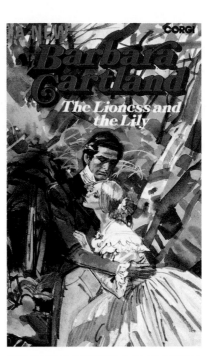

ally; in the former Communist countries, western popular culture was in great demand as a means of satisfying the desire to escape, if only temporarily, from the grey and exhausting grind of daily life.

Even though relations between men and women have changed significantly, millions of readers still dream of a couple who can reconcile sexuality and tenderness, women's work and depth of feeling. "Sentimental" productions are aimed wholly at them, as indeed are romance magazines (cf. p. 222) and television soaps and serials (cf. p. 268). All these help them to build up a world of fantasy and dreams.

1924

JAPAN. *The Love of an Idiot*, Tanizaki Junichiro's masterpiece, causes a scandal by its immorality. The novel is the confession of a young engineer obsessed with modernity and attracted to the Hollywood myth. He does not want an arranged marriage and instead dreams of a woman whom he chooses and who is his equal. He is fascinated by an adolescent girl, manages to oversee her education, and eventually marries her, but she turns out to be unpredictable, lazy, and fiercely independent. Terrified by her threats to leave him, he adopts a perverse reasoning based on humiliation and pleasure. The novel is reminiscent of Pierre Louÿs's *The Woman and the Puppet* and Nabokov's *Lolita* (cf. p. 256). All the author's works consist of gradually breaking down the idyllic images of the serious man and the young, fresh-faced girl, and replacing them with a man who is destroyed by a woman-child.

♡ ♡ ♡

FACING PAGE
Barbara Cartland.

Fritz Lang
& Thea von Harbou

This fashionable couple in Berlin of the twenties produced some of the master-pieces of German cinema.

The year 1925 saw the beginning of shooting for *Metropolis*, one of Germany's greatest ever cinema productions. The film marked the high point of the partnership between the producer, Fritz Lang, and his wife, the scriptwriter Thea von Harbou. After the success of *Doctor Mabuse* (1922) and *The Niebelungen* (1924), both were highly acclaimed in Berlin, whose fashionable places they often frequented. The beautiful Thea von Harbou wore her hair short, a style that was widely copied by Berlin women, and Lang, who was very tall and thin with brown hair, wore a black eye-patch or sometimes a monocle, the legacy of a war wound. Their apartment, where they threw sumptuous parties, was decorated with paintings by Egon Schiele and exotic *objets d'art* that Lang had brought back from his travels round the world.

The son of a famous Viennese architect, Fritz (diminutive of Friedrich) Lang fought heroically in the war and then spent his convalescence writing film scripts. He arrived in Berlin in 1918 and in the following year produced his first film, *The Hybrid*, which relates the story of a man destroyed by his love for a woman; this is a common theme in Lang's works. "I have always been shy and solitary," he told Lotte Eisner later, "and this is why people think I'm aloof. But all I was doing was simply looking into myself." It was producer Joe May who suggested that Lang produce *The Hindu Tomb*, based on the novel by Thea (Theodora) von Harbou, once a child prodigy and now a successful novelist. She combined the modernity of the emancipated and very feminine woman with old-fashioned domestic qualities;

she knitted while dictating her scripts, and she carried on knitting in the studios where the films based on her scripts were being produced.

When they met in 1920 she was thirty-two and he thirty, and an affair soon followed. Both were married, he to Lisa Rosenthal and she to comedian Rudolf Klein-Rogge, who later became Lang's favourite actor and found fame with his portrayal of the fearsome Doctor Mabuse. Some months later Thea divorced and Lang's wife killed herself in mysterious circumstances, the main theme of the famous director's works, that of guilt, can be traced back to this event.

AN EXEMPLARY WORK. In 1921 their first film, *The Three Lamps*, was produced; the film was a major work of the new expressionist movement, recounting the story of a young woman's efforts to "kill her lover with delights". Initially a failure in Berlin, it enjoyed great success in Paris; this success gave it a dramatic new lease of life in Berlin, where Lang was hailed as a "genius". From then on, the influential company UFA allowed him to produce films without financial restrictions, and the couple became extremely successful. They married on 20 August 1922, but had no children. Thea von Harbou worked for other producers, such as Murnau; but from 1923 onwards she wrote only for her husband, without becoming involved in the film production. They shared a common interest in eastern religions, mythology, occultism, and esoteric thought. She introduced him to

German romantic culture and he enjoyed listening to the fruits of her wild imagination. However, their work on *Metropolis*, which appeared in 1927, marked the beginning of a split between them. He was dissatisfied with the conclusion, which proclaimed: "The heart will be the mediator between the arms [the workers] and the mind [the management]." His fascination for his wife began to disappear, and on returning from one of his trips to Vienna, he brought back a twenty-three-year-old comedian Gerda Maurus. While the scandal sheets seized on the relationship between them, they both went on trips on Sundays, frequenting small open-air cafés or dance halls rather than the fashionable locations. After his experience of a powerful and brilliant woman, Lang made himself the "Pygmalion" of his young mistress. Thea von Harbou accepted the relationship and Gerda Maurus, who became a "queen" of Berlin in her turn, starred in two films produced by Lang and based on his wife's scripts: *The Spies* (1928), and *The Woman in the Moon* (1929).

LOST FASCINATION. During the dark years before Hitler came to power, Lang moved towards social realism; his wife, on the other hand, joined the National Socialist party in 1932. For his first "talkie", Lang wished to tell the story of a criminal designed to show the folly of those times; under pressure from the Nazis, its title *The Killers Are Amongst Us* was changed to *M*. While Thea von Harbou wrote the script, Lang visited the seediest parts of Berlin; the experience made him feel more and more alienated from his wife, who kept herself firmly in her strange, outdated world. Both of them worked together on this masterpiece; in fact Lang declared later that Thea had given the best of herself in the film, the great monologue of the criminal (played by Peter Lorre) having been written entirely by her. After the great success of *M* (*The Accursed*) in 1931 and their separation later the same year, their last film, *The Testament of Dr Mabuse*, showed the gulf between their ways of thinking: Lang wanted to denounce Nazism, while Thea von Harbou took pleasure in its curses that deceived with their romantic ring. The première of *M*, scheduled for December 1932, was cancelled, and the film was banned in March 1933. Lang often related how Goebbels, Minister for Propaganda, had summoned him on 30 March to offer him the post of Director of German Cinema; Lang had asked for "time to think about it" and then left on the first train for France that evening. In fact, the stamp on his passport showed that he did not leave Berlin until 21 July 1933; his divorce had come through on 26 April.

Lang took refuge, without Gerda Maurus, in the United States. Here he began a second career, brilliant but not without difficulties, producing several more major films such as *Fury* (1936).

GERMANY. **A love affair between nineteen-year-old Jewish student Hannah Arendt and Martin Heidegger, her philosophy tutor at Marburg University. Heidegger, who was married and very career-orientated, feared a scandal and persuaded Hannah to study at Heidelberg; in 1928 he made the decision to leave her. As Nazism advanced in Germany, she fled to Paris in 1933 and then to the United States in 1941, where she married Heinrich Blücher and wrote a series of important books on political thought. In 1950, during a trip to Germany, she met Heidegger, now a famous philosopher, again; they began corresponding and saw each other regularly. She translated his books in the United States and endeavoured to disprove accusations that he was a Nazi sympathiser. According to him, the best proof that he had no anti-Semitic leanings whatsoever was that he had loved a Jew.**

♡ ♡ ♡

Lang found a new companion, a German *émigré* named Lily Latte. He returned to Germany from 1957 to 1961 to produce a remake of *The Hindu Tomb* and *The Thousand Eyes of Doctor Mabuse*; both of these were highly successful.

After Lang's departure Thea von Harbou tried to produce films on her own, but despite encouragement from Goebbels, her efforts were in vain. Afterwards, she continued writing scripts and novels. She died from a stroke in Berlin in 1954.

♡ ♡ ♡

SENSUALITY
The Dancing Years

In the dance craze of the twenties, many innovations shocked "right-minded" people.

"Yes, Sir, that's my baby": the successful Revue Nègre in Paris was where the Charleston, a wild dance named after the port in South Carolina, was brought to Europe by American dancer Josephine Baker in 1925. Shocked by this mulatto's swaying walk and flimsy costume with its famous belt of bananas, the right-minded sections of the population were outraged at its "indecency", and a show scheduled to be given by her in Munich in 1929 was banned. After the slow, passionate, erotic movements of the Argentine tango, which had already caused a scandal when introduced to Europe (cf. p. 80), this new dance symbolised the dance craze of the 1920s; it was of black origin, like the jazz music that had also provoked an outcry when introduced into Europe through the presence of 360,000 black American combat soldiers during 1917 and 1918.

During the 1920s, Paris was the meeting place for the "lost generation" (cf. p. 52) and for black artists fleeing racial discrimination and prohibition in the United States. Jazz, explained Michel Leiris, "acted like magic, and to come under its influence was like being possessed. That is the best phrase to describe these festivals, which were almost religious in their essence, a kind of communion with dance, eroticism, either hidden or visible, and drink."

Immediately after the signing of the Armistice, the intense desire for peace and harmony showed in a dance craze that broke out in every western capital city. The effect was felt somewhat later in the provinces, where those who introduced the new fashions caused a scandal. In Paris, however, people danced everywhere: in nightclubs, taverns, restaurants, tea rooms, cafés, or even at home. The young bourgeois introduced the "surprise party", an American institution where a person was "surprised" by the sudden arrival of friends with food, drink, and records.

In the same way that the bourgeois had once danced at the Bal Populaire, stylish people now went to the Bal Nègre, the nightclub on Paris's Rue Blomet, with young West Indians or Africans. London abounded with "thés dansants" (tea-dances), "dîners-dansants" (dinner-dances) or "soupers-dansants" (dance-suppers). Berlin's cafés, tea-dances and nightclubs produced German groups with unlikely

Josephine Baker's "lascivious" hip-swaying walk.

FACING PAGE, ABOVE
The Bal Nègre, the nightclub on Rue Blomet, Paris.

FACING PAGE, BELOW
Jean-Gabriel Domergue dancing the Charleston (caricature by Sem).

Le bal de la rue Blomet.

names such as "The Sid Kay's Fellows" or the "Weintraub Syncopators".

Couples danced the Charleston at a furious pace, face to face and without touching, and then came together in a "slow", a dance typified by long, slow, sliding steps. The youthful liveliness of the quick dances contrasted sharply with the elegance of the figure dances; simple steps, like those of the fox-trot, alternated with the fast rhythms of boogie-woogie, well-known Spanish dances such as the rumba, tango, and paso doble, and others of American-sounding derivation such as the one-step, shimmy, Boston and black-bottom, not forgetting of course the waltz, still very popular on both sides of the Atlantic.

Couples formed through dance.

In the Soviet Union, the revolution had, as Joseph Roth commented in his 1926 report, banned public dances in its "desire to see a visible opposition to the bourgeois, capitalist, decadent western life-style manifest itself in Russian life". The same puritanical attitude had led the Danes to ban dance music in Iceland until the end of the nineteenth century, to prevent the staging of balls which had been blamed for "favouring" the births of illegitimate children!

Since it was banned in churches in the twelfth century, western dance has become separated from its sacred origins. Whatever form the dance may take, it is invariably based on a primordial, instinctive energy, which the culture of the time attempts to domesticate and "civilise". The very names of the dances – jazz, samba or, later, rock' n' roll – have sexual connotations; the steps are similar to those of ancient fertility rites, the rhythms encourage the formation of relationships, and the partners play out the eternal game of seduction, pursuit, and possession.

Most young couples met at dances in the 1920s, and this is still true today. Whether the relationship begins in a public place, at the village fête, during the Saturday night disco, somewhere private such as the middle-class ballroom or in a specially licensed dance hall, the language of dance and music is easier to "speak" than words when looking for a relationship. The dance allows a kind of trial relationship, bringing bodies together and firing the imagination, without the necessity of any further commitment.

From chaperon to date.

The developments in dance at the beginning of the century reflected changes both in society and in the perception of the couple. A new phenomenon appeared in the United States, where tradition had previously dictated that middle-class young men visited girls in their homes, with a chaperon present; after the war, however, the new tradition of the "date" developed in the form of two people, or a group, going out together. The "court of love" thus moved from a private location to the rapidly growing world of commercialised leisure – restaurants, cinemas and dance halls – with the young man bearing the cost of the evening out. In the same way, working women went to dance halls where young men bought them drinks and dragged them through the fashionable dances of the time, those that right-minded people thought "unsuitable". These included the slow-rag, the turkey-trot, the bunny-hug, the grizzly bear and the shaking the shimmy, all of which produced a crude sexuality designed to shock; more "acceptable" versions of these dances were produced for the night-clubs frequented by the middle class. Dance clubs also appeared in Manhattan where Rudolph Valentino (cf. p. 118) made his début; here, young men offered their services to chic, modern women who came without a chaperon to dance the tango and Charleston and gave the men very generous tips.

Were they all dancing on a volcano? Perhaps. During the Depression of the 1930s, show managers organised dance marathons that promised a sum of money for the couple who stayed on the dance-floor the longest. The general public watched the contestants dance to exhaustion, as described in Horace McCoy's 1934 novel *They Shoot Horses Don't They*, adapted for the cinema by Sidney Pollack (1969). This was a cruel parody of the liveliness, pleasure, love, and all the other positive things associated with dance.

1925

United States. The sad song *My Man*, sung by Fanny Brice, enjoys great success. Fanny Brice had, since 1910, been the brightest star of the Ziegfeld Follies; well-known for her comic turns, she won the sympathy of the public who identified her with the heroine in the song. At that time her husband, a compulsive gambler, had once again been imprisoned for theft. Unable to bear his broken promises any longer, she divorced him in 1927, but she never stopped loving him despite her subsequent marriage to producer Billy Rose. The life of Fanny Brice was the inspiration for the film *Funny Girl*, starring Barbra Streisand.

"It is not death that takes our beloved ones from us; on the contrary, it keeps them with us and fixes them for all time in their beautiful youth. Death is the salt that preserves our love; it is life that makes it decay."

François Mauriac
The Desert of Love

Kurt Weill
& Lotte Lenya

He was a talented composer whose work with Brecht produced masterpieces; she will always be the touching voice that sang "Surabaya Johnny".

Lotte Lenya, photographed in 1928 by Lotte Jacobi.

Although Kurt Weill married Lotte Lenya in 1926, it is said that he fell in love with her while watching her rowing. The friends with whom she was staying in the country in the summer of 1924 had asked her to look for an invited guest at the railway station and take him to their house on a boat, across the lake. She often said, later, that before they reached the opposite shore he had asked her to marry him and she had agreed.

Born in 1898 to a working-class family in Vienna, Lotte Lenya (real name Karoline Blamauer) was beaten regularly by her alcoholic father. After studying dance in Zurich, she arrived in Berlin in 1920 and became a comedienne. Kurt Weill, who came from a rich musical Jewish family in Dessau, north of Leipzig, had lived in Berlin since 1918. He was already well known as a composer of avant-garde music, which mixed jazz and classical forms.

A small man – he was only 5'2" tall (while she was 4'11") – and bald, with his eyes partly concealed behind thick glasses, Kurt Weill was two years younger than Lotte Lenya, but looked much older. Although his life-style was insular and austere, he was fascinated by her energy, her humour, her carefree yet provocative look, and above all her voice, which was to him, as he described it later, "like a force of nature". In 1925 he dedicated his first opera, *The Protagonist*, to her and wrote her a series of impassioned letters: "I see myself in you, and for the first time I am beginning to understand what I am, like a reflection in a spring." He saw their future as "not paradise, but a fiery and passionate life together".

Lotte's mother had told her: "You are not beautiful, but men will love you." Her modern appearance, with a fringe and straight brown hair, cut short, made her very attractive, which remained with her as she grew older. She was full of paradoxes, being both hard and vulnerable; although independent and contemptuous of conventional morals, she hated being alone. She was impulsive and unpredictable but had a great need for tenderness and looked for it in Kurt Weill. She greatly admired his education, his refinement, his generosity. They always showed great respect for each other. In

1929 he told a journalist that his wife was "hopeless in the home, but a brilliant actress". She made a great impression on the stage, even though she trembled with nerves.

Kurt Weill, who needed silence to compose his music, let Lotte Lenya lead her own life and have numerous affairs, with both women and men. They had no children. She admired his genius and supported him in his ambitions without having any of her own. She enjoyed singing and had a musical ear although she could not read music; he was not anxious for her to learn. Her soprano voice, at once strong and tender, became deeper as she grew older due to her smoking, and was well suited to Weill's dry, syncopated style of music.

MASTERPIECES WITH BRECHT. In 1927 Kurt Weill met Bertold Brecht, a playwright and producer, and together they pioneered a form of modern opera. Lotte Lenya played and sang in their first work, *Mahagonny Songspiel*, written in Baden-Baden in 1927, which was closely followed by a three-act opera (*The Rise and Fall of the City of Mahagonny*, 1929). On 31 August 1928, in Berlin, Lotte created the role of Jenny in *The Threepenny Opera* (an adaptation of John Gay's *The Beggar's Opera*), a masterpiece that combined romanticism and social satire and echoed the uneasy mood of the period. The show is in fact one of the greatest successes of all time, with famous songs such as "Mack the Knife" and "Pirate Jenny".

After the failure of *Happy End* (1929), in which Lotte Lenya sang "Bilbao Song" and "Surabaya Johnny", Weill split with Brecht, who behaved less than professionally over the sharing of royalties. Although Weill became internationally famous, his music was classed as "Jewish and Negroid" in a Germany racked with the upheavals that preceded the rise of Nazism. He carried on composing and worked with other theatre impresarios, while Lotte Lenya acted in plays and in 1930 took up the role of Jenny again, in Pabst's cinema version of *The Threepenny Opera* (1930).

After Hitler came to power, both Kurt Weill and Lotte Lenya left Berlin in March 1933. They had separated early in 1932. Weill worked with Brecht again in Paris, but their work *The Seven Deadly Sins*, in which Lotte starred, was a failure. Although they remained on good terms, Weill and Lenya divorced in 1933, but she remained his obsession. When they met again in 1935, he wrote to her: "You continue to give me things that no other person can, things that are of crucial importance to me." They married again in 1937, a couple held together not by sexual attraction but by friendship and honesty, and they both had fleeting affairs.

A NEW CAREER IN THE UNITED STATES. Weill's work was already well known in the United States, where they emigrated in 1935. He was one of the very few European artists who could adapt to life out there. Always fascinated by American music, he found himself in the land where the inspiration for his style – jazz, blues, and the music of George Gershwin – originated. He worked in Hollywood and carved out a brilliant career in the theatre in New York, writing remarkable melodies for musical comedies; they were very popular stateside but remained unknown in Europe. His greatest successes were *Knickerbocker Holiday* (1938) and the memorable *Lady in the Dark* (1941). Lotte Lenya had a few engagements but then vanished off the scene, while Weill remained snowed under with work. They bought a beautiful house in New York City, where she became little more than a housewife. Just before his death in 1950, Weill asked her: "Do you truly love me?" She answered: "You alone."

Later, Lotte Lenya married the homosexual journalist George Davis, a great admirer of Kurt Weill, out of friendship. She resumed her singing career and channelled all her energies into promoting her first husband's music. She was a success in the United States and later in Europe; she even returned to Germany, where she played, sang, made several records and appeared in a few films. However, she always remained the bewitching voice that sang "Surabaya Johnny, warum bist du so roh? (Why are you so cruel?) Surabaya Johnny, warum bin ich nicht froh? (Why am I unhappy?)."

MAJORCA. **The beginning of the highly eventful affair between English poet Robert Graves and American poet Laura Riding. They lived in Majorca and wrote together, their most notable work being the essay *A Survey of Modernist Poetry* (1928). Graves, who was fascinated by mythology and blessed with a vivid imagination, is hailed as one of the greatest poets of his time. He greatly admired his companion's work, which had an abstruse style very different from his own. For Laura Riding, to be a poet was to live in a search for truth. "The only theme I have ever had", he wrote, "is the impossibility of continued perfect love between man and woman; it can only be achieved by a miracle." His masterpiece, *The White Goddess* (1948) was inspired by the complex, fascinating personality of his "muse". Their literary partnership continued after their separation in 1938, but Laura Riding gave up writing poetry.**

How to Have a Successful Marriage, in Ten Easy Lessons

The Perfect Marriage, credited to a Dutch doctor, was a work of reference for many years before the plethora of "sex guides" appeared.

Unlike the East, where eroticism was widely practised as a slow, gentle art with its "pillow books" rich in poetic similes and sophisticated drawings (cf. p. 68), the West appeared frightened of sex, even in marriage. Until the twentieth century, in fact, sex studies were confined to treatises on anatomy and physiology, with Latin expressions and sketches. The scientific veil allowed intimacy between couples to be examined and discussed only briefly; sexual intercourse was to be practised only in the marriage bed and in total darkness, and the doctor determined which position was

the most conducive to fertilisation. The aim of sex, in the traditional Western marriage, was not to give or receive pleasure, but to produce children.

The Perfect Marriage, published in 1926 by Dutch gynaecologist Theodoor Hendrik van de Velde, was subtitled *A Study of its Physiology and Techniques*. Translated into eighteen languages, it was widely distributed during the half-century that followed and remains a reference manual to this day. During the 1950s, it was the most widely read manual in the United States, particularly because of its detailed description of the various caresses and positions that could be adopted.

Intended for "doctors and husbands who should be their wives' guides", the work was rated very highly by its readers, because of its assertion that "men and women, from the sexual point of view, have the same rights and the same duties". Orgasm was defined as a "physiological necessity" for a woman, who was likely to suffer physical and emotional distress if her excitement was not relieved. The author, however, contradicted himself on some occasions; although he insisted that the woman play an active role, he criticised the position in which the woman sat astride the man, as he believed that it was "inconsistent with natural relations between the sexes". He asserted that if the woman took the initiative, "she should never step outside the bounds of a certain reserve and a certain degree of modesty"; in practice, that spared her the requirement to perform fellatio, the so-called "kiss of excitement", but this was not wrong "from either an aesthetic or a hygienic point of view, provided one kept oneself meticulously clean".

Although van de Velde did not seek inspiration from eastern sophistication – according to him, it was impossible for whites to make

the sex act last without leading to orgasm – he did, however, confirm the scientific conviction that "a good technique will quickly cause the partner's deficiencies to be overcome, unless we are looking at a morbid condition". However, the moralist shows himself through the scientist's white coat, particularly in the frequent use of the word "normal" to mean "moderate" or "reasonable". Van de Velde saw the "climax" of the act as the ejaculation of sperm into the vagina, and the normal procedure consisted of "gradually bringing about more or less simultaneous orgasm in the two partners". These two assertions, dogmatically repeated in every manual, were not called into question until the 1970s (cf. p. 344).

NECESSARY CAUTION. The suspicion surrounding sexual pleasure, which most Christians denounced as an end in itself, has hardly lessened since the times of the early church fathers, when Saint Jerome believed that a man was guilty of adultery if he "loved his wife too passionately". Many writings on married couples warned against "excesses of sensual pleasure", and priests called upon excessively ardent couples to "keep honesty and decency in the marriage bed". The belief was that manliness was characterised by imperious sexual pleasures, and that the wife's duty was to submit to them. Although the more liberal thinkers of the nineteenth century admitted that mutual pleasure was acceptable in moderation, it was only on condition that each partner stay within their role and cultivate the virtues particular to their sex; the onus was on the man, older and active, to introduce the woman, who was passive and modest and knew less, to the delights. Nudity for married couples was ruled out, and the trousseau of young women raised in convents included a nightshirt with openings designed to allow

Êtes-vous l'épouse idéale?

Les tests de «CONFIDENCES»

(Photo Universal-Film)

GRAVE question, en vérité! Combien de ménages, en effet, qui eussent pu connaître un bonheur sans mélange, ont traversé maint orage parce que l'un des deux conjoints ne voulait point se rendre compte qu'à côté des vertus cardinales qui forment la base d'une union solide il devait également posséder un certain nombre de qualités mineures. Ce sont précisément ces qualités qui embellissent la vie, la rendent plus facile, plus harmonieuse. Pouvez-vous affirmer qu'elles ne vous font pas défaut? Il vous sera facile de le savoir en répondant au questionnaire que voici. Munissez-vous d'un crayon et d'une feuille de papier sur laquelle vous inscrirez, chaque fois que vous aurez répondu à une question, le nombre négatif ou positif qui, dans la colonne de droite, correspond à la question envisagée. S'il vous est difficile de répondre par un «oui» ou un «non» catégorique, n'inscrivez rien sur votre feuille. Puis, lorsque vous aurez répondu à toutes les questions, faites séparément le total des nombres positifs et des nombres négatifs que vous aurez obtenus et retranchez la plus petite somme de la plus grande. Si, par exemple, vous obtenez séparément — 18 et + 23, le résultat final sera + 5; si, au contraire, vous arrivez à — 27 et + 14, le résultat final sera — 13 (ce que nous ne vous souhaitons pas). Voyez ensuite dans quelle catégorie d'épouses vous pouvez vous ranger: les excellentes, les bonnes, les passables, les médiocres, les exécrables:

De — 87 à — 40, vous avez certainement tout ce qu'il faut pour n'être pas heureuse en ménage. Il importe de vous réformer d'urgence et radicalement.

De — 40 à — 10, si vous manquez de volonté pour plaire à votre mari, vous semblez discerner ce qu'il faudrait faire pour cela, mais vous ne vous souciez guère de passer aux actes.

De — 10 à + 10, encore un effort, vous êtes sur la bonne voie, mais vous êtes trop hésitante.

De + 10 à + 40, vous possédez d'incontestables qualités qui tendent à s'affirmer de plus en plus.

De + 40 à + 73, bravo! vous êtes certainement une compagne idéale.

	Oui.	Non.
Êtes-vous fidèle à votre mari?	+10	—10
Manifestez-vous des soupçons à son égard s'il lui arrive d'être en retard?	— 6	+ 6
Avez-vous l'habitude de fouiller dans ses poches, de vérifier à son insu le contenu de son portefeuille?	— 7	+ 7
Acceptez-vous de bonne grâce les sorties ou distractions qu'il vous propose?	+ 3	— 3
Vous arrive-t-il fréquemment de le déranger quand il lit pour lui parler «couture» ou lui rapporter les derniers «potins»?	— 5	+ 2
Vous efforcez-vous de n'être jamais négligée en sa présence?	+ 5	— 5
Peut-il «toujours», lorsqu'il le désire, trouver dans votre armoire du linge propre et raccommodé?	+ 4	— 4
Surveillez-vous journellement l'état des boutons de son linge ou de ses costumes?	+ 3	— 3
Souriez-vous avec indulgence lorsqu'il accomplit son «tour du monde» sur le cadran du poste de radio?	+ 2	— 2
Vous arrive-t-il, de temps en temps, de lui tricoter un pull-over, une écharpe, des gants, etc.?	+ 4	— 1
Vous efforcez-vous de varier les «menus» de chaque repas que vous lui servez?	+ 2	— 2
Êtes-vous fréquemment obligée de lui redemander de l'argent une fois qu'il vous a donné votre «mois»?	— 6	+ 3
Dans une discussion, vous efforcez-vous de ne jamais le contredire brutalement?	+ 4	— 4
Faites-vous en sorte qu'il ne trouve jamais votre intérieur en désordre quand il rentre de son travail?	+ 3	— 4
S'il occupe ses loisirs en se livrant à un travail exigeant un certain nombre d'outils (la menuiserie, par exemple), gémissez-vous qu'il va «saccager» tout votre intérieur?	— 5	+ 3
Pour les heures de repas ou lorsqu'il vous donne rendez-vous, vous arrive-t-il fréquemment d'être «en retard»?	— 7	+ 4
Vous arrive-t-il souvent de l'entraîner «dans les magasins»?	— 5	+ 5
Vous récriez-vous que votre mari ne vous aime plus et qu'il vous abandonne s'il manifeste, un soir, l'intention de sortir seul?	— 8	+ 3

Ce test a utilisé un certain nombre d'éléments fournis par M. Jean MALIRY.

the husband to fulfil his "conjugal duty".

A great many wedding nights must have resembled a legalised form of rape! The shorter and more vigorous the act, the less risk there was of the man transforming the pure young girl into a woman of insatiable desires. The "natural lasciviousness" of women had been feared since ancient times, as her capacity for enjoyment was thought to be greater than men's. It was believed that the man, to save his precious substance, should have sex only seldom, not more than three times a week when young, and abstain after the age of sixty. Van de Velde broke new ground by suggesting that men should continue to be sexually active in old age, but he carried on one old prejudice by maintaining that too much sex would cause kidney disease and "a loss of intellectual capacity".

PARTNERS WITH DUTIES. After centuries of sexual repression, a new morality appeared during the 1930s; based on pleasure, hygiene and safety, it carried the new idea of married couples also being lovers. During the decades that followed, the manuals dealt less with marriage than with sex, and modern lovers became "partners", both with a duty to lead the other on to orgasm. The art of loving was even treated like a recipe, as in Alex Comfort's highly successful book The Joy of Sex (1972).

Eroticism is learnt naturally, and herein lies the paradox of such books. The concept of "normality" has changed completely: in the nineteenth century, the application of cold water to the genital organs was recommended if excitement became too intense, but now the practice of masturbation, previously the cardinal sin, is encouraged in young people to enable them to discover their body. Sex is now presented as a physiological need which must be satisfied, in moderation, for the well-being of the individual. As the list of "allowed" practices increases, there is a plethora of books, videos, interactive discs and so on, offering solutions to every problem.

PARIS. The French writer Louis Aragon (cf. p. 140) and the rich English woman Nancy Cunard, begin a stormy relationship. Nancy, fascinated by jazz and black civilisations, supported the avant-garde movement and broke the taboos of her social class. Aragon, like her, hated the middle class, but he allowed her to crush him with her own "prodigal spirit". She founded a publishing house, Hours Press, which published the works of contemporary writers. She was the inspiration for Aragon's work Irene's Cunt, an erotic text with which he subsequently denied any connection, and greatly troubled him with her torments and desires. In 1928, in Venice, she had an affair with the black jazz pianist Harry Crowder and broke with Aragon, who then threatened suicide. On his return from this "journey through hell", he met Elsa Triolet and renounced his former excesses, writing in his Poem to Howl in the Ruins "Spit, if you like, on what we once loved".

♡ ♡ ♡

FACING PAGE
Wedding display cabinet in Leipzig, photographed in 1930 by Herbert List.

Diego Rivera
& Frida Kahlo

"The elephant and the dove": two great Mexican painters combined art, love, and revolution.

When Diego Rivera and Frida Kahlo met in Mexico in 1927, no doubt at the home of their mutual friend, the Italian photographer Tina Modotti (cf. p. 121), he was forty-one and she only twenty. For these two painters, art was inextricably linked with revolution: first, the 1910 Mexican revolution, and then the Russian revolution of 1917. Both were members of the Communist party. The world-famous Diego Rivera was the leading light in muralism, whose heroic frescoes glorified the Mexican people and their indigenous culture. From 1907 to 1921 he visited, in Europe and especially in Paris, great painters such as Picasso, Braque, Derain, Modigliani, and De Chirico.

Rivera, who was something of a ladies' man, had already had numerous lovers. For ten years he lived with painter Angelina Beloff in Paris, and their son was lost in the chaos that prevailed during the war. In 1919 he had a daughter, the future actress Marika Rivera, with Marevna, another Russian painter. On his return to Mexico he married Guadelupe Marin, who bore him another two daughters. This "giant, who unsettled people with his lies and violence and seduced many women despite his spectacular ugliness", had "a face like an Olmec warrior and the body of a Japanese wrestler"; he was often to be seen with Mexico's artistic and cosmopolitan society and was always the life and soul of parties and gatherings. Despite his ogreish appearance he was sensitive; he was bowled over by the beautiful young Frida, who was "dark, brilliant and highly strung" and "seemed to question him with the discon-

certing sincerity of her youth". He was quite taken in by her cheerfulness, eagerness, and courage.

Frida Kahlo was beautiful, proud and possessed of boundless energy. She was close to her father, a photographer who had emigrated from Germany at eighteen, and shared his passion for nature. On the other hand, her taste for independence was a source of grief to her Mexican mother. She walked with a limp, a legacy of polio, and at eighteen she was a victim of a horrific bus crash. The accident affected her for the rest of her life; she endured a string of very painful operations on her spine, and had to wear a corset most of the time. However, she bounced back every time with gusto, elegance, and her own, often black, humour.

PAINS, STORMS, BETRAYAL AND SUFFERING. Frida began her painting career after her accident while confined to bed in the "blue house", her childhood home at Coyoacan, near Mexico City. Using the same realism with which Rivera painted his anonymous people, but in a style more akin to Mexican folk art, she specialised in painting her closest relatives, and, most often, herself. These self-portraits are a study of Frida's hurt, exposed body with its surgical scars, her distress, her loneliness and her hopes; and they show an honesty and courage which forbids any form of voyeurism. "I paint myself because I am alone," she said. "I am the subject that I know best."

The wedding of these two very different people, on 21 August 1929, was dubbed "the marriage of the elephant and the dove" by their friends. They lived both their love and their art with a passion that was often stormy. To please him, she would wear the flounced skirts, caracos and *rebozo* (a kind of cotton shawl) typical of Mexicans. She refused to shave her upper lip, because of his fascination with the shadowy moustache, a sign that she was of Spanish origin and not native Indian. He admired her paintings, believing them to be better than his own. He was the centre of her life, and she often painted him in her canvasses, for example, as a baby in her arms; in one famous self-portrait, his face is superimposed on her forehead.

The United States ambassador gave Diego Rivera the task of restoring Hernán Cortés' house at Cuernava-

México
Frida Kahlo
1949.
Diego y yo

LONDON. **Famous Irish playwright Sean O'Casey, aged forty-six, marries his compatriot, twenty-three-year-old actress Eileen Carey. Thrilled with his plays, she expressed a desire to meet him; and in 1926 she travelled to New York and was successful in an audition for *The Plough and the Stars*. He was so taken with her beauty that he asked her to marry him. After their wedding, she continued her career for some years, and then they bought a house in the Devon countryside, where they lived happily with their three children. Sean O'Casey died in 1964 and she survived him by thirty-one years, refusing all offers of marriage; her long-standing friendship with Harold Macmillan was all she needed. She took a great interest in O'Casey's works and recalled their happy and peaceful marriage in *Sean* (1971).**

♡ ♡ ♡

ca. This commission got him expelled from the Communist party, but did nothing to lessen his convictions. In 1930 the couple visited San Francisco; in 1931 they were in New York, where the Museum of Modern Art organised a retrospective exhibition of Diego Rivera's works; and in 1932 they visited Detroit, where he decorated the Ford factory. At this time Frida suffered one of her many miscarriages and painted a portrait of herself overwhelmed with sorrow and pain; in fact, she never had any children. Although she lived a life of pleasure in evenings spent in Greenwich Village, she longed for the human warmth of her country and adapted less well than her husband to life in the United States. He was dismissed by the Rockefeller Centre in New York in 1933 for featuring Lenin in the centre of the fresco that he had been commissioned to produce.

Back in Mexico, Diego Rivera had several orders from the government, and in particular decorated the National

FACING PAGE

Diego Rivera and Frida Kahlo at their second wedding in San Francisco in 1940.

ABOVE

Diego and Me, Frida Kahlo, 1949.

1930

Dashiell Hammett & Lillian Hellman

"Speak to me of Love"

Anaïs Nin & Henry Miller

Back Street

Vita Sackville-West & Harold Nicolson

"Modesty in Hollywood"

Eleanor & Franklin Roosevelt

Love at the Mercy of Nazism

Gunnar & Alva Myrdal

The Guilty Lovers

Irène & Frédéric Joliot-Curie

The Moustache

The Duke & Duchess of Windsor

Love, War and Tragedy

Margaret Mead & Gregory Bateson

Gone with the Wind

Osip & Nadezhda Mandelstam

The Problem Page

Clark Gable & Carole Lombard

Western Eroticism

Dashiell Hammett & Lillian Hellman

Two American writers, intellectually and politically engaged – devoted to each other, yet wholly independent.

"He was so stylish," wrote Lillian Hellman when recalling her meeting with Dashiell Hammett, one of the masters of the black American thriller, in Hollywood in 1930. Hammett had just published *The Maltese Falcon*, whose hero, the thin, disillusioned, womanising Sam Spade, was an idealised portrait of himself, an image perpetuated by Humphrey Bogart in John Huston's 1941 film.

Hammett was thirty-six, and Lillian Hellman twenty-five; it was love at first sight. After living in poverty for years, he had found success with his detective novels (*The Red Harvest*, 1928; *Cursed Blood*, 1929), and had become the darling of Hollywood, where he had just been hired as a scriptwriter for Paramount. He earned spectacular amounts of money, and his lifestyle was extravagant.

Lillian Hellman, a small and stylish woman, worked as a script-reader; earlier, she had been a theatre production assistant in New York. Born in New Orleans to a family of German Jews, she had an impressive academic record, while Samuel Hammett from Maryland – Dashiell was his mother's maiden name – had worked since he was sixteen. A heavy drinker and a lover of black or Asian prostitutes, he had been very ill with tuberculosis; despite that, however, he had numerous affairs, while continuing to see his nurse wife and two daughters. Lillian Hellman lived apart from her husband, and divorced him in 1932. She had no children and had none with Hammett either, being, as she put it, too busy with her work. They often talked of marrying, but neither one wanted to at the same time!

In 1931, Dashiell Hammett published *The Glass Key*, followed by *The Invisible Man* in 1933. The heroes of these nov-els, Nick and Nora Charles, were very similar to him and Lillian in their respect and mutual admiration, their outspokenness, their acerbic wit as well as their penchant for alcohol and living it up. Hammett was an alcoholic (she was not) and a big-time gambler, who showered her with jewels and furs. She was often away, travelling or working in New York, and the sexual freedom that they allowed each other inevitably led to suspicion and

FACING PAGE
Costumes designed for Vanessa Redgrave, who played Julia in Fred Zinnemann's film of the same name, based on an episode in Lillian Hellman's life.

unease; Lillian, who was jealous, often spoke in a sarcastic tone, asking on the telephone with Hammett, "Is there a woman in my bed?" Hammett, meanwhile, wrote her letters to amuse her, or else stated in no uncertain terms that she had failed him. In 1933 and 1934 they spent several happy months at Key Largo, Florida; while he went off hunting, she worked, under his direction, on her first theatre play, *Children's Hour*. In the autumn of 1934, drinking more heavily than ever, he wrote to her from Hollywood: "I think of you all the time and I love you with all my heart – my pitying heart." She, however, was busy in New York with rehearsals for her play, the première of which, in November 1934, was a success. Although the theme of lesbianism in a boarding school was too controversial to be awarded a Pulitzer Prize, the New York critics created a special award for her. She thus became a star, and Hollywood offered her a fortune to work there as a script-writer.

SHE SHINES, HE DECLINES. The year 1934 was a watershed in their lives. Both Dashiell Hammett and Lillian Hellman were well known, but while she was on the threshold of a brilliantly successful career, his star was fading, beset by an incurable case of writer's block. While he could no longer write novels, he did continue to produce scripts taken from his or other writers' books. He became a recluse, continually listening to the song "Speak To Me Of Love", and was visited by a steady stream of prostitutes. When he was paid his royalties, he lived a life of extravagance and showered Lillian Hellman with presents; but when up to his neck in debt, he vanished and even stopped sending money to his wife and daughters. Because of his alcoholism, he received fewer and fewer commissions; and on two occasions he was taken to hospital, seriously ill.

Meanwhile, in New York, Lillian Hellman was leading a very full life, writing successful plays such as *They Were Three*, made into a film by William Wyler (*These Three*) in 1936, *The Little Foxes* (1939) and many others. Hammett was her best adviser and helped her to adapt the plays for cinema. Both she and he fought for scriptwriters' rights and were actively involved in many

civic rights organisations. The Fascist threat in Europe – the subject of her play *The Guard on the Rhine* (1941) from which Hammett later produced a script – fuelled their activism. He became a member of the Communist party, and both were manipulated by the Soviet secret service. In 1937 Lillian visited Spain and Moscow. On the way she carried out the dangerous task of smuggling money into Germany to enable a childhood friend, to whom she referred in her diary as Julia, to help Jews to flee. (This is the story-line of the Fred

Flat to be lying on table never worn

(9)

Annes Sylbert

blk oxfords dk navy knitted gl cotton stockings.

1930

FRANCE. **The wedding of two painters, Maria Elena Vieira da Silva of Portugal and Arpad Szenes of Hungary. They met in Paris and set up home there; but when war broke out they left for Lisbon, and then fled to Brazil until 1947. Back in Paris, they moved into a small, sparse house, separated from their workshop by a garden. Here they welcomed many of their artist friends. Both were great painters: Vieira da Silva, a leading light in European abstract art, became famous for her stark style of painting, while Szenes produced magnificent variations in light with subtle tones. Their works were exhibited at major retrospectives in Paris (his in 1974, hers in 1988), and a foundation named after both of them was opened in Lisbon in 1994.**

♡ ♡ ♡

Zinnemann film *Julia*, starring Jane Fonda and Vanessa Redgrave, 1977).

THE DELIGHT OF BEING TOGETHER. In 1939 Lillian Hellman bought a huge estate in Pleasantville, New York State, and looked after the farm while continuing to write plays. One evening in 1942, when Hammett was drunk, she resisted his advances and he swore that he would never make love to her again. He was true to his word and she was devastated. In New York, he became the friend and drinking companion of Faulkner, but in 1950 the pair stopped drinking. Lillian Hellman wrote of their relationship, "The excitement that we felt at the beginning had developed into passionate love. Without having to say anything, we knew that we had survived for the best reason of all, the delight of being together." The long-awaited harmony, however, did not last, as the Cold War triggered an anti-Communist hysteria (cf. p. 210) and the couple's magnanimous refusal to denounce anyone earned Hammett six months in jail. They were then blacklisted and banned from working, and in 1952 Lillian Hellman was forced to sell her estate.

Hammett, weakened by the ravages of alcohol, stopped writing altogether. Lillian Hellman took him in until his death in 1961. He lived with her unobtrusively, while she continued to work and have troubled relationships with other men. Before her death in 1984, she published Hammett's previously unpublished works, as well as three autobiographical collections in which she retold her memories in the form of novels, believing that "in literature, it is the everyday that holds the real truth".

♡ ♡ ♡

FEELINGS
"Speak to me of Love"

Many women beg men to whisper them gentle words, while men, even in love relationships, very rarely show their feelings.

"Speak to me of love / Tell me again those tender things / My heart will never grow tired / Of your beautiful words with tender ring." Jean Lenoir's song, sung by Lucienne Boyer, was an international success. People still hum the melody, and the voice of the woman begging the man to say "those words sublime: I love you" has become a part of French culture. It was the beginning of success, fed by a predominantly female public, for a great many singers who crooned their way through various versions of "I Love You", when in reality there was a lack of understanding between the sexes (cf. p. 278).

"Speak to me of love"... It is a rare man who is educated in the fine art of fulfilling this feminine expectation. In the film *The Misty Quay* (1938), the hero says: "A man and a woman cannot understand each other; they speak different languages," and the heroine replies: "They may not understand each other, but they can love each other."

To "love without speaking" is difficult to accept for women who often give precisely what they want to receive: gentle words and signs of love and tenderness. Too often, "I love you" means "Tell me that you love me", with the hope that one day the woman will hear the man say "I love you too". According to Roland Barthes, who analysed this expectation, both declarations of love must necessarily be "made at the same time. The one should not follow the other, as though it depended on it ...; that is what is needed for that one spark to join the two forces."

Too many women expect men to behave in a way that is unfamiliar to them! Ever since the nineteenth century, women have been taught to be prudish about their bodies and men to suppress their emotions. For many men, raised in what might be termed a "culture of efficiency", the telephone is for fixing a meeting time, not for "love talk". Men and women are thus different not only in terms of upbringing and education, but in the way they express their desires. Women are used to expressing their emotions, particularly to each other, and in a couple it is traditionally the woman who takes care of the relationship's affective side. Many criticise men for being frightened of making a commitment, remaining silent, or making sexual demands with no show of tenderness. For some men, desire is enough; as the humorist Coluche said: "I don't need to tell her 'I love you': it shows." Women suffer because of the distinction men draw between sex and love, while men criticise women for seeing sex as a part of love.

Every one needs tenderness in order to "blossom" and words of love produce a sense of well-being.

Lucienne Boyer singing her famous song.

(In Alphaville, the impersonal city of the future in Jean-Luc Godard's film, use of the expression "I love you" is banned.) However, asking the other person to say "tender things" over and over again can kill spontaneity. The same applies to the demand for honesty in the question: "What are you thinking about?" which often means "Are you thinking about me?"

MY HEART TALKS TO YOU. Naturally, there are differences in individual sensitivity; but is the couple of the silent man and the questioning woman a fatal cultural flaw? The question "Do you love me?" seems strange to men for whom the evidence is perfectly clear: "If I didn't love you, I wouldn't be here." When Mabel Dodge (cf. p. 79), the fabulously rich New Yorker who moved to New Mexico in 1918, criticised her Native American husband Antonio Luhan for not saying anything, he defended himself by saying: "My heart talks to you all the time." Smiles, looks, and holding hands are a language all their own, quite independent of spoken words or felt passions. Conversely, nothing has ever proved that the best talkers are the best lovers or even make a better class of lover.

The more intense the feeling, the more difficult it is to describe. Words can often reduce, simplify, or distort reality. However, love blossoms fully when expressed in words. The declaration is one of the tests in the "love initiation process". To say "I love you" for the first time is a creative act; it is an articulation of essential words, words so strong that they transform both the person who utters them and the person who hears them. In *Beauty and the Beast*, it is Beauty's long-awaited words "I love you, Beast" that transform the monster into a handsome young man. Such is the power of words: they are a magic formula which loses its power if repeated.

"Tell me again those tender things." This uniquely feminine request is often interpreted by the man as an expression of the woman's insatiable need to be reassured. It leaves the man confused, wondering why the first avowal of love was not enough. To say "I love you" is to declare love, to express it. To say it again is merely to say it again. Love, which often begins with silence, sometimes tries to survive through a plethora of words.

TALK WHILE MAKING LOVE. "Talk to me in bed." In 1990, sixty years on from Lucienne Boyer, Spanish singer Maria Jiménez made a similar request of her beloved. Are men still just as shy of words? While some fear that talking during love-making will interfere with their concentration, others use very bold words indeed to increase the excitement. During the embrace a whole range of noises, from sighs to groans to screams, combine with movement and gestures to express desire, pleasure or shyness. Most couples, in fact, talk more easily after love-making; this is the time for "pillow-talk", but it is also a time of reckoning. Male clichés such as "are you happy?", or less confident questions such as "how was it for you?", "was it good?" will sometimes bring lavish responses as some women are simply anxious to avoid hurting a man's feelings. Often, however, it causes a new rift, since after love-making, many women wait for tender words while the man simply falls asleep.

And anyway, words are but a small part of the language of love! As Aragon observed in *Elsa's Madness*: "To say that I love you is so little"...

1930

GREAT BRITAIN. **Soprano Audrey Mildmay performs as Blondchen in *The Abduction from the Seraglio*, in the concert hall built by John Christie near his manor house at Glyndebourne, Sussex. She married Christie the following year and together they created the Glyndebourne Theatre, where the famous festival has been staged every year since then.**

PARIS. **Berthe Bovy produces *The Human Voice*, a play by Jean Cocteau which is eventually adapted for the cinema by Roberto Rossellini in 1947 under the title *L'Amore*, with Anna Magnani. A woman racked with despair conducts a long, one-sided telephone conversation in an effort to win back the man who has just broken with her. First she plays a "comedy of detachment" in front of him, and then lets herself go with passionate protestations of love.**

"Love is not an honourable feeling."

COLETTE
Sido

ABOVE

"I love you, Beast," says Josette Day to Jean Marais in Jean Cocteau's film of *Beauty and the Beast*.

Anaïs Nin
& Henry Miller

An affair between two writers who respected, encouraged, and helped each other, in an intimate relationship both sexual and intellectual.

In November 1931 Anaïs Nin, the bored, frustrated wife of an American banker, welcomed Henry Miller, an unknown writer recommended to her, to dinner at her house in Louveciennes, near Paris. She was twenty-eight and he forty, and they took an immediate liking to each other. He was captivated by her reticence and refinement, and she by his hard exterior; in fact, she noted in her diary, "He is like me". She had kept a diary ever since her father, a Spanish pianist, left home when she was eleven. This loss, which traumatised her, along with her strict Catholic education, were determining factors in her complicated attitude towards men. After finding little satisfaction with her husband Hugh Guiler, and feeling the pull of perverse sexual desires after reading D. H. Lawrence (cf. p. 142), she was, as she put it, transformed into an insatiable "Doña Juana" by her meeting with Henry Miller.

Henry Miller, the son of German émigrés from Brooklyn, had led a life of hardship. He was divorced, leaving his wife and daughter to live with a dancing instructor named June; it was she who paid for him to travel to France to take up writing and to start a new life. His relationship with Anaïs Nin began on a purely intellectual level; in Louveciennes or in the cafés of Montparnasse, they spent long hours together, analysing each other's experiences and talking about literature or philosophy. Their affair started in March 1932, when June left for New York; her bisexuality, interest in drugs and pathological lying were a source of fascination to both of them. When she returned to Paris in October 1932, they fell under her spell again and a three-way relationship started; it lasted until June left for good in late 1933.

THEY LOOKED SO DIFFERENT. "Henry was the only man who picked the fruit in me when it was ripe", wrote Anaïs Nin. Lawrence's works may have freed her spirit, but it was Henry Miller who freed her body and released her long-repressed sexual and artistic energy. Soon after their affair began, she went into psychoanalysis. He was as strong and healthy as she was weak and fragile. He was much given to loud talking and coarse language, whereas she always chose her words most carefully. She led an orderly life, he lived in disorder and depravity. "He wanted to explore the depths: I wanted to keep my illusions." She looked for inner truth in beauty and harmony, and adopted a style that was "as polished as enamel", while his style was singularly undisciplined.

In her preface to *The Tropic of Cancer* (1934), Miller's novel financed by Anaïs Nin, she showed great enthusiasm for the book's "blunt description of the body in a world paralysed with introspection and constipated from a surfeit of refined wit".

Anaïs Nin was attracted to Henry Miller's animal qualities, which she called "his ugly, fearless, cathartic strength". She saw a romantic rebel inside the surly, bull-headed man. Henry Miller admired Anaïs Nin's great capacity for feeling, as well as her strength and materialist beliefs behind her reticence and stylishness. Both were obsessed with sex, the legacy of a regimented upbringing. "I want to undress you, coarsen you a little," he wrote to her. "I want my dress to get dirty and torn," she had a character say in one of her novels.

A FERTILE RELATIONSHIP. Henry Miller and Anaïs Nin fulfilled each other's needs: he feared running out of money, she being unloved. She fed him, paid his rent and supported him financially for years. The money came from her husband, to whom she lied, keeping the affair well concealed while maintaining a good relationship with him. She had no plans to divorce, and published only abridged versions of her diary with its analysis of her intellectual and sexual experiences. This was because, while Miller was enjoying "adventures" with prostitutes, Anaïs Nin was collecting a string of lovers: she would make love to Miller, her husband, her cousin and her analyst, before retiring exhausted to her bedroom to write and masturbate, all in one day! In 1933 she found her father again, and started a passionate incestuous relationship with him. However, with help from Miller and her psychoanalyst, she finally broke with him, after getting over the trauma of his departure and her unhealthy desire for his acceptance.

Her relationship with Miller, whom she described as "overflowing with life", was both sexual and intellectual. In 1934 she had an abortion, stating that motherhood would have been "the supreme sacrifice, the ultimate denial of myself". Instead, she and Miller treated Lawrence Durrell, the young British writer whom they encouraged in his work and with whom they discussed things at great length, as their "literary son". Their fertility was reserved for their work: they exchanged hundreds of letters; she published her *Diary* with its remarkable descriptions of him; and he wrote *Black*

PARIS. On 14 July, Giorgio Amendola asks Germaine Lecocq to dance at the Place Beaugrenelle night club. It is love at first sight. He remembers the moment clearly: "Forty-nine years have passed; I write and she paints, we have grown old together, but everything began at that precise moment." Giorgio Amendola was an Italian exile, the son of a prominent politician murdered by the Fascists; Germaine Lecocq was the daughter of a miner, who died in the war, and a factory worker. Amendola was a Communist living in Paris with forged papers; during a secret mission to Italy in 1932, he was arrested and deported to the island of Ponza, where Germaine joined him and they married. Their daughter was born in 1935. After being freed, he undertook numerous missions. When war broke out, he joined the Italian resistance. After being made a minister in 1945, he became one of the leaders of the Italian Communist Party. He died in 1980, and she survived him by only a few hours.

Vita Sackville-West & Harold Nicolson

Two British aristocrats who remained devoted to each other despite a string of homosexual affairs.

In 1932, Harold Nicolson and Vita Sackville-West moved into the dilapidated sixteenth-century house at Sissinghurst, Kent, and created the "garden for all seasons", considered today to be among the most beautiful in the world, with its famous "white garden" and ancient rose trees. He designed the layout, and she chose the plants. They shared a passion for gardening; both were writers, and despite their homosexual affairs, they formed a remarkable couple, remaining very close to each other.

Harold Nicolson, a former diplomat, divided his time between journalism, radio, writing, and politics, but was careful to set aside time for leisure activities and social life. Vita Sackville-West, a successful novelist, was inspired by the garden at Knole, the Kent castle where she was born and lived until her marriage and which she described vividly in *The Edwardians* (1930). She finally lost it because it could only pass to a male heir. Self-willed, and very tall for a woman, she was both passionate and reticent. After first having a lesbian affair, which she described as "purely physical", she married Harold Nicolson in 1913. "Some men," she wrote, "are destined to become lovers, and others to become husbands; Harold is in the second group." For her, what worked about their relationship was that it was "so fresh, so intellectual, so unphysical".

LOVE IN INFIDELITY. After their wedding they lived in Constantinople for a year, where she created her first garden. Their son Ben was born in 1914. In the following year Vita bought Long Barn, a cottage near Knole. While converting its garden, she began her literary career with *Knole and the Sackvilles* (1922). All her novels were inspired by her family history, particularly her best-known work *The Land* (1926). As she clearly did

Vita Sackville-West and Harold Nicolson at Sissinghurst.

FACING PAGE
Orlando, sometimes a man, sometimes a woman, or Vita Sackville-West the temptress.

not follow the advice of her husband, who wanted her to put "a little more eccentricity in [her] work and a little less in [her] life", they are actually quite conventional!

After the birth of their second son, Nigel, in 1917, the couple stopped having sex together and instead found their pleasure in homosexual liaisons. As Nigel later wrote in a book about his parents, they "married for love, and their love grew deeper with each passing year, even though they were both, systematically and by mutual agreement, unfaithful to each other". Vita Sackville-West believed in the existence of "split personalities, dominated alternately by feminine and masculine elements"; and that in the future, "distinctions between the sexes would become blurred because of an increasing resemblance between them" and homosexual relations would no longer be considered abnormal. She had only one affair with a man, the writer Geoffrey Scott, for a few months in 1923.

From 1918 to 1921 she had a passionate but stormy relationship with Violet Keppel, whose mother was the king's mistress. After they fled together to Paris, Violet agreed to marry Denys Trefusis on condition, however, that they have no sexual contact. Vita, alone in England with her lover gone, described her devastation in a letter to her husband, who was in Paris for the Peace Conference; he assured her of his undying love. When the two women ran away a second time, to Amiens in 1920, Denys hired an aeroplane and the two husbands flew out to fetch their wives!

Harold Nicolson also had numerous homosexual affairs in the European capitals where he was sent on assignments; unlike his wife, he believed that the physical element was of secondary importance. Their love was strengthened by the total freedom they allowed each other, and their complete trust in each other. He described her extra-marital affairs as "your complications" and she described his as "your diversions". They often invited their lovers to visit them on the same weekend.

ORLANDO IN THE GARDEN. In 1922, Vita met Virginia Woolf (cf. p. 102), ten years her senior, at Clive Bell's home. Although the two women enjoyed an intensely close relationship, it remained predominantly intellectual. Vita was sensitive to Virginia's genius and vulnerability. "I'm mortified with fear," she confided in her husband. "I'm fearful of awakening physical sensations in her, because of her madness." She came under Virginia Woolf's literary influence and became one of the Hogarth Press's most celebrated writers. Virginia often visited Long Barn and saw Vita as "a real woman", motherly and protective, who wrote "with great skill and confidence". Vita was, in fact, the inspiration for Virginia's 1928 novel *Orlando*, in which the life of the hero, sometimes male and sometimes female, spans three centuries. The relationship between the two women developed into one of loving tenderness, which was not, however, devoid of quarrels; their frequent letters contained advice on writing, personal anecdotes and jealous outbursts. From 1927 onwards, Vita had several more homosexual affairs, all of them passionate rather than intellectual.

From 1925 to 1927 Harold Nicolson was sent to Persia (now Iran), where he had an affair with Raymond Mortimer, and then to Germany. Vita remained in England, concentrating on gardening and writing, and occasionally visited him. The distress that their separation caused them led Harold to resign, reluctantly, from the Foreign Office in 1929; but afterwards he became a journalist and hosted the radio broadcast "People and Things". In this broadcast the couple spoke of their perception

1932

PARIS. **Yvonne Printemps leaves famous playwright Sacha Guitry for Pierre Fresnay, who has just left actress Berthe Bovy. Both highly talented actors, Printemps and Fresnay appeared as the ideal couple in both theatre and cinema. Their private life, however, was both passionate and turbulent. Pierre Fresnay, a severe and very reserved Protestant, with impeccable manners, never stopped loving the beautiful woman who was famous for both her nightingale voice and her terrible outbursts of rage. His love, combined with infinite patience and tolerance, gave him strength to endure the torment to which she subjected him: demanding and terribly jealous, she deceived him and humiliated him in public. When performing, he refused to embrace any other woman but her; and he sent her flowers every day of their forty-two years together.**

of marriage, stating that it needed to be based on "long-lasting love" and guided by "intelligence, mutual respect and a shared sense of values".

As well as embarking on a literary career, publishing essays, novels, and biographies – his book on George V earned him a knighthood – Nicolson also entered the field of politics in 1931, and served as deputy leader of the Conservative Party from 1935 to 1945. During the war, he was governor of the BBC. Vita restored Sissinghurst to its former glory and realised her childhood dream by creating her own private world in one of its magnificent towers. She indulged her passion for gardening, writing several books on the subject. She wore cardigans woven with wool from her own sheep, and during the war helped to organise the Women's Land Army Corps. She wrote a history of the corps and, in 1946, published a major poem *The Garden*.

Nothing ever upset their happy marriage and the rest of their life was peaceful; she passed the time gardening, while he continued his writing and radio broadcasts. They died a few years apart from each other in the 1960s, both at Sissinghurst.

♡ ♡ ♡

IMAGES
"Modesty in Hollywood"

The Hays Code subjected all representations of sexuality to an excessively detailed set of regulations, and studios censored their own productions.

Ever since the beginnings of cinema, censorship has sought to hinder the development of new-found freedom in an art that became popular very quickly. As in other channels of expression, there is a clear demarcation of roles: creators create, right-thinking people protest, censors make heavy moral pronouncements, and bureaucrats draw up rules, which the creators then try to bend by all sorts of different means. In the case of cinema the producers took the initiative by practising self-censorship. In 1922, concerned at the abundance of local censorship measures, they created the National Association of Producers and Film Distributors. The first director of this body was William Harrison Hays, a Republican and former minister with Presbyterian leanings, nicknamed "Mr Clean". His name is enshrined in the infamous Hays Code of 1930, which lists all the scenes deemed "unsuitable" for showing on screen.

Since the beginning of talking movies, in 1927, a wind of freedom had been blowing through the studios with the appearance of female characters embodied by Marlene Dietrich, Jean Harlow, and Mae

West, who advertised their sexuality quite openly. In films by Lubitsch (*Trouble in Paradise, Serenade for Three*) or by Cukor (*Dinner at Eight*), it is the heroines who initiate the sexual encounters, without the slightest hint of guilt. The virtue protection campaigners, however, did not let up, especially as the social and economic crisis that hit the United States during the "Great Depression" of the 1930s reinforced the puritan atmosphere. A "curtain of modesty" was therefore drawn across the screen.

Any mention of sexual urges or sensuality provoked reactions of horror from the virtue leagues, whose obsession with the subject showed in excessively detailed codes for regulating scripts and shooting films; before the film could be approved, every kiss was timed and the cut of every lady's

A makeshift curtain separates unmarried characters played by Claudette Colbert and Clark Gable in *It Happened One Night*.

dress measured to the last millimetre. In particular, kisses lasting over thirty seconds, extra-marital or inter-racial relationships, "ugly" situations (cruelty, rape, prostitution and so on), and "improper" dances and costumes were all banned, as was all bodily representation (the birth scene in *Gone With the Wind*, for example, was shown in shadows). Bedrooms, even those of married couples, were only allowed to be shown with twin beds!

BETTY BOOP AND MAE WEST IN THE STOCKS. The year 1932 saw several scandals in the private lives of stars. One such scandal led Paul Bern, then married to Jean Harlow, to put a bullet in his head. The year also saw the creation of Betty Boop, Max and Dave Fleischer's cartoon character with the seductive wink and sexy swaying walk that raised up her short black dress and clearly showed her ample thighs with their characteristic garter. All this was too much for the Catholic bishops, who formed the Legion of Decency. The major Hollywood studios, fearful that a federal ban would be imposed, applied the Hays Code with greatly increased diligence. Self-censorship was practised on films even before shooting commenced. Already producers were coming under pressure, having been advised not to adapt "immoral" works such as *The Postman Always Rings Twice*.

In 1933, the producers created a new body called the Production Code Administration. Directed by Joseph I. Breen, an Irish Catholic, it had the power to impose a fine on any producer who broadcast a film without its seal of approval. Almost all Hollywood films were controlled by the Administration for the following thirty years, its function being to monitor the social content of the films, while most of its energy was channelled against things that smacked of sex.

Pictures of satin undergarments, and explicit shows of sexuality, especially adultery, were given the axe! Betty Boop's producers were ordered to make her less provocative, and finally compelled to cease producing her in 1939. The axe fell on the antics of the buxom Mae West, who was denounced as a "monster of lechery", but whose greatest offence was unrestrained use of the twin evils of parody and burlesque. She used men either as friends or as puppets, and was not averse to undermining their virility with cheeky remarks; she had al-

The stern Doctor Freud at the bedside of the happy and carefree Jean Harlow, as seen by Miguel Covarrubias.

ready served a ten-day prison sentence in 1926 for her performance, judged "harmful to public morals", in the successful Broadway play *Sex*. In 1932, the appearance of *She Done Him Wrong*, Lowell Sherman's film based on her successful play *Diamond Lil*, made her the target of the censors. Already banned on radio because of its verbal excesses, it was progressively banned from the studios as well.

EROTICISM WITH ELLIPSIS. How could producers who were subject to such narrow-minded censorship escape from the ever-present danger of sterility and mawkishness? Some brought in innovations. While Lubitsch and Capra avoided the full fury of the censors and skirted round the rules by using clever allusions or brilliant metaphors, a new type of heroine appeared, personified by Katharine Hepburn, Jean Arthur, Joan Crawford and Rosalind Russell. Hawks and Capra, for example, showed, in the active and independent characters of their films, images of

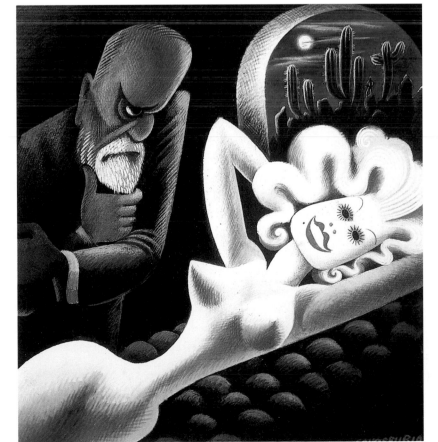

women quite removed from the traditional temptress, and much more interesting. Clearly, self-censorship was not a backward step in every sense! It can even be argued that the Hays Code, over a period of twenty years, facilitated the development of a less direct, more provocative and ultimately more disturbing form of sexuality. The Code, which fell into disuse, was finally replaced in 1966 by a film classification system based on the age of the viewer.

It can be argued that the "sex-bombs" of the 1950s (cf. p. 260), proudly parading their assets across the screen, were not a real victory for freedom of expression. Although similar reservations reared their heads during the "porn wave" of the 1970s (cf. p. 340), two generations of cinema-goers could hardly have been kept ignorant of prostitution, adultery, divorce and, more generally, desire and pleasure as well. The Hays Code was a strange way of going about achieving its noble aims of "social and moral progress, improvements in society, and soundness of thought"!

HOLLYWOOD. **Tarzan, alias Johnny Weissmuller, former Olympic swimming champion, swings from branch to branch with his famous cry in *Tarzan of the Apes*. After saving Jane, played by the beautiful Maureen O'Sullivan, he inspires in her a love so powerful that she chooses to live in the trees with him and Cheetah rather than return to civilisation. The studios' self-censorship (see "Images") only allowed a completely chaste relationship between Tarzan and Jane, and hence their child quite literally falls from the sky. In *Tarzan Finds a Son* (1939), they adopt a baby who is the only survivor of an air crash. In these films of sanitised savagery – Johnny Weissmuller's body is completely hairless – Jane, the subservient woman – most men's dream! –, derives great pleasure, when it is bedtime, from teaching him to say "Hello, I love you."**

♡ ♡ ♡

Eleanor
Franklin & Roosevelt

The couple who moved into the White House were partners in politics but led wholly separate private lives.

In 1933 a new president of the United States, Franklin D. Roosevelt, entered the White House. His wife, Eleanor, was his closest ally in the field of politics, even though they were poles apart in their personal relationship.

The disharmony between them became apparent soon after their wedding in 1905 when he was twenty-three and she eighteen. They were cousins with the same surname, both from a rich New York family who also produced American President Theodore Roosevelt. Eleanor, whose beloved father was an alcoholic and whose mother was a very remote figure, was orphaned at the age of ten and suffered badly from emotional neglect. Tall, unattractive and very shy, but possessed of great zest and vitality, she felt ill-at-ease in public; Franklin, however, was an expert at using his charms on people. She brought him self-discipline, he brought her happiness. Sara Delano, Franklin's mother, dearly loved her son, a lawyer and brilliant public speaker, but she did not relate well to her daughter-in-law. Franklin learned quickly to hide his true feelings in order to appear happy at all times. This did nothing, however, to overcome his wife's fears, particularly her fear of sex; she confessed to her daughter Anna, born in 1906, that she saw it as "a burden that must be borne". Over the next ten years she also gave birth to five sons, one of whom died in infancy. After that she made her husband sleep in a separate bedroom; total separation was the only method of contraception available to her.

Franklin was elected Democratic Senator for New York State in 1910, and in 1913 became Joint Naval Secretary. In 1918 Eleanor discovered that her husband was having an affair with his secretary, Lucy Mercer. She threatened to divorce him, but he made amends in order to save his career, even though the affair carried on in secret afterwards. From that time on, their emotional and social lives were kept completely separate, and their marriage became more of a political alliance.

In 1921 Franklin Roosevelt suffered an attack of polio, which left him semi-paralysed. While being rehabilitated at the Warm Springs spa centre in Georgia, he learned to walk with walking sticks in a show of remarkable determination. He would never appear in a wheelchair before the photographers; if he had to walk a few steps in public, he was always supported by one of his sons. The press respected his demands, and nothing was ever said about the presidential couple's private life, nor indeed about the string of mistresses who passed through the White House.

A PAIR OF PARTNERS. Eleanor Roosevelt found her vocation in social work; working with groups of women gave her confidence in herself. She fought against racial discrimination and defended civil rights. After gathering a network of trade unionists, feminists, and militant anti-racialists around her, she pleaded on behalf of the oppressed, together with her husband, who in return benefited from the support that it brought him from left-wing groups, blacks, workers, Jews, and women.

Elected New York State Governor in 1929, he took exemplary steps to combat the economic depression, poverty, and unemployment that afflicted the state after the Wall Street crash in November of that year. His wife, now indispensable, was by his side in all his campaigns. She represented him everywhere she went, and also travelled widely with him. He made frequent visits to Warm Springs, while she went to New York to teach in a school that she had bought; she lived in a separate cottage at Hyde Park, the family home of her mother-in-law near New York. She also had relationships with two lesbians, Nancy Cook and Marion Dickerman; and in 1932 she met journalist Lorena Hickok, with whom she subsequently had a passionate affair.

In 1932 Roosevelt promised the Americans the "New Deal", a programme based on competence and courage, which would lead the country out of its crisis,

Franklin Roosevelt (centre), supported by his son, and Eleanor Roosevelt, to his right, during the 1932 campaign for the presidency.

FACING PAGE
Eleanor Roosevelt, photographed by Philippe Halsman in 1961.

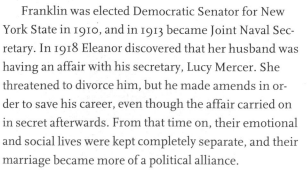

and he was elected President. His style was popular: he was both courageous and accessible, and often spoke on radio, while his wife, the perfect host, broke new ground by serving hot dogs in the White House.

Roosevelt knew how to gather a crowd and was a good listener. Only after listening would he make his decisions, sometimes as a liberal, sometimes as a conservative. In this way he introduced both free enterprise and social planning; and when the continuing crisis forced him to expand on his plans, he introduced social security, unemployment benefits, fair taxation and work organisation schemes. His wife, meanwhile, answered the vast number of letters that she received, always with compassion. As well as fulfilling this traditional role, she published a column known as "My Diary" for forty days in early 1936, gave press conferences exclusively for women journalists, and had a long-running radio show. She was immensely popular, and although her freedom with words and thoughts earned her contempt from conservatives, it also won her admiration from feminists. Franklin and Eleanor Roosevelt were, in short, the most important presidential couple in United States history.

TWO INFLUENTIAL PERSONALITIES OF THE TWENTIETH CENTURY. Franklin Roosevelt owed his great success in the 1936 election campaign to his wife, at least in part, and set great store by her contributions. It was thanks to her that the United States welcomed Europeans fleeing from persecution by the Nazis. According to one witness, Eleanor's method of working consisted of looking her husband straight in the eye and saying: "Franklin, I think you should do this," or even: "Franklin, surely

1933

FRANCE. **Publication of *Commentary*, the only book by Marcelle Sauvageot, who died of tuberculosis in 1934 at thirty-three. Written as a letter to a man she loved and who deserted her in order to marry, this short text contains both the style and the passion of the greatest protestations of love in literature.**

SCREENING *of Ecstasy*, **by the Czech Gustav Machaty, the first cinema film to show a sex act. After leaving her impotent husband, the heroine, played by Austrian actress Hedwig Kiesler (subsequently known as Hedy Lamarr), runs naked through the woods, bathes in a pond and meets a young man, with whom she makes love in a cabin. After finding fame through the "scandalous" film, Hedy Lamarr married a multi-millionaire who wanted to obliterate these "compromising" pictures. He had all the copies of the film confiscated so that he could destroy them, but a few survived.**

"The need to be loved is greater than the need to love."

SIGMUND FREUD
New Lecture on Psychoanalysis

you're not going to do that." It was her influence over her husband, rather than any degree of intimacy, that made her the most influential woman of the time. She described herself as "having the effect of a goad".

With the coming of the war, the couple separated even further. Family troubles afflicted them: their daughter divorced and married again, and they were very disappointed by their younger sons' irresponsible behaviour. Only the eldest, James, remained devoted to his father. Meanwhile Roosevelt, re-elected in 1940 and again in 1944, got the United States involved in the war effort. Together with Churchill and Stalin, he took part in the historic Yalta conference of February 1945. Two

months later, on 13 April, he died suddenly of a cerebral haemorrhage; Lucy Mercer was with him at the time, something of which his wife was unaware.

Until her death in 1962, Eleanor Roosevelt's life was a whirlwind of activity, both journalistic and diplomatic. She supported the creation of the United Nations and of the State of Israel, and was involved in drawing up the Universal Declaration of Human Rights in 1948. Although the great prestige enjoyed by President Roosevelt has lessened with time, his wife remains one of the greatest personalities of the twentieth century. She is buried beside him in the rose garden at Hyde Park.

♡ ♡ ♡

ANGUISH
Love at the Mercy of Nazism

From 1933 to 1945, love and reproduction were both closely monitored in order to further the Nazi regime's racist ideal.

In Germany, where two million men perished during the First World War, Adolf Hitler made a promise that he would give every unmarried woman a husband; it brought him victory in the 1932 elections. As leader of the National Socialist Party (abbreviated to "Nazi"), he was made Chancellor on 30 January 1933, and in order to bring about the "new order" envisaged in his book *Mein Kampf* (1925),

he abolished basic liberties and set up a one-party regime. In November 1933 Josef Goebbels, Minister for Propaganda, declared that "this total revolution has completely changed and reshaped relations between people, relations between people and the state, and relations concerned with the facts of life". Soon the Nazi party was controlling the lives of Germans in every domain; they were trained and supervised in both work and leisure, according to their sex and age, to such an extent that "the only private activity left was sleep". Mixed education was discouraged, and in the processions in support of Hitler, men and women always walked separately.

In an extension of the anti-democratic Prussian tradition of the

nineteenth century, Nazism attached no importance whatsoever to the individual. People counted as a nation, but humans were mere cogs in the machine. In Italy, Mussolini's Fascist regime also denied the individual, and rested instead on a conservative ideology that assigned traditional roles to the sexes. However, while Mussolini appeared in public with his wife and children, the private life of unmarried Hitler remained a mystery; Eva Braun, his young mistress, was unknown to the people. The *Führer* (leader) maintained that "the population fulfils the role of a woman, and like a woman, it does what I want". Love was to be for the fatherland and the Führer, and no one else. Young people were required to be "strong and handsome, with no sign of weakness or tenderness". Of course the home was treated as a haven of love against this background of hatred, but, as Hitler wrote in *Mein Kampf*, the role of women was limited to "bringing real men into the world". Unlike the Fascist view, the vision of Nazism was both pagan and racist in its essence. Political and social life was viewed as a struggle between the weak and the strong, whereby "races" were classified according to their supposed abilities, with the "superior" or "Aryan" race at the top.

At the 1936 Olympic Games in Berlin.

No "MIXED" MARRIAGES. Love and reproduction were strictly monitored, the authority of the state intruding even into marriage and family life. When it came to choosing a marriage partner, maintaining the "purity of the race" was to be more important than individual freedom. As only the "Aryan" race was encouraged to reproduce, the law provided for sterilisation and abortion for Jews and gypsies, who were labelled "inferior beings" and "enemies of the German race". The same applied to the mentally ill and to "deviants", homosexuals, and other "misfits". After the racist laws were introduced, individual acts of violence soon gave way to a collective barbarism, characterised by the mass exterminations in the concentration camps.

Sexual relations with persons of "inferior" race were deemed destructive, and in 1935 all marriages or extra-marital relationships between "Aryans" and Jews were formally forbidden, deemed a "racial crime" punishable by prison and, from 1939 onwards, by death. All "Aryans" already in mixed marriages were required to divorce.

This happened to two famous German actors, both of whom had taken Jewish wives: one was Heinz Rühmann, known for his performance in the film *The Ideal Husband* (1937), who complied but helped his wife to flee to Sweden, and the other, Joachim Gottschalk, who refused to surrender, committing suicide with his wife and family in Berlin in 1941. This is the storyline of Kurt Mätzig's film *Marriage in the Shadows* (1947), which was dedicated to Gottschalk's memory.

ONLY "ARYANS" MAY REPRODUCE. The Hitler Youth Movement believed that "each young man should become a man, and each young woman a mother". Following their logic of selective reproduction, the

Nazis compelled men and women with "Aryan" characteristics to reproduce, and in 1935 the so-called *Lebensborn* (springs of life), a kind of human stud farm, was set up. After the war started, young women with blue eyes and fair hair, who had been selected from occupied countries, particularly Poland, were sent there.

In 1931 Heinrich Himmler, head of the SS, the élite of the Nazi regime, imposed on unmarried SS members the obligation to marry a girl "of good race, the object of the exercise being the preservation of the precious German heritage". All of them were encouraged to produce as many children as possible, legitimate or otherwise. Before leaving for the front, they received an order to "guarantee descendants". This policy led Doctor Walter

Gross, Director of the Department of Racial Policy, to propose, in a secret document produced during the war, the legalisation of polygamy for men in order to compensate for "the weakening of the German people's biological substance". The regime also glorified "male allegiance"; under this arrangement the men, after fulfilling their duty to perpetuate the "race", would meet together in a brotherhood founded on violence and the exclusion of all that was feminine or weak in any way. The official art of the regime was a justification of its inhumanity: nude men and women were shown merely as machines for producing and reproducing, and depicted, with their rigid posture and unwavering forward gaze, as a sexless fraternity devoid of any human warmth or feeling.

1933

GERMANY. **Because of political developments and anti-Jewish policies (see "Anguish"), waves of émigrés leave Germany and, later, territories occupied by the Nazis. The many intellectuals and artists who preferred to flee rather than suffer the terrible fate of being silenced, deported or killed, included couples such as composer Kurt Weill and singer Lotte Lenya (cf. p. 132), playwright Bertolt Brecht and actress Helene Weigel, film-maker Paul Czinner and actress Elisabeth Bergner, and many others including Bauhaus artists such as Josef and Anni Albers, musicians such as Arnold Schoenberg and his family, and so on. Many found refuge in the United States and resumed their careers in surroundings that were often very uncertain.**

♡ ♡ ♡

Propaganda poster for the National Socialist Party.

Gunnar & Alva Myrdal

Two world famous, deeply committed Swedish intellectuals. He won the Nobel prize for economics, and she the Nobel peace prize.

A lamp each, and one desk between them.

In 1934, Gunnar and Alva Myrdal, a married couple, published their *Nation and Family, The Swedish Experiment in Democratic Family and Population Policy* (the title of the book's 1941 English translation), which alerted Swedish public opinion to a drop in the birth rate. He was an economist, and she a psychologist and sociologist. Their assertion that the country needed more children pleased the conservatives, and when they proposed social measures to help families, it was the socialists' turn to show approval. The way to increase the birth rate, they wrote, was not to bring any pressure to bear on women, but to resolve housing and child-care problems. Their plan was a radical one: to create a vast network of crèches and nurseries, increase communal services in high-rise blocks, introduce family allowances, and develop sex education. The book became the reference manual for the Social Democratic party, which held power from 1932 to 1976. It introduced paid maternity leave for public service employees (1936), abolished

the ban on contraceptives (1938), and made it illegal to dismiss an employee for marrying or getting pregnant (1939). Unlike the restrictive measures applied by the authoritarian regimes, such as Italian Fascism, the Swedish attitude was to encourage births in an indirect way, for example by introducing inexpensive accommodation and free school meals. Of course, women still bore the bulk of the burden, but the state helped them to reconcile work with motherhood.

Gunnar and Alva Myrdal met in the summer of 1919, when Gunnar, enjoying a cycling holiday with some fellow students, asked to sleep in a barn owned by Alva's father: he was twenty-one and she seventeen. Alva obtained her parents' permission to accompany them on their travels, and the friends sent their bicycles on by train and constructed a raft to sail down the river. That was just the beginning of the adventure that awaited the young Alva. Her mother had forbidden her to study, saying that a girly had no need to, but her father, a Socialist and atheist with a very open mind, overturned his wife's plan and insisted that Alva study in a university before her wedding, which eventually took place in 1924.

Gunnar was as rational and clear-minded as Alva was full of life and emotion. Both had a strong personality and considerable foresight, and could easily have clashed with each other. Instead, they fitted together hand in glove, combining theory and commitment. He was confident of his own worth, she admired him and was content to help him in his career. She was shy, but he encouraged and respected her and needed her to speak on his behalf and show him the human side of problems. He felt very proud of her when she became a public figure.

WORKING CLOSE TOGETHER. They made a very close couple, warm and tender, and worked together at the same table throughout their lives, co-operating on everything they wrote, either together or separately. They also enjoyed walking, cycling, going for picnics, and having friends to stay.

"We have something we can do together for the world," she wrote, "without giving up having a family." Their three children were born in 1927, 1934 and 1936. For Alva, a woman was not fulfilled through motherhood alone; she also had to be active in society. In 1929 a grant allowed them to study in London, before going to the United States; and when Gunnar took up a teaching post in Geneva from 1930 to 1933, she followed him. Both were opposed to tradition, which they saw as a barrier to progress. At his wife's request, Gunnar studied the economic aspects of an industrialised society and published some important works on monetary and financial theory. Alva, meanwhile, campaigned in favour of contraception and freedom for the individual, without losing her femininity which continued to show clearly in her stylish dress and taste for hats. An article published by them in 1935 argued that "contraception will allow sexual relationships to deepen and thereby lead to a more healthy family morality"; both of them were in favour of sex education beginning at age three.

AN INTERNATIONAL CAREER. Gunnar Myrdal was appointed head of the Housing Commission in 1935, although he protested that Alva knew more about the subject. After being consulted as an expert, she arranged the construction in Stockholm of a communal building for working women only, with priority given to single mothers. A pioneer of purpose-built housing, she designed, together with the architect Markelius, the house that was constructed for them in Stockholm in 1937; the adults had their own area on the ground floor, and the children had theirs on the first. Photographs of the building appeared in the press, with one or two caustic remarks about the bedroom, in which the twin beds were separated by a mobile partition that could be drawn if either party wanted some privacy.

During a second stay in the United States in 1938, Gunnar carried out an in-depth, original study of racism against blacks, with Alva's help, and published the famous book *An American Dilemma* (1944). In 1947 he was appointed to a post in the United Nations in Geneva. Although Alva was frustrated at being kept idle for a while, her appointment to the United Nations in New York in 1949 was the high point in her life. "It was not until 1949 that I truly became a real human being," she wrote later. Sadly, it was Gunnar's turn to suffer, as he complained of being unable to work without her. Therefore in 1955, when she was sent to India as ambassador, he studied the problem of underdevelopment in India in order to join her. He published *Asian Drama* (1968); and she wrote *The Two Roles of Women* (1956, with Viola Klein), about the division between domestic and professional responsibilities in women's lives. While they followed very similar careers, they often lived apart, but were always overjoyed to see each other, because they had so much to share! Both became ministers and were awarded Nobel prizes, he for economics in 1974, and she for peace in 1982. She spent the last part of her life helping the Third World and campaigning for peace and disarmament, becoming the idol of the Scandinavian pacifists. They both died within a few months of each other, she in 1986 and he in 1987.

1934

UNITED STATES. **Bonnie and Clyde, the infamous gangster couple, are ambushed and mown down by the police, after being tailed for many months. Bonnie had announced their death in a ballad she wrote: "One day together they'll die / And in the ground together they'll lie." Clyde Barrow was twenty-five and Bonnie Parker twenty-four; he was brown-haired and she blonde, and they made a very good-looking couple. Since meeting in Dallas in 1929, they spent their time either in prison or on the run. In the spring of 1932, she helped him to escape from prison and together they carried out a string of hold-ups, but not as many as the story about them maintains. Arthur Penn's film *Bonnie and Clyde* (1967) brought their story back to life through the talents of Faye Dunaway and Warren Beatty.**

when she disembarked from the plane she was arrested and spent a night in jail. This move caused a storm of protest. In 1950 her husband was dismissed from the Collège de France and relieved of his duties at the CEA. His pro-Soviet commitment, however, did not lessen, even after Khrushchev made his shocking revelations on Stalin's atrocities in 1956.

While actively campaigning against the military use of nuclear weapons, both Irène and Frédéric worked to make French nuclear research as advanced as that of the rest of the world; he with the CEA, where he launched "Zoe", France's first atomic pile, and she with the Nuclear Studies Centre at Orsay, near Paris, which she founded and directed. Their daughter Hélène taught there later, and married a grandson of Paul Langevin.

Irène Joliot-Curie died of leukaemia in 1956, and her husband survived her by only two years. Both were given a state funeral.

♡ ♡ ♡

IMAGES
The Moustache

A new type of "ladies' man" appears in Hollywood; but the ladies have changed as well.

From Hollywood's early days, the moustache has been an essential attribute of ladies' men such as John Barrymore, or of the heroes of action films: the dashing and charming personalities of Zorro, Robin Hood, or the pirate have become inextricably linked with the fine black moustache worn by Douglas Fairbanks and his 1930s successors Errol Flynn, Tyrone Power or, in Italy, the young romantic star Amedeo Nazzari. For this reason Jean Sablon, when he arrived in the United States from France in 1936 crowned with the international success of the song "Vous qui passez sans me voir" (You who pass without seeing me), was advised to let his moustache grow. However, this charismatic singer, whom the Americans saw as the embodiment of French seduction and sophistication, was snubbed by the French public on his return to Paris in 1945 for looking "too Yankee" and having a "Clark Gable" moustache!

Clark Gable (cf. p. 186), with his protruding ears, ironic expression and dimples, introduced a new kind of ladies' man; unlike the languorous *Latin Lover* personified by the smooth-bodied and graceful Rudolph Valentino and his equals in the 1920s (cf. p. 118), this one was best known for his macho charm. In 1934 Frank Capra's film *It Happened One Night*, a masterpiece of American comedy, won four Oscars, and the overtly masculine attitude of the leading actor, Clark Gable, was like a breath of fresh air in the darkness of the Depression years. It was therefore he who was chosen, without opposition, to play the part of the cruel but sophisticated Rhett Butler, one of the twentieth-century's best known ladies' men, in *Gone With the Wind* (cf. p. 180). This aggressively masculine stereotype dominated the Hollywood screen until the 1970s, when the new, less obviously ladies' men, such as Woody Allen (cf. p. 368) began to appear.

Clark Gable, the crowned king of the moustache, clearly owes some of his tremendous seductive power to this manly attribute. He was advised to grow one because the area between his nose and upper lip was judged too large! In *It Happened One Night* he launched not only the fashion for moustaches, but one which proved disastrous for manufacturers of men's underwear. In the scene where he strips off his shirt, the cinema audience discovered that ... he was not wearing a vest! Vast numbers of men followed in his footsteps, and sales of vests plummeted.

A MANLY ATTRIBUTE. In Britain, the writer Evelyn Waugh was presented with a serious question in 1939: should he let his moustache grow, or not? This accessory was an integral part of a military man, unlike the beard, which was generally banned in the army. Although a great many civilians had worn beards during the latter half of the nineteenth century, numbers had been in decline since the 1914 war. It had suffered a mortal blow in 1917 with the arrival of the Americans, whose clean-shaven faces gave them an irresistible young, handsome look. The safety razor, with its removable blades, had already replaced the cut-throat; and with the coming of the electric razor in the 1930s, the whole matter of shaving became less complicated and the business of the traditional barber declined sharply.

The moustaches, particularly the fine one, has been declining in the West since the 1950s, except where it is a distinctive mark of the British, personified on the cinema screen by David Niven. It is still a mark of manliness in Mediterranean countries, and is grown to impressive lengths. In Italy, several towns even organise moustache contests.

KISS, WITH OR WITHOUT MOUSTACHE? An early twentieth-century proverb says: "A kiss without a moustache is like an egg without salt." Whether it resembles a heady spice or a grater, a soft cushion or a stiff brush, the moustache gives the person being kissed that extra degree of stimulation. It was Maupassant, himself adorned with a magnificent set of "whiskers", who described the irresistibly seductive power of Bel-Ami's moustache in the novel *Bel-Ami*, and its particular delights; the woman being kissed shivers and trembles with delight, as she feels it make contact with her lips. In the same way, Rhett Butler's

GONTRAN

CINÉMA *Éclair*

Aug. loymarie

moustache has a role to play in the famous kiss that reveals the world of pleasures to Scarlett (cf. p. 181). There are, of course, still women who love to shiver at the silken touch of a moustache, and others who jump at the sensation with cries of "Ooh, that tickles!" or "Ouch, that pricks!"

Women have also changed since the 1930s, and the ideal female appearance has altered even more than the male. The motherly figure of the beginning of the century, with her ample body and breasts, has been replaced by an altogether less feminine figure, with small breasts and short hair. The "tart", who caused such a scandal in the 1930s, has gradually taken over in the West, in a revolution unprecedented in the history of feminine dress and hairstyles; not since Spartan times have women shown their calves, for example. The fashion is popular because it has be-

come associated with the new status accorded to women, and the rights they have gained in most countries. Exit the nymphs and beauties of the Edwardian era, and enter the new straight and sober designs, bright colours and make-up. Thanks to the French fashion designer Paul Poiret, who finally freed the female body from the horrible restrictive corset, and to the emancipated women who sacrificed their long hair on the altar of modernity, women have gained a new freedom of style and movement. The seductive lady is no longer a scatter-brained sparrow with a shrill voice; instead, there is a whole variety of different types, and adding the deep voices of Greta Garbo, Marlene Dietrich and Lauren Bacall, female seduction has become imbued with a masculine element never experienced before.

1935

JAPAN. **Publication of Chiyo Uno's book *Confession of Love*,** inspired by an episode in the life of painter Seiji Togo. In 1929 the painter expressed a desire to commit suicide with his then lover; they cut their own throats, and only he was saved. The event caused a great commotion and Chiyo Uno, a modern emancipated woman with short hair and a very free life-style, visited Togo shortly afterwards in order to question him and make the story into a novel. Sixty years later, she recalls their first encounter: "I was irresistibly attracted by the blood-stained bandage around his neck. We fell onto each other like two animals." Both of them made love on the futon which was still stained with blood; a passionate relationship followed and lasted for six years.

FACING PAGE

Seductive moustaches: Errol Flynn (above) and Adolphe Menjou (below).

Duke of Windsor by his brother, the new king George VI, he and his beloved left the country.

This was the beginning of a golden exile, an exile devoted to the cult of love and the cultivation of high-society friendships. After their discreet wedding on 3 June 1937 at Candé castle in France, the Duke and Duchess travelled widely, paying a much-publicised and highly controversial visit to Hitler in 1937. With his pro-German leanings the Duke was sent to the Bahamas and made governor during the war.

In 1953 the couple set up home in Neuilly-sur-Seine, near Paris, throwing lavish parties. At each milestone in their love life, and on every anniversary of their meeting, they sent each other magnificent jewels or precious items engraved with messages. Their happiness was immortalised on innumerable photographs, posing together with their beloved pug dogs and led a life of true style. The Duchess, who repeatedly said "one can never be too thin, or too rich", was voted by the magazines as the best-dressed woman; and the Duke started the fashion of striped socks and excessively wide trousers. As well as publishing his memoirs, he wrote a treatise on horticulture.

Edward, Duke of Windsor, never regretted the choice he made, even though it excluded him from royal events such as the coronation of his niece Queen Elizabeth II. The Royal Family never forgave Wallis Simpson, the "insurgent"; and the queen did not meet her until 1972, when she visited her dying uncle. One concession was made, however, when the Duchess, who died in 1986, was allowed to be buried beside the Duke in the chapel at Windsor Castle.

ANGUISH
Love, War and Tragedy

The dramatic Spanish civil war also saw the defeat of those who had tried to create new relations between the sexes before the retrogression of Francoism.

On 18 July 1936 a military up rising, led by General Franco, was launched against the Spanish Republic. This event marked the beginning of the civil war between nationalists and republicans, which was exacerbated by the in-fighting between revolutionary anarchists, Trotskyites, and Communists. A variety of social issues was at stake in addition to the political conflict, particularly the subject of love, couples, and family life. In 1931, the institution of the Republic, after the left-wing electoral victory and the abolition of the monarchy, caused a tremendous social and moral upheaval in a land shackled by an inflexible form of Catholicism. The Republicans voted for the separation of church and state, proclaimed equality between the sexes, and gave women the right to vote and to receive maternity payments. They legalised civil marriage and made Spain the second country in the world, after the Soviet Union (cf. p. 96), to institute divorce by mutual consent and grant illegitimate children equal rights.

These radical steps further inflamed partisan passions. While republican newspapers carried announcements of civil marriages celebrating the freeing of love – "Congratulations to those comrades who have cast off the yoke of the Church!" – the Vatican backed a conspiracy against the Republic. José Antonio Primo de Rivera, leader of the Falangist Fascist Movement, stated that he was ashamed to hear republican demonstrators cry out "Children yes, husbands no!"; and he denounced the "reign of sensuality" that had been brought in by the new freedom to divorce. His sister Pilar, leader of the women's section of the female Falangist group, declared that "a woman's greatest ambition should be to marry". In the territories recaptured from the "reds" during the first months of the war, the Francoists, whose nationalist Catholicism was based on their reactionary perception of the status of woman and couples, immediately abolished any progressive accomplishments. Amongst the revolutionaries, the Communists advocated a traditional allocation of roles between the sexes, while the anarchists, who opposed the State and were, therefore, on the fringe of the republican movement, were the pioneers of free love. Many libertarian men, however, retained their chauvinist tendencies and saw women merely as sex objects.

FREE LOVE. The magazine *Free Women*, founded in Madrid in 1936, advocated a truly "free" love that allowed men and women to meet completely independently and declared war on prostitution. These militant women, such as the well-known anarchist Hildegart (pseudonym of Carmen Rodriguez Carballeira), issued advice on birth control, believing that ignorance was just one more form of female slavery. Although unanimous in their contempt for the institution of marriage, they were divided on the question of whether a woman needed to become a mother in order to find fulfilment.

The civil war speeded up changes in attitudes, particularly amongst women, and the papers devoted much space to standing up for their rights. While the Republic legalised the issue of contraceptives and even abortion – another innovation – in October 1936, women joined the ranks of men in the mili-

tia and even took part in the fighting. The growing influence of the Communists in the republican camp crushed the local revolutionary activities of the anarchists and Trotskyites. Women were henceforth sent away from the frontline and made to work in the factories. The famous Communist *pasionaria* Dolorès Ibarruri, a miner's widow from Asturias, regularly chanted "men at war, women at work".

While Nazi Germany and Fascist Italy supplied the Francoists with military aid, volunteers came from all over the world to help the Spanish Republic, which received no support from western democracies. Altogether, 40,000 men and women enlisted in the International Brigades, among them Lise and Artur London (cf. p. 242). Ken Loach's 1995 film *Land and Freedom* tells the story of a love between

a young Englishman and a Spanish Trotskyite freedom fighter who leads an independent love life after being freed from traditional female subjugation. In the same way, love was born between the French surrealist poet Benjamin Péret and the Spanish painter Remedios Varo; they left together for Paris in 1937. Another brigade volunteer was the English aristocrat Esmond Romilly, whose romantic leanings were a source of fascination to the young Jessica Mitford; their departure for Spain in 1937 caused a scandal. They were married shortly afterwards.

Among the many foreign observers of the civil war was Ernest Hemingway, who met his compatriot, the American war correspondent Martha Gellhorn, in Spain; they married in 1937 and he dedicated his novel *For Whom the Bell Tolls* (1940)

to her. The novel tells the story of the love between a soldier in the International Brigades and a young Spanish woman who escapes from the Francoists after being raped.

LOVE IN CHAINS. After three years of war and half a million fatalities, the victorious Franco regime imposed a repressive, authoritarian and moralistic regime. The puritan approach of Franco, who had just one daughter and was undoubtedly married to the only woman he had ever really known, was coupled with the Church's strict views on sexual matters. Any woman guilty of abortion, cohabitation or adultery could be severely punished. A kind of sexual asceticism was imposed on everybody, although men were allowed a "safety valve" in prostitution. Boys were only permitted to relate to girls through a long, complicated courtship, without sex; kissing in public was forbidden, and beach wear was monitored by the civil guard. It was not until General Franco died, on 20 November 1975, that Spain at last quietly accepted democracy and modernity.

1936

BERLIN. **An English wedding is contracted between Sir Oswald Mosley and Diana Mitford, in the presence of Hitler. After excelling as an MP and defecting from Conservative to Labour, he founded the British Union of Fascists, turning in the process into the leader of a discredited group. His wife was one of the Mitford sisters, all of whom led very different lives: Unity was also an admirer of Hitler and attempted suicide when war was declared, while Jessica was a Communist who fought for civil rights in the United States after the war. The eldest sister, Nancy, set up home in France near to her lover Colonel Gaston Palewski, and became a novelist. Deborah was happily married to the Duke of Devonshire.**

♡ ♡ ♡

Women at arms and on the frontline: the Spanish Civil War radically altered ways of thinking.

Clark Gable
& Carole Lombard

An ideal Hollywood couple, well-suited and happy, but for all too brief a time.

When David O. Selznick started out on the adventure of producing the film based on *Gone with the Wind* (cf. p. 180), he knew who would be given the part of Rhett Butler: Clark Gable (cf. p. 172) had introduced the image of a new ladies' man, contemptuous, overtly masculine, but always pleasant. The reality was that the actor lived apart from his wife, and his affair with Carole Lombard caused a scandal. He demanded a divorce; and soon after shooting for *Gone with the Wind* started, the lovers were married quietly on 29 March 1939. In order to avoid the press, Clark Gable hid under the back seat of the car while Carole Lombard, in the driving seat, was unrecognisable with plaited hair and an ordinary set of overalls. Their marriage, like that of Douglas Fairbanks and Mary Pickford

in 1919, brought together the two greatest stars of that period. Clark Gable was nicknamed "The King", and Carole Lombard was the highest-paid actress in Hollywood, earning twice as much as he. Slender, blonde and stylish, she was the star of a string of sophisticated and fashionable comedies such as *My Man Godfrey* (1936) and *Swing High Swing Low* (1937). A naturally lively, outspoken and generous person, she swore like a trooper and loved pulling practical jokes.

Their first meeting, during the shooting of *No Man of Her Own* in 1932, was a very brief one, as Carole Lombard was then married to actor William Powell. Clark Gable's life had become very complicated, after the failure of his second marriage, to a rich widow much older than himself, his stormy affair with Joan Crawford, and numerous one-night stands. Underneath his dashing, sophisticated appearance, he was troubled, easily depressed, and unsure of his talent and manliness.

A SIMPLE, SPORTING LIFE. Clark Gable and Carole Lombard did not meet again until 1936, during a party with friends; this time, she won him over with her come-hither attitude and innate charm. At the time, she was twenty-seven and he thirty-five. Initially they saw each other in secret, but then appeared together in public at film premières, night-clubs, race meetings, tennis tournaments, and boxing matches. In him, she discovered an honest, sensitive man, and they never lost their shared sense of humour; after one quarrel, Clark Gable woke up to find himself surrounded by doves, symbolising "Let's forget everything and get back together!" This was the first of many "dove of peace" exchanges between them.

For a year, they lived the society life to which she had become accustomed. Then, to please him, she adopted the simple, sporting life that he preferred, with hunting and fishing. She learned to shoot, accompanied him on duck hunts, and slept outdoors on the ground. He was captivated by her spirit and stamina.

Carole Lombard's rich Indiana family treated her like the boy they never had, while Clark Gable came from a humble farming background in Ohio. Her influence on him was beneficial, giving him confidence in himself and joy in living. Well-matched, they comple-

UNITED STATES. **The writer Erskine Caldwell and photographer Margaret Bourke-White marry with extraordinary suddenness in Nevada. When they met, in 1935, he was well-known for his novels (*Tobacco Road* and *God's Acre*), and she was already famous for her work on *Life* magazine, which chose one of her photographs for the cover of its first edition in 1936. From 1936 onwards, Erskine Caldwell and Margaret Bourke-White both made many important reports from both the United States and Europe; the first was the inquiry into the destitution suffered by the sharecropper tenants in the Southern United States. This inquiry was the subject of their book *You Have Seen Their Faces* (1937) dedicated to Patricia, the daughter they dreamed of having. Margaret was reluctant to marry, but Erskine insisted; she made him promise to stop complaining about the long periods that she spent away on assignments. He was not, however, able to tolerate the absences, and they divorced in 1942.**

♡ ♡ ♡

FACING PAGE
Carole Lombard and Clark Gable at their ranch in the San Fernando Valley.

ABOVE
During a shooting session.

mented each other and agreed to live together in peace and honesty. As they had contracts with different companies, they never acted together, but arranged for their shooting schedules to coincide so that they could be together.

The première of *Gone with the Wind* brought them great public acclaim. In a city where marriages between stars were usually short-lived, they made an ideal couple. They bought a ranch at Encino, surrounded by mountains and vast orchards, forty-five minutes' drive from Hollywood. She decorated the house, preferring comfort to outright luxury, and paid special attention to the dining room; their special delight was to have dinner in evening dress after a day in the open in overalls. When not shooting, they divided their time between breeding chickens, harvesting lemons or going on fishing and hunting expeditions, while trying to dodge the attentions of over-zealous fans. In a location far away from the society life of Hollywood, they organised a great party for all their friends once a year.

They called each other "Ma" and "Pa". Their dearest wish was to have a child, but that pleasure was denied them. In order to keep her husband's spirits up, she had numerous medical consultations, gave up horse-riding,

and finally accepted the diagnosis that she was sterile. The other shadow over their life was Clark Gable's insatiable appetite for seducing young, rising stars; although Carole Lombard pretended not to know, she was in fact intensely jealous of Lana Turner. She realised that her marriage to Clark Gable was not founded on anything sexual, saying "I love him, but he's not much good in bed"; Joan Crawford had already remarked that he was a "second-rate" lover. It appears that he needed all those affairs to compensate for his very low level of self-esteem.

THE DRAMA. In 1941, Carole Lombard starred in Lubitsch's film *To Be or Not To Be* – the high point of her career. Then, on 7 December 1941, the United States entered the war and, like many stars, she used her popularity to help the war effort. On 12 January 1942, she left to shoot a propaganda film, after writing five letters, one to be sent every day to her husband. On 16 January, however, her plane crashed near Las Vegas, and all that Clark Gable got back was the remains of a ruby brooch that he had given her the previous Christmas. Set in a gold medallion, he hung it round his neck and wore it to his dying day. After spending several months prostrate with grief, he took up flying and fought heroically in the war; but he confided to his secretary: "I've got everything I could want in this world, except for Ma." He missed her dreadfully, and found solace in excessive drinking. He had two more marriages, to Sylvia Ashley and Kay Williams, both of whom bore a striking resemblance to Carole Lombard. Kay Williams, who had two children, introduced him to the joys of family life, and their greatest joy was when she got pregnant again; sadly, however, Clark Gable never saw his son, because he died of a heart attack in 1960 as the shooting for *The Misfits* was nearing its end. He was buried in the military cemetery at Glendale, California, next to Carole Lombard.

♡ ♡ ♡

Western Eroticism

The twelfth-century invention of "courtly love" celebrated the cult of the lady and her lover's mastery of seduction.

In his essay *Love and the West*, published in 1939, the Swiss writer Denis de Rougemont offers a whole new vision of European culture by defending the cause of humanism against the threatening shadow of barbarism. In an analysis of the story of Tristan and Isolde, he argues that *Eros*, the love-passion of Eastern pagan origin, imbued love with a tragic element by spreading a new form of idealistic asceticism; *Eros* is marked by suffering and failure, and thrives on obstacles to happiness, leading ultimately to death. Attributing "the crisis in modern marriage" to the fascination with this deadly passion, he contrasts *Eros* with *Agape*, love in action, which thrives on equality between partners forming the only solid foundation for modern Christian marriage.

The term "courtly love" was coined by medievalists at the end of the nineteenth century to refer to the *fin'amor* of which the Languedoc troubadours sang during the twelfth century. This "pure" or "perfect" love was based on the cult of the lady and the championing of male desire, with three key concepts: moderation, expectancy, and chastity. This new love-model, referred to in the Bible in *The Song of Songs* (cf. p. 264), the only truely erotic text in Western literature,

was widespread amongst the minor nobility of Southern France and showed similarities to the closed, aristocratic society of the great Chinese and Japanese love novels. However, while love was written in a context of religious tradition in the East, the Western church denounced the association as heretical; to love a human being with a love that was due only to the Creator was a serious sin.

JOI, LOVE'S ECSTASY. As medieval expert René Nelli shows, courtly sexuality is a combination of influences from chivalry and Arabic poetry, a poetry in which relations between the sexes were reversed, with the vassal lover in service to the suzerain lady. Chastity was championed by Ibn Daoud, who believed that it was capable of raising desire from the plane of time to the plane of eternity.

The troubadours broke with the tradition that dated back to Plato's *Banquet*, according to which love of-fers human beings a hope, either of finding lost unity (Aristophanes's explanation) or of filling a void (as Socrates asserted, quoting Diotymus). In courtly love, the lover, far from seeking union, is anxious to maintain separation, in order to avoid leading to that inevitable religious and social unit, the couple. His love, therefore, is of necessity adulterous; the woman is married to the lord and her lover is the vassal.

Unlike the chivalrous lover, the courtly lover does not seek to "conquer" the woman. For him, desire is an end in itself, and he would rather be loved by the woman without pleasure than experience pleasure without being loved. At the end of his amorous and poetic quest, after passing the tests that the lady sets for him, he discovers the ongoing delight of mutual caresses, and re-

Tristan's Boat, Erté

nounces the climactic pleasure of ejaculation. In this way, he gives in to *Joi*, love's ecstasy, the grace accorded to those who have purified their desires, and then tastes the delight of spending a night with his lady. After this long process of ethical and erotic mastery, the lover embodies love itself and is able to experience *Joi* merely by exchanging glances with the lady.

Joi, which is both a physical and a spiritual exaltation, brings an ecstasy so refined that only poetry is fit to be describe it; often, the meaning of the poem is concealed, because the name of the beloved must remain a secret. For the Italian poets of the *dolce stil nuovo*, who carried on the love-ceremonies of the troubadours, the object of love is the poetry itself. Unlike Buddhism, which encourages renunciation and aims to extinguish all desire, *fin'amor* magnifies desire and makes it shine all the more brightly by freeing it from its illusions. Courtly love is perfect because it is never enacted.

THE LADY, A SNARE IN RELATIONS BETWEEN MEN. The Belgian essayist Suzanne Lilar believed that while courtly love could not unite body and soul in the same passion, modern love came about at the same time, in the life of a real couple, Héloise and Abélard. Theirs was both a physical passion and a conjugal love, moving the immoderate desire of concupiscence onto a spiritual level.

It was in the twelfth century, therefore, that the love-models used in western modernity appeared: the myth of Tristan and Isolde had its genesis in Brittany, and *fin'amor* in the Languedoc area; Héloise and Abélard met in Paris, while Chrétien de Troyes, who praised both heroic achievement and the art of loving, showed conjugal love in a new literary form, the novel. It was the novel that subsequently devel-

oped a completely new concept of the marriage of love (cf. p. 16).

Although "courtly love" altered the image of love, showing it as the ideal of a higher life, it is questionable whether did it improved the image of women. There can be no doubt that Eve, the temptress, became the lady, the inaccessible ideal, and that the Virgin Mary began to be magnified as the "Our Lady" or "Notre Dame" of so many cathedrals during the twelfth century. However, it was Christine de Pisan, the great fifteenth-century French writer, who first rose up against the hatred of women that was implicit in "courtly love". As in Eastern eroticism (cf. p. 68), the point of view was essentially masculine. Although courtly love praised an exceptional, idealised and depersonalised woman, it abandoned every

other woman to her fate, and people remained ignorant of the idealised woman's refinement. It taught young knights to avoid becoming villains, and ultimately led them to serve the suzerain as a good vassal; but are not relations between men given the greatest importance here? And did not the homage paid by the lover and expressed through the mediator of the lady make her husband the true lord and master?

Courtly love developed a code of relations between men and women, and traces of this code are still evident today; it is the basis for the vocabulary of politeness ("my humble respects, Ma'am") and of sexuality (the words "lover" and "mistress"). These are more than merely formal; they are the basis on which the reputation of France, the land of love, is founded, at least in part …

1939

HOLLYWOOD. **First showing of William Wyler's film *Wuthering Heights*, inspired by Emily Brontë's classic English novel of 1847. The writer of this strange story of love, violence and death was a young woman who died in 1848 at thirty. She lived with her two sisters Charlotte and Anne, also writers, in a desolate area of open moor in Yorkshire that forms the backdrop for the novel. The success of the film owes a great deal to Laurence Olivier's portrayal of the hero, the dark, troubled and vicious Heathcliff who, haunted by the memory of his love for Catherine (Merle Oberon), wreaks his revenge on those who despise him and seeks a death that will reunite him with her.**

"To love is not to look at each other, but to look together in the same direction."

ANTOINE DE SAINT-EXUPÉRY
This World of Men

Jean Marais and Madeleine Sologne in *L'Eternel Retour*, Jean Delannoy's 1943 film, based on the story of Tristan and Isolde.

Laurence Olivier & Vivien Leigh

Don Juan

Elsa Morante & Alberto Moravia

We'll Meet Again

Katharine Hepburn & Spencer Tracy

Love Letters

Lucie & Raymond Aubrac

Fifteen Soviet Brides Condemned for Falling in Love

Humphrey Bogart & Lauren Bacall

GIs: Overpaid, Oversexed and Over Here

Benjamin Britten & Peter Pears

Brief Encounter

Juan & Eva Perón

Sex Education

Jawaharlal Nehru & Edwina Mountbatten

The Photo-Romance

Edith Piaf & Marcel Cerdan

The Kinsey Reports on Sexuality

Ingrid Bergman & Roberto Rossellini

The Taboo of Incest

Laurence Olivier & Vivien Leigh

The stormy union of two great Shakespearean actors and screen idols.

"Bless me, reader, for I have sinned!" are the opening words of Laurence Olivier's *Confessions of an Actor*. Son of an English clergyman, his strict upbringing left this private, complex man with a sense of guilt that he could only exorcise through his art. This explains the importance of the theatre in his life. In 1940, he left his wife, the brilliant actress Jill Esmond, to marry another great performer, Vivien Leigh, after both parties had obtained a divorce. Leigh was the wife of a wealthy barrister and had a daughter in whom she took little interest. She had fallen in love with Olivier after seeing him act at a time when he was the fashionable leading man of the day. The marriage regularised a scandalous liaison. No children were born of the union, which ended in divorce after years of torment and mental illness.

Laurence Olivier had been fascinated by the actress with the magnificent green eyes, whom he first saw in London in *The Mask of Virtue* (1935), her stage début. This performance established her reputation and won her a fabulous contract with cinema producer Alexan-

der Korda: "As well as her physical presence, which was magical, her deportment was charming. And there was something else she had: an attraction of the most disturbing kind I have ever known." She described herself: "I swing between happiness and sadness. I am both a prude and a non-conformist." Her relationship with Olivier was intensely professional and passionately physical. Both nourished the same ambition: to tackle the great roles of the Shakespearean repertoire. Korda brought them together on film in *The Invincible Armada* (1936). Their relationship continued, "full of lies and deceit", according to Olivier, especially on his part, despite the birth of a child to his wife. In 1937, at Elsinore, acting together for the first time on stage, the lovers played a memo-

rable *Hamlet*, and took up residence together in London. In November 1938, they left for Hollywood, where he played the role of Heathcliff in *Wuthering Heights* (cf. p. 189), while she was selected for the role of Scarlett O'Hara in *Gone with the Wind* (cf. p. 180). They were soon being cast in the role of romantic couple by the popular press but, while waiting for their divorces to come through, they had to abide by convention and live apart. They toured America performing *Romeo and Juliet*, but the roles were far less suited to them than Heathcliff and Scarlett O'Hara. The production was a flop.

THE IDEAL COUPLE. 1940, when Vivien Leigh finally married her "Larry", was a highly successful year, bringing her an Oscar. Together they acted in Korda's production of *Lady Hamilton*, to immense popular acclaim. Returning to Britain in early 1941, Olivier enlisted in the Fleet Air Arm, but was prevailed on to make a patriotic film. The result was the magnificent *Henry V* (1944), adapted from Shakespeare's play.

The couple set up home at Notley Abbey, a superb country house in Buckinghamshire, within easy reach of London. Leigh decorated it with taste and proved to be a tireless, charming hostess. Her husband was appointed director of the Old Vic, home of English classical drama, where he ruled supreme as the best Shakespearean actor of his generation. He was knighted in 1947. Epitome of beauty, taste and wit, "Larry and Viv" led a life of extreme brilliance. Rich and famous, talented and passionately in love, they seemed, according to their actor friend Douglas Fairbanks Jr, to be the "ideal couple". But cracks were appearing in the relationship. Although they dreamed of working together, Leigh's contract with Selznick, the producer of *Gone with the Wind*, prevented them from doing so. Her subsequent frustration was accompanied by serious health problems: two miscarriages, an attack of tuberculosis and the first signs of a manic-depressive condition. While *Hamlet*, Olivier's second film (1948), was acclaimed as a masterpiece and won him an Academy Award, Leigh, whom he had rejected for the role of Ophelia on account of her age, suffered a setback on screen in the film of *Anna Karenina*.

GREAT BRITIAN.
"He was my North,
my South, my East
and West,
My working week
and my Sunday
rest,
My noon, my midnight,
my talk, my song;
I thought that love
would last forever:
I was wrong."
This extract from the poem
"Funeral Blues"
by W. H. Auden, originally
published in *Collected
Poems*, was featured in the
film *Four Weddings and a
Funeral* (1993). The film's
success aroused a wave of
enthusiasm for Auden's
work.

CANADA. **On 12 July it is officially announced that unmarried men will be called
up on the 15. Throughout
the country there was a
headlong rush to get mar-
ried: couples queued out-
side churches, waiting to
tie the knot; some were
married in batches to
speed things up. In all,
three times as many
people married in 1940
as in 1939.**

DESCENT INTO MADNESS. Concerned for the mental health of his wife and hoping that she would improve if they acted together, Olivier organised a tour of Australia, which was not, however, a great success. She returned determined to play the role of Blanche Du Bois in the London production of Tennessee Williams's *A Streetcar Named Desire*. Directed by her husband, the play was a success, but acting the role of the highly disturbed heroine only made her condition worse. The results were even more disastrous when she played the role again – and won her second Oscar – in Kazan's 1952 film version.

Leigh then entered a vortex of mental illness and violence. She underwent electric-shock therapy and achieved little on stage, while Olivier devoted himself passionately to his work, but was powerless to prevent the gradual collapse of his wife, who engaged in an affair with the young actor Peter Finch. When the couple did act together, the critics reproached Olivier for not rising to his full stature, for not wanting to overshadow his wife. Their estrangement became public and, in 1960, he sued for divorce.

In 1957 Laurence Olivier met the twenty-eight-year-old British actress Joan Plowright. With her, he em-

FACING PAGE
The "ideal couple", by
Ronald Searle.

ABOVE
Photograph by
Philippe Halsman.

barked on a new career, performing plays by young British dramatists. This soon led to a new private life. They married in 1961 and had three children. Olivier ended his career covered in glory: he was made a life peer in 1970, and was eventually buried in Westminster Abbey. Vivien Leigh found some stability with Jack Merivale, a Canadian actor four years her junior. She performed a number of stage roles with him and made several more films. She died of tuberculosis in 1967. Until the very end, she kept Larry's love letters and portrait by her. Douglas Fairbanks Jr reports that, on learning of her death, Olivier murmured: "Poor, dear little Vivien."

♡ ♡ ♡

Don Juan

The Spanish seducer broke every law, ignored love and embodied the absolute freedom of desire.

"Constantly loved, eternally incapable of loving": such is the nature of a Don Juan. This profane seducer is studied by Gregorio Marañon, a Spanish doctor and writer, in *Don Juan and Donjuanism*, an essay published in 1940. His first appearance in literature is as the *burlador* (seducer), hero of the play by Tirso de Molina, *The Seducer of Seville* (1630), which was inspired partly by the life of Count de Villamediana, a courtier of Philip IV, and by a popular legend whereby a certain Don Juan Tenorio seduces the daughter of Commander Ulloa, whom he has just murdered. He comes to his victim's tomb to insult him and is dragged off to hell by the commander's statue.

Although this myth originated in Spain, the male psychological type it represents is universal. What attracts a Don Juan – Marañon explains – is not a particular woman but "woman" in general. Far from being the archetype of virility, as is generally assumed, he is effeminate and immature; nor is he possessive or jealous. "A real man, as soon as he matures, stops being a Don Juan. Those who continue to be Don Juans all their lives retain their indeterminate, juvenile character. And this is one of the secrets of their power and attraction."

The author sees a classic Don Juan in Giacomo Casanova, the famous eighteenth-century Venetian womaniser. In this case, however, he fails to investigate an important aspect of the myth, namely the challenge that Don Juan flings in the face of God and society. This may be the result of self-censorship: in Franco's Spain (cf. p. 176) it was hardly wise to discuss the absolute freedom of desire or the transgression of rules which were the trademark of this free-thinking nobleman.

It is in this guise that Don Juan appears in Molière's play, *Dom Juan ou le Festin de pierre* (1665), and in Mozart's opera, *Don Giovanni* (1787). In these masterpieces, a hero, monstrous in his pride and cruel cynicism, seduces all the women he can lay his hands on – "one thousand and three", according to the list kept by his valet – makes fun of those who warn him of retribution from on high, and defies the commander, symbol of human and divine law. He does not flinch when his victim's statue appears. He agrees to sup with him, rashly offers his hand and is swallowed up in a clap of thunder.

ENEMY OF GOD. Don Juan is the second great masculine figure in Western literature on love. Five centuries after Tristan (cf. p. 188), the personification of passion and fidelity, appears the seducer who sees "nothing so sweet as to overcome the resistance of a beautiful woman". "The pleasure of love is all in change," he says in Molière's play. "Once one has achieved mastery [of a woman], there is nothing more to say or desire; all the beauty of passion has been consummated." According to Kierkegaard, Don Juan "seduces by the sheer energy of desire".

In Stefan Zweig's analysis, "Don Juan is an out-and-out enemy of God". His inconstancy lies not only in his quest for novelty – "tyrant of our soul", according to Casanova – but in his delight in law-breaking. In the view of Denis de Rougement, for whom he is one of the foremost examples of human rebelliousness, Don Juan belongs to "a society hidebound by constraining rules, which is more interested in defying the rules than in actually breaking free of them". Rejecting all values which oppose his desire, Don Juan, who aims to be totally free from perceived mores, believes in neither passion, nor happiness, nor lasting relationships.

The Romantic tradition, from Hoffmann to Baudelaire, has made Don Juan an ally of Satan, a hero of evil, not unlike Faust who sold his soul to the devil not only to satisfy a desire for pleasure, but also for knowledge.

With the decline in religious and moral taboos, the myth has lost some of its power. Apart from the subject of Losey's film *Don Giovanni* (1979), based on Mozart's opera, the character type in the twentieth century lacks the aura of sinfulness and sacrilege, and Don Juanism is viewed as little more than sexual vagrancy. Although such activity is condoned in men, as we see from examples of such seducers like the writer Georges Simenon, the actor Warren Beatty or Prince Francesco Caravita di Sirignano, for whom "the most beautiful is always the next", the same behaviour is severely censured in women.

WHAT SORT OF VIRILITY DOES DON JUAN EMBODY? According to classical psychoanalysis, Don Juan suffers from a hidden anxiety; his moving from one woman to another is the sign of an unconscious search for a mother figure, from which he runs away each time he encounters it. In his illusory, always disappointed quest, his refusal to form lasting relationships, and his need for immediate satisfaction, he is similar, in the view of some psychoanalysts, to a certain type of homosexual. It is interesting to note that Villamediana, the model for the original *burlador*, was involved in a homosexual scandal in Madrid. Tirso de Molina was unaware of this fact, as the king protected his courtier by forbidding discussion of his exploits.

Another example is the writer André Gide. In studying his "Dionysiac nomadism", Denis de Rougemont shows that he made a distinction between love and desire: on the one hand, he projected onto his wife the figure of his mother and was as devoted to her as any Tristan; on the other, he embarked on a Don-Juanesque quest for homosexual pleasure.

The writer Alain Roger even sees Don Juan as a "lesbian": his power of seduction lies in his effeminacy, the "long detour via the other sex", described by Kierkegaard in his *Journal of a Seducer*. According to Georges Bataille, who sees male strength as essentially silent, Don Juan exploits his bisexuality to mobilise the power of words – a feminine characteristic.

We find another literary avatar of Don Juan in Laclos's *Liaisons dangereuses* (1782), which revolves around a depraved pair of social rebels, Valmont and the Marquise de Merteuil, she being the only female incarnation of the myth. But to what sex does she belong when she exclaims of their easily captured prey: "What have I in common with these mindless women?" "Born," she declares, "to avenge my sex and master yours," her aim is not pleasure but power. In this respect, she also challenges the established order.

Few women can resist the fatal attraction of a Don Juan, even in the modern guise of a bronzed beach boy. *Capri, 1935*, Herbert List.

1940

HOLLYWOOD. **Actress Lana Turner marries the band leader Artie Shaw. The film star eventually married eight times in all, twice – in 1942 and 1943 – to the same man, restaurant owner Steve Crane, who subsequently married the French actress Martine Carol. Another of Lana Turner's husbands was Lex Barker, one of the actors who played Tarzan. Artie Shaw later married Ava Gardner.**

GREAT BRITAIN. **Success of the American singer Tessie O'Shea, with the song "I fell in love with an airman who had big blue eyes, but I'm nobody's sweetheart now". The song remained popular throughout the war.**

♡ ♡ ♡

Elsa Morante & Alberto Moravia

The tortured relationship of two great Italian writers.

On Easter Monday 1941, at the church of the Gesù in Rome, Alberto Moravia, thirty-four years old and a celebrated novelist since the publication of *Time of Indifference* in 1929, married Elsa Morante, a staunch Catholic, aged twenty-nine. Four years into their affair, he could no longer bear the thought of returning to his parents' house every night, but was still too poor to buy her a wedding ring. They had met at a friend's house. "When she said goodnight," he remembered, "she handed me her house keys." Not very tall, severe looking, her seducer had been struck by the sulky brunette with the beautiful mauve eyes, with her "bewildered, short-sighted look" and hair already streaked with white.

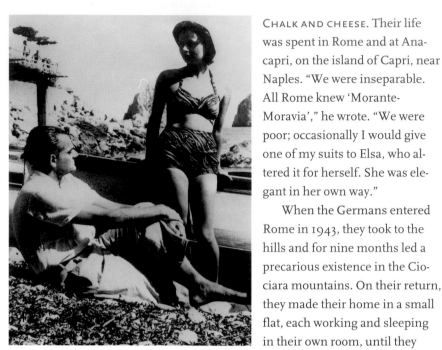

That same year, Elsa Morante published her first book, a collection of essays entitled *The Secret Game*. She was born in Rome, in the working-class Testaccio district, a haunt of drop-outs and vagrants. "Lies were the most important legacy I received from my parents," she wrote. Her mother, a primary school headmistress, told her in adolescence that her real father was a married man. She left home at the age of nineteen. According to Moravia: "She was living alone and literally dying of hunger and loneliness." A scion of the Roman bourgeoisie, Moravia was the son of a Jewish architect and his beautiful Catholic wife, twenty years his junior, who had taken a lover. He drew the conclusion that any married relationship was bound to be unhappy. Confined to his bed for nine years by a form of tuberculosis which affected his bones, he educated himself by reading and, at the age of eighteen, began writing *Time of Indifference*, a cruel portrait of fascist Rome, as was *Disappointed Ambitions* (1935). He denounced the conformism and corruption of the bourgeoisie, and publicly proclaimed his anti-Fascism. As his books were banned, he made a living from journalism, filing reports from all over the world.

CHALK AND CHEESE. Their life was spent in Rome and at Anacapri, on the island of Capri, near Naples. "We were inseparable. All Rome knew 'Morante-Moravia'," he wrote. "We were poor; occasionally I would give one of my suits to Elsa, who altered it for herself. She was elegant in her own way."

When the Germans entered Rome in 1943, they took to the hills and for nine months led a precarious existence in the Ciociara mountains. On their return, they made their home in a small flat, each working and sleeping in their own room, until they could buy a bigger place.

The quarrels of these tormented lovers are well documented. "Brave, generous, cruel, lacking sensuality", is how Moravia described Morante, whom he considered as more talented than himself. "I liked her," he said, "but I was never crazy about her. She always knew it, and that was undoubtedly the main cause of the difficulties in our relationship. I was not in love, but fascinated by something extreme, heartrending and passionate in her."

What a difference in the lifestyles of these two great writers, who soon won recognition and admiration! Up at dawn, Moravia worked from seven o'clock to eleven, while Morante did her writing late at night, smoking, drinking and taking amphetamines. He wrote a novel a year, which were on the short side – fifty in all – the best know of which are *The Woman of Rome* (1947), *Disobedience* (1948), *The Conformist* (1951), *Two Women* (1957), and *The Empty Canvas* (1960). He also worked as a scriptwriter, literary critic and film critic, gave many interviews, and travelled widely. She refused to see journalists and spent her life writing, publishing four long novels in all, each acclaimed as a masterpiece: *House of Liars* (1948), *Arturo's Island* (1957), *History: A Novel* (1974), and *Aracoeli* (1982).

He focused on the middle-class family and the problems of couples, adopting the lucid, ill-at-ease intellectual as his stock character. She, who saw herself as "destined to light up the night", sought in her writing to exorcise "the curse of being born" that afflicted her young heroes. Central to her work are young children, innocent victims. One of her collections of poems is entitled *The World Saved by Little Children* (1968). Nothing could relieve her sense of suffering. She complained that Moravia "hurt her without realising it", while he remembered her as "proud and severe; she did not share her life with anyone, not even me." In daily life, she was so unbearable that, some days, he said, "crime seems easier to her than separation."

ANGUISH AND DESPAIR. In 1955, he sent her a telegram addressed to "Elsa Moravia". She would not forgive him what she felt as an "appropriation" and had a terrible row with him. Their sexual relations ceased at this point. In the same year, she fell in love with the filmmaker Luchino Visconti. Moravia was hurt when she told him of the affair, which lasted two years, conclud-

ing that: "We lived in a strange kind of symbiosis. Anything can find its place in such a relationship, even infidelity." In 1962, Morante, who could not tolerate his relations with other women, demanded that they separate, although she never agreed to a divorce. Moravia left her and, the next year, fell in love with Dacia Maraini, a twenty-seven-year-old novelist – he was then fifty-six – with whom he experienced all the pleasures of eroticism. Sex became his main preoccupation, though it brought no relief to his existential angst.

Fiercely anti-conformist, Morante lived on the margins of society and formed a friendship with Pier Paolo Pasolini. "Three things mattered to me: love, children and cats." She lived surrounded by cats and experienced the pain of being childless. She had short-lived affairs with younger men, and a longer relationship with the painter Bill Morrow, whose suicide in 1968 drove her to despair. She then found she had multiple sclerosis; "all of a sudden," she said, "I had become old." In 1983, she attempted suicide and, until her death in 1985, was confined to a clinic. Moravia spent hours outside her door.

1941

HOLLYWOOD. **A tempestuous relationship between Jean Gabin and Marlene Dietrich. For Dietrich, who was fiercely anti-Nazi and had taken American citizenship, Gabin was "Man, Superman". He had left occupied Paris to make patriotic films. Reserved as to his feelings, he referred to her as "la grande" and preferred her as a housewife making him stews than in the role of "blue angel". When, in April 1943, he enlisted in the Free French forces, she joined the women's corps of the American army. Both covered themselves in glory, eventually meeting up in liberated Paris, but their relationship did not survive the peace. After the failure of *Martin Roumagnac*, the film they made together, Gabin, who wanted to have children, moved away, leaving her three valuable paintings. In 1949, he married the young and beautiful Dominique Fournier. Obsessed by the desire to see him again, Dietrich pursued him for years, but he refused all contact.**

Dacia Maraini left him in 1981. Widowed at the age of seventy-eight, he was at last free to marry again: he chose Carmen Llera, a thirty-one-year-old Spanish woman, with whom he rediscovered his youth – and jealousy. He died in 1990, on the very day he received the proofs of his autobiography, *Vita di Moravia*.

♡ ♡ ♡

ANGUISH
We'll Meet Again

The War came between young lovers. A long wait began. "We'll meet again" was their theme song.

In 1941 the singer Vera Lynn, who recorded the popular hit "We'll meet again", was the "Forces' words of a poem written in 1915 by Hans Leip, a young German soldier on his way to the Russian front. They were later set to music by Norbert Schulze. The soldier remembers saying goodbye to his girl under the lantern, and dreams of one day finding her there again, with the refrain "Wie einst, Lili Marleen" (As in the past).

fate of this song, and the eventful story of Lale Andersen, its creator, inspired the German director, Rainer Werner Fassbinder, to make the film *Lili Marleen* (1980), with Hanna Schygulla in the title role. The heartrending music, associated with images of death and horror, gives the film an apocalyptic dimension.

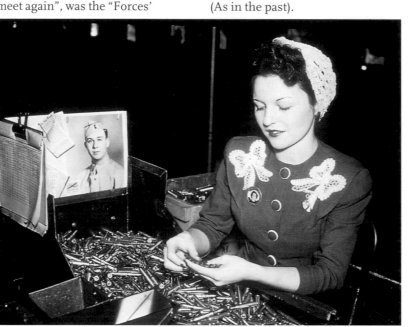

THE PAIN OF WAITING. The war separated many young lovers. Men left their native land to fight across the seas, and had as their only contact letters and food parcels (cf. p. 202). In 1940, the British cellist Kathleen Andersen, whose husband had been taken prisoner at Dunkirk and sent to Germany, founded an association for the families of prisoners of war and organised a big parcel-distribution centre.

sweetheart" in the struggle against Nazi Germany. Like other sentimental melodies frequently broadcast over the radio, this song by Ross Parker and Hugh Charles was intended to comfort those who, at the front or back home, were living a painful separation. It is said that these propaganda weapons were as effective as a speech by Churchill! Vera Lynn was "the voice of home", just as Tessie O'Shea (cf. p. 195) or the Andrews Sisters were for the Americans, who entered the war in December 1941, after the Japanese attack on Pearl Harbor.

"Lili Marleen", sung on both sides, has become something of a legend. "Vor der Kaserne, vor dem grossen Tor" (Outside the barracks, by the corner light) are the opening

When it was recorded in Germany by Lale Andersen, at the beginning of the war, this nostalgic lament immediately became enormously popular and, amazingly, crossed enemy lines. Adapted and translated from Italy to the United States, it symbolised the suffering experienced by war-separated lovers everywhere. In the English version, the refrain was "For you, Lili Marleen". Its interpreter on the allied side was the film-star Marlene Dietrich. German in origin but fiercely anti-Nazi, she had acquired American citizenship in 1939. In Germany, the song was taken up by another star of the silver screen, Zarah Leander. In France, Suzy Solidor sang it for the German officers who frequented her cabaret in Paris. The

Would they be wounded, taken prisoner, killed? Hoping against hope for their return, their loved ones lived in anguished anticipation of news. So painful a separation made it possible to measure the strength of the attachment, and love was often deepened through trial. Except for a few couples who worked together in the Resistance, like the Aubracs (cf. p. 204), a long night began for all who were separated, a difficult life of loneliness, fear, and often deprivation. Horror was the lot of many Jews, hunted, arrested, deported, torn from their spouses and children, and slaughtered (cf. p. 164).

Life went on nevertheless, and love blossomed in unexpected places. Mixing populations, suspending social conventions, the war gave new opportunities for meeting, particularly in the armed forces, where nurses and secre-

Girl working in an armaments factory, her soldier husband's photograph beside her.

FACING PAGE
A man's world: soldiers in barracks.

taries played an important role. Not least, 400,000 American and 45,000 Canadian soldiers served in Europe. Love affairs were commonplace, often in dramatic circumstances; marriages were performed, often with the bridegroom in uniform. Despite the air raids on London between September 1940 and May 1941, Barbara Cartland (cf. p. 126) organised a department at the War Office to lend wedding dresses to those without one of their own.

MEN TAKEN HOSTAGE, WOMEN UNDER SUSPICION. The situation in France was particularly hard after the defeat of June 1940, with the German occupation and the collaborationist regime of Marshal Pétain. The experience of separated couples was very different from that of the First World War (cf. p. 84). A total of 1.6 million prisoners of war, half of them married, spent the best part of five years in captivity, with no leave for brief reunions with their loved ones. Meanwhile, 130,000 young men from Alsace and Lorraine, forcibly drafted into the German army, lived in fear of reprisals against their families, should they decide to "desert". The same was true of the 700,000 men requisitioned for forced labour in German factories. In Germany, these men might get to know other foreign workers or local women, though the latter were forbidden to have sexual relations with non-Germans. *A Love in Germany* (1983, cf. p. 373), by the Polish director Andrzej Wajda, tells the story of a German woman who falls in love with a Polish worker while her husband is away. The lover is subsequently hanged by the Gestapo.

As during the Great War (cf. p. 92), men serving overseas were haunted by the fear of their womenfolk leaving or betraying them. The wives of POWs, who suffered from loneliness and lived in difficult material circumstances, also had to put up with suspicion. Under the Vichy regime, family and sexual behaviour was regulated by the state: the law of 23 December 1942, "intended to protect the dignity of the home", allowed the authorities to intervene, independently of the husband's wishes, to punish "anyone cohabiting with the wife of a person serving at a distance on account of the war". Informers had a field day. As for women who fell in love with Germans, they were seen by some as betraying their country, and received their due punishment when the war ended (cf. p. 211).

In a famous song of the postwar period, the poet Jacques Prévert alludes to couples formed in dramatic circumstances of this kind: "Barbara ... What has become of you now / Under this rain of iron / Of fire, of steel and blood / And the one who held you in his arms / Lovingly / Is he dead, disappeared or still alive?"

1941

NEW YORK. **After some short, unhappy affairs with the writer Samuel Beckett, the painter Yves Tanguy and other artists, the American heiress Peggy Guggenheim finds her mission in life when she opens a modern art gallery in London. She fell deeply in love with a handsome German Jewish painter, Max Ernst (cf. p. 111), who was struggling for a living in France. She helped him leave Marseilles for New York and took him as her husband. In 1942, she opened the Art of this Century gallery in New York, a meeting place for celebrities and talented young artists, where she continued her work of patronage. Max Ernst soon left her for the young painter Dorothea Tanning, with whom he lived happily in Arizona, then in Paris from 1952. Peggy Guggenheim, who went to live in Venice in 1947, never got over being abandoned by Max Ernst, despite subsequent affairs with Marcel Duchamp and others.**

Katharine Hepburn
& Spencer Tracy

The discreet love affair of two legendary stars of the silver screen.

They clash, then make up, in George Cukor's film, *Adam's Rib*.

When Katharine Hepburn, then under contract to MGM, read the screenplay of *Woman of the Year*, in which she was to star, she immediately thought of Spencer Tracy as the man most suited to play the male lead. She had never met him, but had admired his Oscar winning performances in such films as *Captains Coura-geous* and *Boys' Town*. Tracy, an intelligent and cultivat-ed man, had not seen any of Hepburn's films but, on viewing one of her earlier performances, judged her a "damned good actress". This was followed by a chance

John Ford, and the millionaire businessman Howard Hughes.

Son of a middle-class family from Milwaukee, Wis-consin, in 1923 Spencer Tracy had married the actress Louise Treadwell. She gave up her career to look after the elder of their two children, John, born deaf, and to set up a special clinic. Even though he was separated from her, Tracy – a Catholic – never divorced his wife and remained very close to his family. He had a tempes-tuous affair with the actress Loretta Young. A notorious

1942

BRAZIL. **On 22 February, learning of the fall of Singapore, which seems to portend Allied defeat in the Pacific, Stefan and Lotte Zweig poison them-selves. They were found dead on their bed in each other's arms, in their house at Petropolis, to which they had retired af-ter years of wandering. "The world whose lan-guage I speak has disappeared," he wrote in a farewell message, "and Europe, my spiritual homeland, has destroyed itself ... I bid farewell to all my friends. May they live to see the dawn after the long night! For my part, I am too impatient; I go before them." In 1934, having a premonition of the barbarism to come, the great Austrian writer fled his native land. In 1936, he met Lotte Altman, who became his secretary; after divorcing his first wife, he married Altman in 1939. It was in Brazil that he wrote his final master-piece,** *The Royal Game,* **and his autobiography,** *Yesterday's World.*

meeting at Hollywood. He was forty-two, she thirty-three. To make an impression on men, Hepburn, who was 5' 7", would wear platform shoes. "I'm afraid I'm a little tall for you, Mr Tracy," she said, even though he was 5' 10". "Don't worry, Miss Hepburn," he replied, "I'll soon cut you down to my size!" The taming of the shrew had begun: "I knew immediately," she confided, "that I would find him irresistible."

Born in Hartford, Connecticut in 1909, of a wealthy, free-thinking, middle-class family, Katharine Hepburn decided as an adolescent that she would not have children. She contracted a marriage of conve-nience with an insurance broker, Ludlow Ogden Smith, "her best friend", as she claimed, but did not live with him and obtained a divorce in 1934. A big, bony girl with freckles, most at home in baggy trousers and slop-py pullovers, she had decided to be an actress, despite her tomboyish, athletic figure, at a time when the fash-ion was for well-padded women. In 1932, she made *A Bill of Divorcement*, her first film with George Cukor, who became her favourite director, and the following year she was awarded the first of her four Oscars. Dazzling, sophisticated, independent, she had affairs with the theatrical agent Leland Hayward, the director

alcoholic, when shooting a film he would sometimes disappear for several hours, or even days at a time.

HUMOUR AND TENDERNESS. During the making of *Woman of the Year* (a film inspired by the life of journal-ist Dorothy Thompson, cf. p. 141), Katharine Hepburn changed beyond all recognition: giving and receiving love, she shone with a new femininity and even began wearing elegant trouser suits. While the film's spectacu-lar success launched their screen career, they exercised great discretion in pursuing their private relationship. For the sake of Tracy's wife, they never appeared in pub-lic together. This secrecy was perfectly in accord with Hepburn's independent temperament. According to their friend, the scriptwriter Garson Kanin, their rela-tionship was based on "mutual respect, admiration for one another's talents, generosity on both sides, a total lack of possessiveness, and, above all, a gloriously shared sense of humour". This is confirmed by Hep-burn: "What was it about him that fascinated me? A fab-ulous sense of humour."

They lived simply, with great tenderness for each other. When he was making a film, she would take him to the studio and, at the end of the day, drive him to her house; she would prepare dinner, then take him home again. They shared the same simple tastes: weekend walks along the seashore, flying kites, and painting. To distance him from his drinking companions, she would invite a few close friends. Sometimes she would fetch him from a bar in the early hours, take him home, and soothe away his hangover. Always loyal and courageous, she served him as chauffeur, secretary and nurse, and remained a constant companion.

WATCHING OVER HIM. They both pursued their own careers, but she always looked for scripts that would enable them to act together. Between 1942 and 1950, they made six films, including *State of the Union* (1948), Capra's last great classic. However, the male role was always predominant; it was not until *Adam's Rib* (1949), specially written by Garson Kanin and Ruth Gordon, and directed by Cukor, that they achieved a balance. The great success of the film coincided with a difficult phase in their relationship: Hepburn chose to fight against McCarthyism, while Tracy held that actors should not get involved in politics. Also, he would not tolerate her attempts to stop his drinking. Ravaged by alcoholism,

bloated, his sandy hair prematurely white, he was now playing father figures, while she had reached a confident maturity. In the 1950s they were apart for long periods: in 1951 she made *The African Queen* in the Belgian Congo; in 1955 she toured Australia with the London-based Old Vic Theatre Company. Tracy suffered greatly as a result. His drinking increased, and while he was still popular with the public, his health deteriorated. They made another two films together, *Pat and Mike* (1952), a Kanin-Gordon-Cukor joint venture, and *Desk Set* (1957).

To look after him, she declined all engagements after 1962. They made one last film together, *Guess Who's Coming to Dinner?*, by Stanley Kramer (cf. p. 306). Shortly before its release, in June 1967, Tracy died of a heart attack. Katherine Hepburn did not attend the funeral. On receiving her Oscar she preferred to imagine, as she said, that it had been awarded to them both. She continued her brilliant career, enjoying enormous popularity in the United States. The screen duo she formed with Spencer Tracy remains the stuff of legend. *Me*, her autobiography, gives a sensitive account of their great love affair.

♡ ♡ ♡

ANGUISH
Love Letters

Lovers write when they are apart. Letters feed the heart, express the anguish of absence and keep hope alive.

"Of course, I miss your arms around me, but we knew from the beginning that we each had a mission to fulfil." The young American receiving this letter knew where his duty lay. During those terrible years, in most countries of the world, men fought and women contributed to the war effort. Lovers forced to live apart wrote to one another (cf. p. 198). They lived in hope of receiving a letter, which would help them to continue the struggle. Mailing a letter was a sign of life: I write, therefore I am. Receiving a letter had a calming effect: he or she is writing, therefore I am.

Take the example of Bill Cook and Helen Appleton, who got engaged in England in 1942. Immediately separated by the war, they could not marry until 1945. During the three-and-a-half years of their

separation, they wrote a record six thousand letters!

As well as letters, lovers sent poems, dried flowers, parcels, air letters and telegrams. Though they might write every day, like the American novelist Carson McCullers and her husband Reeve, it was not necessarily in reply to an earlier letter received. Postal services were irregular and letters sometimes went astray. Sending words of love and comfort was like entrusting a message in a bottle to the sea, not knowing if it would ever reach its destination. Letters reflected fear, loneliness, and the pain of separation. It was pure anguish to live in ignorance of the other's fate, writing when the loved one might have been killed in battle or during an air raid! On the other hand, if a soldier was wounded, it could mean the hope of his being invalided home.

While many men were risking their lives, making history and having interesting experiences to write

home about, the daily lot of women was anything but exciting. A good wife was expected to say how much she missed her man, but not to make it sound as if her life had dried up. "Everything in my life," wrote Simone de Beauvoir to Jean-Paul Sartre (cf. p. 234), while he was a prisoner of war, "I live to tell you, so it can enrich your life a little." The couple's correspondence, so full of daily details, shows them turned in on themselves and indifferent to the war. What a contrast with the stirring letters of such heroes as the French Resistance fighter Boris Vildé, who wrote to his wife before facing the firing squad in 1942: "I am surrounded by your love, by our love which is stronger than death ... The eternal sun of love rises from the abyss of death."

I LOVE YOU, I AM THINKING OF YOU, I MISS YOU. At the end of the twentieth century, even though the *billet doux* has to some extent been replaced by the telephone call or cassette, the letter – described by Victor Hugo as "a kiss sent through the post" – remains part of the ritual of love, and not just for professional writers. Madeleine Renaud and Jean-Louis Barrault (cf. p. 217), for instance, kept up a daily correspondence for fifty years. The joy of renewed presence often obviates the need for letters and, when a couple normally live together, periods of separation are the only occasion for writing. This is why many love letters express a lament, a sadness, and conclude with the hope of reunion. Even if the writer makes elaborate plans or engages in flights of fancy, what he or she says is born of a sense of emptiness which the silent outpouring of words attempts to fill. To combat their loneliness, each draws on the common fund of memory, recalling the events which led to their union: their first meeting, first confession of love, the first obstacle to be overcome, and so on. All these episodes, seemingly trivial to others, constitute their personal treasure, the secret bond between them. Their litany of love has a charm which may mean nothing to outsiders.

For Roland Barthes, a love letter contains "just one piece of information: I am thinking of you. I have nothing to tell you, except that I am writing this nothing to you." Even though its purpose is to express one's most intimate feelings, the love letter is also a literary genre with a long history, with rules and conventions which change from age to age. According to Raymond Radiguet, it is the least epistolary form, because "all you need is love". But lovers often lack self-confidence when the discovery of strong feelings reveals their heart and are afraid to give free reign to their imagination. If speaking of love is sometimes difficult, especially for men (cf. p. 152), writing about it is even more so. Lovers are steeped in conventional vocabulary: the words

Japanese Love Letters, number 8, Erró.

of popular songs, the captions on postcards (cf. p. 26), the kind of dialogue used in films and novels. If they have doubts about how to behave, speak or write, they sometimes fall back on borrowed models, such as the specimen love letters found in books on etiquette. As a result, each period tends to exhibit a certain uniformity of style, from the "floods of tears" and passionate pledges of the eighteenth century to the more direct declarations of our own day.

At one time, those lacking education could use the services of a public scribe, a traditional practice described by Gabriel García Márquez in *Love in the Time of Cholera*. When one is not sure of one's own powers of expression, there is a great temptation to borrow, without admitting it, the eloquence of another. But there is also the risk of being found out, as in Edmond Rostand's play, *Cyrano de Bergerac*, or in William Dieterle's film *Love Letters* (1945).

Giving and receiving love is a form of exchange. Even death need

not put a stop to the dialogue, and some widows continue to write to the man they love, such as Marie Curie (cf. p. 37), or the eighty-year-old Japanese woman whose husband never returned from the Chinese campaign. In a collection of "beautiful love letters", successfully published in Japan in 1995, we find these touching lines: "Already half a century from the day when my eyes followed you for the last time, our child on my back waving the national flag. I would like to be able to fall asleep in your arms again. Never let go of my hand!"

NEW YORK. **First meeting of two American painters, at a collective exhibition to which they had contributed work. Lee Krasner was attracted to Jackson Pollock's painting by its "force, a living force". All her life, she kept the canvas he exhibited on that occasion, entitled *Birth*. They married in 1945, but remained childless. They shared a workshop, then, having moved to the country, she painted in an upstairs bedroom while he took over the barn. One of the foremost practitioners of Abstract Expressionism or Action Painting, Pollock was one of the century's major painters. Each influenced the work of the other. Following Pollock's death, in 1956 in a car accident, she continued to develop as an artist, showing great inventiveness, but achieved recognition only belatedly, as most of the critics persisted in seeing her merely as "Pollock's widow".**

Lucie & Raymond Aubrac

They loved and fought together: a fearless couple of Resistance fighters.

Seduced then rejected, a girl from a respectable family demands reparation for the affront to her honour. The man she is accusing has been held in prison for the last three months by the Gestapo. No problem! Thanks to her coolness, the pregnant young Frenchwoman who invented this story obtained permission from the German officer to marry her cowardly seducer before his execution. After several attempts, on 21 October 1943, when prisoners were being moved from one location to another, she organised an armed coup and managed to free the man she loved, along with other detainees. The man in question was Raymond Samuel, alias Aubrac, who had been arrested together with the national Resistance leader, Jean Moulin.

Although the story she told the Germans was untrue, her pregnancy was not. Lucie Bernard, aged thirty-one, and Raymond Samuel, twenty-nine, had been married since 1939, and already had a son, Jean-Pierre, born in 1941. They first met in Strasbourg in 1938: she was a young graduate teacher of history; he was doing his military service after completing his studies with distinction at the Ecole des Ponts et Chaussés (national school of civil engineering). He had studied in the United States and she was about to go there, so they decided to get married on her return. But the day before her departure, the war broke out. He was called up; she unpacked her trunk. They were married on 14 December 1939. "I was entitled to ten days' leave," he remembered with a smile. After the French defeat, Raymond was held prisoner in Germany, while Lucie sought refuge in Brittany. Finally, she received a postcard from him, which she then kept through all her adventures. After helping him escape for the first time they went to live in Lyon, where she worked as a teacher, he as an engineer.

Each had decided independently "not to leave France in the hands of Pétain, the 'Vichy clique' and the Nazis". In 1936, she had taken part in the election campaign of the Socialist Jean Zay. In the earliest days of the Resistance, she, Jean Cavaillès, and Emmanuel d'Astier de la Vigerie founded the Liberation group, whose name had been suggested by Raymond. Their first activities were relatively modest: graffiti, writing, distributing leaflets, and publishing the clandestine newspaper *Libération*. Gradually the Resistance became more organised. Ostensibly, the Samuels lived the life of a young couple with a child; under the pseudonyms Aubrac and Catherine, they engaged in intensive clandestine activity and held important positions in the Comité National de la Résistance (CNR). "For both of us, our commitment always grew out of our understanding as a couple," wrote Lucie Aubrac in *Ils partiront dans l'ivresse* (1984), in which she recounts the ups and downs of this double life – the missions and responsibilities, the times Raymond was arrested, and their love, which stood the test and emerged all the stronger.

Their luck, too, it seemed. On three occasions, Lucie helped her husband to escape, without ever being arrested herself. After his last and most spectacular escape from prison in Lyon, they went into hiding for some months, until the Resistance could get them to England. Two days after their arrival in London, in February 1944, Lucie gave birth to a daughter, whom they named Catherine, her mother's *nom de guerre*. They had another daughter, Elisabeth, in August 1946.

AN OUTSTANDING COUPLE. "Without the war," said Lucie Aubrac, "I do not know if our marriage would have lasted. I was independent-minded; I hated housework. But the war welded us together." Whereas many marriages broke up during that tormented period, theirs was strengthened. "Physical desire and sexual pleasure are vital if love is to last," she explained. Faithfulness was, for her, the corollary, and both of them saw esteem and respect as essential aspects of their marriage.

Did their life continue on a similar course once peace was restored? Yes, in the sense that they continued to fight fascism wherever it reared its ugly head and became involved in the anti-colonial movement. After the Liberation, Raymond, whose work brought him into contact with the Far East, cared for Indo-Chinese interned in France, and played an important part in relations with Vietnam and Ho Chi Minh, who stayed with them while the Fontainebleau agreement was being negotiated in 1947. He then organised an association set up to educate Vietnamese children and, much later, a foreign aid organisation. Lucie, having tried publishing a women's magazine, *Privilège de femmes*, was torn between political activity and her profession and family life. In 1943, she had been the only woman appointed by the Mouvements Unis de Résistance (MUR) to take part in the Algiers consultative assembly as a representative of the Resistance on the home front; but she opted to let her husband take her place.

She decided to return to teaching and, passionate about education, taught in an experimental school. In 1958, the Aubracs moved to Morocco, where Raymond worked in rural development. From 1963 to 1975, they were in Rome, where he worked at the FAO, while Lucie, as a teacher at the *lycée français*, was able to indulge her enthusiasm for Etruscan archaeology.

LOOKING TO THE FUTURE. The Aubracs continued to be valiant fighters, not afraid to make their views known publicly. Disappointed by an absence of women on the political scene, Lucie became, as she wrote, "more and more feminist". Always looking to the future, the Aubracs refused to be known simply as former Resistance fighters. They did know a few couples who had been engaged in the struggle against the Nazis but, as they put it, "many Resistance fighters do not show off about it". Another couple as exceptional as the Aubracs were the Lefaucheux, who both performed important functions in the Parisian resistance. Pierre was chief of armed forces until his arrest in June 1944, while Marie-

1943

FRANCE. **The composer Olivier Messiaen writes *Visions of Amen* for two pianos with his pupil at the Conservatory, pianist Yvonne Loriod. He had been appointed professor there on his return from captivity in 1942. Messiaen and Loriod were in love, but their relationship could not be openly avowed: he was a fervent Catholic and already married to the cellist Claire Delbos, with whom he had a son. A brilliant performer and for many years the only exponent of his piano works, Yvonne Loriod inspired and assisted him all his life. In his celebrations of human love, the composer tried to free himself, through music, of his sense of guilt. The song cycle *Harawi* (1945), the *Five Songs for Choir* (1949) and the *Turangalîla-Symphony* (1949), his masterpiece, were, for him, "the three acts of a great *Tristan and Isolde*". Claire Delbos died in 1959; Olivier Messiaen and Yvonne Loriod married in 1961.**

♡ ♡ ♡

Lucie Aubrac was the heroine of an American comic strip, *Lucie to the Rescue.*

Hélène was the only female member of the Paris Liberation Committee. In other marriages – that of Henri and Cécile Rol-Tanguy for example – the woman played the equally dangerous but more traditionally feminine role of courier.

What makes the Aubracs so attractive is Raymond's pride in his wife, and the total absence of jealousy between them. Their secret? "She helped me to live," he said of Lucie. "Our marriage," he wrote in his autobiography, "was, and still is, happy and founded on a deep sense of sharing: there is no important decision which we do not take together."

♡ ♡ ♡

Fifteen Soviet Brides Condemned for Falling in Love

Mixed couples against the State: fourteen tragedies and one miracle.

Of the British soldiers sent to the Soviet Union in 1943 to take part in the struggle against Germany, several fell in love with Soviet women, but their story had a tragic ending. Some worked in Moscow, like Alfred Hall. While on secondment to the British embassy, he met Clara, a teacher's daughter, one evening at the Bolshoi Ballet. There was also William Greenhold, a sailor whose ship brought essential supplies to the northern port of Archangel, where he made the acquaintance of Choura Racheva. In all, fifteen of these liaisons resulted in marriage, duly authorised by the authorities of both countries in October 1945. But things began to go wrong almost immediately. The couples were cruelly separated, and most of them did not even have the opportunity to spend their wedding night together because the husbands were refused leave.

The war ended and the young British servicemen left the country, sick at heart, because they had to leave their young brides behind them, waiting for exit visas. Tears, heartbreak, promises: "I'll wait for you all my life, if need be." They took the train for Leningrad, then the boat for London. Their wives remained in Moscow. Nobody was in any doubt but that they would be given visas: it was a matter of weeks, said their menfolk; months, replied the wives, who were more familiar with Soviet bureaucracy. All they could do was wait, hope, and write.

personal; it had become a state matter. Their visas could not be issued without the consent of Stalin himself and, at a time when NATO was coming into being, he used them as bargaining chips in his negotiations with the United Kingdom, attempting to extort commercial and diplomatic concessions. The British For-

REASONS OF STATE. As the months stretched into years, the husbands kept up a barrage of agitation but, despite press campaigns, sympathetic British public opinion, and the support of their MPs, nothing happened. The only change was the birth of a son, Nicholas, to Clara and Alfred Hall. In 1946, eight of the wives were lodged and employed at the British embassy. The problem they posed was not merely eign Secretary, Ernest Bevin, did not see it this way. As far as he was concerned, the matter was not of great strategic importance: here were just "a few pretty girls who had married British servicemen". The husbands had been sworn to silence but, in early 1947, they could stand it no longer. At the time of an international conference being held in London, they unfurled a banner: "Give us back our Soviet wives".

22 January 1948. Four of the fifteen British servicemen whose Soviet wives were held prisoner behind the Iron Curtain, went to the House of Lords to plead their cause. Alfred Hall (middle, wearing hat) was the only one who would see his wife again.

The press campaign they unleashed forced Bevin to approach Stalin, but it was too late: the Cold War had already begun. Bevin left it to his subordinates to placate the husbands. "You have our profound sympathy; we are doing all in our power" – such was the official line.

CONDEMNED TO DIVORCE. During this time, some of the wives were still sheltering at the British embassy in Moscow, where their husbands were not allowed to visit them. They helped one another and lived on hope, dreaming of "escaping through the sewers or flying like birds". The ambassador would have liked to get rid of these troublesome employees, who created a permanent tension in the daily life of the embassy. In June 1948, he asked them to divorce and told them they would now have to manage on their own. Once it was clear that they were of no more interest to the West, the Soviet machine of repression went to work. Choura Greenhold, who had left Archangel for Moscow, was the first to be summoned by the secret police and imprisoned. She was sentenced to ten years' forced labour in Siberia for residing illegally in Moscow, and left with these words: "Tell Bill I love him and will never forget him." Over the following months, police pressure broke nine of the wives: they agreed to divorce, but, even so, seven of them were condemned to labour camps in Siberia.

This left five determined women, who, refusing to divorce, camped in the embassy. In July 1950, one of them, Lolia, was kidnapped, taken to the Loubianka prison and tortured. For her faithfulness to John Burke, she was sentenced to twenty-five years' forced labour and deported to a camp inside the Arctic Circle. Despite pressure of every kind, she refused to divorce. Each year her husband sent her a telegram for their wedding anniversary, but the embassy claimed not to know her whereabouts and she never received them. The husbands who stubbornly continued to write to the two governments now received one and the same answer: your wife has disappeared. One after the another, the wives had in fact vanished, kidnapped or arrested, except for Clara Hall. Fearing the same fate, she decided never again to leave the embassy compound, where she lived with her son. Thus she survived, a voluntary recluse, until the day in the summer of 1953 when she was summoned by the new ambassador. "I've got your visa," he announced.

The miracle is easily explained: Stalin had died in March. The new Soviet strongman, Malenkov, wanted to make a friendly gesture to the West. After seven years, Clara Hall was at last free to take the plane with her son, free to be reunited with her husband. She was not without apprehension, however: would they not have changed? It was her son who helped to smooth the way: she had always told him about the father he had never known and shown him photographs of him. When the plane doors opened, he recognised him and ran towards him shouting "Daddy!"

Why her? One wonders why was she the only one of the fifteen Soviet wives to come through. Perhaps it was because she was more educated, the most determined, and the only one with a child. She has since had three more, and lives happily with her British husband. And the other couples? Victims of fate, broken lives …

1943

HOLLYWOOD. A sensational marriage between the glamorous redhead Rita Hayworth and Orson Welles, director of *Citizen Kane*. Their daughter, Rebecca, was born in 1944. Timid and anxious, the "love goddess" of the film *Gilda* (1946) admired her husband but found life with a genius exhausting. They decided to divorce while they were making *The Lady from Shanghai* (1948), one of the best detective films ever. To impose his style, he made her cut her hair and have It dyed blond. After their divorce, Rita Hayworth was briefly married to the billionaire Ali Khan. Orson Welles lived with the Yugoslav sculptress Oja Kodar.

BERLIN. On 27 February, 10,000 men, Jewish or half-Jewish, are arrested and held in a transit camp. "Aryan" women – their mothers or wives – protest for several days at the gates of the camp on the Rosenstrasse.

♡ ♡ ♡

Clara Hall with her son Nicky at the airport, shortly after being reunited with her husband.

Humphrey Bogart & Lauren Bacall

A legendary couple who made four outstanding films and enjoyed twelve years of happiness together.

The screen kiss that sealed the couple's real-life relationship (*To Have or Have Not*).

FACING PAGE
Happy family.

HOLLYWOOD. **Smash hit for Vincente Minnelli's film** Meet Me in St Louis, **starring Judy Garland. She was twenty-two at the time, Minnelli forty-one. They married in June 1945. In his autobiography, Minnelli recalls the ceremony, which was attended by their producer, Louis B. Mayer. At the moment when, following American tradition, the priest handed a wooden stick to the bride and groom, Mayer grabbed hold of it, thus giving his own approval! The couple's only child, Liza, was born on 12 March 1946. A brilliant writer of musical comedies, Minnelli cast his wife in three other films:** The Clock, Ziegfeld Follies, **and** The Pirate. **Unstable and miserable, Judy Garland attempted suicide in 1950; they were divorced the following year. She triumphed in Cukor's** A Star Is Born **(1954), but succumbed to depression and alcoholism in 1969.**

QUEBEC. **The Catholic Church organises preparatory classes for couples intending to get married. Some chapters of the handbook, dealing with human anatomy and what is "permitted and forbidden in marriage", were presented with a solemn warning: "You may not in good conscience communicate ...**

"If you want anything, just whistle!" This line by Lauren Bacall to Humphrey Bogart in *To Have or Have Not* was a defining moment in their relationship. On their wedding day, a few months later, Bogart gave her a gold whistle!

In March 1943, director Howard Hawks found the leading lady he was looking for, photographed by Louise Dahl-Wolfe for the cover of *Harper's Bazaar*: Betty Perske, a nineteen-year-old model with chestnut hair and splendid green eyes. Attracted by her charm and deep voice, Hawks signed her up. She took the stage name Bacall, after her mother, who had raised her single-handedly.

As Lauren Bacall, she made her debut in the film inspired by Hemingway's novel, which Hawks shot in 1944. By her own account, it was nerves that made her lower her chin to her chest to look up at the camera – an attitude that became her trademark and earned her the nickname "The Look".

Starting her acting career in the role of an insolent adventuress opposite Humphrey Bogart, who was twenty-five years her senior, was quite a challenge for an inexperienced girl. Just before the whistle episode, for instance, the heroine has to take the initiative of kissing her partner, to find out, "if he would like it".

Bogart, after playing a series of gangsters and private detectives, had achieved stardom in John Huston's *Maltese Falcon* (1941), then Michael Curtiz's *Casablanca* (1942). With his tightly belted trench coat and turned-down trilby, he played the cynic who falls for a pretty girl. Opposite him, Bacall epitomised the new woman,

confident and unattached. Elusive and mysterious, she seemed to conceal a passionate nature beneath her elegant exterior. They made only four films together, each a masterpiece of American cinema: two with Hawks (including *The Big Sleep*, 1946, based on the story by Raymond Chandler), then *Dark Passage* (1947) with Delmer Daves, and *Key Largo* (1948) with John Huston.

THE IDEAL COUPLE. There was nothing "tough" about Bogart in real life: he was tender, restrained and strict in his morals. As soon as they began shooting *To Have or Have Not*, they fell in love, like the characters they were impersonating. For Bacall, who had never known her father, "Bogie" was something of a father figure; he always called her "baby". Bogged down in a third marriage, which again had turned out badly, he wrote her poignant letters: "You are my last love, I will love you till the end of my days, I will watch over you and will always be there to support you."

When he had obtained a divorce, they got married – on 21 May 1945. At his request, she put her career on the back burner, giving priority to the man she was so madly in love with. In her own words: "He was my whole life and I could think of nothing else." She went with him when he was on location abroad, for instance to Africa to shoot *The African Queen*. They were apart only once, for three months in 1953, when she was making *How to Marry a Millionaire*, and he was in Italy for another film.

They were one of the most celebrated couples of the

post-war years, on film and in real life. Bogart had no children from his earlier marriages. Now they had two: Stephen, born in 1948, and Leslie, born in 1952. They lived happily, surrounded by friends such as the Hawks, and Spencer Tracy and Katharine Hepburn.

Success did not blind them to the world's problems. Bogart had already shown courage, enlisting in the navy during the First World War; the scar on his lip was a souvenir. Bacall, meanwhile, was not afraid to mention her Jewish background and her liberal political views. In 1947, when Senator McCarthy began his anti-Communist witch-hunt, they did not stand idly by, but went to Washington and attended the sessions of the senatorial committee tasked with investigating the "Marxist infiltration of Hollywood". They were on the committee set up to protest against abuses of power, organised demonstrations, and petitioned the administration. Despite their efforts, celebrities were imprisoned, reputations destroyed, lives ruined.

While Bogart's career flourished – he played more vulnerable or sentimental heroes, as in *The Barefoot Contessa* or *The Harder They Fall* – Lauren Bacall was offered only the occasional part. She tended to be regarded as "Bogart's wife".

MORE THAN "BOGIE'S WIDOW". In 1956, just as they were preparing to make a film together, Bogart's health deteriorated. After months of suffering, he died of cancer on 14 January 1957. "Bogie had been my reason for living," she wrote. "Was I nothing on my own?"

In 1957, she played a distinguished part in *Written on the Wind*, by Douglas Sirk, and another in Vincente Minnelli's *Designing Women*, followed by several minor films. She did a lot more stage acting and, in 1970, received a "Tony" award for *Applause*, a musical comedy by John Axelrod. She maintained her political commitment and, in 1952, supported Democratic candidate Adlai Stevenson in his bid for the presidency; in 1968, she was a close supporter of Robert Kennedy. She refused to live in the shadow of her late husband, who had become something of a mythical figure. "Being Bogie's widow is not a profession," she wrote in her autobiography, which she entitled *By Myself*. After a brief affair with Frank Sinatra, she married actor Jason Robards in 1961, with whom she had a son, Sam. They divorced in 1969.

"I often think of Bogie. We made a great couple." He had helped her discover a zest for life and the meaning of work. All her life, she tried to follow the advice he had given her: "Never lose your self-respect!"

♡ ♡ ♡

SOCIETY
GIs: Overpaid, Oversexed and Over Here

Embraced by girls everywhere. The war: deaths, encounters, new love affairs.

On 6 June 1944, 132,000 American, Canadian and British soldiers landed in Normandy. Fighting every inch of the way and suffering heavy losses, they advanced through France and on into Nazi Germany, which capitulated on 8 May 1945. In the liberated towns and cities they were met with frenetic enthusiasm; laying aside all inhibitions, delirious girls and young women climbed onto the tanks and threw themselves into the arms of their "liberators". It was a time of celebration, a mad interlude after the long, dark years. Everywhere, an explosion of joy greeted these brave young foreigners. Well equipped and well fed, they shared their rations of chocolate, chewing-gum

and Camel cigarettes.

Amid the jubilation, love blossomed and marriages were planned, particularly with American soldiers, known as GIs from the initials on their equipment (Government Issue). From 1942 to 1945,

three million GIs were stationed in France, Italy, which had been cut in half since the September 1943 armistice, and above all Britain. They offered good prospects, and their country was seen as a land of plenty, a land spared invasion and air raids. In all, 120,000 European girls married GIs. The American law governing marriages of this type did not specify the sex of the foreigner concerned: if a man married an American servicewoman, he automatically became a "war bride", even if he was a British officer – the fate of Cary Grant in Howard Hawks's irresistibly funny film, *I Was a Male War Bride*.

In 1946, Eleanor Roosevelt (cf. p. 162), asked about fraternisation between GIs and foreign women, replied: "A soldier should return home and wait. Passion is not a good counsellor. When he gets back to a normal pattern of life, then he can think of getting engaged." This remark was made mainly with German women in mind: marriages between German women and Americans were forbidden up to 1947. In the following decades, the presence of Allied military bases in Germany, and American bases in France, offered many opportunities for "mixed" relationships.

It was often difficult for "war brides" to adapt to their new country, especially if they had to overcome the language barrier. *Frieda*, a film by Basil Dearden (1947), shows the prejudice faced by the German wife of an RAF officer when she comes to live in a small English town, despite the fact that, as a nurse, she had helped her husband escape from a POW camp. Similarly, young European women arriving in the United States or Canada often faced a rude awakening when their dreams foundered on the reefs of everyday reality.

LOVE YOUR ENEMY. When German-occupied countries such as France, Denmark or the Netherlands were finally liberated, the mob often went on the rampage. As if to avenge the offence to national virility, violence was unleashed against women who had "fraternised with the enemy", which in the case of women had a clear sexual meaning. Thousands of women throughout Europe were publicly shorn of their hair and insulted as "German whores". Because of liaisons with German officers, several celebrities ended up in prison after the war, like the actress Arletty, or were driven into temporary exile, as in the case of fashion designer Gabrielle Chanel. But what crime had they committed in loving a German, whom they had embraced as a man and not an enemy?

Whereas love was accepted between nationals of allied countries, as long as politics did not intrude (cf. p. 206 for events in the Soviet Union), it was disapproved of between "enemies". The point is well

made by actor Richard Bohringer, born in 1941 of a Parisian woman and a young German officer. His father was subsequently sent to the Russian front, and his mother joined him in Germany after the war.

Relationships between prisoners, whether married or not, and "enemy" nurses or local women were not judged by the same standard, as though male "sexual needs" deserved greater indulgence. Similarly, young Frenchmen who seduced German auxiliaries, known as "grey mice" due to the colour of their uniform, were not seen as traitors, but as heroes who had "fucked Hitler"!

FIFTY MILLION DEAD. Although the war provided innumerable occasions for people to meet and fall in love, its main effect was to spread misery. In November 1944, at the annual celebration of All Souls' Day in Germany, the pastor read out the names of the young men who had died – sons, brothers, fiancés. According to Countess Dönhoff: "The young women had dyed their confirmation dresses black; their mothers said that white would never be needed again."

How many women waited for a man who never returned, as in Henri Colpi's fine film, *Une aussi longue absence*, with Alida Valli! In all, the war claimed 50 million lives world-wide, half of them civilians. Millions of married or marriageable women were left to face life alone, especially in the Soviet Union and Germany. In the Soviet Union a new rite emerged: on their wedding day, the bridal couple would lay a bunch of flowers on the tomb of an unknown soldier. Having survived years at the front or in camps, men – and some women – made their way home, on foot, by bicycle, by train or lorry. Of the 2.5 million who returned to France, 40,000 were survivors of the death camps.

Some were all alone in the world, their families destroyed. For others, there were problems of rehabilitation, as after the First World War (cf. p. 104). Some husbands had been reported dead and their wives had remarried. Others found an additional child in their household, or learned by an anonymous letter that their wife had had an affair. Such was the drama of the parents of the German Günter Guillaume (future private secretary to Chancellor Willy Brandt and an East-German police spy): when his father, returning from a British internment camp in 1948, found his wife living with another man, he committed suicide.

Some couples had promised to marry but could not find their loved one after the war, such as Philippus Dierijck from Rotterdam and Janet Münsch from Belfort, who had met in 1944 in Stuttgart. He had been obliged to work in Germany; she survived Ravensbrück. They were finally reunited and married in 1992! "For me," he said with a smile, "Janet is still nineteen!"

1944

... this course to others." Although "birth control" was described as "satanic", the course explained the Ogino method, which might be used without sin in certain circumstances.

FRANCE. Before his execution by the Nazis on 23 February, the French Resistance fighter of Armenian origin, Missak Manoukian, writes a letter to his wife Mélinée saying he feels "no hatred for the German people". "Get married," he tells her, "and have a child who will honour my memory", before signing off: "Your friend, your comrade, your husband."

♡ ♡ ♡

Scenes of joy during the Liberation of Paris (late August 1944).

Benjamin Britten & Peter Pears

A great British composer and the singer who inspired him. The closest of companions, united in their love of music.

"He who despises us / We will destroy," sings the choir in *Peter Grimes*, and the conformist crowd eventually does get the better of the hero, a proud outsider who commits suicide. It was 7 June 1945 when Benjamin Britten's first opera was performed before a London audience. The triumph of the tenor Peter Pears in the title role, written especially for him, eased the controversy surrounding the couple. Not only had composer and performer been conscientious objectors during the war; rumours were also rife as to the nature of their relationship.

Britten was one of the century's great composers. Although he made his name with operas such as *Albert Herring* (1947), *Billy Budd* (1951) and *The Turn of the Screw* (1954), he also wrote symphonies, concertos, cantatas, and a splendid message of peace, the *War Requiem* (1962).

Friendship was a vital part of his creative life: he was very close to his librettists, including the writer E. M. Forster, and the poet W. H. Auden. But Pears was more than a friend, more than the ideal performer of his works and a constant source of inspiration: he was his

alter ego, and the love of his life. When they first met in April 1937, the tenor, an open, warm-hearted man of twenty-seven, was a member of the BBC choir and also sang solo. Britten, with his thick wavy hair, was three years his junior. From middle-class families, they were both homosexual, and both discreet in their individual affairs. Although the scandalous trial of Oscar Wilde (1895) was by now a distant memory, homosexuality was still considered an ignominious perversion. Corrupted innocence is one of the main themes of Britten's operas, which describe a frustrating relationship between a man and a young boy that ends in renunciation or death. This desire tormented him all his life: his diary expresses a sense of guilt, springing from his attraction to young boys. According to several of their friends, the fact that these feelings were never consummated was a factor in the stability of his relationship with Pears.

Initially, the friendship which sprang up between Britten and Pears was not sexual in nature. They were soon sharing a flat, but each kept his independence, his own friends, and liaisons. Both were left-wing pacifists: their first recital together – at Cambridge in late 1937 –

Benjamin Britten and Peter Pears, by Kenneth Green, 1943.

was in aid of the Spanish Republicans. Pears sang and Britten accompanied him on the piano.

MY OTHER HALF. In April 1939, they left Europe, where the storm clouds were gathering, and set sail for the United States. In June, finding its sexual expression, an exceptionally happy and creative relationship began. "It is heaven to hear his voice," wrote Britten, now inspired by the tones which, he said, were like those of his own mother.

When war was declared, they decided to stay in the United States, where they gave recitals. Pears studied, Britten composed, and his work was performed to an appreciative public. He wrote his first song cycle, dedicated "To Peter": *Seven Sonnets of Michelangelo* – love poems celebrating the unity to which their two souls aspired.

In April 1942, returning to England, they were exempted from military service on condition that they gave recitals in aid of war victims. Britten was soon restored to eminence and Pears pursued a brilliant career, with a repertoire ranging from Bach to Stravinsky. Composers like Lutoslawski wrote pieces especially for him. But it was in performing Britten's work, or when Britten accompanied him, that he reached his greatest heights.

They went on many world tours and travelled widely, with a predilection for Venice, where they spent holi-

days with their friends Galina Visnevskaya and Mstislav Rostropovich (cf. p. 334). From 1947, they lived in Aldeburgh, a village on the Suffolk coast, where they organised the now famous annual music festival. As they grew older, Britten preferred to stay at home and write music, but he suffered when Pears was away on foreign engagements. The latter, who loved travelling, deplored the fact that Britten could not tear himself away from his work. The many letters they wrote attest the depths of their love: "I write each note," wrote Britten, "with your celestial voice in mind. My dear, I love you more than you can imagine. I feel incomplete in the absence of my other half." Pears afforded his "Benjie" protection and solicitude, and they supported each other in times of doubt.

Love affairs between men were becoming more common in artistic circles, for instance the relationship between the choreographer Sergei Diaghilev and the dancer Vaslav Nijinsky, the writer Marcel Proust and the musician Reynaldo Hahn, the writer Jean Cocteau and the actor Jean Marais, the choreographer Merce Cunningham and the composer John Cage, or the painters Robert Rauschenberg and Jasper Johns (cf. p. 249); but they were not always publicly acknowledged. So Britten, who was rich – he drove a Rolls-Royce – famous and a member of the establishment, was, nevertheless, always concerned to maintain a certain "decorum". Not until after his death did Pears talk about their homosexuality, though objecting to the word gay, "because it gives a false impression of a situation which is not gay at all".

CELESTIAL JOY. Illness forced Britten to reduce his activities, and in September 1972 they gave their last recital together. Almost exhausted, he composed the opera *Death in Venice*, the first performance of which, in 1973, was a triumph. The following year, when the work was first produced in New York, Pears received these words from the composer before he went on stage: "You are the greatest singer of all time. What have I done to deserve to write for an artist and man like you?" Celebrating "the celestial joy we have known together for thirty-five years", Pears replied: "But it is you who have given me everything. I am only

Benjamin Britten in 1953.

the mouthpiece for your work and I live in your music." Britten said that he should die first, for he would be lost without Pears. Rather than be buried in Westminster Abbey, he asked to rest near his friend in Aldeburgh.

He died in 1976, Pears survived him by ten years. The Aldeburgh Festival and the school of music named after them bear witness to a relationship inseparable from the love of music.

♡ ♡ ♡

MORALS
Brief Encounter

Heartbreak and renunciation: torn between love and duty, modern lovers echo the heroic accents of classical tragedy.

They met, they loved, they heard the voice of duty and separated with an aching heart. The British film *Brief*

Encounter (1945), one of the classics of the post-war era, describes the hopeless love affair between a man and a woman, each of them married. Based on a play by Noel Coward and directed by David Lean, it won the international critics' award at the first Cannes Film Festival in 1946. A tragedy of renunciation, underscored by Rachmaninov's *Second Piano Concerto*, it left its mark on a whole generation of cinemagoers, especially women, for whom adultery was for ever associated with a small station in the London suburbs, and the departure of a bus in the heart-rending finale.

We find the same unity of place

in Vittorio de Sica's film, *Stazione Termini* (1953), in which the lovers bid each other farewell in Rome's main railway station. In *Brief Encounter*, the station buffet, ringing with cheerful conversation between waitresses and customers, is the commonplace setting for the passionate ardour of Alec and Laura – ordinary, middle-class people, nei-

ther young nor particularly good-looking, played by Trevor Howard and Celia Johnson. He is a doctor, she a mother and housewife. Their story, told by Laura, who is going back over the past, is set in the period just before the war.

Laura has a comfortable home, with a maid to do the housework. Her husband is a gentle, kindly man, set in his ways, and they both appear contented. Every Thursday, she takes the train, third class, to spend the day in the nearby town. She goes shopping, borrows books from the library, goes to the cinema. She meets Alec at the station buffet, when he removes a bit of grit

from her eye. Symbolically, he enables her to see something other than her normal routine.

WILL THEY START A NEW LIFE TOGETHER? Both are vaguely dissatisfied with their settled life and partner. Alec is the same age as Laura's husband, but more youthful. When they meet the following Thursday, he rushes towards her like a young man. What does he admire in her? Her large eyes, her shyness, her smile? Her dreams are those of a teenager: she imagines herself with him on a tropical beach, at the Paris Opera, or in a gondola in Venice. She laughs at his jokes and drinks in his words when he talks of his profession, but she has nothing interesting to say.

The relationship is conventional. When they first kiss, for example, they are seated, the man in the dominant position. Suddenly he throws himself at her and kisses her passionately. In their conversation, he denies her any wider ambitions: her role is to be a home-maker. For instance, she tells him she played the piano as a child. He says she is not cut out to be a virtuoso; she protests and he explains that she looks "too sensible". To underline the point, the camera lingers on a trio of rather grotesque café musicians.

Are they "made for each other"? They long to be for a moment, then everything conspires to separate them: their family situation, their sense of duty, and their respect for social convention. Their love is impossible because they feel guilty. Rather than break up two families, they give in to reason and go their separate ways. But not to see each other while living so close together would be insufferable. Alec therefore accepts a post in South Africa. They bid farewell at the station buffet. Their adventure, more poignant than tragic, has lasted just four Thursdays. The husband has a feeling that something has deeply affected his wife, but he keeps his counsel, and remains her solid, affectionate man, calmly doing his crossword puzzles.

TITUS AND BÉRÉNICE IN OHIO. Despite their love for each other, they decide to separate: the conflict between love and duty is the theme of many heart-rending stories, in particular Racine's masterpiece, *Bérénice*, in which the Roman emperor Titus is prevented by reasons of state from marrying a foreign queen. It has inspired many operas. Like their classical counterparts, the lovers in *Brief Encounter* are not the masters of their destiny: for them, after they have been swept off their feet, honour requires its due.

Similarly, in *The Bridges of Madison County*, a novel by Robert James Waller (1992), the relationship between an Ohio farmer's wife and a passing photographer ends in poignant renunciation. This story of a married woman, who experiences a short but passionate love affair, then returns to her husband without ever disclosing what has happened to her, aroused sympathy in readers worldwide. In the subsequent film (1995), which was directed by Clint Eastwood, with himself and Meryl Streep in the leading roles, the hero is not the usual male stereotype: devoid of sexual aggression and possessiveness, he respects the gradual awakening of desire in the woman.

Here again, for four days of tremendous intensity, time stands still. Then the lovers return to their familiar routines again, their illusions lost, bidding a final farewell to youth. The hard-won insight is that

the value of keeping faith with a loving and unsuspecting partner, and children, outweighs that of a brief but intensely passionate affair. We board the train of *Brief Encounter* or take the road to Madison, dreaming of what might have been. Finding the strength to conclude the wonderful interlude also preserves the purity of the memory.

Is an encounter of this kind (cf. p. 356) the product of chance? That is how it appears in works of fiction, where it is often presented as a fateful event, forcing the protagonists to take stock of an emptiness in

them, there is an inner availability, a latent desire for change, a sensitivity to the singularity of the other, and the revelation that he or she may bring.

The encounter often acts as a shock, which leads to self-discovery. It introduces a period of inner disorder, which inevitably leads to a new awareness. For those who choose the way of duty, it leads back to the old order, after an inner upheaval, made all the more acute by secrecy. For the rest of that person's life, the "brief encounter" feeds the nostalgia that was put into words

their lives, of which they were only vaguely aware. The fact that it can happen means that, in each of

by Charles Baudelaire: "Oh, you whom I might have loved; Oh, you who knew it!"

CANADA. *By Grand Central Station I Sat Down and Wept* – a magnificent, moving text, in which a Canadian, Elizabeth Smart, describes her wanderings around New York in search of her lover, the British poet George Barker. Despising "the hatred of the mediocre for all miracles", she proclaimed her desperate adoration of an inaccessible god in a book which caused a scandal, was forgotten, then rediscovered in 1966. She wrote to him after discovering his work, and fell madly in love with him. She invited him to join her in California: he came ... with his wife, whom he loved, but immediately fell for his admirer. Smart was soon torn between her sense of guilt towards his wife "with her madonna eyes", and her suffering at having to share her lover. From then on, he came and went in her life; four children were born of their relationship.

Celia Johnson and Trevor Howard in *Brief Encounter*.

Juan & Eva Perón

In Argentina Fascism was embodied in the double smile of a paternalistic soldier and a beautiful blonde. She saw herself as the "bond of love" between the president and the people.

On 24 February 1946, Colonel Juan Domingo Perón was elected president of the Argentine Republic, and made a general. As minister of war, he had been a member of the government since the putsch of June 1943, when the pro-Fascist military had seized power. However, on 17 October 1945, he was arrested, having been forced to resign by his colleagues in the ruling junta, who resented his popularity. To obtain his release, Perón's companion, Eva Duarte, mobilised the workers of greater Buenos Aires for a massive demonstration in front of the presidential palace. Five days later Perón and Duarte were married.

That night a myth of populist power was born. It was hot on the Plaza de Mayo, and the men took off their shirts. To demonstrate his kinship with the *descamisados* (shirtless ones) – as Perón's supporters became known – Juan Perón always addressed the populace in shirt-sleeves, and for decades this was the custom at Peronist rallies.

Son of a creole servant girl and a middle-class man who later married her, Perón was massively built, with a dazzling smile. On 22 January 1944, he met a pretty radio-show hostess, whose broadcasts in favour of the poor were extremely popular. Eva Duarte was twenty-five; he was forty-nine. He was a widower, and childless. Both were of provincial origin. She was the illegitimate daughter of a land-owner and a peasant woman.

According to a close acquaintance, theirs was a "union of two wills, two lusts for power". Sex was not an important factor in their relationship, and they had no children. Eva, who had not known her father, idealised Perón, seeing him as the people's saviour. Under the spell of Mussolini and Fascism, he cultivated the image of "father of the poor". Shrewd and charming, he embodied a sunny version of Fascism, a mix of social justice and central control. After his election, the regime hardened in its attitude and even welcomed former Nazis.

Energetic and efficient, Eva Perón made herself in-

TIME
THE WEEKLY NEWSMAGAZINE

EVA PERÓN

dispensable, attending political meetings with her husband. Perón used her for image-building purposes. Together they developed a system of social assistance, which won him the support of the working classes. At this time, people were flocking to Buenos Aires, and shanty towns were springing up on the outskirts. To appear in a film, in March 1944 Eva had her hair dyed blonde and arranged in a massive chignon, which framed her face in a luminous halo.

EXERCISING POWER TOGETHER.
Eva Perón regarded her husband as the most brilliant of statesmen, comparing him to the sun. Her idolatry is well expressed in a letter she wrote to him in June 1947, before leaving on an official visit to Europe: "You have made me so happy, it seems like a dream ... I have not stopped adoring you, even for an hour, or thanking heaven for God's goodness in giving me the reward of your love, which I have always tried to deserve by doing all in my power to make you happy."

Although she was sometimes exasperated by the real Perón – relaxed and phlegmatic, and over-fond of long siestas – she constantly strained towards two goals: to demolish her husband's enemies, and to win him the love of the people. Tense and passionate, she was fanatically devoted to the cause of the poor, which she promoted with immense energy and a genius for organisation. She worked without respite, sleeping very little and going to bed at dawn, when her husband was getting up. As this macho Pygmalion wanted to think of her as his creation, she was wise enough to remain in his shadow and not provoke his jealousy by winning more applause than he did.

She secured popular support for the president, and benefited the poorer elements in society. The Eva Perón Association distributed large quantities of clothes, shoes, cooking utensils, and so on. To fund these activities, she held the wealthy to ransom by threatening them with social protest. The official propaganda machine distributed thousands of items decorated with the couple in profile, and hammered home the slogan: "Perón achieves, Evita dignifies."

As far as the people were concerned, this generous, beautiful woman was a queen, a goddess, a saint. The photographs of her taken by Gisèle Freund in 1950 show her immoderate taste for fine clothes and jewellery. Far from tarnishing her image with the poor, this aura of luxury fired the adoration of those who venerat-ed her as "Our-Lady-of-the-Innocent". Her impassioned speeches from the balcony of the Casa Rosada, the government palace, galvanised the crowds massed in the Plaza de Mayo below. Exalting the name of her husband, she would cry: "Violence in the hands of the people is not violence, but justice."

INCOMPARABLE EVITA. Early in 1950, she became aware that she was suffering from cancer, but worked all the

1946

FRANCE. **Two great actors, Jean-Louis Barrault and Madeleine Renaud, leave the Comédie-Française to found the Renaud-Barrault theatre company, which is to leave its mark on French cultural life and be a standard bearer for France on many foreign tours. Madeleine Renaud was divorced and the mother of a son when she met Jean-Louis Barrault while shooting a film. For both it was love at first sight. They married in 1940, but had no children. She was ten years his senior: "Great love affairs are always incestuous" was his comment. Their new career was difficult and tempestuous, and their workload very heavy. Together – he was an avant-garde director, she a consummate actress – they put on some of the great classics and contemporary plays. Until their deaths, a few months apart in 1994, they remained a legendary couple.**

♡ ♡ ♡

harder, helping her husband in his re-election campaign. On 22 August 1951, a million delirious supporters demanded that she be appointed vice-president, but Perón obliged her to refuse. She broadcast a radio message, which might well have been her testament: "I would like people to say this of me: beside Perón there was a woman who devoted herself to making him aware of the people's hopes. All we know of this woman is that the people lovingly called her Evita." Perón expressed his gratitude to "this woman incomparable in every circumstance". Listening in ecstasy, she replied: "I have left fragments of my life along the way." Perón was re-elected on 4 June 1952. She died on 28 July, aged thirty-three, when her reputation was at its height.

Her death deprived Perón of a vital asset. After years of prosperity, the country was hit by economic crisis, brought about largely by his demagogic brand of politics. In 1955 he was overthrown in a military coup and went into exile. In Madrid, he met Isabel Martinez, a twenty-five-year-old Argentine cabaret dancer, whom he married in 1961 and appointed vice-president when he returned to power in 1974. He died soon afterwards, and in 1976 his widow was ousted as Argentina entered its long night of dictatorship.

The cult of Eva Perón remains a vital force among the Argentine people. Abroad, her myth has been perpetuated by a musical, *Evita* (1978), and a film starring Madonna (1996).

♡ ♡ ♡

SEXOLOGY
Sex Education

Educating young people about sex is a difficult issue in a society fearful of adolescent sexuality.

"I dream of the day when all children are wanted, when men and women are equal, and sex is the expression of a true feeling, of tenderness and pleasure." This was the wish of Elise Ottesen-Jensen, who in 1946, with her friend Margaret Sanger, organised the first international congress of the Family Planning Movement (cf. p. 101). A Norwegian married to a Swedish trade-unionist, one of a family of seventeen children, she was deeply affected by the death of her sister, who committed suicide after getting pregnant while still single. She rode around Sweden on a bicycle, speaking about contraception, – illegal until 1938 – and handing out condoms and diaphragms.

In 1933, she founded a national federation for sex education (the RFSU), which aimed to promote "harmonious sexual relations". The idea was not to discourage sex among young people, but to prevent unwanted pregnancies.

The Myrdals (cf. p. 166) also campaigned for sex education and, in 1956, it was made compulsory in

Swedish schools for all children over seven, and broadcast on radio and television. The move led to bitter controversy: conservatives wanted the emphasis to be on moral standards, while liberals, wary of prejudice, insisted that the teaching programme stick to the facts.

What should adolescents be told about sex before marriage? Until 1964, they were advised to abstain; then the emphasis was on certain basic principles: "The act of love should be based on feelings of affection and mutual respect"; sexual violence was condemned; the sexual behaviour of men and women must be judged by the same moral criteria.

IGNORANCE AND TRAGEDY. Everywhere, those opposed to sex education were fearful that it would encourage young people to experiment. Many parents confused ignorance and innocence, and for them, their child's sexual activity always began too soon. Yet, children are more sexually active than their parents imagine (cf. the Kinsey report, p. 226). Jocelyn Elders, responsible for public health in the United States, stated in 1994: "We have refused to acknowledge that young people have a sex life. We have spent more time legislating on morals than teaching responsibility." The result is that the United States has a rate of adolescent pregnancies eleven times high-

er than Holland, where well-presented information is freely available, contraception subsidised and abortion easy to obtain (though not much needed).

In Britain, the 1986 law provides for optional sex education from the age of fourteen, but advice on contraception is not given before the age of sixteen. In France, the aim of the family planning movement is to ensure that every person "is able to live his or her sexuality without repression or dependence, whilst respecting differences, responsibility, and the freedom of others". However, the Fontanet circular (1973), calling for sex education based on "adequate provision of information and the awakening of responsibility", has remained a dead letter. In Russia, China, Japan, India, and other countries, where young people receive no sex education, many adults watch pornographic videos (cf. p. 340) to glean information. In developed countries, children watch such material far more than their parents suspect. Yet people whose only knowledge of sex comes from degrading images of this kind are more fearful about it than those who are given open, reliable information.

In the nineteenth century, the middle classes repressed sexuality in children, which they viewed as dangerous and repugnant. In our own day, the apparent freedom of everyday language, dirty jokes and erotic advertising imagery may give us the wrong impression: the average level of knowledge is still low, particularly when young people embark on their first sexual relationship (cf. p. 294). The success of radio programmes answering listeners' questions reveals both a hunger for information and a basic ignorance of such matters as premature ejaculation, penis size and erogenous zones. Where sex education is concerned, it is almost always a case of too little, too late. Information is acquired mainly from one's peers, to some extent from one's mother, and often from the generally older man or woman with whom a young person has his or her first experience.

LOVE NEEDS TO BE LEARNED. Sexuality is part of the whole person: in focusing exclusively on the physiological, there is a danger of overlooking the relational, erotic, affective, and emotional aspects of sex. But moralising is not an adequate way of giving the necessary guidelines. Sex education is best achieved in a situation of trust and dialogue, where fears, prejudices, and children's anxieties as regards their "normality" can be freely expressed. Their questions need to be answered honestly, using language suited to their age and maturity, avoiding words which are too obscene or technical, and respecting the modesty or freedom of each individual. Should this be done in the family or at school? In Scandinavian coun-

How do you find out? A still from *Tomorrow Is too Late*, an Italian film by Léonide Moguy on the first stirrings of sexuality in a group of adolescents.

tries, it is thought that both have a role to play. The ideal would be for parents to explain bodily development and changes, the feelings associated with intercourse, and ways of avoiding diseases and pregnancy; the role of the school would be to encourage discussion. If things are difficult at home, the school could provide a minimum of information. It is recognised that those who have had the opportunity to talk about sex as children tend to adopt responsible behaviour in later life, and are more able to talk things over with their partner.

Listening to those who claim authority in matters of sexuality, be it the Church, the scientific establishment, or the State, it is clear that every society seeks to promote a "right way" of making love, in moral and therapeutic terms. The fact is that human beings are different and we all seek to develop in our own way, according to our own moral criteria and idea of love.

Some fear that too much talk of sex destroys the mystery of love. But can desire ever be explained? On the other hand, it is just as illusory to think that one can do away with taboos, remove the confusion and abolish the violence associated with sex: there will always be a dark side to it.

1946

VIENNA. **Walter Legge meets Elisabeth Schwarzkopf. A German who had become a British citizen, he was artistic director of the EMI recording company, always in search of new talent. He offered the German soprano a contract, but she insisted on a proper audition. In her he recognised someone of his own calibre. Thus began, he wrote, "the longest and happiest musical partnership of my life". In 1947, Schwarzkopf made her debut in London, then embarked on a brilliant international career. Their marriage, in 1953, was that of two perfectionists. Legge was an extremely demanding producer. Equally devoted to her work, Elisabeth Schwarzkopf was recognised as the ideal performer of Mozart or Richard Strauss. She modestly entitled her autobiography My Master's Voice.**

Jawaharlal Nehru
Edwina & Mountbatten

More than friendship tied the wife of the last British viceroy to the first prime minister of India.

On 22 March 1947, Lord and Lady Mountbatten arrived in Delhi and were met by the head of the provisional government, Jawaharlal Nehru. Mountbatten, the king's cousin, had been appointed viceroy of India and given the task of preparing the country – then in the grip of civil war – for independence. He was forty-seven years old, his wife forty-six, Nehru fifty-eight. The three had already met in 1946, in Singapore, when Mountbatten was supreme commander of allied forces in South-East Asia. Nehru had recently been released from jail for the eighth time: in all, he spent nine years in British prisons. Since 1929 he had been president of the Indian National Congress Party, mainspring of the struggle against the colonial power.

Nehru, who came from a family of Punjabi Brahmins, studied law in England and went into legal practice. With his wife and daughter, Indira, born in 1917, he lived a life of luxury before joining the movement for Indian independence led by Mohandas Gandhi. A reforming Socialist, he was much influenced by the theories of the Fabian Society (cf. p. 60). With his family, he decided to change his life-style: to demonstrate their rejection of British imports, they all burned their finery and took to wearing clothes made of the local *kadhi*, a rough, hand-woven material. Nehru wore a white forage cap, the headgear of Indian prisoners in South Africa, which Gandhi had adopted as a symbol of revolt. Nehru's wife, Kamala, who supported him in this cause, died of tuberculosis in a Swiss clinic in 1936.

Lord Louis Mountbatten, known as Dickie, and Edwina Ashley, a wealthy, elegant heiress, had married in 1922 and were one of Britain's best known couples. They had three daughters. Lady Mountbatten lived extravagantly, taking lovers and dropping them again after a short time. Her husband had homosexual companions and often appeared in public with his mistresses. Edwina was particularly jealous of a beautiful Frenchwoman called Violaine. After a period of tension resulting from a passionate liaison between the latter and Lady Mountabatten, the couple came to an accommodation: they would allow each other complete freedom, whilst taking care to avoid scandal.

In India, Lady Mountbatten was party to the meetings between her husband and Nehru. The viceroy had

to get Nehru to accept the partition of India, demanded by Muhammad Ali Jinnah, leader of the Muslim League, which would create the new state of Pakistan as a homeland for India's Muslims. During their frequent meetings and travels, strong personal ties were established between Nehru, a fascinating, determined man, and the viceroy's wife. They each found the other both disturbing and attractive. Gradually, the frivolous, capricious Englishwoman underwent a transformation. Nehru, who always wore a red rose in the buttonhole of his brown tunic, taught her to know and love India. Lord Mountbatten was conscious of the hold his wife was likely to have over Nehru as a lover. Faithful to their agreement, he behaved as if he were unaware of the intensity of their relationship, but asked his wife to help him persuade Nehru to adopt his point of view. To stop the terrible massacres between Hindus and Muslims, Gandhi undertook long fasts, whilst remaining opposed to partition: "My mother's body cannot be torn apart." But eventually he gave way to Nehru, who had resigned himself to the country being divided. Nehru often took Edwina Mountbatten to visit Gandhi, and an affectionate bond was established between them. He called her "little sister", and gave her a sympathetic understanding of the country's poor and "untouchables", who were his special concern.

SHOCKING VIOLENCE. On 15 August 1947 India achieved independence. Dressed in white, Nehru and Lord and Lady Mountbatten watched as the saffron, green, and white flag of the new nation was raised for the first time. But the next day brought terrible massacres: as many as a million people were killed in the civil strife. While her husband, now governor general, sought to suppress the rioting, Edwina travelled the country in the company of Nehru, organising help for the wounded, the cremation of the dead, and the care of needy children. She arranged for food and medicines to be distributed in refugee camps from one end of the immense country to the other. On 20 September, in a mosque in Delhi that had been attacked by Hindus, Nehru interposed his own body between the fighting parties. When Edwina heard the news, she believed him to be dead; on finding him alive, she threw herself into his arms.

Edwina Mountbatten and her old friend Nehru share a joke. Photograph by Henri Cartier-Bresson.

The violence gradually abated and the Mountbattens returned to England for the wedding of Princess Elizabeth. They were in India again on 30 January 1948, when Gandhi was assassinated by a Hindu fanatic, and attended the cremation in the company of Nehru and his daughter. Indira was aware of the relationship between her father and Lady Mountbatten, and not liking her, preferred to ignore her.

LOVE AND POETRY. The love affair between Nehru and Edwina Mountbatten was painful and difficult. Always surrounded by servants and bodyguards, there were few opportunities for them to be alone. Before the Mountbattens finally left India, they had one last private conversation. Nehru wept and she wiped away his tears. "You are in my life," he said, "like a lighted candle which floats trembling on the water. You will not be ex-

1947

FRANCE. **Publication of *L'Ecume des jours*, a poignant novel by Boris Vian. Through the gaiety and lightness of this verbal fantasy, we glimpse the ghosts of sickness and degradation haunting an absurd world. Death carries off such innocents as the marvellous Chloé, her lungs eaten away by a water lily.**

FRANCE. **Marriage of Pierre Klossowski, a translator and essayist of the philosophical and literary avant-garde, and a beautiful woman with long slender legs and a mysterious smile — Denise Morin-Sinclaire, whom he referred to as Roberte. Claiming that she had restored him to life, he took her for his muse. She was the inspiration for a trilogy of novels, *Les Lois de l'Hospitalité*, beginning with *Roberte ce soir* (1953), and for erotic drawings worthy of de Sade.**

♡ ♡ ♡

Edith Piaf & Marcel Cerdan

The passionate affair of a famous singer and a world boxing champion, immortalised in one of Piaf's most haunting songs.

At Orly, in the crowd coming down the steps of the Constellation from New York, Edith Piaf and Marcel Cerdan, radiant with happiness.

On 14 January 1948, Edith Piaf made a return appearance at the Versailles, a smart cabaret in New York, singing "When he takes me in his arms / Speaks softly to me / Life is a bed of roses." *La Vie en rose*, for which she had written the lyrics, was one of her greatest hits in America.

Aged thirty-two, she was no longer the "kid Piaf", the "back-street sparrow" who had once sung in the streets of Paris. After getting her first night-club job in

1935, she had become a great star in France. In songs such as *La Goualante du pauvre Jean, Les Amants d'un jour, L'Homme à la moto, La Foule* and *Milord*, her theme was love, tragic love, but love nevertheless. With her generous, throaty voice – a voice "bigger than herself", phenomenal, unforgettable – she turned sentimental, sometimes naïve lyrics into hymns to the agony and ecstasy of loving. She also drew tears from her audience because she expressed the world's sorrow, rooted in her own experience. She was born in the gutter, in Belleville, a working-class district of Paris, and had her first lover when she was sixteen. Their baby daughter died at the age of two and, despite her ardent longing, she was never able to have another child.

Piaf was a true man-eater, starting with small-time tearaways, then artists and singers, those who trained her and helped her in her career. Later, she gave a helping hand to up-and-coming singers: Yves Montand, Eddie Constantine, Charles Aznavour, and others. Yet it was not sensuality she was after. What she looked for was the protection of a strong man. As she wrote in her autobiography, *Ma vie*, she felt "a throbbing, almost morbid need to be loved". But she never allowed herself to become enslaved: it was always she who rejected her partners after a few months, or a year or two at most.

PASSIONATE AFFAIR IN NEW YORK. In the boxer Marcel Cerdan, a kind, considerate, sincere man, she found what she was looking for: strength, passion, tenderness. They were both stars at the height of their powers, each worshipped by the public in their own fields, which obviated any sense of competition or critical antagonism.

He was one year her junior, born of a poor family who had emigrated to Sidi-bel-Abbès, in Morocco. At the age of seventeen, he won his first boxing match in Casablanca, where he eventually settled with his wife, Marinette, and their three sons. He had already been to New York, in 1941, for a victorious fight against American boxer George Abrams. He was a fine-looking man, tall, dark and well-built, while Piaf, a brunette with big blue eyes, was frail and tiny by comparison. They had already been introduced in November 1945, in Paris, when she was singing at the Club des Cinq, where her voice had made a profound impression on him.

The decisive meeting took place at a French restaurant in New York in November 1947. Piaf had come with two of her singer friends, Lucienne Boyer and Jacques Pills; the restaurant owner felt it an honour to welcome both Piaf and Cerdan, "two of France's greatest celebrities". They took to each other immediately. The next day he invited her to dinner and spent the night at her hotel. On 6 December, in Chicago, he won a tough match against the Estonian Anton Raadik, so tough that he was discouraged and talked of giving up boxing. She comforted him, just as he consoled her after the failure of her New York début: "You bring them happiness and they don't even realise it." The fact was that, sober and modest in her little black dress, she had a disconcerting effect on the audience, while they applauded Les Compagnons de la Chanson, with whom she sang *Les Trois Cloches*.

In March 1948, Cerdan returned to New York for a fight against Lavern Roach. He met up with Piaf again and they engaged in a passionate affair. After his victory, they returned to Paris. Although they went into hiding, a newspaper revealed their "romance", and Marinette Cerdan threatened to divorce her husband. He managed to dissuade her, but continued his affair with Edith Piaf.

"GOD REUNITES THOSE WHO LOVE". On 23 May 1948, Cerdan lost a fight for the first time in his life, and *France-Dimanche* carried the headline: "Piaf brings Cerdan bad luck." He regained his title in July, and they set off for New York together. On 21 September he became world middleweight champion; the next day she performed to great acclaim at the Versailles. After Cerdan's departure, supported by her friend Marlene Dietrich, Piaf returned to her former restless life-style, taking up, then breaking off, with singer Jean-Louis Jaubet and actor John Garfield.

On 29 June 1949, Cerdan lost his title to Jack La Motta. The return match was scheduled for 2 December. Piaf remained in New York; he returned to Paris. Unable to wait any longer, she asked him to fly back. On 28 October 1949, the plane crashed in the Azores:

"If one day life tears you away from me
If you die when you are far from me,
Never mind, if you love me,
For I shall die, too.
We shall have eternity together
In the immense blue yonder,
No more problems in heaven ...
God reunites those who love."

It was with Cerdan in mind that, in 1948, Piaf had written the words of this splendid *Hymne à l'amour*. On the evening of the tragedy, she found the courage to sing it at the Versailles, in a voice more vibrant than ever. Later she wrote *La Belle Histoire d'amour* in memory of Cerdan:

"I try to forget you
But it is beyond me
I am tearing myself apart
I belong to you only."

Despite passing fancies and excesses, she never again experienced so intense a relationship, nor ever again found love with a man she considered her equal. But she never gave up hope ... and love continued to be her theme. She asked to meet Cerdan's family, and cared for them with real affection. In 1952 she married Jacques Pills, but they divorced in 1956. Her health deteriorated; she became an alcoholic, and addicted to morphine.

Her body deformed by sickness, she sang "Non, rien de rien, / Non, je ne regrette rien", and found consolation in a final love affair with Théo Sarapo, twenty years

1948

NETHERLANDS. At the London Olympics, Fanny Blankers-Koen, the "flying Dutchwoman", wins a record four gold medals in running events. One of the great sportswomen of the century, she had competed in the Berlin Games in 1936. She was trained by her husband, Jan Blankerst. Her selection, at the age of thirty, had sparked off a controversy as to whether a mother of two children should be competing in athletics. Before the final in London, her husband whispered in her ear: "Remember, you are too old!"

"True love begins when you expect nothing in return."

ANTOINE DE SAINT-EXUPÉRY
Citadelle

FRANCE. Choreographer and dancer Roland Petit founds the Ballets de Paris, and makes up with his former companion Zizi Jeanmaire, after a breach lasting two years. They had met at age nine, when they were both in the same class at the Ecole de l'Opéra, in Paris. They never split up again, eventually marrying in 1954. She performed in his ballets, achieving success in London in *Carmen* (1949), with her black hair cut short. *La Croqueuse de diamants* (1950) was the first step in her international career, first as singer then as principal of the chorus line. She was ...

knew it. But it was something we didn't talk about." Their financial position became so extreme that Rossellini finally allowed his wife to act in his friend Jean Renoir's film *Elena et les hommes* (1956), which enjoyed considerable success. But when she agreed to act in an American film, *Anastasia*, it was too much for him. He left for India with a film in mind and, on his return, justified his demand for a divorce with the words: "I do not want to become Mr Bergman."

In October 1957, the breach became irreparable. He returned from India with a new companion; she was

again a big international star and had met a Swedish theatrical producer, Lars Schmidt, whom she married as soon as her divorce came through in 1958. Giving up custody of her children to their father, she pursued her career and was equally successful in films, on television, and on the stage. Rossellini, meanwhile, remained in debt and, though admired by young directors, never again found favour with the general public. Summing up his life, he wrote that he had "kept [his] promise to Ingrid to create a very special form of cinema in fulfilment of the hope that had urged her towards [him]."

♡ ♡ ♡

Morals
The Taboo of Incest

Why is love between close relations outlawed by social convention?

In this context we are not thinking of the criminal abuse of a child, with damage to his or her physical integrity and sense of identity, but of love between adults who are too closely related, for instance a brother and sister.

Disapproval of incest is a worldwide phenomenon, as demonstrated by Claude Lévi-Strauss in his book *Les Structures élémentaires de la parenté* (*The Elementary Structures of Kinship*, 1949). He explains that this rule marks "the progression from nature to culture", and achieves social cohesion by ensuring that women are appropriately distributed among men. Those who justify the incest taboo on the grounds that it obviates the risk of transmission of hereditary diseases forget that our ancestors were unaware of this danger, which in any case is greatly exaggerated.

The word incest comes from the Latin *incastus*, which originally meant "impure". An incestuous sexual relationship is one between a man and a woman who are forbidden to marry because they are too closely related. In some cultures, the taboo may extend beyond blood ties to cover unions with relations-

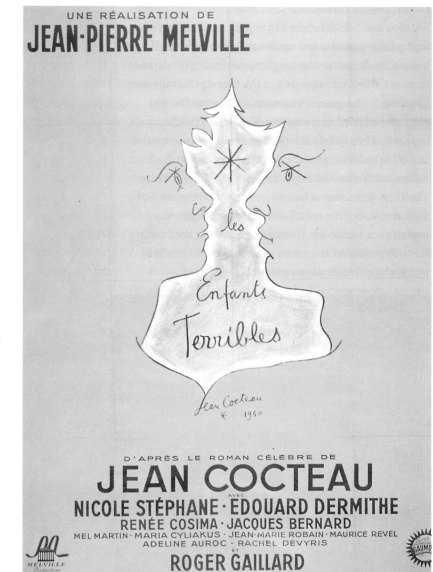

UNE RÉALISATION DE
JEAN-PIERRE MELVILLE

les Enfants Terribles

Jean Cocteau
★ 1950

D'APRÈS LE ROMAN CÉLÈBRE DE
JEAN COCTEAU
AVEC
NICOLE STÉPHANE · ÉDOUARD DERMITHE
RENÉE COSIMA · JACQUES BERNARD
MEL MARTIN · MARIA CYLIAKUS · JEAN-MARIE ROBAIN · MAURICE REVEL
ADELINE AUROC · RACHEL DEVYRIS
ET
ROGER GAILLARD

MELVILLE Productions

by-adoption, godfathers or godmothers, foster parents, and in-laws. On the other hand, endogamy (marriage between close kin) is the rule in many societies. A union between first cousins, for instance, is still the dominant model in the Maghreb countries of North Africa.

In medieval Christianity, the

many impediments to such unions could be overcome by obtaining a dispensation, providing a lucrative income for the church. The scope of the ban has gradually shrunk: since the 1983 code of canon law, it has applied to second-degree kinship relationships (first cousins), but not to the third-degree relationships covered by the earlier code of 1917. The provisions of civil law differ from one country to another. In France, although marriage with a parent, grandparent, brother or sister is illegal, incest between consenting adults is not a crime (it figures in the criminal code only as an aggravating circumstance in the case of abuse of a child by a parent). In Britain, on the other hand, a sexual relationship of this kind, even between consenting adults, is a criminal act punishable by up to seven years in prison.

INCEST BETWEEN BROTHER AND SISTER: A UNIVERSAL PHENOMENON. Incest is an integral part of many of the creation myths by which different cultures explain the origins of our world, and incest among royalty was the rule in many ancient societies, from Egypt to Japan. By marrying his sister, Pharaoh produced Isis and Osiris. Among the Greek gods, Persephone was the daughter of Zeus by his sister Demeter. The Celtic, Nordic, and Germanic myths contain many examples of heroes being born of incestuous relationships between brother and sister: Roland is thought to have been Charlemagne's son by his sister Gisèle, not a nephew; Mordred was the issue of Arthur's union with his sister Morgan le Fay; Siegfried was the son of Sigmund and Sieglinde.

In common parlance, living "like brother and sister" (in the case of non-siblings) means having a non-sexual relationship. It is a way of emphasising the social taboo, which families cope with in different ways. In studying this phenomenon, psychologist René Zazzo makes a distinction between "contact twins", who feel no sense of guilt in playing sexual games, and "avoiding twins", in whom the internalised taboo produces an intense struggle against their natural drives. It would seem that the

prevalence of this taboo – on which Freud's famous "Oedipus complex" is based – suggests that incest itself is universal, along with the fascination to which it gives rise. "My sister, my bride," sings the lover in the *Song of Solomon* (cf. p. 264). Passionate love for a sister is at the heart of the work of Chateaubriand, Byron, or the Austrian poet Georg Trakl. It is also the theme of John Ford's play *'Tis Pity She's a Whore* (1626), or Robert Musil's novel, *The Man without Qualities* (1930), each of which is a quest for "a double of the other sex".

For Finnish ethnologist Edvard Westermarck, very close proximity diminishes sexual interest and acts as a check on incestuous relationships. On the other hand, it often happens that a person abandoned in childhood, when reunited with his or her father or mother, brother or sister in adult life, is attracted by a physical resemblance or identical odour. Typical comments are: "He was me in another body", or "When I see her, it is as if I were looking at myself in a mirror." They seem to believe that they have rediscovered an all-embracing love, that of the father or mother they craved so much.

INCEST OF THE SECOND KIND. The scandal caused in 1992 by Woody Allen's liaison with his adoptive daughter (cf. p. 368) is revealing. As Allen was neither a biological nor an adoptive father to Soon-Yi, this was a case of what anthropologist Françoise Héritier calls "incest of the second kind".

Nowadays, the increase in divorce and reconstituted families has led to many adoptive-parent relationships,

and therefore a growing risk of incestuous liaisons of this kind. The laws on remarriage after a person has been widowed or divorced differ from one culture to another (cf. p. 43). Among Jews, the law of levirate (from *levir*, meaning brother-in-law) requires that a childless widow marry the brother of her dead husband. The Koran, on the other hand, forbids a man to marry his wife's sister. Among Catholics, until the 1917 code was issued, it was even forbidden to marry a fiancée's sister if the original engagement had been broken off. In actual fact, cases of widowers marrying their late wife's sister were very common and subject to a special dispensation.

Love of an incestuous nature is generally met with social disapproval, rather than repression. But another function of the taboo is to affirm an orderly social structure. In the primitive mind, challenging the established order meant risking a return to chaos, and those who committed the sin of incest were believed to be punished with sterility.

Taboos, by their very nature, have a mysterious fascination. As the poet Guillaume Apollinaire wrote: "I wish you were my sister, so I could love you incestuously."

1949

PARIS. Publication of Simone de Beauvoir's seminal essay on women, *The Second Sex* (cf. p. 236), with the outstanding chapter "The Woman in Love" (II, 2). "The word 'love'," she explains, "has a very different meaning for either sex." While there is not a single man "who could be defined as 'a great lover'", for a woman "love is a total surrender of oneself to a master" and, for the woman concerned "he becomes like a religion". Defining true love as being "founded on the mutual recognition of two freedoms", Beauvoir expressed this hope: "The day when a woman will be able to love, not in her strength but in her weakness, not to escape but to find herself, not to surrender but to affirm herself, then love will become for her, as for the man, a source of life rather than a mortal danger."

♡ ♡ ♡

1950

Simone de Beauvoir & Jean-Paul Sartre

Holiday Encounters

Simone Signoret & Yves Montand

Love without Sin

Lise & Artur London

Jealousy

The Rosenberg Affair

Valentine's Day

Federico Fellini & Giulietta Masina

The Story of O

Marilyn Monroe & Arthur Miller

Lolita

Sylvia Plath & Ted Hughes

"Sex Bombs"

Melina Mercouri & Jules Dassin

The Song of Songs

Paul Newman & Joanne Woodward

The Soap Opera

Maria Callas & Aristotle Onassis

"Don't leave me…"

Simone de Beauvoir
& Jean-Paul Sartre

Two leading figures of the intellectual avant-garde in a relationship based on freedom and trust. Fifty years of uninterrupted dialogue.

Jean-Paul Sartre and Simone de Beauvoir, photomontage by Pruszkowski, 1984.

FACING PAGE
Photograph by Robert Doisneau.

MILAN. The Italian composer Luciano Berio marries the American singer Cathy Berberian. Both were twenty-five years old; together they had a daughter. They divided their time between Italy and the United States. She sang material from the classical repertoire and con-temporary pieces. In 1960, she made her début in her native land with *Circles*, a work composed by her husband. Berio, who was fond of Heidegger's phrase: "The voice is the house of the soul", was able to draw a vast range of sounds from her magnificent voice. With and for his wife, he composed *Visage* (1961), *Recital I for Cathy* (1971), and other works. They separated in 1966, but until her death in 1983 she continued to sing for him, as well as performing the works of other major composers.

In 1950 Jean-Paul Sartre and Simone de Beauvoir signed the Stockholm Appeal, calling for an end to nuclear testing. Committed to left-wing causes, they formed a formidable intellectual duo in post-war France. Since they first met in 1929, while completing the state's élite course in teacher training, their relationship had been based on freedom and openness. They maintained their independence in financial, personal, and sexual matters. They scorned marriage, lived apart, and never had children. In their old age, each adopted a daughter.

Both were born in Paris – Sartre in 1905, Beauvoir in 1908 – of middle-class families. Having lost his father, Sartre was worshipped by his mother and brought up to believe in his genius as a writer. Small in stature and cross-eyed, he was ugly to look at but had an attractive personality. Beauvoir was only slightly taller, with a brusque tone of voice and rapid style of delivery. She was determined to make her way in the intellectual world and claimed she could not care less what other people thought of her.

A LOVE BORN OF NECESSITY. They achieved an immediate and total understanding. He was the double of whom she had dreamed, the man with whom she could "always share everything". She recognised his genius and he regarded her as an equal, albeit admitting to "a degree of machismo". In her he found both beauty and intelligence, but he was not a man to settle with one woman and he laid down certain conditions: "The love between us is a love born of necessity; we also need to experience contingent love affairs." She agreed, confident that "no harm would come to me through him, unless he died before me". As time went on, Sartre had affairs with younger and younger women, as if, Beauvoir

wrote, "he could not resign himself to growing up". He enjoyed female company: "I prefer small talk with a woman to talking philosophy with [Raymond] Aron," but added: "I am less interested in sexual intercourse than in caresses." She pointed out to him that he could never let himself go, while she liked to stretch out on the grass after a long walk. He abused his body with stimulants and sleeping pills, smoked, and over-indulged in coffee and alcohol.

Separated in 1931, when they were given teaching posts in different towns, they exchanged letters using the same terms of endearment: "mon tout petit", "cher petit vous autre". They regarded 14 October 1929 as the date of their "morganatic marriage" and kept it as an anniversary. They addressed each other using the formal "vous". She called him Sartre; he called her "Castor" (French for beaver, a play on the name Beauvoir), as did their close friends. Posted to Paris in 1936, they lived in a hotel and did their writing in the café, partaking of a heady mixture of books, discussions, films, German philosophy, and American jazz. They were a source of fascination to their pupils. With one of them, Olga Kosakiewicz, they established a *ménage à trois*, which led to jealousy and almost ended in tragedy.

The success in 1938 of Sartre's first book, *Nausea* (dedicated to "Castor"), led to a flurry of amorous adventures, and in some cases both of them cynically shared the same partners. A kind of incestuous family grew up around them. In 1941, Beauvoir began an affair with Jacques-Henri Bost, with whom she went hiking and skiing. Later, Bost married Olga Kosakiewicz.

Called up in 1939, Sartre was taken prisoner and held in Germany until 1943. "How reassuring it is to think that you exist," he wrote to her, "for me that will always be enough to save the world." Their letters reveal a detachment from everyday reality, absorbed as they were in their writing. In 1943, Beauvoir published *She Came to Stay*, her first novel, based on their triangular relationship with Olga. Sartre brought out *Being and Nothingness*, the first expression of his existential philosophy. They moved in artistic circles and lived in a hotel with "les petits", a group of friends and former pupils, in Saint-Germain-des-Prés. The district became fashionable after the war for its cafés and smoke-filled jazz clubs.

SUCCESS OF A KIND. Plays, essays, novels, articles: Sartre was everywhere, detested by both the right wing and the Communists. He took up the cause of colonised peoples, the working classes, and the Jews. He and Beauvoir were internationally famous and travelled a great deal. In 1946, they and other intellectuals founded the magazine *Les Temps modernes*. Claude Lanzmann, who strove for a rapprochement between Sartre's group and the Communist Party, had an affair with Beauvoir lasting five years. Sartre, who lived with his mother from 1946 to 1962, divided his time between his secretary in the mornings, Beauvoir in the afternoons, and his other women.

Always wearing a turban, Beauvoir was a kind of queen mother. Though Sartre had become the intellectual guide for a whole generation, his fame made no difference to their relationship. They still had first sight of each other's work. She continued to write novels and essays and with his encouragement undertook research on the condition of women. "You are not born a woman, you become one" is the key phrase of *The Second Sex* (1949), the essay which formed the basis of contemporary feminism and unleashed a "festival of obscenities". As a free woman who had refused marriage and motherhood, she met with great opposition, but, as she rightly pointed out, Sartre was not castigated for the same kind of behaviour. She also tackled the subject of love.

At this time, she was exchanging love letters with Nelson Algren, a Chicago writer she had met in 1947, on her first trip to the United States. He wanted to marry her, but she knew she would not be able "to live solely on happiness and love" and that her life was in France. She always wore a ring that he had given her.

In her memoirs, *The Prime of Life* (1960, dedicated to Sartre), Beauvoir sought to present them as a couple who had reconciled the irreconcilable: "In my life there has been one sure success: my relationship with Sartre." For his part, he recognised her pre-eminence over all other women: "I would not have reached the point I have reached in my life without women, especially you." In the 1970s, he flirted with the Maoists; she espoused the feminist cause. He died in 1980. "His death separates us," she wrote. "That is the way things are: it is good enough that we should have lived in harmony for so long." She survived him by six years and is buried beside him in the Montparnasse cemetery in Paris.

♡ ♡ ♡

SOCIETY
Holiday Encounters

The Club Méditerranée introduced a revolution in holiday-making and a new way of finding a partner.

After the privations of the war years, summer holidays made a welcome return. Gérard Blitz, a Belgian diamond merchant and champion swimmer, had a brilliant idea. A former Resistance fighter, he showed a real flair for organisation in his work for concentration camp survivors. Wanting to spend active holidays in a friendly setting on the shores of the Mediterranean, he founded a non-profit-making organisation, the Club Méditerranée, registered in Paris in 1950.

It was an immediate success: a small ad for the first holiday, in Ma-

jorca, attracted thousands of applications from people of all social classes. Inspired by his Tahitian wife's accounts of Polynesian society, Blitz sought to create a relaxed, carefree lifestyle – a return to nature. To encourage contact and "break the ice", the holiday-makers were accommodated in "villages" under canvas, then in straw huts. In the early days, tents were hired from the American army, then supplied by Gilbert Trigano. By creating the conditions for freedom, tolerance and social interaction, Blitz brought about a revolution in people's idea of a holiday, and it gradually spread. The "Club" became a household word, symbolising a new kind of leisure activity.

Wage earners had only recently acquired the right to holidays. The pioneers had been the Scandinavians. The Norwegians, for instance, were first entitled to two weeks' paid holiday in 1920, extended to four weeks in 1947. The French were granted two weeks in 1936, to which a third was added in 1956. The Germans became entitled to two weeks in 1946, increased to three for some categories in 1963, and for everyone in 1974.

Different in atmosphere from popular festivals, Saturday night hops and Sunday leisure activities, there emerged a new form of relaxation which prolonged the pleasures of idleness way beyond the traditional weekly rest. It was paralleled by the development of mass tourism, as charter flights and package holidays enabled the middle classes of Northern Europe to discover the delights of the Mediterranean and in due course more exotic destinations.

FROM "FRIENDLINESS" TO SEXUAL LIBERATION. Overwhelmed by his success, in 1963 Gérard Blitz sought help from Gilbert Trigano. Deploying his managerial talents, Trigano transformed the amateur association into an efficient business, without losing the vision of a "practical utopia". He consolidated the myth of the "Club Med", gave it a world-wide dimension, and ensured that it would endure. Almost fifty years on, it now runs a hundred or so "villages" in fifty countries, has a staff of 25,000, and caters for 1.3 million holiday-makers each year. The original model has been extended to include winter sports holidays in European mountain resorts and stays in sunspots all over the world from Mexico to China. Some of the villages have remained faithful to the original model; while others offer hotel-style comfort. Some are more suited to

families with small children; others attract single people. The Club has responded to changing tastes and a changing market.

For the duration of their stay, the customers – known as "gentils membres" (GM) – form a community in which informality is the rule. This approach was set up in the early days, when they had to put up with Spartan conditions and turn a blind eye to organisational failings. Rather than hang around in their tents, or later bungalows, the clients are encouraged to socialise. Never out of their swimming costumes, they play a range of sports and take meals together around loaded buffets or tables without set places. The "villages", organised by "gentils organisateurs" (GO), are self-contained communities, offering many kinds of entertainment. To complete the illusion of a return to nature, real money is replaced by tickets or bar tokens, which holiday-makers buy on arrival.

No more starchy hotels or never-ending visits to relatives! Here, new relationships could be formed in an intoxicating atmosphere of freedom and good-natured humour. Social distinctions were of little significance and the lonely could find friendship. Far from the tiring reality of work, here was a paradise where city-dwellers could fulfil their dreams of meeting people, communing with nature, and engaging in leisure pursuits.

FINDING LOVE ON HOLIDAY. Holidays devoted to enjoyment and meeting people. This was the formula promoted by the "Club", which soon became associated in the popular mind with the three "S"s: sea, sex and sun. Its reputation for permissiveness, though frowned on by many, only enhanced its popularity.

Holidays are a good time for breaking new ground. People are less inhibited; time is not the usual

tyrant. Anonymity and the informal setting make it easier for people to overcome their natural reserve. The way the "village" is organised, with its rites, welcoming ceremony, fancy-dress evenings and games, encourages interaction. It is something like a traditional country festival, or a Valentine's Day celebration (cf. p. 248), when everyone can find a partner.

The different national origins of the holiday-makers offers a fascinating study in different approaches to seduction: should the man or the woman take the initiative? As amorous and sexual behaviour is very much culturally determined, French or Italian males are often surprised to be accosted by Scandinavian women who are usually used to a more blunt approach to such matters.

Holiday love affairs are often ephemeral, unable to withstand separation and the return of the partners to their normal environment. Yet between 10 and 15 per cent of couples first met in this way. In the 1980s, Gilbert Trigano said he was "proud to have been the cause of two thousand marriages a year". Despite the illusion of a return to nature in which social distinctions lose their relevance, the partners of couples formed at the Club Med are usually of very similar social backgrounds (cf. p. 356). In the course of time, this highly inventive formula, borne along in the 1970s on the wind of sexual liberation, has set into a more conventional mould. But it still offers the opportunity to meet people and find a partner in relaxed and friendly surroundings.

1950

MOSCOW. **Soviet writer Ilya Ehrenbourg falls in love with Liselotte Mehr, wife of the mayor of Stockholm. Aged fifty-nine, he was rejuvenated by this, his last, affair. Both were married, she had two children, and they lived in different countries. They met occasionally and often spoke on the telephone. A source of inspiration, she helped him develop as a writer and persuaded him to write his memoirs. His secret was known only to a few French friends and in 1967, shortly before his death, he made his last trip to France with her.**

"You will find love the day you can show your weakness without the other person using it to affirm his strength," Cesare Pavese writes, shortly before he commits suicide.

♡ ♡ ♡

FACING PAGE
Gilbert Trigano.

BELOW
Drawing by Chaval.

Simone Signoret & Yves Montand

The most popular couple in French cinema, for whom political commitment mattered more than their careers.

Simone Signoret receiving an Oscar for *Room at the Top*, with Yves Montand in Hollywood.

FACING PAGE
Shortly after their marriage.

It was a simple wedding at the town hall in Saint-Paul-de-Vence, witnessed by the poet Jacques Prévert, and Paul Roux, proprietor of the Colombe d'or inn. For Simone Kaminker and Ivo Livi, both aged thirty-one, it was the beginning of thirty-four years of love, argument and political commitment.

They had first met in 1949. Simone Signoret – she took her mother's name – was a cinema actress with a promising career, married to director Yves Allégret, with whom she had made *Dédée d'Anvers* (1948) and had a daughter, Catherine. Yves Montand, of Italian parentage, came from a working-class family in Marseilles. As a singer, he was a protégé of Edith Piaf, with whom he had made his cinema début in 1945. For Montand and Signoret, it was love at first sight. He soon asked her to come and live with him, and she agreed. In 1952, she made *Golden Helmet*, Jacques Becker's masterpiece and her most distinguished piece of acting. While the film was being shot, she missed Montand so much that she decided to give up her career.

Despite her growing celebrity, she refused all further offers of employment. For several months she found fulfilment in the self-effacing role of housewife. In her fascinating autobiography, *Nostalgia Isn't what It Used to Be* (1976), she tells how, but for a row with her husband, she would have become "an old ex-groupie, ex-actress, and probably ex-Mme Yves Montand". Montand challenged her to find work. She remembered the only role it had hurt her to turn down: in *Thérèse Raquin*. It was not too late. "I had almost given it all up. Again

we would know what it was to get all screwed up during our periods of separation, come together again and experience the miracle of being reunited."

Despite difficult and, at times, stormy episodes, Montand and Signoret's love affair lasted until the day of her death. So did their arguments. In "la Roulotte" (the caravan), as they called their Parisian apartment on the Place Dauphine, they began, she wrote "a new life together. That is where we had the piano, received our friends, had our rows." They did not have children, but Montand treated Catherine Allégret as if she were his own daughter. They were always surrounded by crowds of friends, intellectuals and artists, generating a never-ending stream of jokes and discussion.

TWO BRILLIANT CAREERS. In 1954 they bought a large, welcoming house in the country near Paris, where Montand wrote *Battling Joe* and *Feuilles mortes*, two of his greatest hits. Dressed in black, a throw-back to his apprenticeship with Edith Piaf, Montand had a varied stage repertoire, alternating ballads and protest songs. With his southern-French accent and typically Gallic sense of humour, he became an international star, selling thousands of records. As a result of his stay in Hollywood, he also won fame as an actor. For Americans he was the new Maurice Chevalier.

For Montand and Signoret, money was never a problem. Neither was jealousy – even in 1960, when the gutter press seized on Montand's brief liaison with Marilyn Monroe. "She will never know," wrote Signoret with

1951

FRANCE. **Publication of** *Phénix* (Phoenix), a collection of poems by Paul Eluard, one of the century's great poets, inspired by the last love of his life. He had been the first husband of Gala, who left him for Salvador Dalí. In despair at the sudden death of his wife, Nush, in 1946, he wrote of her: "You whom I love for ever; you who invented me." Gradually he rediscovered his zest for life. In September 1949 he met Dominique Laure at the Peace Congress. Two years later they married. He chose the title *Phénix* as a sign that mourning is followed by rebirth. "By a caress we leave our childhood behind / But a single word of love and we are born again." The collection also contains the beautiful poem "Je t'aime", which begins: "I love you for all the women I have not known / I love you for all the times in which I have not lived."

moving dignity, "how much I never hated her." Proud and intelligent, she pursued a brilliant international career, gathering a clutch of prestigious awards (Cannes Film Festival, Oscars). Meanwhile, Montand also made his way as an actor, beginning with Clouzot's *Wages of Fear* (1953), but finding his niche in politically committed roles after the great success of Costa-Gavras's film *Z* (1969). They remained extremely close, professional careers and political interests knit together. For many years they had nourished Communist sympathies without ever joining the Party, but their illusions were dashed in 1956 with the invasion of Hungary. Instead of cancelling a planned visit to Moscow, however, they took advantage of their access to Soviet leaders to express their disapproval in public.

POLITICALLY COMMITTED AND GENEROUS. Although before 1986 it was rare for actors to be committed to political causes, they both took their responsibilities seriously without considering themselves great thinkers. On the contrary, they tended to play themselves down. They preferred indignation to dogma, signing a never-ending stream of manifestos and petitions. With greater lucidity, they henceforth militated in favour of the boat people, Solidarity, and the "mothers" of Argentina. While Montand's sincerity was sometimes misguided,

Signoret was a true "left-wing intellectual". She admitted that her commitment "had its ridiculous side, but was also an expression of generosity".

Only rarely did they perform together, usually in aid of good causes. In 1954, at the height of the Cold War, they acted in Arthur Miller's play *The Crucible*, based on the Salem witch trials, in a plea for tolerance, with special relevance to the Rosenberg affair (cf. p. 246). Though it was a risky stage début, they won tremendous acclaim. They also acted in Costa-Gavras's film *The Confession* (1970), based on the Prague trial of Artur London (cf. p. 242), which they regarded as an act of expiation. As she matured, Simone Signoret gave some superb performances as a strong woman, particularly in films based on George Simenon's novels, such as *Le Chat* and *Etoile du Nord*, and in the television series *Madame le juge*. Old age was cruel to her. She put on weight and her face sagged. She also lost the sight of her magnificent green eyes. Montand, on the other hand, became more seductive as the years went by. In 1980, the readers of *F Magazine* voted him the celebrity with whom they would most like to have a child. After Signoret's death in 1985, this honour fell to Carole Amiel and, as father of little Valentin, Papet (Montand's role in *Manon des Sources*) became the best-known dad in France at the age of sixty-seven. He died three years later.

♡ ♡ ♡

ANGUISH
Love without Sin

The Pope's ban on artificial methods of birth control raised problems of conscience for Catholics. Their only recourse was the Ogino method.

"The importance of the sexual aspect of life is exaggerated," declared Pope Pius XII when, in 1951, he

solemnly repeated the condemnation of contraception promulgated by his predecessor, Pius XI, in the encyclical *Casti Connubii* (1930).

For practising couples, procreation or abstinence would seem to be the only alternative officially permitted by the Catholic Church. "Any conjugal behaviour, in the exercise of which the act is deprived by human artifice of its natural power to procreate life, is offensive to the law of God and to natural law." This is the position of Rome, repeated consistently this century in various forms by successive popes, with the exception of John XXIII.

Practised for purposes other than reproduction, sexual intercourse, they claim, is reprehensible. No mention of desire or pleasure. No questioning of the way in which wives may be forced to submit to their husbands. Not the least indul-

gence for couples fearing an unwanted pregnancy. On the contrary, they are required to exercise almost superhuman self-control.

In traditionally Catholic countries, birth control was not permitted by the state either. It was forbidden in Fascist Italy and Nazi Germany, which demanded that women produce ever more children for the fatherland. It was even banned in democratic France, which was concerned about "depopulation", and in 1920 introduced highly repressive legislation. Everywhere abortion was regarded as a crime, by both law-makers and religious authorities.

The first country to countenance the practice was Britain, in 1967, although as early as 1938 it had been sanctioned in cases of "physical and mental distress". Since the 1920s, progress in this field had come from Protestant,

English-speaking, and Scandinavian countries, where the birth control movement took root, thanks to the initiative of determined militants (cf. p. 218). The Church of England proved far more pragmatic than the pope: the Lambeth Conference, at which Anglican bishops throughout the world meet every ten years, pronounced itself in favour of contraception as far back as 1930.

GETTING ROUND THE PROBLEM. How in fact did Catholic couples in the 1950s avoid having an endless succession of children? Practice varied from country to country. In France, despite papal disapproval, *coitus interruptus* was by far the most common technique, followed by vaginal douching: abroad the bidet is seen as a typically French accessory! In Britain, on the other hand, the use of the condom was far more widespread. The current thinking was that men tended to experience frequent, imperious sexual needs, not women. And what about masturbation? Again, the Church branded it as a sin. So the wife had either to submit or adopt her own solution!

The diaphragm or cervical cap, female equivalents of the condom, were not widely available. Modern methods of contraception, such as the pill or the IUD, were not developed until much later, in the 1960s, despite their condemnation by Paul VI in the encyclical *Humanae Vitae* (1968). It was therefore more often the man who was expected to "take precautions". Forced to choose between early withdrawal or ineffective birth control methods, fertile women rarely experienced satisfaction in sexual intercourse, burdened as they were by the fear of pregnancy. The more desperate, when they did get pregnant, sometimes had recourse to back-street

abortions – distressing, often expensive, and almost always dangerous to health.

PLAYING "VATICAN ROULETTE". Faced with such fraught situations, some Catholic doctors provided information to enable believers to obey the pope and enjoy some sort of sex life. Since the 1930s, there had been an awareness of the rhythm method, with its requirement of periodic continence. It was also known as the Ogino method, named after the Japanese gynaecologist who discovered, in 1929, that ovulation in women occurs halfway through the menstrual cycle. The few days before and after ovulation are the time of maximum fertility. Theoretically, conception can be avoided by not having sex during this period. The difficulty for a woman is that ovulation does not occur with absolute regularity each month and for this reason "Ogino babies" are legion. In Britain the method was nicknamed "Vatican roulette".

In the 1950s, further help came from the temperature method,

whereby the moment of ovulation can be detected by monitoring the woman's temperature, and by the Billings method, which depends on observation of the vaginal mucus. These were slightly more reliable than the Ogino method, but still largely ineffective.

Periodic abstinence was therefore the only solution tolerated by the Church. As it presupposes a sharing of the responsibility for procreation between the partners, it represented some progress over *coitus interruptus*, a source of anguish for many women who had no control over the proceedings. It offered Catholics a way of trying to limit their offspring without being condemned to an inadequate sex life or the commission of sin.

Many couples nevertheless revolted against the pope's inflexibility, torn between the demands of their faith and the burden of bringing up more children than they could responsibly manage. Some came to an accommodation with their parish priest or with their conscience. The intransigence of successive popes and Jean-Paul II's vigorous campaign against condoms undoubtedly caused many believers to leave the Church. Estrangement from the Church or hypocrisy – such was the choice faced by most Catholics.

1951

IRAN. A fairy story comes true for a girl with bright green eyes: Soraya Esfandiari, of mixed Iranian and German parentage, becomes the bride of the Shah of Iran, Muhammad Reza. Sadly, the years went by without the *shabanou* producing an heir to the throne. They were divorced in 1958. Her lucky replacement was Farah Diba who, ten months after the wedding, gave birth to a son.

HOLLYWOOD. *A Streetcar Named Desire*, the play by Tennessee Williams, is adapted for cinema by Elia Kazan, starring Marlon Brando and Vivien Leigh. The heroine is an ageing woman, attracted by the sensual beauty of her young brother-in-law. But in a famous scene Brando, on his knees in the mud in the pouring rain, his T-shirt clinging to his muscular torso, loudly declares his love for his wife.

♡ ♡ ♡

ABOVE
Questioning Children,
Karel Appel.

FACING PAGE
Pope Pius XII.

Lise & Artur London

20 November 1952 saw the start of a sensational trial in Prague, with Rudolf Slansky, the secretary general of the Czech Communist Party, and thirteen other top officials accused of treason. All of them were Jews and former members of the International Brigades in the Spanish civil war. Eleven were subsequently condemned to death and executed, the other three sentenced to hard labour for life. One of the three was Artur London.

Like his wife Lise, London had been an exemplary Communist. Together they had fought for the cause at every opportunity. Elisabeth Ricol, known as Lise, was French, the daughter of an immigrant Spanish miner. She was a secretary at the Lyon office of the Party when, aged seventeen, she married Auguste Delaune, an official of the Paris branch. She followed him to Moscow and worked as a typist at the headquarters of the Communist International. Artur London, known as Gérard, who came from a family of artisans in a predominantly mining region, was already a veteran of the clandestine Czech Party. Having joined the Communist Youth Movement at the age of fourteen and become regional secretary, he fled to Moscow after a number of spells in prison. In the Soviet Union, he was treated for tuberculosis and worked in the youth wing of the International. When they first met in 1934, she was eighteen, he nineteen. In February 1935 she "became his wife", as she put it, and they decided to marry.

Returning to France in 1936, Lise worked for *Main-d'Œuvre Immigrée* (MOI), a Communist organisation established to help immigrants. When the Spanish civil war broke out, she helped organise the International Brigades. She was reunited with "Gérard" in the spring of 1937 in Spain, where both took part in the struggle. Entirely devoted to the cause, they made life-long friends with other militants from all over Europe. In July 1938, she returned to France and in December gave birth to a daughter, Fernande. Artur joined her there in February 1939. After the German invasion of France, they both joined the Resistance, to which Lise's parents were also fully committed. The Ricols' home at Ivry in the Paris suburbs was in fact a nerve centre of the movement. Their eldest daughter, Fernande, was married to the Communist leader Raymond Guyot, while their son, Frédo, was sentenced in 1941 for anti-German activities.

Responsible for propaganda, Lise ran the women's committees of the Resistance in the Paris region with Danielle Casanova, while "Gérard", who since 1942 had been under-secretary for foreign affairs in the clandestine Czech government, was a leader of the MOI.

HEROIC RESISTANCE. Sometimes they had to pretend not to know each other. From time to time they managed to spend time together, such as the night before 1 August 1942 when Lise took part in a demonstration and publicly urged women to join the Resistance. After shots were exchanged between Germans and partisans, the "fury of the Rue Daguerre", as she was described in the collaborationist press, managed to escape. On 12 August, however, both Lise and Artur were informed on and arrested. Before they were separated, "we exchanged a long, very long kiss," she wrote. "The inspector did not intervene, perhaps struck by the obvious intensity of our love." She escaped the death sentence, as she was pregnant with their son Gérard, conceived the night before the demonstration. After months in prison, they were deported in 1944: he to Mauthausen, she to Ravensbrück. When they finally returned to France in the spring of 1945, they worked to rehabilitate victims of deportation and became leaders of the Communist Party.

In 1948 the Londons and their children settled with Lise's parents in Prague, where their son Michel was born, and Artur London was appointed under-secretary for foreign affairs in the Communist government. However, Soviet terror (cf. p. 182) was everywhere and Russian "advisers", sent to sniff out "conspirators", pointed the finger at him. In January 1951, Artur London was arrested. His greatest distress was at being accused of treason by the party to which he had devoted his life. To extort a confession, they threatened him with reprisals against his family, appealing to his loyalty: seeking to prove his innocence was tantamount to doubting the Party. After twenty-six months of interrogation and torture, he finally confessed that he was a Zionist spy and an agent of imperialism. During this time, Lise struggled in vain to dispel what she regarded as a misunderstanding. She lost her job and her flat, and the family barely managed to make ends meet.

FACING PAGE
Artur London with his son in 1950.
Artur and Lise London in 1970.

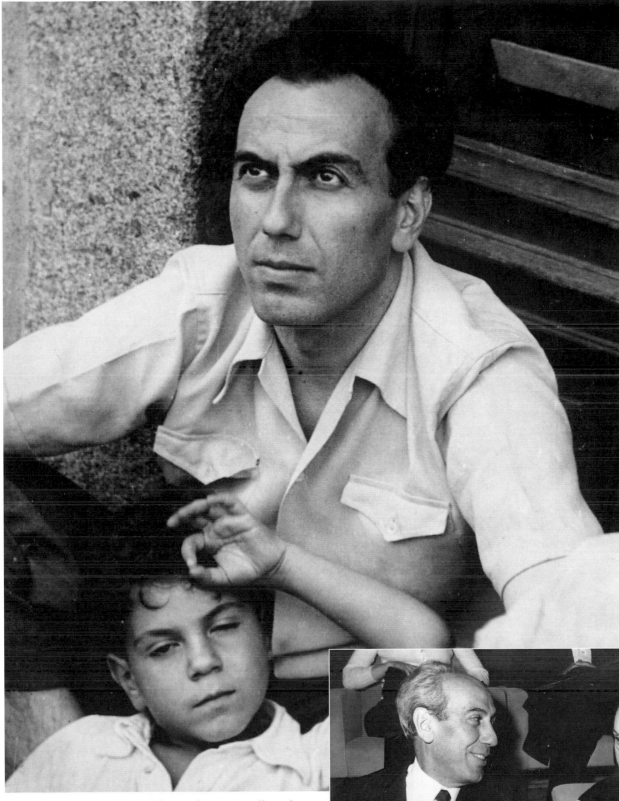

OXFORD. **The American poet Joy Gresham meets teacher and writer C. S. Lewis, for whom she has great admiration. Lewis preferred not to admit that he was falling in love with her, but agreed to marry her so that she could obtain British nationality and stay in Britain. Only when she was struck down with cancer did Lewis face up to his love. The story is sensitively told by Richard Attenborough in the film** *Shadowlands* **(1994), starring Anthony Hopkins and Debra Winger.**

ATHENS. **During an official visit, Alexander Fleming, the discoverer of penicillin, is reunited with Amalia Voureka, a Greek doctor who worked with him from 1946 to 1951 in his London laboratory. At the end of the evening, he murmured: "Will you marry me?" He was ...**

SHE NEVER BETRAYED HIM. The Londons were allowed to exchange letters, but the censors doctored them to make Artur believe that his wife had rejected him. She did in fact write: "I love you, Gérard, but you know that I am first and foremost a Communist. Despite my immense suffering, I will only be able to tear you from my heart if I am certain of your unworthiness." He was torn two ways, because he wanted her to seek refuge in France with the rest of the family. He therefore had to make her believe he was guilty, to get her to dissociate herself from him. In her letter she went on to affirm: "If you

FACING PAGE
The popular view of
middle-class domestic
violence.

were a swine, I would be left with the shame of having been married to a swine. But I am by no means certain that you are." They tried to persuade her to divorce him, but she refused. She was thrown out of the Party. "With or without your card, I am and remain a Communist," was her reply.

She asked for a divorce after hearing London confess his guilt on the radio, but in April 1953 she visited him in prison with the children, who played noisily to distract the attention of the guard while they spoke in French. "From the moment Lise looked at me, I knew I had not lost the love of my wife. And I now realise that she was fully expecting my 'No' to her question of whether or not I was guilty." London's health deteriorated and his wife, having returned to France, moved heav-

en and earth to ensure that he received treatment. After Stalin's death, he was released in 1956, treated in a sanatorium, and returned to France in 1963. He was rehabilitated in 1968 at the time of the "Prague Spring". In August, he returned to Czechoslovakia with Lise for the publication of his autobiography, *The Confession*, in which he exposed the implacable mechanisms used by totalitarian governments to create scapegoats. On the day they arrived, Russian tanks invaded the country. They returned to France, where *The Confession* was finally published. In 1970, Costa-Gavras made a film of it, starring Yves Montand and Simone Signoret. From his exile in France, Artur London worked for civil liberties in his country until his death in 1986, while Lise continued to promote the cause of international Communism.

ANGUISH
Jealousy

THIS PAGE
Othello (Orson Welles)
distraught over the body
of Desdemona (Suzanne
Cloutier), whom he has
just strangled.

"The restless need to tyrannise applied to the things of love" (Proust), but jealousy is no longer viewed with the indulgence it once was.

Jealousy featured prominently in 1952, with the release of two major films on the subject: Orson Welles's *Othello*, based on Shakespeare's tragedy, and *El*, by Luis Buñuel, whose young married hero is constantly asking his wife what, and especially whom, she is thinking about. On their very first night, at a hotel, he believes someone is spying on him and plunges a long needle through the keyhole.

When Desdemona, suspected by her husband Othello, protests: "I never gave him cause," her friend Emilia replies: "But jealous souls will not be answered so. / They are not ever jealous for the cause, / But jealous for they're jealous. It is a monster / Begot upon itself, born on itself." Of course, the traitor Iago skilfully sows suspicion, but Othello would not even have given him a hearing if the poison had not already wormed its way into him, torturing him with doubt: "Desdemona has already deceived her father for my sake; might she not deceive me for the sake of others?"

Similarly, in real life a jealous person is deaf to any attempt to convince him of the vanity of his suspicions. From the very beginning of the relationship, there develops a vicious spiral of questions, insinuations, quarrels and violence. Under pressure, the other partner ends up feeling guilty, while all attempts at justification merely aggravate the morbid tendency to investigate. Not even confessions can placate jealousy. According to Proust, "rather than putting an end to existing doubts, they tend to raise new ones".

A jealous person will sometimes take revenge on his rival, real or alleged, but in most cases, lost in a frenzy of hatred, he turns his anger against his partner, whom he sees as a lustful monster. This ugly

passion may be orientated towards the past – "You were already being unfaithful to me, admit it!", says Julian Barnes's hero in the novel *Before She Met Me* – or towards the future.

JEALOUSY IS NOT LOVE. "The fact that Titus is jealous means Titus is in love," exclaims Racine's heroine, Bérénice. Until the twentieth century, when extreme jealously was finally diagnosed as a sickness, it was seen as an integral part of love. Rare indeed were such enlightened observers as La Rochefoucauld, for whom jealously was more an indicator of pride. Othello kills Desdemona because of an irresistible pas-

sion: he is more in need of forgiveness, was the current thinking, than of treatment for mental illness.

As long as the sense of a husband's ownership of his wife was reinforced by cultural norms, opinion and the law tended to take an indulgent view of *crimes passionnels*. "You are mine, and I would rather see you dead than happy with someone else," was the underlying thinking. A person suffering from obsessive jealousy feels no sense of guilt and presents a skilful defence. In Mediterranean countries, jealously is still an essential component of male identity. In Corsica, it is regarded as a national illness. An Arab lover, according to tradition, who does not experience jealously is neither an Arab nor in love. However, things are changing and on the eve of the twenty-first century, although the incidence of domestic violence is still underestimated, crimes of passion are becoming less common. In France, 80 per cent of such crimes are committed by men. It is not that women are any less jealous, but female hatred finds less violent expression.

"I cannot live with or without you." Losing the love of one's partner means losing one's reason for living. This explains the suicides which often follow a separation or a murder. It would appear that men are more sensitive to sexual infidelity, which explains why some take a dim view of modern methods of contraception (cf. p. 310). Women, on the other hand, often persuaded of the imperious nature of male sexual needs, can more readily tolerate a "purely physical" adventure on the part of their partner, but suffer more when love is diverted elsewhere. Whereas a cuckold feels injured in his virility, for a woman the wound often goes deeper, as her dependence on the man is that much greater and her sense of identity, outside the relationship, more fragile.

Jealousy often provokes the very thing it fears: infidelity or, even worse, separation. The hope that the jealous partner may change ebbs away; fear and the survival instinct get the upper hand. Finally, it becomes clear that jealousy, defined by the Russian writer Ivan Alekseyevich Bounine as "a lack of respect for the loved one", is not evidence of love and can therefore only end in destruction.

AN OLD WOUND. Jealousy is often not caused by an act of infidelity. The recriminations of someone who is obsessively jealous conceal a disorder that is not sexual in origin. His sufferings may mask an older, deeper wound, such as neglect or abandonment by his mother or father. A child marked by a rejection of this kind may grow up to feel jealous of anything in which he does not share, or whenever he feels excluded. His problem springs from a deep-seated insecurity, a mistrust which makes him unable to love and give of himself.

Sigmund Freud showed that jealousy sometimes conceals a homosexual desire for the rival, or a desire for another woman that has been repressed and projected onto the partner. It may even lead to megalomania, as if in his madness a mere mortal aspired to be like the God of the Old Testament, who is described as "jealous" because he demands to be loved and served with total devotion.

If the person one loves wants to break free, the idea that one can hold on to them is an illusion. It is quite impossible to obtain undying love by force. To be healed, one must stop thinking of love in terms of ownership and come to see it in terms of freedom. Far from holding power over another, true love is self-giving, yielding oneself to the other in trust.

1952

... seventy-one, she forty. Amalia accepted his proposal and, until Fleming's death in 1955, they worked and travelled the world together.

CHILE. After a life characterised by violent and impossible love affairs, the poet Pablo Neruda (Nobel Prize for Literature, 1971) marries Matilde Urrutia. He had met her while living in exile in Naples. She inspired the beautiful sonnets of *Cien sonetos de amor* (1959). "I love this piece of land which is you ... It is you that repeat and multiply the universe." In 1953, a selection of poems was published from earlier collections, *Crepusculario* (1923) and the highly popular *Veinte poemas de amor y un canción desesperada* (1924), in praise of the female body and sexual pleasure. "I love love which is shared / In kisses, in milk, in bread / Love which can be eternal / But which may be fleeting / Love which can free itself / To begin to love again / Love, god who draws near / Love, god who draws away."

"FAREWELL"
Crepusculario

The Rosenberg Affair

Found guilty of espionage, Julius and Ethel Rosenberg were executed despite an international campaign in their favour.

On 19 June 1953, Julius and Ethel Rosenberg were put to death in the United States for turning over atomic secrets to the Soviet Union – a charge they always denied. The Rosenberg affair epitomised a period when America was prey to anti-Communist hysteria, stoked up by much of the press. Since the Soviet Union had exploded its own atomic bomb in 1949, the United States had lost its monopoly. Recent confessions by spies working for the Eastern bloc, particularly the East German physicist Klaus Fuchs, who had come to Britain as a refugee, made Edgar Hoover's FBI determined to uncover a corresponding American spy ring.

Having failed to discover the real culprits, some of whom were unmasked at a later stage, they focused their attention on the Rosenbergs, who were arrested in 1950 against the background of the war in Korea. At that time, the most harmless trade-unionist or pacifist was regarded as an accomplice of the "enemies of the West", as Senator Joseph McCarthy conducted his anti-Communist witch-hunt. Middle-class, Jewish, with strong left-wing leanings, the Rosenbergs were ideal scapegoats, domestic victims of the Cold War.

AN EARLY POLITICAL COMMITMENT. Julius and Ethel Rosenberg both came from the Lower East Side, a work-ing-class Jewish Manhattan neighbourhood. Ethel Greenglass, an office worker born in 1915, had been a brilliant student and dreamed of an acting or singing career. At the age of twenty, she was dismissed for having set up a women's union within her company and for organising a strike. She performed as a singer and continued her political activities. In 1936, whilst performing at a meeting of the seamen's union, she met Julius Rosenberg, three years her junior. A militant anti-Fascist, and a practising Jew with a knowledge of Hebrew, he had graduated in engineering from the University of New York. They married in 1939 and had two sons, Michael in 1943, and Robert in 1947. Ethel continued her political activities, despite her poor health and pressure from her disapproving parents.

In 1945, Julius was accused of being a Communist and lost his job as an engineer. With Ethel's brother, David Greenglass, who had been employed at the atomic research centre of Los Alamos, he opened a shop selling army surplus goods, but the business folded and David withdrew.

In 1950, David Greenglass was accused of having passed information to Klaus Fuchs, who had just been unmasked as a spy. To save his skin (he got off with a fifteen-year prison sentence), he pleaded guilty but

Julius and Ethel Rosenberg during their trial.

FACING PAGE
Demonstration in support of the Rosenbergs in Paris, 18 June 1953.

ITALY. **With the marriage of actors Dario Fo and Franca Rame begins a story of love and political commitment that is to revolutionise the Italian theatre. In 1958, after their first production,** *Thieves, Models and Nude Women* **(1957), they founded a company to perform farces and comedies. He wrote and directed the plays, she provided the administrative skills and political leadership. Fo sought to create a genuinely popular form of comedy and to arrive at truth through laughter. His subversive theatre became more and more militant and was one of the most original expressions of the struggle of the new left after 1968. Their productions focused on such burning issues as drugs, feminism (***Let's Talk Women***, by Franca Rame, 1977) and AIDS. In her view, "it is only possible to rebuild our society by starting with the couple, with the love between two people."**

♡ ♡ ♡

claimed he had acted at the instigation of his brother-in-law, Julius Rosenberg, and with the complicity of his sister. He was the only witness against the couple.

The Rosenbergs were arrested and imprisoned. The FBI report states that Ethel reacted "with a typically Communist protest, demanding a copy of the warrant and the right to call a lawyer". The exorbitant sum of 100,000 dollars was required as bail.

While the press stigmatised the Rosenbergs as the "atomic spies", the country was gripped by the fear of nuclear war: fall-out shelters were built, doctors and nurses mobilised, and other militants consigned to prison.

MONOTONOUS DAYS AND JOYLESS NIGHTS. Despite the lack of evidence, on March 1951 the Rosenbergs were found guilty of spying for the Soviet Union. The judge who handed down the death sentence concluded: "Your behaviour in placing the A-bomb in Russian hands has caused the Communist aggression in Korea."

From the time of their arrest, the Rosenbergs resolved not to give way to despair. Separated for the first time in their marriage, they were also deprived of their children, who they did not see for a whole year. Their vibrant love letters, full of comfort and encouragement, and the few visits they were allowed enabled them to hold on. "You are truly a woman of great character," wrote Julius, "worthy and delightful ... Life has been worth living with you at my side."

After their sentencing, the Rosenbergs were transferred to Sing Sing prison, in the state of New York. In May 1951, Ethel wrote: "My dear husband, Sing Sing can offer only monotonous days and joyless nights ... Yet here, held fast in brick, concrete and steel, our love will put down stubborn roots and bear tender flowers; here too, we will challenge our enemies and fight."

In the spring of 1952, after the court of appeals and then the Supreme Court had confirmed the judgement, international public opinion was divided. Rosenberg committees, in which women's groups were particularly active, sprang up everywhere, despite the risks involved in undertaking "Un-American" activities.

In February 1953, President Eisenhower refused to grant a pardon. When there was talk of pardoning Ethel, because of her status as a woman and mother, she rebelled against this "diabolical machination": "I will not dishonour the bond of marriage, the happiness and integrity of our love for each other, to play the role of prostitute for the political prosecutors. My husband is innocent, as I am. No power can separate us, neither in life nor death." For the benefit of their children, the Rosenbergs decided to publish their correspondence, which appeared under the title *Death House Letters of Ethel and Julius Rosenberg*.

Despite appeals for clemency from foreign heads of state, the Rosenbergs went to the electric chair. It was their fourteenth wedding anniversary. "June is ours," wrote Julius, "because it was in June that we became husband and wife, and found the boundless joy of a magnificent, living love. Precious wife, noble wife, until the end I shall be devoted to you, body and soul."

There is still controversy as to the Rosenbergs' guilt. But even if they were guilty, they certainly did not deserve so severe a punishment. The affair still weighs on the American conscience. As well as many books, it inspired Arthur Miller's play *The Crucible* (1953), and Sidney Lumet's film *Daniel* (1983). When, in 1966, a freedom of information act gave access to secret FBI documents, no evidence was found to confirm the Rosenbergs' guilt. In August 1993, in a mock trial organised by the association of American lawyers, they were both acquitted.

♥ ♥ ♥

Valentine's Day

The 14 February, now celebrated throughout the West, has become big business.

14 February, St Valentine's Day, is a time for lovers to exchange gifts. This custom, rooted in European rural tradition, flourishes mainly in Britain and the United States, but since the 1950s it has spread throughout the West. In France, where it had remained alive only in the Vosges and the extreme north, its revival was undoubtedly due to the presence of American troops after the Liberation in 1944.

On 14 February millions of cards bearing such greetings as "Happy Valentine" or "Be my Valentine" are sent by Britons and Americans to the girl of their dreams. The word *valentine* applies equally to the card as to its recipient. The tradition of decorated or embroidered cards is much older than the lovers' postcards of the early 1900s (cf. p. 26). "Valentines", with a decorative border of flower motifs, hearts or pairs of birds, were all the rage as far back as the eighteenth century.

Whether the original intention was to commemorate the Christian martyr Valentine, put to death in 270 AD, or more probably to appropriate a Roman love and fertility festival, the date has always been as-

sociated with birds. This is, after all, the time of year when birds pair off and begin to build their nests. It is also the season for making predictions about marriage. According to a medieval custom, the first bird a girl sees on the morning of 14 February foretells the occupation of her future husband: a blackbird indicates a magistrate, the careless robin a sailor, while the goldfinch, with its beautiful wing bars, presages a wealthy suitor to the lucky girl.

The rural French tradition associated with this day consisted of a game in which boys and girls participated in equal number. Each wrote his or her name on a piece of paper, which was then thrown into an urn.

Lots were drawn to form couples for the duration of the festival. In some regions of France, the young people chose their partners in advance. When each had found his or her valentine, it was time to dance, and each couple was in turn pushed into the middle and invited to kiss in public. As time went by, games of this kind, designed to achieve random pairings, lost their importance and subversive character, and the idea of a valentine was replaced by the more acceptable notion of a fiancé(e).

A WORLD-WIDE PHENOMENON. Nowadays St Valentine's Day, like Mothers' Day, has become very much a commercial enterprise, for the benefit of florists and retailers of greetings cards, chocolates, heart-shaped cakes, household appliances and, of course, sexy underwear! Radio and television broadcasters and daily newspapers are all involved: *The Times* and the *International Herald Tribune*, for instance, publish dozens of lovers' messages in their personal columns.

Peynet's lovers.

FACING PAGE
Valentine's Day,
Erró, 1964.

The custom is spreading: in the Philippines, the day is celebrated with all the fervour of a national holiday; in Poland, Valentine's Day is the name of a collection of romantic novels (cf. p. 126); in Turkey, despite opposition from conservatives, the day was first celebrated in 1993, with hotels offering half-price deals for couples; in Beirut, which first welcomed the occasion in 1985, the embattled city was festooned with garlands of hearts.

Meanwhile, in 1990, the little central-French village of Saint-Valentin (Indre) established a "lovers' garden", where on 14 February couples come to plant a tree in their memory. In Japan, the fashion took off in the 1980s, but only for women: on Valentine's Day they all give gifts of chocolates; the men have to wait until 14 March, "white day", to give sweets in return.

Offering sweetmeats is an old European tradition, as the sweetness of sugar is readily associated with love. Nowadays there is a huge demand for red roses, as giving flowers is another tradition, whereby each flower has its special connotation. In the nineteenth century, it was more appropriate to offer a girl white roses, red having too obvious sexual overtones. Do modern lovers still pluck the petals from daisies to the words: "He loves me – He loves me not" or "This year – Next year – Sometime – Never" as a way of foretelling the future? In any case, it has to be said that sentimentality is the order of the day. Everyone's heart is melted by the timid lovers the cartoonist Peynet has been drawing since 1942: the bowler-hatted poet and his perennial fiancée.

UNUSUAL WAYS OF TYING THE KNOT. As well as these widespread traditions, there are some interesting local customs connected with marriage. On 14 February in New

York, for instance, the winners of a special competition are entitled to marry, free of charge, in a chapel located on the eightieth floor of the Empire State Building. Even more famous is Las Vegas, where 100,000 weddings are performed each year. There are thirty-five chapels reserved for such ceremonies, and you can also get married aboard a hot-air balloon or without getting out of your car. In Nevada, formalities are reduced to a minimum: there is no minimum residence stipulation, nor are medical tests, witnesses or registry searches required. However, for foreigners, such marriages are only valid in their home country after they have been duly authenticated and registered. For the British, the little Scottish village of Gretna Green, located just over the border

from England, is a famous site for marriages and hosts some three or four thousand weddings each year. As a consequence of an English law of 1754, which complicated marriage formalities, couples took to eloping to Scotland, where they could marry in the presence of two witnesses without the involvement of a priest. Although the law has since changed, underage lovers can still marry at Gretna Green without parental consent, as did James Goldsmith and Isabel Patiño (cf. p. 251).

In Scotland, a decree promulgated by Queen Margaret in 1288 allows girls to propose marriage to the man of their choice on 29 February each leap year. In the past, a man who refused had to pay a fine of one pound. The custom continues, apart from the fine!

1953

NEW YORK. **The beginning of a relationship, lasting six years, between the American painters Robert Rauschenberg and Jasper Johns. Rauschenberg helped Johns, six years his junior, to find his way as an artist. They were both opposed to Abstract Expressionism and their work foreshadowed Pop Art. At the time, the hatred of American society for homosexuals, viewed as "perverts", was so strong that they concealed the true nature of their relationship. It was not openly commented on until the 1980s. They engaged in passionate discussion, sharing ideals and exchanging ideas. For both, it was the most intense relationship of their lives and of immense consequence to their art at a crucial point in their careers.**

"I will not describe the reasons you have for loving me, as you have none; the reason for loving is love."

ANTOINE DE SAINT-EXUPÉRY
Carnets

Federico Fellini & Giulietta Masina

Companions for fifty years, a brilliant Italian couple who made two legendary films together.

In Federico Fellini's film *La Strada* (1954), Giulietta Masina was deeply moving in the role of Gelsomina, an innocent who in dying softens the heart of a brutal monster, played by Anthony Quinn. Although the actress had been side-lined into minor roles since her cinema début in 1946, she came to life under the direction of Fellini, who brought out her profound originality, a combination of realism and poetry. The film was an outstanding success and won an Oscar for best foreign film.

In *Notti di Cabiria* (1957), Fellini cast her as another innocent who, despite all evidence to the contrary, insists on believing in goodness and humanity. Again, it was an international sensation and won another Oscar. Masina could identify with Cabiria, the little Roman prostitute with a heart of gold, to whom she lent her exuberance, energy, and unfailing optimism. Small and delicate in appearance, with a round face and bright eyes, she was physically a far cry from the pin-ups and fashionable actresses of the day. Fellini saw her as "a fragile little sparrow, who was yet able to survive the rigours of winter".

THEIR CHILDREN WERE THEIR FILMS. They were both born in 1920, he in Rimini, she near Bologna, of lower middle-class families. In 1942, while studying literature at the University of Rome, she joined the Italian radio drama troupe and was a great hit in a series of sketches, *Cico e Pallina*, written by Fellini. The future director was then a journalist and cartoonist and also wrote screenplays and radio dramas. When they met, in an office of the radio station in the autumn of 1942, she was struck by his height, thinness, pallor, intense gaze, deep, soft, warm voice, and extraordinary sense of humour. Fellini later said that the star of his series immediately became "the star of his life".

He went into hiding to avoid being drafted into the army, and circumstances precipitated their marriage, which took place without ceremony on 30 October 1943.

Giulietta Masina in Federico Fellini's film *La Strada*.

To their great sorrow, their first child – a boy – died at birth and they were told they could not have further children. Later, Fellini said: "Our children are the films we have made together."

After the war, Masina continued to perform on stage and for the radio, then made her film début. Fellini, meanwhile, worked with Roberto Rossellini on the screenplays of his films, from *Open City* to *Europe 51*, and with Pietro Germi and Alberto Lattuada. Fellini and Masina were close friends with Rossellini and Bergman, whom they supported during the scandal of their elopement (cf. p. 228).

Tired of being a scriptwriter, Fellini began directing. After the failure of *The White Sheik*, the international success of *I Vitelloni* (*Spivs*) provided him with the means to make *La Strada*, which was conceived with his wife in mind. With the characters of Gelsomina and Cabiria, they created a modern myth, but there was no further development. Masina remains associated with these roles and with the first period of Fellini's career. She did not shine in the same way when she made films with other directors.

FRESH INSPIRATION. Breaking with neo-realism, Fellini's career took another turn. He had found a double, a brother, in Marcello Mastroianni, and he drew fresh inspiration from voluptuous, well-endowed women, in particular Anna Giovannini, with whom he enjoyed a secret affair from the moment they met in May

1954

SCOTLAND. **On 7 January, after what the newspapers described as the "abduction of the century", James ("Jimmy") Goldsmith, aged twenty, marries Isabel Patiño, aged eighteen, daughter of a very rich Bolivian family, whom he had met in London in June 1953. The lovers had been meeting in secret, as the Patiño parents were opposed to their plans, and the young woman was pregnant. The wedding took place at Gretna Green in Scotland, where formalities are minimal. The newly-weds then settled in Paris, where James Goldsmith was establishing a business with a golden future. In the seventh month of her pregnancy, his wife suddenly died of a cerebral haemorrhage, and baby Isabel was born by Caesarean section. It was less than a year since the couple had first met. Goldsmith and the Patiño grandparents became locked in a legal battle over custody of the child, which was finally awarded to the father.**

1957. He called her "*paciocca*" (chubby), in reference to her generous figure; she was four years his senior, with an opulent bosom and ample hips. He persuaded her to leave her job as a photographer, give up her friends, and sacrifice everything to devote herself to his needs. In his films, now bursting with baroque imagery, his fantasy of a goddess of pleasure first found expression with Anita Ekberg in *La Dolce Vita* (1960). This was followed by other masterpieces, such as *Eight and a Half* and *Amarcord*. There was no place for Masina in films of this kind.

She was well aware of her "Fefé"'s infidelities, but said nothing and waited. Paying the price of fame, the maestro was ruthlessly hounded by the gutter press,

and he and Masina were often obliged to deny rumours of separation. Fellini, who admitted: "I have never been a model husband," confided that he had made love to all the actresses who had featured in his films. Masina, who referred to them as "the courtesans at the court of King Federico", was hurt by Fellini's infatuations; although, according to Anouk Aimée, "this seducer was the man of a single woman – Giulietta."

What a contrast between this little woman, reserved by nature and a fervent Catholic, and her loud-mouthed ogre, anticlerical and renowned for his angry outbursts! He loved the *spaghetti alla bolognese* she prepared for him, or walking with her in the streets of Rome. She accompanied him to all the events held in his honour. For all his flamboyant genius, he needed the daily tenderness she alone could give.

She made two further films with him. In 1965 he cast her in the leading role in *Juliet of the Spirits*, which explores a couple's separation and the resulting liberation of the female partner. But they were not in harmony: whereas Fellini's interest was in fantasy, Masina wanted to act the role of the abandoned wife in a realistic vein. The film was a disappointment and most of her subsequent acting was for television, making her very popular, as did the agony aunt column she wrote for ten years in the daily newspaper *La Stampa*. Twenty years later, Fellini offered her a starring role

opposite Marcello Mastroianni in *Ginger and Fred*, turning his two favourite actors into figures from the past.

A heavy smoker, Masina contracted lung cancer , but it was Fellini who died first, on their fiftieth wedding anniversary in 1993, after a long, painfull illness five months before her. Following a first attack, he deliberately brought forward the celebration of their golden wedding. They are buried together at Rimini.

After so rich a life, their epitaph might well be a quotation from *Ginger and Fred*. Of all her lines, it was the one she loved most: "Everything is a miracle; you just have to realise it."

♡ ♡ ♡

WRITINGS
The Story of O

A woman in love describes her fantasies of being a slave and opens the way to greater sexual freedom.

Dominique Aury, author of *The Story of O*, whose identity remained a mystery for many years, working at the NRF with Jean Paulhan (centre) and Marcel Arland.

The Story of O, published in Paris in 1954 under the pseudonym Pauline Réage, tells the story of a woman who gives herself up to every form of torture and finds mystical bliss in her enslavement.

The enigmatic initial letter of the heroine's name has a timeless quality, distinguishing her from the commonplace Jacquelines, Yvonnes, Anne-Maries, and other nymphets of the 1950s. How old is O? Is she beautiful? Except for her breasts, rather heavy for her slight figure, and her long legs, her body is hardly described at all. "Your belly, your mouth and your loins are open to us." O is all orifices, offered to an endless stream of men: her lover René, the "master" to whom

he delivers her, Sir Stephen, and all those to whom she is presented, like a prize mare, both proud and docile, to be mounted. What humanity is left in O, a slave who submits to the every demand of a lover whom she reveres as a god?

The Story of O is regarded as a masterpiece of erotic literature, a genre whose chief exponents have been men and whose best-known work is Sade's *Justine*. Writing in a highly refined style and describing the heroine's various tortures with boundless imagination, the author manages to avoid almost any concrete reference. Semen spurts forth on every page, but the word is used only once. The term "loins" is preferred to "buttocks", a harmless word until the part in question is branded with a red-hot iron. And, of course, the region conceals what is discreetly described as the "ring of flesh", which is another possible meaning of O.

Prostrate, ecstatic, O has much in common with the sacred prostitute, the recluse, the cloistered nun. The author draws freely on religious imagery, and the way of the cross she describes marks O as a martyr to love. Identifying herself with the "receptacle of impurity, the sewer spoken of in Scripture", she deems herself "abandoned by God in the dark night" and, like St Theresa of Avila, "dies of not dying".

A LOVE LETTER. What distinguishes *The Story of O* from Masoch's novels (cf. p. 50) is that love, not pleasure, is the driving force. While Sir Stephen tells the heroine, "You will obey me without loving me, and without me loving you," she nevertheless ends up falling in love with her tormentor. But this is also a story about men. For O her lover is a god, but Sir Stephen is similarly put on a pedestal by René, and it is his mark that René seeks in O's flesh: "Under the outward appearance of the body they had shared, they were seeking something more mysterious, and maybe more cutting, than an amorous communion."

The Story of O, daringly published by Jean-Jacques Pauvert with an introduction by Jean Paulhan, was well received by a limited circle of intellectuals, while the Catholic writer François Mauriac described it as "an atrocious clinical study of eroticism, unbearable to read". Reading the full account of O's sufferings is indeed a harrowing experience and the book did not reach a wide audience until the 1970s. Even then it did not enjoy the commercial success of more user-friendly erotic novels, such as Emmanuelle Arsan's *Emmanuelle* (1959). Similarly, Liliana Cavani's film *The Night Porter* (cf. p. 337), which explores the relationship between a victim and her torturer, is far more disturbing than the mediocre cinema adaptations of *Emmanuelle* and *The Story of O* itself.

As Pauline Réage was careful to maintain her cover, many doubted whether the author was a woman at all. In his introduction, Jean Paulhan insisted on her "pure and violent spirit" and on the "pitiless propriety" of the work, which he defined as "the most savage love letter a man has ever received". We now know that he was the man for

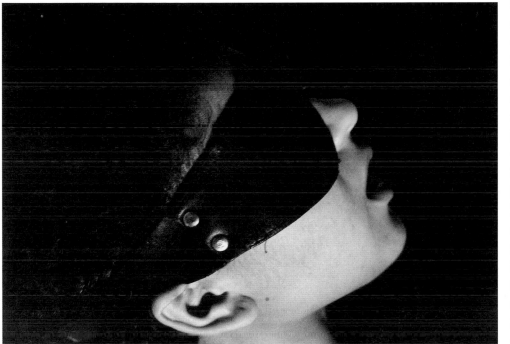

whose eyes the text was written. The author did not reveal her identity until 1994. Her name was Dominique Aury, a translator and literary critic born in 1907, who worked with Paulhan for the publisher Gallimard. Why did she remain silent for forty years? "I waited until my parents had died, for time to go by. The sense of scandal has faded with the years."

She did indeed write *The Story of O* as "a love letter. No more, no less." As she disclosed to Régine Deforges, she did it to safeguard her relationship with Paulhan, who was married: "I was no longer young, not particularly attractive ... I wrote it to keep his interest, to seduce him, because one is always afraid it will not last. And one always looks for a way of prolonging things,

rather like Scheherazade in the *Arabian Nights*." Written at great speed, at night, the text was only published because Paulhan insisted.

THE PLEASURE OF SUFFERING.
"What better can you do than use [your body] to prove to the man you love that you belong to him, and therefore that you no longer belong to yourself," explains the author. "To be killed by the person you love seems to me the height of rapture."

For her, there is something worse than death: "Hell is everyday life when no one loves you, when you are alone." O wants "to reach the end of herself, to attain to the absolute that life refuses her." Just as the masochistic male (cf. p. 51) orchestrates the erotic ceremony in which he is victim, O's story exemplifies a power relationship in which the tormentor is not, in the end, the master. The author supports this interpretation: "Was not O using René and Sir Stephen ... to achieve the fulfilment of her dreams, in other words her destruction, her death?"

Many saw these confessions as belonging to male fantasies. But this is surely a failure to understand the infinite variety of the imagination, the erotic power of literature,

and its capacity to disturb. The alchemy of passion can transform pain into pleasure and apparent enslavement into inner liberation. Violence is part of the mystery of sexuality; and the aphrodisiac properties of a good thrashing are appreciated in all cultures. Even a happy love song may express the pleasure of suffering at the hands of the loved one: "Hurt me," cries Marguerite Burnat-Provins in *Le Livre pour toi* (cf. p. 58), and in the seventeenth century Pernette du Guillet wrote: "In my suffering seeing that he is satisfied, / Satisfied am I at his satisfaction." According to Dominique Aury, who had studied the Marquis de Sade, breaking accepted boundaries is a part of erotic fascination, and you sometimes have to lose yourself to find yourself again. Yielding yourself up in total trust, enables you to find new truths in yourself.

O had a presentiment of the kind of liberation she was making possible: "O, by her existence and behaviour, brought to light an erotic universe as mad and obsessive as that inhabited by men. For centuries silenced, silent out of prudence, out of a sense of propriety, women have in their minds a universe of love, a universe not necessarily that of O, ... but a universe all the same. They have kept silent. Well, that time is over, they will speak, they are speaking." This is indeed true: more and more women are expressing their eroticism in literature (cf. p. 394), revealing the complexity of the sexual power struggle which may be the source of all alienation, but also of total freedom.

1954

FRANCE. **Release of *L'Amour d'une femme*, a superb film by Jean Grémillon, later recognised as one of the great French directors. A young woman doctor (Micheline Presle), devoted to her calling, wins the confidence of the people of the island of Ouessant (off Brittany). She meets an Italian engineer (Massimo Girotti). It is love at first sight, but there is no way forward, as he wants her to give up work and she refuses to forsake her profession. The author drew on sociological surveys on the loneliness of working women. The film was disturbing. The fact that it highlighted the contradictions of French society, in which women's emancipation was often running ahead of the still traditional mentality of many men, was not to the liking of the distributors. Despite its prestigious poster, the film's release was botched. Jean Grémillon never made another full-length feature.**

♡ ♡ ♡

O for offered,
O for oblivious to self,
O for open to everything.
Photograph by Claude Alexandre.

HELL. Her involvement in *How to Marry a Millionaire* (1960) with Yves Montand did not help. Despite a writers' strike, Miller agreed to rewrite some of the scenes, behaving in her eyes as a "scab". She fell into Montand's arms (cf. p. 238), then set off for Nevada to shoot *The Misfits*, based on a screenplay by her husband, who had poured into it all his bitterness and disappointment. Some of the lines, such as "I have never met a girl as sad as you," seem to reflect their life together. Shooting the film in the sweltering heat of the desert was sheer hell. At this juncture, Miller met an Austrian photographer, Inge Morath. Rejected by Montand, Marilyn Monroe was badly hurt by the venomous newspaper reports that followed and by the death of her opposite number, Clark Gable, for which she was blamed. She ended up in hospital again.

Her separation from Miller was formalised and their divorce completed in January 1961. A year later, Miller married Inge Morath, and they later had a daughter. Suffering more and more from depression, Marilyn Monroe had a succession of brief affairs, her partners including Frank Sinatra and President Kennedy. She even took up again with Joe Di Maggio. She began work on another film, but on 4 May 1962 was found dead in her room, having taken an overdose of barbiturates. This led to the most improbable conspiracy theories. Was it that this splendid, yet fragile woman, revered world-wide as a sex goddess, was simply a lost little girl, too unhappy to go on living?

Severely criticised for his play *After the Fall* (1964), whose heroine is a nymphomaniac, alcoholic and drug addict, Miller recovered his creative talent. His famous wife figures prominently in his memoirs, in which he describes her as "seriously neurotic". Since her death, Marilyn Monroe has become one of the legends of the twentieth century.

♡ ♡ ♡

WRITINGS
Lolita

Hymn in praise of "nymphets" or confessions of a paedophile? Nabokov's masterpiece is still a hot potato.

Vladimir Nabokov collecting butterflies.

FACING PAGE
How to avoid parodying a myth?

"Lolita, light of my life, fire of my loins. My sin, my soul." These are the opening words of Vladimir Nabokov's *Lolita*, published in Paris in 1955, after the major New York publishers turned down this tale of a pervert who has sex with a twelve-year-old. The book, covertly passed from hand to hand, soon achieved wide-spread fame. In Britain, Graham Greene defended its literary qualities, and in the United States, where it was published in 1958, it sold so well that Nabokov was able to give up teaching and live exclusively by his pen.

A Russian émigré, after the revolution Vladimir Nabokov lived first in Berlin, then in Paris. He settled in the United States in 1940 and from then on wrote in English. His hero, like him a European exile in the United States, is a murderer who, from his prison cell, addresses a plea to his future jury which is more of a hymn in praise of "nymphets", whose "perilous magic" he seeks to define: aged between nine and fourteen, these "daughters

of the devil", inhabitants of "an enchanted island", bewitch with their dubious grace travellers "twice or many times older than they."

A PRE-PUBESCENT GIRL. Unhealthy confessions of an obsessive paedophile, or an ironic/poetic description of an adult's fascination for a "nymphet"? Now regarded as a masterpiece, *Lolita* has lost nothing of its whiff of sulphur.

Lolita is pre-pubescent, the narrator, Humbert Humbert, is thirty-seven. Marked by his discovery of sexual pleasure as a boy of thirteen with a girl of his own age, he desires the young girl the moment he sees her, while describing her as a vulgar

little idiot. She is the daughter of his landlady, a widow whom he agrees to marry, "thinking of the child while caressing the mother". The mother dies in a providential accident and the narrator sets out, with his step-daughter, on a long motoring holiday. The very first night, at a hotel, they share a bedroom. He gives her a sleeping pill but, though "resolved to pursue my policy of sparing her purity by operating only in the stealth of the night, only on a completely anesthetised little nude", he cannot bring himself to act. "By six in the morning she was wide awake, and by six-fifteen we were technically lovers." His defence: "Had I deflowered this child? Oh, gentle ladies of the jury, I was not even her first lover." Lolita tells him of her sexual experiences with a boy she met at a holiday camp and repeats them with him. Then, during their frequent quarrels, she accuses him of having raped her and calls him a "dirty old man".

He makes no attempt to satisfy her sexually and insists that she keep their relationship secret. Exploiting his position to punish her and prevent her from going out without him, he buys her services

Release of *Stella*, a Greek film by Michael Cacoyannis starring Melina Mercouri. The heroine is a singer whose sensual beauty is irresistible to men. Several times she refuses to marry, rejecting even the man she loves. Finally she agrees to marry him but, on the day of the wedding, fails to turn up at the church. The young man finds her on a beach at dawn and brandishes a knife: "If you will not marry me, I will kill you." She throws herself onto the blade of the knife, deliberately choosing death rather than an unbearable life of conformity.

"Only love ... is able ... to make people whole by reuniting them as one."

PIERRE TEILHARD DE CHARDIN
Le Phénomène humain

♡ ♡ ♡

by giving her pocket money or allowing her out for a walk. He describes himself as "weak and stupid, and the slave of my belle nymphette sans merci". In his jealousy, he persecutes her, only too aware that she does not regard him as "a lover, nor a screen hero, nor a friend, nor even as a human being, but simply as a pair of eyes and a congested prick."

When the girl falls ill and has to go to hospital, he wakes up to reality: "She had never loved me. And I then understood that my love was more hopeless than ever." Lolita runs away from the hospital with another man and the narrator is unable to find her. Five years later, he receives a letter from her, telling him that she is married, pregnant, and in need of money. He goes immediately, but it is too late to offer her his love. "I knew, as clearly as I know I am to die, that I loved her more than anything I had ever seen or imagined on earth, or hoped for anywhere else." Thinking he is looking for sex, she rejects him. He goes off in search of the man who kidnapped her, the only man she claims to have really loved, and kills him. He ends his confession with

the hope that, through his writing, he will have made Lolita "live in the minds of later generations ... the refuge of art. And this is the only immortality you and I may share, my Lolita."

A DEMON CAST OUT. Lolita does in fact live on: her name has become part of the language, but its meaning has changed in the process. A "lolita" is not so much a pre-pubescent nymphet as a precocious woman, a girl who leads men on. In the films based on the novel, the actress is fourteen years old, not twelve, which mitigates the monstrous nature of the incestuous relationship.

Far from identifying with the product of his imagination – like Flaubert, who exclaimed: "Madame Bovary, c'est moi!" – Nabokov distanced himself from the sordid situation he described. A professor of literature, an acknowledged authority on butterflies, and happily married, he described himself as "a gentle old man who cannot stand the thought of cruelty". At his request, the cover of the book did not feature a young girl. "Some of my characters are, undoubtedly, odi-

ous," he wrote, "but that does not affect me. They are outside me, like the doleful monsters on the facades of cathedrals, demons placed there to show that they have been cast out."

In his poetic reconstruction of reality, Humbert Humbert comparing his "idol", his "little mistress" to Dante's Beatrice or Petrarch's Laura, who were also young girls, fails to parody these myths.

As for Humbert's paedophilia, he could not be more severe in his condemnation, describing it as "vile depravity", "desecration of childhood", or "abominable vice". Nevertheless, the author's ironic distance and the virtuosity of his style serve only to heighten the reader's perplexity. The magic of literature has enabled Nabokov to achieve a *tour de force* with one of the most perilous of all subjects. Whether it arouses repulsion or admiration, *Lolita* cannot fail to leave its mark.

Drawing by Loisel.

Sylvia Plath & Ted Hughes

Two great poets who helped and inspired each other, but whose relationship floundered on the rocks of marriage.

On 25 February 1956, Ted Hughes, then twenty-six, and some of his Cambridge friends launched a poetry magazine. Attractive and amusing, always dressed in black corduroys, he was a dynamic figure. Among the guests was Sylvia Plath, a good-looking American student, aged twenty-three. She found him "magnificent, handsome and brilliant". He removed her hairband and kissed her. She bit his cheek, "long and deep", until she drew blood. It was the start of a savage relationship. Four months later they married.

The meeting was a shock for the young woman. She saw Hughes as a "violent Adam", "the only man in the world to equal me". He would, she wrote, "make of me a poet whom the world will gaze upon in wonder." He filled the gap she had felt since the death of her father, the loss of whom, at the age of eight, had been like an amputation. While deploring his insensitivity, she believed he concealed his better side and that she would be able to change him, to tame the "destroyer".

From a working-class Yorkshire family, Hughes went to Cambridge on a scholarship, where he discovered the world of myth and folklore which became his chief source of inspiration. After taking his degree in 1954, he did a number of jobs and published his first poem, *The Jaguar*. He believed in himself and, unlike Plath, cared nothing for social convention. Born in Boston, she was marked by the poverty of her adolescence. Hyper-sensitive and hungry for education – she was an outstanding student at Smith College – she aspired to perfection and entertained great literary ambitions. Since the age of seventeen, she had been publishing short stories and poems in magazines and had won many prizes. In 1953, in a state of depression, she attempted suicide and was subsequently given electricshock therapy.

They saw their relationship as a partnership in the interests of poetry. For Plath, her future life would be "an unbroken song of affirmation and love". They encouraged, inspired and criticised each other. He shared his enthusiasm with her for Robert Graves's book on mythology, *The White Goddess*. She wrote slowly, constantly referring to books. He set her exercises to free her from her inhibitions. Their poems were published in distinguished reviews. Nonetheless, she never felt sufficiently loved or reassured, and spoke of pain "penetrating her heart with the sharpness of a razor". They began to quarrel. She made it a point of honour to succeed in everything, including housework, exhausting herself in the attempt to reconcile her domestic and creative roles. She felt an urgent need to give account of herself: "I am terrified of this dark thing / that sleeps in me."

A CREATIVE PARTNERSHIP. Before settling in London in 1960, they spent three years in the United States, teaching, touring the country, and writing a great deal. Their daughter was born in April 1960. Though delighted to be a mother, Plath was irked by the constraints of motherhood. As they were living in a small apartment, friends lent them a room in which they took turns to write, while the other looked after the child. She was working on *The Bell Jar* (1971), part of her quest for authenticity and integrity, in which she described the period of her breakdown symbolically as a time of death and rebirth. Her first collection of poems, *The Colossus*, was well received. Putting her husband's career before her own, she acted as his typist and literary agent. The two collections of verse published by Hughes won him a reputation as the greatest poet of his generation. He wrote prolifically – poetry, short stories, plays, and criticism – and was especially successful with his animal poems, which celebrate the mystical alliance between the shaman and his companion animal.

Meanwhile, their misunderstandings accumulated. In September 1961, they moved to an old house in Devon, where in January 1962 their son was born. Their partnership continued to be creative. Drawing closer again, they both made progress: he towards self-questioning and greater freedom of form; she towards a fusion with universal forces. Stimulated by motherhood, she wrote more spontaneous, less structured poetry. Her sufferings inspired the bitter poems of *Ariel* (1965). Their marriage was breaking up. Hughes had an affair and was living a lie. In the autumn of 1962, she asked for a divorce and settled in London with the children, with the words: "I shall be a rich, active woman, not a serving shadow as I have been."

LOCKED IN VIOLENCE. According to Hughes, although she was "occupied almost full time by the children and the housework, she nevertheless experienced a sudden and total poetic development virtually without parallel". She wrote rapidly, he remembers, as if being dictated to, through alternate periods of depression and high excitement.

All her major poems date from the last eight months of her life, a gradual unveiling of her hidden truth. In *Edge*, the moon looks down on a perfect woman whose "dead body bears the smile of fulfilment". On 11 February 1963, Sylvia Plath sealed off the children's bedroom and committed suicide by turning on the gas in the kitchen. She was just thirty.

Overwhelmed with grief, Hughes published nothing for the next three years. In 1969, his companion, Assia Wevill, killed herself in the same way, together with their daughter. The following year, he published the sombre poems of *Crow* and married Carol Orchard, who is celebrated in *The Moortown Elegies* (1978). He edited Plath's works

and wrote articles in which he described her as a lark. He saw their relationship as that "of wolves, locked in violence, unable to lower their guard like hounds who hunt in fellowship".

The aura of legend surrounding Sylvia Plath and her early death grew with each posthumous publication. For many people, she embodied the stifled voice of women aspiring to be free, vainly attempting to reconcile the irreconcilable. In 1992, she was posthumously awarded America's most prestigious literary award, the Pulitzer Prize. Ted Hughes, in 1984, was appointed Poet Laureate. In 1998 his collection of poems, *Birthday Letters*, caused a sensation. He had never expressed such poignant emotion as in this *post mortem* dialogue with his first wife.

1956

MONACO. The American actress Grace Kelly gives up film-making to marry Prince Rainier of Monaco, whom she had met the previous year at the Cannes Film Festival. Their wedding was reported by the press as that of Prince Charming and the ideal woman and was accompanied by a campaign to launch the principality as a tourist destination. Thanks to television, the public could admire the bride's sumptuous gown, presented by MGM, her former employers in Hollywood. From a wealthy Philadelphia family, Grace Kelly had received a strict education and little affection. She had played in three films by Hitchcock, who was fascinated by the dynamism of the elegant blonde actress. "Fire is smouldering under the ice," was his comment. Her life with Prince Rainier, then that of their three children, was an inexhaustible source of material for glossy magazines.

IMAGES
"Sex Bombs"

Many men are fascinated by big breasts – a reminder of infant dependency.

Despite the outraged protests of the religious right, *And God Created Woman* (1956) – in which Brigitte Bardot, directed by her husband Roger Vadim, embodies "womanhood" – took America by storm and launched the French actress's career as an international star. Having succumbed to the dark eroticism of the *femme fatale* in the black-and-white films of the 1940s (cf. p, 88), the male public now fell for stars of another kind, whose impressively vital statistics earned them the nickname of "sex bombs". The traditional distinction up to then had been between apple-shaped and pear-shaped breasts, but in the post-war years the fashion was for size rather than shape, and breasts were thought of in terms of explosive projectiles, bombs or artillery shells. The image of a round fruit, symbolising life, was replaced by that of a deadly weapon.

"Bombs away!", shouted an excited spectator at the première of *The Outlaw* (1946), as Jane Russell appeared in a dress displaying her magnificent cleavage. The millionaire Howard Hughes, infatuated with her opulent bosom, had decided to launch her as a film star, focusing the film's advertising campaign on her physical attributes.

The expression "sex bomb" is closely related to the fantasy of American power, associating feminine seductiveness with a destructive capacity, undreamed of in earlier human history. In 1947, the experimental bomb which exploded on Bikini atoll in Micronesia was named Gilda, after the heroine of the King Vidor film (1947), in which Rita Hayworth acted with such smouldering sensuality. The name of the atoll itself was chosen by a French designer for a skimpy two-piece bathing costume, intended to drive men to distraction. In this sense, the word "bikini" has become part of the language.

BREAST FETISHISM. The new filmstars did not cloak themselves in mystery like their counterparts of the pre-war years. They advertised themselves as available, displaying their bodies and making the most of them. Do gentlemen prefer blondes, as the title of Howard Hawks's film (1953) claims? Of course, when they have the radiant sensuality of a Marilyn Monroe (cf. p. 254), who unfortunately was type-cast in the role of a "dumb blonde" with a bird brain and childish emotions. In *There's no Business like Show Business* (1954), for instance, her ambition to become a singer is ridiculed: "Why would a girl with such gorgeous breasts need to take singing lessons?"

According to Jayne Mansfield, akin to May West in her sense of humour: "Men are those creatures with two legs and eight hands." When she flaunts her ample proportions and peroxide blonde hair in Frank Tashlin's film *The Girl Can't Help It* (1956), the milk begins to boil in the bottles of the dumbfounded milkman and the glasses of another astonished ogler are seen to explode. As well as a magnificent bust, Mansfield was gifted with exceptional intelligence; Hollywood nevertheless reduced her to the role of a hothouse plant with sex appeal, devoid of danger or perversity.

"We do not admire big feet or big ears, but we idolise a woman for her overgrown breasts," said Frank Tashlin, criticising the immaturity of the American male, whom he described as a "breast fetishist". The spread of mammary obsession to the rest of the Western world is evidenced by the predilection of photographers for the physical attributes of Sophia Loren or Gina Lollobrigida, or the spectacular apparition of Anita Ekberg, elected Miss Sweden in 1951, in Fellini's film *La Dolce Vita*. Women unhappy with lesser natural endowments cheated by using padding or special bras to give lift to their breasts. Now we have silicon implants.

BACK TO MOTHER. Big breasts evoke the image of the all-powerful mother figure or the buxom femininity celebrated by Rubens and Renoir. However, the ideal woman of the 1950s had neither a rounded belly, nor large thighs, nor imposing buttocks. Rather than homage to female fecundity, this male obsession is considered to reflect a desire for maternal consolation. In *Tess of the D'Urbervilles*, by Thomas Hardy, while Tess is breast-feeding her baby during a break in haymaking, a fellow labourer unconsciously lifts a flagon of ale to his lips.

1956

"When one has
[only love
to share
On the day of the great
journey
Of our great love
... When one has
[only love
To speak to the cannons
And nothing but a song
To speak to the drum
Then, having nothing
But the strength to love
We shall have
[in our loving hands
The whole world."
Quand on n'a que l'amour,
Jacques Brel's first hit
(cf. p. 272).

"When men
[live from love
There will be no more
poverty
Then will begin
[the fine days
But we, we shall be
[dead, my brother ..."
*Quand les hommes
vivront d'amour*,
song by the Quebec singer
Raymond Lévesque

The Art of Loving by Erich
Fromm, an American
psychoanalyst of German
extraction, is avidly read
world-wide. "Love is an art
which demands creativity
and effort. It cannot be reduced to a pleasurable
sensation experienced at
random."

♡ ♡ ♡

With her body crammed into a sheath dress, her waist pulled in to emphasise her breasts, her stomach flattened by a corset, and her long slender legs – another masculine fixation – the film star stood in opposition to the housewife in her practical clothes, the housebound queen bee presiding over an immaculate modern kitchen. In venues such as the Bunny Club, clients were served drinks by topless hostesses, whom they were not allowed to touch, while fantasising over the silicon-inflated creatures displayed in magazines and pornographic films.

Big boobs may give a sense of security to men for whom a generous bosom suggests the supply and shelter of the maternal breast. Some big-breasted women are attracted by men in search of infantile pleasure, that of the replete infant who falls asleep after his feed, head nestling in his mother's breasts. The pendulum of fashion swings periodically between two extremes. Like the flat-chested flappers of the 1920s, apparently devoid of bums and boobs, the rangy, androgynous silhouette fashionable in the 1960s suggests a certain denial of femininity. In the 1980s, big breasts came back into fashion. Admirers of women able to fill out a bra were again free to feast their eyes, with specialised films like *Vixens* and actresses such as Béatrice Dalle, Samantha Fox, and Pamela Anderson, star of the television soap *Baywatch*.

For a real man, the most beautiful bosom is that of the woman he loves. What then is the size of the ideal breast? According to the old French adage: "As much as it takes to fill a gentleman's hand."

ments from 1981 to 1989. She fought lost causes with great panache: for the return of the Elgin Marbles from the British Museum, for Athens to host the Olympic Games in 1996, and to wrest the local government of Athens from the conservatives after their return to power. She also fought a losing battle against lung cancer, but did not give up smoking. She took up her ministry again in 1993, when the socialists came back in, but died on 6 March 1994. She was buried in Athens with the highest honours.

For almost forty years, Mercouri and Dassin lived a relationship of solidarity, sharing the same ideals and enthusiasms: "I am happy to be married, and that amazes me," she wrote in her autobiography.

♡ ♡ ♡

WRITINGS
The Song of Songs

Unique in the Western literary tradition, this song of desire and delight portrays love as a joyful search to know the other, whilst respecting the other's essential mystery.

1957 saw the publication of an illustrated edition of the Bible, with engravings by Marc Chagall. During the same period, the artist painted a series of five pictures inspired by *The Song of Songs*, one of the biblical books. In contrast with the rich Oriental heritage of love (cf. p. 68), this magnificent love song – just a few pages long in Hebrew – is the only such erotic outpouring in early Western literature. Attributed to Solomon, it may well have been written around 450 BC, at the time of Israel's great king. But, apart from his wide culture we know nothing of the author, not even if "he" was a man or a woman.

Is this dialogue between a young man and his "beloved" a hymn in praise of human love or a song expressing the bliss of union between the soul and its creator? Its 117 verses have given rise to passionate disputes between partisans of a "natural" interpretation and those who favour one of the many allegorical meanings. Attempts have been made to reduce it to a collection of chants used in wedding ceremonies; to deny its eroticism in favour of a purely spiritual reading; to tone it down into a romance between a shepherd and a shepherdess; or to transfigure it into a song of the mystical love between the God of Israel and his people, in the case of the Jews, or between Jesus Christ and his Church, in the case of Christians.

"It is not decent for a woman to write about *The Song of Songs*," one of her confessors told St Theresa of Avila. We can only dream of the other writings that might have been inspired by this fascinating text so expressive of desire and delight, if only the scholars had not got hold of it, and puritans had not appropriated it with their own meaning. It shocked our prudish forebears in the nineteenth century, who quoted from it in Latin!

NEITHER LOSS OF IDENTITY NOR POSSESSION. A celebration of erotic love and mystical outpouring, *The Song of Songs* expresses a vibrant passion, a joyful desire for the other: "Draw me after you, let us make haste!" says the young woman. As for her lover, "he comes leaping upon the mountains, bounding over the hills" to meet her.

Those who claim that the Jewish or Christian God disapproves of the pleasure shared by two lovers have lost sight of the essence of this text, buried as it has been beneath so much exegesis. In words beautiful, strong, and simple, *The Song of Songs* praises love as both carnal and spiritual, affecting the whole being without disrupting the unity of body, heart, and mind. Those who disapprove of sex being dissociated from procreation overlook the fact that this sacred poem never once mentions the lovers' fertility, although the fruits of the earth figure prominently in its imagery:

"Your cheeks are like halves of a pomegranate ..., your lips distil nectar, ... your breasts are like clusters of the vine," he says to his beloved who then invites him to come in to her: "Let my beloved come to his garden and eat its choicest fruits." There is nothing blameworthy about their desire, which is unequivocally expressed, and their pleasure is seen as an end in itself. Consent and mutual self-giving are the hallmarks of their love – "My beloved is mine and I am his" – and there is no sense of domination or the will to possess.

Set in springtime, "time of singing", season of awakening and rebirth, *The Songs of Songs* begins in sensual vein: "O that you would kiss me with the kisses of your mouth," she says, "for your love is better than wine, your anointing oils are fragrant." And for him, "the fragrance of your oils [is better] than any spice". Each is a source of wonder to the other: "Behold, you are beautiful, my love. Behold, you are beautiful." Never before in literature had a man and a woman's voices sounded so distinct. Never had a

Marc Chagall,
Song of Songs, IV.

woman spoken on such equal terms with a man. Even though the beloved is a mere shepherdess leading her flocks to pasture, love makes her a queen.

For the first time in history, we hear the song of love triumph, a love which is both fully human and cosmic. Fervent though it may be, this love never aspires to the loss of the one in the other. It is like a third element which prevents the lovers from becoming too self-absorbed. Nor does it represent a withdrawal from the world, an absorption in the miracle of love. Several times, the lovers address themselves to "others", as if to witnesses, inviting them to come and drink with them, to participate in the celebration of universal love.

RESERVING THE MYSTERY. The man hides and the woman searches for him, then it is her turn to hide. The absence of the beloved is a prelude to the joy of rediscovery, to rebirth following death. Seeking out the other is, after all, the essence of love, as the search for God is the essence of faith. Giving up the search is a denial of life, of what is essential in human nature. As philosopher Emmanuel Levinas explains, desire is an approach whose object is constantly moving away. It is the means of access to another, in which the notion of otherness is revealed. "The other must remain absence and mystery," he writes, otherwise eroticism dissipates.

After the waiting and the search for the beloved, the lovers' reunion does not exhaust what will always remain elusive and inaccessible in the other. Far from dispelling it, love preserves the hidden, secret dimension, so long as it remains a bond between two independent beings.

In *The Songs of Songs*, sexuality can be seen as a means of going beyond oneself, of communion with the outside world, of union with God in the case of believers. Pleasure, which provides a release from the body, enables us to experience a kind of resurrection. Love is then akin to death. Is it "stronger than death", "as strong as death", or "strong as death"? The translations differ on this point. In any case, love is birth, awakening, openness to the future. "Your mother conceived you ... I awakened you," says the woman. Just as "nothing, no trial, no flood, can quench the fire of love", so no commentary can detract from the flame of this text, an ever-burning ember which, for 2,000 years, has fed on its own intensity.

[Quotations from the Revised Standard Version]

1957

Doctor Zhivago, Boris Pasternak's masterpiece, appears in an Italian translation because the author had faced insurmountable difficulties in getting it published in Moscow. Forced by the Soviet authorities to refuse the Nobel Prize for Literature in 1958, Pasternak died in disgrace in 1960. Like his hero, there were two women in his life. Their love cost them both dear: his wife was reduced to poverty and his mistress spent a total of eight years in the Gulag. It was his wife, Zinayda Neuhaus, who inspired the collection of poems *Second Birth*. In 1948 he wrote to her: "Do not believe anyone when I die. You alone will have been my life, fully lived until the end, fully led until its conclusion." However, in 1946 he met Olga Ivinskaya, the model for the character of Lara. "If they loved each other," he wrote at the end of the novel, "it was because everything around them wanted it: the ground under their feet, the sky above their heads, the clouds, the trees."

Paul Newman & Joanne Woodward

The exemplary relationship of two great actors with a commitment to political and humanitarian causes.

Joanne Woodward and Paul Newman in the film *A New Kind of Love*.

1958 saw the wedding of two American actors. More surprisingly, their marriage turned out to be lasting and happy.

When Paul Newman and Joanne Woodward first met, in 1952, at a theatrical agency in New York, she was twenty-two, he twenty-seven. "I thought: blow me, what a beautiful girl!" he recalls. For her part, she remembers having "immediately detested this chap; only he was so funny, so sweet, so well-groomed ..." But he was married, with children. From a well-off family in Cleveland, Ohio, he had studied drama. Both athlete and thinker, he was small and handsome, with startlingly blue eyes. Joanne Woodward was from Thomasville, Georgia. Small and blonde, she was of a generous nature, determined, and disarmingly candid. She did not reckon herself beautiful, but had always wanted to be an actress. In New York, she made her début in the theatre and on the small screen.

When they acted together in the play Picnic, their mutual attraction was obvious, but they did not give in to it. They embarked on parallel careers on stage, in films, and on television, determined to accept only quality roles. In 1956, Newman made his name as a cinema actor in Somebody up there Likes Me. Later that year, he was arrested for drunk driving after a car accident, which drew attention to his alcohol problem and to his relationship with Joanne Woodward. Braving the scandal, they began to live together and married as soon as he had obtained a divorce.

Three films released in 1957 enhanced their reputations: The Left Handed Gun in his case, The Three Faces of Eve in hers, and The Long Hot Summer, in which they acted together. Their frankness shocked Hollywood gossip columnists. Newman was reported as saying: "What we do in the evenings and at weekends is our own bloody business." In fact they lived quietly in a simple rented house without a swimming-pool. While he achieved stardom in Cat on a Hot Tin Roof, with Liz Taylor, she became a model wife. Their daughter Nell was born in 1959. "I had a baby because everyone else was having one," she said later. She made far fewer films. "I sit and read cookery books, sew, and wait for Paul. I just love it." While he became a sex symbol, in such internationally successful films as Exodus (1960), The Hustler (1961) and Hud (1963), she gave birth to Melissa in 1961 and Clea in 1964. Wanting to live a "normal" life, they set up home in Connecticut. Making films, however,

was not their only interest. Joanne, who tired of being simply a wife and mother, took up dancing, while Paul went in for motor racing, and both of them became involved in politics. They supported John F. Kennedy and campaigned alongside Martin Luther King. She took up environmental causes.

FILM DIRECTOR AND RACING DRIVER. Newman founded his own production company and began to direct films. For the sake of his wife and because, he said, "she has sacrificed her career for me", he offered her one of her finest roles in Rachel Rachel, which came out in 1968. In a year marked by riots in Chicago, and the assassinations of Martin Luther King and Robert Kennedy, this subtle study of a neurotic woman was warmly received by critics and the public alike, including, to their great astonishment, young people. Their success triggered rumours about Newman's alcoholism and about an alleged misunderstanding between them: "We are not separating," they announced in a large advertisement in the Los Angeles Times. As two strong personalities, they were undergoing some of the classic problems of marriage, but they succeeded in saving the relationship through mutual love and respect. Newman resolved to drink less and in 1970 made his début in motor racing. In 1979, he took second place in the Le Mans Twenty-Four Hour Race.

Paul Newman continued to enjoy success in films (The Sting, 1973; Towering Inferno, 1974), while Joanne Woodward began a second successful career in television. "I have to act," she explained, "otherwise I would become impossible to live with and my family would suffer as much as me." They were both active in social causes: she campaigned for family planning, he against nuclear weapons. They founded the Scott-Newman Foundation to prevent drug addiction among young people. (Scott, his son by his first marriage, drank and took drugs. He died of an overdose in 1978.) To fund his philanthropic activities, Newman marketed a salad dressing, Newman's Own, then other products which brought in handsome profits.

THE SECRET OF A LASTING RELATIONSHIP. He directed his wife in three more films: The Effect of Gamma Rays on Man-in-the-Moon Marigolds (1972), a film sensitive to the problems of women, Harry and Son (1984), a study of a difficult father-and-son relationship, in which he

1958

FRANCE. **First meeting of two actors destined for stardom. Romy Schneider, Austrian heroine of the** *Sissi* **series, made her first foreign film,** *Christine.* **She and her partner, the young French actor Alain Delon, made a superbly romantic couple on screen and fell madly in love. She left everything to go and live with him in Paris, and they became officially engaged in March 1959. Years of stormy passion were to follow for the so-called** *éternels fiancés.* **In 1961, they acted together on stage, in French, in John Ford's play** *'Tis Pity She's a Whore,* **produced by their friend Luchino Visconti. In 1963 Alain Delon met the beautiful Nathalie Barthélémy. On her return, Romy Schneider, who was making a film in Hollywood at the time, found a bouquet of roses and a letter of farewell. They made only one more film together,** *La Piscine* **(1968).**

♡ ♡ ♡

ANGUISH
"Don't leave me ..."

The drama of ending a relationship, the pain of being cut off, but also the chance of a fresh beginning.

"Don't leave me / we must forget / everything can be forgotten / it is already gone / forget the time / of misunderstanding / time lost / working out how / forget the hours / when the whys / sometimes killed / the heart of happiness." The hopeless lament of an abandoned lover, *Ne me quitte pas*, is a heart-rending song of love gone sour. It was written by the great Belgian poet and singer Jacques Brel – who in 1959 gave his first top-of-the-bill performance in a Parisian music hall – at the end of his stormy affair with Suzanne Gabriello, the French singer and actress. He alternates promises ("I will create a land / where love will be king / where you will be queen"), hope ("I will speak to you / of lovers / who have known their hearts / catch fire a second time"), and poetic vision ("when evening falls / do not red and black / combine forces / to set the sky on fire?"), before the final, shameless plea ("I will stop crying / I will stop speaking / I will hide there / to watch you dance and smile / and to listen to you / sing then laugh / Let me become / the shadow of your shadow / the shadow of your hand / the shadow of your dog / Don't leave me").

Brel wrote other magnificent love songs: *Quand on n'a que l'amour* (cf. p. 261), *La Chanson des vieux amants*, *La Quête* (cf. p. 311). At a time when men were supposed to suppress their emotions, he let his vulnerability show: "There is no such thing as armour-plated people," he once said in an interview. In *Ne me quitte pas*, the rejected lover, his poetic powers intact, seeks to seduce with words. But what is the use of humbling oneself, of trying to become "the shadow of your dog"? As

in *The Human Voice* (cf. p. 153), in which a woman begs and pleads, when love is dead, pity will not suffice to re-awaken it.

Love is always a risky business. When couples first meet, each carries within him or her an ideal image of the other person. Then differences, the attrition of daily reality, take their toll. "The ship of love has broken on the rocks of everyday life," wrote the Russian poet Mayakovski, before committing suicide. Failure often results when expectations are too high. Far from solving every problem, love

throws up new ones; a good relationship depends on a shared vision. When desire fades and "love has lost something of its mystery and future" (Bachelard), it easily melts away.

LOVING THE REAL PERSON. A break-up is the result of the disappointment involuntarily inflicted in a relationship when one partner, on whom the other has projected all his or her hopes and desires for some time, turns out to be no more than a human being with all the attendant weaknesses. On the other hand, if the partner is perceived for what he or she really is, there is still hope of building something together. But it is useless to expect a miracle to happen: one does not set out to change the other; that is not what love is about.

Sometimes, the intrusion of a third party acts as a catalyst. The resulting affair is not always the underlying cause of the breach. It merely reveals a dysfunction in an already fragile relationship, which might equally have been shattered by, say, the birth of a child, especially if the woman was hoping that this would put things on a surer footing. People are often slow to see that a relationship has failed, but one day it becomes clear that the bond is broken. It is then evident that love has died or become twisted and the thing they most desire is peace, even at the price of loneliness. The person who takes the initiative in a separation often feels relief, while the other is undermined and completely destroyed, because he or she feels denied, rejected, abandoned, and is often unable to understand why. A deep wound is inflicted, especially in the case of a woman in her forties or fifties who has been abandoned in favour of a younger lover.

Since divorce has become freely available, it is mainly women who apply to the courts, and this tendency is growing. Research has shown that, initially, their chief motive was to escape from male violence. Love is also more important for women, no doubt, while men seem more able to cope with an unsatisfactory marriage, as society allows them to go out drinking with friends or seek consolation with prostitutes. A woman who sues for divorce runs the risk of social ostracism and may well run into financial difficulties. As traditional upbringings taught girls to consider others before themselves, a woman gains confidence in taking a decision which gives her control of her own destiny. She will often analyse the past and see the relationship as doomed to failure from the outset. The man, on the other hand, who often does not see it coming – so blind has he been to their growing lack of understanding – thinks it is possible to blot out the circumstances which have triggered the break-up. As Brel sings, "Everything can be forgotten ..."

REDISCOVERING FREEDOM. Meeting (cf. p. 356) and breaking-up are the two most memorable aspects of a relationship. People break up as they have loved, gracefully or messily, even though the apportioning of shared possessions, the photograph albums, and above all custody of the children, is never achieved without heartache. A right way to separate is for the partners to understand what they have been through without seeking to deny what has happened, blame themselves, or lay the blame at the other's door. Even so, it will always be painful. It is important to find the courage to acknowledge failure, rather than practise self-deception to avoid suffering. An honest break-up, while it cannot wipe out the past – especially for the children who have to maintain their ties with both parents – is more easily accepted on both sides.

The recovery period is often shorter for a man than for a woman, especially if the latter has custody of the children (cf. p. 362). It is tempting to go in search of new experience, to leave the worn-out past for a brighter future. Entering

ABOVE
Drowning Girl,
Roy Lichtenstein, 1963.

FACING PAGE
Jacques Brel.

a new relationship too quickly, however, without first struggling to understand the reasons for past failure, is to risk repeating the same pattern.

Breaking up successfully is possible when a relationship has been lived to the full. Separation sometimes brings atrocious suffering, but the pain eventually diminishes. Mere survival is followed by a rebirth. Though part of oneself has been amputated, one discovers new resources and opportunities. If the former relationship had become a prison, a new freedom is at hand which may be the prelude to a new union. "Don't leave me ...". If one comes to terms with the loss, there may be a chance of rediscovering oneself.

1959

CANNES. *Orfeu negro* (*Black Orpheus*), a film made by Marcel Camus in Brazil, wins the Palme d'Or. It started a worldwide fashion for the bossa nova, the music and movement of which came to be associated in the popular mind with Brazil. Sung by Joao Gilberto, *The Girl from Ipanema* and *Desafinado* were big international hits. The music was composed by Carlos Jobim, the lyrics by Vinicius de Moraes, author of the play *Orfeu de Conceçao*, on which the film was based. In this modern version of the myth of Orpheus and Eurydice, the poet musician is a tram driver whose songs "make the sun rise". During carnival, he meets the beautiful Eurydice. However, his love cannot save her from death, and he also dies, the victim of the jealousy of another woman.

"The only interesting thing about love are the ways of desire. Possession is of little account."

MARCEL JOUHANDEAU
Les Argonautes

1960

Gena Rowlands & John Cassavetes

Unable to Communicate

John & Jacqueline Kennedy

West Side Story

Agnès Varda & Jacques Demy

The Minimum Age for Marriage

Elizabeth Taylor & Richard Burton

Work or Marriage

Sophia Loren & Carlo Ponti

The First Time

Ingmar Bergman & Liv Ullmann

"No" to Marriage!

Niki de Saint-Phalle & Jean Tinguely

Learning to Make Love

Margrethe & Henrik of Denmark

Loving the Other Person

Serge & Beate Klarsfeld

"Sexual Liberation"

John Lennon & Yoko Ono

"69 – An Erotic Year"

Gena Rowlands
John Cassavetes

Surrounded by family and friends, he made films and she acted. A life devoted to love and the cinema.

Shadows is a remarkable American film, which won the Critics' Prize at the Venice Film Festival in 1960. It deals with interracial relationships, a taboo subject at that time, seen from the point of view of black people. John Cassavetes, the producer, was a New York actor and star of a number of television series, including *Johnny Staccato*. He used his own money to finance this film, his first. It was an exercise in improvisation using natural settings, an approach that no large studio would ever have accepted. It took three years to complete. His wife, the actress Gena Rowlands, was at that time having great success on Broadway in *The Middle of the Night*, her first major theatre role. "I saw a lot of the crew," she recalls. "They were always there in our apartment, when I got up in the morning and when I came home in the evening."

They married in 1954 when she was twenty and he was twenty-five. The son of a New York shopkeeper of Greek origin, John Cassavetes trained at the Actor's Studio and became an actor, director, and script-writer. Moving away from conventional techniques he opened his own theatre workshop, where he developed a more natural style of acting. A similar thing was happening in France with the New Wave. Gena Rowlands was the daughter of a politician. She was born into a cultured Wisconsin family of theatre-lovers. It was while she was in New York, following a course at the Academy of Dramatic Art, that she met Cassavetes.

Their relationship was a total fusion of their working and their married lives. Having worked on the theatre fringe, they made their début in the cinema, and did a lot of acting on television, where, she says, live broadcasting made it "the most fearsome and exciting of all fields of expression". It was a happy time: "We did Dos Passos, Hemingway, Faulkner, all the great American authors. John did about a hundred television plays." This "golden age" lasted until 1960, when video-recording started to replace live broadcasting. They then moved to Los Angeles, but remained New Yorkers at heart, retaining an intellectual approach to their work, in contrast to the commercial demands of Hollywood.

LOVE AND CREATION. A recognised film-maker thanks to his success with *Shadows*, Cassavetes was next engaged to direct *Too Late Blues* (1961) and *A Child Is Waiting* (1963). After the failure of these two films, he returned to the independent cinema and his controversial style. He mortgaged their home and sank the money he earned from acting in *The Dirty Dozen* (1967) and *Rosemary's Baby* (1968) into making *Faces* in 1968. "Our whole life was like that," Gena says, "John would start to make a film. Then the money would run out. Everything would stop. I would go back to the theatre, he went to act in some film or other. We would make some money and then re-inject it into our film." In *Faces* he gave his wife a role which was "difficult, strange, and wonderful", attempting to capture the essence of the emotions. The scenes were filmed in close-up as far as possible, because she was pregnant with their first child, Nick. Zoe and Xan would arrive later. Out on the fringe, they were the embodiment of a love story that even Hollywood could only dream about. Both were tall and handsome – she was fair with green eyes, a full face and regular features, he was dark and slim, with a nonchalant elegance. They were united by a deep and implicit love, which was reflected in their professional relationship. They understood each other immediately. One of their friends speaks of the "enormous respect that they had for each other. When Gena was there, John's whole attention was focused on her." The relative success of *Faces* enabled them to make *Husbands* in 1970 with Peter Falk and Ben Gazzara, mainstays of their film-making clique, along with Seymour Cassell, the producer Al Ruban, and many others. For more than thirty years they lived and worked among a "tribe" of friends, technicians, and actors and their families, sharing everything they had – including money, problems and large plates of spaghetti. Their house was the set: "We had no money to go elsewhere. Also we could shoot at all hours of the day and night." Taking care of all their needs Cassavetes had the capacity to develop a creative environment.

1960

ITALY. **General release of a film directed by Mauro Bolognini, *Handsome Antonio*, based on the novel by Vitaliano Brancati. Marcello Mastroianni plays a lady-killer who marries for love but turns out to be impotent. His young and ignorant wife, played by Claudia Cardinale, imagines that he is treating her like "all husbands in the world do" and it requires the indiscretion of a chambermaid for the scandal to be exposed.**

LONDON. **Betty Abatielos slaps Queen Frederika of Greece in public while she is on an official visit. Born in Britain she wanted to draw attention to her husband, the Greek communist Antonis Abatielos. He had been condemned to death in 1948 for his political and trade-union activities during the civil war. His execution was stayed following an international outcry, and his sentence was commuted to life imprisonment. He was freed in 1964 thanks to a number of campaigns and to his wife's publicity stunt.**

CRISES AND STREAMS OF LOVE. In Cassavetes's films, the couples are rarely happy. Their violent crises are due to an excess rather than a lack of love. "I like to show people who really analyse love, by discussing it, destroying it, fighting each other ..." he says. "It is the subject that interests me the most: love, the lack of love, the death of love, the pain caused by the loss of people and things we need the most ...." His highly mobile camera records brawls, drunkenness, unconsciousness, and suicide attempts. Gena Rowlands interpreted the roles he gave her – a hysterical woman (*Minnie and Moskowitz*), nervous (*A Woman under the Influence*), egotistical (*Opening Night*), hard (*Gloria*) or hungry for love (*Love Streams*). According to her, his films always talk about love, "of the suffering which comes from loving a man who also loves you, but with a love that cannot be sustained".

Giving a stunning performance as an ageing actress in *Opening Night* (1978), Rowlands received the prize for best actress at the Berlin Festival. In 1980, *Gloria*, which tells the struggle of a single woman against the Mafia, was the first big public success for Cassavetes. *Love Streams* (1984), in which the hero saves his neurotic sister, is Gena Rowlands's favourite film because, she says, "it's really John and me, as we became in real life: brother and sister." Having chosen to share in her husband's struggles, she acted in seven of the twelve films he made, illuminating them with her courage and inner resources. She made only two films with other directors, Woody Allen (*Another Woman*) and Jim Jarmusch (a sketch in *Night on Earth*). In 1989 when Cassavetes died of cirrhosis of the liver, she felt that a part of herself had been amputated. At first she gave way to despair, then she pulled herself together: "You had so much happiness in your life, why are you complaining? The important thing is to fight, to feel alive." She started to make films again, notably with her son Nick (*Unhook the Stars*, 1996), while contributing with modesty and dignity to keeping alive her husband's work.

BELOW
Jeanne Moreau and Marcello Mastroianni in *The Night*, directed by Michelangelo Antonioni.

♡ ♡ ♡

SOCIETY
Unable to Communicate

Can one person ever really understand the other, even if they are in love? The limits of communication are illustrated by Antonioni and studied by analysing its mechanisms.

"In love," Baudelaire commented, "as in almost all other human affairs, understanding is the result of a misunderstanding. ... The unbridgeable abyss caused by the inability to communicate, remains unbridged." The idea of the inability to communicate existed long before Michelangelo Antonioni showed his film *The Adventure* at the Cannes Festival in 1960, where it was received with violent booing and jeering. However, an open letter signed by many well-known celebrities expressed their admiration for the Italian film-maker. This public reaction brought the subject of the lack of communication between couples into the open. The beautifully-produced film recounts the story of a man and a woman, the boyfriend and a girlfriend of the main character, who fall in love on a yachting trip after she disappears. It is a theme which appears in the novels of Moravia, but, despite his protestations to the contrary, it is to Antonioni that the idea of an inability to communicate is attributed.

Between 1957 and 1964, Antonioni made five important films together with his wife Monica Vitti: *The Cry, The Adventure, The Night, The Eclipse*, and *The Red Desert*. They are about "the instability of feelings," he explains, "about their mysteries". Declaring "I believe in happiness, but I do not think that it can last," he depicts fragile heroes, condemned to drift from one adventure to another, with failure as the only outcome. Having tried to find the love of his youth, the hero of *The Cry* kills himself in front of the mistress who no longer loves him and lets out a never-ending cry; the man and the woman in *The Night* make love even though their relationship is dying, which only serves to accentuate their distress and their solitude; the heroine of *The Eclipse* tries to relearn love, but is unable to grow fond of a mediocre lover; the heroine of *The Red Desert* enters into a relationship which does not save her from a suicide attempt. Faced with the corpse of her husband, the wife of *The Passenger* (1974), when

asked if she recognises him, replies "I never saw him before." With a narrative style that dwells on the fragments of life rather than on the enduring parts, the film-maker explores the secret paths of a different type of communication and reveals hidden truths. "Silences can say so much," he explained in an interview in 1978. "The pictures speak for themselves." Antonioni had chosen, he declared in 1985, to explore the world through the enigma of women, who, according to him, are a more subtle filter of reality, whereas men are looking for the key to understand them. He gives an impression of coldness – but his colleague Alain Resnais compares him to "ice that burns". He knows how to stir the emotions, since the discomfort experienced by his characters finds a resonance in the audience's own sensitivity, although for him "the mystery is more important than any explanation".

Do people have to love in order to understand each other? Are men and women strangers? Is the difference between them incontrovertible? They have neither the same emotional nor sexual needs. Nor do they have the same relationship to power, society, and children. In a love relationship, is it often not the case of loving one's opposite? An analysis of the mechanisms of communication tends to show that each sex functions differently, men with a rational logic and masculine aggression, reinforced by education, women with feminine intuition and feeling. Age for age, it appears that girls have superior verbal skills compared with boys and it is accepted that they are better at communicating their emotions. Each sex can be assumed to have its own emotional culture but it is difficult to assess the effects of nature or nurture since conditioning plays such a powerful role. One of the fundamental differences between

the sexes therefore lies in the expression of emotions, particularly of negative feelings.

These differences between the sexes give rise to many misunderstandings. The words spoken to each other by men and women often have neither the same meaning nor the same function. It is almost as though they do not speak the same language, yet each one thinks that it is the responsibility of the other to try to understand. Communication problems within a relationship often stems from the way in which the relationship has developed, and from the disappointment that often unrealistic expectations have not been fulfilled. Material or psychological dependence also increases the chances of the inability to communicate.

Silence is golden – or like lead. Silence can be golden – when the relationship is very good, partners no longer find it necessary to speak in order to understand each other – or it can be like lead, and on occasion may open the door to violence in a situation where words could have been a substitute for the deed. Where couples are not on the same

wavelength, it can degenerate into domestic squabbles (cf. p. 332). Gregory Bateson (cf. p. 178) studied the way in which partners respond to provocation. He found, for example, that a man who is very attached to his freedom may wish to disengage himself as soon as he identifies what he thinks is a challenge; when the woman sees him maintaining a distance she becomes alarmed, afraid that the bond may give way, and tries to draw closer again. This leads to the man becoming even more anxious.

Each partner has his or her own way of listening to the other, of showing interest and love. Trying to understand what the other person wants to say helps to create an awareness of the differences and to accept them. Each successful dialogue builds a bridge across the "abyss" which Baudelaire described as "unbridgeable". Where good communication has helped to establish a strong and stable relationship, while at the same time giving pleasure in the "collusion", love can become what D. H. Lawrence called "a form of conversation where words are put into action instead of being spoken".

1960

Geneva. Jean-Luc Godard makes his second film, *The Little Soldier*. He extensively filmed the woman he loved, Anna Karina, in amazing close-up shots to "photograph the soul behind". She was Danish, dark with grey eyes, and very tall. She became his muse in a total of eight films. To him, she was a character from Andersen. To her, he had an athletic body and she admired the fact that he could "do anything". They married in 1961. In *It's my Life* (1962) he filmed her face, her smile, her neck, her fragility in long fixed close-ups. "She thought that I made her look ugly, and that was the start of our break-up. We separated, she because of my many faults, I because I could not think of making a film without her." *Pierrot le fou* (1965) strips back the misunderstandings of passionate love. The heroes reproach themselves with "speaking with words" while they "look with feelings." Together with his new muse Anne Wiazemski, Godard made *La Chinoise* (1967).

♡ ♡ ♡

Happiness, 1991–1992, by Florence Chevallier.

John
Jacqueline & Kennedy

An ideal couple moved into the White House, but their apparent happiness eventually proved to be a façade.

In the United States of America, the presidential couple were the perfect embodiment of modernity and youth: John Fitzgerald Kennedy was forty-three and his ravishing wife Jacqueline thirty-one. In a speech at his investiture on 21 January 1961 he declared that "the torch has been passed to a new generation". The new occupants of the White House, parents to Caroline, aged three, and John Jr., aged two months, formed a marked contrast with their much older predecessors. "Mamie" Eisenhower was the model of the self-effacing wife of a famous husband. Only Eleanor Roosevelt (cf. p. 162) had been the exception. Rather than looking toward the "new frontier" referred to in a celebrated speech by the president, Americans focused on an apparently ideal couple. The president, a Democrat and war hero wounded in the Pacific, had a strong and handsome face. As Richard Nixon, the Republican candidate narrowly beaten by Kennedy, put it: "Americans adore him because they would like to look like him. They hate me because I look like them." Dark, slim, and softly-spoken, the new "First Lady" personified the American idea of refined elegance.

John Kennedy, the first Catholic president, and his wife both came from wealthy East Coast families; his ancestors were Irish, his wife's French. As children, neither received the attention from their mothers that they deserved. While she was born to a couple who soon became estranged, and had only one sister, he belonged to a family of nine siblings whose up-bringing was directed toward the pursuit of power. "I only want winners," said the father who saw his dream realised: one son became president and another, Robert, became Attorney-General.

At a dinner in June 1952, John Kennedy met Jacqueline Bouvier who was working as a press photographer. When he introduced her to his parents, his mother Rose thought she was too shy to become the wife of an ambitious politician who had been elected to the Chamber of Representatives in 1946 and to the Senate in 1952. Kennedy was also the author of several successful books – he published *Profiles in Courage* in 1956. But Joseph Kennedy was won over by her charm and the fact that she was a Catholic. The marriage took place on 12 September 1953 in Newport, Rhode Island. In contrast with her mother-in-law, who played an important role during her sons' electoral campaigns, the young Jacqueline was not very interested in politics, preferring art and fashion instead.

NOTORIETY AND DRAMAS. The president's wife renovated the White House with a meticulous attention to detail. Although she was so different from the average American woman, the country liked her: women copied her simple sleeveless dresses, her pill-box hats. Her international reputation was such that when they set out on a trip to Europe in May 1961, the president introduced himself as "the man accompanying Jacqueline Kennedy". A commentator noted that together they were the very image of a European royal couple.

Kennedy put programmes in place to combat poverty and racism and created the Peace Corps to help in the Third World. He gained enormous prestige by persuading Mr Khrushchev, the Soviet Prime Minister, to back down in the missiles-to-Cuba affair and also by displaying firmness in his dealings with the Soviet Union over the second Berlin crisis. He saw himself as the founder of a dynasty, dreaming that when his term of office end-

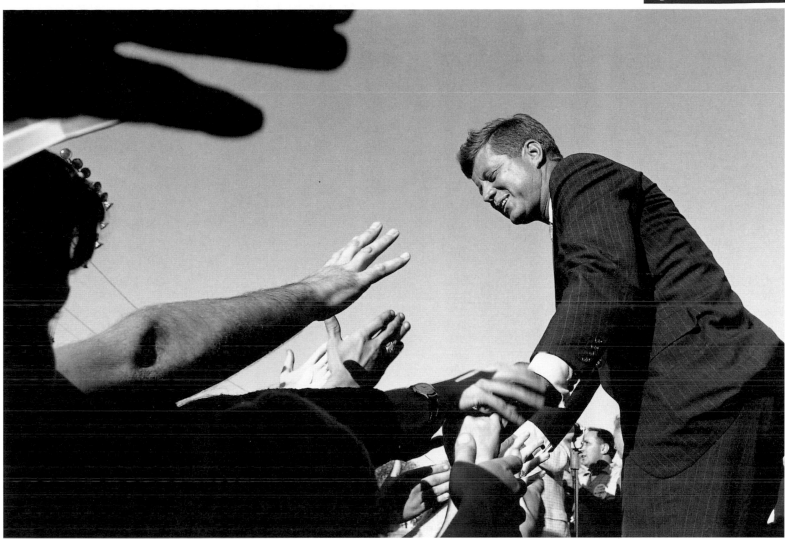

ed, the country would be governed successively by his brothers, then by his son. He wanted to have a number of children, but his wife had several miscarriages. In August 1963 their two day-old-son Patrick died of a congenital abnormality.

Preparing for his re-election in 1963, he asked his wife to accompany him on the campaign trail to Texas. In Dallas on 22 November she was beside him in the limousine when he was shot by an assassin. Pictures of the young widow, dressed in a pink suit spattered with her husband's blood, courageous and proud, rocked the whole world. At her request, the president was buried in the Arlington National Cemetery beside other soldiers who had died for their country "because he belongs to the people". She retained the nation's admiration, behaving in a manner perfectly befitting the widow of a great man. But on 20 October 1968, when the country was still in shock at the assassination four months earlier of Robert Kennedy, a presidential candidate, she married the Greek shipping tycoon Aristotle Onassis (cf. p. 270), who was twenty-three years older than she was. Many people regarded this marriage as a betrayal: "John F. Kennedy dies for the second time" was a headline in

the *New York Times*. Widowed again in 1975 she surprised the nation by embarking on a career as a publishing editor. With her final companion, the diamond merchant Maurice Tempelsman, she enjoyed several happy years before her death in 1994. She was buried, according to her wishes, beside her first husband.

REVELATIONS AND SCANDALS. The fairy story with its tragic ending was only a façade. Gradually the distance between the ideal couple and the sordid reality was revealed, as a number of scandals hit the Kennedy family. The idolised president was shown to have been an unscrupulous go-getter who collected female relationships like stamps, most notably with Marilyn Monroe (cf. p. 254) and who maintained links with the underworld: Judith Exner, his mistress until 1962, revealed in 1991 that he had given her the job of passing money to the Mafia to ensure his victory at the primaries in 1960. If the public at large was ignorant at that time of his unbridled sexual life, it was mainly due to the respect shown to the office of president and to the complicity of journalists with whom he maintained good relations. He was also able to count on his wife's discretion. A ne-

NEW YORK. **Joan Baez and Bob Dylan meet in a Greenwich Village club. He wrote and sang folksongs, she was a singer performing traditional ballads in a compelling but lyrical voice. He was unknown, she was a celebrity following her successful appearance at the Newport Festival in 1959. They set up home together and both became stars, the mouthpiece for an angry generation. They sang about the struggle –** *The Times They Are A-Changing* **– and about love –** *Farewell Angelina.*

♡ ♡ ♡

glected but loyal wife, who forged a perfect, glossy public image for herself, Jackie Kennedy revealed a different aspect in private: those close to her noted that she chewed her nails, drank, and smoked. As an icon of hope and happiness, the Kennedy couple were the living incarnation of a strong and confident America which was poised to overtake the Soviets in the space race, banish poverty, and abolish racial discrimination. The political failures – the blockading of Cuba, the start of the military engagement in Vietnam – and the revelations of private behaviour scarcely dented the myth. It still remains powerful, particularly abroad, where this brief, intense period when everything seemed possible continues to exert a strong fascination.

♡ ♡ ♡

Myth
West Side Story

A modern version of Romeo and Juliet, in which true love is doomed by the hatred of rival gangs.

Beymer and Natalie Wood; an Italian town is replaced by a poor quarter of New York, the East Side, where rival gangs, the Jets and the Sharks, are the modern-day equivalent of the Montagues and the Capulets, noble families of six-

the heart as well as of the body. Similarly, Romeo and Juliet exchange a kiss at their first meeting, desire each other and spend the night together despite the risks. They defy the bans placed on them, since love cannot

Bernardo and his Sharks.

FACING PAGE Maria gives her dead lover, Tony, a final kiss.

West Side Story is the tale of a pure, uncompromising love, a forbidden passion which is held in contempt and ends in death. In transposing the story of Romeo and Juliet it emulates the realism and poetry of the legend of Tristan and Isolde, foundation of the Western concept of love (cf. p. 188). This Robert Wise film, choreographed by Jerome Robbins and with music by Leonard Bernstein, has enjoyed enormous success since it first appeared in 1961. The two young lovers of Shakespeare's play become Tony and Maria, played by Richard

teenth-century Verona. The balcony under which Romeo declares his love becomes a fire escape on which Tony sings of his love in a duet with Maria, in the hit song *Tonight*.

Maria is the sister of Bernardo, leader of the Puerto Rican gang, the Sharks. Tony is the founder and ex-leader of the Jets, who proudly proclaim their all-American heritage. Having come to the United States to marry another Puerto Rican, Maria meets Tony at her first dance; they fall head over heels in love. Their union is one of the soul and

wait or countenance fear or cowardice. "For what love can do, that dares love attempt," Romeo cries. It is the total union of these young two people which allows them to discover and reveal themselves.

OBSTACLE COURSE. The climate of hatred in their respective families makes any relationship between them inconceivable, much less a love affair. The lovers have to resort to various ruses in order to meet. The only freedom they have is that which they win for themselves. Refusing to bend to demands, they face a succession of tests like the stages of a heroic obstacle course. Certain of their love, confident in each other, they are prepared to face anything. "Or bid me ..." pleads Juliet, "Things that, to hear them told, have made me tremble;/And I will do it without fear or doubt,/To live an unstain'd wife to my sweet love." Only doubts about the love of the other partner could undermine their ardour: "Alack, there lies more peril in thine eye/Than twenty of their swords; look thou but sweet/And I am proof against their enmity." Hoping in vain for a reconciliation between their families they see escape as the only way out, and they wed in secret. Likewise, Tony and Maria plan to run away after a bloody brawl in which Bernardo kills the leader of the Jets and is stabbed in turn by Tony.

Discovering the lifeless body of Juliet, Romeo believes that she is dead and poisons himself. Juliet awakes from her drug-induced sleep, sees his corpse and in despair stabs herself with his dagger: "... and lips, O you/The doors of breath, seal with a righteous kiss/A

dateless bargain to engrossing death." Similarly, Tony hears that Maria is dead and believes it to be true. He discovers his mistake too late, as his lover comes running towards him; she embraces him and he dies in her arms, killed by the Puerto Rican whom Maria was intended to marry.

The love which it is hoped will allay conflict and stifle hatred does not succeed in doing so. Does this mean that the death of Romeo and Juliet signifies victory for the murderous inclinations of their families? Lying side by side on a bed which is both nuptial couch and funerary bier, the young lovers remain suspended in the eternity of true love, of promises given and total commitment. As the legendary character Majnoun "crazy with love" for Layla proclaims in the celebrated Arabian tale of *Majnoun and Layla*: "If, beyond death, you said to the lovers 'Spirits, have you found release from your torments?' they would reply: 'It is true, our bodies are only dust, but the flame of love burns in our hearts for ever'."

LOVE RECONCILES ENEMIES. The story of Romeo and Juliet has inspired composers such as Berlioz and Tchaikovsky; Prokofiev brought them to life in a ballet; Rodin sculpted them; film-makers such as Cayatte and Zeffirelli adapted their story, which has been transposed into countless other creative works: in *The Birth of a Nation* (1914) by the American film-maker Griffith, the daughter of a man from the North is loved by a colonel in the Southern army. The tale continues to retain its subversive power; in modern times Romeo and Juliet continue to love each other despite the hatred of their respective groups, whether it be Northern Ireland, Bosnia or Kashmir. In 1993 two directors, one an Israeli, Eran Baniel, and the other a Palestinian, Fouad Awad, tried to establish a dialogue between two communities that are very violently opposed. They mounted a joint production of Shakespeare's play in Jerusalem. The Montagues spoke Arabic and the Capulets Hebrew, with subtitles for the audience.

At the end of *West Side Story* Maria vents her grief and anger, but she does not take her own life. The strength of her love, which is felt by all, dispels the hatred for a time, and the mortal remains of Tony are borne away by members of the two reunited gangs. Maria's survival, an important change to the original story, may perhaps allow us to view the position of those individuals caught up between rival groups in a different light, and convey a message of hope. After the death of the leaders and Tony's sacrifice, will love achieve the miracle of bringing the enemies together?

1961

PARIS. **Marriage of the writer André Schwarz-Bart and a young black woman from Guadeloupe, Simone Brumant. In 1959 Schwarz-Bart received the Prix Goncourt for his novel** *The Last of the Just*. **The subject dealt with Jewish persecution, something which affected him deeply, as half his family died during deportation. He was physically attacked as a result of the book. Unable to finish a book on Black slavery which he had started, he appealed to his wife to finish it for him. It was then that he discovered her talent for writing. Following this joint work,** *Un plat de porc aux bananes vertes* (1967), **Simone Schwarz-Bart had some successful works of her own, including** *The Bridge of Beyond* (1972). **The bonds between the couple went deep; witness the reaction of Simone to a criticism of her play** *Ton Beau Capitaine*. **Since her husband was not black, why did she not write about interracial relationships?** "I wanted to write about love. When I look at my husband I see someone I love. To me he is no particular colour."

♡ ♡ ♡

Agnès Varda & Jacques Demy

Two French film-makers working side by side created powerful and original work.

Two French film-makers made their way to the Cannes Film Festival in May 1962. Agnès Varda, small, with a round face and a mane of black hair was thirty-four; Jacques Demy, thirty-one, was tall and slim with a gentle face. They would eventually marry after living together for three years. Varda had entered her film *Cléo from 5 to 7*, which showed in real time a woman waiting anxiously for the result of a medical diagnosis. From the Cannes casino Demy got the idea for a film about compulsive gambling – *The Bay of Angels* (1963) with Jeanne Moreau.

Born in Brussels to a Greek father and a French mother, Agnès Varda grew up in Sète, close to the Mediterranean, and started her working life as a photographer for Jean Vilar's popular National Theatre. Her first film, *La Pointe Courte* (1954), edited by Alain Resnais, is considered to be the founding work of the New Wave. She lived first with actor (then director) Antoine Bourseiller, and in 1957 they had a daughter, Rosalie. During her pregnancy she made *L'Opéra-Mouffe*, which described reality as perceived by a pregnant woman. Independent in her personal life as well as in her work she founded her own production company, based at her home in Paris in the rue Daguerre.

Demy was the son of a garage-owner and a hairdresser from Nantes, both of whom gave him a love of opera and cinema. He started to make films at the age of thirteen and maintained throughout his life a love of the miraculous and of the mood of the sea. At first he made documentaries, then *Lola* (1961), a romantic love story. Varda wrote the words of the song *C'est moi Lola* sung by Anouk Aimée; Michel Legrand wrote the music and thereafter continued to collaborate with Demy.

WORKING ON IMPORTANT PROJECTS. "Bewitching" was the word Demy used to describe the *Umbrellas of Cherbourg* (1963), the film that made a name for Catherine Deneuve when it received the Palme d'Or at Cannes. The film went on to became an international hit. Demy, who excelled in portraying the promises of a love which fails to blossom, made another film for "the singing cinema", *The Young Girls of Rochefort* (1966) with Catherine Deneuve and her sister Françoise Dorléac. Meanwhile in *Happiness* (1965), Varda described with a mixture of simplicity and studied aestheticism a mar-

ried man who, wanting to enjoy two states of happiness, does not conceal his relationship with another woman from his wife. The wife kills herself. Both film-makers show ordinary people, Demy an umbrella seller, a garage owner, customers in a café, Varda a carpenter and a post-office employee. But beneath the smalltalk of everyday conversation, beneath the colour and the gaiety, serious questions are raised.

Varda and Demy pursued their work independently and made it a rule to visit each other on set only when invited. "You need time to be alone and to be yourself," she said. "I need to have some time which I do not share with Jacques. My artistic world is like my own room." The couple visited other film-makers and intellectuals, such as Jean-Luc Godard and his wife Anna Karina, and their friends from the magazine *Les Cahiers du Cinéma*. Varda trumpeted her ideological views: against the Vietnam war, for women, against the dictatorship in Greece. From 1966 to 1969 they lived in Los Angeles and produced what Varda called "documenteurs" [a mixture of fact and fiction], which sought to get a better grasp of reality. Returning to Paris, Demy had a further success with *Donkey Skin* (1970). Varda filmed the shopkeepers in her street (*Daguerrotypes*, 1974) and then made two important feminist films, *Réponses de Femmes* (1975) and *One Sings, the Other Doesn't* (1976). With vitality and lightness of touch she fought for the right to abortion, denounced inequality, rape, and machismo. She based her work on her own experiences and contradictions: "I like being a feminist and a married woman," she said, "I love this relationship, even though there have been very difficult times when it has nearly broken down."

Their son Mathieu was born in 1972. "When my wife was pregnant she talked endlessly about what was going on inside her. It became the sole topic of conversation and I said, in a sudden outburst, that if it were me who were pregnant, I wouldn't talk about it so much," said Demy, who then made a comedy about the frustrations and pleasures of fatherhood, *A Slightly Pregnant Man* (1973), with Marcello Mastroianni as the "pregnant" father.

"One of the pleasures of living with Jacques Demy," Varda recalled, "is discussion; we shared in events and

FACING PAGE, BELOW
Agnès Varda recounts the childhood of Jacques Demy in the film *Jacquot*. A sick, old man, he sits beside the three young actors who play him at different ages.

FRANCE. **The American actress Jean Seberg, star of Otto Preminger's** *Joan of Arc* **and Godard's** *Breathless,* **expects a child by Romain Gary. She was twenty-four, he was twice her age. Since they were not yet married, they kept the birth of their son Diego a secret at first. Romain Gary, a Frenchman of Russian origin, was a well-known novelist (***Promise of Dawn***). He filmed his wife in** *Birds Come to Die in Peru* **(1968). Jean Seberg, who supported the Black Panther Movement in America was harassed by the FBI; her mental health, which was already fragile, deteriorated. In 1971 she made** *Kill* **directed by her husband, after which they split up. In 1979 after seeing** *Clair de Femme* **based on a novel by Gary which she believed to have been inspired by their life together, she committed suicide. Gary killed himself in 1980, leaving behind a letter saying: "Nothing to do with Jean Seberg. Those looking for a broken heart should go elsewhere."**

our reflections on them." For her, the relationship in a "real couple" was "one of the most exciting adventures you can experience. It can also be difficult and dangerous when it is real. While the couple lasts, so does the adventure."

They went their separate ways about 1980, at a time when they were "raging silently against each other". She then admitted with bitterness that in a book about Demy written in 1982 only three lines were devoted to her.

SORROW EXPRESSED THROUGH CONTINUING CREATION. During another spell in the United States, Varda made more "documenteurs", exploring grief as though it were a place.

Very demanding and fixated on the absolute, Demy failed to regain favour with the public, although he was acknowledged by the critics. While Varda won the Golden Lion at Venice for *Vagabond* (1985), Demy's final films had a darker tone. *A Room in Town* (1982) and *Three Seats for the 26th* (1988), which is dedicated "to Agnès V ...", were commercial flops.

Demy died of leukaemia in 1990. After his death Varda made films using her husband's material, something other creative couples had done before (cf. p. 302).

Three films about him: *Jacquot* (1991), *The Young Girls Turn 25* (1992), and *The World of Jacques Demy* (1995) were, she explained, "my way of mourning". The second film reconciled her with the fact, she said, "that the memory can be warm and smiling, without masking the rest". Into the film she integrated images from *The Young Girls of Rochefort*, such as the long sequence where, like a tender lover, she filmed "my darling putting on a new pullover". In this emotional collage, a delightful mixture of charm and gentle nostalgia, she remembered "Jacques" (Demy), "Delphine" (Seyrig), "Françoise" (Dorléac), but she refused to give in to sadness: "Memories of happiness are perhaps still a form of happiness."

♡ ♡ ♡

THE LAW
The Minimum Age for Marriage

Not a necessity for marriage based on love, but as a safeguard against abuse in traditional, arranged marriages.

In order to combat the practice of child-marriage in under-developed countries, the United Nations, in 1962, requested that its members fix a legal age limit for marriage. It was intended that this would not be below the age of consent (the end of puberty) nor without the partners' full agreement. In the West such a limit has long been in existence, with the proviso that the parents' consent is required until the child reaches the age of majority. In France the Civil Code of 1804 sets this limit at 18 for men and 15 for women. In Germany the law of 1875 stipulated 20 and 16 years respectively which was then raised to 21 and 16 in 1946, with a possible dispensation for men of 18. In Switzerland, the Civil Code of 1908 sets the ages at 20 and 18. In the United Kingdom a law of 1929 sets the minimum age for both men and women at 16. In the Third World, the law is effective from the date of independence. Thus in Tunisia the Code of Personal Status of 1956

adopts French age limits. Senegal did not adopt a code until 1972, fixing the age at 20 and 16, one of the highest in Africa. Around the world today these laws fall into two categories: those which specify different ages for men and women and have their origin in Roman Law, and those which set the same age limit for men and women, generally 18 (northern and eastern Europe) or 16 (English law). In the United States, legislation varies from state to state.

THE FACTS. The minimum age for marriage has nothing to do with the average age of marriage. The facts differ from the law in several respects. Historically, marriage in Europe has always differed from that in the rest of the world. Whereas in other parts of the world it takes place at the age of puberty, the earliest age at which sexual intercourse can take place being difficult to define, in Europe it is somewhat later. In the eighteenth century the average age for a first marriage was 30 for men and 26 for women. At the start of the twentieth century, Europeans got married on average at the age of 26. The proportion of women born around 1880 who remained single was more than 10 per cent in western Europe and more than 20 per cent in northern Europe. In the fifties and sixties the

average age for a first marriage dropped in Europe and the United States: this was the era of the "feminine mystique" denounced by Betty Friedan, where the obsession with finding a husband encouraged many girls to abandon their studies in order to get married. This age eventually rose again in the United States from 22 for men and 21 for women to 26 and 24 respectively in 1990. The fall in the number of marriages in the final third of the twentieth century (cf. p. 298) was accompanied by a rise in age. Thus in France in 1980, a first marriage for men took place on average at 25 and for women at 23; at the end of the century these ages have risen to 29 and 27, the highest in the postwar period.

In Third World countries, however, the law is not always respected. Families decide the fate of their children. Tragically, the practice of allowing child-brides is one of the most significant factors contributing to the inferior status of women, who are often regarded as nothing more than cattle. Consider this answer from a Brazilian girl who when asked "When can girls get married in your country?" replied "When they are thirty kilos!"

Apart from China, where the communist regime maintains rigid control in an effort to reduce the birth-rate by allowing only late marriages, in almost all other poor countries, where the law is flouted, early marriage – indeed very early marriage – is the rule. Thus in Rajasthan in north-west India, one child in two is married before the age of 14. Consummation of the marriage is delayed until the boy reaches physiological maturity. The law is sometimes changed – in the adverse direction. Islamic Iran for example abolished the law permitting child-marriage and polygamy, and fixed the age at which girls can marry at ... 9 years.

At the end of the twentieth century the average age of a woman marrying for the first time is an indication of a country's level of development: 50 per cent of Africans, 40 per cent of Asians and 30 per cent of South Americans are married before the age of 18, the vast majority of them giving birth within two years. What a contrast this makes with Sweden, Denmark or Germany where the average age for marriage is 30!

AGE DIFFERENCE. A factor that seriously affects the status of women is the difference in age between the married couple, particularly in under-developed countries. In the developed countries a man tends to be two or three years older than the woman, although this gap is slowly narrowing. In Kenya, on the other hand, the average age difference is five years and as much as eight in Mauritania. This difference explains the inferior position of women in society, since there can be no equality between a couple where the girl is an adolescent and the man much older. Additionally, there is the continuing practice of polygamy. Although admittedly now on the decline, it still affects more than half of all women in Burkina-Faso or Togo.

Despite some changes to the dominant pattern – where the man is much older than the woman – the majority of marriages still conform to it, reinforcing the traditional view that women are inferior.

In the West, the number of women marrying for the first time, with a man much younger than themselves, are in the minority – about 20 per cent of the total number. This figure has remained constant throughout the twentieth century. But the age difference in the older woman/younger man pairing is much less than in the older man/younger woman pairing. In France in 1980 the man was at least five years older than the woman in 20 per cent of first marriages, whereas the figure for the reverse situation, where the woman was at least five years older, was 2 per cent. The trend towards equality in the West is clear, where currently 90 per cent of couples are in the same age group.

While dissatisfaction with the institution of marriage as yet only affects developed countries (cf. p. 298), marriage at the end of the twentieth century in the rest of the world is rarely a love match (cf. p. 15), much less an agreement based on equality between two adults of similar age.

1962

GREAT BRITAIN. The Beatles (cf. p. 312) sing about love, both happy and sad: *Love Me Do, She Loves You, I Want to Hold Your Hand, And I Love Her* or about past love (*Yesterday*). They proclaim that money can not buy love (*Can't Buy Me Love*), and that quarrels can be sorted out (*We Can Work It Out*). They affirm that *All You Need Is Love.*

UNITED STATES. Success for *David and Lisa*, a first film by Frank Perry, based on a script by his wife Eleanor Perry, which tells the love story of two mentally handicapped adolescents. It is an outstanding film and very original. Far from dwelling on the handicaps affecting the heroes, Perry showed how they were conquered by the power of love and faith in the future.

♡ ♡ ♡

Elizabeth Taylor & Richard Burton

A burning passion punctuated by love affairs, quarrels, and tragicomedy gradually became a pathetic dependence.

Cleopatra, the Mankiewicz film which nearly bankrupted the Fox film company, finally opened in June 1963. The public, whose curiosity had been aroused during the preceding months, were at last able to witness one of the most memorable instances of love at first sight in the history of the cinema. Liz Taylor and Richard Burton were not simply content with playing Cleopatra

and Mark Antony. As everyone working on the film confirmed, they were inflamed from their very first scene together to the point where, according to a stage hand, "it needed a blow torch to separate them". The press immediately started to vilify the "woman who destroys families and eats husbands". The American star Elizabeth Taylor, born in 1932 and with two failed marriages already behind her, had the reputation of being a "home-wrecker". After the death of her third husband she forced Eddie Fisher, husband of her best friend Debbie Reynolds, to divorce in order to marry her. Richard Burton, on the other hand, despite his various infidelities, remained married to Sybil Williams, who came, as he did, from a poor Welsh mining family. They had two children, Liz Taylor had four.

PASSION, QUARRELS AND RECONCILIATION. These "outrageous lovers" were equally impassioned and headstrong. Renowned for her violet eyes and generous bosom, Liz Taylor was an international star whose career began at the age of ten and who won an Oscar for *Butterfield 8* (1960). She typified the feminine woman with a capricious nature who was allowed to have her way, but would ultimately give in to a man. Richard Burton, small, with a powerfully built body and a clear blue gaze, was a great theatrical actor. Hollywood had brought him fame and fortune in the wake of the film *The Robe* (1953). He portrayed himself as aggressively macho, a womaniser, and drinker.

While Liz Taylor was announcing her divorce from Eddie Fisher, Richard Burton, torn between his wife and mistress, started to drink more and more. Hundreds of

articles asked the same question: "Is Liz Taylor going to marry Richard Burton?" She saw herself as the perfect wife. "In the evening, beside the fire, we shall read all the books in the world. That will be Heaven." She quit acting for a whole year in order to follow the man she loved, declaring: "I love not having to work," to which Burton replied, "It's perfect. I make interesting films and Liz sits knitting in corridors." She wanted to have his child – "I love giving birth," she declared – but he refused. She was mad about diamonds, so he covered her with sumptuous gems.

When their divorces were finally announced they married in Montreal in 1964. Film makers offered them fabulous contracts and "the Burtons", who confessed to being lazy, cynically stated that they were only working for the money, which they then spent with the greatest ostentation imaginable. They moved from luxury hotel to luxury hotel giving extravagant parties, while their children followed, with animals, staff, and suitcases.

They made film after film: *The Sandpiper* with Minnelli (1965) was a triumph; *Who's Afraid of Virginia Woolf?* with Mike Nichols (1966), a grandiose squabble between man and wife, marked a high-point in their joint careers and won a second Oscar for Liz Taylor. She had to put on a considerable amount of extra weight for the film in order to play an ageing harpy to Burton's resigned husband. He grumbled at his role which gave him "a poor typecast image of the man who grovels in front of his superior wife". However, in Zeffirelli's *Taming of the Shrew*, based on Shakespeare's play, the wife is humbled and his manly honour is safe. In interviews they talked obsessively about their mutual passion.

Their quarrels as well as their reconciliations were chronicled in the popular press, but in time they ran out of steam and the public got weary. Cocking a snook, Burton bought his wife one of the world's most expensive diamonds; this publicity stunt was enough to sideline the poor reviews of *Boom!* which they made with Losey (1968).

"We can't carry on parodying ourselves," said Burton. The physical pleasure had disappeared and the

The quarrelsome couple in *Taming of the Shrew*, adapted by Zeffirelli from Shakespeare's play.

FACING PAGE
Shortly after announcing their impending marriage, Richard Burton and Elizabeth Taylor attend the boxing match between Cassius Clay and Henry Cooper at Wembley.

household started to go to pieces. They both drank too much, their health was affected; she put on weight, he was never sober and became addicted to cocaine. They separated in 1973 and divorced the following year. In the space of ten years they made ten films together and netted thirty million dollars.

"A great dependence". Despite many passing affairs, Liz Taylor could not forget Burton. She telephoned him every day. "One day," he wrote to her, "something will make you realise that you cannot live without me and you will marry me." They saw each other again, went on a trip together and – got married again in October 1975. But the second marriage crumbled after only a few weeks, and they divorced again in August 1976. They each remarried. But then it was Burton who separated from his wife: when she heard this Liz Taylor left her husband, took a slimming course and returned to the man to whom she appeared to be attached by what the press called "a great dependence". In 1982, they appeared in Noel Coward's *Private Lives* in New York. Despite being savaged by the critics, the theatre was never

1963

The first scene of *Contempt*, Jean-Luc Godard's film, shows Brigitte Bardot and Michel Piccoli on a bed. He is dressed, wearing a hat; she is naked, lying stretched out on her stomach. She asks: "And my feet, do you like them, my feet? – Yes." She works her way up her whole body ("And my thighs?"... "And my bottom?"), eliciting a "yes" each time. The final question is about her face and the last "yes" satisfies her: "Then you love me completely."

"A very simple secret: love. All those things in this inanimate world which fascinate us, the woods, the open countryside and the rivers ... all these things which are ordinary and empty in themselves start to take on a human meaning as, without us realising it, they contain a feeling of love".

DINO BUZZATI
A Love Affair

empty. Would they remarry? They denied all suggestions: "We do not need another marriage. We love each other so passionately that we are burning each other out."

What Burton really needed was a nurse. He married a young script girl and died in August 1984 in Geneva of a cerebral haemorrhage. When she heard the news, Liz Taylor fainted. Ever "the queen in mourning" she visited his grave surrounded by paparazzi. After several affairs she married a construction worker, Larry Forten-sky, in 1991 – twenty years her junior. With eight marriages behind her she equalled the record of other stars, such as Lana Turner (cf. p. 195), who also married the same man twice. This type of remarriage, which is common in Hollywood, is often followed by another separation, as was the case with Natalie Wood and Robert Wagner; Melanie Griffith and Don Johnson.

When Liz Taylor and Larry Fortensky separated in 1995, he remarked that she never stopped talking about Richard Burton ...

♡ ♡ ♡

The Law
Work or Marriage

In the West it is possible both to have a job and to be married, but not in Japan. Are love and work compatible?

What shall I do?
What shall I choose?
What shall I give up?
Why give anything up?

In 1963 air hostesses working for Air France won the right to be married. Previously, their contract required them to quit their jobs if they got married. In a ruling which stated that "the right to marriage is a fundamental right which cannot be restricted or removed", the Court of Appeal in Paris declared this clause of the contract null and void. At a time when it was rare for couples to cohabit (cf. p. 298), marriage was not the sole issue; there was also maternity and age to consider. An image had been created of the smiling, young woman who was also available. From now on, an air hostess was allowed to be married, even though she still continued to represent a popular form of male fantasy.

In Japan in the same year, an *office lady*, the name used by Japanese to designate the employee who brings the tea and does the photo-copying, got married and was forced to leave her job with Sumitomo Cements. She was the first person to bring a complaint of unfair dismissal, which was contrary to the constitution. Since the company had a policy of automatic dismissal for all its female staff in the event of marriage, the young girl had in any case already signed a document agreeing to leave at the age of thirty-five. The employer argued that the efficiency of female employees declines once they marry as "women are not as strong as men" and that housework and family responsibilities which traditionally take up their time "reduce the amount of energy they are able to devote to their work".

The tribunal came to the conclusion that it was a form of sexual discrimination. Despite this precedent, things have evolved only very slowly in Japan, and at the end of the twentieth century, marriage is the main reason why women give up work. The vast majority of Japanese still think that a woman should leave her job when she marries and has a child. While the man is the breadwinner, the wife remains at home, only returning to work, mainly part-time, when the child goes to school. In France where further education is expensive, girls study for a shorter period than boys, then take up temporary work until the age of twenty-five to thirty on average. In cases where they remain single for a prolonged period, and in those companies where women employed largely in junior positions have to be young, they are politely requested to leave. Few of them resist the strong pressure to do so. Since the hours of work are spread over a large part of the day, women are unable to combine the demands of home and job without the assis-tance of crèches, domestic help and a husband. On the other hand, where a married couple are not permitted to be employed in the same company, if work colleagues marry everyone expects the woman to leave, not the man.

A new right. "Female workers claim the right to marry." "Married women claim the right to work." These were the slogans taken up by British women in the thirties. Making a woman sign a contract of work calling for her immediate dismissal without compensation if she got

married was for many years considered to be perfectly fair. This state of affairs did not apply to male employees, since male and female equality had not yet been established in law, much less in customs and manners. Where complaints were made, the law always concluded that there was no violation of a fundamental right, as the employer was not preventing the woman from marrying.

Sweden was a pioneering country. As long ago as 1938 a law was passed to prohibit the dismissal of women who got married or were pregnant. The last two bastions against female equality in the West are the Army and the Church. It is only since 1991 – after 5,700 dismissals due to pregnancy, and many court cases involving large amounts of damages with interest – that women in the British Army now have the right to bear children. As for the law against marriage, it still exists in the Vatican, where female employees are dismissed if they marry.

From time to time, women in the workplace are criticised, particularly when there is an economic crisis. Women are then portrayed as "stealing jobs", as if dismissing some of them would solve the problem of thousands of unemployed men, who, in any case, would be unlikely to fill the same jobs. But times are changing: in the nineties a large majority of Europeans, especially younger people, think that the combination of work and family life is the ideal, for women as well as men.

THE OFFICE ROMANCE. It used to be dancing (cf. p. 130) that offered people the main opportunity to meet. But during the last third of the twentieth century, a period marked by the increase in marriage breakdowns and divorce, the workplace is where many people meet a new partner, rather than during their leisure time (cf. p. 236). Thus 12 per cent of French people met their future husband or wife through their job. Opportunities vary according to the type of work: in addition to work colleagues, there are customers, suppliers or other company connections. The company acts to some extent as a dating agency for people who in effect have already been

through a kind of selection process. Working together can help in the process of getting to know and like each other. Sometimes an incident or misunderstanding is the occasion that enables people to get into conversation and get to know each other.

Nowadays in the West, marrying a colleague does not mean losing your job. However, it is preferable for a couple to work apart, since it is difficult constantly being together, especially in a hierarchical relationship. Where there have been cases of successful collaboration, between artists, scientists or business people, it is often the case that the couple were together before they worked together. In business, matters of the heart have to remain discreet. If problems of jealousy arise or a break-up occurs, the ensuing tensions can threaten to undermine the working atmosphere and affect the career advancement of one or the other. As a personnel manager once said with resignation, "You can't stop people falling in love, so you close your eyes to it, as long as it does not create too many complications!"

1963

COPENHAGEN. A book is the subject of a sensational trial: the translation of the licentious English novel by John Cleland *Fanny Hill* (1749). The case went to the Supreme Court. A new law on censorship was examined, which resulted in the liberalisation of pornography in 1969 (cf. p. 340).

MOSCOW. Marriage of the Bolshoi Ballet stars Ekaterina Maximova and Vladimir Vassiliev. They had known each other since their days at the Bolshoi Ballet school and became a world-famous dance couple. Their quarrels were legendary, but their affection on stage was palpable, where their beauty and grace, combined with their very expressive virtuosity, led to great acclaim in both classical and modern dance. In 1992, at the age of fifty-three, Maximova gave a dazzling performance as Cinderella, full of charm and youth, while Vassiliev dressed as a woman, played the role of the wicked step-mother.

Sophia Loren & Carlo Ponti

A stable relationship between a film producer and an actress whom he made into a star.

A French marriage: this was the solution to a problem that had been facing Italian actress Sophia Loren and film producer Carlo Ponti for a number of years. Divorce did not exist in Italy and Ponti was already married. In 1964 they applied for French citizenship. Ponti was then able to divorce his wife and re-marry in 1966. Similarly Vittorio de Sica and Maria Mercader, in a relationship that had lasted for nearly a quarter of a century and suffered a number of legal ups and downs, married

in France in 1968. Another Italian star Claudia Cardinale married her film producer Franco Cristaldi in 1966, after his first marriage was annulled by an ecclesiastical court. Annulment in the Court of Rome – a very rare occurrence – was in effect the only avenue open to Catholics who wanted to end a marriage.

The film *Divorce Italian Style* (1962) had already drawn attention to the absurdity of a system that refused to allow divorce but treated a crime of passion leniently. Italy did not legalise divorce (cf. p. 42) until 1970. The last Western countries to do so all had a Catholic tradition: Portugal in 1975, Spain in 1981, Argentina in 1987, and Ireland in 1995.

At a time when Sophia Loren was making films in Hollywood, she and Carlo Ponti had married in Mexico in 1957, where the more relaxed legislation allowed him

to divorce. The Vatican then accused Ponti of bigamy. In order to be able to return to Italy he had to apply for the annulment of his Mexican marriage. In Rome he was unable to live under the same roof as Sophia Loren, as they both ran the risk of being accused of adultery. They were never seen together in public. "I dream," she sighed "of being married, having children and leading a normal life." They had to move to Paris and become French in order to do so.

A HAPPY AND ENDURING RELATIONSHIP. Born illegitimately in 1934, Sophia Loren spent a poor but happy childhood in the suburbs of Naples. Withdrawn and lacking in self-confidence, she described herself as being "too tall, hips too wide, nose too long, mouth too large". She started out in Rome as a film extra and posed for magazine photo-stories. "The first time that I noticed Sophia," said Ponti, "I was struck more by her personality than her beauty. She radiated something." She has told the story of their first meeting when she was seventeen. A friend had taken her to see the Miss Rome competition. Carlo Ponti, already a well-known film director, was one of the judges. He noticed her and invited her to his table. "He was very professional, very polite. He asked me why I was not taking part in the competition and said that he was going to enter me. He wasn't the tallest or the most seductive of men, but he had a nice face. I accepted. Since he had picked me out, everyone expected me to win the prize, but I came second. Later he told me that he had launched lots of stars. I though that it was a producer's normal way of sweet-talking. He asked me to go to his office the next morning. I went, but it was not love at first sight. It felt as though we had always known each other. That is how our relationship began." It has been a happy and enduring relationship, despite the obvious differences: he is twenty-four years older than she is, quite a lot shorter, but generous, cheerful and full of energy. "The only person who understands me is Carlo," she says. "If you could see him through my eyes you would see the most graceful man in the world."

Married with two children, Ponti had had several short-lived relationships with other actresses. Having made some outstanding films and numerous hits, in

FACING PAGE
The actress in *Boccacio 70* (1962) produced by Carlo Ponti. She appears in the sketch directed by Vittorio de Sica.

SAINT-PAUL-DE-VENCE.
Art editors, dealers and
friends to three genera-
tions of artists Aimé and
Marguerite Maeght open
the foundation bearing
their name on a hill among
the pine trees in Provence
to exhibit the treasures
of their modern art
collection, with works
by Giacometti, Miró,
Bonnard, Braque, etc.
After the death of their
eleven-year-old son
Bernard in 1953 they decided to show that life and art
are more powerful than
death. Art collectors are often married couples. In the
United States, the names
of Wilhelmina and Wallace
Holladay come to mind.
They were responsible for
the museum in Washing-
ton featuring art works by
women. Or Jean and
Dominique de Ménil, who
opened a large museum
of modern painting in
Houston, Texas. Similarly
in Germany a prestigious
building in Cologne per-
petuates the name of Peter
and Irene Ludwig. In
Switzerland patrons Paul
and Maja Sacher encour-
aged the art and music of
their time.

♥ ♥ ♥

1951 he founded a company with Dino de Laurentiis
which made *Europa 51* with Rossellini, *The Road* with
Fellini, as well as some big international productions
such as *War and Peace*. Sophia Loren made a number
of flops before *Aida* (1953) which launched her career.
Then Ponti took her in hand, giving her the main role in

Woman of the River (1954). He gave her the chance to
work with Marcello Mastroianni in eight successful
films, notably *Scandal in Sorrento*.

AN AFFECTIONATE AND TRUE COMPANIONSHIP. In Carlo
Ponti she found a father-figure, similarly with Vittorio

de Sica, the great actor and producer. After *Gold of Naples* (1954), in which de Sica offered her an enticing part as a pizza seller, she made seven more films with him, of which the best known, *Two Women* (1961), won her the prize for best actress at Cannes, and an Oscar in Hollywood.

Ponti mapped out her international career, made her learn English and transformed an ordinary, pretty girl into a refined and elegant woman. Once she became a star, she found herself in competition with Gina Lollobrigida. From 1956 to 1958 she made nine more films in Hollywood. In the first she fell under the spell of Cary Grant, thirty years her senior, who asked her to marry him. It was at that point that Ponti arranged his divorce and their marriage in Mexico. They smile at the rumours: "If I had really had all the adventures the press ascribes to me, I wouldn't have had time to make a single film," Ponti exclaims. A close friend describes them as a complementary couple: "He needs her high spirits and her vivacity, and she needs his reflective mind and common sense." But they were unhappy at having no children. After infertility treatment, Carlo junior was born in 1968 and then a second son Eduardo in 1973.

Carlo Ponti made an enormous contribution to the renewal of the French and Italian cinema. The success of *Doctor Zhivago* (1965) allowed him to take risks in financing more ambitious films. His films were always conceived with his wife in mind. Her most important work was Scola's *The Special Day* with Marcello Mastroianni. Gradually she made fewer films, spending more time with her sons, while Ponti continued to work and travel widely. Following problems with the Italian tax authorities, in 1982 she returned to Italy to face arrest, which caused a furore. The couple then moved to Los Angeles. Sophia Loren explained their long-lasting relationship by quoting these words from Lawrence Durrell: "The companion takes over from the lover, and affection takes over from love, even from passion."

♡ ♡ ♡

SEXOLOGY
The First Time

When a couple make love for the first time, the dialogue between their bodies has different meanings for each of them.

It can be banal or sublime, but "the first time" is a mixture of love, pleasure, ignorance or fear, as one individual discovers the body of another, and his or her reactions to it. Young people are far more sexually active than adults realise. The age at which sexual activity starts is continually falling and cannot be explained by the earlier onset of puberty alone. In the West during the sixties, the average age of the first experience of sexual intercourse ranged from eighteen to nineteen for boys and from twenty to twenty-one for girls, depending upon the country. This was a reduction of one year since 1900. By 1990 it had fallen further by at least one year: eighteen for girls and seventeen for boys in France, seventeen for both boys and girls in Great Britain. The narrowing of the age gap between boys and girls is largely due to a change in girls' behaviour. The contraceptive pill (cf. p. 310) has not, however, played a significant role.

The most rapid drop in Great Britain, for example, occurred during the fifties, well before wide-

spread use of the pill. Since that time, the interval between the first adolescent sexual experience (kisses and cuddles) and full intercourse has fallen from four years to two.

This figure takes account of a combination of different parameters, with the average age varying according to a number of factors, such as level of education: that is to say, for example, that sexual activity tends to start later in those following prolonged courses of study. In Great Britain and the United States, it has been observed that Asians have their first sexual encounter later than whites, whereas among blacks it is earlier. In the vast majority of cases, most people take the plunge with a partner of roughly the same age and with a little experience. The numbers of young men using prostitutes has dropped markedly.

Old wives' tales still exist, largely because of the inadequacy of sexual education (cf. p. 218). Some people still think that a girl cannot become pregnant when she loses her virginity. Although more widespread information in the fight against AIDS has encouraged the use of condoms among the young, the proportion of unprotected first sexual encounters is still high – depending upon the country this amounts to between a third and a half of young people – with many teenage pregnancies the consequence.

A VIRGIN UNTIL MARRIAGE. Long associated with moral or religious values such as honour and purity, female virginity in the West has tended to be a private matter, reflecting individual responsibility. However, it still remains the object of some social customs such as showing the blood-stained sheet from the marriage bed among Muslims. The deflowering of a young virgin involves rupturing the hymen, the membrane that covers part of the opening of the vagina. This may cause some bleeding. Whereas the virtue of virginity is emphasised in the way a girl is brought up, society on the other hand approves of early sexual maturity in boys. The "sexual apprenticeship" advocated by early pioneers such as Léon Blum (cf. p. 54) was limited for girls to relationships with their future husband, pre-marital sex being more widely tolerated in Europe than in the United States. According to the Kinsey report, (cf. p. 226) 10 per cent of men marrying in the United States in the forties were still virgins when they married, as were 48 per cent of women in the sixties and 20 per cent in 1985. Despite appeals for chastity (cf. p. 404) the proportion today is minuscule in the West, as a result of a rise in the age at which people are marrying (cf. p. 298) and as a result of changing morals.

"Never start marriage with rape," Balzac advocated in *Physiology of Marriage*. At a time when fear and ignorance prevailed, how many wedding nights must have been legalised rape! "Does it hurt?" is the question

Young people at Coney Island, near New York.

most often posed by girls. The answer has already been given in the *Kama Sutra* (cf. p. 68), which advises a man to be patient and gentle. At any age, tenderness, caresses and words of love are essential for a woman.

EMBARKING ON PLEASURE. Often, before the first sexual encounter, a girl does not feel ready and is afraid; the boy, for whom masturbation may have already revealed how the sexual organ works, is shy and does not really know how to begin. Taking the plunge because "it's silly to be a virgin" and giving in to peer pressure do not make him a more mature person.

"The first time" is symbolically important for a boy, because he feels that he has to prove his virility, and may therefore be anxious about his performance. For a girl, who rarely experiences vaginal pleasure right away, but for whom enjoyment is more easily achieved by stimulation of the clitoris, disappointment – which is frequently experienced – is not regarded as a failure: the apprenticeship in pleasure takes longer for a girl and depends chiefly on her readiness to let go. Whether male or female, it takes a

long time to overcome inhibitions, to dare to say what one feels, what one desires, and to guide the other partner in the dialogue of the body.

One third of men and two thirds of women say that they were very much in love with their partner at their first sexual encounter. Traditionally, a girl's upbringing gives priority to the emotional and relational aspect, whereas masculine physical impulses are considered to be stronger. Love, which makes a girl more receptive, can inhibit a boy. If he is worried about the size of his penis or if he is afraid of disappointing or shocking the girl, he may hesitate to get her to part her legs to facilitate penetration. If he loses his erection or suffers from premature ejaculation (after less than about twenty thrusting movements), he may feel humiliated and then suffer a mental block.

"Love makes a virgin," is an old Bantu proverb. Anyone can become a virgin again by discovering true love, which is give and take, respect, and freedom for the other partner. Sleeping together in the same bed, waking up and taking breakfast together – all these other "first time" experiences are important for a couple's future, which will be taken up as much with mundane matters as with sexual pleasure.

1964

VATICAN. **Debate in council about marriage and birth control. Several reforming cardinals asked that love be recognised as the true purpose of marriage. Pope Paul VI made the final decision. The long-awaited document, the encyclical** *Humanae Vitae* **(1968), in which the Pope condemned modern methods of contraception – the pill and sterilisation, which he did not refer to by name – reaffirmed the traditional position of the Catholic Church: the carnal act, when practised for reasons other than reproduction, is a sin.**

FRANCE. **Film-maker Claude Chabrol marries the beautiful actress Stéphane Audran. Up to their split in 1980, Chabrol made nineteen films with his wife, from** *The Cousins* **to** *Violette Nozière***. Combining coldness with sensuality Stéphane Audran was a remarkable interpreter of his best films, notably** *The Unfaithful Wife* **or** *The Butcher***, in which he painted an acerbic picture of the provincial bourgeoisie.**

♡ ♡ ♡

Ingmar Bergman & Liv Ullmann

Life together on an isolated island strained the relationship of a brilliant film-maker and a great actress.

In the summer of 1965, the well-known Swedish film-maker Ingmar Bergman fell in love at first sight twice over as he was shooting *Persona*, one of his greatest masterpieces, on the island of Fårö. He developed a passion for this strange, desolate place, accessible only by ferry from the island of Gotland – "I had the feeling that I was at home here" – and for the Norwegian actress Liv Ullmann, who was playing the leading role. When the day's filming was over, the couple would walk back along the beach. That first summer was, the actress recalled, "a state of pure happiness". Despite being discreet about their relationship, it caused a scandal. Liv Ullmann was childless, married to a Norwegian doctor. Ingmar Bergman, who already had seven children, was married at the time to a well-known Swedish pianist, Käbi Laretei, his fourth wife, not to mention relationships with two actresses who had appeared in his films: Harriet Andersson (*Summer with Monica*, 1953) and Bibi Andersson (*Smiles of a Summer Night*, 1955). Dark and brooding, he was the son of a pastor in Uppsala. Despite an aus-

Ingmar Bergman with two of his favourite actresses, Liv Ullmann (centre) and Bibi Andersson.

tere upbringing by parents who were not very affectionate he was able to remain on good terms with his former wives.

Liv Ullmann was twenty-seven. Coming from a middle-class background she had made her theatre début in Norway and had already made several films. Possessed of a strong, serene beauty, she wore her hair drawn back to reveal a fresh face with deep blue eyes. Ingmar Bergman was twenty years older. Since 1942 he had pursued a career as a theatre producer and cinema director. He had had great success with the films he made in the fifties, *The Seventh Seal* bringing him international acclaim. Death, the existence of God, and the difficulty of communication between a couple are the main themes of a body of work which has been acknowledged as one of the most important of the century. From 1963 onwards he was director of the Theatre Royal. "To me," the young actress wrote, "he was a god. When he spoke to me I blushed."

CREATIVE ISOLATION. Bergman decided to settle on the island of Fårö with Liv Ullmann. It was "a gross error of judgement" he acknowledged later, admitting that he had "quite simply forgotten to ask Liv what she thought". Unfortunately she did not share his enthusiasm for the arid, rock-strewn location on which he chose to build a house of stone and wood in the local style. But Bergman wanted to start a new life. He left the Theatre Royal and settled on the island, alone with Liv Ullmann. She soon became pregnant. "I did nothing to prevent this birth," she said, "because I wasn't afraid. I found it all very normal." Bergman made use of the brief Scandinavian summers of 1966, 1967 and 1968 to make his Fårö trilogy *The Hour of the Wolf*, *The Shame* and *The Passion of Anna* with Max von Sydow and Liv Ullmann. She collaborated on the script writing, as Bergman liked to discuss his ideas with her and call upon their joint imagination to develop his narratives, which also draw on reality. Thus, the hero of *The Hour of the Wolf*, a

FRANCE. **Two teenage "idols" get married: Johnny Halliday marries Sylvie Vartan, who sang the song "This evening, I will be the most beautiful/To go dancing". Her family was Bulgarian, he was Belgian and took an English stage name in common with many pop singers of the time, when English rock and roll was invading France. Their son David was born in 1966. After dramatic separations and spectacular reconciliations their relationship faltered, unlike those of Françoise Hardy and Jacques Dutronc, or France Gall and Michel Berger, but they remained the favourites of a loyal public. Their fans shouted for joy when fate reunited them on stage. An "abandoned singer", Johnny Halliday the rocker was at his best when singing about sadness and solitude. A succession of beautiful young women passed through his life; he had a daughter by actress Nathalie Baye. Sylvie Vartan remarried in the United States, where her career was now based, while the famous "Johnny" rarely ventured abroad.**

famous painter, lives in isolation with an over-attentive wife.

The Lutheran Church refused to baptise their daughter Linn as the mother was still not divorced. "We were not married because neither of us was free and in any case it was unnecessary," she declared. "We didn't need a lawyer or a pastor. We had our friendship and our love."

For several years Bergman, who detested city noise, was content to live a quiet life. He could idle his time away, watching the tides, and write in peace. The child, confined to the other side of the house, did not disturb him. To keep out prying eyes, he built a very high wall around the property, which was situated twenty minutes from the ferry along a rough road. Each morning he took the ferry at a quarter to five to fetch the papers, and by eight o'clock he would be walking along the shore, even if a storm was raging. The wind blew constantly and in winter the temperature dropped to -30° C.

VIOLENCE, SETBACKS, THEN PEACE. This way of life, which was ideal for him, was a nightmare for the young actress. "The island was a prison in which I did not know how to deal with my feelings of solitude and insecurity. I was in a constant state of anxiety and I dreamt of being somewhere else. But I never said anything."

Gradually their life together became the living hell of the couples Bergman had portrayed in so many of his films (cf. p. 332). For him, "we fought our demons both with and without success." One of his demons was violent jealousy. "I was looking for security and protection," she said, by way of analysis, "he was looking for a mother." A couple who could not live without each other, they became engaged in a merciless feud. But their quarrels posed practical problems, with gates to open and close, a ferry with a time-table that never coincided with their disputes, and the long trek to reach the airport: "By the time I arrived, my anger had subsided," she smiled. "I did a hundred-and-eighty-degree turn and went home. Often Ingmar was waiting for me at the gate." During this stormy period, film-making was a parting in the clouds. But in 1969 there was no more shooting, as Liv Ullmann left to make *The Emigrants*, a Jan Troell film. "We knew that it was the end," Bergman wrote. He resumed work as a producer at the Theatre Royal. Despite several attempts at reconciliation they did not succeed in regaining their former intimacy and so they separated. But they remained friends, and Liv Ullmann continued to appear in his films from *Cries and Whispers* (1972) to *Autumn Sonata* (1978), a total of nine in all, and practically everyone a masterpiece. She continued to act successfully in the theatre, she wrote books about her life and also became a director. She married Donald Saunders in 1986.

In 1971 Bergman married again, this time Ingrid von Rosen, who was twelve years his junior and who in future would be involved in the production of his films. They settled in Stockholm, where Bergman divided his time between the cinema, theatre, and writing his memoirs, as well as scripts for young film-makers.

Ingmar Bergman and Liv Ullmann in 1968.

Society
"No" to Marriage!

From marriage without love to love without marriage: as sudden as it was unexpected, one of the major social changes of the century in the West silently took place.

One of the most important social and psychological changes of the century is imperceptibly taking

it enables couples to find a home more easily. Similar practical reasons – in the wake of new positive legislation – explain the sudden but short-lived increase confirmed in Austria in 1972 and 1987, and in Sweden in 1989.

Western countries appear to be evolving on the same pattern, the difference between them being one

the end of the nineties in Scandinavia one child in two is born outside marriage; the figure is one in three in France or the United States.

FREE CHOICE. The movement did not start with the upper classes. The phenomenon of unmarried couples first appeared among the lower classes – they were known as com-

place. While not renouncing living together as a couple, fewer people in the West are getting married. Is this due to an increase in the age at which people marry (cf. p. 286) after two decades of early marriage, or is it a new form of partnership?

The marriage rate began to decline first of all in Sweden, where it fell by a third between 1966 and 1973, and then spread to other countries. In France the number of marriages dropped from 416,000 in 1972 to 265,000 in 1987. This general decline, which is still continuing – 254,000 marriages in France in 1994 – started later in countries with a Catholic or Orthodox tradition. In Socialist countries, marriage is still very popular, since

of time-scale. Today, where the majority of marriages are preceded by a period of living together in a "trial marriage", it is estimated that a third of each new generation will not marry. In France this is already the case in a third of all couples, and in a half of people in the twenty to forty-nine age group. Pregnancy no longer requires a relationship to be "regularised", as was once the case. The stigma of illegitimacy has gradually disappeared as the legal status of so-called "natural" children has come into line with that of legitimate children. This has led to a rise in the number of births out of wedlock: from 6 to 8 per cent of the total in the sixties, it rose to 15 to 20 per cent in most countries by 1985. At

mon-law husband or wife – and was characteristic of large cities; the Swedes called it "marriage Stockholm-style". In the seventies it started to become common among young people and then extended to all levels of society, especially in urban areas and among non-practising Catholics. Far from living together in the poverty so widespread in Latin America, where women are forever subjected to the burden of their inferior status shared with illegitimate children, the situation in the West is the result of free choice in which young women play a decisive role: they are increasing in number, thanks to the growth of sexual equality and financial independence, preferring a private rela-

Marriage, yes or no?
Photograph by
Elliott Erwitt. USSR, 1967.

tionship to a public alliance. More than just an institution in crisis, it is a complete reversal of the notion of a couple (which may also be homosexual, cf. p. 398).

With the growth of sexual relations before marriage (cf. p. 294), the notion of living together, which was frowned on not so long ago, has changed in significance. Society's hostility has given way to a more tolerant attitude, with only a minority of people complaining about the loss of certain "values" (cf. p. 404). In the same way as Napoleon declared "mistresses ignore the law and the law ignores mistresses", the State is now moving toward a more benevolent neutrality. In Sweden, for example, a law passed in 1987 directed that an unmarried couple's property should be shared equally between them in the event of separation or the death of a partner. Everywhere new laws on divorce, marriage, contraception, and abortion show that society is adapting to the changing nature of the "couple".

Marriage has undergone a remarkable evolution during the twentieth century (cf. p. 16). After the "establishment marriage", which was intended to give a woman security, or the "love match", which was an idealised view of the romantic union of two people, the definition of marriage given by a Swedish minister in 1969 – "the voluntary union of two independent people" – marked a change in character. This reference to equality formed the basis of subsequent experiments in new forms of living together in the years that followed (cf. p. 374).

A SILENT REVOLUTION. The "proposal of non-marriage" sung about by Georges Brassens has come about without resorting to violence and has nothing in common with the militancy of the nineteenth-century anarchists who advocated free love. Without taking to the streets,

so to speak, modern couples have forced through a revolution; they think that a love life with its adventures enhances intimacy, and that it is none of society's business. They forget, however, that the state has not renounced its rights regarding sexuality, to condemn incest (cf. p. 230) for example.

The rapid assimilation of this change shows that "the couple" is not in crisis. The couple remains the central focus and a lot is expected of them. There are now two accepted life-styles: one solemn, the other flexible, with both in the end resembling each other. Marriage, as an official rite of passage, remains a voluntary act, with its long-term commitment. The rising divorce rate, however, underlines its fragility. Living together, often criticised

as a union "for better without the poorer", is not unlike marriage when it is a monogamous and stable relationship.

How do we describe these new types of relationship? The English speak of "living together", Australians call it a *de facto* or informal marriage. The difficulty in knowing how to refer to one's partner shows that society has not managed to keep pace with change: "companion" is too long, "mistress" is too bureaucratic, "cohabitant" is too official, "lover" too passionate, "mate" or "buddy" too familiar. While people in Quebec say "chum" and the Germans use "partner", general agreement across the world appears to favour "boyfriend/ girlfriend" to refer to the person one loves but is not married to.

WEDDING ANNIVERSARIES. It is a wide-spread tradition in the West for couples to celebrate their wedding anniversary, either quietly together or among family and friends. They give or receive presents which vary according to the length of time that they have been married. This can range from the "paper (or cotton) wedding" (one year) to the "diamond wedding" (sixty years) with stages along the way, and variations depending upon the country, linking the value of the symbols to the length of the union, as if to underline the value of a stable marriage.

Other anniversaries most frequently celebrated are "wooden" (five years), "tin" (ten), "crystal" or "porcelain" (fifteen), "silver" (twenty-five), "golden" (fifty) and very rarely "platinum" (seventy) and "oak" (ninety).

♡ ♡ ♡

Mujer Esposada, Ouka Lele, 1980.

Niki de Saint-Phalle & Jean Tinguely

Animated sound-emitting machines attached to powerful coloured

The year was 1966, and at the Museum of Modern Art in Stockholm a giant temporary sculpture entitled *Hon* (*She* in Swedish) was on display. It was a giant 30-metre-long multi-coloured figure of a woman lying on her back. Visitors entered through the vagina to discover a maze inside. "I made the original mock-up and painted it," explained Niki de Saint-Phalle. "Jean built a plane-

sculptures in a show of love and life.

tarium in the right breast and a milk-bar in the left. *Hon* was their first joint work. She was thirty-six and her companion Jean Tinguely was forty-one. "We fell in love in 1960," she wrote. "I think it was the day you stubbed out your cigarette in the butter." Tinguely was a man of irresistible charm living in a vortex of energy and ideas. They inhabited a creative world of total freedom, benign madness, and an exuberance which at times was quite frenzied. She was the only woman in the New Realists, a group founded in 1960 by Tinguely with other sculptors such as César and Arman, and painters such as Daniel Spoerri and Yves Klein. She shared with them the spirit of collective entertainment and a taste for being provocative.

Jean Tinguely was born into a working-class Swiss family. From the age of twelve he was making his first working models in the woods near his home in Basle – wooden wheels powered by stream water driving ham-

mers which struck tin cans. Brought up by a violent father, he was a rebel whose art displayed contempt for authority. In 1951 he married the sculptress Eva Aeppli. Their daughter was born in 1953. He moved in anarchist circles. In 1954 the couple settled in Paris, and the following year Tinguely took part in the first "kinetic" (moving) art exhibition. An expert on cogs and gears, and combining humour with eroticism, he constructed grinding, juddering machines, mobile sculptures which with their jerky movements responded to his obsession with death. In 1960 he exhibited at the Museum of Modern Art in New York and became friendly with American pop artists. His marriage to Eva Aeppli eventually broke up; his wife left him, describing him as a "womaniser".

A FEMALE REBEL. "The product of a respectable family and a religious education; escaped into exile at the age of twenty-two, thanks to art," is the way that Niki de Saint-Phalle described herself. She grew up in New York, the daughter of an American mother and a French father. For half a century she harboured a guilty secret so terrible that it nearly drove her mad: her father raped her when she was eleven. She gave vent to her hatred in the film *Daddy* which she made in 1972. Married at the age of eighteen to American writer Harry Matthews, by whom had two children, she was dissatisfied with her life.

Visiting Barcelona in 1955, the Güell de Gaudi park, where she discovered the sculptures of Dubuffet, was a revelation to her. Leaving her family to live with Tinguely, she burst spectacularly on to the art scene. In 1961, to illustrate the martyrdom of St Sebastian, she invited visitors to her exhibition to throw arrows at her paintings which included *Portrait de Mon Amant* (*Portrait of My Love*). In 1962 in the company of Tinguely, Larry Rivers, and Rauschenberg, she fired at paint-filled balloons attached to relief plaster casts because she wanted to "make them bleed". Blatantly sacrilegious, she constructed strange models with dolls' heads and hearts, religious statues, and stuffed animals. Long before the explosion of neo-feminism she was attacking stereotypes by the symbolic use of dolls' tea sets or laundry irons.

The time she spent in Paris, starting from when she

met the New Realists and her collaboration with Tinguely, marked a happy and constructive phase, with *La Mariée sous l'arbre en fleur* (*Bride under flowering tree*) and *La Mariée sur le cheval* (*Bride on horseback*) (1963). In 1965 she was a sensation first in Paris then in New York with her female sculptures – massive exuberant figures, at the same time both clumsy and graceful, with violently coloured rounded shapes which became the symbol of female liberty. "I wanted to make the biggest and, I hoped, the most beautiful sculptures of my generation," she wrote later, "to prove both to myself and to other women that it was possible to do great things with female intuition. I wanted to conquer and I was helped in this by 'knights in armour' such as Jean Tinguely, and others, to realise my DREAMS ... I drew them into a dream world and they gave me the foundations to build my dreams."

JOINT CREATIONS. The anarchic but warm-hearted mechanic, with shaggy eyebrows and a moustache, dressed in dungarees to do his welding, and the beautiful woman with periwinkle blue eyes, delicate yet strong, dressed in extravagant clothes and hats, lived and worked together in an atmosphere of farce and tragedy, where crazy machines joined female bodies to Easter chicks. "Niki is an absolute monster," said Tinguely, "but I like monsters a lot; at least you never get bored with them." "He is my alter ego," she said, "he is unique, he is his own turbo-generator." Between declarations of love and slanging matches, their relationship was that of accomplices, sometimes rivals, of great artists who admired each other and regarded each other as equals. They married in 1971, at a moment when their relationship was at breaking point – Tinguely had a son by another woman in Fribourg in 1973. Despite this they continued to create works together, in a division of labour with Tinguely working on the mechanics, the motor, and the power, and de Saint-Phalle on the figures, shapes, and colours.

The Cyclops at Milly-la-Forêt near Paris is Jean Tinguely's greatest work. In 1969, in the middle of the forest surrounded by four oak trees, he started to build an enormous metal construction in the shape of a head twenty-two metres tall and weighing three hundred tons. Niki de Saint-Phalle coated the rough cement with a skin dotted with a mosaic of mirrors. Through the

FRANCE. *Shabadabada ...* With its sentimental song and romantic shots of the lovers running towards each other along the beach at Deauville, Claude Lelouch's film *A Man and a Woman,* winner of the Palme d'Or at the Cannes film festival, is a huge success. Awarded two Oscars it also had a very successful run in the United States. Jean-Louis Trintignant and Anouk Aimée play two people bruised by life and suffering from loneliness. They each have a child and their partners are dead. Their first encounter is a failure, but they meet again to start a new life together.

SAINT TROPEZ. **Brigitte Bardot accepts a proposal of marriage from German businessman Günther Sachs. To woo her, he flew over La Madrague, the star's home, in his helicopter and dropped thousands of rose petals.**

"You don't have to work to live, but you have to live to love."

JACQUES DEMY
*The Young Girls of Rochefort
(part of the dialogue which does
not appear in the final version)*

♡ ♡ ♡

grinding of rusty gears the visitor gains access to balconies, landings and mezzanine floors where inventions, mobiles, sculptures, and contributions from friends of the couple are displayed. Another well-known work is the Stravinsky fountain in Paris (1982) beside the Pompidou Centre, where moving machines playing with the water are attached to coloured discs. At Garavicchio in Tuscany Niki de Saint-Phalle created the *Jardin des Tarots* (*Garden of Tarot Cards*) where, between the olive trees and Tinguely's sculptures made of scrap

iron, twenty-two Tarot cards are represented by giant sculptures, glinting with flashes of glass, mirror and ceramic.

After the death of Tinguely in 1991 she continued to look after his work while at the same time devoting herself to her own. She painted portraits of him, his head among cogs and bolts, and she wrote to him: "Hymn of love. Cannibalism. Communion. Jean, I am eating you. I am taking on your power. Your soul is joined to mine."

♡ ♡ ♡

Sexology
Learning to Make Love

Masters and Johnson, sexologists and pioneers of sexual therapy, studied sexual intercourse in the laboratory.

Sexual therapy methods advocated by Masters and Johnson spread throughout the Western world.

sixties. They were sexologists, co-workers and a husband-and-wife team (they married in 1971 and divorced in 1993). William Masters was a gynaecologist born in 1915 and his wife Virginia Johnson, ten years younger, was a psychologist.

Americans do not know how to make love. That is the conclusion reached by Masters and Johnson after observing 10,000 sexual acts in their laboratory in St Louis, Missouri. The pioneers of sexual therapy worked as a couple to help those people who came to consult them because love-making was painful or caused anxiety.

Masters and Johnson are the names of the world-famous couple whose work was disseminated widely throughout the United States and Europe at the end of the

Since the start of the century sexuality had begun to shake off the prudery that had previously surrounded it, thanks to the contribution made by psychoanalysis (cf. p. 46). Progressively it became the subject of scientific study, with research work by the German Magnus Hirschfeld (cf. p. 114) making sexology a completely separate discipline. It was during the thirties that the word "sexology" found its way into the language. "Sexologist" is a post-war word. The word "sex therapy" derives from the work of

Masters and Johnson. Since the new discipline was oriented toward the therapeutic, it was quickly hijacked by doctors, gynaecologists and psychiatrists. It did not, however, figure in the official syllabus for medical studies. Even as late as the sixties sexual physiology was not often taught. Given the lack of education on this subject at school and poor communication in the family (cf. p. 218), ignorance and prejudice at all levels of society continues to be widespread. While research into biology and physiology continues to develop, more and more people are seeking help to resolve their sexual problems.

THE FOUR PHASES OF SEXUAL ACT. The first book by Masters and Johnson, *Human Sexual Response* (1966), was the result of eleven years' work in the laboratory on sexual intercourse. With the voluntary participation of 382 women and 312 men of all ages, the authors observed and recorded the reactions of the body before, during and after a sexual act, either alone or as a couple. These are described by defining the four phases of the sexual act: arousal, plateau, orgasm and resolution. One of their most important conclusions concerns female sexuality; in line with Havelock Ellis (cf. p. 62) and Kinsey (cf. p. 226) they emphasise the importance of the pleasure gained from stimulation of the clitoris, which undermines the emphasis placed by Freud and his successors on vaginal orgasm, implying that a woman's pleasure depends on penetration.

Leaving aside the mentally incompetent, the two therapists came to the view that inadequate sexual responses are the fault of poor conditioning and that sexual problems translate into a dysfunctional relationship between partners. Their therapy, which is a form of applied behavioural techniques, starts with teaching about sexual matters. They advocate sexual education and discussion about these matters from childhood onwards.

ACHIEVING SEXUAL HARMONY. Teach yourself love-making. The method used by Masters and Johnson consists of bringing two couples together; one couple are the patients, the other couple are the therapists. The patients are invited to touch each other all over the body at first, then to touch the sexual parts, but avoiding intercourse. Without touching them, the therapists provide verbal encouragement by pointing out the positive aspects

of these exchanges. Gradually the patients work up to full intercourse. This method, which is the opposite of the psychoanalytical approach, has inspired a whole wave of behavioural therapists, notably Helen Singer Kaplan of Cornell University in New York State, who places particular emphasis on the way the symptom is presented. Some sexologists, quoting the German psychoanalyst Wilhelm Reich (cf. p. 310), go so far as to advocate the therapist making direct physical contact with the patient.

In their other books, *Human Sexual Inadequacy* and *Intercourse for Pleasure*, Masters and Johnson analyse recent changes in the role of women, plead for people to stop attributing all responsibility in the field of sexual relations to men, and deal with certain prejudices such as the "automatic" nature of the erection. They also show that male pleasure is not detached from the active participation of a woman. A woman must not try to adapt absolutely to the desires of her partner at the price of inhibiting her own. If there are sexual problems it is generally the woman who seeks help, because she sees herself as being to blame

and also has the courage to ask for help. The international popularity of Masters and Johnson and the spread of their ideas helped sexology to win the right to be quoted in the media. The eighties saw the acceptance of Ruth Westheimer, an American of German origin, who became a star of the small screen in the United States and who went on to give advice on a German television programme – *"Do it"* – starting in 1987, and in Britain in 1993. She also distributed a game, *Dr. Ruth's Game of Good Sex*.

What is "good sex"? The debate is still open, as all "sexperts" fall into the trap of measuring "success" in terms of the obligatory orgasm. Masters and Johnson have a more subtle approach. Having observed how many husbands are poor lovers but refuse to admit it, they suggest that sexual harmony can only come about by sharing responsibility within the couple. This assumes that each partner is aware of his own desires and communicates them to the other. To bring this about, they concede that "the amount of pleasure which equal roles can contribute to sexual relations is unlimited".

1966

JAPAN. A steep drop in the birth rate from 1.82 million in 1965 to 1.36 million was reversed in 1967 to 1.93 million. This phenomenon was due to the popular belief that girls born in 1966 "the year of the horse" would not find a husband.

UNITED STATES. Frank Sinatra has a hit with *Strangers in the Night*, a song about love at first sight. In the same year the fifty-year-old singer married the young actress Mia Farrow aged twenty-one (cf. p. 368).

FRANCE. Orchestral conductor Roberto Benzi, once a child prodigy, marries singer Jane Rhodes. They first met in 1959 when she appeared in *Carmen* under his direction in a memorable production of the Bizet opera.

"In this cruel life which is ours, love is the dream of beauty."

GUNNAR EKELOF
La Légende de Fatumeh

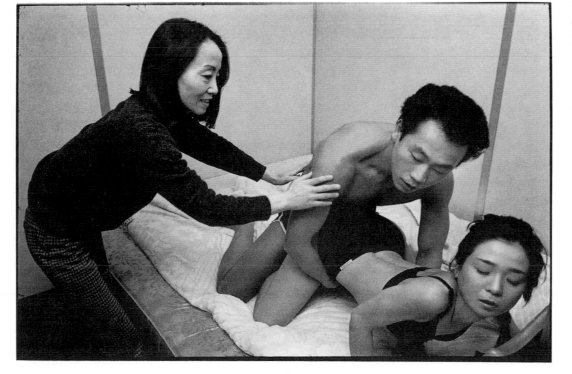

In a club in Tokyo, men can adopt various positions with paid models. Swimming trunks are obligatory.

Margrethe
Henrik **&** of Denmark

Love transformed a French diplomat into a Danish prince. A highly cultured and artistically gifted royal couple were united by their interests.

A royal marriage in Denmark: Princess Margrethe married French diplomat Count Henri de Laborde de Monpezat on 10 June 1967. She was twenty-seven and he was thirty-three. They had met the year before at a reception in London where the count, who comes from south-west France, was working as a secretary at the embassy. The princess is very tall (5'9"), fair, with blue eyes. When this handsome, elegant man, who is a little taller than the princess, was presented to her it was love at first sight. She would later say that she saw "the horizon in flames". The count,

TEL AVIV. **Daniel Barenboim, twenty-five, marries Jacqueline du Pré, twenty-two. They were both child prodigies and acknowledged star performers. She was British and played the violoncello. He was a pianist and orchestral conductor, an Israeli of Argentinian origin. Just when she was at the height of her powers, the young cellist was struck down with multiple sclerosis which forced her in 1972 to abandon her career and devote herself to teaching. They had no children. She was pained by her husband's relationship with Helena Bachkirev, by whom he had two children. She died in 1987. The young couple radiating happiness and talent have left behind some splendid recordings, most notably Beethoven and Brahms sonatas.**

while realising that this marriage would change his life for ever, concluded after mature reflection and in the face of opposition from his father that he had to "take the woman he loved, because nothing is more important than love". On 3 September 1966 in Copenhagen he was introduced as the fiancé of the heiress to the throne. Margrethe was the daughter of King Frederik IX and Queen Ingrid, herself the daughter of the Swedish king. The princess had studied history, political science and economics, spoke several languages and had a keen interest in archaeology.

Bowing to the rules, the new husband changed his name, nationality, language, work and religion. The French count became Prince Henrik of Denmark, and the former pupil of the Jesuits became a Lutheran.

THE ROLE OF PRINCE CONSORT. The Danish monarchy is the oldest in the world. The only queen in its thousand-year history, Margrethe I, reigned in the fourteenth century in place of her son. In 1953 a referendum followed by constitutional reform allowed a woman to succeed to the throne. The princess was thus able to succeed her father, who died in January 1972. At the age of thirty-one she became Queen Margrethe II, a queen with no political power whose chief function is as a figure-head. Along with its Scandinavian neighbours, Denmark is one of the most progressive countries for sexual equality. Women have had the right to vote there since 1915, and child-care provision is so well-organised that the proportion of working women is the highest in the world.

A man who marries a queen is not a king, but a prince consort. When Margrethe II is asked about her relationship, she says, "It is not a very easy life, particularly for my husband, who comes from France, a Latin country, and what is more, from the south! I admire him greatly for his attitude." As for the prince, he declares, "I live in *l'ombre* [the shade] but I do not take *ombrage* [umbrage]. I am content to play the game. But it is difficult for a man not to be accepted on the same level as his wife."

His ideas on child education, where "a little punishment from time to time does no harm", gave him a reputation as a sadistic ogre. His father warned him that he would be "torn to shreds by the public" and more particularly by journalists. The prince jokes: "Sometimes I had the impression that my shirt was in tatters, but they haven't chewed me to bits as yet," and he admits that as he has got older "the bird has developed a thicker skin". The worst thing for him is his financial dependence. He complains that he cannot even buy a packet of Gauloises without the Queen's consent!

In common with his counterparts in Great Britain and the Netherlands, protocol obliges him to walk two paces behind his wife in public. As he sees it, "The prince consort is a strange animal who needs the sensitivity of a seismograph and the hide of a rhinoceros." It is the role of a tight-rope walker. "If he does not do enough, the people say, 'what use is he?' If he does too much, they say 'who does he think he is?'" He helps with the promotion of Danish exports and does a lot for the Danish Red Cross and the World Wildlife Fund, but he feels that the Danes have not totally accepted him. He laments that they still consider him to be an "interloper".

A SIMPLE LIFE WITH A PASSION FOR ART. The queen, who as a teenager thought that she would be merely "one of life's spectators", is one of the most popular people in the country. Always elegant and refined, she can be both serious and light-hearted. Her New Year address always reflects her personal attitude to ethical questions, such as her dislike of xenophobia and intolerance. Together with her husband they form a handsome couple with a stable relationship. They are both talented in the arts, sporty and cultured. The prince plays the piano, paints and sculpts, and is a pilot and sailor. The queen dances and skis, but she is primarily an artist: she illustrates books, designs Christmas stamps, sets and costumes for the theatre, and designs and embroiders religious vestments.

Two sons were born, Frederik in 1968 and Joachim in 1969. According to the queen "each will have to find

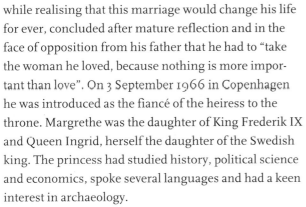

the shoe that fits," that is to say, develop his own personality while at the same time receiving a good all-round education. The family lives in the palace at Amalienborg in Copenhagen and at other royal residences. They spend part of the summer in France in the prince's native region, leading a simple life in the chateau at Caix, near Cahors.

In 1981, the Danish translation of Simone de Beauvoir's novel *All Men Are Mortal* appeared under the name of H. M. Vejerbjerg. This was a pseudonym chosen by the royal couple who had "used the long dark winter evenings in the palace to entertain ourselves by translating this beautiful French prose into Danish". The prince had been struck by this novel when he first read it at the age of eighteen. The queen recounts how, one day, finding herself with not much to do while her husband was away on a trip, she came across the French book and conceived the idea of doing a joint translation.

Their younger son also found love abroad: in 1995 Prince Joachim married a financial consultant four years older than himself, Alexandra Manley. She has a Chinese father and an Austrian mother. He met her while serving in Hong Kong. The royal house of Denmark, with its total absence of scandal, is a disappointment for the tabloid press. Its members convey the image of a united family whose behaviour is impeccable.

♡ ♡ ♡

Society
Loving the Other Person

Cultural differences such as language, colour, and religion add to the problems.

In the Stanley Kramer film *Guess Who's Coming to Dinner* (1967), the daughter of a white middle-class family introduces to her parents the man she wants to marry. They are horrified when they discover that he is black. There is unease in both families, but since it is a comedy everything works out. It was the first time that the American cinema had shown an interracial relationship of this kind. The black actor Sidney Poitier, with his handsome, open face, has appeared in many films to personify the clear conscience of liberal America. He himself married a white woman, the Canadian actress Johanna

Shimkus, with whom he has three children.

The United States is a country of large-scale immigration, where successive generations have integrated and married outside their own racial group; at the end of the twentieth century this melting pot operates mainly between whites of different origins, or between whites, Hispanics and Asians. Marriages between blacks and whites are the most controversial and the fewest in number: 2 per cent of all US marriages. It was not until 1967 that the law forbidding marriage between whites and blacks or between whites and Native Americans was repealed in Virginia, the last state in the USA where the crime of "intermarriage" was still punishable by imprisonment. A similar law was in force in South Africa until 1986, when the son of the white leader De Klerk helped in the dismantling of

apartheid by making a mixed marriage. Elsewhere, there are well-known couples in mixed marriages, particularly in sport and show business, such as Boris Becker and Barbara Feltus in Germany (cf. p. 418), Nastassja Kinski and Ibrahim Moussa in the United States, and formerly John Lennon and Yoko Ono (cf. p. 312).

Outside these spheres, couples who are "different" attract more attention in a small town where everybody knows everybody else than in the anonymity of the city. This was the case, for example, when allied soldiers married a woman from an enemy country (cf. p. 210) or a black African returned home with a white girl from the country where he had been studying. Gaining acceptance by one's future in-laws can be a very tricky matter.

Whereas traditional marriages fit into a pattern of exchange between two social groups, the "mixed" marriage creates an imbalance which can be fraught with problems. The partner who is racially far removed, like the one who is too close, falls foul of a taboo which is the parallel of incest (cf. p. 230). It is true that opposition encountered from those around the couple can make them only more determined, but it also serves to accentuate their isolation and, later, the disapproval which may also affect their children. It has often been the case that mixed marriages between European colonials and native women, for example Anglo-Indians, have been rejected by both cultures.

PARTNERS WITH A DIFFERENT RELIGION. In the West, opposition to marriages based on religion or social class is no longer supported by the law, but occasionally it persists in mental attitudes. It is as difficult to play Romeo and Juliet (cf. p. 282) between Catholics and Protestants in Northern Ireland as it is between Hindus and Muslims in India, where the caste system resists legal abolition. The same applies in Japan, where it is impossible for three million *burakumin*, descendants of those who embodied impurity in feudal times, to contract mixed marriages.

The religious factor remains the most significant problem. As a general rule, one of the partners has to renounce his religion; thus the husband of the Danish princess had to become a Protestant (cf. p. 304). Sometimes even that is not enough. For example, a Muslim man may marry a Jewish or Christian woman, but a Muslim woman may not marry a Jewish or Christian man, because the Koran says that children must take the father's religion. On the other hand, in the Jewish tradition, the man may not marry a *shiksa* [a Gentile woman], since Judaism is transmitted through the mother. In Israel, the law forbids marriage between Jews and Arabs.

A DIFFERENT NATIONALITY. In Europe, marriages with a foreigner represent about 10 per cent of the total, reflecting successive waves of immigration. In France, marriages with Italians, Spaniards and Portuguese fell from 42 per cent in 1980 to 21 per cent in 1991, while marriages with Africans and North Africans represented 40 per cent of the total. In Germany, marriages with Turks are rare; the same applies in Great Britain to people from Pakistan. The situation in France with frequent intermarriage

between French people and North Africans is unique in Europe.

The increased frequency of marriage to a foreigner has led to an evolution of the nationality law. In Sweden, for example, a change in the law in 1951 allowed Swedish women marrying a foreign national to retain their nationality. In 1975 German women were allowed to pass on their nationality to their children. But where frontiers have closed, the problem of marriages of convenience has served to complicate the position of those people marrying for love.

When someone marries a foreigner, the ceremony usually takes place in the home country of one partner, while the friends and family of the other are almost totally absent. In building up a relationship,

the couple has to surmount the obstacles of language, communication, cuisine (where certain foods are forbidden), holidays in the partner's home country, and choice of children's upbringing (such as circumcision for sons of Jews and Muslims). Adapting to each other is both an enriching and painful business. It is very difficult for a couple to successfully invent a new culture without breaking away from their roots. Children are often better at creating a bridge between the two cultures, but if the marriage breaks down, they can be forcibly detained in the country of the mother or the father. Betty Mahmoody, an Ameri-

An enriching and at times painful experience. Photograph by Leonard Freed.

can married to an Iranian, tells of this experience in her book *Not Without my Daughter*. The real dilemma comes as people grow old. Even the best-integrated foreigners dream of dying or being buried in their native country. Contrary to popular belief, a mixed couple is no more likely to break up than any other. The loved person is an individual and at the same time a product of another culture; the differences between the partners add an extra challenge to the problems that already exist in any love affair. A relationship enriched by diversity has a broader foundation and can prove to be more enduring.

1967

FRANCE. **Philippe Sollers marries Julia Kristeva. Coming from Bulgaria to study, she interviewed this brilliant intellectual, novelist and editor of an avant-garde magazine, who recounted: "She was extremely pretty and intelligent. I have no prejudices or inhibitions about intelligent women." She became a university teacher, a specialist in literary analysis, a psychoanalyst, and author of several important papers. Very well known in intellectual circles, particularly in the United States, the couple was often compared to Sartre and Beauvoir (cf. p. 234). The idea itself of a couple horrified Sollers: "It is tacky." From 1958 he had a relationship with a female novelist who was twenty-three years his senior, and who wrote about their "crazy love". He had numerous others affairs. Kristeva described the man for whom "love is the total acknowledgement of the other" as "my best intellectual friend". According to her "we live in the complicity of solitude". "Living with Sollers," she said, "is not easy, but it is never boring."**

♡ ♡ ♡

Serge & Beate Klarsfeld

The son of a French Jew killed in a concentration camp and the daughter of a German soldier united in the fight to ensure that Nazi crimes and their unpunished perpetrators are not forgotten.

Beate and Serge Klarsfeld take part in a demonstration on 10 July 1974 in front of the Federal German Embassy, to protest at her sentence passed by the court in Cologne.

On 7 November 1968 Beate Klarsfeld publicly slapped the West German Chancellor Kurt Georg Kiesinger on the face and accused him of being a Nazi. "I slapped him so that it would leave a mark," she declared, "and to show the whole world that there are still some Germans who have no sense of shame." In 1966, following a political crisis, Kiesinger had replaced Ludwig Erhard, another Christian Democrat, as head of government. The young couple were horrified to learn that during the war Kiesinger had been the assistant director of Nazi radio propaganda beamed abroad. This shock discovery transformed their lives.

Beate Künzel, a German woman, and Serge Klarsfeld, a Frenchman, had been married since 1963. They lived in Paris, where they had first met on a platform in the Metro in 1960. He was then twenty-five and she twenty-one. After studying political science he became a lawyer. She worked at first as an *au pair* then as a bilingual secretary. She was a Protestant from Berlin; during the war her father had been a soldier in the German army. Klarsfeld was Jewish. His father had been deported and killed at Auschwitz. Their first child, born in 1965, was named Arno after him.

Articles by Beate Klarsfeld denouncing the past of the new chancellor were published in the French daily

newspaper *Combat*. As a result she lost her job with a Franco-German youth organisation. Some months earlier Serge Klarsfeld had visited the concentration camp at Auschwitz. "It's there that my militancy began," he said. "It was there that I had the feeling of becoming politically Jewish." His wife took up the story: "We learned from a witness that Serge's father was killed because he protested to one of the guards who had just executed one of his friends. We said to ourselves 'If he could react like that in such a situation, then it is our task to continue his fight.' "

Which one of them was the first to get involved? "Both of us," he replied. "Neither of us would have gone it alone, neither Beate without me nor I without Beate." In her eyes, Kiesinger's appointment symbolised the German nation's willingness to forget about Nazism. In May 1968, in an act of defiance, she threw down a challenge: to slap him on the face in public. She made careful preparations. Using a false press identity card she gained access to the building in Berlin where the Christian Democrat party congress was being held. Sentenced the very same evening to one year in prison without remission for her action, she invoked her French citizenship and was released.

ACTING IN UNISON. Rejected by her mother, a widow, who refused to see her again for a long time before finally having a change of heart, Beate Klarsfeld became in the eyes of some people a disgrace to her country. The slap was resented by many as the equivalent of a daughter slapping her father. Kiesinger was beaten in the 1969 elections and the Socialist Willy Brandt, arch-enemy of Nazism, became chancellor. In 1970, kneeling at the memorial to Jews who died in the Warsaw ghetto, he publicly acknowledged German responsibility for the death of six million Jews.

Of course, the next generation of young people had no reason to be guilty about acts which they did not commit. But Beate and Serge Klarsfeld could not accept that Nazi criminals were able to go on living in comfort without being brought to trial. The couple carried out their investigations supported by the Centre de Documentation Juive Contemporaine [Centre for Modern Jewish Documentation] founded in 1943 and run by Serge Klarsfeld. He devoted himself to this undertaking "like a believer, with absolute commitment." The bonds between the couple were strengthened by their joint involvement. Realising that the judicial path was blocked and that "it became necessary to act with symbolic violence in order to arouse public awareness", the Klarsfelds started to share the work-load. He undertook the legal prosecutions in the name of the Fils et Filles de Déportés Juifs de France [Sons and Daughters of Deported Jews in France], an association of which he became president in 1979. She undertook some dramatic actions which often led to arrests, such as in Prague in 1971, when she distributed leaflets and was held for several days before being expelled. In 1974 they both helped in the attempt in Cologne to kidnap Kurt Lischka, former head of the Nazi police in France, who had been responsible for the round-up at the "Paris Cycle Track" in July 1942 and was now leading the life of a civic worthy. For this latest publicity stunt, Beate Klarsfeld spent two months in prison before the German judiciary upheld their claims and condemned Lischka to ten years in prison.

A STRUGGLE FOR THE TRUTH AND FOR HUMANITY. For many years they had been attempting to track down Klaus Barbie, head of the Gestapo in Lyons from 1942 to 1944, who was in hiding in Bolivia. Arrested by the Bolivian police in 1971, Beate Klarsfeld had a miscarriage, an ordeal she does not talk about. Barbie was not extradited until 1982, when he was sentenced and imprisoned in France. But for every successful prosecution, how many former Nazi torturers have died in their beds without ever having been called to account? How many criminals are receiving protection, such as Alois Brunner, responsible for the deportation of tens of thousands of Jews and now living in Syria? In 1991, she went in secret to Damascus and in the presence of the Minister for the Interior unfurled a banner calling for the extradition of "Nazi criminal, Brunner", but she was expelled without her action bearing any fruit.

In common with Simon Wiesenthal, this intrepid and methodical couple have a self-imposed mission to track down criminal Nazis to the very last one. They want to ensure that not one single person forgets the victims – Serge is occupied with trying to identify them all accurately – nor the atrocities committed in the name of a racist

1968

PARIS. **Serge Gainsbourg meets the young Jane Birkin, who sings in** *Slogan*, **the Pierre Grimblat film: "You are twenty, I am forty/ If you think that that torments me." An actor, painter, later a film-maker, he chiefly composed poetry set to music. The sensitive and fragile English girl fell in love with him, according to her, because of his timidity and awkwardness. She sings his songs. The success of** *Je t'aime moi non plus*, **a passionate declaration full of suggestive sighs, which he had composed for Brigitte Bardot when they were having an affair, made them into a popular couple. Their daughter Charlotte was born in 1971. After separating in 1980, Birkin pursued a career as an actress, in the cinema with** *The Pirate* **by her new companion Jacques Doillon, and in the theatre. Gainsbourg died in 1991. She continued to sing:** *"Je t'aime et je crains/ De m'égarer/ Et je sème mes grains/ De pavot sur les pavés/ De l'anamour"* **[I love you and I am afraid/ Of losing my way/ And I sow my poppy seeds/ Along the road of lovelessness].**

♡ ♡ ♡

Beate Klarsfeld in the dock after famously slapping Kurt Kiesinger.

John Lennon & Yoko Ono

A Beatle married a Japanese artist, a dominant woman who managed his career as a militant pacifist as well as his fortune.

On 18 March 1969, John Lennon married Yoko Ono. She was thirty-six and he was twenty-nine. "Intellectually, of course, we did not believe in getting married," the Beatle declared, "but one does not love someone just intellectually." Shortly afterwards, the couple staged their first bed-in, remaining in bed to receive the world's press who were jostling in their hotel room to hear them launching their slogans for world peace. The Beatle song *The Ballad of John and Yoko* tells the story: "So from Paris to the Amsterdam Hilton/ Talking in our beds for a week/ The newspapers said/ J. what you doing in bed?/ I said we're only trying to get us some peace."

Yoko Ono had not yet become the reviled woman who would later be accused of stealing Lennon from his wife Cynthia and their son Julian, and who caused the Beatles to break up. She was a conceptual artist, com-

bining the art of painting, photography, and film-making. Ono was never short of provocative ideas, such as her film *No. 4* (1967), in which she shows close-ups of bare buttocks. Coming from a wealthy family, she had been married twice and had a young daughter. She was tiny, with a mane of black hair and a high-pitched voice. She met John Lennon on 7 November 1966 in a London gallery and started to pursue him. When Brian Epstein, the Beatles' manager with whom she had been having an affair, died of an overdose several months later, Lennon sought her support.

John Lennon was slim, with a tired, drawn face. He was short-sighted and wore round spectacles with thick lenses. As a child he had been neglected by his mother and deserted by his father. Together with Paul McCartney, George Harrison, and Ringo Starr he formed the Beatles pop group in Liverpool in 1960. The songs writ-

FACING PAGE

John Lennon and Yoko Ono during their celebrated bed-in at the Hilton in Amsterdam in 1969.

ten by Lennon and McCartney are mainly about love (cf. p. 287). The clean, good-humoured image of the Beatles was in stark contrast to the "bad boys" of the Rolling Stones, another well-known pop group. From 1961, Beatlemania gripped Great Britain and later the whole world. It caused a revolution in popular music. With hair that was considered long for that era, the "Fab Four"

became role models for rebellious teenagers. They continue to fascinate the public, as the millions of discs sold to date still prove. After they split up in 1970, only Paul McCartney has had any success with a second musical career. Known for their commitment to vegetarianism and ecology, he and his American wife Linda Eastman were a happily-married couple with three children, until her premature death from cancer in April 1998 (cf. p. 434).

SEX, DRUGS, AND PACIFISM. "I have always refused to grow up," said John Lennon, "normality frightens me." He suffered from self-doubt, was afraid of life and took refuge in drugs. His relationship with Ono was, for him, "a strange cocktail of love, sex, and forgetfulness". He was unable to live without her, and decided to call himself John Ono Lennon. One moment he was completely under the domination of this arrogant and hard woman, the next he insulted her, abused her and threw furniture around in angry rages. She led him toward spirituality, the avant-garde, and political action. In the same way that he alternated between being clean shaven or wearing a moustache and varying the length of his hair, so he varied his choice of debauchery (sex, drugs, alcohol) and abstinence (fasting, drying-out, macrobiotic food). Sometimes he would work at a frenetic pace, at other times he would retreat into silence and sleep. Ono wanted to make a record with him. The cover of their album *Two Virgins* (1969) caused an outrage when it appeared, with a photograph of them both nude taken from the rear.

In 1971 they finally settled in New York and in 1973 moved into an apartment in the Dakota building, a luxury block of flats overlooking Central Park. Lennon recorded several songs (*Imagine*, 1971), some of them with Ono (*Sometimes in New York City*, 1972). His songs dealt with left-wing or feminist causes, such as *Woman is the Nigger of the World*, inspired by an idea from Ono. She tried to become a star but her musical efforts were panned by the critics.

It was during the course of a bed-in that Lennon wrote and recorded his highly successful song *Give Peace a Chance*. His stance against the war in Vietnam brought the threat of deportation. Countless photographs of the couple and their pacifist messages helped to improve their former image as a couple of quarrelsome drug-addicts. Lennon acknowledged his faults: "I am a violent man who has learned not to be violent and regrets his violence." The media readily printed photographs of the affectionate couple as a contrast to the violent behaviour of other rock stars. But Lennon grew tired of his commitment and returned to passivity and drugs, while at the same time swearing blind devotion to his wife. She imposed a separation in October 1973. He then went to live in Los Angeles with a young Chinese girl, but remained in telephone contact with Ono, who was becoming passionately interested in the occult. In the intervals between drugs, alcohol and mad rages, songs such as *Sacred*, where he pleads to be pulled out of the abyss, were a cry of despair.

At the end of 1974 he announced to the press: "Our separation was a failure." It was not long before Ono announced: "We're pregnant." After their re-marriage in a Druid ceremony, he decided to devote himself to their son Sean, leaving his wife to manage his colossal fortune.

THE MISTRESS AND THE PUPIL. For five years, cut off from the world, he returned to alcohol and drugs. "She is the mistress and I am the pupil," he said, "she has taught me all I know." Then he composed some new wave songs for her and together they recorded *Double Fantasy*. On the eve of the album's release, 8 December 1980, he was assassinated in the entrance to the apartment block by a madman, Mark Chapman. A vigil was held throughout the world, and in Central Park a hundred thousand people listened to *Give Peace a Chance*.

On the day of his death, Annie Leibovitz had taken a photograph of the couple which became justly famous. She wanted them to posed naked, but Yoko Ono refused. She lay on the bed on her back, with her hands behind her head and a faraway look in her eyes; Lennon lay naked on top of her in a foetal position, his eyes closed. The photographer recalled that when Ono saw the photograph she exclaimed: "That's really our relationship."

SENSUALITY
"69 – An Erotic Year"

Religious influence waned, and lovers freely enjoyed the infinite variety of sexual practices and erotic games.

It was no coincidence that Serge Gainsbourg and Jane Birkin (cf. p. 309) sang "69, An Erotic Year".

This number, according to Raymond Queneau's lewd, but amusing equation, "1 + 1 = 69", refers to an erotic position, said to be a French speciality, although the same name, sixty-nine, is used in both English and Spanish. In this position, the couple lie head to tail, either side by side or on top of each other, and stimulate each other by kissing or licking each other's sexual organs. When a woman performs this on a man it is called *fellatio*, when a man performs it on a woman it is called *cunnilingus* (cf. p. 386). This form of oral sex which leads to orgasm by mutual masturbation, involves all the senses, but particularly those of taste and smell. Portrayed in sculptures in Hindu temples and in Persian miniatures, it is frowned on by the Church, as is any conduct which does not have procreation as its ultimate goal. Until recent times, people in the West were shocked by this practice, but in the wake of "sexual liberation" (cf. p. 310) it has become more common, particularly among the young.

Unlike animals, human beings vary in the way they have sex. Sexual positions are a cultural matter: each race adopts the position they consider to be the most natural, and they think that the way other people do it is either funny or strange. During the Middle Ages, sexual positions were an important topic of theological discussion. The Church, which proscribed a number of things connected with sex (cf. p. 337), would only condone the position which was the most favourable for conception, that is, the man on top of the woman lying with her legs apart. Taking it for granted that it was "natural for men to act and women to submit", theologians condemned the inverse position (woman on top), asserting that it was this "depravity" which had caused the Flood! As for the rear entry "doggie" position they condemned it as reducing the human being to the level of an animal.

In the Jewish tradition, Lilith, Adam's first wife, rebelled against him. "Why should I sleep with you? I too was made from dust, I am your equal." While rabbis may have threatened gross abnormalities in children conceived in other positions, the sages of the Talmud were more tolerant, provided that the sexual act did not preclude the ultimate aim of procreation. However, they favoured the man-on-top position saying, in that way, a man faced the ground from which he came and the woman faced "the rib of Adam from which she was made".

A THOUSAND AND ONE POSITIONS. The Koran says, "Your wives are for you a field of labour: go about your work as you wish", evidence that Muslim theologians are the most permissive, but they advise against making love with the face or buttocks facing Mecca.

In the East, where sex is not linked to sin (cf. p. 68), traditions have perpetuated some refined techniques, such as the Chinese Taoist treatise describing nine ways of

Photograph by Claude Alexandre.

FACING PAGE
Jane Birkin and Serge Gainsbourg photographed by Gilles Caron in 1968, the year before the "erotic year".

1969

FRANCE. **General release of the Nelly Kaplan film *Dirty Mary*, played magnificently by Bernadette Lafont as an unattached, amoral goodtime girl who devotes herself to a game of attrition on a hypocritical society, where her only friend is the operator of a mobile cinema. She takes revenge on the civic worthies who exploit and despise her; she makes advances, has sex with some of them and ridicules them publicly at the end, before joining up with her friend again.**

moving the "jade rod" by varying the speed and depth of penetration. On the other hand, in the West erotic techniques have long been confined to pornography and, over this century, to sexology. Information has therefore been disseminated under the guise of scientific articles or licentious works circulated clandestinely, as was the case with etchings by Giulio Romano (sixteenth century), which illustrated sixteen positions and inspired the celebrated *Sonnets* of Arétin.

Regardless of how many different positions there may be, according to the Lesbian poet Renée Vivien "there are fewer ways of making love than people say, but more than you might think". The *Kama Sutra* describes eighty-four positions, each of which has a name. The names, many of which refer to animals, are very descriptive in the Arabic (crushing the cockroach, arching the bow, the camel's hump), and comical when used by modern writers Frédéric Dard or Gabriel Garcia Marquez (the Zanzibar wheelbarrow, bicycle on the sea, chicken on the grill). These refer rather to the acrobatic skills required. The large number of positions can be reduced to a few basic types, according to whether the lovers are face to face or not, whether they are lying, seated or standing, with legs bent or straight. Other variants depend upon additional external elements.

CELEBRATION OF THE BODY. The most popular "missionary" position (man on top) is not confined to humans. It has been observed among bonobo monkeys. It is easier to adopt if the woman bends and raises her legs, but it can be uncomfortable in the case of obesity or pregnancy. Other practical considerations are the physical condition of the lovers and the compatibility of their bodies and sexual parts. Thus, in the missionary position better contact is ensured if the woman lowers and closes her legs after penetration. She can also move the muscles of the vagina to vary the pressure on the penis. Depending upon whether the couple wishes to have maximum body contact or whether they want to move apart to look at each other, the position can be changed during union.

Each position involves different areas of the body and allows the hands or mouth to caress other zones; if the same position is maintained, the rhythm of penetration or the intensity of caresses can be modified.

Variety is the spice of (sex) life and renews the expression of love. But the capacity of a couple to become aroused and achieve orgasm, does not depend upon the range of their repertoire. Discovering a new position is a way of making a different approach, of inventing something new together: "It is in the love of caresses," writes Helvétius, "that love can teach." The so-called "perversions" of yesteryear, such as oral sex or sodomy, are now more acceptable, and the only limit between consenting adults is respect of the other person. If the sexual act is seen as a shared pleasure, a celebration of the body, then any caress is a sexual act. The understanding between lovers is translated into a harmony of their movements; it has the beauty of a cosmic dance, such as the union of Shiva and Shakti in the tantras.

FRANCE. **"Does love hurt?" This is one of the closing lines from *Mississippi Mermaid* by François Truffaut, starring Catherine Deneuve. The shooting of this beautiful film about a crazy love affair was accompanied by an affair between the director and the actress. When they split, Truffaut experienced prolonged depression. "I needed a year and a half to get over it," he confided, "and then another three years before I could live normally, which means being able to love without mistrust."**

Pierre & Margaret Trudeau

"Coming Out"

Julio Iglesias & Isabel Preysler

Love at any Age

Andrei Sakharov & Elena Bonner

Last Tango in Paris

Jane Fonda & Tom Hayden

Love in Everyday Life

Galina Vishnevskaya & Mstislav Rostropovich

The Bed

Volker Schlöndorff & Margarethe von Trotta

The Porno Wave

Marina Vlady & Vladimir Vissotsky

Female Pleasure

Arnold Schwarzenegger & Maria Shriver

To Love only God?

Charlotte Rampling & Jean-Michel Jarre

Death of a Loved One

Margaret & Denis Thatcher

Falling in Love

Pierre & Margaret Trudeau

Too many differences shattered the romantic love story of a legendary Canadian couple.

In the autumn of 1970 Canadian journalists were asking: Who was the ravishing young woman sometimes seen with Prime Minister Trudeau? Perhaps she was simply another of the many girlfriends seen with this charming fifty-year-old bachelor, who also occasionally escorted Barbra Streisand. There was great surprise when news came on 4 March 1971 that Margaret Sinclair, dressed in a bridal gown she had made herself, had married Pierre Trudeau in the strictest secrecy in a small church in Vancouver. She was so young – only

twenty-one – and so pretty, with brown curls and lavender blue eyes, that he forgot his motto "reason before passion".

She first met him at Christmas 1968 while on holiday in Tahiti. He was certainly a handsome man – with blue eyes and an athletic physique that belied his age – but she thought he was "very old and very conventional". Eighteen months later he asked to meet her again secretly while on an official trip to Vancouver. A very popular man, he served as prime minister continuously from 1968 to 1984, apart from two breaks of several months. He was bilingual. His father, a wealthy French Canadian, came from Montreal, and his mother was of Scottish extraction.

In Margaret Sinclair he found what he valued most in a woman: grace. She, however, described herself as a "failed hippie". The daughter of a politician turned businessman, she had an abortion at the age of seventeen, then spent seven months in Morocco in the company of drug-addicted "travellers"; she smoked marijuana and tried mescaline; a critic of authority, impulsive, and scatter-brained, she said that her only aim in life was to avoid all forms of conventional social responsibility. Trudeau asked her about her life and her views, and through her seemed to gain an insight into the aspirations of the younger generation. He was inquisitive about everything and she was happy to confide in him. He encouraged her to go and work in Ottowa, where they could see each other. At the age of fifty he had found love, charmed by the spontaneity of this "flower child", but he was full of doubt at the thought of being too old. Vivacious and eager, she had to learn to be discreet and patient. Intimate dinners together and secret trysts in the countryside were not enough to satisfy her. As a Catholic and therefore opposed to birth control, he persuaded her to stop taking the pill. She was afraid of becoming pregnant yet at the same time yearned for him. When Trudeau proposed marriage, he warned her that life would not be easy and he made one condition:

that she stop smoking marijuana. "I have managed to avoid marriage so far," he declared, "because I am very domineering. It is only now that I have accepted that another person can be very different from me and that I can love her despite that. I have decided I am ready to take a chance." For several months he appeared to be very much in love, especially as she became pregnant straightaway. At Christmas she gave birth to Justin; Alexandre was born in 1974 and Michel in 1975.

It was not long before the prime minister's young wife felt imprisoned in the official residence. She discovered that her husband was a loner and loathe to share his privacy. As an observer noted, he "put her under a bell-jar and cut off all her contact with life". In the stiff and starchy atmosphere of Ottawa, her happiness melted like snow in the sun. She hated formal duties and felt terribly alone and unhappy, only managing to escape occasionally on private trips. She recalled with bitterness, some years later: "He always had a very condescending attitude towards me. I never felt his equal. I was never up to it." She described him as "extremely rigid and organised, leading a life shorn of all spontaneity. He came home every day at a quarter to seven and swam in our pool for exactly seventeen minutes." Contrary to all logic, he wanted her to be his opposite: neither disciplined, rational nor intellectual.

HAPPINESS FOLLOWED BY SCANDAL. After being treated for depression in 1974, she gave a television interview which provoked a letter from the writer Gabrielle Roy: "You were not just speaking for yourself, but for all women who are shackled to a greater or lesser degree. When we fall in love, are we not submitting to a kind of slavery? It applies to men too ... but to a lesser extent than to women, who put love at the very centre of their existence."

As the tensions between the couple became increasingly apparent, public criticism began to mount. In public Trudeau defended his wife, declaring that "husbands, when they are as busy as I have been, are less attentive than they ought to be", but privately he heaped reproaches upon her. She started to smoke marijuana again, which he could not tolerate. She then decided to abandon all her official duties: "I had had enough of being a rose in my husband's buttonhole. I wanted to be myself." Six years to the day after their marriage, they began a trial separation. The following day, a night-time incident at a hotel in Toronto caused the final break. In the company of the Rolling Stones, she later recount-

1970

HOLLYWOOD. **General release of *Love Story*, a film by Arthur Hiller from the best-selling novel by Erich Segal. Oliver (Ryan O'Neal) and Jennifer (Ali McGraw) meet at university and fall in love. He is rich and she is poor, but they surmount all the obstacles to get married, living on love and fresh air. After their first argument he says "I am sorry". She replies "Love means never having to say you're sorry." Tragedy overtakes them, as Jennifer is found to be suffering from leukaemia from which she dies. As the film poster says, "She loved Bach, the Beatles and me." Ali McGraw (cf. p. 333) became a star, the embodiment of natural beauty, with her scant make-up and long brown hair parted in the middle. The enormous success of this "weepie" demonstrated that the film-going public likes a love story with a sad ending. But perhaps it was a case of the heroine's death preserving the image of love's youth and eternal beauty.**

ed, she had drunk alcohol, played dice and smoked "a little hash", but certain sections of the press portrayed it as a "sex orgy".

On 27 May 1977 an official communiqué announced that the Trudeaus had decided to live apart "in accordance with Margaret's wish [who] wants to end her marriage in order that she may pursue her own career. Pierre will have custody of their three sons and Margaret will have free access to them." The solitary hero transformed himself into an excellent father and became even more popular as he demonstrated his affection for his sons.

As for his wife, she was accused of "child neglect" and portrayed as a "self-centred career woman". She was undecided whether to become a photographer or an actress, but succeeded only in becoming enmeshed in scandal. She gave ill-advised interviews and published her autobiography during the 1979 election campaign. In 1984, the year that Trudeau retired from politics, Margaret married a Canadian businessman by whom she had a son. She appeared to have reformed. The victims of this noisy and public quarrel were of course the children.

Morals
"Coming Out"

Gays and lesbians exchange shame for pride and gain social acceptance.

To shouts of "Coming out" the first Gay Pride march took place in the streets of New York on 28 June 1970. Thousands of homosexual men and women were commemorating the riot, a year earlier, when police swooped on the Stonewall Inn, a gay bar in Christopher Street, Greenwich Village. Two nights of disturbance marked the emergence of a minority which had until then been both invisible and oppressed.

With its colourful marches, Gay Pride gradually became an annual event in cities in the West. It was a demonstration of power aimed at gaining certain rights, the first of which was the freedom to live openly as homosexuals. The word "gay" came to mean a "male homosexual", while female homosexuals are known as "lesbians". The Women's Lib movement for female equality (cf. pp. 310 and 344), combining boldness with humour, started some months earlier than the homosexual movement. "My body belongs to me" – having claimed the right to contraception and abortion, feminists started to condemn "sexual repression" and the "coercion to be heterosexual". Although their histories had been very different, male and female homosexuals

joined together in a temporary coalition to concentrate their efforts on winning civil rights.

The American Rita Mae Brown stressed the political and non-sexual aspect of the choice of "women who love women", which she described as "the supreme threat to male power". In Paris the banners proclaimed "Quand les femmes s'aiment, les hommes ne récoltent pas" ["When women love each other, men get nothing out of it"]. On the other hand, sex plays an important part for most gays. Frequenting the backrooms of gay bars, with their anonymous encounters and frenetic sex, is a way of life for single gays, who are capable, nevertheless, of forming loving and stable couples.

Although homosexuals tended to be fairly discreet, in large cities

such as San Francisco, around Castro Street, or later in Paris, in the Marais district, gay communities became very visible, with their identifying marks – the colour pink or rainbow-coloured flag – with their own cultural and commercial channels, and in recent years their efforts to combat AIDS (cf. p. 416). As a reaction to the cliché of being called a "failed woman", new types of male homosexual emerged, such as the muscle-bound, moustached macho man hanging around the fringes of drag queen competitions. It was now possible for a male or female couple to kiss in public without causing public outrage. The strength they derived from belonging to a group enabled them to affirm their "sexual preference", as a challenge to society's aversion to homosexuals (known as homophobia).

Couple photographed by Claude Alexandre.

FROM REPRESSION TO ACCEPTANCE. Throughout the world men have been, and indeed still are, punished by laws that make certain sexual acts a crime or an offence, even when they are committed in private by consenting adults (cf. p. 114). This was the case in Great Britain until 1967, and in Austria until 1971. Homosexuality is still punishable by imprisonment in Romania and Algeria. It is punishable by lashes of the cane in Saudi Arabia and by death in Iran. Try as they might, European institutions have failed to persuade all countries of the Union to end legal discrimination; Great Britain, for example, persists in setting the age limit for sexual relations at sixteen for heterosexuals and eighteen for homosexuals. Homosexuals are also discriminated against in the work-place and in the military in the United States.

While Western culture persecutes men who differ from the male stereotype (cf. p. 152), female homosexuality which is either ignored or not taken seriously, causes less of a problem. Militants have tried to raise its profile to make people recognise its subversive political dimension. In the cinema it provoked fascination (Greta Garbo in *Queen Christina*), but it usually involves tragedy, whereas "queers" are ridiculed. The censor cut this pointed reply from *Girls in Uniform* (1931): "In what you call a sin, I on the other hand see the power of love which may take many forms." While Hollywood only offered a choice between suppression and sublimation, European film-makers were more adventurous, such as Visconti, Fassbinder or Schlesinger, who filmed a kiss between two men in *Sunday, Bloody Sunday* (1971).

Is homosexuality a "stain which perverts our society" or "just another way of expressing one's sexuality"? Following on from the work of Hirschfeld (cf. p. 114), the Kinsey Reports (cf. p. 226) played a significant role in decriminalising homosexuality, in the absence of role models for this "obscure love" (Federico García Lorca) "that dare not speak its name" (Lord Alfred Douglas). Of the few couples, particularly artists, who lived together openly (cf. p. 212), many committed suicide or hid themselves away. Marguerite Yourcenar used to refer discreetly to her companion Grace Fields as "the woman with whom I share my house".

THE RIGHT TO LOVE. The shift from shame to pride appears to many Europeans to be a typically American response in a Puritan tradition which lays great store on public approval. It is important to distinguish between *coming out*, which is to reveal one's own homosexuality, and *outing*, which is the practice of exposing or publicising the homosexuality of a well-known person who conceals it. Loving a person of the same sex does not imply a militant attitude. While some people claim the "right to be different", others prefer the "right to be indifferent". It may appear a contradiction to describe a person by his sexual preference while working to abolish discrimination in general against certain groups of people. Over time, homosexuality has become more socially acceptable, particularly in northern Europe, among the young, and in the cities.

At the end of the twentieth century, homosexuals are pressing their main claim for their rights as a couple to be respected (cf. p. 398). During the 1996 Gay Pride march in Paris, the leading banner linked love with rights: "We love each other. We want to be treated as a couple."

1970

PARIS. **"There is no sexual relationship,"** the psychoanalyst Jacques Lacan famously declares in a sentence which ends **"understood:** *that can be formulated* in its structure". According to his colleague J. D. Nasio, Lacan is opposing the popular concept of the bodies of the two lovers being fused into one at the instant of sexual pleasure, which goes back to the theme of a lost unity discussed by Plato (cf. p. 188) in his *Symposium.*.

UNITED STATES. Writers Grace Paley and Bob Nichols set up home together. In 1995, at the age of seventy-two Grace Paley defiantly drew up a balance sheet of the twenty-five years spent together. "We are still married, when the whole world said that it was impossible for two writers to live together; it's true that it has been a little difficult at times."

"Marriage is: the same fear shared, the same need to be comforted, the same futile caress in the dark."

ANNE HÉBERT
Kamouraska

Photograph
by Hans Van Manen.

Julio Iglesias
Isabel &Preysler

A "Latin lover" and a beautiful woman fascinated the Spanish public.

To the great disappointment of all his female admirers, the Spanish singer Julio Iglesias married Isabel Preysler on 20 January 1971 at the chapel of Illescas, a village in the province of Toledo.

He was twenty-seven when, during the course of a party in Madrid in May 1970, he caught sight of a young girl of nineteen with large, mysterious eyes who attracted him with her charm and allure. The following month he saw her again at another event. Although she was not very impressed when he was introduced to her, this Don Juan, who already had a "fiancée" in London where he was recording his new album, fell in love at first sight with the beautiful woman wearing a sari of green silk. He felt that the course of his life was about to change. "From the start, for me she was a different kind of woman, and I knew immediately that it was something more than it had been with any other woman." With his flashing smile and velvety voice, Julio Iglesias was the most famous of crooners, a "Latin lover" (cf. p. 118) who described himself as "the lover all husbands approve of." The family of Isabel Preysler originally came from central Europe, but had

emigrated to the Philippines after living in Cadiz from 1831 to 1860. Her father, who had businesses in Manila, sent her to Madrid in February 1969 to stay with an uncle and aunt. In between two galas, Julio Iglesias saw her as often as he could. He left for a tour of Latin America, but telephoned her every day. He wanted to

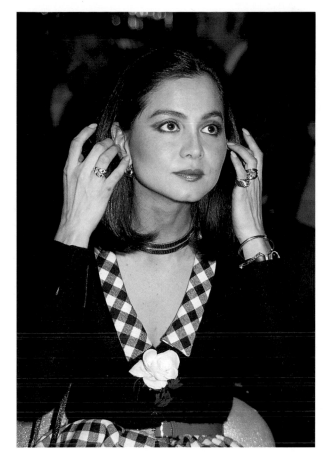

marry her. She refused, he insisted and she ended up by giving in, as a baby was on the way.

The news caused uproar in the Iglesias family: his mother wailed and made scenes in front of her son who remained unshakeable in his determination to marry his "*chiquitaja*" (tiny one). The Preysler parents learned with some satisfaction that their daughter was going to marry into a middle-class family and that the young man, whose father was a doctor, had studied law. But they were unhappy with the fact that he was a singer. Marrying into show business was not the grand marriage they had dreamed of for their daughter. Her aunt reassured them: singing was only a passing fancy and the fiancé had promised to retire in two years' time and open a law office.

ISABEL WANTED HIM TO CHANGE. The honeymoon was spent in the Canary Islands. It was while they were there that the singer wrote *Como el alamo al camino* (*As the poplar tree stands guard beside the road*) which tells of his love: "I cannot live without you/ I do not know who I am/ Nor where I am going/ Nor where I shall go." Isabel wanted him to stop singing but could not extract a definite promise from him. When they returned to Madrid, she continued with the kind of life she loved, trips out and high society parties, especially with her best friend Carmen, Franco's granddaughter, who married the Duke of Cadiz in 1972 (cf. p. 353). But she disliked the fact that their hosts would always ask her husband to sing. After *Gwendolyne* was released, which beat all sales' records, Julio Iglesias remained deaf to his

wife's pleas to keep his promise and become a lawyer. He frequently went on tours of Latin America; in every phone call he promised to come home soon. Devoted to his career, he was convinced that money would make up for his absence. He was scornful of his wife's attitude: "The Julio Iglesias who sang did not interest her the least little bit. Sometimes she came briefly to one of my shows, but with no enthusiasm, completely detached." He reproached her for her "oriental" reserve because she did not readily express her emotions, unlike himself. But he appreciated her influence: "I am a bird, a little crazy, which comes and goes, whereas she is serious and very disciplined." Three children were born: Isabel, called Chabely, in 1971, Julio José in 1973, followed by Enrique in 1975. She was a model mother who lived only for her children, but as "the wife of an idol" she found her solitude bitter, as rumours of affairs reached her. In the spring of 1976 she told him: "I can no longer put up with a situation where I am neither single, married nor widowed," and she proposed a separation. He pleaded with her: "Darling, it's a vital moment in my career, please be a little patient." But the rancour increased and their divorce was announced in 1978.

A COUPLE WITH DREAMS. Julio Iglesias suffered greatly from this breakdown. In the song *Hey* he reproaches a woman boasting that he cannot live without her. Overcoming depression, he decided to become "the Spanish Sinatra" and to conquer the United States. Still as charming as ever, he continued to fly from stadium to concert hall in his private jet, selling a total of two hundred million albums in a thirty-year career. He continued to steal hearts but he never remarried. His love affairs hit the headlines, and in 1992 he was seen with Miranda, a twenty-three year-old beauty with whom he had a child in 1997.

Isabel Preysler embarked on a journalistic career interviewing celebrities and posed for advertisements for Porcelanosa, a brand of ceramic tile. Fulfilling her parents' dream she married Carlos Falco, a Spanish grandee, and so became the Marchioness of Griñon. The marriage took place in 1980, shortly before the birth of their daughter Tamara. There was a scandal when she left her husband in 1985 for the Socialist Miguel Boyer, who gave up his post as Minister of Finance and made their relationship public. He divorced in order to marry her in 1987 and their daughter Ana was born in 1989. The couple lived in luxury and became part of the jet-set. Isabel Preysler is one of the best-known women in Spain, and popular magazines are eager for photographs of her. She continues to be the "different kind of woman" known for her charm and her exceptional attractiveness. Although their marriage lasted for only seven years, the relationship she formed with

UNITED STATES. **General release of the Robert Mulligan film *The Summer of 42*. A man nostalgically tells the tale of his first love; at the age of fifteen he dared to approach a woman on the beach. She was twenty-two and her husband had just left for the front. The boy falls madly in love with her. One day, she receives news that her husband has been killed. She spends the night with the boy. They never see each other again. The climax of this moving and serious film, a love-making scene which lasts for seventeen minutes on the screen, is treated with delicacy and sensitivity.**

JAPAN. **Publication of *Sentimental Journey*, a series of photographs by Araki Nobuyoshi, describing his honeymoon, which starts with ordinary shots of his wife Yoko and then becomes more and more intimate. Like the American Nan Goldin, with whom he made *Tokyo Love* in 1994, he kept a photographic diary of his life. His predilection for young naked girls brought him into conflict with the Japanese censor. In 1990 he photographed the agony and death of his wife.**

♡ ♡ ♡

Julio Iglesias still continues to fascinate the public, who are always delighted to see the former husband and wife together in the same photograph, such as on the occasion of the marriage of their daughter Chabely in 1995.

♡ ♡ ♡

SOCIETY
Love at any Age

The lesson of Harold and Maude shows that love has no age limit. In real life, does an older woman have a right to love and pleasure?

In the film *Harold and Maude*, made by Hal Hashby (1971) and starring Ruth Gordon and Bud Cort, the twenty year-old Harold, obsessed with death and funerals, meets Maude, an unconventional old lady whose unfailing vitality has survived all sorts of tragedies, including deportation. The theme of the film shows how the mischievous, warm-hearted and very liberal Maude teaches a young depressive how to enjoy life.

Maude has decided on an early death, but first of all, armed with her "secret weapon, love", she teaches Harold the pleasures of life. With a spirit for living, "I can't understand why people say 'no' to a new experience," happy to approach others, "The world does not need walls, it needs to build bridges", she deflects him away from death: "It's wonderful, life is. What is even more wonderful is that it does not

last very long." When he touches her, she is rejuvenated – "You make me feel like a schoolgirl again" – and he discovers love. There is a sixty-year age gap between them, but when he plants a kiss on her lips and takes her in his arms, they are a couple united by love.

He wants to marry her and on her eightieth birthday he presents her with a ring. It is then that she tells him that she has taken a drug so that she will die in her sleep. He is desperate:

"You are everything to me, I cannot live without you." – "It will pass." – "I love you." – "That is wonderful. Carry on loving."

The film was a flop when it opened, but its warmth and celebration of the power of love ensured it a lasting reputation. These lovers have become part of a myth, and their Christian names have become the symbol for a couple where the woman is much older than the man. Colin Higgins, the young writer who wrote the screenplay, transposed it into a novel and then a play which has been translated into many languages and performed successfully. In France the

first Maude in the theatre was Madeleine Renaud in 1973; the role was revived by Denise Grey in 1987 then by Danielle Darrieux in 1995.

THE OLDER WOMAN IN LOVE. Is there an age limit for inspiring love or being in love? In all cultures the body of an ageing woman excites horror. Eroticism, both Oriental and Western, places a taboo on showing it engaged in physical acts of love. Ovid is the only author to extol women over the age of thirty-five: "more knowledgeable about love ... they possess the experience which alone makes an artist", and he concludes: "Only the impatient drink new wine!" While we may think that thirty-five is not very old, in Balzac's time, women over the age of thirty were expected to withdraw from their seductive role.

The taboo on sex for old women was so strong for so long that they ceased to have any sex life at all. It was thought that menopausal women should avoid sexual relations to avoid suffering from "congestion of the womb". Similarly, anthropologists have observed in different cultures that the start of the sex life of the children usually coincides with the end of that of the parents.

Although a sex life for "old" people is now less frowned upon than previously, there are many people who think, like the early sexologists (cf. p. 134), that frequency must diminish with age. However, now that female sexuality is better understood (cf. p. 344), it is known that a woman retains her capacity for pleasure throughout her life, especially if she takes hormone replacement therapy at the menopause. Men, on the other hand,

Maude (Ruth Gordon) steers Harold (Bud Cort) along the road of life.

often have problems with erection from the age of about fifty onwards. Drinking, smoking, and stress or drugs for hypertension cause "failures" that are very disturbing for those who see their virility in terms of their performance.

The evolution of sexuality in advancing age is not yet fully understood, given that surveys usually include only the fifteen to fifty-nine age group. However, the search for a partner through classified advertisements or dating agencies is not the preserve of the young. A French survey in 1987 showed that sexagenarians have a sex life which is two to three times more active than was the case twenty years ago, and another study made in Sweden in the year 1996 noted the continuance of sexual feelings beyond the age of eighty-five.

Of the five senses, touch is the least affected by the ageing process; at any age and despite handicaps, it is possible nowadays for human beings to continue to have sexual relations. Throughout the course of our lives, impulses develop and change, and right up to death we are capable of experiencing desires and sensations. With age we have learned to know our own body better and that of our partner; we also know how to take time. Although the pleasure shared with our partner as we grow older may primarily be one of affection and the joy of being together, emotional and sexual relations can help to promote good health and an unfailing taste for life.

A MUCH OLDER LOVER. Statistics show that on average men marry a younger woman (cf. p. 287). A big difference in age is not uncommon and is acceptable when it is the man who is the elder. Rubens was thirty-seven years older than Hélène Fourment, Chaplin (cf. p. 101) or Picasso (cf. p. 97) married very young girls. But the "Harolds and Maudes" of life, even when the age

difference is less than that in the film, can cause outrage, sometimes with tragic consequences (cf. the Gabrielle Russier affair, p. 313). In literature and the arts, the older woman has found a role initiating young men into sex, such as the Colette novel *Ripening Seed*, or in the film *The Summer of 42* (cf. p. 323), but the women of today who become attached to a young lover tend either to be in show business

or successful and wielding power, which increases their sexual attraction in the same way as it does for men. Up to her death in March 1996, Marguerite Duras lived with Yann Andréa; when they met in 1980, she was sixty-five and he was twenty-seven.

Does love have any connection with age? Whether one is old or young, as Pascal wrote: "Love has no age, it is always new-born."

1971

WASHINGTON. **Marriage of Pamela Hayward and multi-millionaire Averell Harriman. He was seventy-nine and she fifty-one. They had both been recently widowed. During the war they had an affair in London, where Harriman had been sent by Roosevelt before being appointed ambassador to Moscow. Pamela Churchill, a member of the aristocratic Digby family, was married at the time to the son of Winston Churchill whom she divorced in 1946. When she met Harriman again she had had several affairs before a happy marriage to the American theatre producer Leland Hayward. Her marriage to Harriman was also happy up to his death in 1986. Having become a prominent figure in the Democrat party, she contributed to the election of President Clinton, who appointed her ambassador to Paris in 1992. She died there in 1997.**

"Love is not placed there like a stone; it has to be worked, fashioned, kneaded like bread, constantly re-worked, rebuilt."

URSULA LE GUIN
The Lathe of Heaven

Photograph
by Elliott Erwitt.

Andrei Sakharov
& Elena Bonner

Two Russian human rights campaigners – a famous physicist turned dissident and his equally indomitable wife.

"How are we living? Tragically. We are the living dead. And yet at the same time, as strange as it sounds, we are happy. On 7 January we celebrated our thirteenth wedding anniversary ..." These words, written by the Russian Andrei Sakharov in 1985 during the couple's enforced exile in Gorki, are a testament as much to the persecution suffered by the great physicist and his wife Elena Bonner as to the extraordinary bond which united them.

The two political opponents were married in 1972 (he was fifty-one and she forty-nine), two years after they met in Moscow at the home of the militant Chalidzé. In his *Memoirs*, Sakharov, who was a very shy man, recalled this "attractive woman" and declared that he had been "impressed with her seriousness, energy, and professional air". He was told that Elena Bonner had "helped prisoners almost all her life". Meeting again at a political demonstration against rigged trials, they fell in love. As a widower, Andrei Sakharov was quite happy to go and live with Elena – whom he called Louissa – and her mother, Ruth Bonner, a Siberian Jewess and one of the party faithful who had experienced the labour camps and exile before being rehabilitated. Her husband, Gevork Alikhanov, executed in 1937, had

been the First Secretary of the Communist Party in Armenia.

Elena Bonner had been a nurse during the war, and had been wounded in the eyes, which was to remain a handicap throughout her life. She became a doctor, married a colleague, had two children, but eventually divorced.

When Sakharov became alarmed at the end of the fifties about the danger of nuclear tests in the atmosphere, he knew what he was talking about. The son of a physicist, the pupil and later a colleague of I. E. Tamm who received the Nobel Prize for Physics in 1958, he had worked for the Soviet Defence Ministry since 1950 at the "facility", a scientific ghetto whose location was a closely-guarded secret. He was one of the "fathers" of the soviet H-bomb, the first of which was detonated in 1953.

In 1963 he helped in the preparation of the Moscow treaty banning nuclear testing in the atmosphere, in space, and under water. His stance became increasingly political and his writings were circulated in *samizdat* [clandestine] editions. The West first heard about him in 1968, with the publication in *The New York Times* of his "Reflections on Progress, Peaceful Co-Existence and

Elena Bonner beside the body of her husband Andrei Sakharov.

FACING PAGE

The dissident couple with Elena Bonner's mother in their small Moscow flat.

Intellectual Freedom". The same year Soviet tanks invaded Prague. The split between Andrei Sakharov and the system was then total. The academician, who had been laden with honours, lost his job as well as a large number of privileges and friends.

SLANDER. Elena Bonner used her invalidity war pension to fight against arrests, detentions and executions. In the tiny two-room flat which her mother had been given after her rehabilitation, they met and drafted their appeals. It was there that foreign correspondents came for news, sometimes little realising the kind of threats being made by the authorities. Elena Bonner faced constant harassment from the KGB with an indomitable spirit inherited from her mother and grandmother, whose name she bears. "I am not a dissident," she said, "I am me."

She admired the calm, clear intelligence of her "Andrioucha", while Sakharov was fascinated by her efficiency, and by the warmth and confidence which emanated from her group of friends, writers, and intellectuals. He adopted her friends and family, while scarcely ever seeing his own children. They were both convinced that there could be no defence of human rights without defence of the individual, and that an appeal to public opinion was worth more than any number of covert actions.

The KGB were on the tracks of the couple. Slander was used, especially against Elena, claiming that she was a CIA agent and an evil Jewess who was suborning her husband. Even the famous dissident Solzhenitsyn, with his misogynist conservatism, called her "a hysterical woman who makes a submissive husband tremble". In 1975 Sakharov won the Nobel Peace Prize while his wife was in Italy. She went to Oslo to read her husband's speech, which talked about *perestroika*.

FROM EXILE TO TRIUMPH. In 1980, Sakharov was sentenced to exile in Gorki, a town closed to foreigners, 250 miles east of Moscow, for denouncing the Soviet invasion of Afghanistan. He was the victim of constant harassment and petty interference. Sakharov's sole link

with the outside world was his wife, who shuttled between Gorki and Moscow, making exhausting trips by train. The KGB filmed the couple but supplied the West with fake photographs. In Moscow, Elena Bonner's telephone was cut off, so she would meet journalists in the street in all weathers. Even after a heart attack in 1983, which she dealt with herself, she went out late at night to pass on the text of the memoirs that she had persuaded Sakharov to write – then re-write, because the KGB had stolen the manuscript as work proceeded. She herself was finally exiled to Gorki in 1984.

Sakharov went on a number of hunger strikes, each one leaving him a little weaker than before. The couple undertook a hunger strike in 1981 to get permission for Elena Bonner's children to emigrate, then again to allow her to go abroad to seek treatment for her eyes and to have a heart operation. It was while she was in the United States in 1985 that she wrote her memoirs, *Alone To-*

1972

UNITED STATES. **Publication of the magazine *Ms.* In everyday use, Ms (pronounced *miz*) gradually replaced Mrs and Miss, allowing women to avoid being described by their marital status. Sanctioned: in 1986 the prestigious daily newspaper *The New York Times* instructed all its employees to use the form Ms. In France, usage has gradually been established by calling all women "Madame", and reserving "mademoiselle" for young girls.**

"No-one will ever know how many novels, poems, analyses, confessions, sadnesses and joys have been heaped upon this continent of love, without it having ever been fully explored."

HEINRICH BÖLL
Essay on the Reason for Poetry

UNITED STATES. **In their successful book *Open Marriage*, psychologists Nena and George O'Neil compare the open marriage, which they define as the relationship of equals, to the closed marriage with its ideal of fusion of the couple. In their view, married love is not based on romantic passion but on deep friendship.**

gether. In the same year, the European Parliament established the Sakharov Prize. An American film *Sakharov*, made by Jack Gold and starring Jason Robards and Glenda Jackson, tells their story.

On 16 December 1986 Gorbachev announced their release to them in person. Returning to Moscow, the couple began their activities again with renewed vigour. Sakharov became the mouthpiece of the liberal intelligentsia. Elected a deputy, he was helping to draft a new constitution when he died of a heart attack on 14 December 1989. His widow continues to fight for human rights and support the Armenian cause.

SENSUALITY
Last Tango in Paris

A perversion or a diversion? Is sodomy a harmless practice?

Spanish men who flocked into the cinemas of Perpignan shouting "butter" ran the risk of disappointment. In the Bernardo Bertolucci film *Last Tango in Paris*, anal intercourse, facilitated by the use of butter, is not meant as a joke. This scene, the most well-known portrayal of sodomy on the screen, represents the abyss of solitude, the tragedies hushed up by the deathly silence of the families, in a rare spectacle of dramatic force.

"*Family ... you, you, you, you, you ... fucking family ... you fucking, fucking family ...,*" repeats the American hero (Marlon Brando) while sodomising the young French girl (Maria Schneider) who is crying. Explaining his behaviour by his loneliness, he says to her: "You won't be able to be free of that feeling of being alone until you look Death right in face. Until you go right up into the 'ass' of Death, right up in his 'ass', until you find the womb of fear. And then, maybe, maybe, then."

In order to free himself, he has invented a whole erotic ritual with this young prostitute, and he offers a pact: "No names, not one name. I want to know nothing, nothing, nothing. We are going to forget everything." She asks, "Can you?"

He replies, "I don't know." The death which he is trying to exorcise is that of his wife, who committed suicide. He discovered then that he knew nothing about her. Beside her corpse he says:"Even if a husband lives 200 fucking years, he's never going to be able to discover his wife's real nature. I might be able to comprehend the Universe, but I'm never going to discover the truth about you, never. I mean, who the hell were you?" When he finally asks the young girl what her name is, the reply has the face of death, for as she shouts her name she shoots him at point-blank range.

MALE FANTASY. Sodomy is rarely as dramatic as this. It was condemned as an "abominable practice" in the Middle Ages, a mortal sin renamed a "major perversion" when religious taboos were relaxed, and was illegal for a long time in Great Britain and Latin America. However, when it appears in advertisements offering a range of other services in the windows of prostitutes in Amsterdam, no one raises an eyebrow. The four letter-word "anal" refers to a practice requested from prostitutes by men whose wives refuse to perform it.

It is solely anal intercourse between homosexuals that appears in the Bible and was condemned as far back as Genesis. Sodomy gets its name from the town of Sodom, whose inhabitants were regarded as "very sinful". When practised between men and women in the

Photograph
by Tono Stano.

FACING PAGE
Maria Schneider and
Marlon Brando in *Last Tango in Paris*.

Christian West it is stigmatised as an "unnatural" practice. On the other hand, it is referred to in Hindu erotic works. The *Kama Sutra* calls it the "lower congress".

The Marquis de Sade, for whom sodomy was a "natural fantasy" (*Philosophy in the Bedroom*), thought that "for the woman this pleasure is the most delightful of all", the initial pain being transformed, according to him, into pleasure. Other erotic authors are less explicit on the subject. There is only an allusion to it in *Lady Chatterley's Lover*: "... softly he stroked the silky slope of her loins, down, down between her soft warm buttocks, coming nearer ... She yielded with a quiver that was like death, she went all open to him."

Sodomy is not referred to by name in *The Story of O* (cf. p. 252). This is in keeping with the elevated style of writing which refers to the anus as a "pink ring". Submitting to all types of male desire, O (the letter is significant) cannot avoid this test: "He wanted to drive his way into

the narrower passage, and pushing hard, violently rung a scream from her lips."

Making love "from the rear", preferably with violence, to humiliate a woman so that she cries with pain and then groans with pleasure, acknowledging the domination of a "true male": this is one of the most common male fantasies, published in millions of copies of magazines or pornographic films (cf. p. 340).

DELICACY AND PATIENCE. In reality, for some women sodomy is a way of avoiding vaginal penetration to preserve virginity, during menstruation or to avoid pregnancy. In its erotic dimension, it has become cheapened by the massive growth of pornographic material since the seventies. While the Kinsey Reports (cf. p. 226) are very quiet on the subject, the Spira report into French sexual behaviour (1992) reveals that 30 per cent of men and 24 per cent of women have practised it.

Curiosity versus repulsion: maybe this is what explains the dif-

ference between the sexes. It often happens that a man may wish to try it but the woman is afraid of pain. In fact she runs the risk of lesions, or even a fistula, if there is insufficient lubrication or penetration is rough. The solution is delicacy and patience. It is one way of gaining pleasure from a practice which is not an obligatory part of the love-making repertoire. To cheapen it is to make it appear harmless. For many people this smacks of heresy, since it remains linked to the dark side of life, if not death itself, which strikes down the desperate hero of *Last Tango in Paris*. Although it may be viewed as an erotic diversion from the ordinary, it does not disguise that fact that it may also come from a fascination for what is forbidden.

1972

UNITED STATES. **Release of the film *All You Wanted to Know about Sex and Never Dared to Ask*, a series of sketches by Woody Allen amusingly adapted from the best-selling book by Dr. David Reubens, set against the background of the 1928 song *Let's Misbehave!* The final scene, which is the funniest of all, is entitled: "What happens during ejaculation?" It shows the greatly magnified insides of a man having sexual intercourse, with Woody Allen hilariously dressed as a bespectacled spermatozoon.**

FRANCE. **The Simon Report on French sexual behaviour, the first of its kind, produces sensational findings: 50 per cent of woman said that they were not sexually satisfied. The average age of the first sexual relationship was nineteen for men and twenty-one for women, which showed a fall of one year since the beginning of the century. Later, it would fall even further (cf. p. 294).**

"Loving – is that not one person making a present of his own loneliness to the other? It is the ultimate thing that one can give of oneself."

CLARICE LISPECTOR
in Jornal do Brasil

Jane Fonda & Tom Hayden

Militancy fit easily into the lives of a controversial couple. Their split was sadly predictable.

In January 1973 two political activists married. At her home in California, Jane Fonda, thirty-five, dressed in a Vietnamese smock, married Tom Hayden, thirty-three. They were surrounded by Vietnamese friends singing folk-songs. The word "peace" in Vietnamese decorated the wedding cake. Six months later their son Troy was born, named after a Vietnam patriot.

Their affair began in April 1972. They met at a conference in Los Angeles where they were both showing slides against the war in Vietnam, one of the many caus-

es adopted by Fonda, who had joined the New Left after spending several years in France. She thought that Tom Hayden, with his beard and long hair, looked like "an Indian, weird but elegant". The marriage united two ambitious people. Jane Fonda had objectives which appeared confused, and she was regarded as a dilettante. Tom Hayden was obsessed by a desire to "get into the history books" and become President of the United States. He gave her political credibility and she gave him her name and her wealth.

Jane Fonda was the daughter of celebrated actor Henry Fonda. From him she inherited the same good-looking oval face and large blue eyes. She became a sex symbol after her Pygmalion-style marriage to Roger Vadim, the French director of *Barbarella* (1967). Beautiful and talented, she suffered nevertheless from a lack of self-confidence, which manifested itself in bulimia and heavy smoking. Shortly after the birth of their

Jane Fonda and her husband Tom Hayden on the campaign trail.

daughter Vanessa in 1968 she left Vadim and made some outstanding films such as *They Shoot Horses, Don't They?* (1969), and *Klute* (1971), for which she won her first Oscar.

Tom Hayden came from a middle-class home in Detroit. With looks marred by a large nose and a pock-marked face, he was highly intelligent and a brilliant orator. He wrote the *Manifesto of the New Left*. Together with Jerry Rubin and Abbie Hoffman he was one of the best-known left-wing activists. Not content with condemning the war in Vietnam, he became a sympathiser of the Communist regime in Hanoi. The wife from whom he was divorced was also a militant activist.

THE BUSINESS WOMAN'S BOSS. In Hayden, Jane Fonda found a new mentor who encouraged her to devote herself exclusively to the Vietnam cause. In July 1972 she left for Hanoi where she was filmed sitting astride an anti-aircraft gun. On Radio Hanoi she read out propaganda literature and incited American soldiers to desert. On her return, "Hanoi Hannah" was received with boos and jeers, as stars of the past went to the front to entertain the troops and keep up their moral. In showing her "controversial side", Fonda broke with the image of Barbarella, but while she did indeed reveal divisions in American society over the Vietnam war, she fell into the trap of a blind, unquestioning acceptance of communism.

In order to maintain their political credibility, the couple moved into an old, ramshackle house in a popular area of Santa Monica, close to Los Angeles. The actress was ridiculed as a Marie Antoinette playing the farmer's wife, but she loved the life which she felt was real. As her career was at a low point, she founded IPC, a company for making political films. The first, shot in Vietnam, was a fiasco. She regained her star status with *Fun with Dick and Jane* (1976), made for Columbia. When it was released, she did not talk about politics, but about more mundane matters, since she was now the wife of a candidate in the Senate elections. Hayden cut his hair, bought a suit and failed honourably in the attempt. The couple started the Campaign for Economic Democracy (CED) and settled on a ranch in Santa Barbara. The film *Julia*, beautifully made by Zinnemann

(1977, cf. p. 152) and which brought together the two most celebrated left-wing actresses of the period, Jane Fonda and Vanessa Redgrave, completed her rehabilitation. She won a second Oscar for *Coming Home* by Hal Ashby (1978), which condemned the folly of war and portrayed the bitterness of its "veterans". The film, produced by IPC, marked the start of her career as a successful business woman. The profits were used to support the ranch and the CED. Tom Hayden was in control of the management and accounts. "He was the boss, the theoretician," a close friend explained. "He told Jane what needed doing and she did it." The couple, who liked to stress the fact that "you can still get rich while having a noble cause", appeared to be motivated particularly by money and power.

PRETTY, RICH AND TOO OLD? "Tom says that in a few years' time I shall be too old and wrinkled and that no one will want me," she confided to a girlfriend. Therefore in 1979 she opened her first gymnasium in Beverley Hills, which was an immediate success. It was followed by others, then books, videos and a whole keep-fit empire which made her a fortune. Afraid that their "past" might be damaging to them, she admitted having made some mistakes in her "radical" period. Although she was the new model of a female militant, she still depended intellectually on her husband. "He is the one

with the intelligence," she said, "I am just a chameleon." Having engaged the best public relations companies to erase his left-wing image, he was elected to the State Legislature in California in 1982. IPC had triumph after triumph with the anti-nuclear film *The China Syndrome* (1978), the feminist comedy *Nine to Five* (1980), and especially *On Golden Pond* (1982) a sentimental film in which Jane Fonda and her father Henry appeared together for the first time.

Despite her insistence that, "Tom is an anchor for me," they were growing apart. While he had numerous affairs, she was preoccupied with growing old. In 1988, when she learned that Tom was having an affair with the young Morgan Fairchild, she cut the lifelines to CED. The divorce went through in 1989. Hayden claimed half of his wife's fortune, but he only succeeded in winning $3 million and an annual allowance. He pursued his political career and, in 1992, was elected to the Senate in California.

Greatly saddened by their break-up, in 1991 Jane Fonda married one of the most important men in the United States, Ted Turner, creator and boss of the CNN television network. At fifty-three she thought of having a child, and then abandoned the idea. Attractive, wealthy, popular, and very actively involved in social and humanitarian causes, they ensure that they still attract attention.

1973

UNITED STATES.
Publication of the novel by Erica Jong, *Fear of Flying*, which became an international best-seller. Henry Miller described it in the foreword as "a work which is undeniably therapeutic", "the feminine counterpart of [his] *Tropic of Cancer*, less bitter and much funnier". The author, an active feminist, shows a cheeky sense of humour in this account, written in the first person, of the eventful life and sexual adventures of Isadora Wing. Married to a psychoanalyst, the heroine is afraid of flying and forces herself to travel by plane in order to conquer the fear. She ends by overcoming her fear at the same time as she becomes sexually liberated. Erica Jong defended herself from what some people described as "pornography" by saying: "There is not all that much sex in my book, but people are enraged because a woman is affirming herself sexually and intellectually by saying, 'This is my life and I shall do what I like with it.'"

SOCIETY
Love in Everyday Life

Those little things which irritate – minor squabbles: are they an art, a ritual, or a way of clearing the air?

In the film *Scenes from a Marriage* (1973) which is partly autobiographical, Ingmar Bergman shows the difficulty of living and communicating as a couple. Liv Ullmann, his own companion (cf. p. 296), and Erland Josephson play an apparently stable couple, but a gulf starts to appear between them which leads from adultery to despair, insults, and divorce. While Antonioni (cf. p. 278) shows the impossible union of two people tormented by the pain of living, for Bergman it is better to share the hell than be alone.

This view is shared by French writer Marcel Jouhandeau, who "lives with Elise on a glacier where we alone are able to withstand the loneliness, the height and the cold". He also used the name *Scenes from a Marriage* for a series of books with eloquent titles from *Domestic Menagerie* (1948) to *The Eternal Process* (1959). Among the many other famous portrayals of home life, there is the play by Edward Albee and subsequent film *Who's Afraid of Virginia Woolf?* (1962) or – in real life – the outrageous lives of Liz Taylor and Richard Burton (cf. p. 288), both stars of the film.

The mythical lovers Romeo and Juliet are spared by death from facing domestic problems, such as running short of money towards the end of the month or the untidy bathroom. For Denis de Rougemont (cf. p. 188) the impossible transition from passion to love can be summed up in two words: "Mrs Tristan". He describes Isolde as being swallowed up in marriage, because it demonstrates the fusion of a woman's identity into that of the man. "The wicked husband kills Prince Charming," sang Claude

Contradictions, love and hate. By Siné and (facing page) by Ouka Lele.

Nougaro. When the lovers find themselves "alone at last", it is then that unforeseen problems arise. If love feeds on the struggle against the obstacles in their path, what happens when there is nothing left to oppose? After the initial idealism (cf. p. 356) there comes a period of disenchantment, of familiarity which often reduces desire (cf. p. 374). When reality shatters the illusions each has of the other, love may become stuck in the rut of daily life.

THE RITUAL OF THE SQUABBLE.
When a relationship forms between a couple, there are two life-histories involved and two different ways of looking at the world. The most crucial event is the birth of a child, when the couple are obliged to unite in a new identity as parents. Children may become the main source of arguments rather than money.

Agreement on the essentials can break down over matters that have differing relative levels of importance for each partner. According to sociologist Jean-Claude Kaufmann, cleanliness and tidiness are the main issues on which couples are at odds: however, the less demanding a woman is in these matters, the more prepared a man is to play a part doing household chores. Unpaid domestic work used to be a woman's traditional lot, and the notion of sharing the household chores is a recent innovation which can be difficult to initiate.

In years gone by, a crisis in the home, even a violent one, did not threaten the couple, as marriage meant being joined for life. Today, where even the most trivial quarrel can lead to divorce, the handling of disputes is more tricky. Most breakdowns come in the early years of living together, when absolute desires lead to withdrawing rather than making concessions. As people mature, they become more flexible,

particularly if they have learned lessons from past experience about how to overcome problems in a relationship. Apart from the scourge of jealousy (cf. p. 244), friction between a couple is inevitable. From annoyance to deceit, from dissatisfaction to resentment, ill feelings mount up until there is a sudden explosion of anger. Quarrels often stem from seemingly trivial incidents or from behaviour which the other partner suddenly perceives as intolerable. They are repeated, about the same issues using the same words. Making a scene is one way of exerting power over a partner who fails to listen or show respect. One pushes the other to the limits, particularly when faced by an exasperating calmness or a partner who avoids confrontation by walking away.

Familiarity provides the knowledge of where to aim in order to injure. Whether it takes the form of jousting in public, or of bitter disputes behind closed doors, interspersed with out-

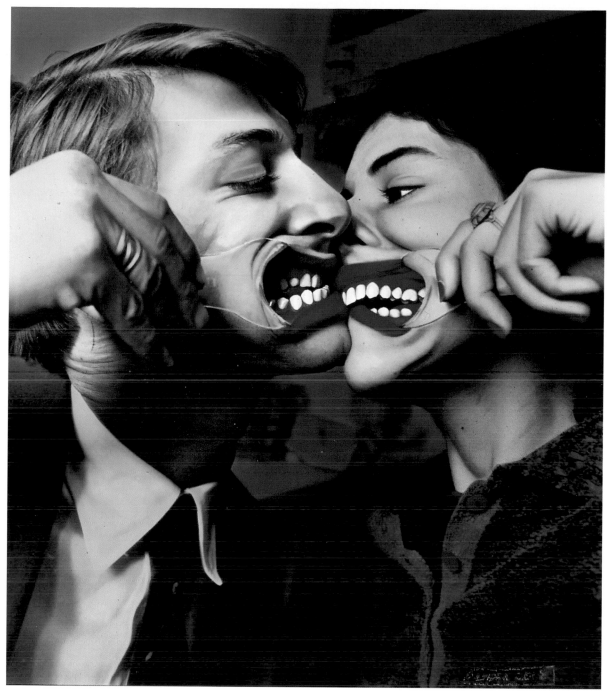

HOLLYWOOD. **Two stars marry – Ali McGraw and Steve McQueen. The attractive young woman who won an Oscar for her role in** *Love Story* **(cf. p. 319) divorced Robert Evans, the film's producer, because she had fallen madly in love with the handsome blond actor who was her co-star in Peckinpah's film** *The Getaway* **(1972). In her memoirs** *Moving Pictures,* **she said that their marriage was hell. Steve McQueen tormented her with his jealousy, prevented her from following her career and deceived her frequently. She became an alcoholic. When Peckinpah offered her a role in** *Convoy* **(1978) she accepted and found the strength to break with McQueen. McQueen remarried and died of cancer in 1980.**

CANADA. **Release of** *Last Betrothal,* **a beautiful and moving film by Jean-Pierre Lefebvre, about the love affair between two old people, married for fifty-five years. Having suffered a heart attack, the old man refuses to be taken to hospital. His wife promises to die at the same time as he does. On a sunny morning, two angels come to fetch them.**

bursts of temper or prolonged sulking, an attempt is made to criticise the other with a mixture of sincerity and bad faith. Insulting a person or wounding their pride is one way of getting at them, goading them, and hurting them. Where individuals have difficulty expressing themselves verbally, or run out of invective, the abuse frequently escalates to shouting and physical violence.

COUPLES WHO STAY COUPLES. Are quarrels between couples a healthy thing? Blowing one's top may be a safety valve. The domestic quarrel where, according to Claude Roy,

"two colluding and interwoven freedoms size up the situation and test each other", sometimes helps to resolve a situation. For some people it revitalises desire and ends in a reconciliation "between the sheets".

Although we all like to have the last word, it is wise to end a quarrel before it is too late and allow our partner to save face. A couple has a better chance of survival if they avoid saying things which are humiliating or should be left "unsaid". They recognise the signals when the other is trying to cool the situation down. The essential thing is to maintain mutual respect and to

keep a good opinion of one's partner. It is no use expecting too much, or making impossible emotional or material demands. Yet sometimes it is necessary to say what one feels, and what wounds, since partners are not always aware of being hurtful. By listening to each other, by trying to understand each other, we learn to negotiate and therefore to overcome problems, to accept each other as we are – warts and all – which of course can be sometimes very irritating, but which all go to make up our personality. A lovers' pact that lasts is constantly being renegotiated.

Galina Vishnevskaya
Mstislav Rostropovich

Two celebrated Russian musicians defected to the West and continued to combine their passion for music with a commitment to freedom.

In 1974 a scandal erupted shortly after the expulsion of writer Alexander Solzhenitsyn from the Soviet Union. Like so many other Russian artists who had "chosen freedom", two distinguished musicians left the country – singer Galina Vishnevskaya and cellist Mstislav Rostropovich.

Galina Vishnevskaya had decided at a very early age that she wanted to become a singer. After an unhappy childhood in Kronstadt, she suffered from starvation during the war and saw the death of her entire family. She started to sing in operettas with a company in Leningrad and married the director. With the help of a teacher who taught her how to make better use of her superb soprano voice, she passed the entrance test to the prestigious Bolshoi Theatre in Moscow in 1952. She sang in Beethoven's *Fidelio* when it was staged for the first time in the Soviet Union and became one of the stars of the Bolshoi. She intensely disliked living in a communal apartment, but she refused to ask favours from the influential people for whom she sang at private functions: "I would rather have cut off my tongue."

In April 1955 she was introduced to Mstislav Rostropovich, known as "Slava", who immediately fell in love with the pretty, dark-haired woman with green eyes. They were both twenty-eight, but she thought that he looked much younger, with the face of an intellectual hidden behind a pair of spectacles. She described him as alert, impulsive, funny, with a steady gaze and very attentive. His mother was a pianist and his father a cellist, while he himself was a soloist and teacher at the Moscow Conservatoire. He treated her in a thoroughly natural way and did not display the kind of slavish devotion shown by her admirers. He did not look upon her as a star; they had never seen each other perform on stage. A short time later they met again on tour in Prague. She became his "wife", as she discreetly put it, and they decided to marry on their return to Moscow. He was in a hurry to get to the registry office and took such long strides that she had difficulty in keeping up.

Their close understanding lived up to expectations. "The only surprise for me was to have married a musician beyond compare, and for him to find himself married to a fairly good singer." Rostropovich later became an orchestral conductor and often appeared abroad.

When she was pregnant, Rostropovich read Shakespeare's Sonnets to her every evening to "help create a unique and beautiful being". Their first daughter, Olga, was born in March 1956, and a second, Elena, in June 1958. Full of energy and living life at a frenetic pace, "Slava" was not easy to live with. From time to time, his wife begged

The World Health Organisation defines sexual good health as "the integration of somatic, affective, intellectual and social aspects of the sexual being in such a way as to allow the enrichment and blossoming of the human personality, of communication and of love."

FRANCE. Enormous success of *Emmanuelle*, a film made by Just Jaeckin, based on the novel by Emmanuelle Arsan (1967). The heroine is encouraged by her husband to make all sorts of sexual discoveries. The more she makes, the more they love each other. The poster, showing a beautiful woman with long legs — Sylvia Kristel — lightly clad and sitting on a large cane armchair, is evidence of the modern acceptability of "soft porn" (cf. p. 340), unlike the novel itself which had been published clandestinely. The same year a new volume of the book appeared, *Emmanuelle IV*, which contains this sentence: "Eternal love can last a whole night, because it is not eternity that makes things last, it is eternity which puts an end to things lasting."

him to take on fewer engagements and spend more time with the children. He would promise, and then promptly forget, and the whirl of activity would start again.

TWO LIVES DEDICATED TO MUSIC. "Everything she touches with her flight/ Suddenly becomes something different," is how poet Anna Akhmatova described the voice of Vishnevskaya. She was without equal in the Russian repertoire, particularly in Tchaikovsky's *Eugene Onegin*. She performed Verdi or Puccini, Mozart's Cherubino or Gounod's Marguerite with singular talent. In 1960 she was the first Soviet singer to appear in the United States. On tour in the West she was described enthusiastically by critics as the "Russian Callas". For his part, Rostropovich is acknowledged as one of the greatest performers of the century. Prokofiev dedicated his *Symphonia Concertante* to him. Shostakovich, who wrote his *Cello Concerto No. 1* especially for him, was very close to the couple and composed several song cycles dedicated to Vishnevskaya. A great friendship also bound them to

Benjamin Britten and Peter Pears (cf. p. 212). They performed every year at the Aldeburgh Festival. It was with "Galia" in mind that Britten wrote the soprano part of his *War Requiem* (1962), as well as other songs. In 1964 he went to Moscow with his *Cello Symphony* written for "Slava". Their foreign tours often obliged them to be apart. In order to spend more time together, they arranged a joint concert in which he accompanied her on the piano, but she was cross because he never found the time to rehearse. They arrived on stage angry with each other, swearing that it was the last time that they would perform together, but, she wrote, "As soon as the first notes sounded, we were fused into a indissoluble whole." The public had no idea of the back-stage disagreements. "On stage, I put on a happy smile of surprise when my husband kissed my hand, but I refused to speak to him during the interval and the next day too."

On 21 August 1968 in London, Rostropovich, greatly embarrassed by the Russian invasion of Czechoslovakia, performed Dvorak's Cello Concerto. The following year he invited Alexander Solzhenitsyn, who had become famous in 1962 for his story about life in the gulag and who was living in wretched conditions, to move to their dacha near Moscow.

COURAGEOUS AND INDOMITABLE. Solzhenitsyn received the Nobel Prize for Literature in 1970. His host, who a short time later became godfather to his son, defended him publicly against the Soviet authorities who started to harass him constantly. Although Vishnevskaya's career was not affected by this commitment, her husband was hounded out of the Bolshoi and his contracts abroad were cancelled. Cut off from his music, he plunged into despair and vodka. Affected in turn by all the humiliations, his wife decided that they had to leave the country. The family received permission to leave from President Brezhnev and they settled in Paris. "Slava" resumed his frenetic pace of life, but his wife, who had left the Bolshoi at the peak of her career, was unable to regain her position as a star. Her troubled life inspired the opera *Galina* (1996), written by their friend Marcel Landowski.

In "gratitude to the West", they turned down Gorbachev's offer in 1989 to restore their nationality which had been stripped from them in 1978. After receiving apologies, they agreed to appear in Russia. This indomitable couple, who chose to leave everything behind rather than surrender their dignity as human beings and artists, remained so deeply committed to each other, to the extent that "Slava" used to carry around with him the love letters he had received from his "Galia".

♡ ♡ ♡

PLEASURE
The Bed

The lovers' domain, a symbol of intimacy and a place for sleep.

Traditionally, in Finland or Russia, peasants used to sleep next to the stove. Further south, curtains were drawn around the bed to retain the warmth in rooms that were poorly heated. The bedroom first began to appear in castles of the Middle Ages. At Versailles, the king's bedchamber is at the centre-front of the building, and the bed is in the centre of the room, like a second throne. Rejecting the aristocratic model of separate bedrooms, King Louis-Philippe, who ascended the French throne in 1830, opted for a shared room. The French subsequently adopted the fashion of a large double bed.

From the eighteenth century onwards, sexual relations were enhanced by the atmosphere of intimacy that had gradually been created, although for a long time it remained a preserve of the rich. Poor people were forced to live communally, with parents and children sleeping in the same bed in the same bedroom – if there was a bedroom. Often there was only a single room, a situation that still exists in the twentieth century when accommodation is scarce.

The "matrimonial" bed unique to Catholic countries, as opposed to "twin beds" which are more popular in Protestant countries, became larger in size in the twentieth century, particularly in Spain where it was the narrowest in Europe – less than 1.20 metres. In the United States there are "king-size" beds which are 2 metres wide. In the thirties, the Hays Code (cf. p. 160) required American films to feature only separate beds, as that was considered to be more decorous. While French Catholics were debating the importance of sleeping separately as a form of birth control (cf. p. 240), Marie Stopes and Margaret Sanger (cf. p. 100), advocates of contraception, condemned abstinence by referring to twin beds as the "enemy of marriage".

In order to combine intimacy and a good night's sleep, one solution is to buy separate mattresses. In countries with a Catholic tradition and double beds, young people are giving comfort priority when choosing the place in which we spend a third of our lives. They are increasingly buying separate beds, Some very wealthy couples go so far as to separate the activities. They have a special bed for love-making and then go to their own rooms, or flats even (cf. p. 374) to sleep. For those people who do not like sharing a bed – which, according to a survey, includes the majority of the French population – it is often too expensive to change, as such purchases are usually made for life.

FUTONS AND DUVETS – A PRACTICAL CHOICE. Replacing the sofa-bed or put-u-up, the futon from Japan is becoming popular with young people, starting in Scandinavia during the seventies, followed by Europe, Britain and the United States. A futon is a mattress that can be rolled up in the morning to make space in small urban flats. Unlike the Arabs, who use their beds for siestas or conversations, the traditional Japanese did not have bedrooms. But from the eighties, it became fashionable among young wealthy Japanese to demand separate space for a bedroom with a purpose-made bed.

In the West, practical improvements for bed-making have come to include fitted sheets which enable the bed to be made more quickly. The duvet, traditional in Scandinavia and Germany, is fast gaining popularity further south, and has virtually wiped out the use of blankets in Britain. Bed linen, which at one time was always white or cream, is now available in a huge range of colours and patterns to suit all tastes and decors.

"The bed is everything in marriage," Balzac wrote. The bed that Ulysses built had one foot made from an olive trunk. The bed symbolises the intimacy between a couple and their union and is evidence of their sexuality. It is more than simply a piece of furniture, it is a place; a place for celebration and discovery; their own island and their ship to Cytherea (the Greek island close to where Aphrodite is) said to have risen from the sea; a place of discord and anguish when a bed of roses becomes a bed of thorns; a place for reconciliations "between the sheets". "Two people who sleep in the same bed ultimately have the same opinion," says a Spanish proverb.

Whereas desire is a form of violence, sleeping side by side, more than the sexual act itself, is a symbol of peaceful intimacy. Don Juan abandons his conquests in the middle of the night. For two people in love, love is: falling asleep in the pleasurable sensation of human physical contact; cuddling up side by side; feeling tenderness while looking at the sleeping partner; the pleasure of waking up together after the separation of sleep. Even when a partner is not there, there remains a comforting reminder of their unique scent.

LOVE IN THE DARK. In earlier times, the body remained clothed both day and night, even for love-making. Sleeping naked has become more widespread since the sixties, with the advent of central heating, and is more popular with men than women and with the young rather than the elderly. The conflict between the erotic pleasure derived from seeing the other's body and shyness at revealing one's own is conveyed by the choice of lighting level. According to the *Kama Sutra*, "women prefer making love in the dark". The poem by Paul Géraldy "Pull down the blind" is an invitation to pleasure. In the Middle Ages, however, the Christian Church forbade making love at night, saying that it would produce children who were blind. With an increasing number of prohibitions, the Church was in the position of imposing 150 days of chastity a year. There were countless other taboos regarding sex, which was forbidden during ritual fasting, such as Lent for Christians, or Ramadan for Muslims. One very widespread and important taboo relates to menstrual blood. In the bedroom of Orthodox Jews there is a special bed for a wife to use during her period of "impurity", that is to say throughout menstruation and the day following. Where there are twin beds, they are moved apart once a month, then pushed together again. However, the Jewish religion recommends husbands and wives to perform the sexual act at the start of the Sabbath (the night of Friday to Saturday), as their union represents the male and female aspects of God.

When we speak of a "night of love" rather than a "day of love", it is because darkness is the lovers' accomplice. At night, Tristan and Isolde sing, love escapes from Time and is transformed into Eternity.

1974

ITALY. **Outrage at the film *Night Porter*, by Liliana Cavani, starring Dirk Bogarde and Charlotte Rampling, which tells a disturbing story. In Vienna in 1957, a former Nazi torturer has a chance meeting with a woman from a concentration camp who was the victim of his sexual brutality and then his partner in sado-masochistic love-games. She joins up with him again of her own free will and they resume their erotic activities. Tracked down by former Nazis and fearing that they will be denounced, they both go to ground, then together they expose themselves voluntarily to death. They come out into the street, dressed as in the old days, he in uniform and she in a girl's shoes. A burst of gunfire kills them as they cross a bridge over the Danube. This powerful and disturbing film sparked off considerable controversy since the shocking images it showed were too much for some people.**

♡ ♡ ♡

I'm hungry,
Gérard Schlosser, 1976.

Volker Schlöndorff & Margarethe von Trotta

Two German film-makers started by collaborating, then found they had to work independently in order to save their marriage.

In 1975 a film by Volker Schlöndorff and Margarethe von Trotta, *The Lost Honour of Katharina Blum*, was the first big success of the new West German cinema. Adapted from a short story by Heinrich Böll, it tells the story of a woman interrogated by the police and harassed by a journalist because she spent the night with a man who had just carried out a hold-up. For Schlöndorff, "everything we do has a political meaning, that is why it is better to be aware of it". They wrote the screenplay and made the film together. It was the first time that Trotta had produced a film, although she had already written several scripts and appeared in films made by her husband.

They first met in 1969 in Munich at the screening of Peter Fleischmann's film *Hunting Scenes from Bavaria*. They promptly fell in love. She was twenty-seven and he was thirty. Trotta left her husband and four-year-old son to live with Schlöndorff. She was the guilty party in the ensuing divorce and as a result lost custody of her son, which caused her much anguish. She never had another child.

Trotta was the illegitimate daughter of an aristocratic Russian immigrant. After an impoverished childhood in Berlin, Bad Godesberg and Düsseldorf, she lived in Paris, where she worked as an *au pair*, and was a frequent cinema-goer. As a young actress, she actively participated in the women's movement.

Schlöndorff brought new life to the German cinema with his highly regarded first film *Young Törless* (1966), based on a novel by Musil. Originally from Wiesbaden he studied cinema in Paris and worked as assistant to Louis Malle, Alain Resnais and Jean-Pierre Melville. In Schlöndorff, Trotta found a man who understood and shared her passion for the theatre and cinema. They both wanted to transform the cinema by drawing attention to political demands, yet at the same time they wanted to work with the film crew in a way that did not reproduce the patriarchal system they were actively criticising. Trotta appeared in *Baal*, a film for television which Schlöndorff adapted from a play by Brecht and in which Rainer Werner Fassbinder also appeared. Fassbinder used the actress in three of his own films, but he was a very possessive man and was annoyed when she married Schlöndorff in 1971.

EMANCIPATION. Their professional life was inseparable from their private life. Trotta wanted to make a film telling her life-story, but her husband was reluctant. He said later: "As a spectator, stories about couples do not interest me, and as a film-maker, even less." However, she managed to convince him and together they wrote the script for *Fire in the Straw*, the story of a woman and her child who are separated after a divorce. The film, in which she played the starring role, appeared in 1972 and the American press welcomed it as "the first masterpiece of Women's Lib". Schlöndorff declared that the film was "a portrait of Margarethe. It is the portrait of a woman who is trying to 'live her life', the equal of a man; on the way she comes up against obstacles put there by society, and prejudice – everything which stands in the way of emancipation of men as well as of women."

Although their collaboration on the script for *The Lost Honour of Katharina Blum* passed without incident, the same could not be said when they were shooting the film: the joint undertaking posed so many problems about who was in charge that they decided to call it a day, afraid that angry repercussions might affect their home life. From that time on, they worked in parallel, each on their chosen path. Trotta starred in another of her husband's films *Coup de Grâce* (1976), based on a novel by Marguerite Yourcenar, and then stopped acting completely except for a film by Krzysztof Zanussi. She collaborated on the script for Schlöndorff's *Forgery* (1980) but, apart from a script for Dagmar Hirtz, continued to write only for her own films.

TWO PRODIGIOUSLY SUCCESSFUL FILM-MAKERS. Devoting herself entirely to her own work, she made nine films in twenty years. Based on personal experiences, and promoting her feminist aspirations, the main characters in her films are largely women, often sisters or friends whose personalities are generally opposites.

"Frau Schlöndorff is becoming liberated" was the headline in the daily newspaper *Die Zeit* when the first film that she made by herself, *The Second Awakening of Christa Klages* (1977), came out on release. She was still far from being recognised as the equal of her husband, who was proud of her but found it hard to accept her independence. They both received prestigious awards: in 1980 Schlöndorff received the Palme d'Or at the Cannes film festival and an Oscar for the best foreign film, *Tin Drum*, adapted from the book by Günther Grass. The following year Trotta received the Golden Lion at the Venice film festival for *The German Sisters*. She was the first woman to be honoured in this way and her success was difficult for Schlöndorff to live with. When *Friends and Husbands* (1983) was released, she alluded to the tensions in their relationship. Meanwhile Schlöndorff, who had made a speciality of adapting great works of literature for the cinema, from *Swann in Love* (1984) to *The Ogre* (1996), was affected by the many criticisms that his films attracted. He went to the United States to make films, and their relationship gradually became strained. They separated in 1989 and made new lives for themselves, but they remained united, she said, by a "fundamental friendship". "We have lived together for twenty years. It was the most important relationship of our life, inseparable from our work, our ideas, the world, and politics."

After *Rosa Luxemburg* (1986), for which Barbara Sukova received the acting prize at Cannes, Trotta made *Three Sisters* (1988). In this freely adapted version of Chekov's *Three Sisters*, she shows that the "only love which resists the test of time is that which has never

1975

GERMANY. **Publication of** ***A Small Difference with Great Consequences*, a book by Alice Schwarzer, founder of the monthly magazine *Emma* (1977). The author describes how the power relationship between men and women is expressed in sex. She condemns the exploitation of women in the name of love and re-affirms the clitoral orgasm and masturbation rather than penetration. Her thesis is that it is in a man's interest to insist on what she calls an "exclusive heterosexuality", because it is only in the male/female relationship that a man can wield power over a woman in the eternal battle of the sexes.**

GREAT BRITAIN. **Marriage of David Gascoyne and Judy Lewis, after meeting in a psychiatric hospital where she was a volunteer reading to the patients. She told of how one day, when she was reading a poem, *September Sun*, she heard one of the patients say, "I wrote it." She thought he was mentally disturbed and did not believe it at first, but it turned out that the patient was indeed the author of the poem. A short time later he left hospital and they got married.**

♡ ♡ ♡

been realised". *The African Woman* (1990) tells the story of two women friends and a man who is married to one before leaving her for the other. The fall of the Berlin Wall was the inspiration for another story about a separated couple, *The Promise* (1995). She has plans for a film about the couples of the Rosenstrasse (cf. p. 207), separated by history, which Schlöndorff may produce in a new-style collaboration between two great artists.

♡ ♡ ♡

IMAGES
The Porno Wave

Pornography, linked primarily to violence, machismo and money, has nothing to do with love.

With the relaxation of censorship throughout the West in the seventies, pornography became big business. Denmark led the way by abolishing all censorship in 1969 (cf. p. 291). Films such as *Deep Throat* (1972) and *Emmanuelle* (1974, cf. p. 335) were international hits. In a move from soft to hard porn, where sexual organs and sexual acts are photographed in close-up in a presence of artistic creativity, the porno cinema offers a crude and stereotypical version of sex – the penis is always erect and revered as an idol, while the female body is submissive and dehumanised by focusing only on its sexual parts.

The word pornography comes from two Greek words, meaning "prostitution" and "writing". In pornography, people are paid to simulate, for the benefit of the voyeur, what is normally hidden from view – the sexual act. Sometimes pornography is distributed clandestinely, sometimes it passes itself off as art, calling itself "erotica". This exploitation of sex debases the human dimension. The French feminist Anne Zelinsky defined it as "that which arouses sexual desire in a way that associates it with violence, for commercial gain". One of the beneficiaries of this market is the state through the taxes it levies.

It is something of a paradox to see the right to the freedom of expression being used to ridicule human dignity. Under the cloak of "freedom" pornography is pro-

duced by and for men. Sexual arousal by sight, which is typical of male eroticism, has a corresponding female version in sentimentality, with love-stories and novels of the Harlequin variety (cf. p. 126). Pornography shows a world of heightened machismo which is stimulated by what is forbidden, where having sex is easy. With an insatiable sexual appetite, the man is an ejaculating machine, while the woman, submitting to all sorts of

humiliation, often plays a passive role.

Whereas the United States replaced the Hays Code (cf. p. 160) by a film classification system based on the age of the audience, France decided in 1976 to impose heavier taxes on X-rated films. But the explosion of the video market and the fall in prices has changed the situation. In the West, from the eighties onwards, pornography represented 40 per cent of video sales and

rentals, not including the black market. Whereas the cinema audience for pornography was male, it now tends to involve a couple, or even makes family viewing. It has become so commonplace that it is now trying to diversify with, on the one hand, an escalation of violence, and, on the other hand, with videos made by amateurs. It is distributed through clandestine channels, either in sex shops or sex supermarkets which offer a whole range of

related items. Customers who are too embarrassed to shop in person can buy through mail order catalogues. A German woman, Beate Uhse, made a fortune with her "love accessories" and Paul Raymond, king of British porn, is one of the wealthiest men in Great Britain.

Today, the United States is the world's main producer of pornographic videos, so-called "blue movies". Millions of cassettes are

Women as Targets, André Fougeron, 1984.

FACING PAGE
Cover page of the German weekly asking: "Do women like pornography?"

available for hire. Films of this type ensure record audiences for Western satellite television channels which can be received as far afield as Arab countries, where they are picked up by dishes described as "paradiabolic" by the Muslims of Algeria. Competition among pornographic magazines in the West is formidable. The best known, *Playboy*, has finally taken off in post-Franco Spain and the former communist countries, after decades of failed attempts.

Traffic in pornography is now growing on a massive, international scale. Culture as a whole is feeling the effects. In the cinema, scenes of nudity have become the norm. Fashion and advertising, hiding behind the cloak of respectability, are having the effect of legitimising sado-masochism or commercial exploitation of the human body.

Throughout the seventies, feminists in the West protested against advertisements or films which they considered to be degrading to women. In Germany the "Red Witches" attacked sex shops. But while overtly racist films were forbidden by law, sexism was protected by the "conspiracy" of public opinion. Charged with being censorious by certain defenders of the freedom of expression, ironically female activists' protests were reinforced by the unwelcome support of organisations promoting chastity.

The Americans Andrea Dworkin and Catharine MacKinnon went so far as to put pornography in the same category as violence. While the link between sex and violence may be disputed, it remains a fact that pornography portrays stereotypical fantasies and perpetuates a misogynist culture. It gives a false and degrading picture of love and sex. As an example, Japanese peasants who are not sufficiently well-off to marry bring in women from the Philippines: conditioned by videos, they are deluded

DER SPIEGEL

Lieben Frauen Porno?

into thinking that they will find a cornered, timid woman. Pornography may act as a stimulus to masturbation and bring temporary relief, but it does nothing to solve fundamental problems. Men watching pornographic films who have problems with an erection are likely to become even more frustrated when faced with apparent acts of sexual prowess.

PORNOGRAPHY RESOLVES NOTHING, CENSORSHIP CONTROLS NOTHING. In 1988 the German Magazine *Der Spiegel* asked whether women like pornography. While the feminists of the monthly magazine *Emma* replied "POR-NO", others were content to simply reject the violent aspect. The Austrian novelist Elfriede Jelinek advocated a style of pornography produced by women which did not debase the female body. A member of the German parliament, Waltraud Schoppe, spoke of an "erotic counter-culture". Some change was noted throughout the eighties, when a number of erotic books were published by women (cf. p. 394). In the cinema, *Seduction: The Cruel Woman* (1984), made by Monika Treut and Elfi Mikesch, dealt with a dominatrix and her masochistic clients; films by the American Candida Royalle show an affectionate and respectful man who is eager to give the woman all the sexual pleasures she wants.

The question, which has to be asked, is whether there are any fantasies which are healthy and natural. To oppose pornography on principle is to fail to understand the complexity of sex and the erotic imagination and to forget that the notion of what is depraved, a subjective opinion, changes with time. To those people for whom pornographic pictures have an aphrodisiac effect, is it a matter of morality or taste? A woman, for example, may be aroused by scenes of rape and humiliation which for her have nothing to do with sex in real life. A married man who is aroused by hard porn pictures which he secretly hides from his wife is able to separate his fantasy life from his married life. Watching a pornographic video together may form part of a couple's sex life and that enhances their freedom. As far as children are concerned, those parents who want to shield them from shocking films and pictures often forget that they see most of them in their own home, on television. Children are less likely to be traumatised if they receive sex education that is both frank and responsible. Seeing what was hidden does nothing to dispel the mystery.

Battles by the censor have been both useless and ridiculous. Examples of this were *Les Fleurs du Mal* by Baudelaire and *Lady Chatterley's Lover* by D. H. Lawrence. Moreover, history has shown that trying to protect public morals often becomes mired in political dogma. We must ask ourselves whether pornography would be less attractive, if it was more widely tolerated. To arrive at a sex culture which is as far removed from prudery as from violence pre-supposes that sex education is widespread and that ideas of what constitutes virility and femininity are changing. A sticker on the window of a sex shop in Copenhagen made the point very neatly: REAL MEN DON'T USE PORNO.

HOLLAND. **Marriage of the young Australian member of parliament Paul Keating with a Dutch air-hostess Anna Van Iersel. He first met her in 1972 on an aeroplane while on a parliamentary trip, and fell in love with her at first sight. He pursued her around the world until she accepted his proposal of marriage. The marriage is a happy one and the politician has had a brilliant career. He was appointed a minister 1975 and became Prime Minister in 1991.**

FRANCE. **"We shall still love each other when love is dead," sings Joe Dassin in *Indian Summer*.**

FRANCE. **Great success of the film *Cousins* by Jean-Charles Tacchella about an adulterous couple who experience happiness but deny being hypocritical. This gentle, but riotous comedy, starring Marie-Christine Barrault and Victor Lanoux, tells the story of a woman and man who meet at a wedding. They have both made a mess of their marriages. Attracted to each other, they keep meeting at family celebrations. Finally they decide to defy opinion and spend their lives together.**

Marina Vlady & Vladimir Vissotsky

A heart-rending love affair with a genius destroyed by drink and drugs.

In 1976, Vladimir Vissotsky, the Russian singer and poet, finally obtained an exit visa to travel to the West. For several weeks he roamed the world with his French wife, actress Marina Vlady, from Poland, Germany, France, and England to North and South America. Everywhere he went he sang his intense songs in a rough, powerful voice which would break into sobs and overwhelm his audience. He was at last able to make records, something he had not been permitted to do in Russia. According to Soviet officials, the poet denounced for his rebellion against tyranny was an "odious personality". Life in the West proved to be a rude awakening for this hyper-sensitive man, and he wept for his beloved Russia. Removed far from his roots, he soon began to suffer greatly and wanted to return home.

When Vladimir Vissotsky and Marina Vlady met in 1967 they were both aged twenty-nine. In a poignant book which she later wrote with the encouragement of Simone Signoret, she told how she had gone to Moscow for a festival and friends had taken her to the theatre to see "an extraordinary actor". She was overwhelmed by the power and cry of despair in his voice. During the party which followed, he came over to her. He was small, much smaller than she was, badly dressed, not very attractive but with magnificent pale grey eyes. "I've met you at last," he said. They met again the next day. He was married with two children and she had three; nevertheless, he said to her that day "you will be my wife".

Marina Vlady, with a pretty, oval face, was the daughter of Russian émigrés. Her career in the cinema began at the age of ten, and she had appeared in more than sixty films, as well as in the theatre and on television. She had been divorced twice, first from Robert Hossein and then from Jean-Claude Brouillet. Vissotsky was an actor at the well-known Taganka Theatre in Moscow, playing major roles such as Hamlet. He was also a singer-song writer, whose songs were on everybody's lips. Despite his great popular success, he was unhappy at the lack of official recognition as a poet – in

his work he expressed challenging ideas which the ruling élite found unacceptable.

In order to meet this "funny little man" again, Marina Vlady accepted a role in a film which was to be shot in Moscow in 1968. Then, "without any real thought," she joined the Communist party, which would later prove to be very useful. And so began a life of separation and passionate reunions. In order to be alone together, they had to hide in friends' houses. In the summer of 1970 they finally obtained permission to marry in Moscow. Since he was still refused an exit visa from the Soviet Union, they spent their honeymoon in Odessa.

THE HELL OF ALCOHOLISM. Vissotsky had been a drinker since the age of thirteen. When he met Vlady he had just left a drying-out clinic. He started to drink again, Russian style: five to seven litres a day of vodka, beer, or 90 per cent proof alcohol when he had nothing else. He even drank eau de Cologne and perfume. His friends had warned her. She took on the challenge to accompany her "Volodia" into this hell, to look after him and to help him fight it. But during periods of crisis there was nothing to be done and crises in general lasted six months, often with a series of tragic complications – haemorrhages, oedema of the brain, accidents, self-mutilation. Sometimes she was in such despair that she left him. When a crisis was over, in an attempt to win his wife back he would swear that he would not start drinking again. But nothing helped: not even courses of treatment or the drugs that she brought for him. During the next crisis, he pulled out the implant and mutilated himself with a knife.

Vissotsky continued to dream of the child they would have together, but Vlady refused saying that she did not want a child to be a "hostage to [their] life".

Between long separations, due to her busy acting schedule in France and abroad and attending to her children in Paris, their strange life together continued when she returned to Moscow. She turned down contracts in order to be with him. They dreamt of having a home together, no matter how simple. But all their requests were turned down. They traipsed from one friend's home to another. In 1978, they were lent a piece of ground on which to build a small house. But how were they going to build it without any materials? After protracted discussions and complicated bartering, they managed to obtain some planks and nails. Vlady brought what she could from Paris. Their home was ready by the spring of 1980, but they were unable to make much use of it. She left for Paris, not knowing then that she would never see Moscow or her husband again. When he died three months later, the house was seized by his family, and then it was torn down by the landowner. "All that effort, all that money wasted, all

that accumulation of possessions will never be of use to anyone," she wrote. "Two miserable nights, several hours of lonely work, a lot of hope and dreams, then for it all to disappear."

GROUNDED. There was only one step left to Vissotsky in his downward spiral: he became hooked on morphine. He admitted it to his wife, he was shaking, he was ill. He promised to stop. He wanted to believe there was life ahead of them. He went to Paris, and tried to dry out, but on 11 June 1980 he left for Moscow.

His final poem is dedicated "to Marina, the love of my life":

"In your care for twelve years of my life, at last I am alive,
When I rise up before the Almighty,
I shall justify myself by the unique virtue of my song."

On 25 July 1980 she was awoken by a telephone call: "Volodia is dead."

"That was all," she wrote, "three short words, mumbled by an unknown voice. The ice engulfs you; you cannot break free of its grip."

On his grave in the cemetery in central Moscow, she wanted to place a meteorite, the "symbol of his brilliant but all too short life". His parents refused. But in 1985 Soviet astronomers named a planet discovered between Mars and Jupiter "Vissotsky" in his honour. From then on, she said, she would smile when she looked at the stars.

SWEDEN. **Shortly after the marriage of King Charles XVI Gustav to Silvia Sommerlath, a young German woman, another wedding takes place, filled with emotion of a different kind, since it had been a long time in coming. After decades of living with his female companion, Prince Bertil, the very popular uncle of the King, at the age of sixty-four married the British woman Lilian Craig, sixty-one. He first met her in 1943 when he was a naval attaché in London. She was a dancer and cabaret singer and already married. The prince's father, the strict King Gustav VI, forbade him to marry a divorced commoner, but promised him that he could marry after his own successor to the throne had married. Lilian Craig went to live discreetly in Sweden in 1957. The press respected the couple's privacy. On the day of his marriage, Prince Bertil proudly declared, "We have been the first royal couple in history to cohabit."**

SEXOLOGY
Female Pleasure

Vaginal or clitoral orgasm? Both are possible, says Shere Hite, but men still have some way to go …

"Nobody ever asked women what they thought of sex." So says Shere Hite, the young feminist born in 1943, who interviewed thousands of women in terms very different from those normally used by researchers. Her book, the celebrated *Hite Report*, caused a furore when it appeared in 1976. It re-

vealed that penetration only result-ed in orgasm for 30 per cent of women, and that 80 per cent reached orgasm by masturbating, which they did regularly.

"For the majority of women, sexual intercourse consists of fore-play followed by penetration and coitus, ending in the male orgasm." Shere Hite condemns this "sexist" definition of the sexual act, which is "cultural, not biological, and only refers to male pleasure". A cartoon from that era sums up the problem: a woman is doing the washing up while her husband reads the news-paper. The child asks "Mummy, what is an orgasm?" to which the harassed mother replies: "I don't know, ask your father." The point is emphasised by many feminists that although caresses may be an end in themselves, the use of the word "foreplay" indicates that the sexual act is considered from a male point of view, with the ultimate purpose being ejaculation. Some women, such as the Swiss writer Alice Schwarzer in her book *A Small*

Difference with Great Consequences (1975, p. 339) advocate sex without penetration.

As a result of Kinsey (cf. p. 226) and later Masters and Johnson (cf. p. 302) disputing the supremacy of the vaginal orgasm so authoritative-ly asserted by Freud, certain femi-nists drew "political" conclusions from affirmation of the clitoral or-gasm; if women can gain enjoy-ment in this way either by mastur-bating or with a male or female partner, is this not a threat to the heterosexuality on which a patriar-chal society is based? Since the function of the clitoris is purely sex-ual and to give pleasure, sex can be separated from procreation. The feminist Anne Koedt, writing in 1968, said that many women ac-cused of being frigid because they could not reach a vaginal orgasm often simulated pleasure in order to please their husbands. Shere Hite demonstrated that sex works for the benefit of men and that women are no more listened to or respected in bed than elsewhere. She explained that pleasure from the cli-toris is no rarer nor more difficult to achieve than the male orgasm. It is different, and from the partner it calls for imagi-nation, gentleness and time, as it requires an average of least ten minutes of stimu-lation.

As far as the more diffuse and less intense pleasure of penetration is concerned, Shere Hite calls it an "emotional orgasm" and attributes it to the joy women feel at being physically united with the person they love. She also shows that female sex is often richer and more satisfying after the menopause. For men, on the other hand, the ageing process can increase anxiety about their "performance".

THE RIGHT TO PLEASURE. Traditionally, a woman has no desire or does not show it; she is passive and does not experience pleasure. In the absence of reliable contraception, many women spend their sex lives worrying about a possible pregnancy. The *Hite Report* indicts the selfishness of many men: failure to caress, and what is worse, to use any form of affectionate words (cf. p. 152). They take their own pleasure without regard to that of the woman, since they either do not know about or scorn the clitoris (cf. p. 386). However, holding back is part of an art scarcely cultivated: the erotic art of the male. Classical manuals teach the male lover to proceed slowly and with delicacy. The *Kama Sutra* (cf. p. 68) advises him to "consider the woman as a flower, and behave towards her so that she does not close and so that she spreads her perfume".

While the feminists of long ago were largely puritanical and favoured abstinence, the women of the seventies claimed the "right to pleasure". In a break with traditional submissiveness and passivity they also affirmed a new female power. "Marital duty" was redefined. Previously it was something submitted to by a wife to whom sexual acts were a chore and a rapidly satisfied husband was an advantage. It became transformed into an erotic pursuit between the couple. "Become your husband's mistress" was the new slogan put out by

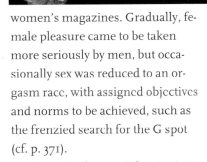

women's magazines. Gradually, female pleasure came to be taken more seriously by men, but occasionally sex was reduced to an orgasm race, with assigned objectives and norms to be achieved, such as the frenzied search for the G spot (cf. p. 371).

Since Ovid wrote "The aim is to get there at the same time," people have extolled simultaneous orgasm. This is difficult to achieve and reinforces the fusion of the couple, but it is something in which not everybody can share. Indeed, it can be a source of pleasure to watch or feel the other person's enjoyment, sometimes giving, sometimes receiving pleasure. Moreover, not all women reach orgasm with the same ease, as that assumes they know all about their bodies and reactions and feel totally at ease with a partner. It is quite a task to get rid of one's inhibitions and anxiety or the disgust and shame about sex which are often inculcated from childhood.

SEXUAL SATISFACTION INCREASES. In the last third of the twentieth century, women have changed more than men (cf. p. 408), and their aspirations to greater equality in sexual relations are better understood (cf. p. 436). Contraception, which has made them mistresses of their own destiny, has modified their attitude to sex, and they have learned to express their desires. The proportion of women who have only ever had a single male partner has diminished, falling in the United States from 42 per cent in 1953 to 11 per cent in 1993. The better informed they are, the more varied their sexual practices. As far as pleasure is concerned, reports on French sexuality published between 1972 and 1992 show that women's sexual satisfaction has grown sharply and exceeds that of men. The higher the age the clearer the difference. Commentators attribute this advance to that fact that female sexual behaviour has become more active and is now more frequent.

1976

JAPAN. **General release of** *Empire of Passion*, **a film by Nagisa Oshima based on an odd incident which caused an uproar in 1936. He tells the story of an affair between an innkeeper and a servant girl. The amorous and sexual passion of the hero, described in the minutest detail with pictures of great beauty, reaches its climax in a closed court and ends in castration of the man, madness, and death. This film, which broke all the taboos on sex, became well-known in the West but the uncut version is still banned in Japan.**

FRANCE. **Publication of** *Archaeology of Knowledge* **by philosopher Michel Foucault, the first volume in an ambitious work** *The History of Sexuality*. **He limits himself to the male point of view and fails to analyse the domination that men exert over women. Challenging the view that sexuality has been repressed in the West, he shows that it is an object of fascination and since the sixteenth century has been the subject of scientific discourse, using the time-honoured procedure of positive affirmation from Christian confession to the statistical surveys of our own time.**

♡ ♡ ♡

Arnold Schwarzenegger & Maria Shriver

The world body-building champion turned actor and a journalist member of the Kennedy clan make a successful marriage.

In 1977, Arnold Schwarzenegger, the famous "Mr. Muscle", took part in the Robert F. Kennedy tennis tournament at Forrest Hill in the presence of the legendary family (cf. p. 280). A world champion weight-lifter, he did not shine on the tennis court, but his antics amused a pretty young girl with dark hair, Maria Shriver, the niece of President John Kennedy. Schwarzenegger was thirty and Shriver was twenty-two. She invited him to spend the weekend at the family "compound" in Hyannis Port, Massachusetts. They left immediately, and the tall sportsman was obliged to borrow a suit to go to church. Although they had opposing political views – he was a Republican – the family gave him a warm welcome. The Shriver brothers were very impressed; in addition to having the physique of a colossus and a face of classical beauty, Schwarzenegger was the author of successful books on body-building, and his career had been portrayed in the film *Pumping Iron*.

Maria Shriver was the daughter of Eunice Kennedy and Sargent Shriver, ambassador to France and unsuccessful Democratic candidate in the 1972 and 1976 primaries. It was while accompanying her father on these campaigns that she decided to become a television journalist. In the bosom of the Kennedy clan, which was Catholic, very rich and where children were raised to be winners, the Shrivers were safe from scandal. Her parents were very devout and went to Mass every day. Endowed with exceptional energy, Eunice Shriver terrorised those around her and pressured Maria to remain slim, but she also managed to convince her that she could do "all that a man can do". It was she who founded the Paraplegic Olympics. Charmed by Schwarzenegger – she was a collector of religious works of art and he collected bibles – she recruited him as a weight-trainer.

Hailing from Austria, the champion dreamt "at the age of ten of being the best at something, and at fifteen of being the most muscular man in the world". His exceptional determination led to him becoming world body-building champion six years in a row. "For me," he said, "winning is an important word. My dream was not to be physically strong, but to be strong in the sense where everybody would listen to me. I wanted to be noticed."

As a child he had another dream. "I wanted to be an American. I believe in the Western philosophy of success, getting on and making money." Arriving in the United States at the age of twenty-one, he was awestruck by California. "There was so much money there, show business, wonderful weather, and the landscape." An intelligent man and a hard worker, he studied management and became a shrewd businessman.

Throughout the years that followed, Maria and "Schwarzie" continued to see each other, but they wanted to make a success of their own chosen professions before taking on a permanent commitment. Their ca-

taking himself too seriously. His other "action" films were successes, almost without exception, from *Conan the Destroyer* to *Running Man*, by way of *The Terminator, Commando* or *Predator*, which emulated, with added humour, the *Rocky* and *Rambo* films starring Sylvester Stallone.

In 1985 Maria Shriver returned to the East Coast to present the CBS morning news in New York, a very prestigious position with an annual salary of half a million dollars. During the summer, Arnold took her to Austria to meet his mother. On a boat in the middle of a lake, he asked her to marry him.

A DREAM REALISED. They married on 26 April 1986 at the church in Hyannis Port. It was a grand affair, with guests includ-

1977

ISRAEL. **Prime Minister Itzhak Rabin resigns his post in support of his wife Leah, who was severely reprimanded by the justice system for a small demeanour: she had not closed the American bank account she opened when her husband was the ambassador to Washington. Publicly demonstrating love and respect for his wife, Rabin also declined to stand in the elections, although he was favourite to win. His party lost. He became prime minister again in 1992 and was assassinated in 1995. Itzhak Rabin was born in Palestine. His wife Leah Schlossberg arrived there with her family from Germany in 1933, the day after Hitler ascended to power. After sharing in the fight for independence in the clandestine Jewish army, they married in 1948. His wife said "He never once reproached me for the bank account business. Never, even during the darkest moments in his passage through the desert, did he accuse me of being responsible for what happened to him."**

reers took them apart; she worked on a television channel in Philadelphia, then in Baltimore. He lived about 3,000 miles away on the West Coast, where he had hopes of becoming a film star. Driven by the same ambition – the pursuit of excellence by their own efforts – they were able to respect it in each other.

A HARMONIOUS RELATIONSHIP. They played sport together, a little tennis, but chiefly horse-riding and winter skiing. He made her laugh a lot. She restrained his impatience and was enthusiastic about whatever he did. He encouraged her in her projects and took an interest in her work commitments. She admired him: "Arnold is a self-made man. He is independent and he has a deep sense of family and religion." In 1980 she helped out with the presidential campaign of her uncle Edward Kennedy, and came together with "Schwarzie" again as she presented a television magazine programme in Los Angeles. They lived together in Santa Monica, although out of consideration for her family, she was said to be sharing an apartment with her brother. Sargent Shriver gave Arnold a labrador and told his daughter, "Watch how he treats it, he will do the same with children."

In 1982, Schwarzenegger had an international success with *Conan the Barbarian*. The public loved this superman, the righter of wrongs, who embodied the American dream of the immigrant who had succeeded without

ing stars from the worlds of Hollywood, the media, and politics. Caroline Kennedy, daughter of the former president, was one of the bridesmaids. The bride wore a sumptuous Christian Dior dress. Since she had broken her toe, she opened the dancing wearing tennis shoes. The groom brandished an American flag and declared "I love Maria and I will take care of her."

According to their friends, they each found what they were looking for – a strong, independent partner. "Before I married Maria, I lived like a gypsy. Now I always have a reason for going home," the actor said. Their home in Malibu was large and luxurious. Maria Shriver divided her time between Los Angeles, where she presented a daily television programme during the week for NBC, and New York, where she made many weekend broadcasts. After the birth of Katherine in 1990, Christina in 1991, and Patrick in 1993, she prepared her programmes at home, while still juggling her commitments, trying to balance her priorities.

Her husband was also conscious of his duties as a parent – their fourth child, Christophe Sargent, was born in 1997. Appointed by President Bush in 1990 to head a presidential committee, he developed a national sports' fitness programme. Alternating action films and family comedies with the same degree of success, he is one of Hollywood's highest paid actors. An "American dream" has become a reality.

Schwarzenegger photographed by George Harrel, and the couple by Annie Leibovitz.

ANGUISH

To Love only God?

The Catholic priest makes no vow of chastity but is committed to celibacy. Frustration and heartbreak are the price he pays.

In *The Thorn Birds* (1977) the Australian writer Colleen McCullough tells the story of forbidden love between Meggie and the priest Ralph, with its tragic consequences. The novel, an international best-seller, was made into a television series with Richard Chamberlain in the role of the priest who became bishop, torn between ambition and love for a woman.

A fascination with what is sacrilegious could explain why people are attracted to others – male or female – who have consecrated their lives to God. Added to that, in the case of a priest, there is the challenge to his commitment and authority. Temptation also exists for nuns; Sister Emmanuelle faced it and said that "the choice was not easy". It happens to monks: in fifteenth-century Florence, the monk Filippo Lippi fell in love with a nun whom he abducted. They were both released from their vows and he painted endless pictures of her modelled on the Madonna. Martin Luther, too, was a former priest, and his wife

Katharine von Bora had been a nun. The Protestant pastor, male or female, the Greek Orthodox pope, the Jewish rabbi, the Muslim imam are all allowed to marry. In the Catholic Church deacons may also marry. The priest, however, unlike a monk or nun, does not take a vow of chastity, yet is obliged to remain celibate. One of the arguments used to support this state of affairs is that with a family a priest would not be

so freely available, and it would cost the Church more to support him. However, in the West, the marriage or cohabitation of priests has long been a reality, and the ordination of married men still takes place in the eastern Catholic church. In the past it was opposed by several Lateran Councils, the Council of 1139 proclaiming the duty of celibacy. One of the aims of this decision was to avoid the formation of a religious class in society where a bishop would be able to pass on his seat to a son.

The celibacy of priests was difficult to enforce. It posed a threat to the social order; as we know from fable-writers who made fun of cuckolded husbands, some priests had affairs with their parishioners. The decisive moment came early in the fifteenth century with the success of Protestantism: faced with married pastors, priestly celibacy became a touchstone of the Counter Reformation.

A VICIOUS CIRCLE. The church thus presented the priest as a man who constantly ran the risk of succumbing to temptation by Woman, the daughter of Eve, who naturally took the blame. In the sixteenth century, Charles Borromée in his *Instructions to Confessors*, stated categorically that priests should not receive

Cartoon by Siné.

FACING PAGE
Cartoon by
Catherine Beaunez:
"Call me Dad."

penitents who wore lace or painted their faces. In the twentieth century, the German priest and psychoanalyst Eugen Drewermann said that "a system which for centuries has forced a man to make a choice between God and human love is both inhumane and contrary to God". This bold and controversial statement describes "the vicious circle of anguish, suppressed desire, regression, dreams of transgression, of new anxieties, and new suppression".

SECRET AFFAIRS. For a long time the law of silence prevailed until in the nineties, when a series of scandals erupted involving priests (and some nuns). They involved misdemeanours or sexual crimes against young children, mainly boys: altarboys, pupils of catechism classes, choristers or scouts. Sentences were passed in France, Ireland, England, Austria and elsewhere.

For some priests, the denial of human love can lead to frustration, which affects them in their ministry. Pursuing a sex life and emotional life in secret can be equally painful, particularly among homosexuals, as told in the fine film *Priest* by English director Antonia Bird (1995). According to a *Newsweek* survey in 1987, 20 per cent of American priests confirmed that they were homosexual. Most Protestant bishops and several Catholic bishops discreetly undertake the ordination of homosexual clergy.

Between 1990 and 1993 revelations of sexual relationships with women accounted for the resignations of the Catholic bishops of Atlanta (Georgia), Galway (Ireland) and Santa Fé (New Mexico). A turning-point was reached in 1995, with the courageous public announcement by the bishop of Basle, Hans Jorg Vogel, of his resignation: he explained that "an emotional problem which was becoming increas-

ingly difficult to bear" had led him into an affair, as a result of which a child would soon be born. According to a survey, 70 per cent of the Catholics in his diocese wanted him to remain in his post. The same year, 400,000 Austrian Catholics, that is to say a third of all

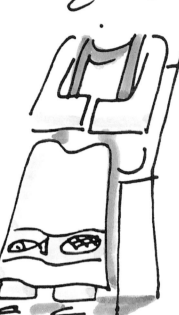

C. Beaunez

practising Church members, signed a petition in favour of married priests. In 1996, 1.5 million Germans voted the same way. But Rome remains obdurate.

The religious hierarchy makes changes only when scandals erupt. It puts pressure on a priest and his companion to end their relationship and to give up any child of the affair for adoption, but ultimately accepts relationships which are conducted discreetly. Some of those people condemned by the hierarchy to a life of humiliation and pretence rebel. For every man like Jean-Claude Barreau who in 1971 announced to a great furore that he was leaving the Church in order to get married, there are many men torn apart and trapped by a psychological and moral dependence who

are reluctant to start a new life without money or a job. Those who make the break join national associations for married priests, which form part of an international federation. According to this organisation, 100,000 priests in total would

renounce their ministry in order to get married. It is estimated that the proportion of practising priests who have a relationship varies between a half and one third, depending on the country. The companions of priests have also formed associations.

It is obvious that it is not the celibate who makes the good priest. Why should love make a man into a bad priest? These views are held by many Catholics, aware of the anguish and pain which this ruling causes. "God is love," wrote Jacques de Bourbon-Busset. "How is it possible to agree with these three words, which summarise everything, if one has never had the real-life experience of a loving relationship?"

1977

"Making love with someone I like" is the way that Woody Allen (cf. p. 368) describes masturbation in his film *Annie Hall*.

"The legs of a woman are the compass which measure the terrestrial globe in all its senses, giving it its balance and harmony."

FRANÇOIS TRUFFAUT
The Man Who Loved Women

FRANCE. Publication of the book *Le Nouveau Désordre amoureux* by two young philosophers, Pascal Brückner and Alain Finkielkraut, which analyses the "power relationship between men and women" represented by coitus. Referring to oriental eroticism (cf. p. 68), they advocate holding back, explaining that by so doing, pleasure becomes infinitely more intense. They see love as an opening on to the world; according to them, "loving the other person is to keep one's uniqueness".

FRANCE. "And you said 'I love you'/ But it is only a word/ It is the custard pie/ Of the photo-romances" sung by *Serge Reggiani*.

Charlotte Rampling
Jean-Michel Jarre

An English actress and a French musician: very different people, but both attached to their "tribe" of children.

"It was a beautiful October day in Croissy and we wanted to have a nice celebration together with our children," Jean-Michel Jarre recalled. On 7 October 1978 the French musician married the English actress, Charlotte Rampling. They were both attractive people, tall and slim, with the same shoulder-length hair. He was thirty and she was thirty-two. Their son David had been born the previous year. She had a five-year-old son by a previous marriage and he had a daughter aged three. They all lived together in a large house near Versailles. "The children have never been a problem between us," he said, "they have welded us together even more."

Jarre first met Rampling in 1976, when his first record, *Oxygène*, was a big international hit. He said "I knew immediately that she was going to be the woman in my life." She said the same thing, "I knew it was Jean-Michel. I was confident in my instincts."

Charlotte Rampling's father was in the army, and she had a strict upbringing – "All my life I have tried to fill the emotional void, the bane of my childhood." She left home at the age of sixteen: "We girls were the pioneers of a generation of women who were experiencing a new kind of freedom." After her cinema début in *The Knack ... And How to Get It* (1964), her career quickly be-

came international. She acknowledged a debt of gratitude to Visconti who gave her a role in *The Damned* (1969): "He gave me self-confidence. He said, 'Don't waste your talents.'" Recollecting that Woody Allen had asked her to play his ideal woman in *Stardust Memories* (1980), she smiled and said, "The ideal woman for Woody has to be seriously cracked."

With her hypnotic beauty, flawless skin, luminous green eyes, and disconcertingly graceful body, she has had a singular career, her charm getting her out of difficult situations with ease. "I have always refused to play women as objects or figureheads. I wanted to play strong roles, rebellious women, because I saw myself in them. I wanted to burn my wings, to throw down a challenge." From the scandalous film *Night Porter* (cf. p. 337) to the risqué *Max my Love*, in which Max is a gorilla, she was acting, she says, "with the permanent threat of falling over". When shooting was finished she needed several long months to recover her sense of balance.

AN INTERNATIONAL STAR. "We are both evolving along rather unorthodox lines," Jarre explained. "My concerts are light-years away from what you normally hear. Charlotte acts in ambiguous, mysterious films. Our marriage is like the carp and the pike, the music and the image, and it is working well."

Jean-Michel, the son of composer Maurice Jarre who wrote the music scores for many films including *Doctor Zhivago*, is known internationally for his electronic music, and his records sell tens of millions of copies. After *Oxygène* he had a further triumph with *Equinoxe* in 1979, the year he arranged the first of his huge spectacular concerts in front of enormous audiences with a mix of music, light, visual displays, and laser projections. He chose open-air venues – "you reach more people that way" – such as the Place de la Concorde in Paris on 14 July 1979. He also celebrated France's national commemoration day in 1990 at the Esplanade de la Défense, and in 1995 by the Eiffel Tower at the request of UNESCO, for whom he is an ambassador of goodwill. This "concert for tolerance," which brought together more than a million people, was accessible all over the world via the Internet. From Houston to London, from China, where he was the first western musician to

JORDAN. **Widowed by his third wife, King Hussein of Jordan marries pretty Lisa Halaby, a blonde American of Syrian and Swedish origin. She was taller than he was and sixteen years younger. A graduate in architecture and town planning, she became Queen Nour-al-Hussein, "light of Hussein", having four children within six years, adding to the eight children from the king's previous marriages.**

FINLAND. **Publication of** *Love Story of the Century,* **a poignant and beautiful poetic work written "in de-spair of love" by Märta Tikkanen, in which she de-scribes the wretchedness of living with an alcoholic husband, writer Henri Tikkanen. "Why is your love for me/ A menacing adoration/ Which I cannot hope to merit/ While my love for you/Would be calm/comfort, commu-nion ..." "I wrote these poems," she decided, "in order to believe – and to gain the strength to believe – that love exists despite everything."**

give concerts, to Mexico, where on 11 July 1991 he greet-ed the total eclipse of the sun with a concert among the Mayan pyramids, not to mention his famous European tour in the summer of 1993 which took in the Mont-Saint-Michel and the palace of Versailles, music has been his way of keeping alive "the utopian flame of the sixties."

A COMPLEMENTARY COUPLE. "Charlotte is my wife, my mistress and my best friend rolled into one. She takes a close interest in everything I do and has done for a long time." She confirmed this by saying, "Jean-Michel needs me when he is working. He is racked with doubt and terribly nervous. My presence reassures him." They see themselves as being complementary to each other.

"The secret of our successful relationship is that we have each found in the other what is missing in ourselves", she has said. He explained, "She is introverted, I am an extrovert." She commented, "He is the voluble Latin, hiding his failures and his disappointments. By day he is anxious and uneasy; at night he metamorphoses: he is sparkling, bursting with energy and creativity. With me it is the other way round." He therefore works at night and has built a studio in an outbuilding beside their house.

They lay great store on the quality of their family life to the point of refusing contracts in order to preserve it. They say that they have professions which are "marginal" and "nomadic", with their small tribe of children and friends as their home port. Jarre says: "At the centre of the clan there is Charlotte." She adds "All five of us, it is what I cling to the most." In order to "stay alive", "Miss Charlie" as her friends call her, became a photographer, taking pictures of concerts, of children, and of her husband who collects robotic machines. As for the rest, she declared: "I am allergic to all housework and anything which is unproductive."

For her, "loving is a daily task, a mutual effort. Loving is accepting someone without making judgements." He says that a relationship has to be worked at every day, in order to keep the mystery alive. Among their principles he lists respect for the other person's secret world, tolerance and generosity. She speaks of the "play of subtleties and re-examining things, so that a couple can weather the storms". They have successfully survived the storms and trials of everyday life. "We have found common ground between our respective weaknesses. You cannot really change anybody," she confirmed. "If you cannot accept the other person as he is, then you have to go."

♡ ♡ ♡

ANGUISH
Death of a Loved One

While some sink into despair, others learn to live with their grief and make a new life.

The French actor Charles Boyer died romantically, aged seventy-nine: the "French lover" (cf. p. 118) followed his beloved wife, Pat Patterson whom he married in 1934, into death. She died of cancer at the age of sixty-eight. He committed suicide two days later. Neither of them had ever recovered from the shock of the suicide of their only son Michael at the age of twenty, in the aftermath of a failed love affair. They were buried beside him in Los Angeles.

Charles Boyer was a charming, elegant man who made his film début in France, but it was in Hollywood that he made a successful career out of playing the screen lover (*Conquest*, 1937; *Love Affair*, 1939). He had held Greta Garbo, Marlene Dietrich, Danielle Darrieux, and other leading ladies in his arms, but after his marriage he loved only his wife. When they first met in Hollywood he fell in love at first sight with the young, fair-haired English actress. They lived contentedly in Phoenix, Arizona, giving the impression of a model couple, a rarity among actors (cf. p. 266).

THE DESPAIR OF "NEVER AGAIN". Whether the death of a loved one comes after a few years or at the end of a long life together, it is always felt to be untimely. The question is how to prepare for this sudden loneliness, this feeling of being abandoned, of emptiness. How does the individual face this "never again", or tolerate living once the reason for living is no longer there? Like Romeo, who kills himself when he thinks that Juliet is dead (cf. p. 282), some people lose their will to live. This is particularly true among women, from the mythical Isolde to Jeanne Hébuterne, the companion of Modigliani (cf. p. 94), Georgette Agutte (cf. p. 117), Dora Carrington (cf. p. 111) or Kay Sage (cf. p. 183). Following a husband into death is a tradition still observed in India and was a custom in ancient China. It was necessary to accompany a master or chief into death, so that he might enjoy the same comforts in the next world as he enjoyed in life on earth. His wives and servants were therefore required to sacrifice themselves during the funeral rites. In India the sacrifice of the Hindu wife is called *suttee*. She throws herself on to her husband's funeral pyre to be burned alive. In the eyes of those who assist in this rite, it is not two bodies which are burning – a dead man and a living woman – but a single entity whose two halves are inseparable, a single offering to the gods. However, the reciprocal action by a widower is completely unheard of.

"The one left behind lives in hell," sang Jacques Brel in *Les Vieux*. Among the survivors, there are those who give in to despair, because they expect nothing more of this world. Lamartine despised this attitude: "A single person leaves you and the whole world is empty!" They are consumed by grief or they let themselves go and succumb to drink or drugs. The grief of mourning is often compounded by a feeling of blame – "I did not love him/her enough" – and a certain shame at being the one to survive, combined with the feeling of being only half-alive. "We were the half of everything," said Montaigne, inconsolable at the loss of his friend La Boétie.

Is love stronger than death, as the *Song of Songs* claims (cf. p. 264)? "... Until death do us part" is the ritual formula of the Christian marriage sacrament. For believers, marriage is only a transient phase, and faith offers the prospect of a reunion on the other side of the grave, thus dying in one's turn means re-joining a loved one. For others, such as Simone de Beauvoir (cf. p. 234), the loss is irretrievable. "His death separates us," she wrote of Sartre. "My death will not reunite us." If love cannot conquer death, it must take its place as part of life. When people love each other, do they not realise that neither belongs to the other for ever and that one day death will separate them, otherwise this is not really life?

Those who want to perpetuate memories do so in different ways. Kings and queens erect buildings, such as the mausoleum at Halicarnassus, the Taj Mahal in India or the church at Brou in Burgundy. Composers compose: *Souvenirs* (Vincent d'Indy). Writers write: *Nous deux encore* (Henri Michaux), *La Plus Que Vive* (Christian Bobin), *Nous ne vieillirons pas ensemble* (Paul Eluard). Eluard, shattered at the sudden death of his wife Nush – "I deny your death but accept mine" – regained his zest for life and fell in love again with Dominique Laure (cf. p. 239).

DYING TOGETHER. Tradition used to encourage widows to devote themselves to the cult of death. Men, however, were not expected to express their grief. Unable to say, as Gérard Narval did, "I am the shadow, the widower, the inconsolable", men are expected to suppress their grief, and often find it difficult to cope with mourning. The Spanish scientist Severo Ochoa, who won the Nobel Prize for Medicine in 1959, never recovered. In every interview he gave he said that he could not have succeeded without his wife. The grief of the duke of Saint-Simon on the death of his wife in 1743 after forty-eight years of marriage was discreet. In his diary, on the day of her death, he drew a necklace of tears around a cross. In his will he asked for their coffins to be attached together as firmly as possible, so that it would not be possible to separate them without breaking them asunder. After long and happy lives together, these elderly couples would certainly have expressed the same wish as Philemon and Baucis, the poor peasants whose story is told by Ovid. In response to the gods who granted them a wish, they both had the same idea, to die on the same day. When the time came, Philemon was changed into an oak tree and Baucis into a lime tree. These trees are not the same species, and in the same way, death does not make lovers identical or fuse them into a single entity. The most that they can do is to mingle their foliage, like the vine and red rose bush planted on the tomb of Tristan and Isolde by King Marcus.

1978

SPAIN. **An unheard-of scandal: Carmen Martinez Bordiu, Franco's grand-daughter, married since 1972 to Alfonso de Bourbon Dampierre, Duke of Cadiz, leaves her husband and their two sons for a Parisian antique dealer, Jean-Marie Rossi, who is twenty-five years older than herself. She divorced in 1983, the first in the family to do so (but not the last). Public opinion was shocked that as a mother she did not claim custody of the children, which seemed inconceivable for a Spanish woman. She went to live in Paris with Rossi and they married in 1984, shortly before the birth of their daughter. One of her sons was killed in a car accident, then her first husband met with a violent death. Jean-Marie Rossi also lost a daughter in an accident. In 1995 there was renewed scandal, but to a lesser degree, when the Rossi couple divorced, Carmen Martinez Bordiu having already gone to live with an Italian.**

♡ ♡ ♡

Until Death Unites Us,
Ouka Lele, 1988.

Margaret & Denis Thatcher

The West's first woman prime minister relied on a husband's discreet support.

The Conservative party won the 1979 general election and Margaret Thatcher, who had been party leader since 1975, became prime minister of the United Kingdom. She was the first woman in the West to rise to such a position and was also the world's first married female prime minister. Women who had been prime ministers before her, Sirimawo Bandaranaike in Sri Lanka and Indira Ghandi in India, were widows or divorced (Golda Meir in Israel). The thorny "problem of the husband" arose. This was a common sticking point where there were female ambassadors and ministers. Protocol dictated that wives of Mrs. Thatcher's colleagues had precedence over her husband. This could have had personal repercussions. Although it is an acknowledged fact that a wife takes a back seat in devoting herself to the greater

glory of her husband, the reversal of these roles has yet to manifest itself. However, in countries with monarchies, such as Great Britain, Holland or Denmark (cf. p. 304), the figure of the prince consort, the queen's husband, is a familiar one.

Mrs. Thatcher was born Margaret Roberts in Grantham, Lincolnshire, in 1925. Her parents were shopkeepers. Her childhood was austere, but she developed a love of work, which taught her that "if you want to, you can". With the help of a scholarship she studied chemistry at Oxford. This brown-haired, open-faced, and energetic woman had a prodigious memory and a phenomenal capacity for work. She had only one real passion, politics, and found her true home in the Conservative party. In 1948, whilst working as an industrial chemist, she stood as an election candidate for Dartford, a working-class area of Kent. It was there, at a party to celebrate her nomination, that she first met Denis Thatcher. The grandson of a farmer turned businessman, he was a divorcee, sporting and rich. After the war, which he spent in France, he became a director of the family paint firm. She admired his presence and his experience – he was ten years older than she was – and thought he was "exceptional". While he drove her around in his Jaguar, they discovered that they had interests in common: reading, music and especially economics. The most important thing was that he supported her in her desire to go into politics.

AFFECTION MOVES UP A GEAR. The projected marriage between the daughter of a shopkeeper and a divorcee did not please either family. Going against her parents' wishes for the first time in her life, Margaret Roberts married Denis Thatcher on 13 December 1951. "We might perhaps have married sooner, but my passion for politics and his for rugby – Saturdays were never available for a date – both got in the way."

"Between us," she wrote, "affection never got in the way of freedom." Their marriage was based on an agreement: they would each give priority to their careers while preserving the family unit. Twins Carol and Mark were

IRELAND. **Contraception is finally legalised, but only for married couples. The very conservative sector of the population of this small Catholic country was obstinately opposed to other "modern evils", such as abortion, which is still illegal, or divorce, which only became legal after the 1995 referendum.**

JAPAN. **The cost of a traditional marriage ceremony escalates. In addition to the number of kimonos which the bride wears on top of one another, all the guests are offered presents. To avoid this problem, many young Japanese adopt another solution – they leave the country separately to marry abroad in a pleasant location, where they then spend their honeymoon, such as New Caledonia, Australia, Tahiti or Hawaii.**

FRANCE. **A married physicist couple at the Academy of Sciences: Yvonne Choquet-Bruhat, the first woman to be elected, joins her husband Gustave Choquet.**

♡ ♡ ♡

born in August 1953 and Margaret Thatcher acknowledges the part played by "Denis's money". She and her husband stick to the same traditional values, but he is more right-wing than she is. Their agreement on the essentials does not prevent them having different interests. He likes sport, especially rugby and golf, which she loathes. He smokes, which she does not like, but tolerates. Also known to like a drink, he enjoys the *bonhomie* of male company. As for her, her only hobby is decorating their succession of homes. She studied law and

stood without success in several by-elections. Her credo was to save the country from socialism and encourage free enterprise. In 1959, she was finally elected MP for Finchley in north London, just after they had bought a house to the south. The children were already in bed when she got home at night from the House of Commons, but she telephoned them every evening. The Thatchers were undemonstrative and strict parents. He travelled a lot, but, according to her, "compensated for his unavailability by helping me enormously in my constituency". In 1963, Denis Thatcher sold his company but retained a directorship, with a Rolls Royce company car. Up until 1979, his wife always made sure that she prepared breakfast for him herself. Refusing to give any interviews he provided discreet and effective support to the "boss", as he called her. She would always ask his opinion. When he was unable to accompany her to a party, she remained isolated, because she was not well liked by her colleagues – although she had her loyal supporters – or even less by their wives; and the feeling was mutual.

AT HER SIDE. In the party leadership campaign in 1975 she wanted to improve her image; she got to work on her high-pitched voice, changed her wardrobe and tinted her greying hair to blond. She started to answer the kind of questions she disliked: how did she combine work and family life, where did she buy her Sunday joint, did she do her own shopping? But when she was advised not to wear a double row of pearls, she retorted angrily, "Denis bought them for me when the twins were born, and I shall wear them, damn you."

The woman whom the Tass news agency called "the Iron Lady" never tried to be popular. As Minister for Education in 1970 she discontinued the traditional glass of milk distributed to school children. She led her government with a rod of iron, applied a policy based on cuts in the social welfare budget and on privatisation, and held to it despite the rise in unemployment and poverty. She saved the country's "honour" by going to war in the Falkland Islands in 1982. She enjoyed the pomp of official visits. After her husband's retirement in 1975 he had more time to accompany her.

"I would never have remained prime minister for eleven years without Denis at my side." She was actually re-elected twice to this high office – a record. But in 1990, dropped by her own party, she took her Denis's advice and, still angry, decided to retire. She remained very active and published her acerbic memoirs.

The effective support of an understanding husband, an asset from which Margaret Thatcher greatly benefited, is what female politicians – and doubtless other women as well – would consider to be absolutely paramount for a woman wanting to pursue a career.

♡ ♡ ♡

FEELINGS
Falling in Love

One out of two people fall in love at first sight, but true love comes later.

In his book *Falling in Love* (1979), Italian sociologist Francesco Alberoni describes the various stages of falling in love. The original Italian title of the book, *Innamoramento e Amore, (Falling in Love and Love)* can be interpreted as the process of "becoming enamoured", an archaic phrase which has been replaced by the modern version "to fall in love". Stendhal used the word "crystallisation" to described this process of idealisation, in which the mind, drawing on all that it knows, discovers that the loved one has other perfections.

Alberoni's book was a best-seller, followed by others, including *Ti amo (I love you)* in 1996. In his opinion, "love is a revolutionary force", and falling in love leads to an extraordinary experience of liberation, fullness of life, and happi-

ness. The emotions felt in the affair produce an immense energy, and this creative shock allows the individual to discover himself.

Making way for love is to accept a new insecurity. As Michel Leiris wrote, "Love: it kills you, it crushes you, it holds you fast, but opens body and soul to you." Some people are afraid to let go in what they consider to be a weakness or danger and try to protect themselves from being overwhelmed. If they have not experienced love during childhood, they find it difficult to cope with love as adults.

A STROKE OF FATE. The experience known as "love at first sight" in English and Spanish, which has formed the basis of endless novels, films and serials, is called "coup de foudre" (the word for "lightning discharge" or "thunderbolt") in French. One person in two claims it has happened to them. Where does this attraction come from, that makes people feel that they are

"made for each other"? It can be explained to a certain extent by biology, by the release of certain hormones as a reaction to the other person. People think that they are in love, when in fact what they are experiencing is desire.

Is love as blind as the old adage says? Carmen sings of it as a "gypsy child who knows no laws". It is said that a prince can marry a shepherdess, and three quarters of the French population believe that they meet their partners by chance. But whom do we meet, and where, and when? What many people assume to be fate is in fact a sociological rule that is being obeyed. Fifty per cent of all marriages are between people from the same social background. This is true particularly of the very poor and the very rich. The greatest social mobility exists among the middle classes. However, in terms of physical differences the range is very broad. The love affair brings together either the ideal, "He/she is all that I ever

wanted", or a double, "another me", or a complementary person, "he/she is everything that I am not". It often echoes a deep experience, linked to early love, of mother or father. The psychoanalyst Karen Horney sees in it "The hope of finding in the couple the fulfilment of all our old desires of the infantile oedipal state". "I fell in love while looking at the sea, I still do not know with whom" the young hero said in the Iranian film *The Age of Love*. Although the infatuations of childhood and adolescence are very strong, a partner can only be, a mirror in the search for oneself.

In the West, the popular concept of love, expounded in Plato's *Symposium*, is that of a creature looking for its perfect other half, in order to become the single entity it was once assumed to be. This was the forerunner of one's "other half", the dream of finding "the man (or woman) of one's life", "Mr. Right". "One day my prince will come" was sung by girls conditioned by an entire culture (cf. p. 126) to await the arrival of their Prince Charming, the only exciting event in life that women traditionally could look forward to. "How will he/she recognise me?", "How will I know that

he/she is the one?" While symbols of professional prestige increase a man's sexual attractiveness, women only have their looks. Good looks in a man are a bonus, and more men than women claim that their relationship began as love at first sight.

TOWARDS A MORE CLEAR-HEADED ATTACHMENT. Can you fall in love before you meet a person? Projecting an ideal image on to an unknown person is to run the risk of ultimately accusing a loved one for not coming up to expectations. In order to establish a long-term relationship, a love affair has to be realistic and take account of the other partner. The philosopher Alain Badiou said, "Love is not the affair itself but what one does and what one thinks, starting from that moment." He defines it as "fidelity to the affair".

Isolated in a kind of bubble, lovers are often intoxicated with the feeling of being in their own world. This sometimes leads them to become totally cut off. Then, if love seems to be impossible, some people renounce it and follow the line of duty, reverting to the old order,

and burying deep within themselves the memory of this "brief encounter" (cf. p. 214). For others, when the attraction fades, clarity of vision can lead to making the break if the realisation is too much to tolerate, but equally this is also the condition for true love to blossom. "People fall in love," explains psychiatrist Boris Cyrulnik, "and when they pick themselves up again, they become attached."

After the illusory initial phase, the partner is "chosen" for a second time, as much for their faults as for their good qualities. Moving from love at first sight to true love is to move from being dazzled to becoming aware, thanks to a clearer vision of what a partner is like. Love at first sight and the turbulence it causes lead to a re-organisation of the internal landscape; after the initial turmoil, a new order can be put in place.

For those who never experience love at first sight there is the reassurance that love can be forged over time, based on respect, affection, and tenderness (cf. p. 378).

1979

ITALY. Publication of *A Man* by journalist Oriana Fallaci, which becomes an international best-seller. It tells the story of the three years she was in love with Alekos Panagoulis, hero of the Greek resistance movement under the dictatorship of the Colonels, assassinated on 1 May 1976. "I chose to look after him, to be his body-guard, his Pygmalion. When he died, I was in New York. It was the first time that I had left him alone. If I had been there, I could have prevented his death." And yet it was his death which revealed the meaning of his struggle to her, "... to change the world, to climb the mountain, to give voice to and return the dignity of the flock which is bleating in its river of wool."

"Sex is not love, it is only a territory which love has claimed for itself."

MILAN KUNDERA
The Book of Laughter and Forgetting

ABOVE
Tango, Isabel Muñoz.

BELOW
Still Life,
by Goran Tacevski.

Petra Kelly & Gert Bastian

Making a New Life

Charles & Diana

Aphrodisiacs

Woody Allen & Mia Farrow

Civil Marriage

Eurythmics

Your Place or Mine?

Vaclav Havel & Olga Havlova

Affection

The Hostage Couples

Erotic Lingerie

Katia Ricciarelli & Pippo Baudo

Devil in the Flesh

Demi Moore & Bruce Willis

Fatal Attraction

Bob Kersee & Jackie Joyner

Salt on Our Skin

Cindy Crawford & Richard Gere

Same-Sex Marriage

Petra Kelly & Gert Bastian

Two important figures in the German Green movement died in unexplained circumstances.

On 1 November 1980, two of Germany's best-known pacifists, Petra Kelly and Gert Bastian, met at a meeting discussing the role of women in the army. He was fifty-seven and she thirty-three. Gert Bastian was a former army general who had espoused the ecologist cause. Disagreeing with his country's military policy, he had just taken early retirement. Petra Kelly, dressed in khaki, was leading from the front in the fight against nuclear arms. She organised demonstrations outside military camps where Pershing missiles were to be stationed under the NATO agreement. They met again several days later to launch the Krefeld appeal, which collected two million signatures in one year, and they decided to stay together.

Petra Kelly, fair-haired and with an intense-looking expression, had taken the name of her step-father, an American officer whom her mother had married after her divorce. In 1959 the family left for the United States. There the young Petra discovered the Civil Rights movement, started by Martin Luther King. Then she took part in student demonstrations against the war in Vietnam. Returning to Europe in 1967, she worked in Brussels for European institutions. She joined the German Socialist party, but was disappointed in it. In 1972 she helped to found the German Green movement, which in 1979 became an "anti-party party", calling herself an

"ecologist, socialist, a practising, non-violent fundamental democrat". Heading the Green candidates for the European elections in 1979, she was elected to the parliament in Strasbourg.

Did she become an idealist because she had missed out on a father-daughter relationship? Her very troubled emotional life appeared to be marked by the search for a father figure. Advocating the ideas of Kollontai (cf. p. 122) on free love, she was of the opinion that young people were dull and lacked experience. She had a three-year affair with the well-known Dutch politician Sicco Mansholt, creator of the "Green Europe" movement who was thirty-nine years her senior; then another with the Irish trade-union leader John Carroll, who was twenty years older. Gert Bastian, a grandfather of two, was an unfaithful husband. He did not seek a divorce, but continued to see his family in Munich while living with Petra Kelly for the rest of his life.

KINDRED SPIRITS. Kelly and Bastian shared the same ideals and devoted themselves to the same causes, writing several books together on Tibet. In addition to their support for the Tibetan resistance against the Chinese, the couple also got involved against French nuclear testing in the Pacific, and for the recycling of household waste etc. Gert Bastian gave the young woman affection

UNITED STATES. **In one of her last interviews, Mae West (cf. p. 160), at the age of eighty-eight, says that she was proud to have contributed, through the parts that she had played in the cinema, to bringing sex out into the open. "I never thought that there was anything shameful about sex. I have never regarded love as a sin. The desire which carries you away is something wonderful. Sex with love, that is the best thing in life. But sex without love isn't so bad either. It's very good for the skin and the circulation, it keeps everything moving."** Having known all sorts of men, she thought that none of them was worth the pain – and therefore the wrinkles – which splitting up would cause. Better to be ready for the next one, not knowing what sort of pleasure he would give: **"A man himself doesn't know what he is capable of, until he gets the inspiration ... from the woman he needs."**

and protection, taking in hand their day-to-day life and her political career, organising trips and interviews. They were both candidates for the Green party in the 1983 elections, and were elected to the federal parliament. At the following election in 1987, a year after the nuclear explosion at Chernobyl, the Greens won 8.7 per cent of the vote and became the third largest party in the country, but in 1990, after the elections following German re-unification, the Greens lost all their seats in parliament. Kelly and Bastian saw this as a rejection of the policy of rapprochement with the Socialists, but within the Green party, their tendency to "fundamentalism" was defeated by the "realists". The couple then withdrew from the political scene, remaining on the fringe of a unified country they continued to condemn. Petra Kelly, who was so popular in the eighties, was gradually being forgotten, in the same way that her pale face and vegetarian diet fell out of fashion. She continued to embody another style of politics, and her idealism was evident in the ambitions she spelled out in 1992: "I want a

society which welcomes children and women, in which everybody would have respect and be responsible." What she wanted for herself was "to live a long life which is creative and productive, together with Gert Bastian, my soul-mate".

On 1 October 1992, they were found dead from gunshot wounds in their bedroom, without leaving any word of explanation. It appeared that Bastian had killed her as she slept and then turned the gun on himself. The police concluded that it was a double suicide, but their friends dispute this. Their replies to Proust's questionnaire were recalled: "How would you like to die?" Bastian had written: "Quickly and with no pain." Kelly had written: "Not alone, close to those who are close to me." She had also declared "If Gert is not there, I don't want to go on living." The questions asked by the leader of the Greens, Lukas Beckmann, in the book of condolence, have no answer: "Dear Petra/ Dear Gert/ Why now?/ Why so soon?/ Why no Goodbye?/ Why no word?"

UNITED IN DEATH. In German culture, a suicide pact is very significant as it recalls the tragic end of the great German author Heinrich von Kleist. After searching for a long time for a woman who would agree to accompany him into death, he committed suicide in 1811 with Henrietta Vogel. Although he had never known this woman, he wanted to leave this world, in which he felt rejected and excluded, by an act which seemed to him to be the only way of yielding to love. This type of pact is also known in the Japanese tradition (cf. for example p. 173), where old love poems paint a world of pleasure and illusion, where everything is transient, unless the couples flee together into another life.

There are few people who make their decision with the same serenity as Laura Marx, the daughter of Karl Marx, and her husband Paul Lafargue. They departed this life, as they wished, in 1911 before reaching the age of seventy. A double suicide is more often an act of despair, such as when love is impossible, like that of Archduke Rudolph of Habsburg and Marie Vetsera at Mayerling in 1889; or when the husband is very ill and the wife cannot bear the thought of surviving him, such as the British writer Arthur Koestler and his wife Cynthia (cf. p. 375) or the Italian couple, actor Tino Schirinzi and musician Daisy Lumini, in 1993. It can also be explained by tragic circumstances such as the Zweig couple (cf. p. 201). This only serves as a counterpoint to the lust for life of the Russian poet Ossip Mandelstam; when his wife, Nadejda, proposed that they die together, as they suffered the most terrible privations (cf. p. 182), he replied: "Life is a gift and no person has the right to take it away."

♡ ♡ ♡

FEELINGS
Making a New Life

Finding a new love can lead to remarriage or living together without formal ties.

In the Europe of the eighties, following the removal of legal obstacles to remarriage (cf. p. 42) and with an increase in the number of divorces, more and more couples included at least one divorced partner. They represented one third of all marriages in Great Britain and in Denmark. In France the proportion increased from 8 per cent in 1970 to 12 per cent in 1980 and 24 per cent in 1994. Slightly lower in Germany (21 per cent in 1994), the figure is the lowest (less than 10 per cent) in countries where divorce has been legalised most recently, such as Italy, Spain and Portugal. However, while the general crisis in marriage (cf. p. 298) does not discourage remarriage, the total number of remarriages is falling, since divorcees finding a new partner increasingly feel that a legal tie is unnecessary. In thirty years, the number of remarriages in France, Denmark, or Germany has fallen by two thirds for people under the age of thirty-five, and by one third for those over the age of thirty-five.

To remarry or not to remarry: the choice depends upon the social acceptability of unmarried couples, which varies according to social group or country. Among other factors to be considered are the presence of children still at home and their ages, and the degree of economic independence of the woman. However, there is a constant factor: men everywhere are quicker to form a new couple than a woman; in France 23 per cent of men and 15 per cent of women form a new couple almost immediately after a separation. In Germany, a study in 1995 showed that one woman in two meets a new companion forty months after separation, whereas 80 per cent of men are no longer alone after ten months. This difference between the sexes can be explained by the presence of children, who are in the mother's custody in 85 per cent of cases. Women without family commitments form a new couple almost as quickly as men. In France, for the twenty-five to forty-four age-group, 51.8 per cent of divorced mothers with children live without another adult, compared with only 8.9 per cent of divorced fathers in the same position. The presence of children has the effect of delaying the point at which a mother feels available for a new relationship. Those women who are coping reasonably well with their situation claim that they want to enjoy their freedom, after years of daily friction and scenes, rather than become encumbered again with a new husband or inflict a step-father on their children. But the statistics show that the probability of a woman remarrying diminishes strongly with age. In addition, divorce brings a fall in income for divorcees, and restricts the network of relationships, more so for a woman than a man, particularly if she does not go out to work.

There is another constant factor: it is the poorest women who remarry or enter a new relationship the quickest. Other women are willing to take a risk and wait for a time to find the right partner. Very often, remarriage for women appears to be a repeat performance, since they tend to marry men in roughly the same social position as their first husband. Husbands and wives are also known to divorce and then remarry each other, such as Elizabeth Taylor and Richard Burton (cf. p. 288).

WIDOWHOOD AND REMARRIAGE. Before the evolution of divorce, it was only widows and widowers who remarried. Today, the number of such unions is very small. In France they fell from 3 per cent of the total in 1960 to 1 per cent of the total in 1990. A difference in the sexes has also been observed – widowers tend to remarry more frequently than widows. Is the reason for this, the fact that traditional mourning rituals exclude men (cf. p. 352). Do they suffer from a greater practical and spiritual upheaval? Or does social pressure play a part? In the romantic novel (cf. p. 126) or picture magazines (cf. p. 222) it is most unusual for the heroine, who is inconsolable at the loss of her only love, to remarry, whereas the widower is always presented as a highly desirable suitor.

In China, widows were traditionally forbidden to remarry. In India, where remarriage has theoretically been legal since 1856 but is condemned socially, the practice of *suttee* – the widow burning herself alive on her husband's funeral pyre – still persists (cf. p. 352). The Indian widow, considered to be an object of repulsion due to her impurity, is forced to lead a life of asceticism and humiliation to expiate the sins she is assumed to have committed in a previous life, and which have brought her this misfortune. In other parts of the world, the patriarchal tradition has forced widows to consider themselves as the "wife of one man", and to devote themselves to the cult of death. Rural Mediterranean societies, which consign widows to being recluses or to wearing mourning in perpetuity, also forbid them in practice to remarry.

NEW DISCOVERY. "Love makes a virgin" is an old Bantu proverb. An individual can in effect feel a new person again, when feelings are reciprocated, and be amazed at the

ability to be happy again, and to give happiness to another person. To build a new life together, to forge new bonds, perhaps even to have a child, it is important to know oneself, and to know how to communicate one's limits. Start a new relationship by all means, but remember the lessons of the old one (cf. p. 273). Finding one's virginity again in a relationship with another person helps to make a fresh start in life on a new basis. Of course, after several years of living alone, the initial sexual encounters may be difficult. There is a lack of self-confidence, there is anxiety that, as one grows older, one's powers may fail. Together, a couple discovers aspects of intimacy and the commonplace: waking up together

for the first time and taking the first breakfast together are both as important for the future, as discovering each other's body and having good sex.

Some couples – generally those for whom this is not the first relationship – reject the illusion of fusing together as one, and decide to "live apart together" (cf. p. 374), either because they do not like having to make the concessions that living under the same roof would entail, or because they both want to preserve the quality of their relationship and enjoy the advantages of being free, not to mention a preference for being alone. Making a new life, or sharing a life with someone else, does not mean that everything has to be done jointly.

1980

LITERATURE. **In "The Word 'Love'", a short article in *Use of Speech*, Nathalie Sarraute clearly shows how between two people, attracted by something which still does not have a name, the word "love" changes everything as soon as it is uttered. "The word 'love' has entered, bringing awareness, destroying innocence … The word 'love' and its derivatives, 'I love you', 'we love each other' … when they are spoken, when they are repeated like the words of a prayer which voices without number have recited across the ages from generation to generation, give a sense of security, calm." She refers to certain religious ceremonies: 'I love you' are the words pronounced as each places a wreath on the head of the other, investing it with a superiority which no one in the world can think of emulating; it is the gift of all gifts, the grace of all graces."**

♡ ♡ ♡

Photograph
by Stanley Greene.

Charles & Diana

A royal marriage which started with pomp and rejoicing ended, like many others, in divorce.

On 29 July 1981 Charles, Prince of Wales, aged thirty-two and heir to the British throne, married a ravishing young aristocrat aged twenty. The wedding was televised across the world. The bride, Lady Diana Spencer, had the charm and distinction befitting a future queen. The popular press portrayed it as a fairy story, stirring the imagination of the nation, including those who until then had no interest in the royal family. The country rejoiced that Charles had chosen a "pure English rose" rather than a European princess, as his ancestors had done. The marriage appeared to be a love match, between a Prince Charming, kind and full of good humour, and a quiet young girl who worked in a children's nursery while she awaited the big day. From the moment that she was seen in the prince's company, the press published pictures of her holding the nursery children in her arms, in photographs which combined beauty and a virginal purity. Her fame was meteoric and the newspapers started to refer to her as the future Princess of Wales.

Lady Diana came from a wealthy family. She was six when her mother left her father and lost custody of her children when they divorced. In 1974 her father married Raine, Countess of Dartmouth, the daughter of Barbara Cartland (cf. p. 126). The teenager reacted violently to her new step-mother. It was through her sister Sarah, one of the many young women whom the Prince of Wales escorted, that she first met him, although he scarcely noticed her. He saw her again several times at official functions.

As the eldest son of Queen Elizabeth II and Philip, Duke of Edinburgh, Charles has said that he received little parental affection in his childhood, but he was given, instead, a sense of duty. The royal family is united but not very warm. As a shy schoolboy he experienced the austere, communal life of a boarding school. Before serving in the Navy, he followed a course of study at Cambridge, interrupted by official duties around the world.

LOVE AND DUTY. When Lady Diana met Prince Charles at a social event in July 1980, she told him that she knew of his grief on the death of Lord Mountbatten (cf. p. 220) to whom he was very close, and who had been assassinated by the IRA. A compassionate person, she knew how to find words of consolation. Charles told his friends that he thought that she was "warm and comforting". She dreamed of marrying him, and he began to give the matter some serious thought. For several years he had been having an affair with Camilla Parker Bowles, married with two children, who was one year older than himself. Her grandmother, Alice Keppel, had been the mistress of Edward VII. In 1936, Edward VIII had renounced the throne for love (cf. p. 174). In 1955, Princess Margaret had yielded to the demands of state (cf. p 255). What would the Prince of Wales do, admitting to a friend that he was tormented by doubt, but adding "I want to do precisely and absolutely what is right for my country and for my family." The public awaited an official announcement with impatience, and he received an ultimatum from his father to make up his mind. It appears that Camilla Parker Bowles advised him to marry the young and innocent Diana. Charles, who later admitted to having been terrified, "of the idea of making a promise and spending the rest of [his] life regretting it," finally gave in.

An explosion of popular joy greeted the announcement of marriage in February 1981. The wedding, an occasion of great pomp, was a heaven-sent commercial opportunity: potteries produced 2.5 million commemorative beakers with the image of the royal couple, and a million copies of the official album were sold. Only a handful of feminists and anti-royalists resisted the "wedding fever", pathetically shouting "Don't do it, Di."

In 1969, television had for the first time shown a film of the royal family going about their daily lives. In the same way that Queen Victoria and Prince Albert had modelled themselves on middle class family values, so the Windsor family wanted to be seen to be adapting to modern times, and at the same time improving their very restrained relations with the media.

A DREAM SHATTERED. Now that she was a member of the "The Firm", the princess worked full time. She undertook hundreds of public engagements a year, became president of a number of charities and made numerous official visits. Prince William was born in 1982, and Prince Harry in 1984. Capricious and easily angered in private, Lady Di remained immensely popular – she was both beautiful and warm, elegant, and a good mother. Far from being a young innocent, she showed herself very adept at using the media, which made her into a celebrity and one of the best-known women in the world. In 1986, for example, she appeared on the front cover of more than 500 magazines. At court, where dis-

cretion and restraint were preferred, tensions began to appear.

Princess Diana was a young woman who loved shopping and dancing at fashionable night spots. The countryside, horses, dogs and hunting, all favourite royal pastimes, bored her to tears. When Charles's brother, Prince Andrew, married Sarah Ferguson in 1986, the new Duchess of York caused a sensation and, later, scandal because of her spontaneity, which many considered vulgar. Defying protocol, the two sisters-in-law had fun together.

The royal couple began to smile less and less in photographs taken of them together on official engagements. Soon rumours started to circulate. Whereas establishment papers took sides with the prince, the popular press spoke up for "Lady Di", abandoned for the "old witch" Camilla. A successful book, published in 1992, then adapted for television, told of the princess's bulimic crises and her suicide attempts.

1981

BEIJING. A diplomatic incident during the visit of Michel Jobert, the French Minister for Foreign Affairs. He was incensed over the reaction of the authorities to the planned marriage of diplomat Emmanuel de Bellefroid and Li Shuang, a Chinese painter. The Frenchman was declared *persona non grata* and his fiancée was sent to a re-education camp. She was finally allowed to join him in Paris in July 1983, when they married. The story of another mixed marriage was resolved after only a six-month wait: the sculptor Wang Keping married Catherine Dezaly, a French woman working in China, in 1981.

GREAT BRITAIN. General release of *The French Lieutenant's Woman*, a Karel Reisz film starring Jeremy Irons and Meryl Streep. It was adapted from the novel by John Fowles (1969), which tells the story of a passionate romance in the nineteenth century between a man who is already engaged to be married and a mysterious woman whose shameful past has made her an outcast. The film superimposes on this tale a parallel love story, between the actors playing the roles of the lovers.

The queen complained in a speech in 1992, that the year had been an "annus horribilis". Her children had shattered the decorous image of royalty which had spanned her forty-year reign. Charles and Diana separated, so did Andrew and Sarah, and their sister Anne divorced and remarried (cf. p. 413). Despite desperate official calls for decency, some newspapers published a transcription of intimate telephone conversations made by Diana, as well as those between Charles and Camilla. Amid sordid "revelations" – Diana's former riding instructor published a book about their relationship – and public confessions, – Charles admitted on television to having committed adultery – the couple moved towards divorce, which was finalised on 15 July 1996. Diana became involved in humanitarian causes. There was speculation about a possible remarriage of the Prince with Camilla, who had also divorced in the meantime. Diana seemed to have found happiness in a new love affair with the wealthy "Dodi" Al-Fayed when on 31 August 1997 the young couple met their deaths in a motor accident in Paris. The tributes from around the world at Diana's funeral, followed by an overwhelming outpouring of public grief, made the woman who wished to be the "Princess of Hearts" into a timeless symbol of beauty and charm.

♡ ♡ ♡

SENSUALITY
Aphrodisiacs

The eternal search for ways of stimulating desire and heightening pleasure.

New "love pills" circulated in the West during the 1980s, but did not succeed in replacing traditional erotic stimulants. The anxiety of "failure" led people to dream of a sexual paradise where the penis would be a magic wand and the vulva a miraculous fountain. Aphrodisiacs have been, and still are, used the world over to promote desire, to prolong it or to revive it. The word "aphrodisiac" comes from the name Aphrodite, the Greek goddess of Love. Throughout history, magic potions have been used to attract, keep or bring about the return of a loved one.

In the Middle Ages, aphrodisiacs were intended for men, as female sexuality, which was considered to be uncontrollable, caused fear. For women, the only admissible stimulants were those of fertility and breast-feeding. Like monks who were obliged to remain celibate, they were administered nenuphar, which "destroyed the pleasures of love", as also supposedly did marjoram, sage and hops. For women there were fresh-water fish, said to be calming; for men salt-water fish, said to stimulate love, as did everything that was associated with Aphrodite, born out of the sea. Similarly oysters and mussels resembled the vulva, while eggs and therefore caviar were linked to procreation.

Among the hundreds of animal, vegetable and mineral compounds renowned for their aphrodisiac qualities, each culture has favoured certain ones, local or imported. Cookery, which brings all five senses into play, has acquired something of the exotic in Europe, with the use of spices such as pepper, cinnamon, cloves or nutmeg. From the Aztecs we have borrowed cocoa, which contains a stimulant, as do tea, coffee, guarana from South America or savory, which was the herb of the ancient satyrs. Other magic herbs are rosemary, basil, and verbena. The Italians have given us *tiramisu* which combines coffee, chocolate, vanilla, egg yolk and rum.

Muslims, copying Muhammad who was advised by the archangel Gabriel to use harissa, a paste with a red pigment, use "facilitators of pleasure", principally the all-purpose henna, which can be applied to the genital organs. Whereas in eastern religions (cf. p. 68) the path to the divine passed through sexual ecstasy, Christianity banned anything to do with sexual pleasure, and persecuted women who concocted philtres or unguents.

Beliefs in the power of aphrodisiacs are often based on the similarity of appearance. This explains, for example, the wearing of phallic-shaped amulets, the use of horn carvings in the West Indies, and in Asia the use of eels and snakes, deer or rhinoceros horn, and the testicles of bulls, tigers or male seals. Certain vegetables such as asparagus or cucumber are recommended because of their shape. There is also the well-known Korean ginseng, and ginger, or mandrake root which resembles the male body with a large penis.

DANGEROUS DRUGS. Do aphrodisiacs work? There is no specific stimulant for the sexual function, but it can be activated by anything which dilates the blood vessels. So there is, for example, yohimbine, extracted from the bark of an African tree called the "tree of strength". In reality, most products have a tonic effect. At best they are harmless, their effectiveness coming largely from the faith that people put in them, but they can often be dangerous, since

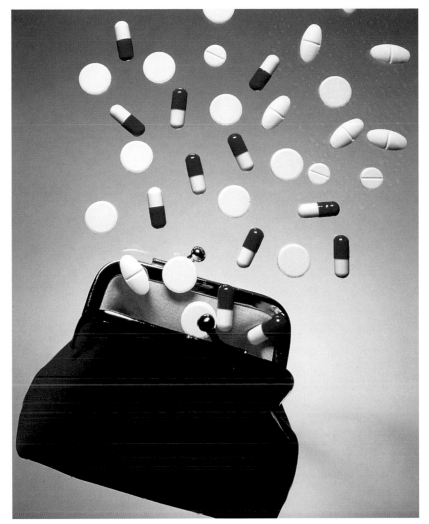

stimulation can be accompanied by toxic or depressive side-effects, or may induce dependence. Spanish fly, for example, a type of beetle used by Sade, is effective but irritates the urinary tract and can be fatal in large doses. As for West Indian "sexy punch" or Chinese "virility wine", the effect of the alcohol depends upon the quantity drunk and the person drinking it. In small quantities it is a stimulant and loosens inhibitions.

One man in two, at some time or other, has problems with his erection, particularly if he is a smoker, as nicotine causes the blood vessels to contract and reduce desire. These problems, which often result in depression or emotional difficulties, increase with age. They may be organic in origin, for example there may be a hormone deficiency, or they may be psychological, or even due to drugs taken for high blood-pressure, or tran-

quillisers. Other drugs may have the opposite side effect on the erection, like Prozac, which causes some people to have an orgasm after a yawn.

Since time immemorial, plants or magic mushrooms containing hallucinogenic substances, which promote feelings of intense pleasure, have been used in initiation ceremonies. Isolation of their active ingredients has made it possible to reproduce them synthetically, so what was once confined to secret rituals has now become general knowledge. These drugs are dangerous, however, because they cause a hang-over, they soon create a dependency, and their effectiveness decreases with use. Hippies of the sixties boasted of "cosmic sex" and "floating" sensations after taking euphoric substances, such as LSD. Twenty years later it is now Ecstasy which is called the "love pill". However, this amphetamine

does not arouse sexual desire; it intensifies tactile sensations and therefore produces the desire to rub against someone. It is dangerous chiefly because it causes a raging thirst and damages the kidneys. It stops people falling asleep, which has led to the growth of all-night rave parties, which are increasing in popularity throughout Europe. Its effects have been felt most in Great Britain where sixty young people have died in ten years. Despite being illegal, it is secretly distributed, along with poppers, based on amyl nitrite, which provoke very intense, but very short-lived, sexual arousal.

THE SCENT OF A LOVED ONE. Desire arouses all the senses, particularly those of smell and touch. There is no need for a charm or a miracle drug, when through the magic of love one can "lead someone by the nose", or "get under someone's skin". The best aphrodisiac of all is the body odour of the loved one, as revealed by the discovery in 1986 of pheromones, secretions which are specific to each individual from puberty onwards.

When a sow finds a truffle, it is because the smell resembles that of a boar. The western predilection for perfumes based on musk, the secretion from a species of male deer in the rutting season, was explained when it was discovered that the odour is similar to that of the male hormone. Musk and other animal perfumes, such as civet, castor, or ambergris (from the sperm whale) were later replaced by floral perfumes. Erotic attraction is a complex phenomenon. Pleasure is at its best when it comes of its own free will, in its own time. Stimulation comes from the brain rather than from the perfume, it is in the head rather than in the action. Surely the imagination, which nurtures expectation and fantasy, is the best aphrodisiac of all!

1981

DUBAI. **In this tiny Gulf state, a sandy desert with enormous oil reserves, a marriage is celebrated which is reputed to be the most lavish of modern times. Mohammed, the son of Sheikh Raschid ben Said Al Maktoum married Princess Salama. In a stadium constructed especially for the occasion a gigantic feast brought together 20,000 guests over a 7-day period.**

SWITZERLAND. **Writer Albert Cohen, author of *Belle de Seigneur* (cf. p. 311) dies several months after declaring in an interview, in a final homage to love and to the woman he loved, Bella Berkowich: "To be loved and to love at the age of eighty-five, whether I die in six months or two years, is for me the only thing that matters, and the only answer." He spent a happy life with this British woman, his second wife, whom he met in London in 1943. She moved in with him in Geneva in 1947. It was to her that he dictated *Le Livre de ma mère* (My Mother's Book) (1953).**

♥ ♥ ♥

Still Life 95,
Goran Tacevski.

Woody Allen & Mia Farrow

One of the most talented contemporary film-makers and his second muse, a pretty actress, made ten films together.

In 1982 the whimsical film *A Midsummer's Night Sex Comedy* appeared on general release. It was the first film made by the New York director Woody Allen with his live-in companion, actress Mia Farrow. In a series of romantic and comic entanglements, Allen plays an inventor who tries to fly, without success, with an engine strapped to his back. When the pretty Ariel appears, with a halo of golden hair, he stammers out that she is charming, but he fails to hold on to her and loses her to another man. Despite the film's lack of success, Woody Allen rejoiced to have discovered Mia Farrow's comedy talents: "I can do a lot more with her than with anybody else," he declared. In his next film, *Zelig* (1983) she plays a psychiatrist, the only person who can understand the hero, played by Allen, and they marry at the end.

From their first meeting at a restaurant in New York in 1980, Woody Allen and Mia Farrow took to each other. She was thirty-five and he was ten years older. They had both been married twice before. For ten years Allen had had a productive relationship with the actress Diane Keaton, with whom he made six films, all of which demonstrate her fine acting talent. He came from a Yiddish-speaking Jewish family, and made her "an honorary Jew" with his customary sense of humour. They lived together briefly and remained very close. *Annie Hall* (1977) was a film inspired by their life together,

and deals with the difficulty of relations within a couple. In one scene, where the screen is divided into two, they are seen talking to their respective psychiatrists about their sex life: "Almost never, scarcely three times a week," he says. She says "All the time, at least three times a week." She starred in other Woody Allen masterpieces, such as *Interiors* (1978) and *Manhattan* (1979), a splendid homage to the New York he loves.

Woody Allen, whose genius is more widely acknowledged in Europe than in his own country, started out as a comic. A solitary teenager, who loved cartoons and jazz clubs – he plays the clarinet,– a self-taught cinema and theatre buff, he started to sell gags to comedians, then performed his own sketches in cabaret clubs, creating a comic persona which he then brought to life in plays and films – that of the skinny bespectacled man, going thin on top, inhibited, shy, and awkward, but who asserts himself by his reason and seduces with his sense of humour. This prolific film-maker, who produced almost one film a year, shifted from comedy to drama, still playing himself: a Manhattan intellectual, neurotic, frustrated and funny, wearing black-framed spectacles and corduroy trousers. However, although he plays a loser overtaken by events, in real life he is very successful. Competitive and well-organised, he has control of his films and has acquired a rare professional indepen-

1982

BROOKLYN. **Marriage of American poets Paul Auster and Siri Hustvedt, who met the previous year in a library at a public reading. They fell in love at first sight. He had already published five collections of poems and she one. They were both good-looking, she was blond and bright-eyed, while he was dark and sombre. Their daughter was born in 1988. Living quietly in Brooklyn, both wrote novels. Siri Hustvedt compared literature to a town in which "we are neighbours, but not living in the same building". In 1985 Auster published** *The Invention of Solitude* **and** *City of Glass.* **After years of living in poverty he became a well-known writer, especially in France. Siri Hustvedt had a success with her first novel, dedicated to her husband,** *The Blindfold.* **This happy couple denied any idea of rivalry and their understanding was expressed, according to Auster, by a "double fictional marriage", which united one of the characters from his book** *Leviathan* **with the heroine of** *The Blindfold.*

♡ ♡ ♡

dence. He has the knack of assembling a talented team around him. He writes or co-writes all his films and takes part at every stage of their production.

MUTUAL ADMIRATION AND SUPPORT. Mia Farrow was the daughter of actress Maureen O'Sullivan, who played Jane in the Tarzan films (cf. p. 161), and of John Farrow, the Australian actor. In a relationship that was rare for Hollywood, her parents loved each other, were fervent Catholics and had seven children. As a child she was delicate, imaginative and mystical. She made her first appearance in the television serial *Peyton Place,* then had her hair cut very short by Vidal Sassoon, in a style which became the fashion. In the cinema she acted in *The Secret Ceremony* (1968) by Joseph Losey and in the

acerbic *Rosemary's Baby* (1968) by Roman Polanski. After a brief marriage to Frank Sinatra, who was thirty years older than herself, in 1970 she married the composer and orchestral conductor André Previn, who was sixteen years older. They lived in the English countryside, had twins, then a daughter. They adopted three Asian children. She divorced him in 1979 and settled with her children in New York in an apartment left to her by her mother.

She met Woody Allen at a time when she felt mellowed by life. Comparing her with Diane Keaton, he said, "Mia does not have the same strength of character, which is a plus for her on the screen, since she adapts much better." He was impressed by her ability to combine work with being the mother of so many children, and at the same time remain so pretty. She admired the fact that he could both act in and direct a film at the same time. She loved only the countryside, but failed to persuade the inveterate New Yorker to live anywhere else. She would have liked to marry, but he was unwilling. They adopted a daughter, Dylan, and a son, Moses. In 1987 their son Satchel was born. While the film *The Purple Rose of Cairo* was being shot, Mia Farrow embroidered a cross-stitch genealogical tree with the couple's first names and those of all their children.

AN UNDIGNIFIED BREAK-UP. The couple lived apart in a rigorously organised set-up: Woody Allen would get up early, cross Central Park to have breakfast with Mia Farrow, then go home to work and return again to his family in the evenings. He said, "I probably see as much of Mia as anybody might who was married to her." He rarely left New York, where he makes all his films, and this allowed Mia Farrow to stay close to her children and give them a secure homelife. He was assured of her permanent availability, as she made films for no other director. In

their mutual need for a secure and stable environment, they used up their emotional reserves supporting each other. Their collaboration was productive, a total of ten films in all, nearly all of them successful. In *Alice* (1990) Mia Farrow never looked so attractive nor was filmed so beautifully, but it marked the end of a happy period.

In 1992, the public was wondering where his autobiography was leading in *Husbands and Wives*, the story of a couple who separate. Then a scandal broke: Woody Allen was having an affair with Soon-Yi, Mia Farrow's adopted daughter. The age difference caused outrage – he was fifty-seven and Soon-Yi twenty-one – but it was the "incestuous" nature of the relationship (cf. p. 231) that was even more shocking. The couple self-destructed in a most undignified manner. When Woody Allen asked for custody of their three children, Mia Farrow accused him of sexually abusing Dylan. It would take more than this to stop the film-maker working, and Diane Keaton replaced Mia Farrow at short notice in *Manhattan Murder Mystery*. Woody Allen married Soon-Yi and continues to write, act and make films.

♡ ♡ ♡

THE LAW
Civil Marriage

Greece was the last European country to have introduced civil marriage. There is now a choice between church or civil ceremony.

When Greece joined the European Union in 1981, it was forced to modernise and secularise its legal system. Civil marriage was instituted in 1982, nearly two centuries after France. The following year, the dowry was abolished, and divorce by mutual consent and sexual equality were introduced. Married women were allowed to keep their maiden name.

In Europe, civil marriage started to develop in the nineteenth century, with the emergence of the new value called "freedom of conscience". It was introduced in England in 1836, in Holland in 1838, and in 1874 in Germany and Switzerland. For Italians it was the subject of Lateran accords in 1929. In Spain, however, it was not until 1979 that the concordat removed the obligation to marry in church.

Greece was the last European country imposing a religious form of marriage on the whole nation, no matter whether they were believers

or not. With a population which is still 96 per cent Orthodox, the Church continues to exert such a massive influence that change comes about only very slowly. Civil marriage, which has been adopted by secular parts of society, still accounts for only 10 per cent of all marriages.

In the rest of Europe, which is in general experiencing a fall in the number of marriages (cf. p. 298), the reduction in the number of church marriages is greater than that for civil marriages. In Catholic countries this is due to the large number of couples in which one partner is divorced (cf. p. 42) and who are prevented from remarrying in a church ceremony.

Catholic or Orthodox marriage does not differ from the Protestant ceremony simply in the rite. In the eyes of the Church, although its members may undergo a civil ceremony, it is the religious ceremony which is all-important, as it constitutes one of the seven sacraments. It is the most recent of all sacraments, not being instituted until 1439 at the Council of Florence, and

did not appear in its current form until the Council of Trent in 1563. A union made in this way is indissoluble. The Protestant churches, on the other hand, which allow divorce, also allow the remarriage of divorcees. The ceremony in the church is not a sacrament, but a blessing. For the Protestant churches, what constitutes marriage is the free will of two people to sign up in human society to a lasting and loving relationship.

IN CHURCH, TEMPLE OR SYNAGOGUE. On average, 60 per cent of marriages conducted in Europe in 1990 were religious ceremonies. The situation varies greatly from one country to another. In France, the percentage fell from 90 per cent in 1950 to 70 per cent in 1977, and to 50 per cent in 1992. Men working in agriculture and manual workers are the most likely to marry in church, the least likely are female employees.

In northern Protestant countries the ideological implication of marrying in church is weak. Since 1980 the proportion of church weddings has settled around the 55 per cent mark for Denmark, 65 per cent in Sweden and Norway, and 80 per cent in Finland. The purely civil marriage, which in Denmark was linked to a social and religious protest movement, became widespread in that country much earlier than in the neighbouring countries, starting in the towns – particularly in the capital – and among the working class. While the proportion of religious marriages in Great Britain is around 50 per cent, in Northern Ireland getting married in church to affirm one's religious affiliation goes without saying. Church weddings are also *de rigueur* in the staunchly Catholic Republic of Ireland, where in 1990 marriages were 94 per cent Catholic, 2.5 per cent Protestant and only 3.5 per cent purely civil.

The only western democratic country not have a civil ceremony is Israel, although more than half of the Jewish population describe themselves as non-religious. The rabbinate, which exercises its monopoly over marriage, refuses to marry people subjected to a religious prohibition, such as women who have committed adultery or who are presumed to have done so, or the descendants of illegitimate children. Each year, 2,000 Israeli couples resort to a subterfuge which the state then endorses – they marry by post, by sending the papers to Paraguay, which duly sends them a marriage certificate in return, or they make the trip to Cyprus.

NEW RITES. Whether civil or religious, the traditional purpose of the wedding ceremony was to show publicly who would be the father of a woman's future children. Up to the Middle Ages, it was an informal contract: the couple's agreement, symbolised in Roman times by the joining of hands, was sufficient. Likewise, modern civil marriage ignores the idea of transcendence. As with any contract, it can be revoked, which implies the possibility of terminating it through divorce.

In France, civil marriage and divorce were instituted by the law of 20 September 1792. The Revolution was inseparable from the secular, that is to say, inseparable from a political concept implying separation of civil and religious society. The law therefore ensured that the National Assembly would not "prejudice the freedom of citizens to sanctify their marriage by ceremonies in the sect to which they are attached". Church marriage became a private affair, preceded by an obligatory civil ceremony. When marriage became de-sanctified and secularised it did not lose anything of its solemn character. Far from returning to a simple union based on mutual agreement, the revolutionaries conceived of a civil ceremony, at which the mayor would officiate. The same thing happened in Russia in 1917 (cf. p. 96) or China in 1949. In some countries, civil marriage has been reduced to a simple form of registration. In others, new rites have been established. Thus in the Soviet Union, since the Second World War, all weddings take place beside the tomb of the Unknown Warrior, where the married couple place a spray of flowers.

While a church wedding retains its importance, particularly in Catholic countries, it is also still favoured by couples who are neither church-goers nor believers, because it gives a solemnity and sense of ritual celebration (cf. p. 30), for which the civil marriage is only a pale substitute.

UNITED STATES. Publication of the book *The G-Spot* by Alice Kahn Ladas, Beverly Whipple and John D. Perry encourages many couples in, often anxious, research. In 1950, the discovery of this female erogenous zone by the German doctor Ernst Gräfenberg – hence the letter G – had gone unnoticed. This well-known point is in reality a zone located on the anterior wall of the vagina. Some feminists condemned this as an attempt to rehabilitate the vaginal orgasm, and therefore the penis as an instrument of male domination. The real question was, how to find the G-spot. The authors replied that the best position was in the "doggie" position (cf. p. 314), using the fingers or penis. Women who have found this point confirm the intense pleasure which it can arouse.

♡ ♡ ♡

ABOVE
Wedding in Havana, the Palace of Weddings.

FACING PAGE
Marriage under water.

Eurythmics

The stormy but creative relationship of a musical couple produced a series of hits.

Sweet Dreams Are Made of this ... in 1983, the British duo Eurythmics had two international hits with *Sweet Dreams* and *Here Comes the Rain Again*. Annie Lennox, the singer, wrote the words, while Dave Stewart, combining melancholy, sensuality, and electronic sounds, wrote the music. Videos, which at that time were becoming essential promotional tools, showed a beautiful, androgynous woman with an ice-cool exterior. Her cropped hair could be bright orange one day, ash blond the next, or jet black yet another. With long, straggly hair and a beard, Dave Stewart was the stereotypical

scruffy rock musician; chubby and taciturn, with chunky rings on his fingers and sandals on his feet, he wore old jeans and a shabby leather jacket. Couples have rarely featured in the history of rock music, and when they split up, all collaboration ceases, as in the case of Ike and Tina Turner. The story of the Eurythmics, with its prodigious musical and commercial success which lasted until 1990, is even more surprising, given that its

fame grew from the time they announced the end of their love relationship. Describing themselves as a "working team", they kept their private lives secret. It is known that they first met in 1976 in a London restaurant where Annie Lennox was working as a waitress. She was twenty-two and Dave Stewart twenty-four. Born into a modest Scottish family in Aberdeen, she owed her musical skills to her studies at the Royal Academy of Music in London. She abandoned classical music for pop, and scraped a living working in a variety of jobs. A delicate and hyper-sensitive person, she was a troubled soul. Dave Stewart came from a middle-class family in the north of England. He dreamed of becoming a pop star and started to learn the guitar at an early age. At sixteen he left home and formed pop groups which failed, lived on his wits, became hooked on drugs, and begged his way around Europe with a friend.

Not long after they met, they set up home together and made music. After the failure of their first group they founded the Eurythmics. The name is a fusion of the word "rhythm", "Europe" and a particular form of gymnastics. In 1981 their first album *In the Garden* passed unnoticed. Two years later they triumphed with *Sweet Dreams*.

"WE TOO ARE ONE". The macho world of rock music attributed all the originality of the Eurythmics to Dave Stewart, but the public perception of the group's image was based on Annie Lennox, a star who was both cool and sensual, and in perpetual motion like their music. In reality, despite their private separation – they each had a love life – their relationship was very strong, often stormy, and was the stimulus for their creative activity. "We have spent hundreds of hours in the studio so that the sound is perfect," she revealed. Stewart said, "Annie and I, in the end, are just one person, and we understand each other instinctively. We share an identical musical vision and we collaborate in writing the lyrics." She described their work as "creative ping-pong, batting an idea to and fro," but also as a "succession of mental and nervous crises," adding, "It's a miracle that Eurythmics has lasted longer than a week!" One hit followed another. After *Sex Crime* (1984), their album *Be Yourself Tonight* (1985) revealed an evolution towards rock. Their

GERMANY. **General release of the film *A Love in Germany* by Polish director Andrzej Wajda. In 1941, in the German village of Brombach, Paulina (Hanna Schygulla), a grocer's wife whose husband is fighting at the front, falls in love with a Polish prisoner. The Nazi legal system (cf. p. 164) severely punishes sexual relations with a foreigner. The woman pursues her passion right to the end and defies the ruling. The Pole is hanged.**

HOLLAND. **Installation of "family rooms" for men serving prison sentences. "Love rooms" allowing detainees to have sexual relations with their wives or partners during visits were opened in Sweden in 1970. Venezuela, a pioneering country, opened them in men's prisons in 1968 and in women's prisons in 1993. They also exist in Spain and Russia. There is no such thing in France, where the subject remains taboo. In 1993, the French prison warders' association condemned the "shame on human dignity" which the existence of these rooms represented, since some couples make love during visits, unable to enjoy any privacy.**

♡ ♡ ♡

song *There Must Be an Angel Playing with My Heart*, where the dizzy vocals of Annie Lennox blend with the harmonica of Stevie Wonder, was an international hit. The album *Revenge* (1986) and the world tour which followed marked the high-point of the group's success. Their concerts, which often ended in over-heated venues with the singer taking off her shirt, were moments of intense communion with the public. But she refused to be treated as a star: "I am no more or no less happy than the woman who works in a bank, who is a secretary, model or whatever. The only difference is that

I am doing what I want to do." She sang feminist songs such as *Sisters Are Doing It for Themselves* with Aretha Franklin.

STOP BEFORE DESTRUCTION. Despite their success, the group did not take the easy route. In a break with the rock machine, they headed off in a new direction with electronic pop music in *Savage*, their next album, with lyrics which were overtly sexual. On the cover, Annie Lennox is unmistakable as a blond-haired Marilyn figure, with a studied vulgarity.

Having become a sought-after composer, Dave Stewart collaborated with Mick Jagger, Bob Dylan and the group Bananarama. He married one of the singers from the group, Siobhan Fahey, and they had a child. Even more discreet about her private life, Annie Lennox had a brief marriage with a German Krishna devotee, and then married an English documentary-maker. After the traumatic still-birth of her first child in 1988, she went on to have a daughter.

The album *We too Are One*, with its clever pun in the title, was released in 1989. It was the last and least successful of the Eurythmics albums. A final concert in Rio de Janeiro in 1990 marked the end of the duo. "The atmosphere was very tense," Stewart recalled: "Working with Annie is an irreplaceable experience, but in the long term it affects the system." She explained further, "It was going to become black, evil, vicious; it was better to stop."

They continued to pursue separate careers. Dave Stewart formed a new group with other musicians called The Spiritual Cowboys, which stalled after some initial success. Annie Lennox was disorientated at first, because she did not think that she could work without him, then she brought out *Diva* in 1992 and *Medusa* in 1995, but neither met with the success formerly enjoyed by Eurythmics. Although their names are still remembered, they are now largely unproductive. Their story – personal relations in perpetual crisis and overlapping creative collaboration – is encapsulated in one of their songs, "Better to have lost in love than never to have loved at all."

♡ ♡ ♡

Society
Your Place or Mine?

Couples find a way of life and a way of loving to fit in with their needs.

In 1983, British demographers started to include a new category of couple, whether married or not, in their statistics. These were people who had a stable love relationship but did not live together permanently. They were known as LAT (Living Apart Together). The French called them semi- or non-cohabitants. They comprised mainly young people, although they did include some older people with grown-up children, and occasionally families with children still at home.

The proportion of couples not living under the same roof, which continues to grow, reached 7 per cent of French couples in 1996, of which 1 per cent were married and 6 per cent unmarried. The law has taken this fact on board by ceasing to insist on "living together" in the marriage vows. Conversely, it is possible to share a home with someone without forming a couple. Multiple occupancy of flats and apartments is common in Germany, Britain and America, and is a growing phenomenon in large towns where rented accommodation is expensive.

The individual urban home has gradually replaced the home in the country which housed several generations. Single-person occupancy, which varied in 1950 from 6 per cent in Canada to 20 per cent in western Europe reached between 25 and 35 per cent, and up to 50 per cent in capital cities, forty years later. However, one third of all people living alone have a stable love relationship. The same applies to a proportion of the women bringing up children on their own, and whose numbers are rising in the wake of divorce and separation.

NECESSITY OR CHOICE. In the West at the end of the twentieth century, one adult in three is not part of a couple. Among those people who have a love relationship, many are forced by necessity to live apart. Obstacles standing in the way of living together often cause too many complications. For young people (cf. p. 428), prolonged study and the difficulty of finding a secure job mean that financial independence and settling down with a partner is delayed. Continuing to live in the parental home is no longer as painful as it used to be in the seventies, when the generation gap was more pronounced than it is now. It is common for young, middle-class people to continue to live with their parents up to the age of twenty-five, with girls leaving home earlier than boys. Sometimes they return home again after a divorce or separation, and particularly if they are out of work. Other constraints on living together may involve employment. In an area of mass unemployment or where there is no prospect of promotion, some people are willing to take up posts a long way from home, which means a *de facto* separation from the partner who may already have a job. Other couples opt voluntarily for the testing and very often costly situation of living apart during the week, and spending only the weekends together.

In some circumstances, this way of life is not the result of a choice made equally by both partners. Bigamy (cf. p. 420) means that one individual imposes a restricted life on the other or others. As in *Back Street* (cf. p. 156), the most independent member of the couple comes and goes as he pleases, while the other one, or two, wait. As for those people who have lived with several partners, and had their fingers burned, they often embark on a new

LONDON. **The Hungarian-born British writer, Arthur Koestler, author of *Darkness at Noon* and his wife Cynthia commit suicide (cf. p. 360 for other cases of double suicide). They had known each other since 1949 when the writer engaged the young woman to be his temporary secretary. They lived together from 1955. This experience transformed his life. He wrote: "It is to her that I owe the peace and relative happiness which I have enjoyed in the latter part of my life – and never before." He was vice-president of Exit, the association which supports voluntary euthanasia. At the age of seventy-eight, Arthur Koestler was suffering from leukaemia and Parkinson's disease. His wife was fifty-five and in good health, but in her last letter she explained her decision in these words: "I cannot live without Arthur."**

relationship in order to ensure that they have somewhere to live. In the same way that cohabitation may serve as a trial run before marriage, so a period of separation can also test a relationship before a total commitment is made. It has been observed that more and more couples are opting for this way of life, as an interim measure – for example before having a child – or as a permanent arrangement. There are people who think that they are too set in their ways to make concessions to living intimately with another. Others want to avoid the status of being step-parent to children whom the (usually female) partner is bringing up alone. Many people say that they want to maintain the quality of their relationship while at the same time protecting their independence and keeping their network of friends. They want to hang on to their freedom and solitude afraid that, after the thrill of meeting and falling in love (cf. p. 356), everyday life will destroy the magic. Although this attitude sometimes masks the fear of taking on responsibilities or of entrapment, the relationship is no less real, and any break-up that may occur causes just as much pain.

CHANGE OF LIVING PATTERNS. "Living apart together". Although not on the same scale as the massive disaffection with marriage (cf. p. 298), this new phenomenon is evidence of a new pattern of living as a couple. In order to avoid not only the social constraints of marriage, but also the routine, the "couple living apart" are attempting to reconcile love and independence, fidelity and freedom.

This was precisely the bohemian arrangement adopted by the privileged people who took Nietzsche's advice: "If husbands and wives did not live together, there would be more happy families." Among these were Fannie Hurst, author of *Back Street*, Jean-Paul Sartre and Simone de Beauvoir (cf. p. 234) who never took breakfast together, Michèle Morgan and Gérard Oury who called each other on a telephone line reserved for their use, or the Austrian novelist Elfriede Jelinek for whom "writing necessitates a monastic life", and

spoke of being "married for twenty years to a computer expert who lives 500 kilometres way and whom I see for ten days a month".

In the same way that Virginia Woolf demanded "a room of one's own" for women, Rilke (cf. p. 146) started to get a hearing, the man who reproached young people for letting their precious solitude be submerged and of not retaining "anything of their own any more". "Living apart together" allows individuals to alternate periods of doing what they want, when they want, with the benefits of a love life. For example, there are people who think that reading in bed and sleeping are private and solitary activities, and prefer to sleep in their own bed, without marital constraints. Modern couples, living together under the same roof or not, learn to respect each other's autonomy whilst at the same time preserving their own. Between the risk of alienation by living too closely together and becoming strangers because they are so far apart, the relationship between loving partners is a subtle matter of distance.

With their own Homes, Christine Touzeau.

Vaclav Havel & Olga Havlova

From prisoner to president, a Czech, dissident, author, playwright and philosopher was supported by a courageous and combative wife.

"If there is any certainty in my life, it's Olga," Vaclav Havel, the most famous Czech dissident, declared in 1989. "We have known each other for thirty-three years, and we have lived together for thirty, sharing moments of happiness and sadness." His *Letters to Olga,* written during four years of imprisonment and signed "Your Vasek" or "Your V. who loves you" were published after his release in 1983. The collection was distributed secretly in Czechoslovakia and translated into a number of languages. In an admirably high-minded tone, he ended with these words: "It's strange, but it may be that I am even happier than before. In short, I feel good and I love you."

When they first met in 1956 in the Slavia café in Prague, a well-known meeting place for intellectuals, Olga Splichalova was twenty and Vaclav Havel seventeen. They discovered a mutual passion for the theatre: "She acted in amateur groups and often went to the theatre. She knew this milieu much better than I did." Burdened with family responsibilities through her teens, the young woman who dreamed of becoming an actress

was forced to work as a stocking-mender at the Bata factory. When Havel found employment as a stage-hand at the avant-garde theatre La Balustrade, she also found a job there as a theatre attendant. They married in 1964, but remained childless. "I was a middle-class child," he related in 1989, "an intellectual who was always indecisive; she came from a working-class family, completely natural, realistic and unsentimental, occasionally with too much to say for herself and intolerable ... Brought up in the loving arms of a domineering mother, I needed a strong wife ... In Olga I found exactly the woman I needed. She answers my uncertainties, corrects my slightly mad ideas with her clarity of mind, and is the private support of my public actions. I have always asked her opinion in everything I do. ... Olga and I scarcely express our feelings, although it is for different reasons. For her it is her pride, for me it is shyness."

She described herself as a "combative woman", and was the first person to read his youthful poetry, his plays in which he condemns the absurdities of society, his political essays, and later his presidential speeches.

Returning to the prison where he was detained.

"Sometimes, Vaclav wakes me in the night to read out something he has just finished," she said. "We have always done everything together."

He asks her to stay cheerful. In 1968, after the "Prague Spring" was crushed by Soviet tanks, a pacifist resistance took shape. Hounded from the theatre, the Havels became dissidents. They organised meet-

bread and signed himself, "your faithful travelling companion along the road of life". He complained that his "dear grouser" wrote so infrequently and in a "telegraphic style". He reproached her for being a "miser with letters", and that they were his only information on the "other world". The "spiritual" parcels were for him as important as those containing food or tobacco.

Whenever she made one of her officially permitted

1984

Release of the film *Carmen* by Italian director Francesco Rosi, with American soprano Julia Migenes-Johnson in the title role. The film was based on Georges Bizet's opera (1875) which tells the story of a Spanish gypsy, a cigarette factory worker and fiery, fickle woman. It is one of the world's most frequently performed operas, and has often been adapted for the cinema or ballet. Now out of copyright, the work is in the public domain and there are no fees to pay. Many directors have used the theme, including Peter Brook, who filmed three versions in 1983 with different actors. Jean-Luc Godard won the Lion d'Or at the Venice film festival with his free adaptation *First Name: Carmen*, played by Maruschka Detmers. Carlos Saura used the story for a flamenco ballet danced by Laura del Sol and the Antonio Gadès troupe. There is continued audience fascination for this heroine of disorder and death, who sings: "If you do not love me, I love you. And if I love you, watch out!"

ings of human rights campaigners at their country home in Hradecek (north-west Bohemia). After the publication in 1977 of Charter 77, Havel became a prime target for the police. In 1979, with five other signatories, he was sentenced for subversive activity against the state and thrown into prison. His wife became his only link with the outside world, "the only hope, the only certainty that life has a meaning".

The letters which he wrote to her and in which he questioned the meaning of life and the search for truth were for him "the most important event of the week". He was entitled to only four sheets of paper, which he filled with tiny handwriting, happy to be able at last to put on to paper the philosophical ideas that he had been marshalling and polishing in his head. He also gave her instructions for this period while a "grass widow", and recommended her to find something interesting to occupy her time. "Live harmoniously," he advised her, "be cheerful and stay sane. That is how you can help me the most, if I know that you are well and that I do not have to worry about you." "Blame me," he wrote elsewhere, "but not so much, so that you become sad; don't lose hope and love me!" Although he may have forgotten to wish her a happy birthday, he made her a pendant out of

four annual visits, and which for him were "points of anchorage", she made herself up carefully, and at his request wore bright clothes, to introduce some light into the greyness of prison. She continued to pass on information about other dissidents and secretly to edit documents. This brought accusations of subversion against her, and she was forced to submit to long interrogations.

She regrets that he is elected president. "Truth triumphed in the end, but it was so late in coming." This was the slogan of the great reformer Jan Hus, which was taken up by the Prague Spring. On 17 November 1989, eight days after the fall of the Berlin wall, the "velvet revolution" started. In only a matter of days, and free of violence, the Communist regime was overturned. On 29 December 1989 Vaclav Havlova was elected president of the Republic. Olga Havlova, who was opposed to his candidacy, won the right not to live in the presidential palace in Prague, preferring their apartment on the banks of the Vltava, which for her was "more civilised, normal and democratic". She preferred her own career to official duties, and in 1990 she created a foundation bearing her name to help the sick.

Vaclav and Olga at the window of their house in Hradecek.

Despite disappointments in the days which followed, the president-philosopher enjoyed immense popularity. The man for whom politics was the "art of the impossible which consists of making us better" did not cease to urge vigilance, condemning totalitarian authority, including the western model of consumption, which ignores all moral and spiritual standards. He was re-elected twice. Each time the ever-reticent Olga said, "I do not think you ought to stand again." He was very affected by her death in January 1996, and had also to suffer an operation for lung cancer the following December. On 4 January 1997 he married a forty-three year old actress, Dasa Veskrnova, a divorced mother with a child. In a radio interview he said: "Olga is, and will remain for ever, an irreplaceable and essential part of my soul. Before her death she told me to get married again ... she was sure that I was incapable of living alone. She was clearly right."

♡ ♡ ♡

FEELINGS
Affection

Neither high-flown sentiment nor love-substitute, affection is a form of happiness unrelated to passion.

After unbridled sex, a return to romance? As a reaction to the sexual excesses (cf. p. 310) brought about, in some quarters, by the change in social mores, a new aspiration to traditional values such as fidelity and affection started to emerge in the eighties. Rejecting the "dictatorship of the orgasm", people started to re-appraise the merits of caressing (cf. "The New Chastity" p. 404). Others, distrustful of passion and the havoc it wreaks, limited themselves to a gentler form of love and the aspect of a dramatic and tormented desire, affection is reserved for relations between parents and children. A discreet refuge for lovers, it offers them a private world of unrecognised delights, where each can soak up the essence of the other. It is expressed by a look, a smile, extended arms; in demonstrations of love, couples hug each other, and embrace in an act of complicity, sometimes in silence, sometimes whispering confidences, and inventing gentle words in the language of love.

From sexual ecstasy to peaceful attachment, the word "love" covers a variety of very different conditions that can exist between two people.

ferent order from desire. According to the moralist Joseph Joubert, it is the "home of passion". Does this mean that it is merely the residue of pleasure, like warm ashes after a fire? For the majority of women, affection is an emotional sharing of trust which leads on to the flowering of a sexual exchange, whereas conversely for many men it is the sexual act which leads on to a stage of relaxation and affection. While eroticism, in an emotion linked to arousal and discovery, requires elements of surprise and variety, even violence, affection belongs to the world of the familiar. Whereas the first is intermittent and "for the moment", the second belongs to a continuum, to constancy, the long-lasting, and acquires a richness of meaning in the repetition of everyday life. According to writer Jacques Bourbon-Busset, it transfigures and illuminates eroticism by its inventiveness, and "does not frighten strong men". The difference between affection and desire could be compared to the difference between happiness and pleasure. Its gentle presence is connected to a deep modesty, but the caress, which endlessly retraces the silhouette of a lover's body, is neither asexual nor fragile. The softly stirring airs of affection warm without burning. Poets compare its taste to honey, its perfume to that of the rose of love. The opposite of passion, it is compassion. "Phèdre does not have the slightest hint of affection for Hippolyte," wrote Julian Benda. "If he

to "being spoiled". "Fondling" a phrase used with children in the past, has now become a weak synonym for making love. Affection between adults has not been seriously studied. In works of fiction, which tend to describe love from

Kollontai sees in it multiple facets of the same feeling (cf. p. 122): that is to say, why compare love-affection with love-passion? For some people affection is a preliminary to erotic play, whereas for others it is an end in itself, since it is of a dif-

Illustration taken from
AIDS, you won't catch it,
1990, Niki de Saint-Phalle.

378 · THE 1980s

is ill, she does not make him a cup of tea. She is the true lover." The opposite of indifference, it is devotion, attending to the other person, and disinterested giving. It is what Albert Cohen describes as: "The wife pressing her husband's boil gently to remove the pus, is far more meaningful and beautiful than all the thrusting of the loins and the somersaults of Karenina."

EVERYONE NEEDS AFFECTION. The skin is for caressing. In childhood, the affectionate bonding which comes from gentle, continuous stroking, helps to relieve our anxieties and teaches us to open out to others. Young children denied this kind of affection tend later to exhibit behavioural problems, and become emotional cripples as adults, because they have not learned how to give. In order to develop the skills essential for such exchanges, the "milk of human kindness" is as necessary to children as is water to a plant. Those who have been deprived lead a neurotic search for love, when they become adults, in order to compensate for what their parents failed to provide (cf. p. 390).

In days gone by, fathers were in general not expected to cuddle and kiss their children, such excessive affection was frowned upon. Times have changed. Reserve and rigidity are valued less, and expressing the emotions is not restricted to women. As a result of changes in social attitudes, affection in the family is now encouraged. Many men, however, are still afraid of intimacy. The products of a traditional upbringing, they believe that giving vent to their feelings or emotions is a sign of weakness. This is the source of their inability to communicate their feelings and their lack of skill in love-making. However, Jacques Brel sang, "For a little tenderness/ I would exchange my face/ I would exchange my drunkenness/ I would exchange my language."

Women are more ready to identify their hunger for affection, which they dream of reconciling with sex. "Speak to me of love, Tell me again those tender things," they plead (cf. p. 152). Nothing is more seductive to a woman than a man who can combine strength with gentleness (cf. p. 58). Throughout the world people speak of French gallantry; however, the quality women desire most in a future partner is kindness.

FEELING GOOD TOGETHER. Speaking of the man she loves, Oprah Winfrey the American television chat-show host explained, "He made me discover affection." This came first in many couples, such as the Webbs (cf. p. 60), Katharine Hepburn and Spencer Tracy (cf. p. 200) or Sophia Loren and Carlo Ponti (cf. p. 292), where the relationship was interwoven more with

an emotional accord and understanding than with sexual drive.

One person in two has never experienced love at first sight (cf. p. 356). Love can equally be based on esteem, affection, and respect, with the same pleasure of sharing a bed (cf. p. 336) or cuddling up in someone's arms bringing feelings of well-being and security. Far from the cannibalistic type of passionate love which says "I want to eat you, I want to devour you with kisses", this gentle sensuality reinforces the bond of love, and encourages people to relax with confidence, and to relive those feelings of childhood. Affection is a comfort against the hardships and injustices of life, and helps people to find serenity and joy. Its "I love you" is the antithesis of possession: it does not mean "I want you, I want to take you", but "I want you to feel good, I feel good with you."

1984

"The heart has its reasons which reason knows nothing of."
BLAISE PASCAL (1623–1662)
Pensées

"She is all states, and all princes, I, Nothing else is. Princes do but play us; compared to this, All honour's mimic; all wealth alchemy."
JOHN DONNE (1572–1631)
The Sun Rising

PARIS. Re-opening of the Pont des Arts, a favourite meeting-places for lovers. Planted with shrubs and flowers, this foot bridge crossing the Seine between the Institute and the Louvre, was inaugurated in 1803. Damaged several times by boats colliding with the piers, it was pulled down in 1979. It has been re-built exactly as it was.

PARIS. Première of *Délices*, a ballet by Régine Chopinot, with one of the longest kisses in the history of choreography: while dancing to the theme from Orpheus and Eurydice, Philippe Decouflé and Michèle Prélonge embrace for ten minutes.

Sardine Fishing, Colas, 1996.

The
Hostage Couples

Families of westerners taken hostage in Lebanon fought for their release. After such long and dramatic separation, reunion can be difficult.

During the early months of 1985, in a Lebanon which was in the grip of civil war, Britons, Americans, and French were kidnapped by terrorist groups linked to Iranian fundamentalists. A total of seventy-one foreigners, including diplomats, university lecturers, and journalists were taken hostage and became pawns in long drawn-out deals. For months which extended to years, they were held in abominable conditions, with no link to their families. The fear of death haunted them constantly. The American, William Buckley, head of the CIA in Beirut, was executed in front of his companions. The French research worker Michel Seurat died from an illness after nine months.

The survivors have told of how they were held, with their feet in chains, the privations, and the torture. But how could they explain the mental pain, the humiliation and above all the denial of themselves, which was the most destructive element? Nelson Mandela, they recalled, knew why he was in prison; as far as they were concerned, they were deprived of freedom, sunlight, love – for nothing. Of what use was their suffering? Some of them began to feel that they were losing their minds, when despair or hatred was so strong that it overwhelmed them, but others, in this test, found a way to serenity and light.

THE WIVES' STRUGGLE. These men had families and many were married with children. The women were deeply affected too, and the descent into despair was suffered by both, like Terry and Madeleine Anderson, who called their book of *Den of Lions*. Anderson, an American and Associated Press Agency correspondent, was kidnapped when his partner was six months pregnant. He knew nothing about the birth of their daughter Salome. For several years she was brought up by her mother who had no idea whether the man she loved was dead or alive.

Other wives shut themselves up in their grief, and not knowing what to do, put their faith in official statements. For others, it was the start of a long battle. Although government objections and diplomatic advice were put in their way, they fought like lions, knocking on doors and calling on all their contacts. Many of them had strong personalities; before the kidnap they had been more than simply "the wife of ...". They were also supported by collective action, since their cause received popular support. In Great Britain, the courageous Jill Morrell who fought for John McCarthy, was still being named in a 1996 poll as one of the country's five most admired women. In France, a public television channel kept the memory of the French hostages alive by showing pictures of them every evening.

Joëlle Brunerie-Kauffmann with her sons Grégoire and Alexandre watching a video of Jean-Paul Kauffmann.

FACING PAGE
John McCarthy freed largely due to the actions of Jill Morrell.

A RADICAL CHANGE. When these men returned several years later (it ranged from three to seven years), there was the problem of how they would fit in again. They had not been living, they had been surviving, with their horizons restricted to the walls of a cell. This was bound to leave its scars. Those who had faith had run out of strength. Some had mystical experiences, and discovered God. They all changed radically. "A part of him has definitely stayed behind," Joëlle Brunerie-Kaufmann confirmed, adding later, "The thing that causes me the most anxiety, is his need to be alone. It needs a lot of love to be able to accept that."

With their return, new trials started for many couples. Terry and Frances Waite had difficulty in readjusting. John McCarthy and Jill Morrell finally went their own ways. For others, each day was greeted as a new miracle. For these people, they felt that henceforth, between them, it was "for life, what is left of it", which was one year in the case of Jackie Mann. This Briton, kidnapped at the age of seventy-five, was the only person to be held in solitary confinement for more than two years. He returned to Sunnie, his wife since 1943, and called his book of memoirs *Yours till the End.*

As in other hostage cases, such a test of faith can be a revelation, a chance to ask questions, to adopt a new scale of values, and sometimes to save love. This was the view expressed by Gerhard Vaders, travelling on a Dutch train which was stopped and searched by Moluccan independence fighters in 1975. "I had a lot of ambition, but I lost it in the train." His wife confirms, "My husband was consumed by his work. He became a new man. He discovered those about him. We would doubtless have got divorced but this incident saved our marriage. We are richer and happier today, because we have rediscovered love and affection."

As for Terry Anderson, father of a little girl he did not know, a bible which he finally obtained helped to give him patience. The one certainty which supported him throughout this terrible ordeal was that Madeleine still loved him and that she would never lose hope of his return. "In the dead of night," he wrote, "it is you

Among these courageous women was the American Jean Sutherland, wife of the Beirut University Dean, who decided to remain where she was – "I felt closer to him" – and continued teaching. Tom Sutherland later recounted how he had twice tried to commit suicide, but it was the vision of his wife and three daughters which deterred him at the last moment. Similarly, Joëlle Brunerie, the French wife of journalist Jean-Paul Kaufmann, spent each Christmas in Beirut with their two sons, and addressed her husband on television. This small, dark, and energetic gynaecologist and women's rights activist was one of the most battle-hardened, but everything that had filled her life previously suddenly seemed trivial in comparison. Her status, her work and even her maiden name which she gave up became, in her words, completely "kaufmannised". A woman proud of her independence and well-established, was now only a wife who was suffering, and fighting to achieve a single goal – to get back the husband she loved. She promised to change. "Before, I was always on the go, I only ever offered him tiredness. When he comes back I will give him my time."

1985

MADRID. **Multi-millionaire German Baron Hans Heinrich Thyssen-Bornemisza, owner of the largest private collection of western art, marries for the fifth time. His wife was the pretty Spanish woman Carmen Cervera, Miss Spain in 1961, who had already been married twice. This marriage was a great asset to Spanish cultural life, since it was in that country that he decided to place his prestigious collection on permanent exhibition. Previously stored in the Villa Favorita, near Lugano in Switzerland, it was to be housed in a new museum in Madrid, the Villahermosa Palace, opened in 1992.**

LITERATURE. **In *Love in the Time of Cholera*, the Colombian novelist Gabriel García Márquez tells the story of a patient, crazy love, which is fulfilled after a wait of fifty years, "as intense as if he was awaiting death."**

who have saved me, you and your vigil." In *Fidelio*, Beethoven's opera which glorifies married love, Florestan finally released from prison as a result of his wife's perseverance, sings, "I owe my life to you" and Leonora replies, "It is love which has guided me, it is love which has released you."

♡ ♡ ♡

IMAGES
Erotic Lingerie

Sexy underwear shapes women's bodies to men's desires.

After twenty years of tights, which became fashionable in the wake of mini-skirts, and practical underwear which represented good value for money, exotic lingerie is now back in fashion, thanks to designers such as Chantal Thomass, a Frenchwoman who has been attempting since 1980 to re-introduce stockings and lace. This sector of the economy has moved up a gear, into mass-production: the American company Victoria's Secret, which distributes more than 200 million copies of its catalogue each year, offers an enormous variety of styles and colours. Customers are received in boudoir-style shops, to reinforce the image of lingerie as a product which is exciting and refined. Men shop there too. Their purchases represent a half of all sales. "Let silk do the talking," advertisements whisper in the run-up to Saint Valentine's Day (cf. p. 248).

"The Silk Road has reopened," announced the headline in a women's magazine. This "new femininity" refers largely to suspenders and uplift bras, symbols of an old order which the rebels of the American Women's Lib burned on the fire of freedom in 1968. These items of female apparel are now worn by a generation of young women ignoring what their mothers fought for. In France in 1985 two thirds of women under the age of twenty-five owned exotic lingerie, many saving it for special occasions. Synthetic materials provide stretch and comfort. In 1986, hold-ups, held in place by means of an elasticised top, have helped to stimulate the sales of stockings, which were thought to have been replaced by tights. Hemlines are getting longer, and underwear is changing. Shops are full of broderie anglaise and basques, and department stores compete by opening "lingerie rooms" to offer styles and designs combining the charm of yesteryear with today's easy-care.

MALE FANTASIES. In the old days, any garments coming into contact with the skin had to be white for practical reasons – they had to be boiled – , and for moral reasons – colours were deemed to be improper. From the 1850s, underwear was coloured, with pastels at first, followed later by deeper shades. In the social code, colours had a symbolism according to the era, social class, country, age, or sex. For example, in the nineteenth century, black underwear was associated with prostitutes, along with make-up and dyed hair. Today, these practices, which together with others once constituted "bad form", such as smoking in the street – wearing lipstick or black stockings – are now not only acceptable, but *de rigueur*. Whether it is a matter of appearance, behaviour or certain sexual practices (cf. p. 386), the evolution of fashion as a means of seduction has entered the arena previously reserved for prostitutes, whose "offer" has now been adapted to the permanent "demand" of masculine eroticism. It took several decades for middle-class women to adopt these fashions, which young girls, impatiently trying to achieve adult status, interpret as the sign of being up-to-date and emancipated.

Black has lost its attraction as a "wicked" colour, since it is now so often worn; at the end of the twentieth century red is now reputed to be the most seductive colour. As for white, it is the colour which men say arouses them most on a woman's body.

Although for everyday wear, women prefer to wear clothes and shoes which are comfortable, they are surrounded everywhere by messages seductively advertised by models.

Gypsy Temptation, Yves-Marie Pinel, 1992.

Unlike men (cf. p. 432), the female identity is bound up with making themselves look desirable and conforming to stereotypes of male desire. While men will fantasise about

a hint of thigh glimpsed under a skirt or pert breasts supported by a Wonderbra, advertisements invite female consumers to buy sexy underwear in order to fulfil an erotic "conjugal duty". Some women even give men a present of a suspender belt, which they will wear to give him the pleasure. In the film *Annie Hall*, the hero (Woody Allen) gives his girl-friend a birthday present, a little something in pink lace edged with black, and she asks incredulously, "It's for you?" Later, he

brings out his intended gift. Underwear, a traditional method of stimulation in male eroticism, draws attention to those parts of the body which are erotically arousing – the breasts, thighs, legs or pubic area –, yet teases by covering them up, much as Eve's fig-leaf did. Worn in advertisements by models with perfect bodies, underwear trivialises the aspects of feminine nudity. Unfortunately, the female body, with its ability to seduce, will always be commercially exploited, and in the end reduce the infinite nuances of desire to the hackneyed stereotypes of the male imagination – the tart or high-class woman, the little girl or the femme fatale (cf. p. 88) with its vari-

ant, the dominatrix with her whip satisfying the masochistic male (cf. p. 50).

DESIRE AND PLEASURE. "Your barrier/ Of frills/ Has to be crossed/ But it's nice/ Pretty lady," sang Léo Ferré. Those little hints of fabric glimpsed indiscreetly between skin and clothing arouse the desire to look or touch. By playing on a woman' shape, with curves accentuated or disguised, shadows thrown between the breasts, lingerie has a role in love-making to stir and excite. It is the final refuge of modesty in front of a partner, where the boundaries of intimacy are pushed back, delaying the moment when the body is revealed. The woman can be viewed as naked while at the same time being clothed. The poet Lucien Becker speaks of "your lingerie which you use to offer yourself and to colour my desire". By virtue of its colour, its tactile softness, rustle, and intimate aroma which is an aphrodisiac permeating this second skin, underwear offers a whole range of pleasures to the eye and, later, to the hands and lips.

Today, women can vary the erotic signals they wish to send. From white lace to black leather, or the formality of dress for an evening engagement, they can construct different roles in the game of seduction. They can openly indicate their desire to a partner, or surprise him and stimulate his imagination, in a continuous renewal and enrichment of the erotic game. There are occasional hurdles which can stand in the way – unfastening of a bra by novice hands! – when the instant of total contact is delayed and desire becomes more acute. Lovers go from discovery to discovery and give free rein to their fantasies.

1985

BONN. **Arrest of Margaret Höke, a secretary to the president of the German Republic, who was responsible for having secretly photocopied documents over a period of fourteen years and passed them to her lover, a spy from the East. She was sentenced to eight years in prison. During the cold war, such affairs regularly hit the headlines in federal Germany. It was always the same scenario: a secretary working in an office connected with national defence, generally a lonely spinster, was seduced by a spy and persuaded to hand over copies of important documents.**

UNITED STATES. **Publication of *Women who Love too Much* by Robin Norwood, which beat all sales' records. The author, a female psychotherapist, describes "love druggies", women suffering from emotional dependence, and "hooked" on men who make them submit to violence. Inspired by Alcoholics Anonymous she proposed a regime to "find the child in oneself" and to grow up spiritually.**

Katia Ricciarelli
& Pippo Baudo

A television presenter and a famous singer, Italy's most popular engaged couple, get married.

On 8 January 1986, the eyes of Italy were on Militello, a Sicilian castle near Catania. Amidst great pomp, a local man, Pippo Baudo, forty-nine and a star television presenter married an internationally famous opera singer, Katia Ricciarelli, thirty-nine. The popular press headlined it "the love story of the year" and it was covered by all the television channels.

The son of a lawyer, Pippo Baudo studied law in Catania, at the same time writing songs and plays. He also acted in the theatre and tried his hand at journalism. In 1959, having submitted his thesis, he left for Rome and found work in television, compering shows. He worked on radio, in the theatre, in the cinema, and he wrote songs. He produced variety shows which became very popular viewing on Saturday evenings or Sunday afternoons on the public television channel. After "Settevoci" came "Canzonissima", then "Un colpo di fortuna", "Domenica in" and "Fantastico". He introduced games shows and quiz shows. He sang, he danced, he acted in sketches; his talents extended to presenting a book programme, which he made interesting as well as entertaining. He was credited with the phenomenal success of a history of Greek philosophy. With his agreeable, average looks, the multi-talented Pippo was successful because he was ordinary. He was acknowledged as a great professional, all-round entertainer. In 1963 he presented the song festival from Naples and from 1984 the famous festival of song in San Remo.

He divorced Angela Lippi, whom he had married in 1970, shortly before the birth of their daughter Tiziana. He had several affairs, most notably with the theatrical actress Maria Grazia Grassini, then with Alida Chelli who declared, "He was married to television. He lived only for his work and the telephone. He never gave presents or surprises, never wrote love-letters, was always tired and fell asleep as soon as his head touched the pillow."

A MEETING WHICH CHANGED THEIR LIVES. Tall and blonde with beautiful green eyes, Katia Ricciarelli, originally from Rovigo in Venezia and fatherless, had earned a living since the age of fifteen working in a circus. Her fine soprano voice also made her in great demand for family and village celebrations or parish recitals. She worked hard at her music and in 1971 became a star overnight when, singing the aria from *Le Corsaire,* she won the Verdi prize in a live television broadcast. La Scala in Milan, the Metropolitan Opera in New York, and Covent Garden in London were now open to her. Wherever she went she was acclaimed in the Italian opera repertoire, in *Otello,* for example, or *La Bohème*

which she performed with the famous tenors Placido Domingo, Luciano Pavarotti and José Carreras. Her voice, said a critic, resembled "rose petals, air-borne, light, and velvety".

In 1977 she bought a fifteenth-century manor house in Spoleto, which she decorated in Renaissance style. She had several affairs, notably with Paolo Grassi, director of La Scala, then with José Carreras. Of the latter she said, "Since he could not decide to leave his wife, after twelve years I got angry and said 'That's enough!'"

Pippo Baudo, who had invited her on to his programme in 1985, asked her in the autumn of 1986 if she would be a sponsor for young singers. "I went to see her and we had dinner," he said. "Like all the magazine stories, we discovered that we were made for each other." He learned how to woo a woman. "I had never been in the habit of sending flowers, but now I was constantly phoning Katia and giving her presents." When he introduced her to his parents, she said she was "nervous, just like going on stage for the first time". In Pippo she was sure of her choice, "This time it is for real. He really is the man of my life and I want to have a child."

GETTING TO KNOW EACH OTHER. Love, money, beauty, fame: all the ingredients which make money for popular magazines were there. Only four months after they fell in love, they got married. When reporters, quoting the last words of Othello beside Desdemona's dead body, shouted "Another kiss," they responded with good grace. "I would have preferred a quiet wedding," Baudo confided, "but in the end I decided to do it in public to avoid speculation and the chase for exclusive pictures." Why this marriage, was the question on everybody's lips. "I am marrying Baudo because I love him," declared "La" Ricciarelli. For the couple it was the "normal course of events", and they added, "If we ever

1986

FRANCE. Sitting at the controls of a helicopter, Nadine Vaujour snatches her husband from prison. As soon as he was sentenced, she learned to fly with this single aim in view. Since then, French prisons have been fitted with equipment in case anyone else has the same idea.

GERMANY. A bill is passed concerning the name of a married couple, enabling them to choose to use the woman's name, the husband's name or a combination of the two. Whichever, the couple were each obliged to use the same. Over the next ten years, ten per cent opted to use the wife's name. In Britain and France (cf. p. 115) there is nothing in law to prevent a woman using her own name, but custom has dictated that she takes her husband's name, something that some younger women are starting to rebel against.

CANADA. Release of the Denys Arcand film *Decline of the American Empire*, in which four men and four women talk about sex, in sparkling dialogues, which are by turns provocative and moving. They tackle each other about the failure of sexual liberation, hypocrisy and the lies in love, described as a "feeling which lasts for four years". They are all obsessed by pleasure, ...

have children ..." The singer defended herself against insinuations, "I am nearly forty, it's a time for calm reflection not adventure. I have my career and Pippo has his. They may cross, but they will never conflict nor one rely on the other."

However, Baudo's life changed, he left the television studio to be with his wife. He accompanied this hard-working artist, whose diary was full three years in advance, on tour. In 1986 he declined to present the San Remo festival. "Today we are still discovering the joy and pleasure of getting to know each other," he said, a year after they were married. To their great disappointment they did not have any children. They had a house in Rome, but preferred to live in Spoleto. In 1990 she explained that they had found a *modus vivendi*. "Not liv-

ing together all the time makes the relationship stronger," she said. She travelled the world while he was busy between Rome and Milan. They arranged to meet almost every weekend. Sometimes he travelled with her, sometimes they joined up where she was performing.

In 1987, tempted by an offer from Silvio Berlusconi, Baudo left the public broadcasting service for a private channel, then alternated between the two. Despite professional problems which troubled the couple, their relationship appears to be stable and rumours of discord without substance. Katia Ricciarelli is at her husband's side when he is ill and when her voice is giving her trouble. "Pippo's simplicity and humility are moving," she declared, and said that she was touched by his "continued desire to study and improve himself".

♡ ♡ ♡

Sensuality
Devil in the Flesh

Oral sex becomes more widespread, despite reservations.

Marco Bellocchio's film *Devil in the Flesh* (1986) with its famous scene of fellatio, brought this sexual practice out of the pornographic ghetto, as actress Maruschka Detmers was forced to explain these 17 scandalous seconds in 857 interviews!

Stimulation of a man's penis by using the lips or tongue leading to ejaculation is properly known as fellatio (from the Latin word meaning "to suck"). It is known in the vernacular as a "blow job". The corresponding practice with a woman is called *cunnilingus*, formed from two Latin words literally meaning "vulva-licker". In the so-called '69' position (cf. p. 314), the lovers lie head to tail and caress each other's genitals with the mouth.

Dismissed by those people who associate sex which is not aimed at procreation with obscenity and sin, oral sex practised in private between consenting adults is still condemned in many countries at the end of the twentieth century as an

act against nature, for example in Singapore, or in certain southern states of America. In Virginia, a woman living together as a couple with another woman was forced in 1994 to fight for custody of her child because of their "immoral" sexual practice. Is the caress given by Isis to arouse Osiris, shown in an illustration in the Egyptian *Book of the Dead*, to be condemned? In a world which has forgotten the link between eroticism and the sacred (cf. p. 264) are poets the only people to believe that love makes the loved person divine? The Belgian writer Suzanne Lilar celebrates "the most humble of caresses, ... that, when feelings of shame are replaced by worship, is turned about and rapidly transformed into supreme veneration."

"I kissed you like a robin redbreast in my hand"; for the poet Marie Dauguet it was a palpitating bird, but the penis has been described also as a sacred pillar, a root of life, a trunk, a tree whose sperm is the sap, or even a ripe fruit ("My stem bursts out beneath your lips like a plum in July," wrote Apollinaire). As for the vulva, from the *Song of Songs* onwards (cf. p. 264), it has been compared to a flower or a

fruit (cf. pp. 58 and 395). Reference is also made to its salty aroma.

FOR PLEASURE. Surveys on sexual behaviour carried out since the forties (cf. p. 226) show that the practice of oral sex is on the increase. It grows with the level of education, and in the United States is more prevalent among whites than blacks. It also varies with age, and is favoured more by the young. Age is no bar however: to quote an old Roman saying "Thaïs, why do you keep telling me that I am too old. You are never too old to lick."

A man differs from a woman in that the penis can be regarded as distinct from the body, whereas fondling a woman's sexual parts implies an invasion of her inner self. For both, however, these are the most sensitive erogenous zones. For a man, pleasure is prolonged by varying the intensity of the caress, and breaking off from time to time. The clitoris, on the other hand, which is the size of a grape stone and endowed with extraordinary sensitivity, means that the minutest movement or slightest pressure is sufficient to provoke a range of sensations. In both cases, rough treatment can be painful.

Sex and Death Double 69, Bruce Naumann, 1985.

The reactions of the person being caressed allows the giver to make subtle variations, but the same caress may elicit differing degrees of pleasure, depending upon the particular occasion. Initiation into the pleasures of sex can be compared to an apprenticeship which the couple undertakes together, at the same time giving free rein to the imagination.

FEAR AND IGNORANCE. Oral sex features heavily in pornography (cf. p. 340) and is often associated with prostitution and homosexuality. Individuals react differently to what is taboo. While some may be aroused others may be shocked. Since oral

sex involves all the senses, including taste and smell, there are people who may find the sexual organs of the other repugnant. Equally, if a person is not comfortable with his own body, and is ashamed of the way the sexual organs look or their scent, it is sometimes difficult to relax and enjoy the pleasure of being fondled: the individual only "lends" himself, instead of "giving". In order to surmount these psychological barriers, it requires patience and subtlety, to promote confidence and communication. It sometimes happens that a new approach can dispel an old inhibition.

Ignorance and taboos always have a severe impact on sexual be-

haviour. Ovid's advice in *The Art of Loving* remains invaluable: "When you find the place that a woman likes to be fondled, modesty should not prevent you from fondling it." The majority of men do not know where the clitoris is (cf. p. 344) and many women do not even know that they have one. In western culture, which is very misogynist, the vulva is devalued, as use of the word "cunt" in a pejorative sense shows. For many men, female sexuality is a "dark continent" as Freud called it, which they make no attempt to explore. If they fondle a woman, it is to arouse her and prepare her for penetration, rather than for bringing her to orgasm.

Some men prefer fellatio to penetration, because they are subconsciously afraid of the vagina, or because they want a more passive role. Conversely, men who like to keep control are embarrassed by a woman taking the lead. Depending upon the power relationship within the couple, oral sex can be interpreted as the act of appropriating the other's sexual organ, or on the contrary of submitting to his desires. What is pleasurable for some may be humiliating for others.

The meaning of sex is limited to whatever interpretation an individual chooses to place on it. Respecting the other person is to take account of their desires, their contradictions and their personal history. Loving the sex organs of the other person and to show it by means of the mouth is one way of demonstrating love for the whole person. Deriving pleasure from this method of fondling leads to a feeling of being recognised and accepted in the totality of one's body.

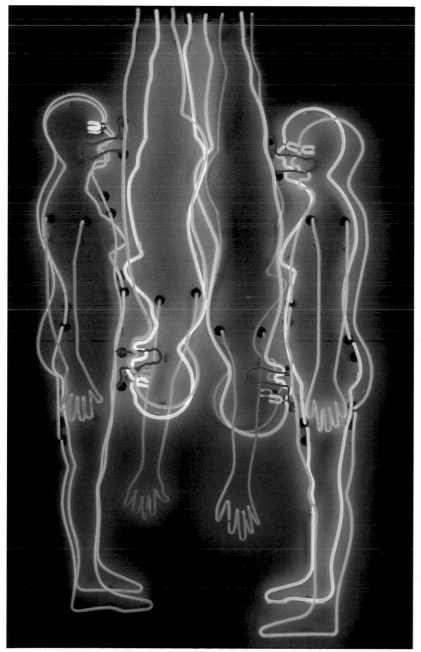

... the men talk about the G-point, and one woman says that she cannot bear "the condescension of men who have made [her] enjoy it". Very funny in parts, the film leaves a bitter taste of disappointment.

HOLLYWOOD. Release of the film *Children of a Lesser God* by Randa Haines, based on the play by Mark Medoff, telling the awe-inspiring love story which develops between a young deaf girl (played by Marlee Matlin who was herself deaf) and her teacher (William Hurt) through his original methods of teaching. Performed in France in 1992, the play saw the emergence of the pretty, deaf actress Emmanuelle Laborit. She married Jean Dalric, who both directed the film and played the part of the teacher.

FRANCE. "Love stories usually come to a bad end," the Rita Mitsouko duo sings. The singer Catherine Ringer and guitarist Fred Chichin had their first hit in 1984 with *Marcia Baïla*. They lived together and composed their own songs, such as *Little Darlings* (1993), dedicated to their daughters.

Demi Moore & Bruce Willis

Two Hollywood stars married, formed a model family, and continued to be provocative.

"I was not expecting to fall in love when I met Bruce Willis," Demi Moore recalled. "After splitting up with Emilio Estevez, I decided to stay on my own for a year. When Bruce came to a viewing with a mutual friend, although he was interested in me I stayed aloof, because he had a reputation as a ladies' man. But when he asked me for my telephone number I forgot my vow to stay single.

He called me the next morning and we have been together ever since. We got married on impulse on 21 No-

vember 1987. Later I remembered that it was exactly a year to the day that we had first met."

Bruce Willis was thirty-two and Demi Moore twenty-five. In the public's eyes they soon became a model couple. "Bruce gives me the strength that I lack, and I do the same thing for him." They both built up their careers with determination, and their success stems solely from their own efforts. They both came from poor, small-town families, he from New Jersey and she from New Mexico. He said: "What has happened to me is the

Photograph
by Annie Leibovitz.

very epitome of the American dream. The person who gets off his butt and works hard can make it." At first, Bruce Willis was a workman, like his father, and although as a teenager he was afflicted with a terrible stammer, he wanted to become an actor. He went to New York, where he played small stage parts, and in 1984 landed a role in the Sam Shepard play *Fool for Love*. He became involved with alcohol and drug abuse. It was the success of the television series *Moonlighting* which launched his career in 1985. In the cinema he appeared in *Blind Date* and, as an accomplished musician, he had a hit album with *Return of Bruno* (1986). From then on Bruce Willis was able to command astronomical sums to appear in films. As his hair began to thin, he established himself in *Die Hard* and *Sunset* as an action-film hero, in the mould of Sylvester Stallone or Arnold Schwarzenegger.

Demi Moore, born Demetria Guynes, explained that her driving force came from her difficult childhood, with unstable parents and a serious eye problem which was resolved only after two operations. At the age of nineteen she married the rock star Freddy Moore, whom she divorced. She later had an affair with the actor Emilio Estevez. Small, dark and pretty, with expressive green eyes and a husky voice, she made her first appearance in the television series *General Hospital* and later appeared in several films. She drank and took drugs, but in 1985 she gave them up for good, which demonstrated, according to her friend Tom Cruise, her unusual strength of character.

PREGNANT AND SEXY. Bruce Willis also stopped drinking after they got married. They had three daughters, Rumer Glenn, born in 1988, Scout LaRue in 1991, and Tallulah Belle in 1994. In order to experience "all the sensations of motherhood", she gave birth without the use of anaesthetics. She blossomed when she became a mother, "I said that I would improve with each baby, and I have proved it."

Willis was present at each birth and said that they would continue to have children until they produced a son. He was a caring father, and quite at home with nappies and feeding bottles. The couple made it a rule never to be apart for more than two weeks when they were shooting a film. As far as the other aspects of their life are concerned, they are "like everybody else. We go to the cinema at the weekend, we rent videos, we lounge about at home, we go swimming, we go to the beach."

Their daughters played with the Schwarzenegger children, their neighbours in Malibu (cf. p. 346). Bruce Willis went skiing with "Schwarzie". As fathers aware of their responsibilities, they discussed the difficulty of combining professional and family life. As for Demi Moore, she said, "I am madly ambitious, and without a

career I would feel frustrated. I would not be complete without my children, so I do things in double quick time, so that I can have both." She became a star with her part in *Ghost* (1990), and caused a furore in August 1991, when she was photographed by Annie Leibovitz, posing for the cover of *Vanity Fair* magazine naked and eight months pregnant. "Bruce supported me 100 per cent, telling me that I was beautiful and that I had never looked so sexy. People said it was indecent. What was indecent about it? It was an ad for family values!"

Involved with women's rights – in 1996 she made a film for the right to abortion and also acted in it – she said of this photograph, "I like to think that I created an awareness of the repressive attitude towards women's bodies." As someone who kept in shape with intensive training, she wanted to remove the barriers, both objective and subjective, which are an obstacle to women. She played roles as a mother ready to do everything for

1987

LONDON. **Kenneth Branagh and Emma Thompson meet while shooting the BBC series** *Fortunes of War*, **and they marry in 1989. She is the daughter of well-known actors, and he is a brilliant Shakespearean actor. Young, talented, and good-looking, overflowing with energy and joie de vivre, they made a dream couple. The English newspapers compared them to Laurence Olivier and Vivien Leigh (cf. p. 192), without the madness. Branagh directed his wife in four films, in which he also starred: Shakespeare's** *Henry V* **and** *Much Ado about Nothing*, *Dead Again*, **and** *Peter's Friends*. **Emma Thompson was a feminist, who said that there were no interesting roles for actresses over the age of thirty. She was the first person to win two Oscars, one as an actress for Margaret Schlegel in** *Howard's End*, **and the other for her screen-play for** *Sense and Sensibility*. **Kenneth Branagh continued a dual career as actor and film-maker (** *Mary Shelley's Frankenstein*). **They divorced in 1995, announcing that sadly their busy working lives had kept them apart too much.**

♡ ♡ ♡

her children, and also as strong-willed heroines in *Indecent Proposal*, *Disclosure* or *In Pursuit of Honour*, where she plays a lesbian GI with a shaven head. She formed a production company and looked for "projects which create parts for other kinds of women, and role-models for young girls". She co-produced *Mortal Thoughts* (1991) in which she starred with her husband.

ENERGY AND SENSUALITY. Demi Moore said of herself that she was not a very good actress. Her phenomenal success has irritated more than a few people. When she became the highest paid actress in Hollywood she declared that it would "help women. The gap with what men earn is closing." Bruce Willis meanwhile made a number of Hollywood blockbusters, and had an enor-

mous success with *Bonfire of the Vanities*. In order to expand the range of his repertoire he also starred in independent films, such as *Pulp Fiction*, which brought him the title as the world's sexiest man. Are they rivals? "There is no room between us for fear or insecurity due to the other's success. We don't need competition. What a waste of time, what a waste of one's life," she said. When Donna Karan, the New York dress designer, asked them to pose for an advertisement for her in 1996, it was, she said, because "nobody embodies energy, emotion, and sensuality better than they do." Would they be spared the jealousy and bitterness that plague Hollywood couples? Rumours have been denied, but rows have been followed by rows and the reconciliations have been ever shakier. The split came in 1998.

♡ ♡ ♡

MYTH
Fatal Attraction

The return of the bitch to the screen provokes a strong reaction among male film-goers.

Sharon Stone and Michael Douglas in *Basic Instinct*.

If there is anything worse than the "bitch", Hollywood's latest dramatic creation, it is the "bitch" who is proud of it. From *Fatal Attraction* (1987) to *To Die For* (1994) by way of *Basic Instinct* and *Last Seduction*, the main characters played by Glenn Close, Nicole Kidman, Sharon Stone or Linda Fiorentino, could be described by the last-named's stark observation: "I am a total fucking bitch."

The vamp of the early cinema (cf. p. 88), then the tart of the wicked films of the forties (cf. p. 168) disappeared as the emancipation of women brought more complex characters to the cinema. This shift gave the impression that the idea of equality between men and women in work as well as in love, was more widely accepted. It was an illusion, as this series of successful films demonstrates, contrasting the "good wife" who stays at home to look after the children, and the "bad wife", whose aggressive sexuality threatens the

"supreme value", that is to say, the family. Has the "battle-axe" of the old days become the ice-pick of *Basic Instinct*?

In this film, a praying mantis in a chic suit and high heels, a career woman crazed with ambition, appears to have planned the destruction of the male, whom she sizes up with a carnivorous smile. Before her is a man, slightly weak and who does not punch his weight; perfectly suited to this role, Michael Douglas embodies in *Fatal Attraction*, *Basic Instinct*, and *Disclosure* the decent sort of man, hypnotised then destabilised, a powerless victim in the clutches of an authoritarian and predatory woman.

MEN HATE HER. The ordinary man at close quarters with a possessive female psychopath is a classic theme in psychological dramas; Clint Eastwood dealt with the theme subtly in *Play Misty for Me* (1971). If *Fatal Attraction*, a succinct psychological film, was a success, it was because the moral ending shows the mood of the moment: the legitimate couple facing the infamous female home-wrecker; during a bathroom scene of hair-raising tension, the husband tries to drown her, but it is finally the wife who

kills her with a bullet to the heart.

Glenn Close played the main role and, according to one magazine, she was "the most hated woman in America". The character she plays is what the adulterous husband thoroughly deserves. The man, who thought he was having a short-lived fling, sees her transform herself into a "Venus attached to her prey," then in a fury thirsting for blood. He repulses her in vain, she attacks him and destroys what she believes to be the obstacles to their relationship. Overwhelmed with cruelty she cooks his son's pet rabbit which she has stolen from the garden. There is a reference to this scene in the British film comedy *Four Weddings and a Funeral* (1993, cf. p. 421). The main characters spend a night together, and when they wake up, the woman announces that they are going to get married. When he thinks that she is joking, he says, "I thought I was in *Fatal Attraction* ... and I was going to get home and find my pet rabbit on the stove."

Although there were parallel films with male heroes involved in spectacular violence, such as Rambo and Terminator, the Hollywood cinema appeared to be taking up again the old themes of the fear of maternal and female omnipotence. When *Fatal Attraction* was released in the United States, men hurled abuse at the evil woman when the wife killed her. "I have never seen such aggression in the cinema," said film director Adrian Lyne, "Once, I was so afraid that I left."

More than the fear of AIDS (cf. p. 416) which is never referred to, or the condom, the return to the screen of the *femme fatale* can be explained by the panic of men faced with a "new woman" (cf. p. 408). The proliferation of monstrous female characters reflects the anxiety of the average white male whose status is under threat. By applauding when they are punished, a man is avenging his own frustrations, identifying with the victim in the

clutch of harpies ready to do anything to achieve their ends.

HAVE WOMEN TOO MUCH FREEDOM? It would be possible to argue that far from encouraging monogamy, as some observers of social trends maintain, films such as *Fatal Attraction* produce a dislike for sex. The message is quite clear, a single passing fancy can unleash catastrophes, because sex is a serious and even dangerous affair. Female desire is assimilated into absolute evil and the modern-day Circe or Lorelei who use their sexual power to attract men, are very often portrayed as "bitches" out to destroy them. According to one female script writer, "American society is resisting modern women's

way of life, and it wants to punish "new women". This is translated in Hollywood to mean, if single women are unhappy, it is because they have too much freedom. Freedom has deprived them of the joys of marriage and motherhood. In the mind, "mother" is always taken to mean the opposite of "bitch", and in real life, women are called upon to make a choice between the two, which are presented as radical and irreconcilable models.

In reality, the majority of sex crimes are committed by men, although there are members of both sexes who are "hooked" on love or sex, or the mentally ill who harbour delusions of being loved by the person they stalk, such as a film star. Such people have often been deprived of love in infancy and are ready to do anything to get it. Conversely, a pathological mistrust leads some people, who are always on the defensive, to feel that they are under attack at the least hint of an approach. Misunderstandings can poison a relationship when a person like this who feels "stifled" (cf. p. 383) is reluctant to make a clean break, leaving an ambiguity which encourages the other in a vain hope. In the Hollywood tradition, these are women who are the victims of screen violence; the brutality they tolerate is a constant ingredient, and is depicted with complacency in other films such as *Silence of the Lambs*, *Batman*, or *Dick Tracy*.

According to some feminists, the uncommon figure of the "bitch", who turns the moral code on its head and makes an object of the man, offers a different perspective: seeing Sharon Stone grab the castratory ice pick could provoke a secret pleasure of revenge. As far as this is concerned, *Last Seduction* is the most immoral of all, as the heroine, with superior intelligence, manipulates men but evades any form of punishment.

1987

UNITED STATES. **Love at first sight during shooting of the film *Bull Durham* between Susan Sarandon, forty-one, and Tim Robbins, twenty-nine. Brought up by a feminist mother, the actor said that he was not afraid of women with strong personalities. They have a happy marriage with two sons, and continued to follow their separate careers.**

CHINA. **Release of *Red Sorghum* by Zhang Yimou. This film brought the famous Chinese filmmaker to the attention of the West, together with his very pretty and talented leading lady, Gong Li. They made ten films together (notably *Wives and Concubines*, *The Story of Qiu Ju* and *To Live*). Their love affair was opposed by the Chinese authorities. Although he was separated from his wife, Zhang Yimou was not allowed to live with Gong Li. The couple enjoyed great notoriety among Chinese around the world, for whom Gong Li was both an idol and a symbol of the new China. During shooting of *Shanghai Triad* (1995) she split up with Zhang Yimou. In 1996, she married a businessman from Singapore.**

"Love is a dream in the sun, but a night-time reality."

JULIA KRISTEVA,
Black Sun

Bob Kersee
& Jackie Joyner

A successful coach marries one of his athletes and makes her into a great champion.

The winning jump by Jackie Joyner, gold medallist in the heptathlon at Seoul.

Two magnificent black American women athletes, Florence Griffith Joyner ("Flo-Jo") and Jackie Joyner Kersee, caused a sensation at the 1988 Olympic Games in Seoul. Joyner won gold medals in the 100 metres and 200 metres, both in new world record times. Kersee was long jump champion and also established a new world record in the heptathlon, which involves seven disciplines. These two athletes were sisters-in-law. Florence Griffith was married to Al Joyner, Jackie's brother, himself the winner of three gold medals in track and field at the 1984 Games. All three athletes had the same coach, Bob Kersee, who married Jackie in 1986. Always dressed in dark colours, bearded and wearing a baseball cap nearly all the time, he used to watch them from the stands.

Bob Kersee was also coach to Ben Johnson, the sprinter disqualified from the 100 metres after a positive dope-test. Suspicions therefore fell on the female medal-winners in his stable, whose overt femininity in the stadium with their long hair, jewellery, make-up, lacquered nails and sexy outfits in bright colours, could not disguise their impressive muscular frames. However, all their dope-tests proved negative. Bob Kersee defended himself saying, "A lot of things have been written about me. They said I was a guru, a slave driver, a chemist, but no one wrote that I was simply a *good coach*." According to him the only secret of "his" athletes is their capacity for hard work.

Born in 1952, Bob Kersee was the son of a Baptist preacher, and he too started out in the same vocation. Obstinate and rigorous, terribly demanding of his athletes, he obtained spectacular results: with his wife and sister-in-law, with the equally famous Valerie Briscoe-Hooks who won the 200 metres gold medal at the 1984 Olympics, and with Gail Devers whom he encouraged to carry on with her career despite serious illness and who won the 100 metres gold medal in 1996.

He trained his athletes on the campus of UCLA (University of California in Los Angeles), where he was in charge of athletics. Noticing Jackie Joyner's diverse talents on the basketball court, he directed her towards the heptathlon. Born in 1962 to a poor family in East Saint Louis, Illinois, she was called Jackie after Jackie Kennedy. She was a very restless child. Her father, a

railway employee, devoted all his time to her elder brother Al. Later it was Florence Griffith the "100 metre-tigress" who cast a shadow over her, since Jackie Joyner, smiling and calm, was more reserved.

"Defeat has its good side, it gives you a goal," Jackie Joyner said in 1984 when she was a few points short of the gold medal in the heptathlon, which she went on to win in 1988 and 1992. Thanks to the stimulating competition of the German Heike Drechsler, she enjoyed twelve years of glory. With her many wins and world records in the heptathlon and long jump, she compiled an impressive honours' list.

TRAINER AND HUSBAND. Jackie Joyner and Bob Kersee had been such close friends for a long time, that no one noticed that they had fallen in love. He asked her to marry him while they were watching a baseball match. "I knew it was serious, " he said, "because we were not paying any attention to the game." They then discussed the possible repercussions of their relationship. "We were afraid that if things did not work out, our wonderful friendship might be at risk," she recalled, "and we did not want that to happen."

When Kersee was at home he refused to discuss work, and when he was at the track he was no longer a husband, Jackie is reported as saying. In Tokyo at the 1991 World Championships, when she hurt her ankle, he ran towards her to console her. "For a moment he was my husband, then he decided that I could continue, and he told me to put on a bandage and carry on. That's what I did." He explained: "The coach took over from the husband. I would never tolerate the presence of a husband or wife while I was busy with an athlete. Therefore I had to push the husband aside."

In 1988, the International Athletics Federation awarded Jackie the title "Athlete of the Year", and again in 1994. The public admired her as much for her performances as for her generosity, when she consoled her unfortunate rivals. At the Games in Atlanta in 1996, she was injured in the first event of the heptathlon and had to abandon it, but she continued to compete in the long jump, and won the bronze medal on one leg. She retired at the age of thirty-four, having thought about it for several months, and deciding that the time had

quent in mixed disciplines such as skating. It is not often that athletes of completely different disciplines marry, as in the case of Michelle Smith, the Irish swimmer, and Erik de Bruyn, the Dutch discus thrower, who both won gold medals at Atlanta in 1996.

The wife a star, the husband in the shade, a Pygmalion (cf. p. 76) proud of a success to which he has contributed: like Jackie Joyner and Bob Kersee, other couples have met in a woman's sport, or in other fields (such as the singer Elisabeth Schwarzkopf and her "master" Walter Legge, cf. p. 219).

Who better than a husband-cum-coach can help his wife to excel, and use her for his own self-esteem, as in the case of Fanny Blankers-Koen (cf. p. 225)? At the Atlanta Olympics there were a number of couples, such as athlete Gwen Torrence and Manley Waller, cyclist Jeannie Longo and Patrice Ciprelli, and athlete Ludmila Engqvist, who joked about the position: "Johan is my husband, my agent and my trainer rolled into one. A single person with three functions, it's much cheaper that way."

come to start thinking about a family. Pointing to the track, Bob Kersee said, "One day, I want to be at the finishing line with my children and say 'Look, I saw your mother win here.'"

WINNING TEAMS. Love stories between athletes of the same discipline are not uncommon, but are more fre-

♡ ♡ ♡

WRITINGS
Salt on Our Skin

Erotic literature used to be a male domain. Now it is the turn of women to put their fantasies on paper.

While the novel *Salt on Our Skin* published by Benoîte Groult in 1988, celebrating female pleasure with a cheerful candour, was moderately successful in its home country, France, in Germany and Scandinavia it was an outright winner. Born in 1920, the author, an established novelist happily married to writer Paul Guimard, was also known as a feminist activist since her vigorous essay *So Be It* (1975). Her novel, which is a defence and an illustration of the "sin of the same old thing", is written in the first person by a woman describing with accuracy and without crudity, the pleasure which her lover gives her. In a story intercut with sections in italics, her inner voice of reason represented as a cantankerous chaperone, who pours cold water

over her amorous ecstasies, George, a female Parisian intellectual, tells of her secret affair with Gauvain, a Breton sailor. It is a story which lasts throughout their lives, running in parallel with their married lives. Their social differences are so great that it is impossible for them to be together in any other way, so they meet in places all over the world, for brief and splendid sex. This "bumpkin conceals the most delicate of experts", he is "intelligent in love, unlike most men", but he is more than just an accomplished lover, as this description of the loving man shows: "The only man who truly loves you is the one before whom you can show your superiority without dashing his self-esteem or causing bitterness."

For Benoîte Groult, "feminism has broken the moral yoke which was suffocating women. They have won a freedom of movement which would have been unthinkable years ago. I wanted to write a story where, for once, a woman would be free of all moral strictures without being

punished for it. My heroine is not punished for loving or being loved." At the end it is Gauvain who dies, leaving George, "the certitude of having received from him all that was capable of radiating love."

FEMALE FANTASIES. While deploring that "the vocabulary describing female pleasure is revealed even among the best authors as being amazingly impoverished," Benoîte Groult was aware of the risks she was taking: "When a woman talks about sex, it always seems to be obscene." She took up the challenge and dared to use the appropriate words for clear and strong images. By comparing the vulva to a flower or fruit, she was following in a rich poetic tradition. In the world of the imagination, the vulva has sometimes been taken to resemble a terrifying crevice opening on to a "vagina with teeth". Whereas in the West it has provoked so much hypocrisy and fear, oriental art (cf. p. 68) has praised it as a lotus flower or peach. Western poets, in the tradition of the *Song of Songs* (cf. p. 264) also describe it as a flower – often a rose – or a fruit. For Marguerite Burnat-Provins (cf. p. 58) it was a fig, for Apollinaire or Francis Ponge it was an apricot. Paul Eluard wrote: "And you open like a ripe fruit, oh, delicious one." For other women it is "my nest of flesh" (Andrée Chédid), "the hungry flower" (Olympia Alberti) and "my anemone with petals of flesh" (Céline Willocq), whilst the penis is seen as "the root of the world" (Violette Leduc), "the living cigar" (Joyce Mansour) or the "fabulous serpent" (Emmanuelle Arsan).

In the early twentieth century, female poets (cf. p. 58) were breaking new ground in their lyrical invitation to pleasure. Whilst not forgetting the power of erotic evocation of texts such as the novels of Colette (cf. p. 34), *Anna Soror* by Marguerite Yourcenar or most of Marguerite Duras' work, it has to be accepted that erotic literature was effectively the preserve of men. At the end of the twentieth century, the prophecy of the author of the *Story of O* (cf. p. 252) has come true: "Women, these silent creatures ... had nothing to say. Well, that is over, they are going to speak, they are speaking." In reality, they expressed their erotic fantasies in increasing numbers. Publishers welcomed their bold imagination and the public followed in droves.

From the eighties onwards, young female novelists started to use crude language to describe the violence of desire and sex. Books written by new authors, such as *The Ages of Loulou* by the Spanish writer Almudena Grandes, or *Butcher* by French woman Alina Reyes, were very successful. In *Dirty Weekend* or *True Romance*, the English writer Helen Zahavi describes sexual ad-

ventures and a destructive madness with excoriating humour, whilst the Austrian Elfriede Jelinek, author of *The Pianist* and the licentious *Lust* showed a ferocious bitterness, completely lacking in affection.

Apricot, Nelly Trumel.

WRITING ABOUT DESIRE. Before censorship was relaxed, erotic books circulated clandestinely. Today they are sold by reputable publishers, most of whose novels contain sex scenes. "There is no more perturbation, because there is no sin," claimed Jean-Jacques Pauvert, an expert on de Sade. New novelists often have a very hard view of human relationships and their descriptions have a clinical precision, but they do not challenge the order. They publish under their own names, their heads held high. Amazed at their apparent knowledge and well-ordered lives, men tend to attribute the adventures of the heroines in the books to the writers themselves, who are irritated and disconcerted at the suggestion.

In addition to these novels, volumes and anthologies of erotic texts have also been very successful in the West, as well as cheap reprints and collections with provocative titles such as *The Vertical Smile* in Spain or *Black Lace* in Great Britain. Men usually form the largest part of the readership. Fantasies sometimes have "local colour", such as the

tendency to sado-masochism in Spain and an attraction to prostitution in France.

Some female authors use the male stereotype in their account of the progress of a heroine who is free, or who liberates herself by a series of sexual adventures in which, by submitting to the whims of the man, she becomes the mistress of the game. Other have fresh ideas, such as Benoîte Groult, whose writing avoids the tyranny of physical beauty and youth. According to Régine Deforges, a publisher of erotic books in the sixties who became a very popular novelist, women write in a more natural way, their descriptions are more closely linked to real life and their affairs are more complex. While visual methods of arousal such as pornographic films (cf. p. 340) appear to be a masculine approach, female writing gives an insight into the twists and turns of desire. "What is the point of seeing, and seeing what you already know," wrote Alina Reyes, "when you can enjoy mystery?" Times have changed (cf. p. 408), men have in turn become objects of desire and women are not afraid to show it. For a woman, wrote Annie Ernaux, "the freedom to write without shame far exceeds that of being the first woman to touch, with desire, the body of a man."

A good erotic book is a good short book. It requires talent on the part of the author to maintain the tension and hold the reader's interest. Women add an additional perspective; in common with the author of *Story of O*, who wrote to please Jean Paulhan – the first person to read the manuscript of what he called a "love letter" – so the books of young female novelists are very often dedicated to the man they love.

1988

"He entered into the spirit of love, of claiming to love for ever, but knowing that he would only love once; showing that the *truth* of love does not accord with the *experience* of love."

CLÉMENT ROSSET
The Principle of Cruelty

SWEDEN. A law is passed to put cohabitation on a par with marriage, including the division of assets. The following year a law was passed saying that childless couples had to be married for the survivor to receive a retirement pension, which provoked a doubling in the number of marriages from 42,000 in 1988 to 106,500 in 1989. In France, a provision of the 1996 Finance Act produced a rise of 10 per cent in the number of marriages, from 254,600 in 1995 to 279,000 in 1996. The reason was that single parents with children who cohabited would receive only one half of the tax allowance calculated on their income. Cohabiting couples were therefore encouraged to "regularise" their situation, since for the year in which they married, there was favourable tax treatment.

♡ ♡ ♡

Cindy Crawford
& Richard Gere

A Hollywood star and a famous model made a dream couple who did not survive the times or the pressure.

In Hollywood in 1989, Herb Ritts the fashion photographer introduced his friend the actor, Richard Gere, to Cindy Crawford, one of the models he was working with at the time. "It was not love at first sight," she recalled, "we

friend Jody Foster, "he hates talking about himself." He became a Buddhist, and since 1978 he has supported the Tibetan resistance, and is involved with the protection of indigenous peoples and the environment.

Cindy Craw-

saw each other once. Then again another time. We started to get interested in each other." On their first dinner engagement, Gere arranged to pick her up from home. With his usual annoying habit, he was an hour late. This was not the style of a young woman who was always punctual and well-organised, but that day it worked out well, she said later, as she could not decide what to wear. Nominated "the sexiest man in America" in 1985 by *Newsweek* magazine, Gere was thirty-nine, slim, and softly-spoken. Cindy Crawford, with a distinctive facial beauty-spot, was already famous at the age of twenty-three. Handsome and wealthy, they made a perfect couple whose photographs were always eagerly seized on by magazines.

Richard Gere was born in Philadelphia, Pennsylvania, but the family moved to Syracuse in upstate New York when he was a boy, after his father left the family to sell insurance. He made his début in the theatre at a very early age, and inevitably then moved on to Hollywood. In 1980 *American Gigolo* established him as a sex symbol, whether he liked it or not. "If the role demands it," he said, "I am not embarrassed about undressing, but to call me a sex symbol, that's crazy." He had some successes – *Yanks, An Officer and a Gentleman* –, but other films were less well-received before the blockbuster triumph of *Pretty Woman* (1990). A lady's man, he has often had stormy relationships with the press and gives few interviews. "He's a big baby," said his

ford was born in De Kalb, Illinois. Her father was an electrician. Her parents divorced when she was seventeen. "At fifteen I was already grown up, I earned pocket money doing housework and working in the cornfields." She went to New York in 1986 and embarked on a career as a model, which rapidly took off: in 1988 her photograph appeared on the covers of 250 magazines around the world.

Marriage and rumours. Crawford wanted to get married and have children, but Gere resisted. On 12 December 1991 they had it out. "Your family is coming for Christmas," she pleaded. "That makes twenty-five people. I shall be doing the cooking and looking after everybody. Why should I put myself to so much trouble if you refuse to marry me?" He was convinced, and two hours later they flew off quietly to Las Vegas to get married.

As in similar cases in Hollywood, the tongues started to wag. Was it a marriage of convenience? Richard Gere and Cindy Crawford were a "committed" couple like actors Susan Sarandon and Tim Robbins (cf. p. 391), which was rare in this industry. In particular they were both activists for homosexual rights. For a long time Gere had been the subject of rumours: his many female conquests were regarded as a cover; gay activists wanted to "out" him. The same kind of rumours targeted other star couples, including illusionist David Copperfield, the "fiancé" since 1993 of top model

Cindy Crawford, photograph by D. Fischer.

FACING PAGE
Richard Gere, photograph by Annie Leibovitz.

Claudia Schiffer. "I am proud to be heterosexual," he declared, while Gere's explanation was somewhat ambiguous: "I cannot say that I am not homosexual, because that would appear that I am defending myself against a moral defect. However, for me, there is no shame in it." As for Cindy Crawford, she posed in *Vanity Fair* in August 1993, bending over the lesbian singer kd lang, and shaving her head. When she was asked about it, she was as evasive as her husband had been, saying that this photograph had merely been a job of work.

In 1992 Cindy Crawford was the highest-paid model in the world. A prudent business woman, she presented a television show, posed for advertisements and launched a series of keep-fit videos. "Nothing has happened to me by chance. All that I have, I have worked for." Wanting "to be a role model for the young girls who admire me," she refused to pose for photographs in a manner she considered undignified, and asserted that she was a feminist, which meant taking her own decisions, including those to pose for *Playboy*.

No RIGHT TO PRIVACY. When Richard Gere was asked if he had a normal life with one of the world's reputedly most beautiful women, he replied with a disarming smile, "What is a normal life?" As for Cindy Crawford, who regarded men as "teenagers with credit cards", she told how once "I was talking to Richard and suddenly he turned his head: I knew that a pretty girl in a short skirt had just come into the room. It's like a reflex with him."

They promised each other not to stay apart for more than a week at a time, but they lived life at a frenetic pace. Their secretaries used to call each other to find where they would be spending the night. The press did not leave them alone, one day announcing a pregnancy, the next day a separation. On 6 May 1994, in exasperation the couple took a whole page in *The Times*, to announce: "We got married because we love each other and we decided to make a life together. We are heterosexual and monogamous and take our commitment to each other very seriously." Referring to the number of causes they supported, they claimed a "basic right to privacy".

Despite all this, their marriage failed, and they divorced in 1995. They each claimed to have learned a lesson: Cindy Crawford believed, wrongly, that marriage would conquer her fear of being abandoned; Richard Gere came to realise that a woman "could not be the key

1989

EUROPE. The collapse of the Berlin Wall marks the same fate for the entire Communist culture. In countries which were fundamentally disorganised, deprived of their moral and ideological benchmarks, and falling prey to the worsening situation of old-style shortages and new miseries such as unemployment, the balance of relations between men and women was bound to be catastrophic; a surge in prostitution and pornography was duly observed.

FRANCE. Release of the Coline Serreau film *Mama, there's a man in your bed*, a fable superbly acted by Daniel Auteuil and Firmine Richard. He plays a white company president and she is a black servant. When he becomes the victim of a swindle, she saves him and takes him in. At first he is ungrateful and egotistical, but he comes to appreciate her generosity. Love opens his eyes and it all ends in a happy marriage.

HOLLYWOOD. Success of the Rob Reiner film *When Harry Met Sally*, starring Billy Crystal and Meg Ryan, which describes with affectionate good humour a couple who are hesitating to become engaged. In a memorable restaurant scene, Harry boasts about his talents as a lover, which are manifested, according ...

to happiness. I have to find it, alone." He then had affairs with other beautiful women. As for Cindy Crawford, after the failure of her film *Fair Game*, she celebrated her thirtieth birthday with Val Kilmer.

Marriages between celebrities and models are not always destined to fail, as those between David Bowie and Iman, David and Estelle Hallyday, and Barbara and Boris Becker (cf. p. 418) prove.

♡ ♡ ♡

SOCIETY
Same-Sex Marriage

Denmark was the first country to legalise same-sex marriages.

On 1 October 1989, Axel and Eigil, two old gentlemen known by the name of Axgil, left the town hall in Copenhagen in triumph, filmed by television crews from around the world. In 1948, having spent time

in prison for immorality, they formed an association for homosexuals claiming their rights. Forty years later, they were at last allowed to marry when Denmark, a pioneering country, legalised "marriage" between homosexuals. The question was raised of why marry and conform to a traditional model. The American homosexual magazine *Outlook*, which claimed to subvert the patriarchal order, asked its readers in 1989, "Since when has marriage led to liberation?" However, a large number of homosexuals are trying to integrate rather than innovate. According to surveys in various countries, the proportion of homosexuals in the population varies between 4 and 8 per cent for men and between 2 and 4 per cent for women. About one third of them live as a couple. What do these candidates for marriage say? "We are a couple with a normal life and aspirations. We want to do the same as everybody else." In a society where the number of marriages is falling (cf. p. 298), what is the significance of the desire to make official and public a bond which is individual and private? "Living in secret makes it fragile, living openly makes it strong." The symbolic aspect counts for a lot. Getting married means winning respectability; solemnising a commitment can change attitudes. There is also a practical consideration in marrying, as the law provides no protection for people living together without a legal agreement. There are no social security entitlements, no benefits from company schemes such as those available to employees' spouses. In the event of death – and the AIDS epidemic (cf. p. 416) has shown what tragedies can occur in the legal void – there is no right of residence for the survivor if a property is not in his name, no right of inheritance, and, if named in a will, a possible tax liability. The sole material advantage is that the partners are not responsible for each other's debts.

AN EVOLVING EUROPE. Condemning the effects on public order of this "triumph of Sodom", opponents of homosexual marriage are afraid that the institution of marriage, "the symbolic foundation of society", will be weakened. For a long time, the law has only recognised homosexuality by repressing it (cf. p. 320). The countries of Scandinavia, which are pragmatic and tolerant when it comes to moral attitudes, were the first to accept homosexuality as a fact. After Denmark it was the turn of Norway: on 1 August 1993, to the acclaim of the assembled crowd and in the presence of the Minister for the Family, the first five gay and lesbian couples were married at the town hall in Oslo. In 1995, Sweden subsumed homosexual partnership into the civil law. Three years later, Kent Carlsson, a promising young social-democrat deputy dared to *come out* and publicly reveal his homosexuality in parliament. "I explained how it was important for homosexual couples to have their relationship legally recognised, and I said that our love is as strong as the love between two heterosexuals."

In the Netherlands, the Supreme Court ruled in vain in 1990 that homosexual marriage was contrary to the law, as militants addressed themselves directly to the municipalities. The law permitting persons of the same sex to register legal partnerships came into force in January 1998. About a hundred Dutch lesbians take advantage each year of artificial insemination. They are forbidden to adopt children, as in Scandinavian countries.

In France, where companies have a social insurance arrangement, the right to benefits was granted in 1993 to any person of the same sex as the insured, provided that he or she was supported finan-

FACING PAGE
The Happy Couple, 1992, photograph by Pierre and Gilles.

cially by the insured person. In 1995, the town hall in Saint-Nazaire, followed by others, started to issue a certificate of cohabitation to homosexual couples, which enabled them to obtain a property lease. Since 1994, officially registered homosexual couples in Spain are entitled to the same rights as married heterosexual couples including paternity leave, a right secured by lesbians in a court case in 1996.

As far as the European institutions are concerned, there are inconsistencies. On the one hand, the Court of Justice confirmed in 1993 that in order to be recognised as a cohabitant and to benefit from rights attached to this status, it was necessary for the partners to be of a different sex. On the other, the European Parliament made a recommendation in 1994 to ensure that homosexual couples are treated equally in matters of adoption, social security, inheritance and housing.

NEW PARENTAL COUPLES. In the United States, San Francisco has been registering "domestic partners" since 1991. "Our town is humane," declared an elected representative, "and respects all people and their love relationships." A positive decision was given in Hawaii in December 1996: following an action against the state, Nina Baehr and Genora Dancel won the right to the same legal and financial benefits as a heterosexual couple. But in Washington the Republican majority pre-empted this move by passing a law some weeks earlier in the defence of marriage, defined as the union of a man and a woman, which allowed each state to refuse to recognise homosexual marriages registered in another state.

Since 1989 several thousand same-sex marriages have been celebrated around the world, 3,000 in six years in Denmark, of which

more than two thirds were between men. In Europe, especially in the north, new battles are currently being fought: for the right to marry in church – 59 per cent of Danes are in favour – and for the right to have children, either by adoption, or by insemination in the case of lesbians. In the United Kingdom there have been some pioneering decisions: in Manchester in 1994 two lesbians were recognised as a "legal parental couple"; in Edinburgh, the first gay couple was allowed to adopt a child in 1996.

Although it is possible to count a thousand such families in San Francisco, the Appeal Court in New York in 1995 recognised the right of homosexuals to adopt the biological child of their partner. According to a judge in Hawaii, "the sexual ori-

entation of the parents does not prevent them from being loving and competent with their children"

Experience has shown that there are all kinds of families, and that heterosexual parents are no guarantee of stability or success. The essential requirement is for children to be brought up by adults between whom there is a rich, long-term relationship which will see them through the whole of their childhood and well into adulthood.

... to him, by the way his girlfriends react. Sally then demonstrates that women can fake an orgasm, which is so convincing that the other diners watch her in wonder, until one female customer says to the waiter, "I'll have what she's having."

UNITED STATES. The Glaser family tragedy rocks the country. Paul Glaser played Starsky in the popular television serial *Starsky and Hutch*. In 1986 his wife Elizabeth revealed that she had contracted AIDS from a blood transfusion she received shortly after the birth of Ariel in 1981, and that she had transmitted the virus to her daughter while she was breast-feeding. Ariel died in 1988. A second child, John, born in 1984 was similarly affected. Only Paul Glaser himself remained free of the infection. His wife wrote of him that it was his "wonderful love" which had helped her in her crusade for the victims of AIDS. She created a foundation for these afflicted children. Admired for her eloquence and her energy, she helped to change the way in which the public viewed AIDS. She died in 1994 and her last words to Paul were: "You and John, make sure that my battle helps the helpless of the world."

Nelson & Winnie Mandela

A glittering image was soon tarnished; after twenty-eight years' separation, the reunion of South Africa's golden couple soon broke down.

FACING PAGE
Nelson Mandela as he leaves the Victor Vester prison after twenty-seven years of incarceration.

In February 1990 the longest serving political detainee in the history of the world, the black opposition leader Nelson Mandela, imprisoned in South Africa since 1962, was released, and returned to his wife Winnie. The photograph of them hand in hand was seen around the world, as a symbol of their country freeing itself from apartheid. But this perfect image was shattered before Mandela could be elected president of the Republic in 1994.

Nelson Mandela and Winnie Madikizela married in 1958. They had two daughters. During the first six years of their marriage, periods of separation for reasons of secrecy or terms in prison meant that they spent a total of only six months together.

They first met in Johannesburg in 1957, when he was thirty-eight and she was twenty-two. For him it was love at first sight for this pretty woman with a gentle face. "Her spirit, her passion, her youth, her courage and her wilfulness – I felt all these things the first moment I saw her." Winnie, for her part, was impressed by his imposing height and his natural air of authority. They both came from Transkei, in the south-east of the country, and belonged to the Xhosa tribe. Winifred Zanyewe Madikizela was the daughter of teachers, and was encouraged by her father to study. She moved to Johannesburg and became the first black female social worker. Nelson Mandela, of princely origin, was brought up to be a future chief, but he left his family in order to escape an arranged marriage. He settled in Soweto, a black township near Johannesburg, where he finished his law studies in extreme poverty. He married Evelyn Mase, a midwife, and they had three children. He was an activist against white power, and beside Walter and Adelaide Sisulu, he became involved in the African National Congress (ANC). He founded the Youth League, the radical wing of the ANC, and became its president. His militant activities took him away from his wife, and they divorced in 1955.

The apartheid regime ("apartheid" means "separation") established in 1948 by the white minority who were in power, legalised discrimination against black people. Nelson Mandela, who had opened the first black lawyers' office in Johannesburg with his friend Oliver Tambo, launched actions of collective civil disobedience, inspired by the non-violent approach of Gandhi. He was brought to trial, where he conducted his own defence. He spent several terms in prison.

CONDEMNED TO LIFE-LONG SEPARATION. "I knew that in marrying him I was espousing the cause of my people," Winnie Mandela said. At their first meeting he asked her to collect money for his trial defence fund. In March 1960 the police fired on the black crowd in Sharpeville demonstrating against the pass laws. Nelson Mandela, acquitted after proceedings lasting four years, went home to collect a suitcase and then disappeared from sight without any explanation being given. "I think that he found it too difficult to tell me, " she wrote. "Despite his power and strength, inside he was very sensitive. When I was washing one of his shirts, I found a piece of paper in the pocket: he had paid the rent for six

months." The ANC, of which he now became leader, was on the point of being banned, and the movement decided to turn to violent action.

Constantly monitored by the police, Winnie Mandela continued to work, and to meet her husband in secret on rare occasions. "I had such little time to love him." In 1962 he made a six-month trip abroad. On his return he was arrested with other leaders of the ANC and sentenced to life imprisonment. "A part of my soul went with him," she wrote. Every six months she travelled nearly a thousand miles to the prison on Robben Island, situated off the Cape, in order to visit him for half an hour, separated by a pane of glass. As the target of constant police harassment, she was arrested several times, and imprisoned and tortured. In 1976, when the police fired on youths in Soweto demonstrating against the compulsory use of the Afrikaans language in schools, which caused outrage world-wide, she came out of the shadows and immediately became the symbol of resistance and the mouthpiece of the ANC. Interviewed by the foreign press, the "mother of the nation" received world-wide support. In 1977 she was forced to live in internal exile at Brandfort, in the Orange Free State. In 1982 Mandela was transferred to prison on the Cape. They were then permitted to see each other once a

month, and, after twenty years of separation, to touch each other.

A WIDENING GULF. When Winnie returned to Soweto in 1985 she lost all sense of proportion. Regarding herself as untouchable because of world opinion, she thought that she could do anything. She became an alcoholic and surrounded herself with a band of gangsters called the Mandela United Football Club, which perpetrated a reign of terror in Soweto. She had a luxurious house built. She inflamed the youth of the townships by violent speeches. In 1989 she was accused of several violent incidents, notably the death of a young militant in the ANC.

International pressure, backed up by economic sanctions as well as the accession to power of Frederick De Klerk in 1989, transformed the political situation and led to the release of Nelson Mandela. After a brief period of euphoria, the husband and wife discovered that they had become strangers. From November 1991 they lived separately, she in Soweto and he in a residential quarter of Johannesburg. Nevertheless, he contin-

ued to support her, and financed her extravagant lifestyle. After a trial in which she caused a furore, she was sentenced to complicity in the murder. The prison sentence was commuted to a fine, which he paid.

Mandela announced their separation "for personal reasons" in April 1992, at the same time declaring that for him she had been an "indispensable support" during his detention, and that his love for her was undiminished. One month later, the press published a letter from Winnie Mandela to her young lover, the lawyer Daluxolo Mpofu.

In 1993, Nelson Mandela and Frederick De Klerk jointly received the Nobel Peace Prize. Winnie Mandela, accused of the misappropriation of funds, stuck to her hard political line, with the support of radicals in the ANC who opposed power-sharing with whites. In 1994 Mandela appointed her to the post of deputy minister, but relieved her of it shortly afterwards. Their divorce was announced in March 1996. After that time he was seen in public with Grace Machel, widow of the president of Mozambique, whom he married in 1998.

♡ ♡ ♡

MORALS
The New Chastity

After sex without love, now love without sex? Young and old learn to wait, and have respect for each other.

A movement advocating sexual abstinence before marriage, and presenting itself as a reaction to the "sexual liberation" (cf. p. 310), developed in the West, particularly in the United States. Many saw this as the way to reduce teenage pregnancies, others saw it as a way of promoting loving relationships which were not sexual. Love without making love? Would this "chastity wave" – "chaste" comes from a Latin word meaning "pure" – turn out to be a cultural revolution or a puritanical tidal wave?

In the United States, the success of this "moral recovery", combined with a rejection of alcohol and drugs, was due to a collective "detoxification". People were forced to admit that self-interested sex, the route to orgasm and sexual frenzy often ended in a feeling of emptiness. A surfeit of sex does not com-

pensate for a lack of love any more than sexual activity in itself makes up for a need for love. "We have nothing against virtue," said the American feminist Kim Gandy, "provided that the "virtuous" do not try to impose on us their idea of good and bad." Also, powerful religious groups, dismayed by widespread acceptance of pre-marital sex (cf. p. 298), condemned the loss of "values", and "sexual promiscuity", preached against pornography (cf. p. 340) and "sex in everything". According to these groups, sexual freedom is only an illusion, because it creates a need for sex.

In the young, a greater sexual precocity (cf. p. 294) is no substitute for a gentle awakening of young love. The person who satisfies his own desires without being able to wait or to give way to those of a partner, through lack of self-control, is immature. Making love because "that is what people do" runs the risk of reducing sex to a habit, to a technique, or to a bulwark against loneliness. Each new sexually-active generation is now faced with the threat of AIDS (cf.

p. 416), and people are encouraged to protect themselves. Far from safe sex, some individuals are tempted to behave in suicidal fashion, and others to take refuge in the kind of bonding relationship, seen between adolescents in German night-clubs, where they dance around slowly for hours on end, entwined together.

AN EFFECTIVE CAMPAIGN. From "chastity clubs" in Spain, where abstinence is presented as the "key to happiness", to the vows taken in public by South Korean students who receive a silver ring as a token of their commitment to abstinence, the "chastity wave" is breaking everywhere, but it is in the United States where "virgin clubs" are being formed, that it has the most popular support. Calls for "sexual and moral purity" take the form of publicity campaigns – "It's good to wait!" – or lessons in abstinence. At a demonstration organised in Washington in 1994 by the *True Love Waits* movement, 200,000 adolescents committed themselves to remain "sexually pure" until marriage. Hillary Clinton herself advocated abstinence until the age of twenty-one: for her it was a way of saying to young people that "they are not always ready to take on the consequences of an early active sex life". Among the stars who signed up to the "new chastity" was the actress Brooke Shields, who said that she would remain a virgin until her big romance came along; she appeared to find it in 1994 with tennis champion André Agassi.

The campaign appears to be working: whereas 54 per cent of college students (aged from sixteen to twenty) in 1990 said that they had an active sex life, the number dropped to 36 per cent in 1994. In the world as a whole, the proportion of young people aged eighteen to twenty-four who have stated their intention to await marriage before sexual relations, is growing. According to a survey in 1994, it reached 19 per cent in the United States, 12 per cent in Australia, 9 per cent in Japan, 6 per cent in Great Britain and Sweden, 4 per cent in Germany and 3 per cent in France.

NO TO SEX! Why is it necessary to have sex, even after marriage? Japan, the country of "love hotels" and porno bars is also a country of "sexless couples". The number of people who are happy in a marriage without sex are neither rare, nor confined to Japan. According to the *Kinsey Report* (cf. p. 226), 2 per cent of couples never made love. Some chose to forego it for mystical reasons, such as the followers of Maritain (cf. p. 51) or like the Woolfs (cf. p. 102) who renounced it after a few years, the Dalís (cf. p. 144) or Aragon and Triolet (cf. p. 140). Where there is abstinence, a loving dialogue may follow, with the bond of marriage remaining strong provided that it is interwoven with mutual understanding and affection (cf. p. 378). There is no risk to the couple unless one of them feels frustrated, ending in a so-called "Narita divorce". Narita is the airport in Tokyo and the phrase was coined to describe couples who decide to get divorced as soon as they return from honeymoon.

With the importance attached nowadays to sexual performance (cf. p. 344) there has been a tendency to regard the absence of a sex life as something of a failure. But it may only represent a temporary phase, as the fashion in California grows for couples to find other forms of intimacy, when the stress of daily life (cf. p. 332) adversely affects sexual relations or the arrival of a baby upsets desire. Could this signal the return of flirtation? There could be a re-learning of how to make love (cf. p. 302), with respect and self-control, which starts with caresses and taking one's time.

The West has been influenced by Plato's notion of a spiritualised and ideal love, which came to be known by the term 'platonic' from the seventeenth century onwards. Restraint, lengthy anticipation and chastity were the keys to courtly love (cf. p. 188). An echo of this is found in the works of Jean Giraudoux, whose heroine Ondine says to the knight: "It is so sweet to wait. We shall remember this time, later on. It is the time when you did not kiss me."

According to whether coitus is seen as a terrifying threat or as the climax to an embrace, chastity may be immoral, according to Otto Weininger who advocates it for a man so that he may avoid "the fatal ascendancy of women", or healthy, since eroticism is inseparable from self-discipline (cf. *Story of O*, p. 252). In *Lady Chatterley's Lover* (cf. p. 142), Lawrence defines it not as a lack, but as a fullness. For lovers who are separated, it is "the peace which comes from having made love together".

1990

CANADA. **"Your back is perfect like a desert/ When the storm has passed over our bodies ... /You are so, so, so, beautiful/ A gift of death/ Sent from heaven"** sang the Quebec singer **Richard Desjardins** in *Tu m'aimes-tu?*

UNITED STATES. **"They turn their back on us in the street/ because we do not come from the same world"**: Selena Quintanilla, an American singer from Houston, singing in Spanish has a hit with *Amour prohibido* (Forbidden Love).

HOLLYWOOD. **Daniel Day Lewis receives an Oscar for his role in *My Left Foot*, an Irish film by Jim Sheridan, based on a book of the same name by painter Christie Brown, in which he tells the story of his life. Born into a working-class Dublin family and paralysed from birth, he has the use only of his left foot. The love which he feels for a young woman doctor helps him to make progress, but she marries someone else. He falls in love with another young woman who learns to love him through his book, and they marry.**

Followers of *True Love Waits*.

Kurt Cobain & Courtney Love

Two "grunge" singers identified with revolt and despair.

Violence, despair and world-weariness: these are the feelings expressed in *Nevermind*, an album by the American band, Nirvana. In 1991, it was a world-wide hit, and started a rock revival. The anger of *Smells Like Teen Spirit*, which criticises young people who have no opinions, and the anxiety of *Lithium*, in which Kurt Cobain repeats in a low-pitched, raucous voice. *"I'm not gonna crash"*, were the negative feelings which helped to create the "grunge" movement. The "grunge look" was characterised by torn clothes, and a filthy and neglected appearance. A whole generation of troubled adolescents empathised with this singer and guitarist, a small man of slight build, with stubble on his cheeks, and straggly hair, who hurled abuse at society, and said that he wanted to change the world. The lyrics, which he wrote himself, were really cries for help.

Kurt Cobain's relationship with Courtney Love began several months earlier. "She and I," he said, "have never had any love in the whole of our lives." He was born in 1967 to a working-class family from a small town near Seattle. His childhood was "immersed in racism and sexism", and he suffered from humiliating treatment by his father. After his parents divorced he became a depressive, but rock music gave him a reason for living. Together with some friends he formed the group Nirvana (Nirvana is the state of supreme happiness in Buddhism, a name which they used tongue-in-cheek). Their first album in 1989 made no impression. The group claimed to be radical, pro-feminist and anti-sexist. With a hyper-sensitive and unstable personality, Kurt Cobain suffered greatly with stomach ailments and was addicted to heroin.

Courtney Love, born Michelle Harrison, was two years older than Cobain. She was the daughter of a San Francisco feminist, Linda Carol. She talked about her father's abuse of her as a child, accusing him of giving her drugs from the age of six. After her parents' divorce, she ran away from home, drifted about, took drugs and became a well-known figure in hippie communes. She was bisexual, had lots of tumultuous love affairs and was married briefly. Domineering and with a violent temper, she invited scandal as an outrageous poseur, with tousled bleached hair, bright red lipstick thickly applied, and short, little-girl dresses which showed her suspenders and plump thighs. She sang with a male band, then, growing tired of its machismo, started the group called Hole in 1990. *Pretty on the Inside*, their first album appeared at the same time as *Nevermind*. It was characterised by the same hysterical rage, but it was badly produced, and met with little success.

PROVOCATION AND HATE. At the end of 1991 Kurt Cobain and Courtney Love made their relationship public. The singer discovered that she was pregnant, and they married secretly in February 1992. He was in tears, she was wearing a dress that had belonged to actress Frances Farmer – their daughter was named after her – whose career was cut short by a stay in a mental hospital, followed by suicide. The provocative behaviour of the mother-to-be – she boasted of taking heroin and continuing to smoke because she wanted "a small baby" – unleashed a campaign against the couple. Social services took their child away, and the parents were able to regain custody only after a court hearing. The media started to pillory Courtney Love: they said that she was responsible for Kurt Cobain's problems, she was called a "junkie mother", and a "tart and groupie with no tal-

JAPAN. **Maurice and Katia Krafft, vulcanologists, are killed on the slopes of Mount Unzen by the cloud of gas preceding an eruption. They were enthusiastic, generous, and intrepid geologists, who came from Alsace. They shared their passion with the public at large through their photographs, lectures, books, and films. They married in 1970 and renounced parenthood in favour of devoting themselves to the "birth of the Earth". They lived by the rhythm of the planet, dashing from one volcanic eruption to another, with the exciting feeling of "sitting on the back of a giant dragon".**

FRANCE. **Publication of *Simple Passion*, a bestseller by Annie Ernaux, about the amorous obsession of a woman. "From the beginning of September, last year, I did nothing apart from wait for a man: to telephone me or visit me." Making herself totally available, the narrator lives through the mystery and the martyrdom of a burning passion, which is a long series of vain waits and ephemeral embraces with a man who finally disappears.**

ent". In between drug-induced collapses and drying-out treatments, they managed to play some improvised music together. Overwhelmed by the success of *Nevermind*, Cobain talked about leaving the group and going to sing with his wife and Hole, or about combining the two groups. Nirvana was working on a new album. Cobain wanted to call it: "I hate myself and I want to die." He gave a characteristically contemptuous reply when he was asked how it was going. The title finally chosen, *In Utero*, demonstrates a desire for regression. One of the

tracks, *Rape Me*, caused such an outrage that many shops refused to sell it.

DESPAIR AND ANGER. Kurt Cobain said he was "gutted by the macho rubbish of rap lyrics" and criticised Guns and Roses, another successful group, for their sexism. Condemning the compromise of "Coca-Cola rock" with the "star system", he was reduced to conceding that the rock rebellion was in vain, since it always ended up being taken over and commercialised by the multinational companies. An idol of the young, whom he condemned for their apathy, he was far from becoming a mouthpiece of his generation, unlike Bono of the Irish group U2. He distrusted the public and the effects of popularity: "Fame is the worst thing that happened to me."

"Every day I think of killing myself. I can't imagine that ten years from now I shall still be here playing songs on stage with Nirvana." On 4 March he tried to kill himself and was saved just in time. He was persuaded to take another drying-out treatment, but escaped from the clinic and, while his family were away, spent several days at home in Seattle, completely alone. Then he shot himself in the head on 8 April 1994, leaving a long message behind, in which he talked about his unhappiness: "I'm pretty much of an erratic moody person and I don't have the passion anymore. Since the age of seven I've become hateful toward all humans in general. [Perhaps] it is because I love and feel for people too much." Many other rock musicians before him came to

a similar tragic end, such as Jimi Hendrix, Janis Joplin, Jim Morrison or Sid Vicious. In the way that they became cult figures after their death, the same happened to Cobain. Before the mourning vigil, Courtney Love read extracts from his farewell note, and described as "total rubbish", the line by Neil Young which he had quoted, saying that it was better "to burn out than to fade away." Several days later, the second album by Hole was released, with the title *Live through this*. Love called it "angry vaginal music", in which she bellows: "You want me to take precautions/ Go on, try to shut me up." She refused to accept the blame for Cobain's suicide: "He would never have found anybody who could stop him dying. He wished that he had never come into the world, that's what he told me from the beginning." Love is still making records with Hole and appeared in the film *The People Versus Larry Flynt* (1996), in which her talent as an actress was recognised.

♡ ♡ ♡

Pravda, the Survivor, Guy Peellaert, 1967.

Society
Men
Suffering ...

... from women's "revenge", or the search for new benchmarks in a changing society.

In our rapidly changing world, a large-scale redistribution of male and female roles is taking place. This is not achieved without some pain and disruption. Many women aspire to a more equal relationship in a couple than was the case with their parents. Thanks to the freedoms and rights gained by the actions of feminists, and the control they exert over their own reproductive systems using modern methods of contraception (cf. p. 310), many women now have the power, independence, and ability to make their own plans for the future, a factor which has a big impact on their love relationships.

People are asking whether women are taking the place of men. Is the emancipation of women undermining a man's sense of worth? A fear of the blurring of male and female roles is a thread running throughout society. During the

First World War, for example, when women were compelled to perform men's jobs, newspapers railed against the "topsy-turvy" world, and were suspicious that women were taking "revenge". Even today, there are men who interpret the desire for justice and equality as a desire for revenge.

CHANGING AND SUFFERING. From Spain, to the United States, to Japan, the male role model is in crisis. A man is no longer the "head of the family" in legal terms, and his traditional supremacy has been challenged. The shift has become obvious as the media talk about "the new woman", who is often perceived as a victor. Whereas men of all ages can discuss the same sort of topics, the sexual behaviour and love relationships of many younger women, particularly when they earn their own living, have changed: women are far more prepared to say what they want, so confirming their new power, and sending out confusing sexual signals. Countless magazine surveys discuss this "male angst": "She makes the first step and he feels that his manhood

is threatened." Thrown off balance by this evolution which they had no part in initiating, men no longer know who they are or what they want. Girls brought up in co-educational establishments are less intimated by boys than earlier generations of women educated in single-sex schools. In addition, young men frequently lack a masculine role model, for despite the fashion for fathers to take a more active part in child-rearing than during preceding decades, they still do not take such a large part in their children's upbringing. Worried by women's demands, men are trying to find their way. Some adopt an attitude of withdrawal, a wait-and-see policy, or insist on the right to do nothing. Others have ceased to play a macho dominant role, but are having difficulty finding their bearings in the game of seduction. Many are reluctant to become involved with a woman, afraid either that unemployment will hamper their plans, or that they will not be equal to the task.

"Men!" is an exclamation often heard from women, who deplore the fact that the traditional male has been replaced by an irresponsible, infantile being, lacking self-esteem. With the rise of divorce and separation, one home out of two in large towns comprises a single person. "Where are the men?" read the magazine headlines, underlining the contradictions of what women want today. They would like men to be manly, but not macho. They dream of a man who is a good lover, strong and tender, and who is confident in all aspects of his life. According to sociologist Jean Baudrillard, after taking on powerful roles which were traditionally male, women are now becoming disillusioned and showing resentment at men's feebleness.

"What do they really want?" Faced with demands from women, whose earning power now gives them independence, there are still men who continue to claim a position of dominance, although it is crumbling. The more frustrated they become, the less able they are to adapt. Instead of proposing alternatives, they simply resist change, like those men yearning for the good old days of patriarchy, who send away for docile wives by mail order from Third World countries.

It is difficult to be a man in the present world. In the old days, to be born a man was sufficient in itself to guarantee superiority over a woman. Today, for many of them, the loss of power, whether real or apparent, constitutes a loss of face. In the workplace, women have become their equals, if not their bosses. The conservative male reaction, for example, those "angry white Americans", or black men looking for "pride", stems from economic insecurity and fear of losing their identity. Those who suffer the loss of privilege, resent even the slightest female advance, interpreting it as a symbolic form of castration. Women have acquired the right to say "no", and men feel threatened if women appear no longer to have need of them. As men see it, any

woman who decides how to run her own life, in a way which does not conform to the pattern of traditional male domination, is actively trying to "dispose" of them. So, a man who needs to rely on his wife's in-

come feels diminished and, in trying to restore his manhood and his image among his peers, often resorts to violence.

The change is perceived as being greater than is actually the case. Society in fact still treats men and women differently (cf. p. 432) and household chores are still not shared equally. The asymmetry is also apparent when it comes to seduction: if power can increase a man's sexual attractiveness, the same has to be true for a woman. Seen as all-powerful, women who take the sexual initiative frighten some men, as the Hollywood cinema's portrayal of them as demonic Furies demonstrates (cf. p. 390).

MEN RE-INVENT THEMSELVES. The nature of the lack of understanding between the sexes has changed. Yesterday, women complained of brutality and the male ego; today it is men who accuse women of being "in a hurry", while some women are disappointed at reaching their goals

easily: "I would like him to make himself desirable." Disoriented by female partners who are more demanding in sexual matters, some men now ask "how was it for you?" Prepared to give pleasure, they ap-

ply themselves to the task, and if they allow spontancity to take over, can forget the cult of performance, and its corollary, the anxiety of failure. When men who have been brought up to control their emotions discover that being in love means overcoming the fear of appearing weak and vulnerable, they can contribute to building a new image for men, such as Woody Allen, (cf. p. 368), whose trump card is daring to expose their fragility.

To accept another person's freedom, requires maturity and self-assurance. Far from being the stuffy couple of old, a new style of relationship is appearing (cf. p. 374) which promotes the independence of each partner, while still linked to a culture of intimacy, sharing, and communication. In the social mores being established for tomorrow's world, which are more demanding and based on adult choices, the love relationship becomes one of equality and good relations, founded on mutual trust.

1991

ITALY. **Release of the Marco Ferreri film, *House of Smiles*, about the love affair of two old-age pensioners in a residential home, which shocks the staff. While the world which surrounds them is sad and cynical, the amorous and sexual passion of Adelina (Ingrid Thulin) and Andrea (Dado Ruspoli) saves them.**

GREECE. **A net increase in the number of marriages, which fell in 1992 to avoid a leap year, said to be unlucky according to superstition, and rose again in 1993.**

Girls in a Taxi,
Beryl Cook, 1991.

Hillary
Bill & Clinton

For the first time in American history, the president's wife is a successful career woman. The First Lady has to ensure that she does not outshine her husband.

"Vote for me and you will get two Clintons for the price of one," declared Bill Clinton, the Democrat candidate in the 1992 presidential election. His victory was also a victory for his wife Hillary, his closest ally and campaign organiser. He was forty-six and she forty-five. Their love and mutual esteem are apparent. According to one of their friends, each thinks that the other is the "most intelligent and most formidable person in the world". Hillary Roddam Clinton not only pursued a career as a lawyer, but also earned far more money than her husband. Did this change in the White House reflect the changes taking place among couples generally, where the husband and wife were also partners? Would the traditional role of First Lady be transformed by this "new woman", who had the photograph of Eleanor Roosevelt (cf. p. 162), her role-model, hanging in her office?

Bill Clinton and Hillary Roddam met in 1970 at the prestigious Yale University, where they were both outstanding students. They shone at their law studies, and at the same time were militant activists. Passionate about politics, with a talent for leadership, and equally ambitious, they understood and complemented each

other. The cool logic of the serious-minded Hillary combined well with the intuition of the fun-loving Bill, a warm and gifted communicator.

William Jefferson Clinton came from a modest, Baptist family living in Hope, Arkansas, a poor rural state. He never knew his father, who died in a car accident on the day he was born. His mother remarried and he took his step-father's name. A Rhodes scholar, he studied first at Oxford then at Yale, and aimed at a political career in his home state. Hillary Roddam came from a solid middle-class home in Chicago. The family was Methodist and supported the Republican party. While studying at the smart Wellesley college, she espoused left-wing views, supporting the struggle for the rights of black people, and protesting against the war in Vietnam. She dressed in sweaters and baggy skirts, and wore large spectacles. Her fellow students thought that she would make a future senator or female president, but her love for Bill Clinton changed everything.

In 1971 they took the bold step of living together while still unmarried. When their studies finished in 1973, they chose separate paths. Clinton returned to

Arkansas, while Roddam went to New York to start a promising career, but in August 1974 she left everything behind to go and rejoin him. "You are mad," a girl friend said; "I love him," she retorted. She later analysed their situation, saying, "Bill's desire to enter politics was much more clearly defined than my desire to change the world." She worked as a lawyer, first in Fayetteville and later Little Rock, the state capital. They also both taught at the university there. In order to avoid any scandal, they lived apart until their marriage in 1975. Chelsea, their only child, was born in 1980. They remember those years as being very happy. They shared the domestic chores and lived a full social life.

PRESENTING A UNITED FRONT. Hillary Roddam specialised in women's and children's rights, but also defended traditional values, advocating abstinence rather than condoms to prevent teenage pregnancies. She orchestrated her husband's election campaigns: elected governor in 1978, he was very disappointed by his defeat in 1980. Some people attributed this to his wife; a partner in the Rose Law firm, she neither used make-up nor spent much time on her appearance. Nor did she take her husband's name. For the new campaign in 1982, she started to wear contact lenses, and took care over her clothes and hair-style; more importantly, she started to call herself Hillary Clinton. "However," he told her, "I am not asking you to do it. I would prefer to lose the election than to lose you." As soon as he was elected, he entrusted her with reform of the educational system, which she carried out energetically and with great success. Their opponents said she was cold and too powerful, and that he was shifty and spineless. Despite rumours of her husband's extra-marital affairs, she stood by him.

She faced criticisms again in 1991 when they were running for the White House, and the press made revelations about a former mistress. On 26 January 1992, the couple appeared live on television. Clinton said that he loved his wife. She explained: "All couples have their moments of crisis, and we have surmounted them together." Pressed on the subject, she said, "What you see here this evening is what you get. Take it or leave it." This appearance saved the campaign, but made her a target for the conservatives, who called upon this capable woman to prove that she did not dominate her husband.

The Clintons are loving and affectionate parents. They have brought up their daughter strictly and, taking Jackie Kennedy's advice, have protected her from the public. Alongside the Clintons there is another stable and very popular couple, Vice President Al Gore and his

1992

PALESTINE. Yasser Arafat always said that he was "married to Palestine". On 17 July 1990, it was announced that at the age of sixty he had married Soha Tawil, twenty-six. They first met in Paris in May 1989, when the PLO chief was making an official visit, and she went to work for him in Tunis. The daughter of a wealthy banker, Daoud Tawil, and of a journalist and well-known activist, Raymonda Tawil, she was a Christian Palestinian who converted to Islam. Arafat wanted to keep their marriage secret – "my people will not understand that I am married" – and asked her not to tell her family, but her mother found out and demanded an official announcement. When the Arafats' daughter, Zahoua, was born in July 1995, they left Tunis to live in Gaza, Palestine. In 1994, Yasser Arafat and Itzhak Rabin jointly received the Nobel Peace Prize.

wife Tipper, with their three children. The Clintons talked about adopting another child, but eventually gave up the idea.

LOW PROFILE. After his election, President Clinton handed his wife an explosive brief – reform of the social welfare system. Although her magisterial presentation to Congress was highly praised, its failure was a bitter disappointment. Thereafter, she remained in the background and found a niche for herself. Bill Clinton's first term in office was clouded by a number of financial scandals, and an accusation of sexual harassment dating from 1991, for which the legal costs ruined him financially. After the Republicans' electoral triumph in 1994, Hillary Clinton was deemed to be his evil genie, although she continued to be very popular with women of the political Left. Vilified by Republican sexist insults, which aroused the president's anger, she adopted a low profile for his re-election in 1996. She published a successful book on children, *It Takes A Village: And Other Lessons Children Teach Us*, but was not in a position to be able to protest publicly against the cuts in the social budgets and reacts with dignity to the revelations made about his irregular sexual life. She no longer said "we", but referred to "my husband" or "the president", compared with the Republican challenger's wife, Elizabeth Dole, who spoke of "Bob" and "The man I love". What a contrast these two wives made in such a conventional role – brilliant women who were both capable of standing as candidates in their own right. Bill Clinton was re-elected in 1996. His wife appeared to have successfully modified her role: did she agree to make the traditional sacrifices a wife makes, in order to advance her husband's career?

♡ ♡ ♡

SOCIETY
Virtual Love

The Internet helps lonely hearts to meet globally.

Cupid is now "on-line". People looking for a kindred spirit or a sexual partner can now meet others via computer, instead of replying to the lonely hearts' column in a newspaper. The Internet, which initially served to link American information centres from as early as 1969, became a world-wide network in 1992. The World Wide Web now connects millions of computer-users. In 1996 the number stood at 10 million, and a figure of 200 hundred million is predicted by the year 2001. With the establishment of "newsgroups" and "E-mail", people can meet and communicate on an international scale.

For the public at large, "cybersex" or "virtual sex" is one of the attractions of the Internet. After the excesses of the "sexual liberation" (cf. p. 310), the time has now come for substitutes. With the fear of AIDS (cf. p. 416) contributing to the movement for "new chastity" (cf. p. 404), many people are now adopting "no risk" practices. No aroma, no perspiration, no sperm: the other person is simply reduced to a projection on the screen, like the enemy during the Gulf War. It may only be an image, but it can nevertheless provoke intense feelings, not unlike those Japanese video games which offer a virtual love relationship to boys afraid of contact with real girls.

On the Internet, freedom of expression is totally unconstrained. Those who were alarmed at some of the early signs of abuse – such as prejudice, racism, or pornography – tended to forget that all tools of communication when they first appeared had a parallel, "clandestine" use: photographs, postcards, films, telephone, video, cable television, etc. With the advent of the Internet, men are able to select a "submissive wife" by mail order from Asia, Latin America, or eastern Europe, from among women who want to escape poverty. On the "Net", it is possible to procure sex, virtual or real, with just about anybody, including children. Where is the novelty in this, apart from the speed and international scale? Efforts are being made to break up prostitution rings and to protect minors, but no method of censorship – by banning the servers or increasing charges – has been shown to work on the "Net". It is difficult to detect obscenity and filter the millions of messages. Moreover, the ingenuity of these traffickers is limitless, as demand will always create supply. Although pornography does not resolve the problems of loneliness and unhappiness (cf. p. 340), there still remains an immense craving for it.

IMPOSSIBLE MEETING. The Internet serves as an enormous lonely hearts' meeting-place, with love at first sight and even marriage. There is the initial curiosity, the pleasure of discovery and excitement at breaking the rules, as one's desires are projected on to the screen. "Surfing the Net" allows the user to talk to people who may live around the corner or on the other side of the world, without any of the usual risks associated with talking to strangers. These meetings give rise to new forms of wooing through the ether, but the strategy is nonetheless a traditional one: men still have to compete for a woman, as women are in the minority on the Internet. In the United States women form 30 per cent of "Net" users, and 20 per cent in the rest of the world. In addition, the women are usually single, dreaming of their big love affair, while the men tend to be already attached and are merely looking for a bit of an adventure.

On screen, a meeting is public and can be under an assumed name. People sometimes choose to conceal their social status, play games with their identity, and even change their age and sex. There is no way of knowing for sure with whom one is actually in communication; seduction techniques rely purely on words, writing and personality rather than physical appearance.

More adept at their skills on the keyboard than in their inter-personal relationships, virtual-reality "druggies" can avoid sexual and intimate exchanges. They may use crude language, but are reluctant to arrange a face-to-face encounter. The illusion for them is sometimes so powerful and their relations so intense, that they claim to have "made love". Why then trouble to confront real life? Do these voluntary recluses really want to meet a partner? As the Hal Salwen film *Denise Calls up* (1995) demonstrated, they affect to believe in it, protecting themselves from the world by the screen, which is their shield, or the mirror which reflects their fantasies. Their "exchange" is rather a form of masturbation for which the other person

provides the support. Only very strong feelings for a person can give them courage to leave their "bubble" and arrange a real meeting. It is only then that those who have fallen in love with a person's style go on to discover a voice on the telephone, and finally a face and a body, at their first meeting face-to-face.

DISAPPOINTMENTS. While the match-maker of former times has been replaced by friends who organise "blind dates", electronic messages are no competition for newspaper advertisements, singles' clubs or matrimonial agencies. These traditional methods of meeting people continue to thrive, despite their high cost and low success rate. The basic rule is knowing how to "sell oneself" with a sense of humour, but many clients – up to 70 per cent of which are men – are often too hampered by their own personal hang-ups to be successful. Women are often looking for the man of their dreams, and their high expectations combined with the

mental picture they have formed of him are often at odds with the reality when they meet.

In 1995, in Birmingham, Michigan, the photograph of a pretty, young woman appeared on a large advertising hoarding, with the message: "I am fed up with being alone. Creative, graduate, refined." Is this the best way of finding the love one is looking for? Questions which are too direct or too urgent may scare away a potential partner, especially someone who is just beginning to open up, but is afraid at the same time of appearing vulnerable. Whereas solitude sometimes becomes a position of retrenchment for reassessing the past, reaching out to another person implies a level of self-confidence, an acceptance that such meetings may come to nothing, and that one is prepared to give without expecting anything in return. Love does not follow any rules, and has little to do with reason or calculation. In real life, as on the Internet, it often comes unexpectedly, at no cost.

1992

LAS VEGAS. **Marriage of the German film-maker Barbet Schroeder and French actress Bulle Ogier. They fell in love when they first met in Paris in 1968, but they never lived under the same roof. "Fidelity is finding oneself," she explained. They travelled together, sometimes united by work, and when they were apart they telephoned each other every day. After the wedding ceremony, which was a sudden decision by Barbet Schroeder: "He said to me one day, 'We are going to get married tomorrow' ," he left for New York and she for Los Angeles. "We carried on with our lives. Perhaps now is the best phase of our love, the most unselfish. Some couples stay together because they have common interests, but our love is quite free."**

GREAT BRITAIN. **Divorced from Mark Philips, Princess Anne marries Timothy Laurence in a Presbyterian church in Scotland. The Anglican Church forbids the remarriage of divorcees, under the Royal Marriages Act of 1772.**

♡ ♡ ♡

Photograph by Bernard Descamps.

Prince Naruhito & Owada Masako

A modern woman renounced a brilliant career and disappeared behind stultifying ceremonial when she married the Japanese Crown Prince.

A royal wedding ceremony without a carriage or retinue, presents or honeymoon: the marriage of Prince Naruhito, son of the Japanese emperor, and Owada Masako (the surname comes first in Japanese) took place on 9 June 1993, shorn of the pomp normally associated with royalty. The ceremony was reduced to its essentials: out of sight of the television cameras, the couple observed secret rites in the temple of the goddess of the Sun. The groom wore an orange kimono and traditional black headgear. The bride had to support the weight of twelve kimonos worn one on top of the other, and a large hair-piece. Although the costumes have a tradition going back to the tenth century, the marriage ceremony itself is only a hundred years old. It was established in the Meiji period, at a time when the country was first opening up to westerners.

The new princess is a commoner, like her mother-in-law Empress Michiko, who married Prince Akihito in 1959. On the death of his father Hirohito in 1989, Akihito became the 125th. Emperor of Japan, descended from a long line whose ancestor, according to legend, was the Sun goddess, Ameratsu.

Owada Masako, who speaks five languages, was the daughter of a former diplomat who became a deputy-minister for Foreign Affairs. She was the first princess to graduate from Harvard and Oxford, and the first to have earned a living. She met the prince, who is a gentle and considerate man, and himself an Oxford graduate, at a reception in 1986, when she was twenty-three and he was twenty-six. The princess had just embarked on a career in the diplomatic corps, with an ambition to be appointed Japan's first female ambassador.

Prince Naruhito wanted to marry her. However, contrary to tradition, she was a little taller than his 5'3". Like many other young women before her, who had been selected as possible partners for the prince, she was frightened by the formality of the court and her principal purpose, which was to produce a son and heir. She respectfully declined the offer and her father sighed with relief, "I hope that he will give up the idea and pay attention to someone else. It is so difficult to say 'no'." In 1987 she left for the United States, where she became involved in trade relations with Japan. The prince repeated his request several times. Finally she gave in, won over by his ultimate argument, that she could serve the country just as well as a member of the royal family as in the role of a diplomat.

BETWEEN TRADITION AND MODERNITY. At the press conference to announce their engagement in December 1992, the prince declared that he had promised his future wife to "protect" her for life. The opportunity soon presented itself, when conservative critics referred to the "condescending" tone of the young woman, who said that she had accepted, saying "if I can be of use". On the other hand, she gained wide public sympathy, which was sustained by numerous pictures in the me-

self-effacement and self-sacrifice, the supreme virtue of Confucianism.

The new princess reflected the ambiguity of a country split between tradition and modernity. Her wedding day marked the end of her social and civic life. She was removed from the civil and electoral registers. Educated to become a twentieth-century woman, she entered a closed, archaic world, with strict rules, whose language is ancient Japanese. Cut off from politics and business, this isolation helped to guarantee the integrity and popularity of the imperial family. Similarly, the British monarchy was also once a model of isolation, but the well-publicised marital problems of the queen's children (cf. p. 364) are scarcely a good advertisement for a more open approach.

After the Japanese surrender in 1945, the emperor was no longer considered to be a living god. Under the

1993

SARAJEVO. **In the besieged capital of the war-torn country, two lovers, Admira Ismic, a Muslim, and Bosko Brkic, a Serb, both aged twenty-five, want to marry and leave the country. For weeks on end they negotiated their departure with the Bosnian and Serb headquarters. The siege of the town was lifted for them for several minutes around the Franz-Ferninand bridge, which formed the front line. On 19 May 1993 with their papers in order, they passed through the checkpoint. When they were only a few metres away from freedom, a burst of gunfire from a sniper mowed them down. They died in each other's arms. For eight days their bodies lay on the ground, as no-one dared to risk an enemy bullet. Finally, two Serbian soldiers removed them under cover of darkness, and buried them in a Serbian military cemetery closed to Bosnians.**

ITALY. **The new highway code comes into force. It formally bans kissing while driving a car.**

dia showing her as an exemplary student. She was presented as a modern young woman, who would perhaps help to re-invigorate the court.

Japanese journalists, subjected to rigorous monitoring by the office of the Imperial Court, practised their own censorship, but foreign journalists were able to escape such constraints, and the *Washington Post* newspaper was first to announce the engagement of the crown prince. There was an immediate chorus of lament from the world's press about the "sacrificial princess" (in the French magazine *Elle*) or the "reluctant princess" (on the cover of the American magazine *Newsweek*). In contrast with western "egotism", Japan lays great store on

constitution, he now symbolises the country and the unity of the people. The sacred aspect of the imperial system has become absorbed into the culture of a country which owes its dazzling economic success to the dynamism of its businesses.

Japan too, is undergoing social change. Despite the fact that Owada Masako has conformed to the tradition of young girls giving up work on their marriage (cf. p. 290), times are changing. The number of Japanese working women has almost reached the European average, but they are confined to inferior jobs, with a salary which is between 30 and 50 per cent lower than for a man in comparable work. Although tradition makes a

"Love is born of an involuntary attraction, which our free will transforms into a voluntary union. This is the necessary condition — the act which transforms servitude into freedom ... Sex is the root, eroticism is the stem and love is the ...

Elizabeth Glaser and
the children (cf. p. 399)

BELOW
Obelisks, 1987,
Niki de Saint-Phalle.

FACING PAGE
Extract from *AIDS,
you won't catch it*,
1990, Niki de Saint-Phalle.

distinction between love and marriage (cf. p. 16), marriages on the western model are on the increase: only 13 per cent of marriages in 1993 were arranged.

No heir in sight. With her head gently bowed, Princess Masako, silent and smiling, follows behind her husband with short steps. She only speaks in public when he invites her to. She whispers and keeps her eyes lowered. She is not allowed to leave the palace alone, and may only see old friends and relations in the presence of a functionary. The members of the imperial family spend their lives in each other's company; it is known that they play western chamber music and that their favourite sport is tennis. Three years after the marriage, *Newsweek* magazine asked questions about the "princess in a gilded cage", and commented on the fact that she had practically disappeared from sight. In December 1996, in the first news conference she gave alone, the princess complained of the "skewed" portrait which journalists painted of her, without denying her difficulties in adapting to the way of life. She did not utter a word about the topic which preoccupying the nation: time was passing and there was no sign of a pregnancy. The Japanese popular press, however, raised the tension. In reply to a question, the prince said, "The stork needs peace and quiet to bring his gift."

♡ ♡ ♡

MORALS
Love in the Time of AIDS

AIDS kills through ignorance, but precautions can be taken.

In 1993, Cyril Collard died of AIDS at the age of thirty-five, several months after the discussion provoked by his autobiographical film *Savage Nights*. Fascinated by the passion for living of this "wild angel" – the title of his posthumous book – many young people recognised themselves in what he said: "I am made from pieces of myself which have been assembled at random" or, "I am trying to make the world bearable." The hero, – he plays the role himself – is handsome and bisexual. He lives life at a frenetic pace, and risks causing the death of a young girl, since he knows that he is HIV-positive and did not wear a condom when he made love to her. Shocked when he first tells her, she chooses danger: "I love you, I want to share everything." She is not infected. He concludes, "I am probably going to die of AIDS, but it is no longer my life; I am a part of life". AIDS is neither a romantic "love sickness" nor

a "punishment" for homosexuals and drug-addicts. It is a fatal viral illness, transmitted by body fluids or blood. It attacked four million people in 1993, and killed one and a half million in 1996. From 1993, heterosexuals formed the majority of infected cases. The number of women infected through sexual relationships is greater than the number of women drug-addicts infected through shared needles. New HIV-positive cases are distributed equally between the sexes. Since there is no antidote, the only course is prevention. The male condom, which appeared to have gone out of fashion with the advent of female methods of contraception, is now back in use. The female condom, a Danish invention, went on sale in several countries in 1992.

Between consenting adults who face up to their responsibilities, only the foolhardiness of putting another person at risk without his knowledge is a fault in moral terms. Despite the Pope's ban on the use of condoms, many Catholics think that although wearing a condom may be a sin, not to wear one is a crime when it may put another person at risk of infection. AIDS revives the virtues of caution and precaution, and curbs the unrestrained sexual activities of certain groups. According to sociologist Jean Baudrillard, however, the "sexual disaffection" had begun well before the appearance of AIDS. After the "liberation" phase of the seventies (cf. p. 310) the lack of restraints revived the desire to find out where the boundaries of behaviour lay.

The appearance of AIDS also encouraged a new solidarity. While homosexuals at first refused to accept the reality of the AIDS' scourge, they then started to organise themselves by helping the sick, and fighting the ostracism which AIDS' victims encountered. Elizabeth Taylor, Line Renaud and other stars lent their support to this cause. The wider public, shocked by the Glaser family tragedy (cf. p. 399), was moved by films such as *Philadelphia* with Tom Hanks, or *Silverlake*, which demonstrated the power of love between homosexual couples.

DON'T CARE OR WON'T CARE? "Don't die of ignorance" said the slogan. The sex lives of millions of people were thrown into confusion by the spectre of AIDS. It now became necessary to protect themselves not only from life, in the form of an unwanted pregnancy, but from death, too. The first generation of women to take control of their own reproductive systems through the contraceptive pill and the coil, now faced the prospect of their lives being potentially threatened by their partner. Women were often afraid to insist on a man wearing a condom if he was unwilling to. The women who said nothing were often more afraid of a relationship failing and remaining single, than of contracting AIDS. In France, the Spira report revealed that for people who had had more than one partner in the preceding twelve months, one man out of two, and two women out of three had not used a condom at their first sexual encounter with a new partner. As far as contraception is concerned, it is difficult to reconcile desire and reason. How can condoms – and with them, fear – be introduced into an intimate relationship where spontaneity implies trust? There are people who carry the virus without being aware of it, but for a couple who are about to have sexual relations, such a test of honesty at the outset can compromise a relationship, by introducing an element from the past history of one partner or the other.

The opponents of "permissiveness" or "sexual promiscuity" can take comfort in the evolution towards more thoughtful or wiser practices. Indeed, "new chastity" (cf. p. 404) coexists with a modernised form of pornography, cybersex (cf. p. 412), which avoids not only all risk but also all contact. Conservative attitudes, which link death and sex (cf. the "femme fatale", pp. 88 and 390), condemn pre-marital sex, and advocate monogamy – " to browse in your own field" as they say in Uganda – as the only method of safe sex. This does not take account of supposedly stable couples where one of the partners may be deceitful, for it is a fact that the majority of prostitutes' customers are married men or men in a relationship, and many are prepared to pay extra for unprotected sex.

PROTECTED LOVE? Freedom coupled with a sense of responsibility is developing among the young, where, in France, three quarters used a condom the first time they had sex, whereas twenty years ago, no contraceptives were used for the "first time" (cf. p. 294) in a half of all cases. Will this new concern with safety alter the importance of penetration, and help to re-establish the merits of fondling? It could change our perceptions about the emphasis we place on sex at the present day, and teach to us be in control of it, rather than it being in control of us.

An element of risk is inseparable from human life, and that includes loving and sexual relationships. Eroticism has always pushed against the barriers. Desire has always tried to evade scientific or moral taboos, but the risk-taking here is of a completely different order: it often manifests itself by an inconsistency between knowledge and behaviour. Based on the available information, it is the responsibility of each individual to work out his or her own strategy for prevention, using dialogue as well as condoms. This emphasises the need to educate the young about responsible sexual behaviour (cf. p. 218). In developed countries, the total number of new AIDS' cases is falling, while new forms of treatment allow existing cases to be held in check. As vigilance is relaxed, a new threat grows. It is a fact that 90 per cent of carriers of the virus live in Third World countries.

1993

... flower. And the fruit? The fruits of love are intangible. That is one of its mysteries."

OCTAVIO PAZ
The Double Flame, Love and Eroticism

DENMARK. For the first time in history, a government led by Social-Democrat Poul Nyrup Rasmussen counts a married couple among its ministers: the husband is Mogens Lykketoft in charge of Finance, and his wife, Jytte Hilden, of Culture. Denmark was the first western country to appoint a female minister, Nina Bang, in 1924.

GREAT BRITAIN. Anthony and Maggie Barker celebrate their Golden Wedding with their family. Both doctors, they spent their working lives in South Africa before returning to England. The following day they got on their tandem and rode off toward the Lake District, as they had done fifty years before, on their honeymoon. A lorry ran them down and they were killed instantly.

♡ ♡ ♡

Boris Becker
& Barbara Feltus

A white man and a black woman married in defiance of nationalism and racial hatred.

The birth of Noah Gabriel Becker on 18 January 1994 was an important event not only on the "Announcements" page. In Germany, his parents, tennis champion Boris Becker and the fashion model Barbara Feltus, were the most famous couple of the time. While criminal racist elements were burning down the homes of Turkish immigrant workers, the love story of this mixed marriage (cf. p. 306) – he was white and she was of mixed race – was moving because of their political stance in favour of tolerance and human dignity.

Since winning the Wimbledon Tennis Championship in 1985 at the age of seventeen, the youngest winner in the history of the game, Boris Becker, a great favourite with the crowd, became a national German hero. In 1991 he headed the world rankings in a career which was brilliant, if at times somewhat erratic. The victories gained by this good-looking man with sandy-coloured hair and blue eyes, nick-named "Boom boom" for his cannon-like service, symbolised, according to some magazines, "the renaissance of a Germany which dares to win." Unlike Steffi Graf, Germany's other tennis champion, who was a perfect role model for young girls, Becker proved to be a rebel; he refused to do military service, and settled in Monaco to avoid paying taxes. Instead of mollifying his fellow countrymen, he laid the blame for the country's Nazi past at their door. He said

that, at first, he was proud when Germans, who had long been ashamed to admit it, said that they came from the same country as Becker. But he gradually became disgusted by the fanatical cheering his victories brought, and said he was frightened by the "zombie look" of his fans. He asked himself about the meaning of life, had nightmares about a career shattered at the peak of its glory, and dreamt of "simply being a man". In interviews he confided his anxieties – "I was afraid of that abyss, that deep trough which follows euphoria" – and said that he experienced "the loneliness of being at the top". During the Gulf War, shortly before his victory in the Australian Championships, he declared: "I would willingly march with the young people in Germany demonstrating against this war. Tennis has never seemed so futile as it does now."

RACISM IN DAILY LIFE. Becker was not short of success with women. He was often seen with skating champion Katarina Witt, then it was Karen Schultz, who helped him to mature and contributed to his political awareness. In the autumn of 1991, in a fashionable Munich café called Harry's New York Bar, he met a famous model called Barbara Feltus. It was love at first sight. She was twenty-six, a year older than Becker and of mixed race. "When I saw her, I said to myself, 'I hope she speaks German.' In fact, she speaks German better than I do." They started to chat to each other about their childhood, spent in the same area near Heidelberg. Becker's father was an architect in Leimen. Feltus was the daughter of a German woman from Karlsruhe and a black American from Los Angeles serving as a GI in Heidelberg, who then settled in Düsseldorf as a photographer. She had just embarked on a career as an actress, appearing in a television series.

On 5 March 1992, dining alone together in a Munich restaurant, he proposed to her. She discovered a diamond ring which he had dropped unobtrusively into her wine-glass. He asked the pianist to play "their" song – *Summertime*. "Summertime, and the living is easy ... " But could life ever be easy for this couple, when photographs of Becker had appeared with the caption "Boris likes chocolate"? For Becker, racism was no longer a distant enemy; from that time on he experi-

POLAND. **Danuta Lutoslavska does not long survive her husband, the composer Witold Lutoslavski. They married in 1946. She always helped him in his work. As he composed, she transcribed each page and resolved any complex problems affecting technique.**

ALGERIA. **Cheb Hasni, a very popular singer from Oran is assassinated by fanatics. His love songs upset Muslim fundamentalists. His** Beraka **(1987) sung as a duo with Chaba Zahouania, was an enormous success, but the "bearded ones" exhorted retailers not to sell this "impious" cassette. Singing about love, is that not also singing about freedom?**

"What we ask of love, perhaps above all, is to reconcile us with ourselves."

CHARLES JULIET,
Accuells

HOLLYWOOD. **Love at first sight between Antonio Banderas and Melanie Griffith while shooting** *Too Much*, **the film directed by Fernando Trueba. The Spanish public, proud that its "Latin lover" had dazzled an American film star, made a success of both the film and its stars. Two matters remained to be sorted out. Banderas was married to actress ...**

enced it on a daily basis, and fought against it, not afraid to shock people: "I had never noticed that Barbara was black before I discovered how beautiful her skin looked against white sheets." The tabloids published a photograph of the scantily dressed young woman, and called her "Babs the suspenders." In spring 1993, the couple counter-attacked with another photograph, on the cover of *Stern* magazine: they posed in a tender embrace, naked but chaste, with Becker's engagement ring clearly evident on his left hand. "Our love, our life, our plans," they announced in the caption. While some people applauded him as a champion of anti-racism, others fulminated against the left-wing provocation.

STRENGTH OF CHARACTER AND HAPPINESS. "What has she done to deserve this?" Becker asked. Why the hate mail? Why the insults in the street? A group of skinheads called her a "filthy negress", and told her to "go back to the jungle". Another passer-by yelled, "Black witch, you only want his money." In an interview however, she said "I feel more German than Boris with his fair hair and blue eyes." She related how, in Germany, people had refused to serve her, because she was black. The next minute she was called "Frau Becker" and treat-

ed like a queen. "Sometimes," she said, "I find both attitudes just as difficult to understand."

Deciding that life in Germany was "unbearable because of the xenophobia," they settled in London in 1994, after the birth of their son – they had married a month earlier. They returned to Germany in 1996, the year that Becker won the Grand Slam. Barbara Feltus was seen in the front row at all the tournaments he played, giving him her fierce support. "When he is playing," she said, "I am as tense as a bow-string; I can sense his energy." Becker's friends, who recognised his wife's strength of character and genuineness, confirmed, "she loves him for himself, not for his fame". As for the champion himself, he enjoys a strong and solid relationship with her. "She was the first person to say, 'I want to see you win again.' Thanks to her I have regained my spiritual equilibrium. I have at last learnt to live and pursue my career conscientiously. 'Babsi' has made me strong, she has been good for me." Of course, he has continued to find his way; "tennis never has been and never will be my whole life". He is interested in jazz, poetry and ecology. But he knows that henceforth, "love is more important than all the tennis tournaments in the world". Love is also a little boy, who looks like his mother.

♡ ♡ ♡

SOCIETY
"I Love Two People ..."

How to live a lie without causing pain?

She is twenty years old, pretty and intelligent, and has just passed a difficult college entrance examination. Mazarine is a love-child, the illegitimate daughter of a great statesman. Since her birth she has lived in obscurity with her mother. In 1994, her father, François Mitterrand, fulfilled a final duty to her, and brought her out of the shadows. Several months after his period of office ended, he knew that cancer would not give him long to live. He appeared with her in public and allowed the press to reveal his "secret". Few French people were shocked.

"I married a seducer, and I had to put up with it," Danielle Mitter-

rand, his wife of fifty years and mother of their two sons, confessed at an early stage. She described herself as an independent woman, and proved it by valiantly fighting for human rights with her foundation called France-Libertés. Her husband's private life had always been troubled, but the press were scarcely aware of it, since, in France, it is the financial dealings of politicians which scandalise public opinion, rather than their intimate private life. Danielle Mitterrand recalled, "Mazarine's birth was neither a revelation nor a drama for me: I assumed it." She said that as husband and wife they had respected each other's freedom while remaining interdependent. Mazarine's mother, Anne Pingeot, an expert on nineteenth-century sculpture, was a conservator at the Orsay museum leading a quiet, simple life. The president spent the last Christ-

mases of his life with them in Egypt, returning to his official family to celebrate the new year. He died in January 1996. Danielle Mitterrand, with great dignity, invited Anne Pingeot and Mazarine to join the funeral cortège. The two women and their three children were united in mourning, with a moving dignity. She then continued to see the young woman on a regular basis: "François loved her dearly. She is very engaging. I am very happy to have inherited a daughter."

The same thing happened in 1902 after the death of writer Emile Zola, when his wife Alexandrine greeted Jeanne Rozerot and her children as his coffin was being transferred to the Panthéon. At the end of his life, Zola had two homes. After reacting violently at first, his wife, who was barren, came to accept his second family, which included a son and a daughter. She asked to meet the children, and cared for them affectionately, finally succeeding in winning permission for them to bear their father's name. In Zola's time, "bastards" had to pay for their parents' indiscretion, and were compelled to live with public opprobrium and the stigma of illegitimate birth. Times, and morals, have changed (cf. p. 298), although hypocritical attitudes still persist.

MALE POLYGAMY. "The freedom to love is no less sacred than the freedom to think. What we call 'adultery' today is identical to what used to be called 'heresy'," declared Victor Hugo, justifying his own polygamy. Sartre made the same sort of distinction, between "necessary love" and "contingent love" (cf. p. 235), or Philippe Sollers (cf. p. 307), who was in favour of secrecy and against control, each individual, according to him, being responsible for his own sexuality. Conversely, there have been men who have lived a double life full of guilt and remorse, in particular Catholics such as Spencer Tracy (cf. p. 200) or Olivier Messiaen (cf. p. 205).

Freud explained this incapacity of a man to choose between two – or several – women by the distinction a man is forced to make between love and desire, between the mother figure and the prostitute. In real life, as in fiction, "bigamy" committed by women – a situation found in *Jules and Jim* (cf. p. 110), is much rarer, and the happy "double life" of the heroine of *Salt on Our Skin* (cf. p. 394) is exceptional. Throughout the world, polyandry (a woman with several husbands) is extremely rare, whereas male polygamy is very widespread, particularly in Africa, even among Christians. The Koran restricts a man to four wives, who must be treated equally. Polygamy (cf. p. 287), far from being justified by a high ratio of women in the population, serves to bring a wealthy man social prestige.

The relationship between his wives is one of both rivalry and mutual support, their internal conflicts reinforcing the husband's authority. In the West, the last group of people to practise polygamy were the Mormons, a Christian sect based in Utah. Their attempt to gain statehood in the United States was turned down by the federal authorities until they officially renounced the practice in 1890.

LIES, SUFFERING AND A "DOUBLE LIFE". The French nation's tolerance of their leaders' private lives lies in stark contrast to the outrage caused in other countries by the misconduct, even if discreet, of well-known people. "Revelations" by the British tabloids have forced many politicians out of office. The writer Julian Barnes said, "Al-

Moon, Francesco Clemente, 1996.

though sex outside marriage in itself is not enough to send a minister to the stake, it makes very good kindling." It is traditional for a wife who has been deceived to continue to support her husband publicly: this was the case in the United States with Hillary Clinton (cf. p. 410) or Eileen McGann, the wife of Dick Morris, Clinton's political adviser whose relationship with a prostitute hit the headlines in 1996.

Today there are women who, more independent or having a

sense of their own worth, are no longer willing to accept this support role. In 1996, German public opinion was on the side of the very popular Hiltrud Schroeder against her unfaithful husband Gerhard Schroeder, the Minister-President of Lower Saxony, who saw his career compromised. The film comedy, *First Wives' Club*, by Hugh Wilson, a hit first in the United States then abroad, is about the vengeance wreaked by three "first wives", abandoned in their fifties for "something a bit younger". Similarly, many women in the shadows are no longer happy with their *Back Street* (cf. p. 156) situation, with its snatched moments together and suffering linked to a "double life". For "new women" (cf. p. 408), love is based on freedom, not lies.

1994

... Ana Leza; Melanie Griffith had divorced the actor Don Johnson, then remarried him. After a double divorce, the marriage took place in 1996.

GREAT BRITAIN. Following the triumph of the Mike Newell film *Four Weddings and a Funeral*, the actor Hugh Grant becomes a star. With the appearance of an overgrown schoolboy, his charm contributed greatly to the success of this brilliant comedy, which ends in the marriage of the hero and a beautiful American (Andie MacDowell). In real life, Hugh Grant, the companion of Elizabeth Hurley, a well-known model, revealed in interviews that he jibbed at such "adult acts" as marriage and fatherhood. The couple were severely tested by a well-publicised scandal in June 1995, when Hugh Grant was arrested *in flagrante delicto* in Hollywood. He paid a prostitute for oral sex in his car. They were both fined for "vice". Contrite and repentant, Hugh Grant was forgiven by his girlfriend and found favour with the public once again.

Christo
& Jeanne-Claude

They design and organise together. This couple has invented an art-form and created artworks that are equally monumental and ephemeral.

Wrapped Reichstag in Berlin, June 1995.

In June 1995, the Reichstag (parliament) in Berlin was wrapped up in 100,000 square metres of aluminized fabric using 15 kilometres of blue rope. Twenty-four years of preparation and negotiation had gone into the two-week show. After they had convinced the members of Parliament individually, a vote was taken, to permit this "contemporary work of art *Wrapped Reichstag, Project for Berlin*". The Christos were American artists. He came originally from Bulgaria and she from France. Through their efforts, the German people regained pride in a building burdened with a tragic history, which stood in the centre of a city preparing to become once again the capital of a unified Germany. "The fabric will create an energy, smooth out the details and increase the mass," the artists announced. They had already done the same thing with the Pont-Neuf in Paris in 1985, and were now recreating the astonishing spectacle. There were those who thought that it was magnificent, but it was a sight which everyone would certainly remember, as it attracted spectators from near and far. Three million visitors had seen the Pont-Neuf in Paris and five million came to the Reichstag.

Christo declared, "I do all my projects for Jeanne-Claude first of all, then for the whole world." They married in 1960, the year their son was born. Surnamed Javacheff – Christo is his first name – he arrived in Paris in 1958. Not long after, while painting the portrait of the wife of General de Guillebon, he met her daughter, Jeanne-Claude, a young married woman leading an ordinary middle-class existence. It was love at first sight. Discovering that they were both born on the same day, 13 June 1935, they took it as a good omen. Everything happened very quickly. Jeanne-Claude changed the lock on her apartment, separated from her husband telling him, "Your key no longer fits my lock," and left him to spend her life with Christo.

DETERMINED AND INDEPENDENT. At the age of sixty-four, the couple are still tall and slim. Christo's hair is pepper and salt, Jeanne-Claude's is red. They like to be known as "the Christos", and are one of the most fascinating of couples in the art world. He is the visionary, and she is the "band leader". Either he or she dreams up the project, and together they organise the financial and technical support with a prodigious tenacity. They do need this, as it takes years, and sometimes decades, to bring a project to fruition.

They began by wrapping up objects in Paris, bottles

or boxes, and dreamed of doing it on a larger scale with buildings. In 1964, they settled in New York in a small, run-down apartment, with a studio for him on the fifth floor where there was no lift, and living and office space for both of them downstairs. In 1968, at the Documenta 4, the big contemporary art show in Kassel, they showed 5,600 *Cubicmeter Package*, on "air package" surrounded by canvas 82 feet high. Their work became accessible to a wider public when they wrapped up a medieval tower in Spoleto, Italy, and the Kunsthalle, in Berne. Gradually their determination and perseverance opened up the whole world; they covered an Australian coast with fabric, stretched an orange curtain across a valley in Colorado, ran a canvas fence to the north of San Francisco, which ended in the ocean, and surrounded eleven small islands in Florida with pink material. In 1985 they wrapped up the Pont-Neuf; in 1991 they arranged thousands of giant umbrellas in the open countryside, blue in Japan, yellow in California, before triumphing in Berlin in 1995. "We stimulate interest, we have to explain clearly what we are doing and why we are doing it." They were forced to become diplomats, accountants, entrepreneurs, philosophers – "all our projects offer a continual 'presence in the absence'" – and finally, in Berlin, choreographers for the ballet of climbers who glided across the façades of the building, unrolling kilometres of fabric, which would later be recycled.

The Christos make it a point of honour not to ask for money from anyone, nor for the cost to be met from the public purse. Their works have been entirely self-financing from the sale of either preparatory work – sketches, drawings, collages, original lithographs and models. Working in total freedom, these two creators take decisions purely for aesthetic reasons, since they are accountable to nobody but themselves. Do they call themselves artists, who start from the concrete then work towards the theoretical? "We are questioning the notion of art. Our projects contain elements of painting, sculpture, town-planning, and architecture."

EGYPT. **The marriage of two Muslims, Hamed Nasr Abou Zeid a teacher of Arabic, and Ebtehal Younes, a teacher of French, is declared null and void on the grounds of "apostasy" (abandonment of one's religion). Abou Zeid's writings were considered to be incompatible with the doctrine of Islam. In reality, the "crime" of this intellectual was to have applied modern methods of criticism to sacred texts. Fearing for his life – the death of an apostate was actively encouraged by some extremists – Abou Zeid fled to exile in Holland together with his wife. In 1996, a second Egyptian court granted him an unlimited stay of execution and therefore the right to remain married.**

FRANCE. **The resumption of French nuclear testing in the Pacific triggers an international campaign of opposition. T-shirts sold in Australia carried a list of "Ten reasons to hate the French." The fourth reason read: "They make love better than we do"!**

♡ ♡ ♡

COMPLEMENTARY PARTNERS. There is no division of labour, except for two things, as Jeanne-Claude says, that each does alone. Jeanne-Claude doesn't make drawings or collages, and Christo has never touched a tax form. The project are like presents for each other: "It makes me much happier to see Pont-Neuf wrapped up for me, than when he gives me a diamond," declares Jeanne-Claude proudly. Christo readily acknowledges the debt he owes to his wife, admiring her capacity for work, but also watchful when she is tired, gently persuading her to pace herself. Their relationship is tense, passionate, explosive, with great shouts and expansive gestures, which are sometimes brusque, sometimes affectionate, but always prodigiously effective thanks to their complementary personalities. Their life is devoted to work.

The Reichstag was the first project to carry both their signatures. Up to that point, Jeanne-Claude had always been content to be the originator of the various photographs of projects they had realised. "We have put a 30-year-old mistake right," says Christo. Henceforward, they were both in the limelight. In a different way to Niki de Saint-Phalle and Jean Tinguely (cf. p. 300), whose work was quite different, or the Lalanne couple or the Poiriers who worked closely together, the Christos's work is a joint effort, pursuing apparently crazy ideas, which they succeed in bringing to fruition. Their extraordinary success, based on passion and tenacity, combines the magic of the ephemeral with an unbounded ambition: "Throwing down a challenge to the idea of immortality".

♡ ♡ ♡

MORALS
Bisexuality

We all have bisexual thoughts. Does the fashion at the end of the twentieth century reflect the eternal fascination with androgyny and all its possibilities?

Bisexuality, which means having sexual relations with members of both sexes, gained extensive media-coverage in 1995. In the United States, it prompted self-publicising claims; "Be bi" was the slogan used by Pleasure Chest, a Los Angeles sex supermarket. The movement started to gain ground on the Los Angeles university campus from about 1990, and received a boost in 1995 with publication of the book *Vice Versa*, by Marjorie Garber, a teacher at Harvard. In this book she made a defence of "sexual fluidity". According to her, this showed that "sexuality is a process of growth, transformation, and surprise, and not a stable or knowable state." Many bisexual activists carried the idea of non-discrimination to the extreme, saying that "we do not fall in love with a man or a woman, but with another person; the sex of that person is just another characteristic such as age, hair type or skin colour."

The fashion to be "bi" grew rapidly, following the publication in 1996 of the *Bisexual Resource Guide*, which identified more than 1,400 groups in 20 countries. In the United States, the topic was featured on popular television programmes. As happened in the gay community (cf. p. 320) years earlier, a "bi" culture grew up, with its own clubs, magazines, specialised cable channels, and icons, some drawn from the past – such as Marlene Dietrich or James Dean – or from the present day, such as singer Ani DiFranco or poet June Jordan. Among the celebrities supporting the movement, some actively cultivated scandal, such as Madonna or, to a lesser degree the outrageous couple Courtney Love and Kurt Cobain (cf. p. 406). Others preferred ambiguity, such as the singer Prince, who abandoned his name in 1994, and insisted on being known by the symbols for male and female superimposed on each other.

WHO IS WHAT? According to Freud (cf. p. 46), at birth the human being is naturally bisexual and desire may be directed at either sex. Upbringing and resolution of the Oedipus complex cause us to abandon one of our love objects in favour of the other, to become, usually, heterosexual. Experience has shown that a love triangle between the sexes rarely lasts. Bisexual practices, restricted largely to artistic circles (cf. pp. 34 and 111), remained a private affair until the seventies, when rock idols Mick Jagger, David Bowie, and Elton John broke new ground with their aggressively provocative behaviour. Elton John, who talked about his bisexuality in an interview with *Rolling Stone* magazine in 1976, had a hit with *Daniel*, a song about homosexual love. "What sex do you belong to?" sang David Bowie. Like Jagger, Bowie was also married to a very beautiful woman, and both singers appeared at wild events in London, wearing extravagant make-up to make them appear more effeminate, and took pleasure in their ability to shock or excite their audiences with their sexually suggestive gestures. In the nineties, the cinema frequently showed bisexual themes: the stand taken by Cyril Collard in *Savage Nights* (cf.

p. 416), a lesson in tolerance in the play *Bushwhacked* by Josyane Balasko, where a pretty woman married to a macho man is seduced by a female lorry-driver; the joys of lesbianism in *When Night Is Falling* by Patricia Rozema. Was the public at large impressed? Their feelings were reflected on the whole in the following dialogue in the Rolph Silber film *Regular Guys*, between two police inspectors worried by the announcement of a colleague's bisexuality: "The world has become very complicated nowadays! – Yes, it's hard to keep up." With the media saturated by sex and its extremes of behaviour – by those who think of "nothing else but that", and the proponents of "the new chastity" (cf. p. 404) – this era could turn out to be an age of confusion.

THE ANDROGYNOUS DREAM. The word "bisexuality" combines what reality separates. Leaving aside group sex, a bisexual person has sexual relations with men or women. Kinsey (cf. p. 226) coined the name "bisexual" to describe the 4.6 per cent of men in his survey who had had partners of both sex.

But this applies to the majority of homosexuals at some point in their life. Bisexuals are therefore a fluctuating population, which is impossible to quantify without a strict system of identification. They are not inventing a third form of sexuality; they alternate, flitting between two well-defined set categories. As they move from one partner to another, from one sex to another, they enjoy an ambivalence which prevents them from forming a stable and lasting relationship. In their relations with a partner, bisexuals are looking less for genital sex – they usually have recourse to masturbation – than for the pleasure of intimacy. With the exception of activists, bisexuals do not define themselves by their practices, and are often torn by doubt, as homosexuality or what looks like sexual promiscuity elicits even stronger disapproval. Their refusal to make a choice, to be pigeon-holed with a label, brings the accusation that they are deceiving themselves, for example in not admitting to their homosexuality. After pornography (cf. p. 340), books and magazines present bisexuality as a symbol of liber-

ation and being fashionable: hence the label on Calvin Klein's unisex perfume with young androgynous models, or advertisements for jeans, showing mixed groups of young girls and boys. Although these images may have helped to relax the rigid classification of sexual roles, when it comes to real life, these trailblazers come up against practical difficulties. Liberated fantasies become grotesque when they are put into practice. Inciting people to satisfy all their desires on the premise that "everything is possible", is to go too far along the road of irresponsibility, and loses sight of the value of fantasy. "There are no heterosexuals, only guys who have mistakenly learned to chase women," says a character in the film *What a Drag!* This is to trivialise the situation.

Sometimes people dream of being themselves and the opposite of themselves, at one and the same time, of being a double, of being a whole, the sum total of their parents, to be self-sufficient, and extinguish desire for ever. This amounts to a denial of pleasure, as Greek mythology teaches: the soothsayer Tiresias, having experienced pleasure as a man then as a woman, told Zeus that female pleasure was nine times more intense. This revelation incensed Hera, who took away his sight. The hermaphrodite, a product of Hermes and Aphrodite, is therefore only an ideal, a dormant sculpture, a dream of androgyny, the myth found in "the conjunction of opposites", adopted by the alchemists. The psychoanalyst, Carl Gustav Jung, their modern successor, described how the "knowing" is joined to the "unknowing", the *animus* [mind] joining with the *anima* [soul] to produce a psyche which is in equilibrium. For the British critic John Cowper Powys, "all genuine human genius is, to some extent, bisexual", demonstrated by the Denishawn dance couple (cf. p. 87).

1995

JAPAN. A lavish and spectacular wedding of two celebrities takes place: the most popular sumo wrestler Takanohana, twenty-two, marries television presenter Kono Keiko, thirty. In 1992, his engagement to the young actress Rye Miyazawa had already hit the headlines, as did their split after the champion suffered a series of defeats. Awarded the title of *yokozuna* (grand champion) in 1994, this 142 kilogramme-heavyweight celebrity (height 6'1") became the idol of young Japanese girls. The wedding preparations and ceremony of this giant of a man with the slightly-built Kono Keiko were broadcast live on television.

"And I confess my love was too remiss
That had not made thee know how much I priz'd thee,
But that mine error was, as yet it is,
To think love best in silence."
Extract from a funeral elegy discovered and authenticated in 1995 as being written by Shakespeare.

Photograph by Isabel Muñoz.

Roberto Alagna
Angela & Gheorghiu

A love duet between two young, handsome opera singers, who are a perfect match both on stage and in real life.

In New York, Rodolpho married his Mimi: on April 26 1996, between two performances of *La Bohème* at the Metropolitan Opera House, the French tenor Roberto Alagna, thirty-two, married the Romanian soprano Angela Gheorghiu, thirty. The next day, during an interval in the opera, they signed the final official document in the presence of the mayor who had gone to the opera house especially for that purpose. Puccini's opera is integral to the story of this couple, who radiate youth and good looks, and who have become the latest favourites among opera-lovers. They first met in London in 1992, playing Rodolpho and Mimi, roles they later performed at the "Met". Roberto Alagna made his first appearance in New York, where the event was announced by a spectacular press campaign, with his picture on countless billboards introducing him as the "tenor of our generation".

The newly-weds left for a honeymoon in Venice, then they appeared together in *La Traviata* in London, and in *The Elixir of Love* in Lyons. Their recordings of songs and duets were eagerly snatched up by the public. They sang of their love for each other through the medium of their roles.

WILD APPLAUSE. This was the first time that such a well-known tenor and soprano had fallen in love on stage, as people do on the street. The legendary pairings of earlier times, such as Maria Callas (cf. p. 270) and Guiseppe di Stefano, Renata Tebaldi and Mario del Monaco, or Joan Sutherland and Luciano Pavarotti, lasted only for as long as the performance.

When Roberto Alagna and Angela Gheorghiu sing together on stage or in a recording, the admirable thing about them, more than the sum of their talents, is their deep mutual understanding combined with a strong stage presence. Their voices harmonise superbly, with a sumptuous tone, clear diction and a feeling for the music. Alagna's voice has been greeted by his fans as a

"miracle of nature". In addition, the young man with fine green eyes has none of the corpulence associated with certain tenors of the preceding generation! Although his parents were Sicilian, he was born in a suburb of Paris. His father and uncles, all endowed with fine singing voices, perform at family gatherings. He discovered opera at the cinema when he saw a film about Caruso, and listened passionately to his records. He studied accountancy. "I started to get seriously interested in opera at the age of seventeen. Before that, I thought it was out of the question." Singing in a cabaret show, his talents were recognised by a music teacher. He was brought to the attention of Gabriel Dussurget, founder of the Aix-en-Provence music festival, who introduced him to an agent. Alagna began to pursue his studies with an iron discipline, and fame soon smiled on him. In 1988, he sang the role of Alfredo in *La Traviata* at Glyndebourne, and won the prestigious Pavarotti competition. Engagements quickly followed. Invited by Riccardo Muti to sing Alfredo at La Scala, Milan in 1989, he went on to tour the world in this role. Criticism was sometimes harsh, but the public applauded him wildly. However, music lovers were unaware of the drama in the young man's life. Not long married, and with a young daughter Ornella, his wife was suffering from cancer. She died in 1994. "When I lost my wife, I took refuge in my work," he said. "It was a drug, a way of forgetting." Then life resumed afresh, and a new love was born when the tenor, returning to London for another engagement, met Angela Gheorghiu again.

The beautiful Gheorghiu, with a flawless complexion and long black hair, was born into a humble family in Adjud, a small Romanian town, where her father was a train driver. She always wanted to be a singer, and received a thorough training at the Bucharest Music Academy. She left her home country after the 1990 revolu-

Roberto Alagna and Angela Gheorghiu in Donizetti's *Elixir of Love*.

FINLAND. **Riitta Uosukainen, the parliamentary president, increases her popularity by publishing a book** A Flickering Flame, **in which she describes the intimate details of her married life. Married for thirty-five years to a professional soldier, she praises his talents as a lover. In an interview, she declared: "I wanted to show that eroticism is a source of energy for me, and that it forms a part of normal life. There should be nothing strange about older women having pleasure."**

ATLANTA. **At the Olympic Games, Donghua Li, a Chinese-born Swiss rider, wins the gold medal for show-jumping. In 1988, in Tienanmen Square, Beijing, he fell in love at first sight with Esperanza, a Swiss German tourist who asked him the way. They married, and he went to live in Switzerland, where he was able to obtain Swiss nationality only after five years of marriage. On the podium in Atlanta, he dedicated his victory, "after so many difficult years", to his wife, the child she was expecting and his new country.**

LIMA. **During the course of a reception at the Japanese ambassador's residence, a unit of the Tupac Amaru movement took hundreds of hostages; for ...**

tion, and made her first appearance in London in *Don Giovanni*. She was successful in *La Traviata*, and sang the role of Violetta in Europe, then at the "Met", where she made her début in 1993 in *La Bohème*. She played the role of Mimi again in 1996, with the man who became her husband.

PLEASING THE PUBLIC. Roberto Alagna and Angela Gheorghiu never tire of praising each other. According to her, he possesses "an extraordinary instinct, which al-lows him to approach the great roles of the repertoire in a very realistic way". He says of her, that he is "moved by her singing, both as a partner and spectator". Each is the other's principal fan and teacher, as they both strive for perfection. "Angela and I listen to each other and criti-cise each other. She had a proper musical training and her judgement is very important to me." Their married life is organised around their work. They want to be to-gether as much as possible, and juggle their many en-gagements, so that their timetable, worked out months in advance, allows them to sing, if not together, then at least in the same city at the same time. In common with other internationally famous artists, they spend a month in London, or a month in New York, between a tour to Japan and an engagement in Paris or Vienna. They spend their rare free time going to the cinema or museums. "We are very lucky," they say, "our repertoires are very close, our voices and temperament are complementary. Our great driving force is constantly having to change character, role or story." They know that nothing can be taken for granted, that the least fault will be noted, but they say that they are "happy to have such a voice, this gift from heaven, and to offer it to the public to make them happy in turn." As Norma sings, they live "on art and love", but without the tragic fate that befalls many of the couples in opera.

♡ ♡ ♡

Society
No Home of their Own

Feeling grown up, but without the financial independence, necessity forces many young people to live with their parents.

An amusing definition offered by novelist Janine Boissard to parents in their fifties reads: "A baby-couple is made up of a boy and a girl, usually adults, who have decided to spend their lives together, especially for the better, under the same roof: yours." In the West at the end of the twentieth century, several generations living together is a different structure from the traditional rural family of years ago. In times of economic recession and social break-down, some young people are forced out on to the streets after being turned out of the house or because they leave home of their own volition, while for many others family support comes into full play: family members contribute to help a young couple who have no money; they club together to give them a home, and are also prepared to accept children.

For those people who do not do well at school and end up in jobs with no prospects, this situation is one of necessity, not choice. The price of a couple's independence – rent, furniture, and fittings – is high, and the only alternative is to invite themselves to live or "squat" with the family. Other people often have no alternative but to return to the parental home, albeit only as a temporary measure. Given all the uncertainty, many young people are afraid to take the plunge and leave home. By keeping a foot in the door, they can come and go, holding on to their keys as a kind of insurance. This does not help them to develop their independence, rather it tends to hold them back. The reaction of parents, mindful of the harshness of life in the outside world, is to resist pushing the fledgling out of the nest. When offspring do make the break, most parents leave the door open, for the home to continue to act as a safety-net. This insecurity impacts on the feelings of young people, as the difficulty of finding their first permanent job makes it difficult to plan for the longer term. Today, setting up as a couple is of less significance and a less definitive step than thirty years ago, when there was great rejoicing at crossing the threshold and being "alone at last". In this day and age, when love affairs are often short-lived and splitting up is frequent, returning home is regarded as a backward step, to be sure, but also as a time of solace and repose, preparing for the next departure.

GROWING UP. In most countries, even when a girl has a responsible job, she gives it up more readily than a man, in order to run a home or to get married. The number of sons continuing to live at home is highest in Italy, where 70 per cent of single men, including those with permanent jobs, still live in the family. Even those men who have left their *mamma* to live with another woman, go back home in 25 per cent of cases when the marriage

The Youngest Parents,
Jocelyn Lee, 1996.

breaks down. In Germany, where the system of apprenticeship means that adolescents enter the workforce at a young age, independence comes earlier. In France, among the urban middle classes, children stay at home until the age of twenty-five on average, and longer where the family is better off. Even if they live elsewhere, such as students in a university town, they go home at weekends to do their laundry.

The increasing difficulty faced by young people wanting to set up home together is demonstrated by the reduction in the number of marriages (cf. p. 298), the increased age of the parents when the first child is born, and the fact that more and more couples are opting to live separately (cf. p. 374). For cohabiting couples it is desirable for at least one partner to have a fairly secure job. However, the number of obstacles continues to increase. In France, for example, 30 per cent of young people have temporary or part-time jobs in the service sector, which require few qualifications and offer no future prospects. The gap is increasing between the most able students, who study in the best establishments where competition is tough, and those who leave school early without any qualifications, and who are often steeped in a culture of physical or verbal violence.

More than half of French people aged between eighteen and twenty-two are in further education, stimulated either by the fear of unemployment or the desire to get on. According to the researches of sociologist Olivier Galland, although students consider that financial independence is a true measure of being grown up, many still regard themselves as grown up while continuing to live at home with their parents. This contradiction marks a change which cannot be explained by the recession alone. The delay between finishing a course of study and obtaining a first permanent job

continues to grow, with independence coming later and in a different way. The traditional stages of growing up towards adulthood are now less well-defined and less certain than before.

NEW RELATIONS BETWEEN THE GENERATIONS. In France there are approximately 400,000 homes where parents accommodate their grown-up children with partners. The French refer to them as "baby-couples". This situation can be explained to a large extent by the "generation gap" which has become less of a problem in recent years, as parental authority has become more relaxed, and the social and cultural revolution has brought more tolerant attitudes, where children are freer to speak out.

Despite the threat of AIDS (cf. p. 416), the younger generation leads a freer sexual life from an earlier age (cf. p. 294). Sex has always been a sensitive subject to broach with parents, whose role is to set limits for their children, and to provide emotional and practical support when required. Where people live together, it is important for them to have their own space, so that intimacy does not become confused with immodesty. When

young couples are obliged to live with parents, it is essential that their private life is restricted to the confines of their room. The two generations have to learn to adjust to a new type of relationship. Some parents find it difficult to accept that their son or daughter is having a sex life under their roof. When the living arrangements are permanent, friction can increase, and accusations of "sponging" can arise. If a son or daughter returns home from a broken marriage, the parents must avoid the censorious "I told you so", since the individual's self-esteem has already been sufficiently wounded. While acknowledging that it is experience of life which enables young people to mature, parents still tend to treat their offspring as children, and fail to recognise the importance of granting them their own space, and respecting their need to be alone. The best way for young people to ensure their own freedom, is to contribute to living costs, do their own washing and ironing, and share in the household chores. By so doing, the homeless young couple grows up in an atmosphere of tolerance and love.

1996

... seventy-four of them the ordeal lasted for several months. Nestor Cerpa, leader of the terrorists, wanted members of his movement to be released. They had been arrested in 1995 and sentenced to life imprisonment, where they were detained in inhumane conditions. His companion, Nancy Gilvonio, was among them. Living together as guerrillas since 1983, this Latin-American "Bonnie and Clyde" hid in the Peruvian jungle or at the home of accomplices in Lima between kidnaps and bank raids.

FRANCE. Release of the film *The Seducer's Diary*, directed by Danièle Dubroux, who took as her theme the book of the same title by Danish philosopher Sören Kierkegaard. Analysing the fatality of the love process, the film-maker contrasted calculated seduction with romantic passion. In 1843, Kierkegaard wrote, "Love is everything; also for those who love, everything loses its real meaning and only takes on the interpretation which loves gives it."

♡ ♡ ♡

Tony Blair
& Cherie Booth

Britain had a new prime minister. For the first time in the country's history, the prime minister's wife, an eminent lawyer, pursued her own career as a judge.

On 2 May 1997, Tony Blair and Cherie Booth walked triumphantly hand in hand along Whitehall. Then, on the steps of 10, Downing Street, the prime minister's official residence, they posed for the photographers, embracing each other affectionately. Slim and elegantly dressed, they made a handsome couple, he with brown hair and blue eyes, she dark and with a direct gaze. Earlier that morning, and still half-asleep, Cherie Booth had opened the door of their home in Islington, a sought-after area of the capital, to a delivery man brin-

THIS PAGE
Tony Blair.

FACING PAGE
Cherie Booth with her daughter Kathryn and one of Kathryn's friends.

ging flowers. Behind him, flash bulbs popped and photographs of the new First Lady in her night attire, with nothing on her feet and her hair dishevelled, winged their way around the world.

At forty-four, Tony Blair is the youngest prime minister for a century and a half. At a time when the Conservative government had been undermined by a series of scandals involving sex and money, he campaigned on the theme of "things can only get better", and led the Labour Party, which had been in opposition since 1979, to a resounding victory. With his youthful appeal, his warm, relaxed, and easy manner with people, he is a man out to make changes, whilst at the same time providing reassurance by putting the emphasis on modernity and the family.

His private life reflects his own set of values: Cherie Booth, his wife since 1980, continues to use her own name; she had a glittering career as a barrister prior to her appointment as a judge, and earns four times his salary. As caring parents, they take a deep interest in the education of their children, two sons aged thirteen and eleven, and a daughter aged nine.

PROFESSIONAL SUCCESS. Tony Blair belongs to a new generation of politicians, something he shares with Bill Clinton (cf. p. 410). Blair, too, is a political animal, but his disarming smile disguises a tough and authoritarian personality. Cherie Booth is two years younger than her husband. They met in 1977 when they were both students in legal chambers. He specialised in labour law. He admires his wife: "She is naturally brilliant. I have to work much harder than she does." Tony Blair is the son of a lecturer in law from Durham, a conservative (with a small "c"), who instilled in his children a sense of justice and duty. As a student at Oxford, Blair wore his hair long and played the guitar. His youth was carefree, but he was already characterised by a deep religious faith – he is an Anglican – and moral values which he defended with tolerance. Attracted by a socialism based on Christianity rather than Marxism, he joined the Labour party in 1975.

Cherie Booth comes from an impoverished, Catholic, Labour background. She and her sister were raised by their mother Gale Smith, a strong-minded and hardworking woman, in a working-class district of Liverpool. She scarcely knew her father, actor Tony Booth, who abandoned them at an early age and later went on to produce five more daughters during a turbulent life. Always an achiever, she won various scholarships and in 1995 reached the peak of her profession, with the prestigious appointment to Queen's Counsel.

The following year she became a judge, donning the traditional black robe and full wig. In Britain, the independence of the judiciary from political power is such

that her function is compatible with her husband's position as prime minister. A confirmed feminist, Cherie Booth often represented victims of sexual or racial discrimination, and supports measures designed to improve educational opportunities for young girls and members of ethnic minorities.

AN IDEAL MODERN COUPLE. The Blairs both had a desire to be involved in politics, but they made a pact, she recounts: only the first of them to be elected would become a career politician. In the General Election of 1983, however, he was elected to Parliament, while she was defeated. Tony Blair quickly became a spokesman, then a member of the Shadow Cabinet. When party leader John Smith died unexpectedly in 1994, Blair succeeded him and continued the rebuilding of the party commenced by his predecessors. He manoeuvred skilfully to dissociate himself from the Labour old guard, and oriented the party towards the centre. He succeeded in appealing to the middle classes, and gained substantially from the powerful support of *The Sun* newspaper, which, in a spectacular move, withdrew its support from the Conservative party.

During the 1997 campaign, Cherie Booth retreated behind a smiling reserve. In public, this lively-natured woman became the silent and smiling admirer of a distinguished husband. However, she who stated: "I live in the real world", does not intend being dictated to, either in the way she acts or the way she dresses – she

1997

SPAIN. **Cristina, the king's daughter, marries Basque handball player Iñaki Urdangarin in Barcelona cathedral. He is a champion sportsman and star of the Spanish team. They had met fifteen months earlier, in Atlanta, as the princess congratulated him after the team had won a bronze medal at the Olympic Games.**

UNITED STATES. **Kelly Flinn, a lieutenant in the American air-force, and the first woman to pilot a B52 bomber, is accused of adultery and insubordination. She had "fraternised" with a man who had lied to her, pretending that he was legally separated from his wife. To avoid appearing before a court martial which could have resulted in a heavy prison sentence – she resigned her commission. The affair aroused fierce debate about bigotry in the armed forces.**

ITALY. **The Marquis and Marchioness of Ripa di Meana, well-known as ecological activists, pose for a publicity photograph, financed by the World Wildlife Fund, opposing the use of fur. They lay naked on a bed, wrapped in each other's arms. The picture of their bodies, barely concealed by a sheet, carried the slogan: "Women, poor things, buy furs because they have no-one to keep them warm."**

wears trouser suits to work. Alluding briefly to her husband she said: "I could not say that he knows how to operate a washing machine, but at least he knows where it is!" She stands aside from politics and tries, she says, "to lead a normal life". While party strategists would like to present her as a home-loving type, the popular press sees her as a new Hillary Clinton.

Speaking at the funeral of the Princess of Wales (cf. p. 364) when he had been prime minister for only four months, Tony Blair found the words to touch a nation in mourning. In a matter of only several months more, he began to acquire the stature of a statesman, with the successful referendum on Scottish and Welsh devolution, and particularly with the delicate negotiations on Northern Ireland, which ended in the accord signed on Good Friday, 10 April 1998, a critical stage in the peace process.

Another of Blair's expectations is to boost the economy and lower unemployment. He is pushing for job creation, putting the emphasis on jobs for women, even if they have young children. He wants to give priority to education and to reduce the "dependency culture" associated with social security. He defends his European convictions, as well as feminist causes, such as the fight against marital violence. Although he has disappointed some Labour voters, particularly over restrictions on invalidity and single-parent benefits, he continues to enjoy great popularity. For a large portion of the population, Tony Blair, Cherie Booth and their children embody the ideal of a modern, responsible and caring family.

♡ ♡ ♡

SOCIETY
How to Maintain Good Relations with an "Ex"

Does splitting up mean that the break has to be total? Is it possible to remain friends when a love affair ends?

Bill Gates, head of the Microsoft Corporation, and one of the world's most powerful men, has come to a very strange arrangement with his wife, Melinda. Every spring, with her agreement, he goes to spend a long weekend with Ann Winblad, a woman with whom he once had a relationship. He is thereby keeping a promise he made to his ex-lover when they split up in 1987, to remain friends. Bill Gates described to a journalist from *Time* magazine how he spends this, immutable, weekend: it is he who goes to visit Ann Winblad at her home in North Carolina; they spend the time in conversation, walking along the beach, and playing mini-golf.

The ex-lovers are thus able to come to terms with their separation, by meeting and continuing their conversation where they left off. What is their secret? They continue to be interested in each other. Is this expecting too much? Is it possible to remain on good terms after a split? One thing is certain:

Andrew and Sarah with the Prince's new girlfriend, Sally Prosser.

even if it applies to only a minority of the couples who separate – the most frequently-used procedure is divorce on the grounds of the other's unreasonable behaviour, and not by mutual consent – the phenomenon exists and appears to be a growing trend. However, even when the decision to split is taken amicably, and the two partners remain on moderately good terms with each other, it may take quite a time for the sadness of loss or desertion to diminish. For it is only in learning to live without the other, by assimilating the memory of a shared life, and not by trying to erase it, that a person becomes capable of regarding it, not as a failure, but as an enriching experience.

FOR THE BETTER … At the end of the twentieth century, people typically have two or three long-term relationships in the course of a lifetime, whether legally binding or not. The most clear-headed of lovers no longer marry "for life", but for as long as the desire to live together continues. Attitudes have changed, and there is no stigma attached to being divorced, since at least one third of the population finds itself in this situation. In the West, on average, one marriage in three ends in divorce, in cities the rate ist one in two. Separation affects unmarried couples to an even greater extent. Some become declared enemies – old-style hate relationships still survive – while others succeed in remaining polite, outwardly even cordial, particularly if they are trying to avoid creating "scenes", which would affect their children.

If the stormy period of breaking up has not swept all away before it, ex-partners may still retain positive thoughts. "We were married for so long," one woman said, "and we shared so many happy times together. He is not a monster. He is still the father of my children." And her former husband said, "I still re-

spect her. Love has turned into something more serene. I no longer feel jealous or insecure."

Jane Birkin (cf. p. 319), speaking of Serge Gainsbourg said: "He never really went out of my life." Carole Bouquet claimed: "Neither in my heart nor my actions did I abandon the men I had loved." Or there is the case of the Duke and Duchess of York, divorced from each other but posing for photographs with their two daughters, who continue to live together under the same roof from time to time at the family home in Sunninghill. When the Duchess extolled the virtues of this arrangement in a televised broadcast in America in April 1998, she aroused protests from the more conservative sector of the population, but gained support from the Association of Stepfamilies.

Maintaining a relationship as parents rather than as a married couple appears to be the preferred option for many ex-partners, who, having made a new life for themselves, wish to maintain their responsibilities towards their children and their upbringing. They conceive innovative solutions, such as alternating care, in order to meet the emotional needs of their children. Instead of sacrificing a part of their own lives, they attempt to "have the best of both worlds". Some divide up their formerly joint home into two separate units. There are increasing numbers of people who celebrate Christmas with their new partners and their children from various relationships, in a joyous mix, the comical aspect of which – who is who? – has been exploited in a number of films. The essential thing is that each member succeeds in finding his or her place in this family mosaic and clearly identifying the others.

… AND WITHOUT THE WORSE. Relations between ex-partners therefore fall between two extremes, hate – or

indifference – and friendship. The friendship may be discreet, or even clandestine when it is unacceptable to a new partner, who finds any form of comparison disagreeable. It may also take the modern form of a friendship with three or even four participants, where an ex-partner is sometimes invited to act as godfather or godmother to the child of the new couple, or with joint agreement, sharing leisure pursuits and sometimes even holidays taken together. Without denying or regretting the past spent with an "ex", a new style of relationship develops, integrating the past into the present, combining affection and complicity. Such an approach is only possible, however, when all the participants have mourned the love that was, without malice or bitterness, and have forged new relationships, while taking account of their fragile nature. This approach also assumes a respect for the other person and a fine balance, in which the current partner recognises the importance of a previous relationship, and accepts that the loved person is a product of this previous relationship, and of the transformation which evolves from it.

Is friendship all that is left when love, sex and the daily routine are removed? Can mutual attraction, and hence temptation, be eliminated from the relationship between men and women? This dilemma was illustrated in the 1995/1997 Nescafé advertising campaign, which showed a divorced couple who had split up, but had not been able to make the final break: she calls him to rescue her when her car breaks down, and he compliments her on her attractiveness. The scene ends with the interesting question: "What about starting again?"

1997

AUSTRIA. **Viktor Klima succeeds to the post of chancellor after Franz Vranitzky's resignation. Klima, who was divorced, had been a minister since 1992 and had remarried in 1995. He declared on several occasions that he wanted to avoid sacrificing his marriage to his work once more, and that he would quit politics in 1999.**

"Love is a long and wonderful apprenticeship of the spoken word. Love is this elementary, silent kindness, starting from which a solitude can speak to another solitude and, if need be, accompany it to the end."

CHRISTIAN BOBIN
Diary

Novelist Noëlle Châtelet **recalls her marriage. She was twenty. Her husband, philosopher François Châtelet, said to her at the time, "I love what you are going to become." Widowed in 1985, she added, "Those words have never left me, they reconciled me with myself, and I know that this peace will accompany me to the end of my life."**

Paul Linda
& McCartney

A happy couple who defied the times. Only death has separated the former Beatle from the woman who inspired his love-songs.

"He held her pressed closely to him all night long, and she died in his arms," a woman friend of the McCartneys is reported as saying. On 17 April 1998, at the age of fifty-six, Linda McCartney succumbed to a relapse of the cancer from which she had been suffering. After her cremation, Paul brought his wife's ashes back from the United States to Britain, to Peasmarsh, their farm in East Sussex.

Two days before her death, they had gone for a final horse-ride close to their ranch in Arizona. They were both still hoping to attend the wedding of their daughter, Mary, the following month. Linda had been unable to attend the ceremony at Buckingham Palace when the former Beatle was knighted by the Queen, but she was at the première of *Standing Stone*, composed by her husband and performed at Carnegie Hall, New York, in November 1997.

PRIORITY GIVEN TO A PRIVATE LIFE. "Linda was, and still is," Paul declared, "the love of my life. The two years we have just spent battling against her illness were a nightmare." After twenty-nine years, this compatible and long-lasting couple – a rarity in show-business – have been parted only by death.

Their first meeting goes back to 1967, at a press-conference held by the Beatles on the release of their album *Sergeant Pepper's Lonely Hearts Club Band*. Paul McCartney was then twenty-five, a year younger than Linda Eastman. The daughter of a New York lawyer – her name led people to believe, erroneously, that she was an heiress of the Eastman Kodak company – she was a divorcee and mother of a four-year-old daughter, Heather. She worked as a photographer for a music magazine. Unlike the group's fans who followed them around with a crazed adoration, she was spontaneous and displayed a refreshing exuberance. Paul had just announced his engagement to actress Jane Asher, but was attracted to this pretty, blue-eyed blonde who laughed good-naturedly at his jokes and was very proud of smoking "pot". Was this just another passing infatuation for a man who until then had been fickle and not very faithful? In a shrewd move, Linda Eastman returned to the United States. It was he who followed her there. Several months later she became pregnant and they announced their marriage. Paul tried to console his weeping fans: "Come on girls, cheer up! I have to get married some day." That day was 12 March 1969. Their first daughter, Mary, was born the following August. Two years later Stella arrived; finally in 1977, a son, James Louis. They raised their four children – Paul adopted Heather – ensuring that they led a well-balanced life, because Paul wanted them to have as happy a childhood as his own.

For a long time, British pop music fans were very bitter at the fact that foreign women had got their claws into two of the country's national assets. Lennon and McCartney, who wrote all the group's songs, had married a Japanese, Yoko Ono (cf. p. 312) and a left-leaning American respectively. The two women disliked each other. In the opinion of many inconsolable fans, it was they who were responsible for the group breaking up. In reality, although the break-up did not become common

knowledge until 1969, it in fact went back much further than that, the final concert by the "Fab Four" being staged in September 1966.

After the Beatles split up, Paul went through a period of depression, then, at his wife's insistence, started to compose songs again and formed a new group called Wings. To avoid being separated from her, he insisted that she become a member of the band, and taught her to play the piano. The results were unconvincing, as the public was not slow to make clear. They decided to move to the countryside, in Scotland; they lived there happily, raising sheep. Paul dedicated all his love-songs to his wife; some are criticised for their lyrics, but "Silly Love Song", which they sang together on stage, was a great success. His most recent recording, *Flaming Pie*, was also inspired by his wife.

Linda accompanied her husband on all his tours – they had sworn to each other never to spend a night apart. They managed to keep their promise, with few exceptions, one of which occurred during a tour of Japan in 1980. Arrested by customs officials for being in possession of marijuana, the singer spent ten nights in prison.

"Can't Buy Me Love" the Beatles sang. Neither fame nor money – he is one of the wealthiest men in the United Kingdom – could have brought Paul the joys he shared with his wife: three fine children and serene happi-

1998

World-wide success for *Titanic*, the film by James Cameron. The hero – played by the young, good-looking Leonardo di Caprio, who subsequently became an international idol – gives a lesson in courage to the girl he loves: "Never give up."

UNITED STATES. **Renewed scandal after the release of Mary Kay LeTourneau. This primary schoolmistress from Seattle (Washington State), aged thirty-six, and married with four children, had received a jail sentence for having an affair with a thirteen-year-old boy, as a result of which a baby girl was born. Although she undertook never to see the boy again, she did so, and was returned to prison. In a televised interview, she declared: "I regret nothing. Risking seven and a half years in prison to see him again was worth it."**

ROMEO AND JULIET **in Pakistan: Kanwar Ahsan and Rifflat Afridi married in secret because the girl's parents were opposed to her marriage to a man from a different ethnic group. In a country where arranged marriages are the norm, the affair upset public opinion and unleashed violent demonstrations in the streets of Karachi. When the young man was brought before the court under police protection, he was seriously injured ...**

ness. Their secret? The priority they gave to their marriage and their family: a simple, ordinary way of life; very few staff, no ostentatious spending, the knack of enjoying the small pleasures and the big occasions in life. "We love each other," he said frankly, with no sense of conceit.

"LET IT BE." After Wings disbanded in 1979, Linda started a campaign against the ill-treatment of animals. She was not a drinker, gave up smoking and became an outspoken vegetarian. She made a fortune from a cookery book, *Home Cooking*, and from a line of frozen products, Ready Meals. She resumed her profession as a photographer and exhibited her work.

In December 1995, she discovered that she had breast cancer. When she lost her hair from the chemotherapy treatment, Paul cut his own hair very short in sympathy. Sustained by the unwavering love of her husband, she displayed a great moral fortitude. "A catastrophe such as this makes you aware of what is really important in life," said Paul. They both found the strength to go to Paris to attend the first fashion show of their daughter Stella, who succeeded Karl Lagerfeld as designer for the Chloé fashion house. In March 1998, at the show's opening, Stella McCartney chose to use the Beatle theme-song "All You Need Is Love". This was her mother's last appearance in public. Looking drawn and with her hair very short, Linda McCartney beamed with pleasure.

"Let it be" Paul had once written in a song dedicated to his own mother who died of cancer when he was fourteen. "Whisper words of wisdom, let it be": words of resignation, words of wisdom indeed.

♡ ♡ ♡

SOCIETY
Double Standards

A woman's sexual behaviour is judged more severely than a man's, and love plays a greater part in her life.

"A woman who drinks too much at a party and finds herself making love with two men runs the risk of feeling very guilty the next day, saying 'I was stupid, I behaved like a whore.' A jack-the-lad who has sex with two girls is not ashamed afterwards, and for a couple of weeks is something of a hero among his mates." The young man who made this comparison is making the point very well that the system – alive and kicking despite claims that steady progress is being made – still operates a set of double standards: traditional sexual roles are so ingrained that the same type of behaviour can be interpreted in two different ways, depending upon whether a man or a woman is involved.

In the sexual domain, women are judged more severely than men. At the end of the twentieth century this "double standard", exposed by nineteenth-century feminists, and later by Léon Blum (cf. p. 54) or Alexandra Kollontai (cf. p. 122), still persists. It is based on old beliefs about the differing natures of men and women: a man is made up of good and bad and his sexual needs assumed to be "natural"; a woman is either all good or all bad, that is to say, a virgin and mother figure, or a prostitute. Whereas men are free to indulge their desires, women are forced to choose between one of two irreconcilable models, the "mother" or the "whore". Regarded as potential mothers, girls are expected to remain chaste, or at least display greater self-control than boys.

In legal terms, equality between men and women has come a long way in the West. Nevertheless, it is far from being effective in concrete ways (cf. p. 408), such as sharing household chores, or symbolically, as in assigning different meanings of sex and love to each of the sexes. Contraception has helped women to become mistresses of their own destiny, and has contributed to changes in their sexual behaviour. While women are now more sexually active and enter more freely into relationships of their own volition (cf. p. 310), society as a whole is slow to adapt and social restraints are still influential.

A VIRILE MAN. Discrimination starts at a very early age, from school-days onwards. The "lady-killer" who goes out with three girls gains a flattering reputation, while the girl who kisses three boys at a party is treated as a flirt, or even a "tart". This reputation stays with her throughout her life. Although the taboo surrounding female virginity may have lost its force in the West, the contradiction revealed by the difference in attitude to a "Don Juan" character and the "woman of easy virtue" has not disappeared. While a man may boast of his sexual conquests in order to enhance his standing, women underplay anything which could lead to the accusation of being "easy". This goes a long way to explaining the surprising results of surveys into sexual behaviour (cf. p. 226)! When the time came to draw up the balance-sheet, the biographers of multimillionaire Howard Hughes, for example, used a hunting analogy to describe the number of beautiful women in Hollywood that he "bagged", whereas Pamela Harriman (cf. p. 325) was described as a "courtesan".

Despite changing morals, male and female adulterers are still treated unequally: greater indulgence is shown to the unfaithful husband (cf. p. 42); the male bigamist (cf. p. 420) is tolerated, esteemed even, as a symbol of great virility; there are also double standards when it comes to the choice of a much younger partner (cf. p. 324), or on remarriage after being widowed (cf. p. 352).

For a man giving free rein to his sexual desires passes as a proof of virility, whereas the equivalent behaviour in a woman is considered degrading. A woman who refuses to be hunted, and turns into the hunter, is soon treated as a slut. She runs the same risk if she is a woman with a taste for power, or if she simply wishes to affirm her independence by acting in a non-conformist way. No term is more calculated to insult a woman who departs from the norm than that of "tart", a word which has no masculine equivalent and which is used to condemn the aspiration to sexual emancipation by many modern, independent women.

The female identity, unlike that of the male, is based largely on a desirable appearance: the female body is scrutinised for sexual messages, hence the erotic characteristics attributed to women's clothing – transparency, décolletage, fit – and underwear (cf. p. 382). Undeniably, women's freedom has increased enormously, but the requirement to conform to a physical norm, that is to say, a slim figure or hair dyed to hide the greying streaks, is more important than for a man. Those women who deviate from the norm come in for criticism. The same inconsistency in attitude applies to sexual attraction: power increases a man's sexual allure, and may be reinforced by the symbols of professional status; on the other hand, a woman in a high-powered job, in addition to being suspected of owing her success to sexual favours granted, arouses fear rather than desire, and her sexuality is seen as a threat (cf. p. 390).

While our culture has accustomed men to dissociate love from sex, for the majority of women feelings, whether of love, tenderness, or affection, condition sexual relations. This difference is clear in the first sexual relationship (cf. p. 294): generally speaking, girls make love for the sake of love, and boys do it out of desire or curiosity. Ultimately, girls want lasting relationships, while boys tend to shy away from commitment. This quid pro quo is repeated when a man has a fling with a woman who imagines that the fact that she has "yielded" to him confers rights, and marks the start of a relationship.

LOVE IS THE OPIUM OF WOMEN. Despite an apparently growing freedom, old traditions die hard: most girls still dream of a big romance, the opiate distilled by sentimental novels (cf. p. 126), even though today's Prince Charming may be described by a supermarket cashier in somewhat different terms, as "a big hunk of man, who will take care of me". Men are not waiting for a princess: after a youth of sexual promiscuity, the majority of them "settle down" with a female companion who is prepared to devote herself to material and emotional comfort. The same inconsistency applies to infidelity. some men will not tolerate a woman's extramarital sex, but tolerate an affectionate friendship, whereas women, convinced that a man's desires are "imperative" often allow their partner to have a "purely physical" affair, but are much more upset if he actually loves the other woman.

At school, boys who are in love are made fun of. Later on, as a result, saying "I love you" constitutes an admission of weakness for many men (cf. p. 152). Whereas films and novels show that love is the most important aspect of a woman's life, it is conceded that a man views love in quite a different way. A man without a woman remains a man; a woman without a man is regarded as being somehow incomplete. If a man fails in his love relationship, he can fall back on his professional success; conversely, a woman is always judged on her private life. Similarly, a woman's biography gives plenty of space to her marriage and love life, but that of a man glosses over such details. Throughout the course of the twentieth century, women have changed more than men (cf. p. 408), and their aspiration to more equal relations is being acknowledged, even if poverty and unemployment mean that there has been a backward step. Nevertheless, progress would not have been made were it not for the fact that love, for women, is "like a religion" (cf. p. 231), nor were it for the fact that women, more than men, put the success of their love life and family life at the very centre of their existence. In renouncing a very demanding career, by "opting" for a career which is compatible with looking after children, women allow men to continue to give priority to their professional life and neglect family commitments without any sense of guilt.

Some men are starting to change: they take care over their appearance, try to become better lovers and fathers. Those who try to reconcile their professional and emotional lives have, it appears, heard this eighties' message from an official Swedish agency: "On your deathbed, you will not regret having missed a promotion, but having not spent enough time with the people you love." Come the twenty-first century, shall we see love occupying a comparable position for both men and women? Although a life without love is a life which is incomplete, love alone is not sufficient to give an absolute meaning to life; to succeed in it, also implies opening up as a human being.

Love remains a mystery ...

"Love has to be re-invented."

(Arthur Rimbaud, *Illuminations*)

... by an unknown gunman. His wife has gone into hiding, as they both try to leave the country to live and love in safety.

UNITED STATES. **Phenomenal success of Viagra after the introduction on to the American market of this vasodilator, which facilitates an erection without provoking it. The laboratory's share-price leaps in value, and a black market is created in those countries where Viagra is still not available over the counter. It is also sold on the Internet. The Vatican approves its use, for married couples only. The small, blue tablet, sometimes called Sextasy, is the first rapidly-acting pharmacological product to deal with the physiological problems of erection. At least 10 per cent of men suffer from impotence, but the potential market is much larger. Many men associate virility with the ability to have an erection, and are prepared to do anything to improve it, even where there are contra-indications. The risks, however, are serious, sometimes fatal, particularly for men with heart conditions.**

♡ ♡ ♡

BIBLIOGRAPHY

Unless otherwise stated, the works listed below were published in Paris.

GENERAL WORKS

Christine Bard, *Les Filles de Marianne, Histoire des féminismes 1914–1940*, Fayard, 1995

Miguel Benasayag and Dardo Scavino, *Le Pari amoureux*, French trans. Monte, La Découverte, 1995

Pascal Brückner and Alain Finkielkraut, *Le Nouveau Désordre amoureux*, Le Seuil, 1977

Collectif Clio, *L'Histoire des femmes au Québec depuis quatre siècles*, Quinze, Montreal, 1982

André Comte-Sponville, *Petit Traité des grandes vertus*, PUF, 1995

Courrier international (French weekly publication)

Norbert Elias, *La Civilisation des mœurs*, Calmann-Lévy, 1973

Jean-Louis Flandrin, *Le Sexe et l'Occident, Evolution des attitudes et des comportements*, Le Seuil, 1981

Shere Hite, *Women and Love, A Cultural Revolution in Progress*, Knopf, 1987

Laurence Klejman and Florence Rochefort, *L'Egalité en marche, Le Féminisme sous la Troisième République*, Presses de la Fondation nationale des sciences politiques / Des femmes, 1989

Anne Martin-Fugier, *La Bourgeoise*, Grasset, 1983

André Miquel, *Deux histoires d'amour, De Majnûn à Tristan*, Odile Jacob, 1996

Florence Montreynaud, *Le XXe Siècle des femmes*, Nathan, 1995

Félicie Nayrou and Alain Rudy (ed.), *La Rencontre, figures du destin*, Autrement, 1993

Pascale Noizet, *L'Idée moderne d'amour, Entre sexe et genre: vers une théorie du sexologème*, Kimé, 1996

Octavio Paz, *La Llama doble, Amor y erotismo*, 1993

Antoine Prost and Gérard Vincent (ed.), *Histoire de la vie privée*, vol. v, Le Seuil, 1987

Phyllis J. Read & Bernard L. Witlieb, *The Book of Women's Firsts*, Random House, New York, 1992

Claude Roy, *Le Verbe aimer et autres essais*, Gallimard, 1969

Jacqueline Rubellin-Devichi (ed.), *Des concubinages dans le monde*, with postscript by Marie-Thérèse Meulders-Klein, CNRS, 1990

Edward Shorter, *The Making of the Modern Family*, 1975

Françoise Thébaud (ed.), *Histoire des femmes, Le XXe siècle* (series edited by Georges Duby and Michelle Perrot), Plon, 1992

Theodore Zeldin, *France 1848–1945*, vol. 1 (*Ambition and Love*) and vol. 5 (*Anxiety and Hypocrisy*), Oxford University Press, 1973 and 1977

SEXUALITY

Jean-Claude Bologne, *Histoire de la pudeur*, Olivier Orban, 1986

Jean-Claude Bologne, *Histoire du mariage en Occident*, Lattès, 1995

Alain Corbin, *Le Temps, le Désir et l'Horreur*, Aubier, 1991

John d'Emilio & Estelle B. Freedman, *Intimate Matters, A History of Sexuality in America*, Harper & Row, New York, 1988

Catherine Desprats-Péquignot, *La Psychopathologie de la vie sexuelle*, PUF, Que sais-je?, 1992

Barbara Ehrenreich, Elizabeth Hess, Gloria Jacobs, *Re-making Love, The Feminization of Sex*, Anchor Press, New York, 1986

Jean-Louis Flandrin, *Le Sexe et l'Occident, évolution des attitudes et des comportements*, Le Seuil, 1981

Michel Foucault, *Histoire de la sexualité*, vol. 1: *La Volonté de savoir*, Gallimard, 1976

Harriett Gilbert (ed), *The Sexual Imagination*, Jonathan Cape, London, 1993

Jane Mills, *Sexwords*, Penguin, London, 1993

Florence Montreynaud, *Amours à vendre. Les dessous de la prostitution*, Glénat, 1993

Dr June M. Reinisch & Ruth Beasley, *The Kinsey Institute New Report on Sex*, The Kinsey Institute for Research in Sex, Gender and Reproduction, 1990

GENERAL BIOGRAPHICAL MATERIAL

The Europa Biographical Dictionary of British Women, Europa, London, 1983

Barbara Sicherman, Carol Hurd Green et al., *Notable American Women*, Radcliffe College, The Belknap Press of Harvard University Press, Cambridge, 1980

Jennifer S. Uglow, *The Macmillan Dictionary of Women Biography*, Macmillan, London, 1984

Biographical information in *Universalia*, annual supplements to the *Encylopaedia Universalis*

CINEMA

Chronique du cinéma, Chronique, 1992

Gilles Horvilleur (ed.), *Dictionnaire des personnages de cinéma*, Bordas, 1988

Edgar Morin, *Les Stars*, Galilée, 1984

Vincent Pinel, *Le Siècle du cinéma*, Bordas, 1994

Marion Vidal and Jean-Claude Glasser, *Histoire des plus célèbres répliques du cinéma*, Ramsay Poche, 1993

BIBLIOGRAPHY BY YEARS

1900 *Le Soir*, illustrated: special number to cover the death of Prince Albert, 1934

Lionel Giraud-Mangin, "Une reine humaniste: la reine Elisabeth de Belgique", *Texts & Documents*, January 1966

Carlo Bronne, "Hommage à la reine Elisabeth", *Revue des Deux Mondes*, December 1976

Claudine Chevrel and Béatrice Cornet, *Affiches et images d'amoureux*, Edita, Lausanne, 1990

Geneviève Grimler, *Le Livre des amoureux*, Du Rhin Publications, Mulhouse, 1994

1901 Sophie Laffitte, *Tchekhov par lui-même*, Le Seuil, 1955

Vive la mariée!, an exhibition on marriage in the civilised world, staged in the Kunsthalle, Cologne, August – October 1985

Arnold van Gennep, *Manuel du folklore français contemporain*, Picard, 1943; reprinted 1982

Martine Segalen, *Amours et Mariages dans l'ancienne France*, Berger-Levrault, Paris, 1981

Claudine Fillion, *Souvenirs de mariage*, a leaflet available at the Abbey of Saint-Arnoult at Crépy-en-Valois (Oise), showing a collection of bridal bouquets collected by M. and Mme Fillion

Tad Tuleja, *Curious Customs, the Stories behind 296 Popular American Rituals*, Harmony Books, New York, 1987

Michel Pastoureau, *Dictionnaire des couleurs de notre temps*, Bonneton, 1992

1902 Karen Monson, *Alma Mahler, Muse to Genius*

Colette, *Œuvres complètes*, Gallimard, coll. La Pléiade, Vol. 1, 1984 (preface by Claude Pichois, critique de Paul d'Hollander)

1903 Marie Curie, *Pierre Curie*, republished by Odile Jacob, 1996

Susan Quinn, *Marie Curie*, Simon & Schuster, New York, 1995

Louise Nyström-Hamilton, *Ellen Key, Her Life and Her Work*, translated from the Swedish, Putnam, New York and London, 1913

Gabriel Monod, preface to the French translation of Vol. 1 of *Lifslinjer, On Love and Marriage*, 1907

1904 Claudine Brécourt-Villars, *D'Annunzio et La Duse*, Stock, 1994

Ernest Glasson, *Le Mariage civil et le divorce dans l'Antiquité et dans les principales législations de l'Europe*, Pédone, Paris, 1880

Françoise Héritier, *Les Deux Sœurs et leur mère*, Odile Jacob, 1994

Alfred Dittgen, "La Forme du mariage en Europe", *Population No. 2*, 1994

1905 Desanka Trbuhović-Gjurić, *Im Schatten Albert Einstein*, Paul Haupt, Berne, 1983; *Mileva Einstein, Une vie*, Des femmes, 1991

Albert Einstein and Mileva Marić, *The Love Letters*, Princeton University Press, 1992

Interview with Freud by *Kulturpolitische Gesellschaft* in the context of inquiry into reforming marriage lines, 8 February 1905, in John W. Boyer, "Freud, Marriage, and Late Viennese Liberalism: a commentary from 1905", *The Journal of Modern History*, Vol. 50, No. 1, March 1978

Gérard Lauzun, *Freud et la psychanalyse*, Seghers, 1962

Sarah Kofman, *L'Enigme de la femme*, Galilée, 1980

Roland Jaccard, *Freud*, PUF, Que sais-je?, 1983

Paul-Laurent Assoun, *Freud et la femme*, Calmann-Lévy, 1983

Sigmund Freud présenté par lui-même, Gallimard, 1984

Michael Pollak, *Vienne 1900*, Gallimard, 1984

Laurence Paton and Gisa Llobregat, *Freud, prénom Martha*, Renaudot et Cie, 1989

1906 Emma Goldman, *Living my Life*, 1932

Alice Wexler, *Emma Goldman*, 1984

Wanda de Sacher-Masoch, *Confession de ma vie*, republished Gallimard, 1989, preface by Jean-Paul Corsetti

1907 Shari Benstock, *Women of the Left Bank*, University of Texas Press, 1986

Andrea Weiss, *Paris Was a Woman, Portraits from the Left Bank*, Pandora, London, 1995

Grete Schiller, *Paris Was a Woman*, film documentary, 1995

Alice B. Toklas, *What Is Remembered*, 1963

Ernest Hemingway, *A Moveable Feast*, 1964

Jean Lacouture, *Léon Blum*, Le Seuil, Paris, 1977

Francine Muel-Dreyfus, *Vichy et l'éternel féminin*, Le Seuil, 1996

1908 Arthur Gold and Robert Fizdale, *Misia. The Life of Misia Sert*, Knopf, New York 1980

Marguerite Burnat-Provins, *Le Livre pour toi*, La Différence, 1994

Claudine Brécourt-Villars, *Ecrire d'amour, Anthologie de textes érotiques féminins*, Ramsay, 1985

1909 Carole Seymour-Jones, *Beatrice Webb, Woman of Conflict*, Pandora, London, 1992

Ruth Brandon, *The New Women and the Old Men: Love, Sex and the Woman Question*, Norton, New York, 1990

1910 Dominique Desanti, *Sonia Delaunay magique magicienne*, Ramsay, 1988

Hajo Düchting, *Robert and Sonia Delaunay. The triumph of colour*, Cologne, 1994

Max-Pol Fouchet, *L'Art amoureux des Indes*, La Guilde du Livre, Lausanne, 1957

Vatsyayana, *Kama Sutra*, English translation by S. C. Upadhyaya, Taraporevala, Bombay, 1961

Kalyana Malla, *Ananga Ranga, traité hindou de l'amour conjugal*, Cercle du livre précieux, 1963; republished by UGE 10/18, 1995

Françoise Couchard, *Le Fantasme de séduction dans la culture musulmane*, PUF, 1994

Ibn 'Arabî, *Traité de l'amour*, translated by Gloton, Albin Michel, 1986

1911 Jean Chalon, *Le Lumineux Destin d'Alexandra David-Néel*, Perrin, 1985

Alexandra David-Néel, *Journal de voyage*, Plon, 1975; *Lettres à son mari*, Plon, 1976

Sandor Kuthy, *Sophie Taeuber – Hans Arp, Dialogues d'artistes*, Kunstmuseum, Berne, 1988

Alexandre Lavrentiev, *Varvara Stepanova, Une vie constructiviste*, Philippe Sers, 1988

L'Avant-garde russe 1905 – 1925, a catalogue of the exhibition staged in the Musée des Beaux-Arts de Nantes, 1993

1912 Katherine Mansfield, *Journal*, translated by Duproix, Marcel et Bay, Stock, 1932

Michel Dupuis, *Katherine Mansfield*, La Manufacture, 1988

Pietro Citati, *The Short Life of Katherine Mansfield*, Rizzoli, 1980; translated by Pérol, Quai Voltaire, 1987

Marcel Proust, *Le Côté de Guermantes*, 1920

Martin Green, The von Richthofen Sisters, 1974

Ruth Brandon, *The New Women and the Old Men: Love, Sex and the Woman Question*, Norton, New York, 1990

1913 Gordon N. Ray, *H. G. Wells and Rebecca West*, Yale University Press, 1974

Rebecca West, *Family Memories: an Autobiographical Journey*, Viking, New York, 1988

Michael Coren, *The Invisible Man: The Life and Liberties of H. G. Wells*, Bloomsbury, London, 1993

Nina Berberova, *Histoire de la baronne Boudberg*, Actes Sud, 1988

Horacio Salas, *Le Tango*, translated by Morvan, Actes Sud, 1989

1914 Jean-Denis Bredin, *Joseph Caillaux*, Hachette, 1980

Edward Berenson, *The Trial of Madame Caillaux*, University of California Press, Berkeley, 1992

Françoise Thébaut, *La Femme au temps de la guerre de 14*, Stock/Laurence Pernoud, 1986

Anne Martin-Fugier, *La Bourgeoise*, Grasset, 1983

Stéphane Audoin-Rouzeau, *L'Enfant de l'ennemi 1914–1918*, Aubier, 1995

1915 Suzanne Shelton, *Divine Dancer, A Biography of Ruth Saint Denis*, Garden City,

New York, 1981

Mireille Dottin-Orsini, *Cette femme qu'ils disent fatale*, Grasset, 1993

Hans Meyer, *Les Marginaux: Femmes, juifs et homosexuels dans la littérature européenne*, 1975

Claude Frioux, *Maïakovski par lui-même*, Le Seuil, 1961

1916 H. R. Lenormand, *Les Pitoëff, Souvenirs*, Odette Lieutier, 1943

Aniouta Pitoëff, *Ludmilla ma mère: Vie de Ludmilla et Georges Pitoëff*, Julliard, 1955

Svetlana Pitoëff, article on Ludmilla Pitoëff, in *Les Femmes célèbres*, Mazenod, 1960

Jacqueline de Jomaron, *Les Pitoëff, Un roman théâtral*, Champion, 1996

Françoise Thébaut, *La Femme au temps de la guerre de 14*, Stock/Laurence Pernoud, 1986

Sandor Kuthy, *Sophie Taeuber – Hans Arp, Dialogues d'artistes*, Kunstmuseum, Berne, 1988

1917 Billy Klüver and Julie Martin, *Kiki's Paris, Artists and Lovers 1900–1930*, Abrams, New York, 1989

Doris Krystof, *Amedeo Modigliani 1884–1920. The Poetry of Seeing*, Cologne, 1996

C. Schweisguth, "Modigliani", in *Encyclopaedia Universalis*, 1974

André Salmon, *La Vie passionnée de Modigliani*, Gérard, Verviers, 1957

Jeanne Modigliani, *Modigliani sans légende*, Gründ, Paris, 1961

Françoise Navailh, "Le modèle soviétique", in *Histoire des femmes, Le XXᵉ siècle*, directed by Françoise Thébaud, Plon, 1992

Karl Marx, *L'Idéologie allemande*, 1845

Friedrich Engels, The Origin of the Family, Private Ownership and the State, 1884

August Bebel, *La Femme et le socialisme*, 1883

Wilhelm Reich, *La Révolution sexuelle*, 1930

Youki Desnos, *Les Confidences de Youki*, Fayard, 1957

1918 Karen Blixen, *Out of Africa*, 1937

Karen Blixen, *Letters from Africa 1914–1931*

Judith Thurman, *Isak Dinesen, The Life of a Storyteller*, St Martin Press, New York, 1982; Karen Blixen, translated by Raciquot-Loubet, Seghers, 1986

Errol Trzebinsky, *Silence Will Speak* (biography of Denys Finch Hatton), Heinemann, London, 1977

Marie Carmichael Stopes, *Married Love, A New Contribution to the Solution of Sexual Difficulties*, Putnam, London, 1918

Biography of Marie Stopes by Ruth Hall, Virago, London, 1977; by June Rose, Faber and Faber, Winchester, 1992

Germaine Greer, *Sex and Destiny*, Secker & Warburg, London, 1984

Annette Kuhn, *Chronik der Frauen*, Chronik Verlag, Dortmund, 1992

1919 Virginia Woolf, *A Writer's Diary*, 1953

Virginia Woolf, *Letters*, 1975–1980

Phillys Rose, *Virginia Woolf*, 1977

Jean Blot, *Bloomsbury, Histoire d'une sensibilité artistique et politique anglaise*, Balland, 1992

Françoise Thébaut, *La Femme au temps de la guerre de 14*, Stock/Laurence Pernoud, 1986

Dictionnaire de la misogynie, preface by Benoîte Groult, Albin Michel, 1994

Phyllis J. Read & Bernard L. Witlieb, *The Book of Women's Firsts*, Random House, New York, 1992

1920 Matthew J. Bruccoli, *Some Sort of Epic Grandeur: The Life of F. Scott Fitzgerald*, Caroll & Graf, 1993

Ernest Hemingway, *A Moveable Feast*, 1964

Geneviève and Michel Fabre, *"Tender is the Night" by F. Scott Fitzgerald*, Armand Colin, Paris, 1989

Henri-Pierre Roché, *Jules et Jim*, 1953

Elisabeth Weyer, *L'Histoire vraie de Jules et Jim*, film documentary, Hessischer Rundfunk/Arte 1994

Helen Hessel, *Journal*, followed by *Lettres à Henri-Pierre Roché*, translated Raybaud, André Dimanche, 1992

Franz Hessel, *Romance parisienne*, translated Marcou, Maren Sell, 1991

Henri-Pierre Roché, *Carnets*, André Dimanche, 1990

Manfred Flügge, *Le Tourbillon de la vie, La Véritable Histoire de Jules et Jim*, translated Bary, Albin Michel, 1994

François Truffaut, *Jules et Jim*, film, 1962

Colette, *Le Pur et l'Impur*, 1932

Lawrence Joseph, *Catherine Pozzi, Une robe couleur du temps*, La Différence, 1988

1921 Serge Esenin, *Poèmes*, Lenizdat, 1965 (in Russian), translated by Florence Montreynaud

Pierre Pascal, Article on Esenin in *Encyclopaedia Universalis*, 1974

Anatoli Mariengof, *Un roman sans mensonges*, Le Seuil, 1992

Annette Baxter, Article on Isadora Duncan in *Notable American Women*, Harvard University Press, 1971

Maurice Lever, *Isadora*, Presses de la Renaissance, 1987

Magnus Hirschfeld, several books are still available in German. *Berlins Drittes Geschlecht* (1905), *Die Transvestiten* (1910), *Die Homosexualität des Mannes und des Weibes* (1914). Other books: *Liebesmittel* (1926), *Die Weltreise eines Sexualforschers* (1932). Titles of revues published by Hirschfeld: *Jahrbuch für sexuelle Zwischenstufen* und *Zeitschrift für Sexualwissenschaft*

Freud's assessment of Hirschfeld appears in a letter to Karl Abraham dated January 1909

Havelock Ellis, *The Task of Social Hygiene*, 1913

Günter Grau et al., *Homosexualität in der National-Sozialistischen Zeit*, Fischer, 1993

Marie-Jo Bonnet, *Les Relations amoureuses entre les femmes, XXIᵉ–XXᵉ siècles*, Odile Jacob, 1995

Carrington, film de Christopher Hampton, 1995

1922 Charles W. Ferguson, "Unforgettable DeWitt Wallace", *The Reader's Digest*, February 1987

Press File, *The Reader's Digest*

1923 Anna de Noailles and Maurice Barrès, *Correspondance 1901–1923*, published by Claude Mignot-Ogliastri, L'Inventaire, 1994

Claude Mignot-Ogliastri, *Anna de Noailles, une amie de la princesse de Polignac*, Méridiens-Klincksieck, 1986

François Broche, *Anna de Noailles, Un mystère en pleine lumière*, Robert Laffont, 1989

Maurice Barrès, *Un jardin sur l'Oronte*, preface by Emilien Carassus, Gallimard, 1990

Françoise Navailh, "Le modèle soviétique", in *Histoire des femmes, Le XXᵉ siècle*, directed by Françoise Thébaud, Plon, 1992

Alexandra Kollontaï, *Marxisme et révolution sexuelle*, texts presented by Judith Stora-Sandor, Maspero, 1973

Myriam Revault d'Allonnes, "Alexandra Kollontaï", in *Femmes et histoire*, Martinsart, 1980

Arkadi Vaksberg, *Alexandra Kollontaï*, translated by Dimitri Sesemann, Fayard, 1996

Georges Bardawil, *Inès Armand*, Lattès, 1993

Clara Zetkin, *Lénine tel qu'il fut*, 1934

Joseph Roth, *Croquis de voyage*, Le Seuil, 1994

Wilhelm Reich, *La Révolution sexuelle*, 1930

1924 Jack Cowart and Juan Hamilton, *Georgia O'Keeffe, Art and Letters*, National Gallery of Art, Washington, 1987

Britta Benke, Georgia O'Keeffe 1887–1986. Flowers in the Desert, Cologne, 1994

Dorothy Norman, *Alfred Stieglitz*, Aperture Foundation 1976; Nathan, 1989

Georgia O'Keeffe, *Alfred Stieglitz*, The Metropolitan Museum of Art, New York, 1978

Benita Eisler, *O'Keeffe and Stieglitz: An American Romance*, Doubleday, New York, 1991

Gwen Robyns, *Barbara Cartland*, 1984; Tallandier, 1988

Bruno Péquignot, *La Relation amoureuse, analyse sociologique du roman sentimental moderne*, L'Harmattan, 1991

Michelle Coquillat, *Romans d'amour*, Odile Jacob, 1988

Annick Houel, *Le Roman d'amour et sa lectrice, L'exemple d'Harlequin*, L'Harmattan, Bibliothèque du féminisme collection, 1997

Marie-Victoire Louis, *Le Droit de cuissage, France 1860–1930*, L'Atelier, 1994

Hildegard Brenner, *Asja Lacis, Profession: révolutionnaire*, trad. Ivernel, Presses Universitaires de Grenoble, 1989

1925 Lotte Eisner, *Fritz Lang*, Secker & Warburg, London, 1976

Gilbert Guilleminault and Philippe Bernert, *Les Princes des années folles*, Plon, 1970

Georges Sturm, *Fritz Lang Films/Textes/Références*, Presses Universitaires de Nancy, 1990

Sara M. Evans, *Born for liberty: A History of Women in America*, Macmillan, 1989

John d'Emilio and Estelle B. Freedman, *Intimate Matters, A History of Sexuality in America*, Harper & Row, New York, 1988

Michel Bozon and François Héran, "La Découverte du conjoint", in *Population*, No 6, 1987

Anne Martin-Fugier, *La Bourgeoise*, Grasset, 1983

Michel Leiris, *L'Âge d'homme*, 1939

John Fuegi, *Brecht and company*, Grove Press, New York

Joseph Roth, *Croquis de voyage*, Le Seuil, 1994

Barbara Grossman, *Funny Woman: The Life and Times of Fanny Brice*, Bloomington, Indiana University Press, 1991

1926 Donald Spoto, *Lenya, A Life*, Little, Brown, Boston, 1989

Jean-Michel Palmier, *Weimar en exil*, Payot, 1988

"Meine Frau", inquiry published in *Münchner Illustrierte Presse*, 14 April 1929

John Fuegi, *Brecht and company*, Grove Press, New York

Barrie Gavin, *Lotte Lenya*, television broadcast, Arte, 1994

Theodoor Hendrik van de Velde, *Le Mariage parfait, Etude sur sa physiologie et sa technique*, Albert Müller, Rüschlikon, 1970

Jean-Claude Bologne, *Histoire de la pudeur*, Olivier Orban, 1986

Alain Corbin, *Le Temps, le Désir et l'Horreur*, Aubier, 1991

John d'Emilio and Estelle B. Freedman, *Intimate Matters, A History of Sexuality in America*, Harper & Row, New York, 1988

Barbara Ehrenreich, Elizabeth Hess, Gloria Jacobs, *Re-making Love, The Feminization of sex*, Anchor Press, New York, 1986

Hubert Aupetit and Catherine Tobin, *L'Amour déboussolé*, François Bourin, 1993

Marie-Laure de Folin, "Robert Graves", in *Encyclopaedia Universalis*, 1968

Christine Jordis, "Robert Graves", in *Encyclopaedia Universalis*, Universalia, 1986

Deborah Baker, *In extremis: The Life of Laura Riding*, Grove Press, New York, 1993

1927 Rauda Jamis, *Frida Kahlo*, Presses de la Renaissance, 1985

Andrea Kettenmann, *Frida Kahlo 1907–1954. Pain and Passion*, Cologne, 1993

Andrea Kettenmann, *Diego Rivera 1886–1957. A Revolutionary Spirit in Modern Art*, Cologne, 1997

J. M. G. Le Clézio, *Diego et Frida*, Stock, 1993

Xavier Fauche and Christiane Noetzlin, *Le Baiser*, Stock, 1987

Maryam Sachs, *Der Kuss*, Wilhelm Heyne, Munich, 1991

Yannick Carré, *Le Baiser sur la bouche au Moyen Âge*, Le Léopard d'or, 1993

Ibn 'Arabî, *Traité de l'amour*, trad. Gloton, Albin Michel, 1986

Desmond Morris, *The Naked Ape*, Grasset, 1967

Hitchcock, *Notorious*, film, 1946

Dante Alighieri, *Inferno*

John d'Emilio and Estelle B. Freedman, *Intimate Matters, A History of Sexuality in America*, Harper & Row, New York, 1988

1928 Louis Aragon, *Le Roman inachevé*, 1956; *Les Yeux d'Elsa*, 1942; *Cantique d'Elsa*, 1942; *Le Fou d'Elsa*, 1963

Dominique Desanti, *Elsa-Aragon, Le Couple ambigu*, Belfond, 1994

Pierre Daix, *Aragon*, Flammarion, 1994

Diane de Margerie, article on Lawrence in *Encyclopaedia Universalis*, 1974

Simone de Beauvoir, *The Second Sex*, Part 3, Chapter II: "Myths"

Christine Jordis, *Le Paysage et l'amour dans le roman anglais*, Le Seuil, 1994

Elaine Feinstein, *Lawrence's Women, The Intimate Life of D. H. Lawrence*, Harper Collins, 1993

1929 Chantal Vieuille, *Gala*, Favre, Lausanne, 1988

Robert Descharnes u. Gilles Néret, *Salvador Dalí*, Cologne, 1994

Dominique Bona, *Gala*, Flammarion, 1995

Marc B. de Launay, preface to the bilingual edition of *Letters to a Young Poet*, Gallimard, 1993

Rainer Maria Rilke, *Oeuvres en Prose*, edited by Claude David, Gallimard, la Pléiade, 1993

Billy Klüver and Julie Martin, *Kiki's Paris, Artists and Lovers 1900–1930*, Abrams, New York, 1989

1930 Diane Johnson, *Dashiell Hammett – A Life*, 1983

Stephen Koch, *La Fin de l'innocence: Les*

Intellectuels d'Occident et la tentation stalinienne, trad. Saporta, Grasset, 1995
Natalie Robins, *The FBI and Writers*, translated "Le FBI et les écrivains", Saint-Jean et Kern, Albin Michel, 1997
Roland Barthes, *Fragments d'un discours amoureux*, Le Seuil, 1977

1931 Noël Riley Fitch, *The Literate Passion of Anaïs Nin & Henry Miller*, in Whitney Chadwick & Isabelle de Courtivron (ed.), *Significant Others*, Thames & Hudson, London, 1993
Anaïs Nin, *The Unexpurgated Diary*, Vol. 1 1931–1932: Henry and June, Harcourt Brace Jovanovitch, New York, 1986; Vol. 2 1932–1934: *Incest*, 1992; Vol. 3 1934–1937: *Fire*; Stock, 1997
Noëlle Riley Fitch, *Anaïs: The Erotic Life of Anaïs Nin*, Little, Brown, 1993
Entry on Fannie Hurst in Barbara Sicherman, Carol Hurd Green et al., *Notable American Women*, Radcliffe College, The Belknap Press of Harvard University Press, Cambridge, 1980
Cinema Adaptations of *Back Street*: films by John M. Stahl (1932), with Irene Dunne and John Boles; by Robert Stevenson (1941) with Margaret Sullavan and Charles Boyer; by David Miller (1961), with Susan Hayward and John Gavin
Giorgio Amendola, *Un'isola*, Rizzoli, Milan, 1980
Sally Festing, *Barbara Hepworth, A Life of Forms*, Viking, London, 1995

1932 Nigel Nicolson, *Portrait of a Marriage*, 1974
Victoria Glendinning, *Vita, The Life of Vita Sackville-West*, Weidenfeld & Nicolson, London, 1983
Cécile Wajsbrot, *Violet Trefusis*, Mercure de France, 1989
Gerald Gardner, *The Censorship Papers*, Dodd & Mead (Hays Committee archives containing 5,000 files)
Claude Dufresne, *Yvonne Printemps*, Perrin, 1988

1933 Blanche Wiesen Cook, *Eleanor Roosevelt: A Life*, Viking, New York, 1992
Karl Dietrich Bracher, Kiepenheuer & Witsch, Cologne, 1969: *La Dictature Allemande*, translated by Strachitz, Privat, 1986

Rita Thalmann (ed.), *Femmes et fascismes*, Tierce, 1986
Joachim Gottschalk's dramatic life is retold in the film *Mariage dans l'ombre*, Kurt Mätzig, 1947
Victor Klemperer, *Ich will Zeugnis ablegen bis zum letzten Tag*, Aufbau Verlag, Berlin, 1995
Walter Gross, in *Le Monde*, 5 April 1995
Jean-Michel Palmier, *Weimar en exil*, Payot, 1988

1934 Sissela Bok, *Alva, Ett Kvinnoliv*, Bonniers, Stockholm, 1987; *Alva Myrdal: A Daughter's Memoir*, Merloyd Lawrence, Reading, Mass., 1991
Kaj Fölster, *De Tre Löven; Sprich, die du noch Lippen hast: Das Schweigen der Frau und die Macht der Männer; Annäherung an Alva Myrdal*, Hitzeroth, Marburg, 1993
Kris i befolkningsfragan English translation: *Nation and Family, The Swedish Experiment in Democratic Family and Population Policy*, Harper and Bros, New York & London, 1941
François Duchêne, *Jean Monnet: The First Statesman of Interdependence*, Norton, London, 1994

1935 Noëlle Loriot, *Irène Joliot-Curie*, Presses de la Renaissance, 1991
Chiyo Uno, *Confession Amoureuse*, Denoël, 1992
James Kirkup, Obituary on Chiyo Uno, *The Independent*, London, 12 June 1996
Obituary on Chiyo Uno, *The Times*, London, 13 June 1996

1936 *Wallis & Edward, Letters 1931–1937*, Michael Bloch (ed.), Weidenfeld & Nicolson, London, 1986
Duchess of Windsor, *The Heart Has Its Reasons*, McKay, New York, 1956
Duke of Windsor, *A King's Story*, Putnam, New York 1951
Stephen Birmingham, *Duchess, the Story of Wallis Warfield Windsor*, MacMillan, London, 1982
J. Bryan III & Charles J. V. Murphy, *The Windsor Story*, Granada, London, 1979
Bartolomé Benassar, *Histoire des Espagnols*, Armand Colin, 1985
Marie-Aline Barrachina, "La section féminine de la Phalange espagnole", in Rita

Thalmann (dir.), *Femmes et fascismes*, Tierce, 1986
Danièle Bussy Genevois, "Femmes d'Espagne, de la République au franquisme", in Georges Duby and Michelle Perrot, *Histoire des femmes, Le xx siècle*, directed by Françoise Thébaud, Plon, 1992
Note on Ruth Rohde, in Barbara Sicherman, Carol Hurd Green et al., *Notable American Women*, Radcliffe College, The Belknap Press of Harvard University Press, Cambridge, 1980

1937 Mary Catherine Bateson, *With A Daughter's Eye*, William Morrow, New York, 1984
Margaret Mead, *Blackberry Winter, my early years*, 1972
Josyane Savigneau, *Carson McCullers, Un cœur de jeune fille*, Stock, 1995

1938 Nadezhda Mandelstam, *Hope Against Hope*, Atheneum, New York, 1970 & 1973
Nicolas Werth, "Goulag, les vrais chiffres", *L'Histoire*, No. 169, September 1993
Lydia Chukovskaya, *Entretiens avec Anna Akhmatova*, translated Nivat & Leibrich, Albin Michel, 1980
Pis'ma o liubvi (Letters on Love) collected by Julia Voznesenskaya, Lev Roitman, Munich, 1987
Evelyne Sullerot, *La Presse féminine*, Armand Colin, 1966
Marcelle Ségal, *Mon métier: le courrier du cœur*, Pierre Horay, 1952
Luisa Passerini, "Société de consommation et culture de masse", in Georges Duby and Michelle Perrot, *Histoire des femmes, Le XXᵉ siècle*, edited by Françoise Thébaud, Plon, 1992
Farid Chenoune and Jean-François Poirier, *Le Divan radiophonique*: by Ménie Grégoire au Doc, in *Encyclopaedia Universalis*, Universalia, 1996
Harriet Gilbert, *The Sexual Imagination*, Jonathan Cape, London, 1993
Judith D. Suther, "Separate Studios, Kay Sage & Yves Tanguy", in Whitney Chadwick & Isabelle de Courtivron (ed.), *Significant Others*, Thames & Hudson, London, 1993

1939 Jean Garceau and Inez Cocke, *Dear Mr. G.*, 1961

Warren G. Harris, *Gable and Lombard*, Kassel, London, 1976

Jane Ellen Wayne, Simon & Schuster, New York, 1987; *Clark Gable's Wives*, Carrère, 1988

Octavio Paz, *La llama doble. Amor y erotismo*, 1993

Georges Duby, *Mâle Moyen Âge, De l'amour et autres essais*, Flammarion, 1988

René Nelli, *L'Erotique des troubadours*, Privat, 1963

Suzanne Lilar, *Le Couple*, Grasset, 1963: republished by Les Eperonniers, Brussels, 1988

1940 Alexander Walker, *Vivien Leigh*, Weidenfeld & Nicolson, London, 1987

Laurence Olivier, *Confessions of an Actor*, Weidenfeld & Nicolson, London, 1982

Gregorio Marañon, *Don Juan et le donjuanisme*, 1940

Søren Kierkegaard, *In vino veritas*

Stefan Zweig, *Casanova*, 1930

Denis de Rougemont, *Comme toi-même, essai sur les mythes de l'amour*, Albin Michel, 1961; republished as *Les Mythes de l'amour*, 1996

Alain Roger, *L'Art d'aimer ou la Fascination de la féminité*, Champ-Vallon, Seyssel, 1995

Prince Francesco Caravita di Sirignano, in *Bas les masques*, programme produced by Mireille Dumas, France 2, 1994

1941 Alberto Moravia and Alain Elkann, *Vita di Moravia*, 1990

Carlo Sgorlon, *Invito alla lettura di Elsa Morante*, Mursia, Italy, 1972

Clio n°1 *Résistances et Libérations (France 1940–45)*, Presses Universitaires du Mirail, Toulouse, 1995

Sarah Fishman, *We will wait: Wives of French Prisoners of War 1940–1945*, Yale University Press, 1991

"Barbara", by Jacques Prévert, in *Paroles*, 1949

André Brunelin, *Gabin*, Robert Laffont

Marlene Dietrich, *Marlène D.*, Grasset

1942 Garson Kanin, *Tracy and Hepburn*, 1973

Anne Edwards, *Katharine Hepburn*, New York, 1985

Katharine Hepburn, *Me*, 1991

Judy Barrett Litoff & David Smith, *We're in This War, Too: World War Two Letters From American Women in Uniform*, Oxford University Press, New York, 1994

"Forces' Sweethearts": Wartime Romance from the First World War to the Gulf, exhibition held at the Imperial War Museum, London, from Feb. to Oct. 1993

Boris Vildé, *Journal et Lettres de prison*, Allia, 1997

Josyane Savigneau, *Carson McCullers, Un cœur de jeune fille*, Stock, 1995

Simone de Beauvoir, *Lettres à Sartre 1940–1963*, Gallimard, 1990

Jean-Philippe Arrou-Vignod, *Le Discours des absents*, Gallimard, 1993

Claude Roy, *Le Verbe aimer et autres essais*, Gallimard, 1969

Roland Barthes, *Fragments d'un discours amoureux*, Le Seuil, 1977

Raymond Radiguet, *Le Diable au corps*, 1923

Philippe Pons, article on a collection of Japanese love letters, *Le Monde*, 5 July 1995

1943 Lucie Aubrac, *Ils partiront dans l'ivresse*, Le Seuil, 1984

Raymond Aubrac, *Où la mémoire s'attarde*, Odile Jacob, 1996

Catherine Bayley, British documentary: *The Secret History of the Soviet Wives*, produced by Juniper, 1993

1944 Lauren Bacall, *By Myself*, Knopf, New York, 1978

Alain Brossat, *Libération, fête folle*, Autrement, 1994

Le Monde, special issue, 4 June 1995

Annick Cojean, feature on the Normandy landings, *Le Monde*, May 1994

Hiroshima mon amour, film by Alain Resnais, screenplay by Marguerite Duras, 1958

Alain Brossat, *Les Tondues*, Manya, 1992

Richard Bohringer, interview, in *Télérama*, 13 July 1994

Howard Hawks, *I Was a Male War Bride*, 1949

Comtesse Marion Dönhoff, *A childhood in Eastern Prussia*

Robert Sabatier, *La Souris verte*, Albin Michel, 1990

Gena Turgel, *I Light a Candle*, Grafton Books, 1987

What Did you Do in the War, Auntie?, televi-sion series, BBC 1, May 1995

Vincente Minnelli, *I Remember It Well*, 1974

Collectif Clio, *L'Histoire des femmes au Québec*, Quinze, 1982

1945 Humphrey Carpenter, *Benjamin Britten, A Biography*, Faber & Faber, London, 1992

Christopher Headington, *Peter Pears, A Biography*, Faber & Faber, London, 1992

Charles Baudelaire, "À une passante", *Les Fleurs du mal*, 1857

Elizabeth Smart, *By Grand Central Station I Sat Down and Wept*, 1945

1946 Alicia Dujovne Ortiz, *Eva Peron*, Grasset, 1995

Birgitta Linnér, *Society and Sex in Sweden*, The Swedish Institute, Stockholm, 1971

Antoine Prost and Gérard Vincent, (ed.) *Histoire de la vie privée*, vol. v, Le Seuil, 1987

World Network of Women for Rights over Reproduction, *Report of the Campaign against Maternal Mortality and Morbidity*, Amsterdam, 1992

Elisabeth Schwarzkopf, *On and Off the Record: A Memoir of Walter Legge*, Faber & Faber, London, 1982

Elisabeth Schwarzkopf, *My Master's Voice*

Noëlle Loriot, *Madeleine Renaud*, Presses de la Renaissance, 1993

1947 Catherine Clément, *Pour l'amour de l'Inde*, Flammarion, 1993

Roland Barthes, *Fragments d'un discours amoureux*, Le Seuil, 1977

Serge Saint-Michel, *Le Roman-photo*, Larousse, Idéologie et Sociétés collection, 1979

Françoise Cavé, *L'Espoir et la Consolation*, Payot, 1981

Annie Guédez, "Presse: la presse du cœur", in *Encyclopaedia Universalis*, *Universalia*, 1986

Sylvette Giet, "Vingt ans d'amour en couverture", *Actes de la recherche en sciences sociales*, n° 60, Nov. 1985

1948 Edith Piaf, *L'Hymne à l'amour* (extracts from her songs, trans. S. Knight, 1998)

Claude-Jean Philippe, *Edith*, Carrère-Kian, 1988

Dr June M. Reinisch & Ruth Beasley, *The Kinsey Institute New Report on Sex*, The Kinsey Institute for Research in Sex, Gender and Reproduction, 1990

Wilhelm Reich, *The Function of the Orgasm*, first published in Germany, 1927

Georges Bataille, *L'Erotisme*, Ed. de Minuit, 1957

Roland Petit, *J'ai dansé sur les flots*, Grasset, 1993

Interview with Zizi Jeanmaire, in *Libération*, 29 January, 1985

1949 Roberto Rossellini, *Fragments of an Autobiography*, Ramsay, 1987

Ingrid Bergman (with Alan Burgess), *My Story*, Delacorte Press, New York, 1980

Laurence Leamer, *As Time Goes By*, Leda, New York, 1986

Françoise Héritier, *Les Deux Sœurs et leur mère: anthropologie de l'inceste*, Odile Jacob, 1994

Miguel Benasayag and Dardo Scavino, *Le Pari amoureux*, French trans. Monte, La Découverte, 1995

Jean-Claude Bologne, *Histoire du mariage en Occident*, Lattès, 1995

Agnès Fine, *Parrains marraines*, Fayard, 1994

Bertrand d'Astorg, *Variations sur l'interdit majeur, Littérature et inceste en Occident*, Gallimard, 1990

André Langaney and Robert Nadot, "Génétique, parenté et prohibition de l'inceste", in *La Frontière des sexes*, Albert Ducros and Michel Panoff (ed.), PUF, 1995

René Zazzo, *Le Paradoxe des jumeaux*, Stock, 1984

Guillaume Apollinaire, "Ombre de mon amour" 1947

1950 Simone de Beauvoir, autobiographical works: *Memoirs of a Dutiful Daughter*, 1958, *The Prime of Life*, 1960, *Force of Circumstance*, 1963

A Farewell to Sartre, an account of Sartre's last years, 1981

Letters to Nelson Algren, 1997

Letters to Sartre, 1990

Jean-Paul Sartre, *Lettres à Castor et à quelques autres*, Gallimard, 1983

Annie Cohen-Solal, *Sartre 1905–1980*, Gallimard, 1985

Liliane Siegel, *La Clandestine*, Maren Sell, 1988

Toril Moi, *Simone de Beauvoir, The Making of an Intellectual Woman*, Blackwell, Oxford, 1994

Gabriel Wackermann, Biography of Gérard Blitz, in *Encylopaedia Universalis, Universalia*, 1991

Lily Marcou, *Ilya Ehrenbourg*, Plon, 1992

1951 Simone Signoret, *Nostalgia Isn't What It Used to Be*, 1976

1952 Lise London, *La Mégère de la rue Daguerre, souvenirs de résistance*, Le Seuil, 1995

Lise London, *Le Printemps des camarades*, Le Seuil, 1996

Artur & Lise London, *L'Aveu*, Gallimard (Folio), 1968; English title: *The Confession*

Marcel Proust, *Un amour de Swann*, 1930

Julian Barnes, *Before She Met Me*, 1991

La Rochefoucauld, *Maximes*, 1665

Malek Chebel, *Encyclopédie de l'amour en islam*, Payot, 1995

Alain Roger, *L'Art d'aimer ou la fascination de la féminité*, Champ-Vallon, Seyssel, 1995

Ivan Bounine, *Le Sacrement de l'amour*, 1925

Gwyn MacFarlane, *Fleming, The Man and the Myth*, Berlin, 1990

1953 Julius and Ethel Rosenberg, *Letters from the Death House*, 1953

Arnold van Gennep, *Manuel du folklore français contemporain*, Picard, 1943; reprinted 1982

Martine Segalen, *Amours et Mariages dans l'ancienne France*, Berger-Levrault, Paris, 1981

"Les Nouvelles Langues de l'amour", *Courrier International*, 1st August, 1996

Article on Dario Fo and Franca Rame, *La Repubblica*, 3 February, 1987

Interview with Franca Rame, *Corriere della Sera*, 7 August, 1995

Jonathan Katz, "The Art of Code: Robert Rauschenberg and Jasper Johns", in Whitney Chadwick & Isabelle de Courtivron (ed.), *Significant Others*, Thames & Hudson, London, 1993

1954 Bertrand Levergeois, *Fellini, La Dolce Vita du maestro*, Ed. de l'Arsenal, 1994

Charlotte Chandler, *I, Fellini*, Herbig, Munich, 1994

Régine Deforges, *On m'a dit*, Pauvert, 1975

Interview with Dominique Aury, FR3, 22 October, 1994

Ivan Fallon, *Billionaire, The Life and Times of Sir James Goldsmith*, Arrow, London, 1991

Geneviève Sellier and Noël Burch, *La Drôle de Guerre des sexes dans le cinéma français*, Nathan, 1996

1955 Donald Spoto, *Marilyn Monroe, The Biography*, Harper Collins, New York, 1993

Arthur Miller, *Timebends*, Grove Press, New York, 1987

Marjorie Rosen, *Popcorn Venus*, Coward, McCann & Geoghegan, United States, 1973

Vladimir Nabokov, *Lolita*, 1955

Maurice Couturier, *Nabokov ou la Tyrannie de l'auteur*, Le Seuil, 1993

Jean Blot, *Nabokov*, Le Seuil, 1995

Christine Raguet-Bouvart, *Lolita, Un royaume au-delà des mers*, Presses Universitaires de Bordeaux, 1996

Lolita, film directed by Stanley Kubrick with Sue Lyon and James Mason, 1962; another version was made in 1996 by Adrian Lyne, with Dominique Swain and Jeremy Irons

1956 Ronald Hayman, *The Death and Life of Sylvia Plath*, Heinemann, London, 1991

Margaret Dickie Uroff, *Sylvia Plath & Ted Hughes*, 1979, University of Illinois Press, 1979

Sylvie Doizelet, *La terre des morts est lointaine*, Gallimard, 1996

Marjorie Rosen, *Popcorn Venus*, Coward, McCann & Geoghegan, United States, 1973

Evelyne Caron-Lowins, *Hollywood Falbalas*, Pierre Bordas, 1995

Jeffrey Robinson, *Rainier and Grace*, 1989

1957 Melina Mercouri, *I was born Greek*, Observer, 1971

Fabien Siclier and Jacques Lévy, *Jules Dassin*, Edilig, 1986

Jacques Séguéla, *Vote au-dessus d'un nid de cocos*, Flammarion, 1992

Jean-François Six, *Le Chant de l'amour, Eros dans la Bible*, Desclée de Brouwer / Flammarion, 1995

Julia Kristeva, *Histoires d'amour*, Denoël, 1983

Emmanuel Levinas, *Totalité et Infini; Le Temps et l'Autre*

1958 Joe Morella and Edward Epstein, *Paul and Joanne*, Delacorte Press, New York, 1988

Mary B. Cassata, "The Soap Opera", in *TV Genres, A Handbook and Reference Guide*, Brian G. Rose (ed), Westport Greenwood Press, 1985

Mary Ellen Brown, *Soap Opera and Women's Talk*, Sage, London, 1994

Articles on South American soaps, in *Courrier International*

1959 Jacques Lorcey, *Maria Callas*, Ed. de Paris, 1977

Renzo Allegri, *La Véritable Histoire de la Callas*, French trans. Laget, Belfond, 1992

Olivier Todd, *Jacques Brel*, Robert Laffont, 1984

Irène Théry, *Le Démariage*, Odile Jacob, 1993

1960 *John Cassavetes, Self Portraits*, selected by Ray Carney, trad. Grünberg, Cahiers du cinéma, 1992

Dough Headline and Dominique Cazenave, *John Cassavetes, Portraits de famille*

Charles Baudelaire, *My Heart Laid Bare*

Deborah Tannen, *You Just Don't Understand*, William Morrow, New York, 1990

Alain Braconnier, *Le Sexe des émotions*, Odile Jacob, 1996

D. H. Lawrence, *Lady Chatterley's Lover*, 1928

1961 André Miquel, *Deux Histoires d'amour, De Majnûn à Tristan*, Odile Jacob, 1996

Joan Baez, *Daybreak*, Summit Books, New York, 1987

Ronnie Scharfman, "André and Simone Schwarz-Bart", Whitney Chadwick & Isabelle de Courtivron (ed.), in *Significant Others*, Thames & Hudson, London, 1993

1962 Jean-Pierre Berthomé, *Jacques Demy, Les Racines du rêve*, L'Atalante, Nantes, 1982

Anne Andreu, "Agnès Varda" in *Femmes et arts*, Martinsart, 1980

Agnès Varda, *Varda par Agnès*, Les Cahiers du cinéma, Paris, 1994

"Mariage (droit du)", in *Encyclopaedia Universalis, Universalia*, 1974

Michel-Louis Lévy and Jean-Paul Sardou, "L'écart d'âge entre époux", *Population et sociétés*, No. 162, October 1982

Jacques Véron, "Inégalité des sexes, inégalité des femmes", *Population et sociétés*, No. 305, September 1995

1963 Alexander Walker, *Elizabeth: The Life of Elizabeth Taylor*, Weidenfeld & Nicholson, London, 1990

Muriel Jolivet, *Un pays en mal d'enfants, Crise de la maternité au Japon*, La Découverte, 1993

Christine Bard, *Les Filles de Marianne, Histoire des féminismes 1914–1940*, Fayard, 1995

Eliane Vogel-Polsky, "Les Impasses de l'égalité", *Parité -Infos*, No. 1, May 1994

1964 Sophia Loren and A. E. Hotchner, *Sophia Living and Loving: Her Own Story*, William Morrow, New York, 1978

Alfred Spira, Nathalie Bajos et al., *Rapport sur les comportements sexuels en France*, French Public Records, 1993

Kaye Wellings *et al.*, *Sexual Behaviour in Britain*, Penguin, 1994

Hugues Lagrange and Brigitte Lhomond (ed.), *L'Entrée dans la sexualité, le comportement des jeunes dans le contexte du sida*, La Découverte, 1997

Martine Sevegrand, *Les Enfants du bon Dieu. Les catholiques français et la procréation au XXe siècle*, Albin Michel, 1995

1965 Ingmar Bergman, *The Magic Lantern: An Autography*, 1987

Liv Ullmann, *Changing*, Knopf, New York, 1977

Peter Cowie, *Ingmar Bergman*, Secker & Warburg, London, 1982

Thérèse Hibert and Louis Roussel (ed.), *La Nuptialité: évolution récente en France et dans les pays développés*, INED, Congrès et colloques No. 7, PUF, 1991

Sabine Chalvon-Demersay, "L'Union libre", in *Encyclopaedia Universalis, Universalia* 1985

Jacqueline Rubellin-Devichi (ed.), *Des concubinages dans le monde*, postscript by Marie-Thérèse Meulders-Klein, CNRS, 1990

id. *Des concubinages en Europe*, 1989

1966 Jill Johnston, "The Cyclops of Fontainebleau", *Art in America*, June 1996

Niki de Saint-Phalle, *Mon secret*, La Différence, 1994

Text written by Niki de Saint-Phalle on a wall at the Fémininmasculin exhibition, Pompidou Centre, Paris, 1995

1967 Danish public records: "Queen Margrethe II", "Prince Henrik", publications by the Ministry of Foreign Affairs

Henri de Montpezat, *Destin oblige*, Plon, 1996

Augustin Barbara, *Les Couples mixtes*, Bayard, 1993

Barbara Chase-Riboud, "Métissage", *Vogue*, February 1996

Michèle Tribalat and Francisco Munoz-Pérez, "Les mariages d'immigrés avec des Français. Leur évolution depuis quelques décennies", in Thérèse Hibert and Louis Roussel (ed.), *La Nuptialité, évolution récente en France et dans les pays développés*, INED, PUF, 1991

Gérard Neyrand and Marine M'Sili, *Les Couples mixtes et le divorce. Le poids de la différence*, L'Harmattan, 1996

Yehudi Menuhin "Jacqueline Du Pré", in *The Dictionary of National Biography*, 1986–1990

Philippe Lançon, interview with Philippe Sollers and Julia Kristeva, *Libération*, 5 August 1996

François Armanet and Sylvie Véran, "Quand l'infidélité sauve les couples", interview with Philippe Sollers and Julia Kristeva, *Le Nouvel Observateur*, 8 August 1996

1968 *Beate Klarsfeld*, film for television by Michael Lindsay-Hogg, 1986, produced by William Kayden and Orion Television for ABC

Serge Klarsfeld, film for television by Gloria Campana, Michkan World Productions, 1995

Claude Bochurberg, *Entretiens avec Serge Klarsfeld*, 1997

Wilhelm Reich, *La Révolution sexuelle*, 1930

Octavio Paz, *The Double Flame, Love and Eroticism*, 1993

Martine Sevegrand, *Les Enfants du bon Dieu. Les Catholiques français et la procréation au XXe siècle*, Albin Michel, 1995

Sandrine Treiner and Catherine Valabrègue, *La Pilule, et après? Deux générations face au contrôle des naissances*, Stock, 1996

Gérard Lenne, *Jane Birkin*, Henri Veyrier, 1985

1969 Albert Goldman, *The Lives of John Lennon*, William Morrow, New York

Paul Du Noyer, "Macadam Cowboy", trad. Bonnin, in *Les Inrockuptibles*, 26 July 1995

Renée Vivien, in Colette, *Le Pur et l'Impur*, 1932

Jean Gondonneau, *Techniques de l'amour physique*, Balland, 1971

Chen Heng, *Le Tao de l'amour*, Albin Michel, 1994

'Abd al-Rahmane al-Souyoûti, *Nuits de noces ou Comment humer le doux breuvage de la magie licite*, trad. Khawam, Albin Michel, 1972

Malek Chebel, *Encyclopédie de l'amour en islam*, Payot, 1995

Renée David, *Les Femmes juives*, Perrin, 1988

Gabriel Garcìa Márquez, *Love in the Time of Cholera*

Helvétius, *Pensées*

Raymond Jean, "Pour Gabrielle", in Gabrielle Russier, *Lettres de prison*, Le Seuil, 1970

Gilles Cahoreau, *François Truffaut*, Julliard

1970 Richard Gwyn, *Le Prince*, France-Amérique, 1981

Margaret Trudeau, *Beyond Reason*, 1979

Frédéric Martel, *Le Rose et le Noir, Les Homosexuels en France depuis 1968*, Le Seuil, 1996

Lionel Povert, *Dictionnaire gay*, Grancher, 1994

Marie-Jo Bonnet, *Les Relations amoureuses entre les femmes, XVIe–XIXe siècles*, Odile Jacob, 1995

Vito Russo, *The Celluloid Closet*, 1981; film by Rob Epstein and Jeffrey Friedman, 1995

Leontine Sagan, *Jeunes filles en uniforme*, film, 1931

Didier Eribon, "L'Affirmation homosexuelle", *Le Monde diplomatique*, June 1996

Virginie Mouseler, *Les Femmes et les Homosexuels, la fausse indifférence*, Calmann-Lévy, 1996

Geneviève Sellier et Noël Burch, *La Drôle de Guerre des sexes dans le cinéma français*, Nathan, 1996

Jean Cocteau, *The White Book*, published anonymously in 1928

J. D. Nasio, *Five Lessons on the Psychoanalytical Theory of Jacques Lacan*, Rivages, 1992

Interview with Grace Paley, in *Libération*, 31 August 1995

1971 Paloma Barrientos, *Isabel Preysler reina de corazones*, Ed. B, Barcelone, 1991

Julio Iglesias, *Julio raconte Iglesias*

Ovid, *The Art of Love*

Françoise Héritier, *Masculin / féminin, la pensée de la différence*, Odile Jacob, 1996

Pascal, *Discours sur les passions de l'amour*, 1652

1972 Elena Bonner, *Alone Together*, Knopf, New York, 1986

1973 Ingmar Bergman, *Scenes from married life*; television series and film (1973)

John Gottman, *Why Marriages Succeed or Fail*, 1994

Irène Pennacchioni, *De la guerre conjugale*, Mazarine, 1986

Deborah Tannen, *You Just Don't Understand*, William Morrow, New York, 1990

Jean-Claude Kaufmann, *Sociologie du couple*, PUF, 1993 (and bibliographical references)

Jean-Claude Kaufmann, *La Trame conjugale, Etude du couple par son linge*, Nathan, 1992

Claude Roy, *The Verb To Love*, Gallimard, 1969

Martine Trittoleno, interview with Erica Jong, *Libération*, 10 March 1995

1974 Galina Vichnevskaïa, *Galina*, Harcourt, Brace & Jovanovitch, New York, 1984

Pascal Dibie, *Ethnologie de la chambre à coucher*, Grasset, 1987

Rêves d'alcôves, la chambre au cours des siècles, catalogue accompanying the exhibition at the Musée des Arts décoratifs, Paris, January-April 1995

Balzac, *Physiology of Marriage*, 1834

Richard Wagner, duet, *Tristan and Isolde*

Martine Sevegrand, *Les Enfants du bon Dieu. Les catholiques français et la procréation au XXe siècle*, Albin Michel, 1995

Anne Carol, *Histoire de l'eugénisme en France*, Le Seuil, 1995

1975 Alice Schwarzer "Margarethe von Trotta: das bisschen Leben, das ich brauche", *Emma*, January 1982

Conversation between the author and Margarethe von Trotta, 23 February 1997

Peter Buchke, *Il vaudrait mieux être un autre*, video film on Volker Schlöndorff, Kirch-Film, 1991

Bonnie Sher Klein, *C'est surtout pas de l'amour*, Canadian film

Antoine Rakovsky and Daniel Serceau (ed.), "Les dessous du cinéma porno", *Cinémaction*, No. 59, April 1991, Corlet

Catharine MacKinnon, *Only Words*, Harvard University Press, Cambridge, Mass., 1993

Diana Russell (ed.), *Making Violence Sexy: Feminist Views on Pornography*, Teachers College Press, New York, 1993

Lynne Segal & Mary McIntosh (ed.), *Sex Exposed: Sexuality and the Pornography Debate*, Rutgers University Press, New Brunswick, New Jersey, 1993

Jean-Claude Bologne, *Histoire de la pudeur*, Olivier Orban, 1986

Lindsy van Gelder, "When Women Confront Street Porn", *Ms.*, February 1980

Louise Briceno and Françoise Foucault, "Le Porc-no!", *Cahiers du féminisme*, No. 40

Simon Garfield, "*Deep Throat*, twenty years on", *The Independent on Sunday*, in *Courrier International*, summer suppl., August 1992

"Lieben Frauen Porno?", article in *Der Spiegel*, 31 October 1988

The marriage of David Gascoyne and Judy Lewis, *Le Monde*, 8 March 1996, literary supplement

The marriage of Paul Keating and Anna Van Iersel, *Courrier international*, suppl. *Ces fous qui nous gouvernent*, 1994

1976 Marina Vlady, *Vladimir ou le Vol arrêté*, Fayard, 1987

Shere Hite, *The Hite Report: A Nationwide Survey on Female Sexuality*, 1976;

The Hite Report on Male Sexuality, 1981;

Women and Love, Knopf, New York, 1987;

Anne Koedt, *The Myth of Vaginal Orgasm*, 1968

Michel Foucault, *Histoire de la sexualité*, vol. I: *La Volonté de savoir*, Gallimard, 1976

Josée Néron, "Foucault, l'Histoire de la sexualité et l'occultation de l'oppression des femmes", *Nouvelles Questions féministes*, 1996, vol. 17, No. 4

1977 George Butler, *Arnold Schwarzenegger, A Portrait*, Simon & Schuster, New York, 1990

Michel Cieutat, "Stallone et Schwarzenegger, les messieurs musclés du cinéma", *Positif*, February 1994

Laurence Leamer, *The Kennedy Women*, Villard Books, Random House, New York, 1994;

Tom Green, *Arnold!*, St. Martin's Press, 1987

Susan Price, "Maria Shriver, No Kennedy Clone", *McCall's*, October 1988

Sylvia Stein, interview with Sister Emmanuelle, *L'Express*, 29 June 1995

Jean-Claude Bologne, *Histoire du mariage en Occident*, Lattès, 1995

Jean Delumeau, *La Peur en Occident*, Fayard, 1978

Eugen Drewermann, *Psychoprogramm eines Ideals*, München, 1995

Odette Desfonds, *Les Rivales de Dieu*, Albin Michel, 1993

Jacques de Bourbon-Busset, *L'Amour durable*, Gallimard, 1969

1978 Interviews with Charlotte Rampling and Jean-Michel Jarre in *Paris-Match*, *Marie-France*, *Femme*, from 1982 to 1994

Item on Charlotte Rampling, in the programme of the 17th International Women's Film Festival, Créteil, March 1995

Entries for Charlotte Rampling and Jean-Michel Jarre, *Who's Who*, 1994 edition

Catherine Weinberger-Thomas, *Cendres d'immortalité, La Crémation des veuves en Inde*, Le Seuil, 1996

Ovid, *Metamorphoses*, VIII

1979 Margaret Thatcher, *The Path to Power*, Harper Collins, 1995

Carol Thatcher, *Below the Parapet*, Harper Collins, 1996

Hugo Young, *One of Us*, Macmillan, London, 1989

Leo Abse, *Margaret, Daughter of Beatrice, A*

Politician's Psycho-biography of Margaret Thatcher, Jonathan Cape, London, 1989

Francesco Alberoni, *Falling in Love*

Stendhal, *Love*

Michel Leiris, *Langage tangage ou ce que les mots me disent*, 1985

Georges Bizet, *Carmen*, 1875

Véronique Nahoum-Grappe (ed.), *Rêves de rencontre*, Textuel, 1996

Félicie Nayrou and Alain Rudy (ed.), *La Rencontre, Figures du destin*, Autrement, 1993

Jean-Claude Kaufmann, *Sociologie du couple*, PUF, 1993

Boris Cyrulnik, *Les Nourritures affectives*, Odile Jacob, 1993

Pascale Noizet, *L'Idée moderne d'amour*, Kimé, 1996

Time of Love, film by Mohsen Makhmalbaf, 1990

Interview with Alain Badiou, in *Le Monde*, 31 August 1993

1980 Sara Parkin, *The Life and Death of Petra Kelly*, Pandora, London, 1994

Item on the death of Petra Kelly and Gert Bastian in *Der Spiegel*, 20 October 1992

Sigrid Latka-Jöhring, *Frauen im Bonn, 12 Porträts aus der Bundeshauptstadt*, J. Lather Verlag, Bonn, 1988

Martin Monestier, *Suicides: histoire, techniques et bizarreries de la mort volontaire des origines à nos jours*, Le Cherche-Midi, 1995

Catherine Villeneuve-Gokalp, "Du premier au deuxième couple: les différences de comportement conjugal entre hommes et femmes", in *La Nuptialité: évolution récente en France et dans les pays développés*, Thérèse Hibert et Louis Roussel (ed.), INED, Congrès et colloques No. 7, PUF, 1991

Jean-Yves Raulot and Elizabeth Brown-Demonet, "Nuptialité et formation des couples en Europe: évolution récente et comparaison internationales", *ibid.*

1981 Jayne Fincher/Judy Wade, *Diana. Portrait of a Princess*, Cologne, 1998

Andrew Morton, *Diana, Her True Story*, 1992

James Hewitt, *Princess in love*, 1995

Claudia Müller-Ebeling & Christian Rätsch, *Isolden Liebestrank*, Kindler, 1986

Cheng Hen, *Le Tao de l'amour*, Albin Michel, 1994

William Shakespeare, *Macbeth*

Diane Ackerman, *A Natural History of Love*, Ramdom House, New York, 1994

Ronald Nossintchouk, *L'Extase et la Blessure, Crimes et violences sexuelles de l'Antiquité à nos jours*, Plon, 1993

Malek Chebel, *Encyclopédie de l'amour en islam*, Payot, 1995

Diane Ackerman, *A Natural History of Love*, Ramdom House, New York, 1994

1982 Jonathan Moor, *Diane Keaton*, St. Martin's Press, New York, 1989

Sam Rubin, *Mia Farrow*, St. Martin's Press, New York, 1989

Bertrand Tavernier and Jean-Pierre Coursodon, *Cinquante ans de cinéma américain*, Nathan, 1991

Jean-Philippe Guérand, *Woody Allen*, Rivages, 1989; reissued 1995

Giannalberto Bendazzi, *Woody Allen*, Liana Levi, 1991

Eric Lax, *Woody Allen*, 1991

Maria Paradisi, "Femmes et droits en Grèce, Les réformes du droit de la famille" in *Actes*, "Quels droits pour les femmes?", No. 57–58, winter 1986–1987

Jean-Claude Bologne, *Histoire du mariage en Occident*, Lattès, 1995

Jean Baubérot et al., *Religions et laïcité dans l'Europe des douze*, Syros, 1994

Alfred Dittgen, "Les mariages religieux en France. Comparaison avec les mariages civils", in *La Nuptialité: évolution récente en France et dans les pays développés*, Thérèse Hibert et Louis Roussel (ed.), Congrès et colloques No. 7 INED / PUF, 1991

Alfred Dittgen, "La forme du mariage en Europe. Cérémonie civile, cérémonie religieuse. Panorama et évolution", in *Population*, March-April 1994

Alice Kahn Ladas, Beverly Whipple et John D. Perry, *The G Spot and Other Recent Discoveries about Human Sexuality*, Holt, Rinehart & Winston, New York, 1982

1983 Articles on Eurythmics in *Rock & Folk*, Nos. 204, 237, 247, 267 (October 1989) and 297 (May 1992)

Catherine de Guibert-Lantoine et al., *La Cohabitation adulte*, INED, *Population et sociétés*, No. 293, September 1994

Nicole Czechowski (ed.), *L'Intime*, Autrement, 1986

Interview with Elfriede Jelinek, in *Télérama*, 13 April 1994

1984 Vaclav Havel, *Letters to Olga*
Vaclav Havel, 1987; *Interrogatoire à distance*, conversation with Karel Hvizdala, ed. of l'Aube, 1989
Eda Kriseova, *Vaclav Havel, la biographie*, ed. of l'Aube, 1991
Joubert, *Pensées*, V, LIII
Albert Cohen, *Belle du seigneur*, Gallimard, 1968
"The milk of human kindness", William Shakespeare, *Macbeth*, I, 5
Mario Mercier, *La Tendresse*, La Table ronde, 1995
Anne Muxel, *Individu et mémoire familiale*, Nathan, 1996
André Comte-Sponville, *Petit Traité des grandes vertus*, PUF, 1995
Nicole Czechowski (ed.), *L'Intime*, Autrement, 1986
Jacques de Bourbon-Busset, *L'Audace d'aimer*, Gallimard, 1990; *La Tendresse inventive*, Gallimard, 1996

1985 Jean-Claude Raspiengas and Patrick Volson, *Paroles d'otages*, film, 1990
Tom Sutherland, *At Your Own Risk*
Jackie Mann, *Yours Till the End*
Michel Pastoureau, *Dictionnaire des couleurs de notre temps*, Bonneton, Paris, 1992
Florence Montreynaud, *Amours à vendre. Les dessous de la prostitution*, Glénat, 1993
John d'Emilio & Estelle B. Freedman, *Intimate Matters, A History of Sexuality in America*, Harper & Row, New York, 1988
Léo Ferré, *Jolie môme*, 1961
Lucien Becker, *Le désir n'a pas de légende*, ed. La Dérobée, Le Relecq-Kerhuon, 1996

1986 Pippo Baudo, *Intervista col successo, A cura di Paolo Butturini*, ed. Reverdito, Coll. I grandi dello Spettacolo, Trente, Italy, 1987
Suzanne Lilar, *La Confession anonyme*, 1960; reissued Suzanne Lilar, *Benvenuta*
Guillaume Apollinaire, *Les Exploits d'un jeune don Juan*, 1907
Marie Dauguet, "L'Amant", in Claudine Brécourt-Villars, *Ecrire d'amour, Anthology of female erotic texts*, Ramsay, 1985

1987 Interview with Demi Moore and Bruce

Willis, "How They Met", *Cosmo*, September 1992
Susan Faludi, *Backlash, The Undeclared War Against Women*, Crown, 1991
Julianne Pidduck, "The 1990's Hollywood Fatal Femme: (Dis) Figuring Feminism, Family, Irony, Violence", *CinéAction* No. 38, Canada
Interview with Adrian Lyne, in *Us*, August 1992
Zhang Yimou and Gong Li, article in *Sunday Times*, in *Courrier international* 7 September 1995

1988 Frank Deford, "The Fastest Woman Ever", in *Newsweek*, 24 June 1996
Benoîte Groult, *Salt On Our Skin*
Histoire d'une évasion, Grasset, 1997
Claudine Brécourt-Villars, *Ecrire d'amour, Anthology of female erotic texts (1799 –1984)*, Ramsay, 1985
Pierre Béarn, *L'Erotisme dans la poésie féminine des origines à nos jours*, Jean-Jacques Pauvert / Au terrain vague, 1993
Annie Ernaux, *L'Infini*, January 1997
Abramovic and Ullay, in the programme for the 3rd Biennale of contemporary art, Lyons, RMN 1995

1989 Barbara Findlen, "Is Marriage the Answer?", *Ms.*, May-June 1995
William Raspberry, "Why Are We So Scared Of Same-Sex Wedlock?", *The Washington Post*, in *International Herald Tribune*, 28 January 1997
Frédéric Martel, *Le Rose et le Noir, les homosexuels en France depuis 1968*, Le Seuil, 1996

1990 Nelson Mandela, *Long Walk to Freedom*, Little, Brown, Boston, 1994
Ronald Harwood, *Mandela*, film, Channel Four Books, Boxtree, London, 1987
Winnie Mandela, *Part Of My Soul Went With Him*
Jean Giraudoux, *Ondine*, 1939
Otto Weininger, *Sex and Character*, 1903

1991 Philippe Ducayron, *Nirvana Testament*, Albin Michel, 1994
Michael Azerrad, *Come As You Are; Nirvana, histoire d'un mythe*, Lieu commun, 1994
Sébastien Raizer, *Nirvana, romance sans sens*, Camion blanc, 1994

Interview with Kurt Cobain, *Rock & Folk*, No. 300, August 1992
Interview with Courtney Love, *Les Inrockuptibles*, March 1997
Jean Baudrillard, in *Libération*, 4 December 1995
Hubert Aupetit and Catherine Tobin, *L'Amour déboussolé*, François Bourin, 1993
Susan Faludi, Backlash, *The Undeclared War Against Women*, Crown, 1991
Shere Hite, *The Hite Report on Male Sexuality*, 1981
Mariages en Grèce in Alain Monnier et Catherine de Guibert-Lantoine, "La conjoncture démographique", *Population* Nos. 4–5, 1994

1992 Judith Warner, *Hillary Clinton, The Inside Story*, ed. Signet / Penguin, New York, 1993
Hillary Clinton, *It Takes a Village: And Other Lessons Children Teach Us*
Christian Huitema, *Et Dieu créa l'Internet*, Eyrolles, 1995
Sherry Turkle, *Life on the Screen: Identity in the Age of the Internet*, Simon & Schuster, New York, 1995
Martine Vantsès, *Sexe et mensonge*, Joëlle Losfeld, 1993
Josiane Jouët, "L'amour sur minitel", in *Paroles d'amour*, Family Planning Colloquium, Isère, Syros, 1991
Gérard Sebag, *Soha Arafat, enfant de Palestine*, Michel Lafon, 1995
Marie-Claude Treglia, Barbet Schroeder and Bulle Ogier, *Marie-France*, March 1993

1993 Luc Lamprière and Patrick Sabatier, "Le mariage dont le Japon fait toute une histoire", *Libération*, 9 June 1993
Philippe Pons, "Rite sans romance", *Le Monde*, 10 June 1993
Jeffrey Bartholet, "Princess in a Gilded Cage", *Newsweek*, 3 June 1996
Frédéric Martel, *Le Rose et le Noir, les homosexuels en France depuis 1968*, Le Seuil, 1996
Jean Baudrillard, in *Libération*, 4 December 1995
Jonathan Demme, *Philadelphia*, 1994
Tom Joslin and Peter Friedman, *Silverlake*, 1993
Hugues Lagrange and Brigitte Lhomond (ed.), *Enquête de l'Agence nationale de recherche contre le sida*, 1995

Alfred Spira, Nathalie Bajos et al., *Rapport sur les comportements sexuels en France*, French Public Records, 1993

Admira Ismic and Bosko Brkic, *Actuel*, July–August 1993

Florence Hartmann, in *Le Monde*, 11 December 1994

Obituary of Anthony and Maggie Barker, in *The Independent*, September 1993

1994 Pam Lambert, "The Course of True Love", *People*, 30 August 1993

Claude Askolovitch, "La Trahison de Boris Becker", *L'Evénement du Jeudi*, 6 January 1994

Laurent Rigoulet, "Becker terroriste sur court", *Max*, April 1994

Georges-Marc Benamou, *Le Dernier Mitterrand*, Plon, 1997

Danielle Mitterrand, *En toutes libertés*, Ramsay, 1996

Interviews with Danielle Mitterrand, in *L'Express*, 2 February 1996; in *Libération*, 5 March 1996

Victor Hugo, *Tas de pierres*

Julian Barnes, *Letters from London*,

Gérard Pommier, *L'Exception féminine*, Aubier, 1996

Cécile Abdesselam, *Les Aventuriers de la double vie*, L'Archipel, 1995

Sylvie Fainzang et Odile Journet, *La Femme de mon mari. Anthropologie du mariage polygamique en Afrique et en France*, L'Harmattan, 1988

Claudia Roth, *La Séparation des sexes chez les Zara au Burkina-Faso*, L'Harmattan, 1996

Obituary of Danuta Lutoslawska, in *The Independent*, London, May 1994

1995 Lucas Delattre and Serge Belet, article on wrapping the Reichstag and interview with Christo, *Le Monde*, 18–19 June 1995

Jacob Baal-Teshuva, *Christo et Jeanne-Claude*, photog. by Wolfgang Volz, Benedikt Taschen, Cologne, 1995

Conversation between the author and Leïla Voight, February 1997

Marjorie Garber, Vice Versa, *Bisexuality and the Eroticism of Everyday Life*, Simon & Schuster, New York, 1995

Interview with Ani DiFranco, in *Ms.*, November 1996

Robyn Ochs, *Bisexual Resource Guide*, 1996, quoted in *Lesbia* No. 151

Interview with June Jordan, in *Ms.*, March 1996

Nicole Loraux, *Les Expériences de Tirésias*, Gallimard, nrf esssais, 1989

Jean-Luc Hennig, *Bi, de la bisexualité masculine*, Gallimard

Gabriel Aghion, *What a Drag*, film, 1996

Carl Gustav Jung, *Psychology and Alchemy*, 1944

Shakespeare: *Funeral Elegy* by William Shakespeare

Gilles Kepel, "Frémissements sur le Nil", l'affaire Abou Zeid, *Le Monde*, 12 April 1997

1996 Conversation between the author and Marinella Alagna, 21 March 1997

Janine Boissard, *Bébé couple*, Fayard, 1997

Jean-Claude Kaufmann, *La Trame conjugale, Etude du couple par son linge*, Nathan, 1992

Olivier Galland and Marco Oberti, *Les Etudiants*, La Découverte, 1996

Olivier Galland and Alessandro Cavalli, *L'Allongement de la jeunesse*, Actes Sud, 1993

Riitta Uosukainen, in *Courrier international*, 10 October 1996

Nestor Cerpa and Nancy Gilvonio, *Newsweek*, 20 January 1997

1997 Bill Gates, in *International Herald Tribune*, December 1996

Sarah Ferguson, Duchess of York, in *The Guardian*, 7 May 1998

Carole Bouquet, in *L'Express*, 31 July 1997

Noëlle Châtelet, in *Marie-Claire*, May 1997

1998 Statement by a young man, in Janine Mossuz-Lavau and Anne de Kervasdoué, *Les femmes ne sont pas des hommes comme les autres*, Odile Jacob, 1997

Survey by the Economic and Social Research Council, in *The Independent*, 25 February 1997

Dominique Frischer, *La Revanche des misogynes, Où en sont les femmes après trente ans de féminisme?*, Albin Michel, 1997

Index

Numbers in bold refer to pages where the subject in question is treated in depth. Numbers in italic refer to the column on the right on a page.

Names of works, periodicals and fictional characters, and foreign common nouns, are in italics.

Names in small capitals indicate the couples and social phenomena studied in the chapters. Dates of birth and (where appropriate) death for each member of the couple are shown in brackets.

At the end of the entry for each country, after a dash (–), the numbers of the pages dealing with couples originating from that country, both in the chapters and in the column on the right. Sometimes the number relates to only one member of the couple. The numbers of pages dealing with social phenomena relative to that country, both in chapters and in the column at the right, are also shown.

CREDITS

© Adagp, Paris, 1997
pp. 33, 35, 43 © Svein Andersen / Sidsel de Jong, Munch Museum, 46 © Demart Pro Arte B. V., Geneva, 47, 56, 73, 81, 102 © Man Ray Trust, Paris, 112, 115, 131 t and b, 143, 145 © Man Ray Trust, Paris, 147, 185, 203, 241, 248, 249, 265, 273, 301 t and b, 340, 378, 387, 406 b, 407 t.

© Vega, 1997, p. 132.

© AFP, pp. 240, 297, 309, 318, 354, 380.

© A. K. G., pp. 128 r, 129, 133, 212 t, 361.

© Claude Alexandre, pp. 253, 294, 314, 320.

© The Anaïs Nin Trust – Reproduced by permission of Gunther Stuhlmann – All rights reserved, p. 155.

© Gérard Ansellem, p. 426.

© Archive Photos, Paris, pp. 34 b, 78, 109 t, 162, 186, 187, 196, 197, 210, 211, 243 b, 246, 270, 272, 289, 292, 306, 308, 350.

Art Curial, pp. 66 b, 67 t and b. © L & M Services B. V. Amsterdam 961 204.

© Artothek, Munich, p. 80.

© Associated Press, p. 405.

© August Sander Archive, Cologne, p. 115.

© Cecil Beaton, courtesy of Sotheby's London, pp. 52, 174.

© Catherine Beaunez, pp. 349 (D. R.), 417 b (D. R.).

© Heiner Becker, pp. 48, 62.

Bibliothèque Nationale, pp. 66 t © L & M Services B. V. Amsterdam 961 204, 70 (courtesy Galerie Michèle Chomette, Paris).

© Bibliothek der E. T. H., Zurich, p. 44.

© Romaine Brooks, p. 53 (D. R.)

© Leo Castelli Photo Archives, New York, p. 387.

© Cat's, pp. 118, 157 © National Film Archive, Still Library, 160, 169 t, 172 t, 189, 230, 231, 278, 282, 285 b, 296, 324, 329.

© Jean-Loup Charmet, pp. 222, 223, 243.

© Cnac / Béatrice Hatala, p. 241.

© Chaval, p. 237 (D. R.)

© Florence Chevalier, p. 279.

© Christie's Images, p. 95

© Francesco Clemente, p. 421 (courtesy Galerie Jérôme de Noirmont, Paris).

© Club Méditerranée, p. 236.

© Colas, p. 379 (D. R.)

© Laurent Condominas, p. 416 b.

© Contact, pp. 315, 347 (Annie Leibovitz), 369 (A. Reiniger), 388 (Annie Leibovitz), 397 (Annie Leibovitz), 410 (Thomas Muscionico), 411 (David Burnett).

© Beryl Cook, 1991, p. 409 (courtesy Rogers, Coleridge and White Ltd, London).

© Corbis-Bettmann, pp. 49 (UPI), 57 (UPI), 136 (UPI), 150 t (Springer), 150 b (Pach), 178 (UPI), 198 (UPI), 201 (Springer), 213 (UPI), 259 t (UPI), 269, 394 (Reuters), 403 (Reuters).

© Cosmos, pp. 285 t (Pierre Boulat), 351 (Pierre Boulat), 373, 376 and 377 (Anzenberger / Nemec), 384 (Grazia Neri / Mencarini), 396 (LFI / David Fisher), 402 (J. B. Pictures / L. Gubb), 423 (Gorgoni), 427 (Grazia Neri / G. Arici).

© Descharnes & Descharnes, p. 46.

© Di Marco, pp. 169 b, 245.

© Dite / Usis, p. 86.

© Documentation Musée National d'Art Moderne, Pompidou Centre, pp. 94 (photo Marc Vaux), 340.

© D P A, p. 360.

D. R., pp. 26 t and b, 27, 36 b, 50, 51, 53, 68, 69, 72, 79, 88, 89, 97, 100, 113 t l, 119, 122, 126, 127 t and b, 131 t, 138, 139, 151, 154, 161, 165, 166, 167, 179, 184, 188, 204, 205, 226, 227, 237, 273, 432.

© Edimedia, p. 81.

© Emipress, Zurich, p. 250.

© Enguerrand, p. 385.

© Erró, pp. 203, 249.

© Explorer, pp. 31 b (Mary Evans), 85, 92 (Archives), 93.

© S. Fischer Verlag, Frankfurt, p. 32 t.

© Fondation Alexandra David-Néel, pp. 70, 71.

© Gisèle Freund, p. 217.

© Fundación Colección Thyssen-Bornemisza, Madrid, p. 56.

© Gamma, pp. 319 (Owen Franken), 330, 331 (Shapiro), 334 (Apesteguy), 335 (Sola).

© Claude Gassian, pp. 372, 407.

© George Eastman House, Rochester, p. 76.

© Norbert Ghuisoland, p. 101.

© Giraudon, pp. 143 (Lauros), 144 (Lauros), 146 (Alinari), 147 (René Magritte picture library), 185 (René Magritte picture library).

© Graphische Sammlung Albertina, Vienna, pp. 47 © Bild-Kunst, Bonn, 63.

© Graphische Sammlung der E. T. H., Zurich, p. 55.

© Photothèque Hachette pp. 24, 31 t, 34 t, 36 t, 37, 40 t and b, 41, 82 b, 83, 104–105 b, 105 t, 111 t and b, 113 r, 120 t and b, 130 (Wallery), 131 b, 153 (G. R. Aldo), 170 (Palais de la Découverte), 171, 180 (MGM), 181 (MGM), 199 (Jean A. Fortier), 215, 228.

© Sam Haskins, p. 345.

© Verlag Paul Haupt, Berne, p. 45 (in *The Tragic Life of Mileva Einstein-Maric*, 1993).

© Herbert List Estate, Max Scheler, pp. 134, 195.

© Hulton Deutsch / Getty Images, pp. 60, 61, 74, 103, 128 l, 158, 159, 175, 181, 206, 207.

© Imapress, pp. 323, 364 (Camerapress), 365 (Camerapress), 381 l (Camerapress), 381 r (Camerapress), 418 (AP), 419 (Richard Open).

ILLUSTRATIONS

1902
Gustav Mahler, Historisches Museum der Stadt Wien, Vienna.
The Bride of the Wind, Oskar Kokoschka, 1914, Kunstmuseum, Basel.

1903
Hope, Gustav Klimt, 1903, National Gallery of Canada, Ottawa.

1904
Separation, Edvard Munch, Munch Museum, Oslo.

1905
Freud, Salvador Dalí, 1938 (private collection).
The Great Head, Alfred Kubin, 1899, Graphische Sammlung Albertina, Vienna.

1907
Young Girl, Egon Schiele, 1913, Graphische Sammlung der E. T. H., Zurich.

1908
Portrait of Misia Godebska, Pierre Bonnard, 1908, Fondation Thyssen-Bornemisza, Madrid.

1909
Woman in Repose, Gustav Klimt, 1913, Historisches Museum der Stadt, Vienna.
Self-Portrait of the Artist Masturbating, Egon Schiele, 1911, Graphische Sammlung Albertina, Vienna.

1910
Dress Simultaneous, Dancer, Sonia Delaunay 1917 (private collection).

1912
Pygmalion and Galatea, J. L. Gérôme, The Metropolitan Museum of Art, New York.

1913
Dance in Baden-Baden, Max Beckmann,

Bayerische Staatsgemäldesammlungen, Munich.
The Archangel's Tango, Kees van Dongen, Musée des Beaux Arts, Nice.

1915
Pornocrates, Félicien Rops (private collection).

1918
Karen Blixen c. 1922, Karen Blixen Museet, Rungsted Kyst, Denmark.
Denys Finch Hatton c. 1931, Karen Blixen Museet, Rungsted Kyst, Denmark.

1921
Manuscript of a poem by Esenin, Literature Museum, Moscow.
Wife of the painter Peter Abelen, August Sander Archiv, Cologne.

1924
Georgia O'Keeffe painting a flower, photograph by Alfred Stieglitz, National Gallery of Art, Washington D. C.
Stieglitz, photograph by Imogen Cunningham, The Imogen Cunningham Trust.

1926
Lotte Lenya, photograph by Lotte Jacobi, Berlinische Galerie, Landesmuseum für Bildende Kunst, Berlin.

1928
Louis Aragon and Elsa Triolet, Paris 1945, Boris Taslitzky, Musée d'Art et d'Histoire, Saint-Denis.
Return of the Beautiful Gardener, Max Ernst, Menil Foundation, Houston.

1929
Portrait of Gala, Salvador Dalí, 1935, The Museum of Modern Art, New York.
Young Woman Crouching, G. Schrimpf, 1923 (private collection).
Reproduction Prohibited (Portrait de M.

James), René Magritte, 1937 (private collection).

1934
Gunnar and Alva Myrdal, Gripshoms Slott, Mariefred, Sweden.

1938
The Link, René Magritte (private collection).

1945
Benjamin Britten and Peter Pears, Kenneth Green, 1943, National Portrait Gallery, London.

1957
Song of Songs, IV, Marc Chagall, Musée message biblique Marc Chagall, Nice.

1959
Drowning Girl, Roy Lichtenstein, 1963, The Museum of Modern Art, New York.

1975
Women as Targets, André Fougeron, 1984 (private collection).

1986
Sex and Death Double 69, Bruce Nauman, 1985, Gallery Leo Castelli, New York.

My thanks to Monique Perrot-Lanaud, whose friendly help and support have been so precious to me, and to Claudia Binet, Raphaëlle Branche, Blandine Houdart, Madeleine Miloutinovitch, Laurence Klejman and Julien Théry for their assistance;

to Léonore Branche, Renaud Branche, Dominique Candellier, Gaëlle Lassée, Alexander Scarlat, Maria-Grazia Tajé and Marianne Vergne for their documentary research;

to Elise Aubly, Françoise Audé, Virginie Barré, Caroline Boucher, Aurélie Branche, Jean-Paul Branlard, Pierre Bréchignac, Jackie Buet, Mark Carlson, Yvonne Charles-Minet, Yves & Sylvain di Maria, Yvane Dréant, Géraldine Dubois de Montreynaud, Nicole Duplaix, Catherine Durand, Sylvie Escat (SOS Translations), Catherine Gonnard, Martine Guillon, Sara Gutierrez, Alexandre Hayoun, Caroline Helfter, Natacha Henry, Ellen Hinsey, Jean-Claude Kaufmann, Hugo Marsan, Evelyn Mesquida, Eva Orue, Florence Rochefort, Renée Théobald and Leïla Voight for their help and advice;

and to Muriel Jeancard (iconographer) and Marthe Lauffray (graphic designer) for their highly talented work.

I owe a great deal to Colette Véron, who worked with me with careful and loving attention and thanks to whom this book was completed in harmony.

Thanks to you all, to all who have given me confidence in myself, who have taught me to love words, pictures and the search for truth ...

Florence Montreynaud

Illustrations on the back cover:

Petra Kelly & Gert Bastian © D P A

Margaret & Denis Thatcher © Magnum (Archives)

Katharine Hepburn & Spencer Tracy © The Kobal Collection

Gertrude Stein & Alice Toklas © Cecil Beaton, courtesy of Sotheby's London

Gala & Dalí © Télimages / Man Ray Trust

Clark Gable & Carole Lombard © Archive Photos, Paris

John Lennon & Yoko Ono © Azoulay / Paris Match

Sonia & Robert Delaunay © Bibliothèque Nationale / L & M Services B. V. Amsterdam 961204

Christo & Jeanne-Claude © Wolfgang Volz, Düsseldorf

Simone Signoret & Yves Montand © Keystone

EVERGREEN is an imprint of Benedikt Taschen Verlag GmbH.

© for this edition: 1998 Benedikt Taschen Verlag GmbH

Hohenzollernring 53, D-50672 Köln

© 1997 Editions du Chêne-Hachette Livre, Paris – Aimer, un siècle de liens amoureux

Text: Florence Montreynaud

Preface: Yves Simon

Editor of the French edition: Colette Véron

Layout: Marthe Lauffray

Picture research: Muriel Jeancard

Typographic design: Catinka Keul, Cologne

Cover design: Angelika Taschen, Cologne

Translation from the French: Simon Knight, Jean Pitt and Mark Pallant Tripp

in association with First Edition Translations Ltd, Cambridge

Printed in Italy

ISBN 3–8228–7645–3

GB